THE SHAPE OF MEANING IN THE POETRY OF DAVID JONES

THOMAS DILWORTH

The Shape of MEANING in the Poetry of DAVID JONES

UNIVERSITY OF TORONTO PRESS
Toronto Buffalo London

© University of Toronto Press 1988
Toronto Buffalo London
Printed in Canada
ISBN 0-8020-2613-3

Printed on acid-free paper

Canadian Cataloguing in Publication Data

Dilworth, Thomas
The shape of meaning in the poetry of David Jones

Includes bibliographical references and index.
ISBN 0-8020-2613-3

1. Jones, David, 1895–1974 – Criticism and interpretation. I. Title.

PR6019.053Z57 1988   821'.912   C87-095196-3

For Kate, Alison, Molly, and Christine

Contents

PREFACE ix
ACKNOWLEDGMENTS xi
ILLUSTRATIONS xiii
ABBREVIATIONS xiv

1 Introduction 3

In Parenthesis

2 Genre and technique 38

3 Secular mythos 62

Utility and Gratuity 64
Disaccommodation 72
Friendship 80
Sex and Death 83
Natural Order 91
The Tradition of War 94
Dai Greatcoat 107

4 Sacred mythos 119

Ritual Motifs 121
The Queen of the Woods 139
Dialogic Tension 146

The Anathemata

5 Form 152

Movement 158
Structure 168
Physical and Semiotic Continuings 174
Timescape 181

6 Typology 201

Coupling 206
The Lady of the Pool 215
Gwenhwyfar 228
Voyaging 234

The Sleeping Lord

7 Sequence 258

'A, a, a, Domine Deus' 261
'The Wall' 263
'The Dream of Private Clitus' 273
'The Fatigue' 284
'The Tribune's Visitation' 294
'The Tutelar of the Place' 309
'The Hunt' 321
'The Sleeping Lord' 330
'Balaam's Ass' 343

8 Conclusion 360

NOTES 369
INDEX 395

Preface

My chief concern in this book is interpretation. This is largely, therefore, a prologue to critical assessment of the poetry of David Jones, which is of necessity a collective enterprise and will be the work of a generation of critics. But interpretation always implies evaluation, and I shall on occasion enter into critical debate. In my judgment the poetry of David Jones is a major contribution to English literature. For readers new to his poetry this judgment can only be a hypothesis, but an important test of this hypothesis is the fullness and accuracy of my analysis, which attempts to demonstrate how thoroughly the language, the imagery, the allusions, the intermediate forms, and the inclusive structures of Jones's poetry convey meaning. To the extent that this analysis avoids being shallow, selective, forced, or subjective, it supports a claim for Jones's place among the most important poets of this century. My approach is deliberately flexible, altering to suit the different works and different aspects of each work. It is, for example, 'biographical' when biography serves interpretation. While this book is not intended to be introductory in the sense of merely describing the surface of the poems, it is meant to help the reader understand what is often difficult poetry – difficult because the poet loads 'every rift with ore.' This initial cause of difficulty enriches and prolongs the pleasure of reading his work beyond what is usually experienced with easier poetry. Other books – descriptive, appreciative, and critical – have been written on David Jones, but as the first inclusive attempt to interpret the poems in depth, this book is meant to meet a critical need. It should supply a basis for assessing David Jones's stature relative to that of the high modernists, with whom, as T.S. Eliot noted, he has affinity – and, ultimately, relative to authors of epics and epic-length works throughout literary history. This is a 'basic' book also in that it makes extensive use of previously unpublished manuscript material.

The primary focus of my interpretation is symbolic form, which involves the relation of form to content. On one side of the relationship are forms ranging from verbal juxtaposition to structure; on the other side is content ranging from autobiography to an interpretation of culture. I hope to demonstrate that David Jones is an important innovator in poetic form and that his analysis of culture is an original intellectual synthesis that illuminates the cultural circumstances of our past and present.

Acknowledgments

In reading David Jones's poetry and in writing this book I have been helped by many people. The trustees of the estate of David Jones have generously given me access to unpublished material and have permitted me to quote from it. Over the years I have read the long poems aloud with William Blissett, Robert Barringer CSB, Vincent B. Sherry Jr, William J. Keith, Daniel DeMatteis, Herb Batt, Douglas Lochhead, and George Johnston. I have had many long talks with Vince Sherry about *In Parenthesis* and with Bob Barringer about *The Anathemata* and have discussed *In Parenthesis* and *The Sleeping Lord* with my students at the University of Windsor. At various stages of composition, my manuscript was read by Barringer, by Blissett, by John Reibetanz, by Colleen Cassano (who also helped me create the index), by Mary Baldwin, and parts of it by my wife Kathleen. I owe much to Barringer, much also to Blissett, who introduced me to Jones's work and then to the poet himself, and who has shared with me (as with many others) the treasure trove of his encyclopaedic memory. I am indebted to Daniel Huws, Huw Ceiriog Jones, and Philip Davies of the National Library of Wales – which, along with the University of Toronto Library, the Beinecke Library at Yale, and the Burns Library at Boston College, has granted permission to quote from its holdings. In various stages of development, parts of this book have appeared in or as essays in the *University of Toronto Quarterly*, *English Language Notes*, *Mosaic*, *The Anglo-Welsh Review*, *Poetry Wales*, *The Georgia Review*, *The Southern Review*, *Papers of the Bibliographical Society of America*, *Renascence*, and *The Journal of Modern Literature*. Quotations from *In Parenthesis*, *The Anathemata*, and *The Sleeping Lord* by David Jones are reprinted by permission of Faber and Faber Ltd.

My work was generously supported by the Canada Council and the Research Board of the University of Windsor and assisted by the Word Processing Centre of the university. It is published here with the help of a grant from the Canadian Federation for the Humanities, using funds provided by the Social Sciences and Humanities Research Council of Canada.

Illustrations

David Jones *The Garden Enclosed* (1924)
Oil on canvas, 35.6 × 29.8 cm (Tate Gallery)
15

David Jones *Petra im Rosenhag*
Pencil, watercolour, and bodycolour, 76.2 × 56 cm (Janet Stone)
22

David Jones *Melpomene*
Ink sketch on the back of a manuscript page of Part 7 of *In Parenthesis*,
32 × 19 cm (National Library of Wales)
143

Ebenezer Bradshaw
A photograph of the poet's maternal grandfather
(National Library of Wales)
165

Tellus Mater on the Ara Pacis (Museum of the Ara Pacis, Rome)
275

Abbreviations

I IDENTIFY unpublished letters by David Jones to Tom Burns, Jim Ede, Harman Grisewood, and René Hague by the initial of the surname of Jones's correspondent and the date of the letter. The letters to Ede are at Kettle's Yard, Cambridge; those to Grisewood, at Yale; those to Hague, at Toronto. When I quote from a published letter, I cite it as such, but whenever I have had access to the original and have noticed discrepancies I silently restore Jones's punctuation and abbreviations and otherwise correct transcription. The following books by David Jones are identified by the abbreviations shown (the 1972 edition of *The Anathemata* and the 1978 edition of *In Parenthesis* are used because they incorporate the poet's latest corrections):

A *The Anathemata* (London: Faber and Faber 1972)
IP *In Parenthesis* (London: Faber and Faber 1978)
RQ *The Roman Quarry* ed Harman Grisewood and René Hague (London: Agenda Editions 1981)
SL *The Sleeping Lord* (London: Faber and Faber 1974)
DG *The Dying Gaul* ed Harman Grisewood (London: Faber and Faber 1978)
DGC *Dai Greatcoat* ed René Hague (London: Faber and Faber 1980)
E&A *Epoch and Artist* ed Harman Grisewood (London: Faber and Faber 1959)
IN *Inner Necessities* ed Thomas Dilworth (Toronto: Anson-Cartwright 1984)
LF *Letters to a Friend* ed Anerin Talfan Davies (Swansea: Christopher Davies 1980)
LVW *Letters to Vernon Watkins* ed Ruth Pryor (Cardiff: University of Wales 1976)

Biblical quotations are from the Authorized Version unless otherwise indicated, but references follow the usage established by the Vulgate.

THE SHAPE OF MEANING IN THE POETRY OF DAVID JONES

1

Introduction

THE YEAR IS 1938. The guests assembled for tea fall silent at the sight of W.B. Yeats towering in the doorway, searching the room. He spots the one he wants and, making a profound bow from the waist, intones, 'I salute the author of *In Parenthesis.*' The author of *In Parenthesis*, embarrassed by the dramatic gesture and by Yeats's prolonged, effusive praise, is David Jones, reputed to be one of the best painters in England. He has published nothing prior to this long poetic narrative based on his experience as an infantryman in the Great War. After its acceptance for publication at Faber and Faber by Richard de la Mare, T.S. Eliot reads it in typescript and considers it 'a work of genius.' In 1954 W.H. Auden declares it 'the greatest book about the First World War that I have read,' and in 1962 he calls it 'a masterpiece.' In 1980 Graham Greene judges it to be 'among the great poems of this century.' In 1952 Jones's second long poem, *The Anathemata*, is published. Eliot, who accepted it for publication, now considers Jones a figure 'of major importance.' This poem, on the meaning of Western culture, is more fragmented in form than *In Parenthesis* and even greater in scope and range of allusion. William Carlos Williams recommends it in a letter to Ezra Pound as 'tough but rewarding' though 'too much for me.' We do not know whether Pound read it. In 1954 Auden judges it to be 'one of the most important poems of our time,' and in 1971 he calls it 'probably the finest long poem in English in this century.' David Jones himself considers it, in 1972, 'a lot better' than *In Parenthesis*.[1] In 1974 *The Sleeping Lord* appears, a collection of Jones's middle-length poems set in Roman-occupied Palestine, in sixth-century Britain, and in the modern West. Most of the reviews are celebratory. On

4 The Shape of Meaning

19 October 1974 Hugh MacDiarmid announced at a poetry conference in London that David Jones is the greatest native English poet of the twentieth century.

Few poets have been so highly praised, especially by fellow poets. And few poets who have been so highly praised have been so long neglected by the academic establishment. This is partly because David Jones is not easy to read. His major works are epic-length, fragmented in the modernist mode, and highly allusive. His allusions to Welsh literature and legend, classical and Norse myth, anthropology, geology, folklore, and the Catholic liturgy involve what is, for many readers, unshared background. Realizing this, David Jones supplies his own annotations. For some readers, notes to poems are off-putting, though these notes do help the reader into the poetry. And once in, most readers quickly realize that David Jones has not merely researched material for use in poetry but is writing about what he knows and loves.

The difficulty of understanding the unfamiliar references can be overcome. And the process is educational, since everything Jones refers to has historical or cultural significance. In this respect his allusions are more intrinsically rewarding, for example, than many of those by James Joyce, who so often engages the reader in playing turn-of-the-century Dublin trivial pursuit. As with Joyce, however, the allusions are essential to meaning and aesthetic effect. They are not mere borrowings from sources but generate a rich subtext that requires reading on more than one level. The allusions may, however, involve difficulties of emotional response. While the genuineness of Jones's feeling is unquestionable, most readers do not respond with equivalent feeling to the Welsh allusions and, especially in the later poems, to the explicitly Christian or Catholic allusions. The extraordinary demands that such references may place on a reader can only be justified, for that reader, by their importance to poetic statement and by the significance of that statement. In this regard, Jones's private apologia for *The Anathemata* may be taken as applicable in various degrees to all his poetry:

> I know it's a bit of a bugger on the surface; but underneath it's pretty straightforward really, compared with most modern 'personal experience' and 'psychological' kinds of poetry. I tried very hard to make a lucid, impersonal statement with regard to those things which have made us *all* – of this island. Even its 'Welsh' stuff is not there because I happen to be in part Welsh, but because the Welsh mythological element is an *integral* part of our tradition. Nor indeed is even the 'Catholic' element there

because I happen to be a Catholic, but rather because historically speaking (and leaving aside the truth or untruth of the Christian religion) it is the Catholic thing which has determined so much of our history and conditioned the thought of us *all*. (DGC 155–6)

Wales or 'the Matter of Britain' is far more than the insular concern which Jones here, like many of his English commentators, seems to consider it to be. The Arthurian cycle belongs to the whole of the West because, as he writes in one of his essays, it 'is, in some ways, and so to say, an *Iliad-Aeneid* of the Celtic-Germano-Latin Christian medieval West' (E&A 204). Moreover, the mythos or significant pattern of the prolonged defeat of Celtic Britain provides Jones with analogues to modern warfare, to modern cultural decline, and – paradoxically, in his later poems – to the possibility of spiritual renewal. The universal appeal of the Celtic myth lies in its being redolent of mutability and personal mortality. The Matter of Britain is first of all, therefore, a means to what T.E. Hulme calls the 'realization of the *tragic* subsurface of life, which makes it legitimate to call all other attitudes shallow.'[2]

David Jones's preoccupation with Wales extends the historic range of his poems and makes possible a symbolic tension of epochal proportions. I remember him saying, 'Most people think of history as Churchill did, as extending from Marlborough to himself.' This is the period of the first and second British empires, against which Jones places the centuries-long defeat of Celtic Britain as a moral and imaginative antithesis. The symbol of the doomed Celtic cause is Arthur. He is imperial Britannia's proper opposite, her Yeatsian mask. That partly explains the popularity of *The Idylls of the King* at the height of imperialist expansion. In the twentieth century, imperialism emanates from other centres, but the dying Gaul remains a potent symbol of its cost and so retains a haunting appeal. As David Jones says, moreover, in the realm of imagination 'nothing succeeds like failure' (DGC 75).

In the letter quoted above, Jones also argues that Catholicism is historically important. True enough, since it alone defined western Europe during the first millennium and a half of modern history, but in his poetry it is also a medium of perception and devotional feeling. Like Hopkins, therefore, and in contrast to Joyce, David Jones does require of the non-Catholic reader an imaginative suspension of religious disbelief. Unless such a reader can make this adjustment, he cannot fully appreciate the poetry, for Catholicism is integral to what Arnold would call Jones's 'criticism of life.' On this score Basil Bunting writes that in *The Anathemata* David Jones makes 'the Mass a complex of symbols

6 The Shape of Meaning

capable of ordering and interpreting pretty well the whole of the history of the world and the whole order of nature.' And with a sense of how some Catholic and Anglo-Catholic critics might attempt to parochialize Jones's reputation, Bunting adds, 'I can say that because I am not a Catholic and am thoroughly out of sympathy with Catholicism.'³ Not that Jones's beliefs are the sort that non-Catholics are most likely to feel out of sympathy with. He is the least ultramontane of literary Catholics, closer to the Church fathers than to the Council of Trent, more sacramental and contemplative than juridical, ascetic, or adversarial. His is a religion not yet torn to pieces by the Reformation. It is a religion directly continuous, furthermore, with the religious aspirations and rites of paganism. While the basic Catholic teachings are, in sections of the later poetry, recounted in a way that introduces a doctrinal stridency, Catholicism is, nevertheless, a huge asset to Jones as a poet. It supplies an all-inclusive vision of life and a sense of integral relationship between matter and spirit that helps interpret the content of his poetry and even places poetry itself in a metaphysical context.

After becoming a Catholic in 1921, Jones was deeply influenced by certain Catholics he read and came to know personally. First among these is Eric Gill. Jones had been 'inside a Catholic' since 1917, but Eric Gill convinced him of 'the truths of the [Catholic] Church.'⁴ A later acquaintance but greater in influence throughout Jones's life is the historian Christopher Dawson, who stresses in his writings the centrality of religion to culture and of Christianity to western culture. Dawson was a friend, but Jones also read everything by him he could lay his hands on.⁵ Close to Dawson and Gill in importance is Baron von Hügel, to whom Jones was 'quite addicted... in the late '20s and early '30s' (*IN* 90).⁶ Other Catholic influences are the second-century bishop Irenaeus of Lyons; Maurice de la Taille, whom Jones calls 'my theologian'; G.K. Chesterton, whose poetry Jones thinks formally 'bad' but full of wisdom; and his close friends Martin D'Arcy, Tom Burns, Harman Grisewood, and René Hague. The secondary-school and university educations of these men rubbed off on Jones, who had only an elementary-school education before entering art school at the age of fourteen.

Add to these Catholics the art critic Roger Fry, the cultural historian Oswald Spengler, and the classicist W.F. Jackson Knight and we have most of the influential figures behind the intellectual form (as distinct from the aesthetic form) of the content of Jones's poetry. All of these figures 'seemed to provide a kind of "unity of indirect reference,"' Jones writes, 'which seemed to tie-up with what little artistic perceptions one had by nature oneself, and gave edge and certainty and conviction to one's work' (DGC 185).

The content of Jones's poems derives from his experience in the trenches, from his reading of classical, English, and Welsh literature and history, from his reading of European anthropology and folklore, and from his experience of the liturgy, his knowledge of London and its people, his visits to Wales, his 1928 visit to France, and his 1934 visit to Jerusalem. The impressions made by these experiences began to receive interpretative form as they mixed in his preconscious mind and were ordered by relative strengths of feeling. His feelings were heightened in certain areas by his sublimation and repression of sexuality and his persistent neurasthenia, which in 1947 he came to understand in Freudian terms. By 1930 his experiences began to make intellectual sense to him. By 1950 their meaning reached more or less finished form in a coherent philosophy of life and of history.

Preconscious synthesizing is also the first stage in the creation of a poem. From his reading of John Livingstone Lowes' *The Road to Xanadu* (1927), Jones became fully aware of the aesthetic importance of this preconscious activity and of the early, uninhibited stage of writing that some authors call free fall.[7] Because the kind of preconscious activity that begins to give intellectual shape to a lifetime's experience also begins to give aesthetic shape to a poem, the two shapes are related in important ways. But they are not the same shape.

The intellectual form of content must be considered in any critical evaluation of poetry. Language means something, after all, and most of us still read to discover what a writer has to say. But even if it is intellectually shaped by a coherent interplay of philosophy, anthropology, and psychology, content is not poetry. 'Subject is *everything* in one sense,' Jones writes, 'and nothing in *another*' (DGC 138). It gives a literary work much of its significance, but a poem is poetry only because of its technique, which is the union of form and content.

We know from his letters to friends that with regard to each of his poems and paintings what matters 'above all else' to David Jones is the 'wedding of "form" and "content"' (to H 15–19 July 1973). The consummation of this union he calls 'shape.' He himself attributes his preoccupation with shape to his exclusive artistic concern, from about the age of five till the age of thirty, with visual art (to H 15–19 July 1973).[8]

David Jones is first of all a visual artist. He first experiences the creative process and develops his understanding of form and technique in his childhood drawing, and later in his art-school training and his

8 The Shape of Meaning

painting and engraving. This sets him apart from all other important modern poets. His aesthetic sensibility is already mature by the time he begins to write. Nothing else explains how he can produce *In Parenthesis* without serving a literary apprenticeship. His switching from paint and line to language without loss of technique is nevertheless remarkable and suggests an unusual analogical sensibility that is worth investigating.

Visual and literary art are analogous because space and time are analogous. Since Lessing's *Laocoön*, painting and poetry have tended not to imitate one another. Allegorical painting and pictorial poetry have been considered second-rate because each limits itself by a generic metaphor in which space pretends to be time or time pretends to be space. But this metaphorical exchange elevates to the status of content an analogy that nevertheless always operates on the level of form. The primary indication of this formal mirroring is the technical vocabulary shared by the critics of visual and literary art – terms such as imagery, pattern, allusion, fragmentation, juxtaposition, structure, tone, and point of view. Because most of these terms belong more properly to visual art than to literature, their use in literary criticism suggests that works of literature, while they exist primarily in time, are generally regarded spatially, at least in the purview of memory. Furthermore, certain metamorphic aspects of literary form which are primarily temporal – such as shifting viewpoints and alternation between mimetic modalities – have analogues in the perception of pictures, which is an act in time affected by complexities of spatial image.

David Jones certainly thinks of poetry as analogous to painting. His first published work began as an exploration of the analogy. About *In Parenthesis* he writes:

> In 1928 at Portslade in Sussex I began to find out for myself in what way the making of a writing presented the problems of 'form & content' as compared with those same problems that I had every reason to know constitute the main, or rather the whole, problem in the visual arts. I began what ultimately came to be *I.P.* with no other idea than to find out in what fashions these problems of 'form & content' cropped up in this totally different medium of written words.

He goes on to say that *In Parenthesis* actually began as a drawing with some writing to go with it, though he 'soon gave up that idea & got enmeshed in the difficulties inherent in the writing.'9

9 Introduction

In Parenthesis began and proceeded, he says, 'as an experiment' (to G 22 May 1962). Its composition coincides with the period of pictorial experimentation that culminates in the early 1930s in his mature style of painting. In its movement from realism to symbolism and from narrative continuity to fragmentation, the poem seems to reflect his development as a visual artist. *The Anathemata* – which is, Jones writes, 'in no sense' an 'experiment with words, with forms' – is written at the height of his development as a painter and is a straightforward reflection of his mature visual style (*IN* 24). The poem is a radically innovative work. If, as he says, it is not experimental, it must owe a great deal to his visual art having been for the previous thirty years continuously experimental. A few months after the publication of *The Anathemata*, he writes about its composition:

> Nearly all the time I had to think of how, in certain juxtapositions, *this* word rather than *that* would best call up the somewhat complex image required. My 'method' is merely to arse around with such words as are available to me until the passage in question takes on something of the shape I think it requires & evokes the image I want. I find, or think I find, the process almost identical to what one tries to do in paintin' or drawin'. Having tried, to the best of one's powers, to make the lines, smudges, colours, opacities, translucencies, tightnesses, hardnesses, pencil marks, paint marks, chalk marks, spit-marks, thumb marks, etc. evoke the image one requires as much as poss., one only *hopes* that some *other* chap, someone looking at the picture, may recognize the image intended. It seems to me, *mutatis mutandis*, just about the same process as writing. (*IN* 24)

The first stage of Jones's mature development as an artist includes his years at Westminster School of Art (1919–21) and his early acquaintance with Eric Gill, until about 1924. During this period of his development, he was mostly influenced by modern – or what was then known as post-impressionist – painting and theory, from which he acquired permanent convictions about the importance of objectivity and structure in a work of art. These convictions were strengthened in the early 1920s by his exposure to Eric Gill and to the writings of Aristotle, Jacques Maritain, and T.E. Hulme. Before the war, at Camberwell Art School, his approach to art was basically illustrative and modelled on the work of nineteenth-century illustrators and the Pre-Raphaelites. Now he became convinced that his art should not be illustrative but 'associative' (see E&A 98) – in other words, that the relation between his art and the objects it depicts should cease being mimetic and become symbolic.

Though not abstract in the strict sense, the work of the major post-impressionists – Cézanne, Gauguin, Van Gogh, Matisse, Bonnard, Picasso, and Braque – is obviously not primarily concerned with imitation. The chief English theorist of the movement and the one who named it in 1911 is Roger Fry. He claims that a post-impressionist work is what a painting should be, not an impression of an object but an object in its own right, a thing-in-itself. It is 'an equivalence, not a likeness.'[10] This was reaffirmed for Jones by his reading of Maritain in 1923. Maritain too is a promoter of the modern movement as representative of the essential nature of art. He writes that, without slavish imitation, art 'manifests or expresses *in a material* a certain radiation of Being, a certain form, a certain soul, a certain truth' that belongs to the object depicted. An art work is therefore a 'sign' – Maritain's equivalent term for 'symbol,' which Jones adopts in all his writing, probably to avoid Yeatsian Neoplatonic connotations.[11]

The notion of art as essentially symbolic has affinity with Joyce's theory of epiphanies, but Jones, who had not read Joyce at this time, found a different liturgical metaphor. While still at Westminster School of Art and before officially becoming a Catholic, it occurred to him that the equivalence of an art work to its object resembles eucharistic transubstantiation: the Mass has 'by analogy a very similar intention' to 'what we, or anyway what "Post-Impressionists" & "significant form" wallahs' claim:

> 'This [picture] may be made of pencil or paint or what you will but it is in fact such & such a human body or a hill slope under the form of those materials.' This was thought a pretty far-fetched & rather dangerous idea, more especially by my two Catholic friends because, they said, 'but in the Mass a change of substance is actually effected ...' To which I replied, 'Of course but *by analogy* they are speaking in not dissimilar terms. The desire is to make the flesh & blood Dorothy Price,' a model we sometimes had or her sister (Anita, I think) – 'a Miss Price under the appearance of chalk or paint.'   (to H 19 January 1973)

When he later writes of poetry as a re-calling or *anamnesis* (A 21), David Jones's use of eucharistic sacramental terminology presupposes a poetic 'transubstantiation' analogous to that which he strives for in painting.

The ontological separation of a work of art from its object, which is prerequisite to the work's being a symbol, has its corollary in the independence of the work from its maker. In his preface to *The Anathemata*, Jones writes that

> the workman must be dead to himself while engaged upon the work, otherwise we have that sort of 'self-expression' which is as undesirable in the painter or the writer as in the carpenter, the cantor, the half-back, or the cook. (12)

While this passage was still in typescript, he commented to Harman Grisewood:

> I am pleased with the bit ... about the Aristotelian conception. That is my main conviction. Anything that I may have partly achieved seems to me to be rooted in that conception of a work. That I owe I suppose almost entirely to those contacts round about 1920–30s: the Church, Eric, Maritain, Fry & the main Post-Impressionist conception of making 'things' – all that & Joyce-Hulme-Hopkins-Eliot as to the other art, writing, my conversations with you, all that fruitful & exacting period of the '20s & 30s. I remain *totally* & more & more convinced about the validity of all that. (14 February 1951)

Certainly his conviction about objectivity owes something to Eric Gill's assertions that a work of art should have the objectivity of a good piece of carpentry. And it reflects T.S. Eliot's theories about objectivity in poetry – though Jones thinks that '*at bottom*... the trouble with Tom E[liot]' is subjectivity. 'In fact, in one form or another, it holds the field. At base, I suppose, it is this subjectivism that separates them *all* from Joyce' (to G 10 January 1954). If the separation of a work of art from its object makes it a symbol, the degree of its independence from the artist largely determines its validity as a symbol.

In post-impressionist theory, structure is closely related to the objectivity and essential symbolism of an art work. Throughout his career, Roger Fry insists that what makes a work of art successful is 'logical structure' (1912) or 'structural design' (1917). 'Formal design,' he writes, 'had been almost lost sight of in the fervid pursuit of naturalistic representation' (1920), especially at the height of this pursuit in impressionism, with its 'continuous patchwork or mosaic of coloured patches without architectural framework or structural coherence' (1917).[12]

While Jones never speaks of structure as such, the concept seems to be included in his term 'shape.' And since structure is that aspect of form which is most readily abstractable – because it can be visually or spatially imagined – it seems to be included in what he means by abstract form, which he considers the most important aspect of an art work. He regards 'the assertion of total distinction between "Abstract Art" & "re-presentational art" as fundamentally untenable ... because there must be an "abstract quality" in any work, otherwise it would have no "being"' (to H 19 January 1973). He asserts, furthermore, that 'it is an abstract *quality*, however hidden or devious, which determines the real worth of any work' (E&A 265). In *Speculations*, a book which Jones said influenced him very much during this period, T.E. Hulme insists on the equivalence between abstraction and structure. Hulme argues for 'a tendency to abstraction ... in all art' which results in the 'geometrical form' of primitive art and of the post-impressionist works, which he heralds as a 'new complex geometrical art.'[13] And apropos of primitive art he says that geometric form is potentially symbolic.

The adjective 'geometric' may not seem to apply to Jones's poetry, or to his later visual art, which is nearly chaotic in its floriation of organic forms. Even the word 'structure' seems too rigid in its connotations, and that may explain why Jones avoids using it. But, as I hope to demonstrate in later, detailed analysis, the poetry is structured, and structured in a way that is usually conceptually geometrical. I do not mean that other aspects of form are geometrical. There is always in his poetry and paintings a vital tension between spatially conceived structure and the other aspects of form which are the organic details in the large design. This tension between symmetry and variation probably originates in an early appreciation of abstract Celtic art. Jones was especially fond of the La Tène bronze Battersea shield in the British Museum. His mother first took him to see it when he was about eight, and when he was about fifteen he saw it a second time with his art teacher A.S. Hartrick, who, as they looked at the shield, said of the Celts, 'They knew what they were up to, Jones.' The shield, Jones writes, 'looks at first sight wholly symmetric but actually each of the applied "decorative" spiral floriations etc. are other from each other' (to G 17 December 1970). In his poetry too, form is ambiguous in this way, but in reverse: everything seems various but behind the variety is a symmetry that is more or less geometrical. Any other kind of structure would be obscured by such a complex variety of forms. In this respect, moreover, the poems are structurally related to the paintings and engravings. From the mid-1920s onwards these latter are, as Paul Hills writes in an excellent essay, 'nearly all similarly organized around a powerful central shape.'[14] Basically the same organization informs the two long poems and half of the later, middle-length poems. Structurally, the poetry is almost always centred.

Structure is not, of course, the first thing a reader notices in a poem by David Jones. It is, rather, the last aspect of poetic form to reveal itself. And even then awareness of structure requires of the reader an imaginative quantum leap from the strategies of linear, temporal composition – linking word to word and passage to passage – to a simultaneous, spatially visualized sense of the emerging whole. When this occurs in the memory and imagination of the reader, the poem's diachronic or temporal sequence reveals its synchronic or spatial structure. This is not the 'spatial form' that Joseph Frank sees as characterizing literary modernism, and which consists mainly of the fragmentation of historical chronology – though this too characterizes Jones's poems.[15] Instead it is an abstract, visualized shape which emerges for Jones himself during the middle phases of composition, when he is juxtaposing passages or intermediate shapes, and which, once discovered, influences the subsequent composition and arrangement of material.

Deriving as it does from his experience as a painter, Jones's sense of structure is more visual or spatial, less musical than that of other poets. And because a poem, like a picture, is for him an 'associative' sign, its structure – in conjunction with its representational content – often has symbolic meaning. This too sets him apart from other poets. Yeats, Eliot, and the other modernists are chiefly indebted to the French symbolist poets, for whom the symbol is an image within the poem. For Jones, shape itself is symbolic.

By the mid-1920s the formation of his mature visual aesthetic reached a plateau. During these years his paintings are fairly realistic, though stylized. Objects and figures securely located in uniform perspective are solid, weighted, and somewhat tubular, with heavily defined and shaded, hard outer edges. These paintings seem indebted to the vorticist combination of solidity and linear thrust, and probably reflect the influence of Bernard Meninsky, who exhibited with the vorticists and taught Jones at Westminster School of Art. I remember Jones saying, furthermore, that he admired the work of Wyndham Lewis.

An example of this middle style is the 1924 oil painting *The Garden Enclosed* (Tate Gallery), which depicts a young man embracing a young woman and is based on Jones himself embracing Petra Gill in a garden at Ditchling. Its title alludes to the Song of Songs, in which 'a garden inclosed is my sister, my spouse' (4:12). The allusion suggests Jones's 'associative' sensibility – but while the verbal association is archetypal, the pictorial image does not pass beyond the typical. To do that he needs a different style.

At Capel-y-ffin in the Breconshire mountains where he stayed with the Gill family in 1925–6, his work began to undergo a transformation that would eventually make it capable of expressing archetypal 'association.' The change was gradual. It continued through the five years of his active membership in the Seven and Five Society, to which Ben Nicholson had him elected in 1929. Jones was now in distinguished company, which included the Nicholsons, Christopher Wood, Frances Hodgkins, and, from 1931, Barbara Hepworth and Henry Moore. The society was in close touch with the European modern movement. Nicholson and Wood knew Picasso. Jones himself met Braque. During these years, Jones's style reached its maturity in watercolour paintings that are semitransparent and multilayered, with surfaces fractured or bent by multiple perspective. In them colour and line separate so that they complement, and no longer restrain, one another. Jones's years in the Seven and Five Society include the four years in which he wrote the first complete draft of *In Parenthesis*. During this period, all the changes in his visual style have the effect of diminishing perspective.

Not all, but many of his later paintings are done in the multiple or free perspective that Jones considered characteristic of post-impressionist painting (see DG 141 n14). Unlike Cézanne and the cubists, however, he seldom breaks perspective into more than five points of view, and they are never very far from one another on the picture's imaginary window pane. For example his 1932 watercolour *Curtained Outlook* (British Council) has four distinct viewpoints, all within about fifteen degrees of one another. In his 1931 bodycolour painting *Merlin Land* (reproduced facing A 185), there are eight different viewpoints, almost one for each figure or grouping in the picture, but they are all within about ten degrees of each other.

In 1967 Jones writes that the main influence behind the free perspective of *Merlin Land* is that 'I along with most, if not all, visual artists & art-students felt the imperative need to break away in this manner or that from the academic "laws of composition" etc. in which we had been trained previous to the 1914–18 War.' He adds that in his own case a secondary influence was the Celtic aesthetic, which differed from that of 'Classical art & also from Gothic art' in that 'its method of making a unity was other ... not "architectural" *in the same way*' in that 'there

15 Introduction

The Garden Enclosed (1924)

was not a "centre" so to say but many "centres."[16] It must be emphasized that he is writing here not about abstract structure but only about centres of perspective. In freeing perspective, furthermore, he may owe something to the landscape of Capel-y-ffin, a place of huge irregular hills in which spatial planes at various heights slope in wildly different directions. Even landscapes painted here in strict, uniform perspective tend to appear to be done in multiple perspective.

The literary analogue of perspective is point of view. Strictly speaking, they are not the same thing, of course. Literary point of view is more complex and variable, involving emotional tone, degrees of knowledge, levels of psychological involvement, and variations in literary modality – as well as the viewpoint from which an object or event is perceived. But equally subtle differences may occur in a picture. And although in art criticism they are not considered under the rubric of point of view, these differences do determine how a picture is perceived. In actual fact, therefore, visual perspective has as many facets as literary point of view, and, as we shall see, these facets are analogous to those that determine literary point of view.

With regard to optical perspective, there are basically three kinds of picture: those in single perspective, those in multiple perspective, and those with no perspective. With regard to point of view, there are basically three corresponding kinds of literary work. Each kind of picture achieves a distinct relationship with its viewer. The corresponding kind of literary work achieves an analogous relationship to its reader.

Single or uniform perspective was introduced into visual art in the Renaissance. It brings the object depicted into an order external to itself. The ordering principle is the position first of the painter, then of the viewer, outside the picture and opposite to the vanishing point on the picture's horizon. The hidden meaning of every picture in uniform perspective is consequently the viewer's sense of himself as a distinct individual.

A picture in multiple perspective has several vanishing points, so that its viewer is forced mentally to shift about. His points of view alternate. If he can perceive the whole picture at once, his unfixed viewpoint becomes simultaneously multiple. Either way, the consciousness evoked is that of a plurality. It may be that of a social collective or, because time tends to become unstuck along with space, it may be the historical consciousness of a folk with a common culture. The nature of the plurality largely depends on subject matter. Cubist cityscapes evoke, for example, the collective consciousness of modern city-dwellers.

17 Introduction

If a picture has no perspective it is an icon. The early wood engravings Jones did at Ditchling in 1922-3 are icons. They are flat, without depth or vanishing point, and therefore without viewpoint. The object's location in space vis-à-vis the viewer is indeterminate. Imaginatively, the psycho-intellectual definition that makes him an individual is annihilated. Instead of regarding what he sees from a fixed mental distance, the viewer is drawn into contemplation or reverie. With the dissolution of spatial relationship, the entire space-time continuum is undermined, and time also tends to become meaningless. A Russian icon or a medieval stained glass window is timeless in a way that a Vermeer, for example, is not.

On a psychological sliding scale, single perspective is displaced by multiple perspective which is displaced by non-perspective. Single perspective involves the viewer in individual perception of which the proper object is any realistic particular. Multiple perspective evokes collective knowledge or memory and its proper object is the general type. Iconic non-perspective invites the viewer to contemplative reverie. Its proper object is the archetype.

About his poetry, Jones writes, 'I deal almost only with the typic' (to H 9-15 July 1975). As this suggests, his dominant literary mode is the equivalent of multiple perspective. This is true, for example, of *In Parenthesis*, where most characters are types and where multiple viewpoints generate a collective consciousness which corresponds first to that of infantrymen and then, as allusions accumulate and transform subject matter, to what Eliot calls 'the mind of Europe.'

Because poetry is temporal in a way that painting is not, multiple perspective in poetry is more properly called shifting perspective. The cumulative effect is multiple, but the immediate experience is initially of single perspective or of iconic non-perspective. Without changing voices, however, viewpoint often changes as tone changes. Most of *In Parenthesis* and *The Anathemata* is written in editorial omniscience, which is the free verse of points of view and the viewpoint of meditation and daydream. Frequent alternation of tone within editorial omniscience approximates the effect of the multiple-perspective paintings whose angles of refraction are minimal. In all the poems, of course, viewpoint also shifts radically as one voice replaces another. And in both long poems, point of view sometimes loses itself in iconic non-perspective. In the first poem this happens in Dai Greatcoat's boast and the concluding visitation of the Queen of the Woods. In the second poem it happens in the numinous description of Gwenhwyfar in the section entitled 'Mabinog's Liturgy.' Among the poems in *The Sleeping Lord* it happens most strikingly in the description of Arthur in 'The Hunt.'

In strict literary terms there is no such thing as absence of viewpoint. But the effect can be approximated through various literary techniques that resemble the visual techniques Jones uses to neutralize perspective so that his pictures can depict archetypes.

The example of his favourite painter, Pierre Bonnard, encourages him to paint window views. The window frame within the picture frame is a direct assault on perspective. It allows an abrupt juxtaposition of foreground and background that eliminates intervening space and therefore largely circumvents the operation of perspective. Near and far remain distinct but no longer continuous in depth. Their broken spatial relationship is ambiguous and therefore potentially metamorphic because, in the viewer's perception, secondary depicted space can become primary. In terms borrowed from Gestalt psychology, this means that the ordinary figure-ground relationship of painting is reversible, and the foreground can become the ground against which the background figures. We will see that Jones achieves such an inversion in *In Parenthesis*. But the chief effect of the window paintings is a flattening of perspective.

Transparency also has this effect. It transforms space and swallows point of view. Elements in the background that would ordinarily be blocked from view can be seen through objects in the foreground. Perspective is multiplied, therefore, not only across the picture's window plane but in depth. While remaining before the foreground, the viewer is also behind it, at once outside the picture and within it. Jones does not render everything transparent, even in his later paintings. But the effect is of general transparency, owing in part to his increasing use of watercolours, the most transparent medium. Literary allusion, evocation, and connotation achieve an effect similar to visual transparency. Because Jones's poetry is always highly allusive, it is always, in this sense, transparent. Each poem is a layered text-in-depth and, consequently, any interpretation of his poems must involve explication of its allusions. Such explication is rarely mere source study, however, for when Jones alludes to a text it is usually to incorporate in his poem the meaning of that text. He does this to generate what he calls 'association-perceptions' (*E&A* 98), which require comparisons between surface text and allusive subtext.

A corollary of transparency in visual art is the elimination of *chiaroscuro*, which is, like perspective, a Renaissance technique that situates objects in space with reference to something other than themselves, in this case a single source of light. With the elimination of this single source, light shines from or through the object in the picture. Because *chiaroscuro* also models figures, its absence tends to flatten them, rendering them iconic. The freeing of light from shading seems, furthermore, to involve a sort of iconic timelessness. H.S. Ede writes, 'Monet painted his haystack a dozen times, each time from a different light; Jones paints all the lights in the same picture. The Cubists have a variable perspective point. Jones has a variable time point.'[17] This temporal indeterminacy reaches its apex in *Tristan ac Essyllt* (1962, National Museum of Wales), in which the two lovers are depicted on a ship at sea. Jones says, 'I wanted it to be neither light nor dark, not night, not day, but all of one tonality.'[18]

Chiaroscuro subordinates the tonal qualities of colour to gradations of light and dark. The absence of *chiaroscuro* frees these tonal qualities for a greater interplay, which contributes to the effect of iconic immediacy. Tonal values (warm or cool) may be said to radiate temperature and therefore engage the tactile imagination. As recipient of light, the viewer is a sort of temperature-sensitive screen on which the painting is projected and takes place. This complements transparency in its effect on perspective. From two of the painters he most admired, Turner and Bonnard, Jones may have learned to order composition by tonal values instead of the graduated shading of light and dark that gives solidity to mass in his early paintings.

Chiaroscuro has several literary analogues. One is the consistent use of the past tense, which orders narrated time to a narrative future. In Jones's poetry, tense is variable and continually shifts between past and present. This is most noticeable throughout *In Parenthesis* and in 'The Hunt.' Another analogue to *chiaroscuro* is the subjectivity that orders experience to the implied author or narrator. The elimination of *chiaroscuro* has an analogue, therefore, in objectivity or authorial invisibility. In both of Jones's long poems, the implied author and even the implied primary narrator are barely, if at all, defined. Rarely and only briefly does Jones appear in person, like Alfred Hitchcock, as a minor figure in his own work (see *IP* 108, *A* 216). The primary voices of the long poems are not dominant but chameleon-like, which is why the poems modulate easily between soliloquy, objective narration or description, and dramatic monologue. By contrast, the voice in most of the poetry of Yeats, for example, is highly defined. It rhetorically engages the reader and therefore defines the reader's viewpoint. That is partly why readers react personally and so strongly to Yeats and not just to his poetry. The same is true for Pound in the *Cantos*. In literature as in life, Yeats and Pound are ego-filled, the major difference being that Yeats's poetic ego is largely an artefact. The reduction of subjectivity frees poetic tone, which is analogous to visual tone. It varies, therefore, more often and through a greater range in the poetry of Jones than in that of Yeats. It varies a great deal in the *Cantos* too, because Pound employs techniques to neutralize his poetic ego much as Jones uses techniques to neutralize point of view.

In painting, tone ordinarily supports perspective by varying in strength with distance from the viewer; the nearer the object, the stronger its tone. Jones eliminates this gradation by flattening tone to create a field on which tonal variations play with little or no reference to location in space. Often a distant object is stronger in tone than a nearer object. Sometimes this has the realistic justification of back-lighting, which makes a distant object in partial silhouette – a ship against the sea, a tree against the sky – darker than anything closer to the eye. But usually the effect diminishes realism. In any event, the conventional ratio of tone to distance, which complements perspective, is confounded. The effect is metamorphic; the painting seems in the process of turning inside out.

In poetry, the analogues to tonal free play include modulation between lyrical and prosaic language, between narrative and dramatic fictional modes, and between levels of mimetic modality, such as the alternation in the middle and later parts of *In Parenthesis* between realism and myth. Verbal connotation is also involved in changes of tone, as is the ability of unusual language to focus the reader's imagination. In *The Anathemata*, for example, a ship in dangerous waters heads for safe harbour as 'a sky-shaft brights' the shoreward rocks (108) and later during an account of the crucifixion, a 'dark cloud brights the trembling lime-rock' (237). Jones deliberately uses the unusual verb-form 'to strengthen... the archetypal meaning' (*IN* 45). Here verbal echoing also helps to enrich tone, since the repetition of 'brights' implies a symbolic correspondence between haven-finding and the death of Jesus.

Related to tonal free play and likewise contrary to perspective is the separation of line from colour. Usually line and colour combine in a painting to give some objects high definition while others are suggested only by colour or by a hollow linear cartoon. Between these three possibilities are partial combinations and degrees of variation. As Kenneth Clark writes of one of Jones's later pictures, 'The sharpness of focus with which details are seen varies from inch to inch.'[19] Since such variation has very little to do with the distance of an object from the viewer, again perspective is undermined.

In the poetry, an effect similar to this variation in focus involves variation in narrative time or in degrees of descriptive concentration. As a work progresses, degrees of telescoping or summary alternate with zooming forward for detailed close-ups like the slow-motion account of a shell-burst at the end of Part 3 of *In Parenthesis*. The explosion is instantaneous in narrated time but occupies almost a full page of frenetic lyric description. Sometimes there is a real sense of spatial movement in varying descriptive concentration, as in the movement into and out of the cock-thrush simile in 'The Hunt' in which near-microscopic detail implies a myopic visual viewpoint (*SL* 68). (Because it is short and immediately rewarding, 'The Hunt' is probably the best introduction to Jones's poetry.)

As a result of the visual techniques that neutralize perspective and diminish the imitative factor, Jones's later pictures draw the viewer into the iconic range of consciousness where type becomes archetype. If *The Garden Enclosed* does not live up to its title's allusive advertisement, the watercolour *Petra im Rosenhag* certainly does. There sits Petra Gill, virginal enough to sustain the verbal allusion to Renaissance madonnas in rose arbours. With flowers on her dress to match the cut flowers beside her, she is also Flora, goddess of springtime, as Botticelli depicts her in *Primavera*. But that is an allegorical reading. What makes her also symbolically archetypal is the diffusion of light shining through her, and the fractured perspective in which her physical context is depicted, so that she is the only uniform wholeness in the picture. Because she is tonally weaker than her rocking background, she seems to sink back into it, to become part of it, and to calm it. (A very close literary equivalent is the unifying of diverse Celtic factions and personalities by Arthur's godlike presence in 'The Hunt.') Added to this is a facial expression half-way between outward regard and profound inwardness, with a mouth that welcomes and eyes that warn you to keep your distance. The painting captures her in the act of revealing her archetypes. There are two, in paradoxical double exposure – Diana and Flora, virgin and mother. The archetypal identity of an individual is an important factor in Jones's literary portraits – of Gwenhwyfar, for example, and Arthur – but it is first of all important in his painted portraits. He writes about trying to do a picture of Jack Hanson's wife in about 1932:

22 The Shape of Meaning

Petra im Rosenhag (1931)

He reckoned she was jolly beautiful, but I remember I found her jolly hard to draw because I could *not* beat up any real feeling about her, for some reason. I didn't know what she was – Athena, Diana or Persephone or whatever & if you don't know the archetype, how can you draw the type? (to G 5 August 1952)

If he wanted simply to paint archetypes, he could have done away with perspective altogether and painted icons. But he wanted to capture the full range of perceived reality, from individual to archetype. In 1930 Eric Gill writes about Jones, 'What concerns him is the universal thing showing through the particular thing, and as a painter it is this showing through that he endeavours to capture.'[20] He does not want to dispense with material reality any more than he wants merely to render or imitate it. And he wants the viewer to retain some sense of corporate, and sometimes even individual, identity. So he retains perspective, which is perhaps the most powerful of pictorial techniques and is therefore never completely neutralized by the means he uses to counteract it. Everything he does is an attempt to make pictures that achieve the full range of visual modality.

This involves the fullest possible fidelity to the object he depicts, which always includes the physicality of the object. To switch for a moment to poetry, he once told me 'there's something missing' in the poems of Yeats, and when I asked what, he referred to 'the Plato-Aristotle thing.' By this he meant that, unlike Aristotle, Plato and Yeats discount the material world. Similarly, Dante's poetry suffers, Jones thinks, from the fleshlessness of Beatrice (to G 6 April 1973). But if matter is important, it is not everything, for he also sees something missing in the 'yards of "able" paintings of various kinds that seem only seen with the eye of the flesh' (*DGC* 46). There are immaterial aspects of people and things which he believes do not originate in the imagination of the perceiver. With initial reference to his poetry, he writes in 1962:

> It's largely the same over my watercolours. Chaps refer to the 'mystery' or 'subtlety' or 'illusiveness' or 'fragility' or 'waywardness' or 'complexity' or 'fancifulness' etc. etc. – Well, Christ almighty! what else is there in a bunch of flowers or a tree or a landscape or a girl or a sky, but these qualities? By the severest logic one must somehow, if possible, capture *something* of these qualities if the thing is going to be any damn good. It isn't the artist's 'fancy' or 'imagination' that imposes these qualities on a work – the blasted stuff is there as plain as a pikestaff – the bugger of it is

how to 'transubstantiate' these qualities into whatever medium one is using, whether paint or words or whatever. (*DGC* 189)

It is tempting to call these immaterial qualities spiritual and to consider Jones a visionary artist and poet, but these adjectives are not very helpful. A man may be a visionary, but an artist never is, and David Jones once denied being in any sense a mystic (adding, 'I wish to God I were'). In addition to Turner, Ben Nicholson, and Bonnard, the painters he especially admired are El Greco, William Blake, and Samuel Palmer. As men they may have been visionaries – El Greco probably not – but as artists they are all mannerists. Among contemporaries, the painters Jones considered himself closest to are Stanley Spencer and Ben Nicholson.[21] The former a mannerist in the traditional sense, the latter a post-impressionist who becomes increasingly an abstract painter. Post-impressionist art, including that of David Jones, seems to have its roots in European mannerism. Both movements have the distinctive characteristic of distortion.

In 1933 Jones happened on a musical analogue to visual distortion – the early eighteenth-century innovation in the tuning of keyboard instruments called 'equal temperament' tuning. This innovation makes it possible to play in the twenty-four keys in which Bach composes his preludes and fugues. In a letter, Jones transcribes the words of a published lecture in which Bach is imagined saying

'Don't try to put anything exactly in tune; put everything a little out of tune; make the octave consist of twelve exactly equal semitones; we know that's wrong, but we shall get accustomed to it.' Such was his advice, and all the advances of orchestral music since his day have been rendered possible through everything being a little out of tune.[22]

If Jones does something similar in his paintings, he also does it in his poems and for basically the same reason. He wants to maximize the potential of the art form.

In poetry as in painting, this means expanding the range of modality of truth to content. About *The Anathemata* he writes that 'the images used are meant to mean as much as you can make them mean' (*IN* 69). As this suggests, he also wants to prolong the reader's perception and force it to be more actively co-creative. Pictorial distortion achieves these effects by making images play against familiar conceptions and expectations and by making the entire work dynamic. This dynamism

Jones places second only to unity as necessary to good art. About composing his lettered inscriptions, he says that

> most of the corrections and changes are in order to get the unity that is essential in any art work of any sort; also a feeling of movement, for I know of no picture or other art work, if it's any good at all, that has not this feeling of not being stuck still.²³

He admires this sense of movement in the language of Pound's *Cantos* (*IN* 81). He obviously considers it impossible to achieve or sustain within the constraints of conventional prosody. That is partly why he dislikes the poetry of Stephen Spender and is amused at his friend Roy Campbell keeping 'all the rules.' But he is well aware of the dangers of his own 'catch-as-catch-can,' free-verse method of composition. 'Just as in painting,' he writes, 'our old and familiar friend "distortion" has to be infallibly right & requisite to the occasion or it is *worse* than all the academic tediums' (*IN* 50).

There are affinities between the work of David Jones and that of other painters and writers. His visual techniques are not his alone, nor are their literary analogues unique to his poetry. But his poems – like his engravings, his inscriptions, and his later paintings – are distinctively his own and in no essential sense derivative. His combination of literary techniques, while typically modernist, is also original, and this is partly because the greatest influence on his poetry is his visual art. To a large extent he translates painting into poetry, doing with time in his poems what he does with space in his pictures. Yet in achieving the transition to literary art, he doubtless owes a great deal to certain practitioners in that art. In 1961 T.S. Eliot writes in his introduction to *In Parenthesis*:

> The work of David Jones has some affinity with that of James Joyce ... and with the later work of Ezra Pound, and with my own. I stress the affinity, as any possible influence seems to me slight and of no importance. David Jones is a representative of the same literary generation as Joyce and Pound and myself. (viii)

But as Eliot goes on to say, Jones was 'the tardiest to publish,' and this inevitably gives rise to questions of literary influence.

The first things the reader of David Jones's poetry notices are the breadth of its vocabulary and its rich variety of sound. These characteristics place Jones's work in a tradition of modern poetry that begins in the poems of Hopkins, though it has affinity with Keats's verse and roots in the alliterative patterns of Welsh poetry. For his place in this tradition, Jones is not indebted exclusively to Hopkins. Before reading Hopkins for the first time in 1926 or 1927, he read Middle Welsh and later Welsh poetry and, like Hopkins, he read it (with difficulty) in Welsh.[24] Basil Bunting thinks Jones has an advantage over the other modern poets 'in his familiarity with the complicated skills of Welsh poetry, which he never seems to imitate but which yet permeate' his poetry.[25] He also has the further advantage of seeing in the poems of Hopkins how the old Welsh verbal richness can be reproduced in English. Jones said he once talked for several hours with Dylan Thomas about Welsh poetry. It must have been a one-sided conversation, for when I asked how much Dylan Thomas knew about the subject, Jones replied, 'Not much. What he knew he mostly got from Hopkins.' On another occasion Jones told me, 'If you want to know what old Welsh poetry is like, don't read translations, read Hopkins.'

Hopkins is also important for him as someone who liberates poetry from prosody so that meaning instead of convention determines form. In the poetry of Hopkins language is a revelation of 'design, pattern ... *inscape*.'[26] Jones writes in 1949 that Hopkins is 'more interesting to me than almost any poet for centuries ... He really understood what poetry is all about and how it is a made thing with a shape – he really "makes" his poems in a way that can be said of few poets.'[27] Probably more than any other poet, Hopkins influences Jones's own definition of poetry as 'language at a heightened tension' with 'a sense of form and shape, an exact and evocative use of *each* word' (DGC 155). Jones may also owe to the example of Hopkins his use of ellipses, his asyntactical formations, his use of epithets and unorthodox compounds.

Hopkins influences his sense of local or immediate form, the shape made by a phrase, a clause, a series of lines. The poets from whom Jones derives a more extensive sense of form, especially when he is writing *In Parenthesis*, are St John Perse and T.S. Eliot.

I remember Jones saying with reference to Eliot's 1930 translation of *Anabase*, 'If anyone has influenced me in the deepest sense, it's St John Perse.' Jones acquired his copy in 1931, though he may have read the poem in the previous year. It is a series of fragmentary interior monologues chronologically arranged but separated by temporal ellipses. The resemblance between its organization and that of *In Parenthesis* suggests one way in which Perse's poem influences Jones. Even more important, *Anabasis* (the title in English) is devoid of the pervasive equivalence begins to take place as fields of reference break the narrative surface. This happens at the end of the poem's Part 3, in Dai Greatcoat's boast in Part 4, and in the sustained montage of the poem's conclusion, Part 7. In Dai Greatcoat and in the figure of the Queen of the Woods, who moves among the dead, a full reversal of figure and ground occurs as myth subsumes realism. This is a literary equivalence to the inversion in Jones's paintings. The movement inside out from narrative realism to myth takes the poem through the full range of literary modalities. Formally, *In Parenthesis* begins, as it were, as *Ulysses* and ends as *The Waste Land*. Jones maximizes the literary potential of his poem, therefore, just as he maximizes the visual potential of his pictures.

The final part of *In Parenthesis* certainly seems to owe something to *The Waste Land*. In the concluding section of Eliot's poem, montage speeds up, voices speak out of delirium and hallucination, and archetypes become autonomous – Christ on the road to Emmaus, Buddha preaching. Similar things happen in Part 7 of Jones's poem, and even though differences far outweigh them, the similarities are striking.

Eliot is probably the greatest literary influence on David Jones, especially since, after meeting each other about 1930 in Tom Burns's flat in Chelsea, they occasionally met to talk about poetry.[30] Moreover, the example of *The Waste Land* must underlie the greater fragmentation and broken chronology of *The Anathemata*. But by the time David Jones writes his second long poem, Eliot has relinquished his pre-eminence in Jones's estimation to James Joyce.

In 1930 Jones heard and was astonished by the 1929 recording of Joyce reading from *Anna Livia Plurabelle*. Subsequently his Irish friend René Hague read more of *Anna Livia* to him and Jones read the two-shilling 1930 Faber edition. In 1939 he acquired his own copy of this *Fragment of a Work in Progress* – the subtitle of the Faber edition and a phrase that influenced Jones to refer to his own poems from then on as 'fragments.' By this time he also had the recording of Joyce's reading. He memorized the section Joyce reads and used to recite it to himself as he walked by the sea at Sidmouth. 'How good it is,' he writes. 'Authentic, that's what it is ... Like looking at some *natural* beauty, in a way. A bloody sight different to the general bulk of "the English Poets"' (to G 14 April 1939). By the mid-1940s he had thoroughly assimilated at least the *Anna Livia* fragment. This is indicated by the frequent punning in the 'Balaam's Ass' fragment (SL 97–111) and by its anatomical form.[31] It is the most nearly Joycean of his writings.

He said he never read *Ulysses*. If that work influenced *In Parenthesis*, therefore, it did so indirectly, through its influence on *The Waste Land* and owing to the widespread knowledge of how *Ulysses* is written even among people who have not read it. In the twenties and thirties Jones was aware of the pervasive influence of Joyce as someone solving 'in a specially valid manner' the 'problems of an artistic nature which many, many artists find themselves faced with' (*DGC* 174). And during this period, Joyce's reputation was based primarily on *Ulysses*.

It is *Finnegans Wake* that exercises a direct influence on Jones's writing. This is apparent first of all in the use of symbolic personal names throughout *In Parenthesis* and, later, in the catalogues of images and place-names in *The Anathemata* – though, with regard to this aspect of form, the anatomical chapters of *Moby-Dick* may also exert an influence. Jones once said that Melville's novel, which he read twice, had 'a great impact' on him. Joyce's Anna Livia partly accounts for the association of Jones's Lady of the Pool with the city of London and its river, even though Jones's Lady is very unlike Anna Livia. (She is, in fact, more like Molly Bloom.) The overall shape of *Finnegans Wake* may influence the circular shape of *The Anathemata*; Jones writes that his poem 'returns to its beginning' (*A* 33). Like *Finnegans Wake*, *The Anathemata* takes place in the mind and generates its form with the complete freedom that the mind as setting affords. *Finnegans Wake* is in almost constant metamorphosis, with figures and occasions melting into one another without gap or seam. *The Anathemata* consists of fragments that are rhetorically or dramatically more unified and distinct. The difference is owing largely to different fictional occasions: *Finnegans Wake* is a dream; *The Anathemata* modulates between meditation and daydream.

Joyce joined Hopkins in possessing a sense of language that David Jones admired above that of other writers. In his own poems, as in his paintings, Jones seeks 'recession ... undertones & overtones' (to G 23 March 1961). It is in the connotations of words that the layering of *In Parenthesis* and the symbolic associations of the later poetry usually begin. We saw that for Jones the verb 'brights' has 'archetypal meaning.' This is because he knows from having read *The Golden Bough* that the Aryan *Di*, meaning 'bright,' is the root of Greek, Latin, and modern European words for 'divinity.'[32] Connotations arise from etymologies in Hopkins, of course, and in Joyce who, Jones once said, 'gives his words so many facets.' Except to allude to them, however, Jones never imitates Hopkins or Joyce. He seldom puns, seldom invents new words. But in his own way he works language so as 'to lose as little as possible of the overtones & undertones evoked by the words used' (*IN* 24). His '*first requirement*' is that 'the words appear ... to include the various allusions'; his second is that 'they ... have a sound that tallies with, or better still re-inforces, the meanings & feelings both proximate and more remote' (*IN* 38). In addition to this allusive quality and its auditory complement, he wants to achieve a richness of texture that is perhaps best illustrated by his expression of disappointment with the flat prose of the New English Bible, which, he writes, is 'rather like being given processed cheese when you have ordered Double Gloucester' (to G 23 March 1961).

The one modern poet with whom he is often compared (I have already done it) but who has no influence on his poetry is Ezra Pound. Before completing *In Parenthesis*, all Jones had read by Pound was *The ABC of Economics* – 'which I approve of,' he said – and *The Spirit of Romance*. He first saw the *Cantos* and began reading them in November of 1952, after *The Anathemata* had been published. He himself was struck by the similarities with his own poem, which he ascribed to 'the common tongue of the Zeitgeist.'³³ In some respects those similarities are owing to a formative influence shared by Jones and Pound.

From very early on, Robert Browning was one of Jones's enthusiasms. His monologues are 'the start of it all,' Jones used to say, because they introduce colloquial speech to poetry. They also achieve objectivity or independence of the poem from the poet. Browning is especially congenial to Jones, furthermore, because Jones is a talented mimic. In his letters he recreates the spoken language of his parents, his maternal grandfather, his English and Welsh uncles, a local parson, military officers, Cockney and Welsh infantrymen, and the Dickensian Cockney sailor-persona of Hamish McLaren's *The Private Opinions of a British Bluejacket*. In 1921, when he stayed with Fr John O'Connor (the prototype of Chesterton's Father Brown), the two of them occasionally discussed 'Bishop Bloughram's Apology,' 'The Bishop Orders his Tomb,' and 'The Grammarian's Funeral.' In the 1930s Jones and his friends used to recall these poems and laugh together 'with pleasure at their form-content' (to G 12 December 1970).

Aside from his use of colloquial language, Browning has little direct influence on the form of *In Parenthesis*. Dai Greatcoat's boast is a dramatic monologue, though unlike anything Browning (or anyone else) has written. Dai is not a realistic persona; he begins to speak as a type and very soon becomes an archetype. Most of the other voices in the poem are not those of specific, dramatized personae. Instead, they constitute a kind of anonymous chorus mediating between soldiers and the reader.

It is only in about 1940 that Browning's dramatic monologues began discernibly to exert an important influence on Jones's poetic form, and then it was a case of Browning to the rescue. After finishing *In Parenthesis*, Jones began to founder in the manuscript material he was struggling with. He needed an equivalent to the organizing gravitational force exerted by his first work's realistic narrative. That poem, he writes, 'was chained to a sequence of events which made it always a straightforward affair whereas this effort is, I fear, about "ideas", the *one* thing I have always disliked in poetry' (*DGC* 86). And about the manuscript of *The Book of Balaam's Ass*, which is nearing completion at this time, he writes, 'It tends to be descriptive in a way that bores me, also rhetorical, my chief fear & danger ... This bloody difficulty of writing about ideas & somehow making them concrete is a bugger to surmount, but I believe it can be done' (to G 19 March 1940). It is significant that the only section of this manuscript he subsequently considered worthy of publication is the 'Balaam's Ass' fragment – a dramatic monologue.

Because a dramatized persona and his auditor situate ideas in 'concrete' reality, the dramatic-monologue form makes possible much of Jones's later poetry. Located in space and time, the monologue's persona is a functional equivalent to chronological narrative sequence. Even if the monologue is interior, so that the persona is his own auditor, his historical setting and psychological integrity preclude authorial subjectivity. They also provide a realistic basis for recession from the individual person to the type or beyond to the archetype.

Browning emerged as an important influence on his poetic form as Jones began to base his writing on recollections of his 1934 visit to Jerusalem, which, he says, lies behind most of his later poetry.[34] The place drew his imagination back to the time of Christ. The remembered soldiers of the British mandate reminded him of Roman soldiers and recalled his own time in the army. By analogy with the experience of the Romans, his military service provided an experienced, and therefore imaginatively secure, entrance to the biblical setting. Thinking of this setting, he probably recalled Browning, who in 'Cleon' and 'Epistle of Karshish' is the only other English author to have done anything like what he was attempting. These poems by Browning are set immediately after the life of Jesus and are spoken by personae unaware of the religious and historical significance of what they say. Jones's Roman monologues intensify the irony by being set, most of them, in Jerusalem at the time of the Passion.

In their movement away from strict dramatic realism, of course, Jones's monologues differ from those of Browning. And his monologues are more transparent to the present than Browning's. The images and language of Jones's Roman poems frequently imply the reader's modern perspective, in allusions to Spengler, for example, and paraphrases of St Paul. In this way Jones may be influenced by Eliot's late experiments with dramatic monologue, though unlike the speaker in 'Journey of the Magi,' for instance, Jones's personae, with the possible exception of the Lady of the Pool in *The Anathemata*, never become transparent to the point of losing credibility as realistic dramatic characters. And unlike monologues by Browning or Eliot, those by Jones are often set within soliloquies or other dramatic monologues. They are to their respective host-poems what the play-within-a-play is to a drama. As the reader regards the literary background, he becomes part of the foreground and does not so much see it or see through it as see from it. Set within larger poems these monologues recall the window paintings in which a landscape is framed by a still life in a way that tends to swallow point of view.

Browning, Hopkins, Eliot, Joyce, and Perse: these are the principal modern literary influences. Jones is also influenced by the free verse and the long line of Walt Whitman.[35] But to be complete, the search for influence would have to reach back through Coleridge and Christopher Smart (favourites of Jones) to the Renaissance and beyond. At such distances it is often difficult to differentiate between direct and indirect influence or to ascribe influence at all. Does he owe the mixing of verse and non-verse in his work partly to Shakespeare's history plays? (Grisewood recalls that when writing *In Parenthesis* Jones was reminded of this aspect of these plays.)[36] How much does he owe to Shakespeare's language and to the powerful colloquial speech and sprung rhythm of another of his favourites, John Skelton? We know Jones considers the chief precedent for his own kind of free verse to be medieval plainchant with its interior rhythms and modal notation.[37] But to what extent do other liturgical forms influence his poetry? He borrows imagery from William Langland and the Pearl poet. Does he borrow anything else? What does he owe to the Anglo-Saxon poems he alludes to, and to the language in which they are written?[38]

And how much does he owe to Welsh poetry? We considered his unusual, verbal use of the adjective 'bright.' Such asyntactical usage may derive from Welsh. Apropos of Hopkins, he writes in a letter to Vernon Watkins, 'that verb-noun thing they go in for in Welsh – and noun-adjective (is it?) seems to have the most valuable... influence on the English speech-form' (17 April 1962). We considered the matter of alliterative language. In the traditional Welsh poems, alliteration proliferates in patterns called *cynghanedd*, a paradigm of ordered variety which is the aural equivalent of visual Celtic interlace. This kind of complex pattern may well – I think probably does – influence the complex symbolic interrelationships that comprise a rhyming of images throughout *The Anathemata*. Jones's basic sense of imagery may also owe something to Welsh poetry. He once said that the early oriental war poetry which Arthur Waley translated is 'like all early poetry, very curt and powerful,' and, to illustrate, he improvised:

> The wind blows. The reeds bend.
> Men go to war. I am not going.
> Blast it! My wound won't let me.

His model is not oriental but an *englyn* in the ninth-century Welsh poem *Claf Abercuawg* which he quotes (in Skene's translation) in *Epoch and Artist*:

> The snow falls, the plain is covered.
> Warriors hasten to battle.
> I go not, my wound will not let me.   (257)

This stanza possesses the sharpness of image and absence of sentimentality that T.E. Hulme, Pound, and the other imagists found in Japanese haiku and in Chinese poetry and introduced to modern poetry.

Almost as important as Welsh poetry for Jones, and related to it in his mind, is the poetry of the English metaphysicals. He may have become aware of them through Eliot's famous essay, 'The Metaphysical Poets' (1921); he probably discussed them with Eliot in the thirties. He mentions them frequently in conversation and in correspondence, and in his preface to *The Anathemata* he refers to their wedding of 'widely separated ideas' (17). The distinctive use of incongruous images by these poets seems reflected in the problematic correspondences of *In Parenthesis*: those, for example, between military life and the Christian liturgy, between infantrymen and the knights of medieval romance, and between a battlefield and the imaginary worlds of Lewis Carroll. In *The Anathemata* the incongruities are even more extreme. For example, Christ is symbolized at one point by a hard-drinking Greek sea captain of lecherous reputation and elsewhere by a moving glacier. Always there is some precise point of overlap which sparks a clear insight. The incongruity, which usually delays insight, serves to keep the image independent of what it signifies. This prevents a coalescing of image and 'reality' in which symbolism would revert to metaphor and myth to allegory. The independence maintained by incongruity allows the layers of allusive reference in *In Parenthesis* gradually to equal in force the narrated action. In *The Anathemata* this independence preserves the looseness and sense of motion that David Jones rightly values so much. Whether explicit because of juxtaposition or implied by connotation and allusion, his heterogeneous correspondences block sentimental stock response and preclude conventional moral judgment. They deepen experience and freshen perception of traditional images and concepts by removing the shell of cliché that often obscures archetypes. Because of their incongruity, these correspondences are, in their effects, the literary equivalent to distortion in his pictures.

In his characteristic choice of incongruous images, he may also be influenced, as the metaphysical poets are, by the fifth-century mystical theologian Dionysius the Pseudo-Areopagite. Jones read him around 1928 and again in 1940 and counts him among his own 'formative' influences (*DGC* 188, 104). Dionysius writes about biblical symbols of God. In one of his works, he states that 'the Divine manifestation is twofold — one, indeed, as is natural, representing through likenesses that are similar, and of a sacred character, but the other, through anomalous shapes, fashioning them into entire unlikeness and incongruity.' The latter, he adds, are preferable: 'the dissimilar representations elevate our mind rather than the similar.'[39] That is, they are unlikely to be confused with what they symbolize. The examples Dionysius gives of such incongruous images for God are fragrant ointment, the cornerstone, the lion, the panther, and the worm. He practises his interpretation of symbols in *The Divine Names*, which we know David Jones read (*DGC* 104).

In Jones's mind, the incongruous imagery of the metaphysical poets is part of a continuity that reaches from the startling imagery of the early Welsh poetry attributed to Taliesin forward to the poetry of Hopkins. Partly what suggests this continuity to him is that Traherne, Donne, Herbert, and Vaughan all descend from Welsh families.[40] It is significant that the affinities he sees, which are certainly valid, range across thirteen hundred years and two linguistic traditions. Hopkins, the metaphysical poets, Taliesin, and Dionysius the Pseudo-Areopagite influence David Jones because, like them, he has a profoundly analogical sensibility. He can see resemblances where few others can, and as a result his poetic output constitutes what is probably the most far-ranging intellectual and imaginative synthesis in modern literature.

In considering form, as we have throughout most of this introduction, it is easy to forget about meaning or statement, which is form's complement in what Jones calls 'shape.' In itself, form may be complex or simple; it may be beautiful, but it can only be significant in relation to content. And while a poem's importance necessarily involves considerations of form, it is largely determined by its statement. That is partly why *The Waste Land* is more important than *Paterson*. That is why we know how important *Ulysses* is but we are not sure about *Finnegans Wake*, whose meaning we do not yet fully comprehend.

The rest of this book is about the relation of form to meaning, but leaving aside considerations of form, we can say at the outset that what David Jones has to communicate is important. Just as he refused to follow his contemporaries and friends among visual artists into purely abstract painting, he resists the movement towards autonomous literary works. While certain romantics, symbolists, post-symbolists, and now post-modernists – in their reaction against the increasing positivism and materialism in the modern world – have de-signified language in order to produce literary heterocosms, David Jones refuses to write poetry that is 'purified' of existential, historical, and cultural meaning.[41] No other writer in the English language has tested traditional values as he has in the face of political totalitarianism, technological pragmatism, and modern mechanized warfare. His subject is vast in scope, opening to Europe as a whole and extending beyond the European West to human culture in general. David Jones places what he sees as the crisis of modern civilization in the context of a coherent cultural analysis involving an original combination of aesthetics, metaphysics, and political morality. This analysis may be gleaned from various of his published essays, but he develops and tests it in detail in the poetry.[42] It is mainly this analysis of culture that prompts the American critic and fiction writer Guy Davenport to write in 1982, 'Every so often there comes along a poet or scientist who can realize for us the new configuration, which only our time can see, into which culture seems to be shaped, and the historical processes that shaped it. Jones is one of these.'[43]

In Parenthesis

2

Genre and Technique

In language, modality, and content *In Parenthesis* is so varied that it is difficult to classify. Most of it is printed in run-on lines, though after Part 2 much of it is in free verse. Whether in verse or not, its language almost always approaches the maximum aural and connotative potential of poetry, so that while it does contain prose, the work as a whole should be considered a poem. As a poem it undergoes continual subgeneric metamorphosis. It modulates between the narrative mode, in which events are related in the second or third person; the dramatic mode, in which infantrymen speak or think; the lyrical mode, in which images are vividly perceived, sometimes with subjective intensity; and the associative or allusive mode, in which a personal or cultural past is evoked. In various ways these modalities accommodate and blend into one another so that modulation between them is generally fluid. Even drama and narrative sometimes merge as narration achieves camera-like objectivity or when it combines the second-person pronoun and present tense to approximate consciousness of present action. Content varies with modality, of course, but also, and in an elemental sense, with type of modality. Narrative, dramatic, and lyric modes are mimetic. The sequence of events they convey in *In Parenthesis* is partly documentary – as is attested to in the preface and in the work's concluding claim to the authority of 'the man who was on the field' (187) – and the conveyance is fictional realism. The associative mode blends with the mimetic fictional modes but is expository in direction and reaches beyond mimesis to metafictional meanings. The nonmimetic pole of the associative mode appears in its pure, anatomical form in the poem's notes. Basically the aesthetic of the poem is a Gestalt configuration with a ground of fictional realism and, figuring against it, analogues from general experience and tradition.

The analogues occur within the fictional progression like flashbacks. Their content is the past. But the consciousness that mediates them sometimes passes from the events in the narrative present to a later, meditative present in which the poet attempts 'to appreciate some things, which, at the time of suffering, the flesh was too weak to appraise' (x). In some degree, then, the poem is a postwar meditation as well as a fictional narrative. The poet implies this in his preface when he declares that 'this writing is called "In Parenthesis" because I have written it in a kind of space between' (xv).[1]

Even if an association begins, as it were, in the narrative present, it may involve meditative extrapolation so that, while its content is rooted in the narrative present, the imaginative process grows to include the narrative future. Associations take us into the future, for example, in the lyrical meditation that occurs as the poem's main figure, Private John Ball, gazes at Biez Copse:

> To groves always men come both to their joys and their undoing. Come lightfoot in heart's ease and school-free; walk on a leafy holiday with kindred and kind; come perplexedly with first loves – to tread the tangle frustrated, striking – bruising the green.
> Come on night's fall for ambuscade.
> Find harbour with a remnant.
> Share with the proscribed their unleavened cake.
> Come for sweet princes by malignant interests deprived.
> Wait, wait long for –
> with the broken men, nest with badger and the marten-cat till such time as he come again, crying the waste for his chosen.
> Or come in gathering nuts and may;
> or run want-wit in a shift for the queen's unreason.
> Beat boys-bush for Robin and Bobin.
> Come with Merlin in his madness, for the pity of it; for the young men reaped like green barley,
> for the folly of it.
> Seek a way separate and more strait.
> Keep date with the genius of the place – come with a weapon or effectual branch – and here this winter copse might well be special to Diana's Jack, for none might attempt it, but by perilous bough-plucking. (66)

40 The Shape of Meaning

A striking instance of movement into the narrative future is the evocation of Edward VIII's abdication in the reference to 'sweet princes by malignant interests deprived,' though that is a secondary evocation.[2] More important, the poet articulates what the infantryman doubtless feels at some level but in terms he probably would have been incapable of, at least at the time. In its early drafts this meditation belongs entirely to Private John Ball and is fairly commonplace, but in the process of twenty rewritings the poet takes it over.[3] He does not so much make it his own, however, as objectify it. In its final form the meditation is a sequence of associations ranging respectively through the typical-real (youth on holiday, youth in love) to the vaguely historical to literary romance to myth. This progression resembles on a small scale that through which the poem as a whole passes. Something like this meditation also occurs in Dai Greatcoat's long boast (79–84), which far exceeds in allusive variety what any infantryman, even a Welshman, could have managed spontaneously.

Meditative extrapolation is subtle and in its initial stages barely noticeable. It is usually an expansion of a metaphor or simile. It occurs on a minor scale in the rapid montage of familiar associations that conveys the full physical and emotional experience of being wounded (182–3). In its elemental form, meditative extrapolation takes place when 'a rifle bullet raw snapt like tenuous hide whip by spiteful ostler handled' (42–3). It might be objected that the notion of meditation applies no more to this poem than to any well-crafted literary work. But the poet does sometimes carry the poem in his mind *within* the conventional fiction of the poem, and he sometimes refers to himself in the first person (see, for example, 154). Perhaps the clearest indications of meditative agency – I do not think we can call them authorial intrusions – are the Christmas-morning memory of a night patrol in no-man's-land, which none of the poem's principal figures, who are its narrative reflectors, has yet experienced (70–1); and the parenthetical reference during the concluding assault in 1916 to a story told in 1917 (170). In narrated time as well as narrative time, these are 'flashforwards.'

But associations do not necessarily, or perhaps usually, originate in the narrative future. When, for example, in Part 6 an extended seaside metaphor is used to describe artillery fire falling on the valley of bivouac (140), we may assume we have moved completely into future meditation, but Jones writes that the analogy came into his mind 'at the time ... of the action, July 1916' (to H 24 September 1974). As we move backwards into childhood summer holidays, we move inward, not forward in narrative time. We do not, however, know this from the text. Similarly, many associations involving allusions to Welsh history and tradition, to *Henry v* and to the *Morte D'Arthur*, seem to originate in postwar meditation, but may not. Jones knew a lot about Welsh history and legend before the war.[4] By 1910 he had memorized passages from *Henry v* (DGC 48), and in that year he began to read the Everyman Library edition of Malory (to B 17 October 1971). Jones admits that 'subsequent apprehensions' influenced the poem 'a good bit,' though, he insists, 'the general attitude was not distorted' (to H 7 May 1960). 'True enough,' he writes, 'I not infrequently made explicit what had been implicit, but I was careful to have a foundation, maybe a chance word remembered or a lengthy conversation, or some attitude of mind detectable enough even if not verbally expressed. In fact those "subjective" data were, I should say, more easily remembered than the purely physical or material data.'[5] Malory, *Henry v*, and the Welsh past certainly belong, to some degree, to that remembered 'subjective' data. They must have informed some of the prolonged daydreaming that occupied Private Jones during the long hours of inactivity, which we get a glimpse of in the reverie-filled morning of the poem's Part 4. In specific instances it is impossible, however, to determine the temporal origin of an association and whether, or to what extent, it involves meditative extrapolation.

The fictional time of most associations is indeterminate because their fictional medium is imagination. We know only that we share an analogical awareness active sometime between perception and the conclusion of meditation. This associative ambiguity has its corollary in the alternation in the narrative mode between the past tense, which implies a narrative future, and the present tense. The constant shifting of tenses combines with the temporal indeterminacy of associations to establish the poem's fictional time as the split presence of reverie.

As in most reveries, the poem's narrative or narrated present largely displaces its later, meditative present. This is achieved partly through the dramatic mode, in which soldiers speak in the narrated present. It is also achieved through a lyrical immediacy which locates point of view in the narrated present by making events directly experienced imaginatively, instead of reported as in most conventional narration. During a night march, for example, pools suddenly glimmer and barbed wire glistens (34–5). We are not told, as we are in an early draft, that 'the moon's disk' emerging from behind clouds has this effect. We experience the visual transformation of the landscape and can only infer its cause. Later, tattered canvas falls through the air, and we may assume, but are not told, that a shell has destroyed a stretcher bearing a soldier named Dai (177). We have none of the privileged information that usually separates readers from the fictional participants in narrated action. In this respect, Jones's poem is characteristically modernist.

Whether in the narrated present or in the meditative present, the poem is chiefly anamnesis. Its sense of nowness precludes retrospective emotion and keeps the poem from being – like *The Gododdin*, the sixth-century source of its epigraphs – largely an elegy. The sense of presence also accounts for an emotional objectivity that is missing in much of the literature of war written by combatants. True, such objectivity may be possible for Jones only because he begins to write a decade after the end of the war. But objectivity does not come to those who merely wait; it is an achievement of technique. Technically, the emotional objectivity of the poem is a product not of distance but of the elimination of distance. In this respect, the poem supplies its analogue in its prelude, where the opening of a legendary door causes warriors to be 'conscious of... all the misery that had befallen them, as if it had happened in that very spot.' *In Parenthesis* is charged with feeling – but the nostalgia, anxiety, bitterness, and horror felt at the time of action, not the pity and irony of subsequent reflection.

As we have begun to see, the poem's sense of immediacy is achieved largely in its narration of events. It is on the level of narrative, furthermore, that Jones makes most of his decisions about selection, arrangement, point of view, and tone. In addition to immediacy, the main considerations governing these decisions are the accommodation of analogues and the achievement of a universality of experience to sustain the mythic dimension that these analogues bring to the narrative. The poem is more than a narrative, but as narrative it is a model of technique. Here we come again to the question of genre, or subgenre, but in a dimension that involves matters of content and organization.

In Parenthesis derives from David Jones's experience on the western front during the eight months that culminate in the battle of the Somme. He writes that 'each person and every event are free reflections of people and things remembered, or projected from intimately known possibilities. I have only tried to make a shape in words, using as data the complex of sights, sounds, fears, hopes, apprehensions, smells, things exterior and interior, the landscape and paraphernalia of that singular time and of those particular men' (ix–x). This combination of projection and memory results in the hybrid form of fictionalized chronicle. It is a form involving a generic tension that complements the temporal tensions we have been considering; chronicle corresponds to the narrative future, since it presupposes a future perspective, while the fictional component largely corresponds to narrative presence.

The narrative's relative accuracy in sequence and detail can be gauged by comparison with two books David Jones read while writing the poem. One is *A History of the 38th (Welsh) Division by the G.S.O.S I of the Division*, edited by Lieutenant-Colonel J.E. Munby (London: H. Rees 1920) – a brief history of Jones's division, which he read and annotated in July 1928.[6] The other is Llewelyn Wyn Griffith's *Up to Mametz* (London: Faber and Faber 1931) – a memoir of the period covered in the poem by an officer in the poet's battalion.

On the first of December 1915 Jones's battalion, the 15th Royal Welch Fusiliers (London Welsh), marched from Winnal Down through Southampton and then embarked for Le Havre. On the fifth they arrived at Warne, and after a period of further training they marched down La Bassée road towards the trenches, resting on the way at Riez Bailleul. The dates and place-names are not given, but this is the exact sequence and setting to the end of Part 3. The battalion occupied the area in the Richebourg sector described in Part 4. Part 5 telescopes actual events of the spring and summer of 1916: the first, ominous issuing of metal shrapnel helmets; the 'quite successful raid'; the general alert during an unsuccessful German offensive; the outdoor concert, at which someone really did sing 'Thora'; the long march south to the Somme; an officer's reading of 'the good news' of initial British success – this took place on July first and infantrymen actually were 'permitted to cheer' (*DGC* 72). Also in Part 5 are the night march and reversal of direction that robbed the men of sleep and the subsequent marching that brought them weary into the field of bivouac on July ninth. 'Part 5 has nothing in it,' Jones writes, 'that was not actually experienced.'[7] In Part 6 is the subsequent confused marching around Mametz village which further robbed the battalion of sleep and brought it, exhausted, into battle. In Part 7 is the assault on Mametz Wood on July tenth commencing at 4:15 AM from an immense ditch called Queen's Nullah and, that afternoon, the digging of the trench at map coordinates 'V,Y,O & K.' (The Nullah is still there today and so is the shallow trench in the wood, among other trenches, shell-craters and occasional, still dangerous, unexploded artillery shells.)

To some extent, then, the poem is a chronicle with its scope determined by memory. Of the time leading up to the Somme offensive, Jones writes:

> While that first few months was for me patient of being, so to say, unrolled almost day by day, in 1928, the period from my return to France in Oct.

1916 (after being wounded in July 1916) was much more vague & simply repetitive, even apart from the more wholesale & impersonal, more 'mechanized' nature of the war. It may have been that the earlier bit remained more vivid just as memories of childhood remain vivid, I don't know. But I do know the thing became terribly tedious and repetitive.[8]

He remembered the early period more vividly also because he had already recorded part of it for himself in a diary, which, he says, 'chanced to be blown up in a dug-out along with much else when I was on some fatigue or other (rather luckily) ...' The recording and possibly the rereading of diary entries must have helped to etch events in his memory. After the diary was destroyed, he sometimes made brief entries in 'a pocket-diary or calendar, only three pages of which survived.' These too aided memory:

> One of them was pencilled, 'Blankets taken in – rotten to find none when we came out of line.' I cannot recall the whys and wherefores of this, but I do recall how damned annoyed we were and by the sheerest accident this surviving page of a pocket calendar gave of course the date and, though meagre & unimportant in itself, helped me to recall other matters relating to that period.[9]

He reconstructed parts of specific days which he was eventually able to join together in a fragmentary sequence (to H 9–15 July 1973). Part history, part autobiography, the remembered material gives the poem a documentary dimension that may partly account for Jones's original intention to print it 'in long columns like a newspaper.'[10]

In *David Jones, the Man Who Was on the Field: In Parenthesis as Straight Reporting*, Colin Hughes uses Griffith's book and divisional diaries to chart the events behind the poem.[11] It is a historically valuable account, but has led one literary critic mistakenly to assume that *In Parenthesis* is a 'marvelously exact, even literal record ... of the 15th Battalion's experiences ... down to the most insignificant details ...'[12] Jones's narrative is not strictly accurate. He says himself, 'I have not hesitated to change the chronology when it appeared to serve my purpose.'[13]

There are two important changes in chronology. Jones's battalion spent two weeks, not three (15), training in France, so that his battalion first entered trenches on the night of December nineteenth. In the poem, this is moved to Christmas Eve, so that the first day in trenches is Christmas. The change compresses the action to accommodate more effectively the poem's seasonal and liturgical imagery. The other change in chronology occurs at the end of Part 6 on the afternoon before the assault, when John Ball and some friends watch waves of infantry going forward to attack what must be Mametz Wood: they

> wondered for each long stretched line going so leisurely down the slope and up again, strained eyes to catch last glimpses where the creeping smoke-screen gathered each orderly deployment within itself. (150)

The terrain is right. To reach the wood the assault-force had to cross over five hundred yards of no-man's-land which dropped steeply fifty feet into a valley and then rose for four hundred yards to the edge of the wood. But the time is wrong. The wood was not under attack on the ninth. It had last been assaulted, unsuccessfully, on the seventh, when Jones was not in the vicinity to observe. But he did see what he describes.[14] And the only time he could have done so is the morning of the tenth, during the assault he took part in. From inside Queen's Nullah he could not have seen the first wave (the 16th Battalion RWF) attack the wood, and he recalls that he 'had little or no information of the previous assault' (DGC 225). He could only have seen the lines of walking men as he himself walked toward 'the creeping smoke screen,' which had in fact been laid down that morning. In the poem a description of the sight is placed in the previous afternoon where it becomes an objectively perceived, distant image of things to come and affords no alleviation of the next morning's emotional intensity. In the early drafts, which probably correspond more closely than the later ones to actual memory, there is no assault at the end of Part 6. The poet is certainly being over-careful when he writes in his preface that no 'sequence of events' in the poem is 'historically accurate' (ix), but he is not primarily recording history. He does not intend to write 'a description of the Battle for Mametz Wood, so the sequence of events was not meant to be accurate – but typic' (to Colin Hughes, 24 March 1971).

In other, more autobiographical respects too, the narrative is fictionalized. As the principal narrative reflector, John Ball is the poem's human centre and a focus for Jones's own remembered experiences. But Ball does not merely relive those experiences. On Christmas morning, for instance, Ball's section journeys away from the front line to a nonexistent fatigue duty and then back into the line again. We shall return to the symbolic and structural importance of this journey. Its historical basis is the whole of Jones's battalion marching out of the trenches that morning and proceeding two or three miles up La Bassée road to reserve billets for a few days rest (see A 216; DGC 47). But fictional John Ball is not with his entire battalion, and he and his section do not move down the road but only cross it with 'a toward-home glancing, back down the broken avenue ... To the reserves, to billets ...' (92), and they return to the front line that morning. The difference here between fact and fiction is greater than might be inferred from the poet saying that Part 4 is 'virtually a pretty exact chronicle.'[15]

Later, on the eve of the assault, Ball visits two friends on a grassy knoll. Reggie 'with the Lewis guns' (139) is Reggie Allen – R.A. in the poem's dedication. Olivier is Leslie Poulter. They were Jones's closest friends in the army. Like him they were middle-class, not Cockney. Although the poet describes their conversation in the poem as 'straight reportage,' John Ball takes an active part in it (142), whereas as far as he can recall Jones himself 'said nothing' (to G 15 November 1970).

Even when it is accurate, disguised autobiography is subordinate to fictional intention. At the end of Part 2, for example, the shell-explosion, which Ball experiences in vivid slow motion, is a 'Pandoran' epiphany of 'all unmaking' (24). The poet told me he actually witnessed this explosion as Ball does in the poem. Like Ball, he had just given matches to a lieutenant whom he had failed to address properly as 'sir.' So the ironic contrast between a breach of etiquette and a breach in ontology is remembered, not invented. And after the explosion, he said, the blood-red sap of mangolds really did slobber 'the spotless breech-block' of a nearby artillery piece. The image is remembered but included primarily for its contribution to the antithetical significance of artillery within the poem's fertility motif. The dramatic and symbolic impact of this explosion is partly owing to its being the first one in the poem. But in early drafts, and therefore probably in actual fact, the marching column comes under repeated artillery fire earlier. This historical shellfire was deleted to emphasize the single archetypal shell-burst.

During the subsequent night march into trenches, Ball experiences dream-confusion of obstacles in the route of march with the obstacles of an art class:

> wooden donkeys for the shins of nervous newcomer to the crowded night-class, step over to get your place beside Mirita; it's a winding mile between

47 Genre and Technique

hostile matter from the swing-door, in and out the easel forest in and out barging ... Stepping over Miss Weston's thrown about belongings. (32–3)

As a former art student, Jones had such memories, of course: not from his years at Camberwell Art School but from an after-hours life class he attended in 1914 (and again in 1919) in which 'one just walked in, gave a chap a bob or something, signed the registry (I think), tried to get hold of an easel or at least a stool and started to paint after saying... "Good evening gentlemen, good evening miss"' (to G 24 August 1956). The memory of the chaotic prelude to the making of significant artistic order is recorded primarily to contrast with the current chaotic prelude to further and more inimical chaos.

Similarly, on Christmas morning Germans sing the carol 'Es ist ein' Ros' entsprungen' and the British irreverently counter with 'Casey Jones' (67–8). The singing is an ironic pastoral song contest that heightens the morning's violation of the conventions of classical and Christian pastoralism. The poet told me that on Christmas morning in 1915 the Germans really did sing that carol and the British really did try to drown it out with 'Casey Jones.' These songs are recorded, however, not merely because they are remembered but for the contrast they imply between the symbolic rose and the utilitarian, man-killing machine. They were not, of course, the only songs he heard that morning. In an early draft, the English sing 'Tipperary.' Its replacement by 'Casey Jones' heightens symbolic tension.

During the assault at the end of the poem, Ball's experiences are generally those of the poet, but even here autobiography is to a large degree fictionalized. Jones remembered the 'green-gilled' corporal restoring order (172), and he along with other men was withdrawn to an assigned position. In the poem an officer says, 'I say Calthrop, have a bite of this perfectly good chocolate you can eat the stuff with your beaver up' (173). What the poet actually heard was, 'I say, X, have a bit of this, old man, it's a perfectly good sandwich (or whatever he was offering).' The reference to chocolate comes from a 1918 memory (to H 9–15 July 1973). The Shakespearean echo recalls another occasion, during a barrage, when Leslie Poulter answered Jones's question about the safety of a mutual friend named Harry Cook with the quotation, 'I saw young Harry with his beaver up' (to H 4 March 1974). (At the time, Jones did not recognize the allusion [to H 9–15 July 1973].) The poet does accurately record having heard someone with a very English public-school voice 'shouting rhetorically about remembering your nationality'

(180), but he decides not to record a Welshman's response, '*What nationality?*' (to B 2 July 1971). Like the poet, Ball is wounded in the leg early the next morning after over twenty hours of close combat. And like him, Ball crawls away, reluctantly abandoning his rifle. In the poem, Ball does not, however, share Jones's experience of being helped through the woods by someone until they met an officer named Jack Edwards, who 'commanded, quite rightly... "Put the bugger down, Corporal Davies, – there's a sod of a war on"' (to Hughes 24 March 1971).

John Ball is not synonymous with David Jones even though, in a physical and emotional sense at least, he is the poet's proxy most of the time. Next in importance to Ball are Lieutenant Jenkins and Lance-Corporal Aneirin Lewis. Together these two epitomize the battalion's dual Welsh and English character. More than John Ball, they are fictitious, yet they too have historical counterparts.

If there is a single figure in the poem whose sensibility corresponds to that informing *In Parenthesis*, it is Aneirin Lewis. He is an associative, rather than a narrative, reflector. Even more than Dai Greatcoat, he perceives and meditates fully in the poem's allusive mode. If Ball is a focus for Jones's bodily sensations, Lewis reflects Jones's imaginative life. But Lewis is not modelled on the poet. When I asked him whether Aneirin Lewis, with his thorough knowledge of Welsh tradition, was a real person, Jones answered, 'Yes, as with other characters, a combination of people: he may have been Aneirin Evans and Cadwaladr Lewis.' In his first appearance in the earliest draft of the poem, Lewis is Lance-Corporal Evans. Before reaching its final form, his name changes to Pryce, Evan Hughes, Owain Evans, John Merddyn Johns, and Merddyn Prys-Jones. The last two of these names suggest that the poet was conscious of his affinity with this figure.

Like Lewis, Mr Jenkins represents a combination of prototypes. Jones writes that one of these was 'an attractive man, very absent minded, and also fair-haired like the squire for the Rout of San Romano' to whom he is likened in the poem, but without 'the "elegance" intended to be implied by my choice of the names Piers, Dorian, Isambard.'[16] The prototype of Jenkins is also the prototype of Talbot Rhys – Jenkins's friend in the poem who is killed in the raid in Part 5. (The raid corresponds to an actual raid in which the prototype of Rhys and Jenkins actually was killed.) The other model for Jenkins is an officer who fell during the assault immediately in front of the poet soon after leaving Queen's Nullah and not, like Jenkins in the poem, close to the edge of the wood.[17] In a draft of a letter to John H. Johnston, the poet explains what Jenkins represents: 'I know it's a far cry from Brooke to Graves, but still *in the main* these men, including Sassoon, Blunden etc. are representative of an educated, variously sophisticated, certainly cultivated, more or less upper middle-class, *very* English group of chaps. My "Mr Jenkins" was *very* typic of all that: cultivated, considerate, liberal, humanistic, gallant' (27 April 1962).

The derivation of fictional characters from remembered people is characteristic of the poem and indicates that, while not a chronicle, it nevertheless remains commemorative. In this respect especially, it is conventionally bardic. 'Usually in *IP*, apart from change of name,' Jones writes, 'I have in mind two, or sometimes three, persons, mixing some of the characteristics of one with something typical of the other' (*DGC* 257). But certain figures are based on single prototypes. These include Bomber Mulligan and Runner Meotti, Joe Donkin and Captain Elias.[18] Corporal Watcyn is based on Harry Cook ('with his beaver up'), who was repeatedly promoted for his enthusiasm and demoted for drunkenness.[19] Fr Martin Larkin is based on Fr Daniel Hughes SJ MC, whom Jones first met late in October 1916 after returning from recovery leave to the Boesinghe Sector north of Ypres. Colonel Dell represents Lieutenant-Colonel J.C. Bell, called Dell to preserve the incongruous rhyme, 'Well Bell' (cf 154), which Jones actually heard as he lay face down in the Nullah. (At the age of seventy-six, the poet remembered Bell as 'a lovely old man of about fifty.') Sergeant Snell, he said, 'really was my sergeant – he was terrified, poor thing.' That explains the reference to Snell as 'a windy tripehound' (42) and the snippet of conversation overheard in an estaminet: 'it's the Minnies [*Minnenwerfer*, German trench-mortars] what gets you down – yes, Ducks Bill, same as where old Snell went sick from –' (103) from fright. 'The little Jew' wounded in the Nullah and crying for Debora his bride, offering bearers 'walnut suites ... from Grays Inn Road' (155) commemorates Lazarus Black who, Jones said, 'attached himself to me.' Before the war he had been an antique dealer in Grays Inn Road. He had a wife named Rebecca and four children. Later in the poem Lazarus Cohen also partly commemorates him. The 'fussily efficient' brigade commander known to the men as 'Aunty Bembridge' has his surname, Jones said, from a staff officer, but his personality is based entirely on that of Brigadier L.A.E. Prise-Davies. In *Up to Mametz* Griffith writes, 'his mind was slow ... but tenacious to the point of obstinacy. He spoke slowly, in a prim way – his fellow regular officers called him "Jane"' (124).

There are two figures through whom the poet makes cameo appearances in the poem. In what resembles the depiction of quattrocento painters in their own works, we see for a moment "'79 Jones, in his far corner, rearrange and arrange again a pattern of match-ends' (108). David Jones once said, 'There were three Joneses in my regiment; I was '79 Jones.' The other figure is David Jones not in 1916 but at a later time. Temporarily attached to headquarters as a typist, Private W. Map (127) evokes Walter Map, the medieval Welsh politician attached for a while to Henry II's court, also a sort of headquarters.[20] But the name is also a cryptogram for that of the poet, whose first name was officially Walter and who was assigned to headquarters from September 1917 to March 1918 to draw maps for the battalion intelligence officer. According to the Welsh colloquial practice of calling a man by what he does professionally, Walter David Jones who draws maps would be called 'Walter Map.' The correspondence is clinched by the fictional figure (at headquarters in July 1916) being '79 Map and, like the real '79 Jones, of '6 Pla. "B" Coy' (125). In both instances, the poet seems to be autographing parts of the poem to give them quasi-documentary authority.

Part of technique is knowing what not to include. Jones excludes anecdotes. He himself was an inveterate teller of war stories. In a letter to Harman Grisewood, for example, he writes:

> I remember going on a patrol party early in 1916 to examine Jerry's wire. It was a small party, 4 men including myself, a sergeant & I think a corporal under the command of a Lieutenant Best, for whom I had a liking. He wore a beautiful British Warm & a light Khaki muffler & when we got to the German wire immediately before the glassis [sic] of the front trench where the ground was soggy with mud we had to lie down as low as possible, Best whispered to me (I chanced to be next him), 'Blast this wet mud, I simply loathe putting my chin into the stuff,' and then with great deliberation he drew out from the left-hand cuff of his British Warm a silk handkerchief (purple as far as I could see) and spread it carefully & squarely over the mud & then put his chin & indeed half his face on the handkerchief. (12 January 1974)

The memory of Lieutenant Best's incongruous fastidiousness may account for the surname of Veronica Best at the canteen (4). (In early drafts she is Veronica Smythe.) Jones used to relate how his Colonel, Bell, once caught him carrying on his back half a barn door, which he had taken from a farmhouse:

51 Genre and Technique

As I went, the door got heavier and I got more bent over. Suddenly I saw a pair of spotless boots. 'What are you doing with that door?' 'I'm going to make a fire with it, sir.' 'We pay rent to the French.' It's true, we did pay rent, for the trenches. 'I'm not saying your regiment isn't brave,' he said, enjoying himself very much, 'but you've got a bad reputation for *stealing*! Take it back where you got it.' I did, and found some sticks somewhere instead. The next day the house was blown to buggery.

This farmhouse may be the one whose destruction is foretold at the end of Part 4, but the personal anecdote is not recorded. And there are other anecdotes, about J.C. Bell, Lazarus Black, General Prise-Davies, and about a night patrol Jones was part of, whose members suffered a dangerous attack of nervous giggling within a few feet of an occupied German trench.[21] Nothing like any of this gets into the poem. Such miniature dramas would distract from the larger pattern. You cannot plant little plots in a work that has no plot without the little plots dominating the whole. Anecdotes also round out character, and for reasons we shall consider later Jones wants his characters flat.

Although aspects of commemoration permeate the narrative, the overriding criterion governing selection is tone, particularly the relationship of narrative consciousness to narrated event. Jones consistently ensures that this relationship is immediate, sometimes at the expense of broad historical perspective.

This is evident, for example, in the selective naming of places. While places are not named early in the poem, in mid-poem they are – the Lys River, le Plantin, Croix Barbée, Gorre, Guinchey – because the Richebourg sector is inhabited for many months and fully comprehended imaginatively. Even here, however, meditation mixes with narrative realism, for places are named early in Part 4, before the poem's infantrymen become familiar with the area. From this known landscape the battalion passes in Part 5 through and into virtually unnamed territory as the poem enters a more intense, universal dimension of experience. The field of bivouac in Part 6 was called Happy Valley. Jones knew this but sacrificed the name's tempting irony for anonymity of place.[22] Mametz Wood, which the 15th Battalion attacked, is unnamed and referred to merely as 'the dark wood' (165). Acid Drop Copse, from which German machine guns sprayed the British flank, is called, simply, Acid Copse (168). This, says Jones, is 'so as not to tie it [the battle] down to a particular action' (to H 14 June 1970). The word 'Acid' is retained more for symbolic than documentary reasons. The great summer battle is obviously the Somme offensive, and he indicates this in the preface, but it is not named in the poem – partly, no doubt, because, at the time, common soldiers did not think of their action as 'the Battle of the Somme' but also because the universality of battle experience takes priority over a particular historical event.

A very important decision for immediacy over broad historical perspective involves the waves of men walking 'so leisurely' (150) towards the anonymous wood. The usual and much safer tactic was (and still is) to assault in short rushes between cover. Old Sweat Mulligan refers to this standard procedure (117), and it is used once the men are in the woods (168). But on July tenth, crossing no-man's-land towards the woods, the infantry walked slowly in 'admirable formation / and at the high-port position' (162), four paces between each man, a hundred yards between each line of men. This carefully rehearsed slow walk was especially invented for the Battle of the Somme by General Henry Rawlinson, who believed the new recruits of his Fourth Army would not otherwise keep ranks in a frontal attack on strongly fortified enemy positions. And so line after long line of infantrymen walked slowly into the devastating fire of enemy machine guns. They were, in fact, forbidden to run until within twenty yards of enemy trenches. Seeing them coming so slowly, the Germans thought them mad. The number of British casualties was high, as Jones suggests: one-third of Ball's section reaches the wood, and of his platoon of sixty, only nineteen. But he does not inform us in the poem or in its notes that the lines of walking men are disciplined against their own safety on this occasion only and by their own commanding officer. If he had told us this, he would have generated a bitter irony and gained historical perspective, but at the expense of immediacy and narrative consistency.

A final, all-pervading indication of the poem's relation to chronicle is the language of its dramatic mode. This is Jones's greatest technical achievement, for it is a language invented, not remembered. As he tells us, the speech of the army is Cockney (xii). His infantrymen speak something like it but not the faithfully reproduced Cockney of the poem's early drafts, which recalls the ludicrous colloquial speech of Kipling's verse. While reworking the drafts of the poem, Jones describes the problem he faces:

> The real thing I'm afraid of is this business of Cockney speech. It's the very devil to try & make a *real enduring shape that won't be embarrassing* with

the stuff – dropped 'h's & 'yers' & 'bloody' & all that are *so* difficult. And yet you've got to get across that form of speech somehow because so much of the feeling of the sentences depends on all that. How to make it not *realistic* is the bugger.   (to H 2 December 1935)

An example of undesirable realism is Sergeant Snell's complaint about Mr Jenkins in an early draft of Part 2: 'too damned heasy wiv the men – they take hadvantage.' As the poet works through his handwritten draft foliation, he tones down the Cockney by diminishing orthographical notation of Cockney pronunciation while preserving Cockney syntax, rhythms, and vocabulary.

He also eliminates most of the coarse vocabulary, which pervades the early drafts. As he told William Blissett, its impact in print is greater than in spoken language, especially language in which its use has become conventional.[23] What began, in an early draft, 'Fucking obliged ...' is now 'signally obliged to yer, Jerry-boy' (138). So the most common of Cockney (and soldierly) expletives survives only, encoded, as 'the efficacious word' (53; see 201 n45).

A language that is only suggestive of Cockney sustains intimacy with the reader. For the sake of a closer approximation of the effect of reality, the poet dispenses with strict imitation. As a result of his meticulous adjustments, furthermore, the poem's spoken language is closer than it would otherwise be to the broad middle range of its narrative language. This closeness allows for easy modulation between the coarse, lower-class eloquence of the dramatic mode and the more formally composed styles of the lyric and associative modes. The narrative mode consists, then, of a medial language like the unrealistic middle tone that unifies his paintings by serving as a basis for variation.

In Parenthesis demonstrates both the validity and the limitations of the poet's favourite words of Picasso, that the artist 'does not seek, he finds' (*E&A* 99). The poem is faithful to remembered experience in a way that anticipates modern documentary fiction, which recreates experience. Its dramatic speech has an authenticity reminiscent of the spoken language in Joyce's *Ulysses*, and its descriptive vividness recalls that of Hopkins in his poetry and journals. The physicality of Jones's poem bears out his commitment to an Aristotelian conception of reality. As one of his favourite Welsh proverbs expresses it, 'Truth is the best muse.' But we have also seen that the poem is more radically fictionalized than the conventions of documentary fiction allow.

Its creative fidelity to historical truth helps to establish *In Paren-*

thesis as an epic. In one of the finest essays written on the poem, John H. Johnston convincingly argues that it is an epic.[24] Generically, in this respect, Jones's poem is a rarity. While modern definitions of epic vary, they all concentrate on subject matter, so that non-narrative poems and even novels concerning 'the extensive totality of life' are said to qualify as epics.[25] They may well be 'epic' in that they resemble epics, but subject alone does not a genre make, and, strictly speaking, an epic must first be a long narrative poem. *In Parenthesis* is such a poem, and it also conforms to the various modern, content-oriented definitions of the genre. We have seen that *In Parenthesis* is, in the words of Ezra Pound's definition of an epic, 'a poem including history.' In ensuing chapters we shall see that it also conforms to the following, more exacting criteria. C.M. Bowra defines an epic as a long narrative about important events, especially those of war, which conveys the dignity of man. E.M.W. Tillyard adds that epic must involve a crisis that tests man to the uttermost and must express the feelings or values of a large group of the poet's contemporaries. Within an ordered structure, he continues, it must have 'amplitude, breadth, inclusiveness' — what Northrop Frye calls 'encyclopaedic range of theme,' what Paul Merchant calls a concern with 'a civilization.'[26] In this last respect, the allusive analogues of *In Parenthesis* take it far beyond the quasi-realism of conventional epic, even 'secondary' or 'literary' epic, into imaginative regions that expand the limits of the genre — as all the great epics do. *In Parenthesis* is an epic but also, in large part, a critical anatomy capable of altering western cultural consciousness.

Although the poem's associations may be personal, they are never private in an exclusive sense. And very often they evoke the collective consciousness that is contained in history, literature, folklore, scripture, and liturgy. For the figures in the poem, in varying degrees, and for many readers, associations of this sort involve a cultural buried life and articulate a collective unconscious. Such associations summon to the present the values of a culture or cultures, which are in any event implicated in the present conflict and are therefore at risk. Interrelated associations evoke myths or significant, trans-fictional patterns to which the poem's events conform and which lie at the heart of the identity of the battalion, the British nation, and the western world. Moreover, while cultural associations have an expository, anatomical dimension, they also nearly always provide images that serve as correlatives to emotion — so that, by objectifying them, associations often intensify feelings that belong to the narrative present. In this poem,

55 Genre and Technique

associative bridging inward and backward through collective cultural experience takes the place of conventional exposition, which, in most narratives and dramas interprets realism for the reader.

In his preface, the poet writes that 'at no time did one so much live with a consciousness of the past, the very remote, and the more immediate and trivial past, both superficially and more subtly' (xi). Elsewhere he elaborates:

> My impression is (and was at the time of that war) that there existed a sense of continuity with history in a fashion hard to convey to those who did not experience that particular time ... There was a very widespread, however unspoken or even unconscious or sub-conscious feeling of 're-entering history' or something of that sort. The thing I mean is not at all the Julian Grenfell thing nor the Rupert Brooke thing, though I suppose there are affinities – but it's something far deeper, elusive and very difficult to state. It wasn't 'patriotism,' still less 'jingoism.' It was something more to do with being linked with the whole past.[27]

This linkage receives mythic expression at the centre of the poem in the boast of Dai Greatcoat, who claims to have served in the historical and legendary campaigns he commemorates. He is the mythic personification of the split presence of reverie. The synthesis of past and present is especially strong in the Welsh who, consciously or not, retain an identity rooted in pre-Roman Britain. It is a synthesis captured syntactically in the poet's claim that Welsh soldiers 'are before Caractacus was' (x) – a reference to the son of Cymbeline who fought invading Romans.

Imaginative synthesis in the poem is a product not of historical imagination, which insists on the pastness of the past, but of ritual imagination, which conjures its presence. History allows for continuity, not contemporaneity. To be contemporary, the past must be imagined as present in literature, legend, or myth, or imagined in equivalent terms. Historic time is capable of being so imagined, and therefore of being transformed – though the more distant the time, the more susceptible it is to imaginative transformation. The process involves the mutation of realistic figures and landscapes into romantic or mythic archetypes, which possess psychological value that is innately contemporary. Time prior to the seventeenth century seems especially amenable to such transformation, perhaps because, before then, time was not generally conceived of as purely historical. In any case, it is significant that most of the history to which the poem alludes is mediated through scripture or through literature – Shakespeare's history plays, for example. And, like the *Morte D'Arthur*, most of the literary matrices, while they have historical connotations, are essentially ahistorical. They make possible what Thomas Mann, echoing Freud, calls 'lived myth.' For the most part, the poem's associations are English and Welsh. This reflects the poet's being a Londoner by birth and maternal heritage and his being Welsh by affinity and paternal heritage – a mixed cultural consciousness which corresponds to the racial mixture of his battalion, which was made up of Londoners and Welshmen. Its collective consciousness is the objective justification for the expression of his own binary imagination.

Throughout the poem, associations are activated, as it were, by the presence of figures who serve as associative reflectors. Chief among these is John Ball, who most often justifies the English associations. But the balance between the two cultural traditions is symbolically kept by Mr Jenkins and Lance-Corporal Lewis. One whistles, the other sings – as if to suggest the difference between English culture, which is possessed unconsciously, and Welsh culture, which is deliberately retained and consciously articulated.

English and Welsh cultural associations differ in their significance within the poem. The English associations are more historical and therefore emphasize continuity. The Welsh associations are imaginatively much more powerful and directly illuminate the present. This is evident even in the associations triggered by personal names. Throughout the poem, culturally evocative names comprise a scattered, anatomical list that recalls the past. The English names include those of poets: Wyatt (1); Donne (8); Herbert of Cherbury (127); and Hopkins (172); historical figures: Wat Tyler who, with the original John Ball, led the fourteenth-century Peasants' Revolt (73); and John Hales, who was beheaded by the mob during the Revolt (173); and fictitious characters: Dickens's Dick Swiveller (17) and Job Trotter (110); and Shakespeare's Master Shallow (138), whose garrulousness Jones's Corporal Shallow inherits. Welsh names evoke a very different tradition: Cadwaladr, the last Welsh king to claim lordship over Britain (181; E&A 43); Goronwy ab Heilyn, devoted seneschal to Llywelyn and then to his brother in the last fugitive Welsh court (185; E&A 221); Thomas Cantelupe, Llywelyn's bitter opponent (48); and Adam of Usk, the fifteenth-century chronicler (52).

The full names of Mr Jenkins and Lance-Corporal Lewis are themselves abbreviated anatomical lists. The patronymic of 'Piers Dorian

57 Genre and Technique

Isambard Jenkins' (34) recalls Joseph John Jenkins of London, the Victorian engraver and watercolour painter. Isambard is the name of the great Victorian civil engineer, Isambard Brunel (see A 38). Dorian is the name of the central character of *The Picture of Dorian Gray*.²⁸ And Piers, in modern times an upper-class name, recalls the hero of Langland's *Piers Plowman*, a medieval literary counterpart of Wilde's moral allegory. Mr Jenkins is a 'Mercian dreamer' (35) like Langland and Langland's fictional narrator, each a native of Shropshire in what was ancient Mercia. Similarly with 'Aneirin Merddyn Lewis' (1), who lacks a confirmation name because he is a nonconformist: his first name is that of the sixth-century author of *The Gododdin*; his middle name is that of a Welsh bard (see Triad 87) who became the Merlin of Arthurian romance; his last name is a modern form of Llywelyn, the name of the last native Welsh prince, whose death in December 1282 Aneirin Lewis remembers in December 1915. Like that of Mr Jenkins, Lewis's name is related to his native place. At the end of the poem the mythic Queen of the Woods bestows on his mutilated body 'a rowan sprig, for the glory of Guenedota' – the Gwynedd of his birth, which Llywelyn once ruled.

Jenkins is Anglo-Welsh but psychologically English. His name embodies recent history mostly, though it begins with a medieval echo of which he is probably unaware. In contrast, the native Welshman's name embodies a more ancient tradition, on which he habitually meditates. Each man's name proceeds, as it were, in chronological order, with Jenkins's English forenames picking up where Lewis's Welsh names leave off. The English names connote a cultural amalgam of visual art, technology, literature, and ethics rooted in Christianity. The Welshman's name connotes a culture enriched by poetry, romance, and political calamity.

In so far as the traditions are distinct, there is much more potential for mythic identity in that of Wales. In some respects the traditions are antithetical, since England conquered Wales, but the imaginative power of loss compels a sort of synthesis. The Welsh are obsessed, and the English haunted, by an awareness of the 'lost causes of Western Britain that has given [British] national tradition its distinctive character' (xiii). The centuries-long defeat of the Celts in Britain has its mythic expression in the tradition of Arthur. This tradition is 'the common property of all the inhabitants of Britain' (E&A 216) and comprises its trans-racial cultural inscape (E&A 243). Another mythos common to English and Welsh cultures is Christianity. The traditions of Arthur and Christ are wed in Jones's poetry, as in fact they are in the collective consciousness of the island and the European West. Through allusions to these married traditions, *In Parenthesis* acquires its mythic order and significance.

The reciprocity between narrative realism and the associative mode is facilitated by the narrative's being written to accommodate associations. This involves a sort of narrative self-abnegation for the sake of a larger effect.

An important example of this self-abnegation is flatness of character. The main characters are types. John Ball is inefficient. Little else can be said about him. Because he has no personality to react to, Ball is the poem's Anyman, with whom the reader can thoroughly identify. He does not so much engage the reader as absorb him. The other important characters are equally flat. Mr Jenkins is kind and a daydreamer. Aneirin Lewis remembers his heritage. Flatness of character is true to life, of course; most of us seem two-dimensional even to those who know us fairly well, and flat characters help populate realistic fiction. But, as can be seen in the novels of Dickens, they have a special relationship to their fictional contexts. Flat characters blend into setting and accommodate the symbolism that emerges from setting. In Jones's poem, flat characters serve as associative reflectors to trigger or justify allusions which often have a symbolic effect that rounded characters would eclipse or displace to the periphery of narrative. With reference to psychological displacement, furthermore, type is only one step removed from archetype. More easily than fully developed characters, therefore, types mix with, and correspond to, the archetypes of myth. So the flat characters in the poem facilitate its overall movement from realism to myth.

Flatness of character was not an easy achievement for the poet. In its early drafts the work's central figure is not John Ball but Bobby Saunders – a fairly rounded character by virtue of an elaborate flashback to his Kipling-conditioned, childhood patriotism and his sexual interest in his sister's girlfriend. In the last of six drafts, this flashback fills seven typed foolscap pages. When Jones deleted these pages, he eliminated roundness of characterization. In so doing he also eliminated the potential for tragic feeling, which requires free and consequential action originating in character. In Saunders' case this action was his volunteering for armed service. The deleted material begins with a reference to 'the tricky question of the relative tragedy of Bobby Saunders.'

Economy of characters, such as unifies action in drama, also accommodates the associative mode. The principle of economy governs the poem's revisions, during which, for example, Corporal Quilter absorbs the role of a second corporal named Sprangler. And originally at the end of Part 3 an anonymous Englishman instructs the night sentry, who is not yet Ball but merely the pronominal 'you.' Near the end of the first set of drafts, the instructor becomes Aneirin Lewis speaking in a very Welsh intonation. Like the flattening of characters, their limitation to a half dozen interacting figures frees narrative from the need to sustain and order a complexity of human relationships.

Narrative progression also accommodates the associative mode. There is no plot, no important causation stemming from character. Infantrymen are 'pawns' (165); they do not initiate or control the main action. Events merely happen, but in the process the narrative gathers momentum and emotional resonance. In this regard *In Parenthesis* resembles *The Waste Land*. Jones indicates other literary analogues and possible models when he writes in 1941 that 'the *Morte Darthur* ... gathers depth and drive as it proceeds toward the final disaster, as do few writings, including individualistic works of peculiar genius, such as *Moby-Dick* or *Wuthering Heights*, works famed for this quality' (E&A 248). *In Parenthesis* proceeds at varying speeds, moving most slowly in Part 4 and gaining much of its momentum, because of quick-paced editing, in Part 5, in which an extended allusion is made to that section in Malory where, Jones says, 'the smouldering begins to break flame' (E&A 248). He goes on to suggest that this sort of progression also characterizes the liturgy – a subject we will return to in a later chapter. As the narrative accumulates its 'depth and drive,' it also accumulates associations and analogues. Because they too add up, they do not so much interrupt narrative accumulation as complement it. Plot and the rounded characterization it requires dominate everything else in literary works; because *In Parenthesis* is plotless, association and narration are equal partners in its overall aesthetic. This subgeneric co-ordination is particularly evident in the poem's shape, which is the consummation of technique but which we must postpone considering until we have dealt with the motifs and associations that help determine structure.

The occasion of the poem is its appraisal of war. The juxtaposition of narrated events with cultural analogues is the means of this appraisal. But more than war is appraised. Because of what has been called the 'hermeneutic circle,' interpretation moves in two directions. If cultural tradition interprets war, war forces a reinterpretation of cultural tradition. The lack of attention to this reciprocity by critics has led, in many cases, to inadequate and mistaken readings of *In Parenthesis*. All perception involves what Heidegger calls 'pre-knowing.' Allusive writing is especially dependent on it. But each act of perception alters pre-knowledge, and not only by adding to it. To interpret an allusion in its current context, you must understand its matrix, but by approaching the matrix you necessarily reinterpret it in the light of your tentative understanding of the current context. This means that by evoking tradition Jones calls it into question. He tests its values against the immense calamity and apparent absurdity of modern war. Through an accumulation of allusions, therefore, the whole of western culture eventually becomes the poem's subject in a metamorphic reversal of figure and ground. As Marshall McLuhan once said to me about the title of this poem, 'Parentheses are metamorphic.'

We get our first sustained exposure to the ambiguous relationship of allusive figure and realistic ground at the end of Part 3, as John Ball stands night watch during his first evening in the trenches. What takes place here in the consciousness of the narrator is the cultural counterpart to the artillery shell's physical explosion that opens the day at the end of Part 2. Each is a moment of revelation that transforms human experience. Together they contain in parentheses this first day in the combat zone.

It is dark. Ball looks and listens. Aneirin Lewis is nearby and awake. A picket iron in a flooded shell-hole recalls Arthur's sword sinking into the lake. Sleeping infantrymen are compared to the *sidhe* underground and then to Mac Og, a mythic Celtic prototype of Arthur sleeping. Then Aneirin Lewis consciously alludes to 'Kulhwch and Olwen' in *The Mabinogion*, and a Celtic floodgate opens. The narrator refers to the Celtic god of the underworld, and to Arthur's harrowing of the underworld in the ancient Welsh poem *Preiddeu Annwn*, 'The Harrowing of Hades.' He refers then to the hellish antarctic seascape in 'The Rime of the Ancient Mariner' and to Christ's agony in the garden. Then old Adams sings. He is an ex-miner, come from the modern industrial underworld of South Wales to this watery and now myth-charged underworld. Before English Ball falls asleep, the narrator alludes to the Anglo-Saxon poems about the battles of Maldon and Brunanburh, to establish essential continuity and accidental discrepancy.

The entire account of Ball's night watch, most of it in free verse, is riveting in its physical description, which culminates in the unforgettable 'scrut scrut sscrut' of rats in no-man's-land that 'furrit with whiskered snouts the secret parts of us.' The allusions mine both English and Welsh traditions and identify this place with resonance and precision as a hellish underworld. Although the reader does not realize it until the early pages of Part 4, this is Christmas Eve. All the more so, then, the place cries out for redemption of the sort provided by 'Arthur and his men' in *Preiddeu Annwn* who 'went, like our blessed Lord, to harrow hell' (200 n42). Is there a counterpart to Arthur here and now? The corpse-eating rat recalls him. 'By a rule of his nature' he 'saps his amphibious paradise' and therefore does 'redeem the time of our uncharity' (54). This may seem a damning with faint redemption. But, in addition to the rats, a collective counterpart to Arthur may be implied through the allusions to the Celtic *sidhe* and to Mac Og. The latter is, like Arthur, a healer, and his epithet is Oenghus, 'the Young Man.' Like him and like the *sidhe*, most of the infantrymen are sleeping and so, through allusion to these mythic figures, they have a certain corporate affinity with sleeping Arthur. Later in the poem, moreover, infantrymen are compared to 'rodents' (70, 85). Can the infantrymen who contribute to its dereliction bring healing or redemption to this place? Through the human feeling objectified and magnified by the poem's associations, these circumstances and the very landscape cry out. They issue a challenge to the moral and cultural values of the traditions made present here. And the metaphysical juxtaposition of incongruous images provides a literary challenge for the reader. Suddenly, in the night, we are deep in the poem's mythic substrata. Partly because the reader has never, in any work of literature, been anywhere quite like this, it is not a comfortable place to be. No simple set of stock responses, no easy interpretive way out, present themselves.

3

Secular Mythos

'MYTHOS' IS THE WORD in Aristotle that is usually translated as 'plot.' Because the Greek word does not, like its English counterpart, denote causality, we may adopt it as applicable to the overall form of *In Parenthesis*. 'Mythos' also denotes archetypal meaning, and it is in this sense that David Jones uses the word in his own prose, preferring it to 'myth' because 'mythos' lacks any connotation of falsehood. *In Parenthesis* has a sacred mythos and a secular mythos, though the distinction is sometimes blurred because time is the necessary context for intimations of meaning beyond time. Nevertheless, each mythos is generally distinct, and we shall see that the distinction generates a broad dialogical tension. Each mythos consists of interrelated motifs. These motifs have formal significance because here, as in Joyce's *A Portrait of the Artist*, the generation of motifs replaces the development of plot and produces the conceptually musical formal element of theme and variation. Motifs also constitute the meaning of the poem in that they express and imaginatively assess the experience of war. The motifs that comprise the secular mythos do this within the range of direct physical and emotional experience.

These motifs all begin in the narrative realism of the poem's first three parts and continue on that level throughout the rest of the poem, where they open through allusions and associations to the more deeply felt levels of romance and myth. In all of their dimensions, these motifs identify and interpret military experience as either peculiar to warfare or continuous with ordinary life. In either case a continuity is established with the past. Most literature of the First World War asserts the war's discontinuity with the past and the non-military present. Though it has a certain emotional appeal, such discontinuity impoverishes literature. More than any other war poet, David Jones manages to see the horror and destruction of war as part of universal human experience. In this he is also exceptional among modernist writers, for whom the present primarily contrasts with the past. If for Jones war is ultimately mythic, so is the rest of life. And their underlying myths are identical. He implies this when he writes that the poem has its title partly because 'the war itself was a parenthesis' but 'also because our curious type of existence here is altogether in parenthesis' (xv). The difference is that war abbreviates the pattern and intensifies the experience.

The main theme uniting the poem's secular motifs is the degradation of human life. The primary symbol of this degradation is the Waste Land or, as it is called on the title page of Part 4, 'King Pellam's Launde.' The image comprehends the poem's full secular mythos since it is a landscape at once external and internal, social and personal. The human equivalent of the Waste Land in Malory is the Maimed King, a figure repeatedly evoked, in Jones's poem, by wounded and dying soldiers. In early editions, the devastated forward zone is initially humanized by Jones's frontispiece, a drawing of a maimed foot soldier who is tonally at one with the landscape.[1] In his psychological and physical desolation, the infantryman personifies the landscape. His living archetype is Dai Greatcoat, the poem's universal foot soldier, who forces the question which the Maimed King is meant to raise in Malory and which would lead to the restoration of the land.

As invoked in this poem, the image of the Waste Land broadens in its connotations to include the current condition of western civilization. And, even beyond that, it symbolizes human life as it has always been – an experience involving suffering and death, in a 'Vale of Tears' (xii). David Jones lets Mandeville speak for him: 'Of Paradys ne can I not speken propurly I was not there' (xiii). In theological terms – and Jones was convinced of this – life is partly spoiled by original sin. In the poem, the mythic prelude to the fall is Lucifer's unsuccessful rebellion in heaven: 'That caused it,' says Dai Greatcoat, 'that upset the joy-cart' (84).

I said that the poem's motifs are interwoven. The metaphor is appropriate because it implies intermittent disappearances and reappearances of the various thematic strands. It is an image of depth and movement – qualities which probably account for the poet's fondness for wattling wherever he saw it, in baskets, in Welsh weirs, in sheepfolds, in the revetments of French army trenches. He confessed to 'having an apparently innate affection for any kind of plaited or twined thing' (to G 7 July 1971). The themes of *In Parenthesis* are woven through the warp of narrative, sometimes disappearing, sometimes visible below in the allusive substrata. But the pattern, if there is any, is asymmetrical as in Celtic interlace. What follows is a disentangling of strands, all of which run from realism into myth. By separating them, we shall see how they combine to make a multilayered, composite myth which identifies the forward zone as 'a place of enchantment' (x), a word which is – often in Malory, always in *The Mabinogion* – negative. The only benign enchantment in Malory to which the poem alludes is Excalibur rising from the lake, but it is evoked by a 'corkscrew-picket-iron ... by perverse incantation twisted' (50). As Jones, quoting Malory, says in his preface, 'the landscape spoke "with a grimly voice"' (xi).

UTILITY AND GRATUITY

An important aspect of desolation in the poem has to do with a cultural shift in modern times away from gratuitous activity towards functionalism. Jones refers to this shift as a crossing of a rubicon (xiv), 'the Break' (*A* 15), 'the "Positivist" Hegelian turn' (to H 8 June 1966) that characterizes the age. War 'accelerates' this change and therefore epitomizes it (*DG* 133). The poet's perception of this widespread transition rests on a distinction between utility and gratuity. He sees these as antithetical characteristics constituting a fundamental duality in human behaviour. They correlate with Spengler's distinction between civilization and culture. Utility is essential to civilization, gratuity to culture. The purpose of utility is always an effect outside itself, and its sole criterion is efficiency. In contrast, gratuity is intransitive, and its main criterion is delight. A bicycle pedal or screwdriver is essentially utile; a bouquet of flowers or birthday cake is essentially gratuitous. Art is gratuitous because form is 'good in itself' (*DG* 134), and even though the making of art involves technique, it 'is essentially "play"' (*DG* 164). Furthermore, only gratuitous acts or objects can have positive symbolic value, although things made for use may be endowed with significance by gratuitous imagining. John Ball's rifle is an example: he feels so much affection for it that after being wounded he hates to abandon it. But, as the poet writes with reference to mortar fire and aerial bombing, it is 'difficult ... to recognize these creatures of chemicals as true extensions of ourselves, that we may feel for them a native affection, which alone can make them magical for us' (xiv). The distinction between utility and gratuity is the foundation of all Jones's analysis of culture and history and the key to understanding his poetry.

Although it is rooted in ancient and medieval philosophy, this distinction receives its most influential exposition in Kant's aesthetics, from which it passes into post-impressionist art theory, which is where David Jones first encountered it. In 1909 Roger Fry distinguishes between objects created 'for use,' and art, which is made 'not to be used but to be ... enjoyed.'[2] In 1926 he contrasts 'emotions which lead to useful action' with 'feelings which have a high intrinsic value.'[3] Clive Bell makes similar discriminations.[4] The thinking of these Bloomsbury critics was subsequently reinforced by Jones's reading of Jacques Maritain, who also maintains that 'taken in itself' fine art 'is not done to be used as a means, but to be enjoyed as an end.' Its 'mode of being is contemplative.'[5] Here Maritain is indebted to Aquinas's distinction between art and prudence, which derives from Aristotle's distinction between *poiesis* (making) and *praxis* (doing) in an important chapter of the *Nicomachean Ethics* which Jones once urged me to study (6.4–6, 1140a1–1141a14). Clive Bell claims, furthermore, that quite apart from an art work's specific symbolic content its 'significant form' implies 'the essential reality ... which lies behind the appearance of all things,' and Maritain claims that art's 'splendor of form' implies God's 'Creative Intelligence.'[6] This is going farther than many may be prepared to follow. But David Jones writes in 1943 that art is the 'normal "sign" of the existence of absolute values, of "heaven"' (DG 151), first because as 'a thing ... good in itself it must be part of the whole good and that good is clearly not "of this world"' of relative values (DG 134), and second because it reminds man of 'that perfection which is unity.' In this respect, he says, art manages to evade 'the consequences of the "fall"' (DG 156).

Of itself and regardless of its content or object, then, gratuitous activity, and art especially, expresses man's spiritual nature and metaphysical affinities. Because of accelerating technological development in recent times, man has become increasingly pragmatic, and this has resulted in an imbalance or distortion in his character. We are limited more and more by 'our new media' to narrowly utile, merely functional extensions of ourselves' (xiv). In his provocative essay, 'Art in Relation to War,' the poet writes that

> if the situation is such that men can no longer regard what they do as though it possessed this quality of 'art' – then indeed he is of all creatures

most miserable, for he is deprived of the one and only balm available to him, as a worker. 'Good man' he can still be, and heroic may be, but a complete man he cannot be. And that is the kind of deprivation which the conditions of our kind of age seem to impose upon great numbers of people, upon most people. This deprivation is, in the sphere of art, analogous to a sterilization or a castration in the physical sphere. (DG 150)

It is just this deprivation that the forward zone in *In Parenthesis* has in common with the larger Waste Land of modern western civilization. In the modern world, the poet says, no work of art expresses our 'present world-feeling' as well as does 'a bomber plane, or an electric elevator' (DG 137).

Jones began to experience this deprivation in the trenches, especially from the time of the Somme offensive. 'From then onward,' he writes, 'things hardened into a more relentless, mechanical affair ...' (ix). But only after the war did he gain the perspective that allowed him to see this mechanization as part of an 'unprecedented metamorphosis in human society all over the world and at every level' (E&A 173). He was probably helped to this perception by Spengler's judgment that the war itself marks 'a historical change of phase' from a culture with artistic possibility and interior dimension to a hardened civilization of only 'extensive' or 'practical potential.'[7]

In *David Jones Mythmaker* Elizabeth Ward emphasizes the importance to the poem of the dichotomy between utility and gratuity, but – and this seems to me a basic flaw in her discussion of all his poetry – she does not consider the dichotomy valid and so tends to reduce it to its affinity with the 'rural/industrial myth' and 'the cult of primitivism.' She also underestimates the variety of the poem's motifs and discounts the poem's retrospective, meditative dimension when she claims that in the poem warfare tends to become 'a metaphor' for postwar industrial civilization.[8] The cultural change Jones notices is not a postwar phenomenon; it has its beginnings in the Renaissance and was widely recognized throughout Europe by the mid-nineteenth century, though not in the terms of the poet's analysis. The dichotomy that underlies his cultural phenomenology is, of course, profoundly valid and perennially applicable, though the poet was able to articulate it only after the war.

The relationship between utility and gratuity becomes a subject of the poem on page one, when John Ball has his name and number taken for being late for parade. In a small way he is a victim of what Jacques

67 Secular Mythos

Ellul calls social technology. Then Aneirin Lewis quips to Ball, 'there was a man in Bethesda late for the last bloody judgment.' His words involve significant irony, of which Lewis may well be aware, but the remark is primarily a joke deflating Ball's infraction by mock apocalyptic comparison. It 'brings in a manner, baptism, and metaphysical order to the bankruptcy of the occasion' (2).

While they undergo further training in France, the men hear lectures by two officers who further exemplify the difference between gratuity and utility. We may assume that both men are efficient. One is a medical officer lecturing about hygiene who glosses 'his technical discourses with every lewdness' and so balances utility with gratuity. In this respect, the narrator says, his 'heroism and humanity reached toward sanctity' (13). In contrast, a bombing officer speaks 'lightly' of the 'efficiency' of his trade and contrasts the 'supremely satisfactory' Mills Mk IV grenade with earlier 'inefficiencies' (13). His vocabulary may seem appropriate to his topic – though we shall see that it really is not – but he then goes on to use the same language to speak about cricket: 'He took the names of all those men who professed efficiency on the cricket field – more particularly those who claimed to bowl effectively' (13). Here his terms are obviously inappropriate. Cricket is an essentially gratuitous activity, perhaps the quintessentially gratuitous activity, and whatever utility or technique is involved in bowling, it is basically, as Jones insists, an intransitive act:

> Persons at cricket-matches are sometimes heard to exclaim 'Beautiful!' of a ball ... the cricket-fan's exclamation corresponds to a reality. It is an excellent example of the dictum, *Id quod visum placet*. The beauty seen by those who can tolerate this game is an objective beauty which the activity of art has made to shine out under the form of bowling. (E&A 152–3)

When utility excludes gratuity it displaces other values as well. That is why the bombing officer's lecture on the new grenade is, finally, appalling. It is part of a widespread technological hypocrisy that morally justifies the whited-sepulchre image evoked later, when sappers disinter victims of artillery shelling and the narrator comments, 'They bright-whiten all this sepulchre with powdered chloride of lime. It's a perfectly sanitary war' (43). Excessive emphasis on efficiency masks the violation of more important values.

Not that efficiency is bad. It is praised when men 'dyke and drain' trenches (88), and even during a murderous barrage, technology receives its due, for human

> inventions are according to right reason even if you don't approve the end to which they proceed; so that there was rectitude even in this, which the mind perceived at this moment of weakest flesh and all the world shrunken to a point of fear that has affinity I suppose, to that state of deprivation predicate of souls forfeit of their final end, who nevertheless know a good thing when they see it. (154)

The social technique of military life partakes of this utile 'rectitude' and under pressure of combat its 'unlovely order' (27) makes sense, though it remains 'singularly inimical, hateful, to us' (xiii). It is hateful largely because infantrymen are alienated from their labour by what one of them calls the army's 'not-ter-reason-why techniques' (114). Men function quantitatively as replaceable parts in the war machine. For efficiency's sake, numbers replace first names, as with 25o1 Ball at the beginning of the poem. Marching men go 'unchoosingly as part of a mechanism' (19) and resemble puppets whose 'stiff marionette jerking' (37) has suggested dehumanization at least since Stravinsky's *Petrushka*:

> Wired dolls sideway inclining, up and down nodding, fantastic troll-steppers in and out the uncertain cool radiance, amazed crook-back miming, where sudden chemical flare, low flashed between the crazy flats, flood-lit their sack-bodies, hung with rigid properties –
> the drop falls,
> you can only hear their stumbling off, across the dark proscenium. (37)

But dehumanization owing to the demands of corporate efficiency is not peculiar to the army. Soldiers resemble civilians detailed 'to captain Industry' (161):

> You aren't supported as you spend yourself in this blind doubling on your bleedin' tracks by the bright reason for it, they know about back there.
> You know no more than do those hands who squirt cement till siren screams, who are indifferent that they rear an architect's folly; read in the press perhaps the grandeur of the scheme.

Clarence was on that remarkable job.
Dai clickt for that do.
Clarence knows little of the unity for which his hours are docketed –
little more than bleating sheep the market of her fleece.   (87)

What aggravates this fundamental form of alienation is that strict discipline allows for little compensatory gratuity.

The exceptions that prove the rule are the signallers, who know what they are doing and why and are freed by their work from military discipline. Finding and fixing breaks in telephone lines above ground at night, 'they kick tins gratuitously, they go with light hearts' and one of them sings the sexually suggestive music-hall song,

Kitty, Kitty, isn't it a pity
in the City you work so hard
with your 1, 2, 3, 4, 5, and 6, 7, 8 Gerrard.   (47 n31)

(The telephone number is listed here with the exchange at the end.) Signallers sing freely, unlike Aneirin Lewis who can only 'sing low' (42, 45, 53), because of 'the Disciplines of the Wars' (42). Habituated to freedom, signallers are frequently 'warned for Company Office' (47). Ball, too, is so warned but only once (1) because, down in the trenches and in the grip of authority, he learns to obey – unlike these freer men, who 'despise a fenced place' (47).

A measure of the ordinary infantryman's resilient gratuity is the moon. As the men march toward the trenches, the visual effect of moonlight receives a lyric celebration which implies in at least one of these men an appreciation of beauty. Emerging from obscuring clouds, 'she'

... frets their fringes splendid.
A silver hurrying to silver this waste
silver for bolt-shoulders
silver for butt-heel-irons
silver beams search the interstices, play for breech-blocks underneath the counterfeiting bower-sway; make-believe a silver scar with drenched tree-wound; silver-trace a festooned slack; faery-bright a filigree with gooseberries and picket-irons – grace this mauled earth –
transfigure our infirmity –
shine on us.   (34–5)

Inwardly, someone responds with the words of a popular song 'I want you to play with / and the stars as well' (35). Here the moon evokes biblical Wisdom, personified in Proverbs 8:31, which Jones quotes elsewhere in the Knox translation: 'I made play in this world of dust, with the sons of Adam for my play-fellows' (E&A 154). A pragmatic antithesis of lunar Wisdom is Brigadier Bembridge, under whose 'fussily efficient eye' infantrymen chafe and complain (18). Seated on his horse, Aunty Bembridge views his troops from a green which is also occupied by a 'stone shrine in 1870 Gothic.' In an early draft this is specified as a shrine 'of our Lady, Seat of Wisdom.'

Man projects onto the moon his desire to play and to make beauty. Such projection becomes problematic when directed to events of war. An enemy barrage that breaks off a Sunday football game seems to manifest an artistic bent: 'he cuts the painter properly – flames uncontrol over the whole subsector.' But this 'nasty type of flamboyance' is not really gratuitous, like the football game it terminates. And it is only metaphorically artistic, unlike the real, though more chaste, artistry of '79 Jones arranging and rearranging 'a pattern of match-ends' as he waits for the barrage to let up (108). The false art and the true are linked here by the relationship of 'flames' to 'match-ends.'

On the level of strategy, war is an art. The poet argues this convincingly in 'Art in Relation to War,' where he also speaks of the ordinary soldier's 'art' (DG 147). The latter includes the basic tactics of staying alive and perhaps marksmanship. Jones himself was a first-class shot in 1915. His affection for his rifle – and that of John Ball for his – may have to do with its being an instrument of gratuitous expression, in so far as shooting is an art. In the poem the rifle is called 'the Last Reputable Arm' (186). Elsewhere Jones writes that, like the longbow, it was a weapon 'of the individual foot soldier' (to G 21 May 1940). But the end to which the art of shooting is directed in war cancels or complicates any pleasure taken in it. And art that serves a larger pragmatism is compromised. By the end of the war, David Jones ceased to care about it: in 1918 he was rated a third-class shot.[9]

Throughout the poem the contrast between war and art is implied by metaphors in which artillery is compared to band music (108), to a 'show' (111), to an orchestral performance (98). Someone comments on the tremendous British bombardment at the Somme, 'Good show boy ... couldn't beat it at *The Alexandra*' (136). When a candle accidentally goes out, someone says, 'Let it bide – let's keep the auditorium dark like a pukka gaff' (Indian army for 'smart entertainment'). A human audience derives entertainment from what is only accidentally entertaining. The appreciation of accidental form is a valid exercise but here is implies its own peril. This beauty is killing, and is merely the incidental byproduct of a widespread, functional, corporate activity which relegates gratuity to uncreative, private fancy. A soldier must be a dilettante, and his gratuity is more than a little pathetic.

In striking contrast is the poem's only real show, in which Company Sergeant-Major Trotter sings 'Thora.' 'A' Company's concert is less spectacular than artillery fireworks and maybe less beautiful, but in a strict sense, it is artistic. And throughout the amateur concert 'their applause filled the night and the orchard' (110). For a moment, it also fills an ontological void in their collective life.

The imbalance between utility and gratuity involves an imbalance between 'Use and Sign' (*DG* 177ff). Things made or done for themselves come to symbolize one another and sometimes explicitly evoke a spiritual economy that underwrites the other values implied by gratuitous making. This contrast between use and significance is symbolized in the Christmas song contest, in which the song about the technician, 'his orders in his hand,' makes inaudible the religious carol about the symbolic rose. The cancellation of one song by the other is an accident of proximity, of course, but it suggests that the symbolic rose has no chance against the mighty engine Casey rides (68). A similar imbalance occurs when the 'regular discharges' of a nearby artillery piece 'made quite inaudible the careful artistry of the prayers' of an Anglican Sunday service (107).

There are other examples of this fundamental antithesis, of which the most elaborate and symbolically charged is the juxtaposition of two buildings described on facing pages. One is the ruined cemetery chapel west of 'the broken village on the hill' (149). The other, further west, is a German dugout captured in the previous days' fighting (148). Like the chapel, but metaphorically, the dugout is dedicated to a 'God' – Mars, at some level of meaning – and its description establishes a significant correspondence with the ruined Christian chapel. Still in perfect condition, the dugout is an 'awfully well made place engineered deep in the gleaming chalk' with 'white walls,' and the Christian chapel displays 'its engineered masonry' and 'white inner-plaster.' The German gothic 'black script' seen in the dugout matches the 'heavy script' on markers over fresh German graves near the cemetery chapel. The dugout is, as it were, the Christian chapel turned inside out. The graveyard of the chapel is desecrated by artillery so that 'civvy dead' are 'churned and shockt from rest all out-harrowed and higgledy-piggledy' along with the fresher German dead buried there before the British took the village. In contrast to this macabre disorder, the dugout, underground, is quite tidy: 'Everything well done and convenient electric light fittings. Cosy, too, and nothing gimcrack and everything of the best.' Yet 'you felt faint for the noisomeness sweated up from the white walls.' The dugout is another whited sepulchre of military-technological hypocrisy. It tries to hide, and to hide from, the purpose of its neat efficiency. It de-signifies. Even in its original condition, the Christian chapel may have been no more beautiful than the dugout, with its proto-Bauhaus utility, but it differs in its essential revelatory intention. Behind the broken symbol of Christian order are the prayers of 'all the old women in Bavaria' who pray novenas, recite the *Salve regina,* and superstitiously practise sympathetic magic to make life less horrible for young Josef at the front. Nothing is more gratuitous than love, and nothing is more dependent on signs for its expression.

John Ball's Christmas reading of Dunbar's 'Lament for the Makers' (95) must be interpreted only partly with reference to the war. As Jones writes elsewhere, 'the lament for the makers is a world lament, like the weeping for Thamuz' (*DG* 155). And like that weeping, it mourns the wasting of the land.

DISACCOMMODATION

Dehumanization owing to the diminishment of gratuitous, significant life is part of a larger frustration of the desire for accommodation. The realistic symbol of this desire is John Ball's latch-key, whose 'complying lock' is far away in a London suburb. As he searches his pockets for matches for Mr Jenkins, he places the key on the ground, and together they regard it. Ball's carrying it would make better sense if he were among the 'gentlemen of the 6.18 [a commuter train], each with a shining key, like this strayed one in the wilderness' (23). The entire movement of the poem is a leaving home, which begins before the poem opens in 'the unnamable nostalgia of depots' (28). But even at home man is not entirely accommodated.

One reason is class, reflected here in the military hierarchy. Soon after they gaze together at the key, each in his own reverie, Ball fails to call Jenkins 'sir,' a word of address used for persons of higher military rank or social class. Jenkins doesn't mind, or doesn't notice, but Sergeant Snell notices and minds, and subjects Ball to a verbal reprimand. Then the shell explodes, suggesting, among other things, a common peril which renders class distinctions profoundly ridiculous.

We have already seen allusions to the Peasants' Revolt, of which Private John Ball's namesake was the chief fomenter. Private Ball is not himself rebellious, but throughout the poem he and others resent the military caste system, which institutionalizes inequality. Ball first feels this resentment when he is charged for being late for parade: 'a sense of ill-usage pervades him' owing to 'the inequity of those in high places' (2). During the night march into trenches, Ball dreams that a 'Gorilla-sergeant ... claps his hands like black-man-master' to make him jump (32). Later he overhears the 'white-man talk' of officers (155). Awaiting a message at brigade headquarters, Bobby Saunders sees the 'admirable tailoring and ... laundered shirts' of officers and becomes 'conscious of his soiled coat's original meanness of cut and the marks of his servitude' (137). Private Walter Map types orders at headquarters on a hot day while cool drinks are served to officers but not to him:

> That syphon's cool release let drive in him a reflex kick for the prick, and when all's done and said there are an amenity or two making bearable their high stations – that's why their wives have puddings and pies. (127)

And, as the song alluded to continues, that's why the common 'soldiers' wives have sweet fuck-all to fill their empty bellies.'

Officers are 'the slingers' who drink gin slings. They are 'the selected ones – an ecclesia who have special meats – off the Q.M.' (128). During the assault, while ordinary infantrymen long for 'water from a well / rooty and bully for a man on live' ('rooty' is regular army for bread; 'bully' is beef), supply details 'bring meats proper to great lords in harness and: I say Calthrop, have a bite of this perfectly good chocolate ...' (173). The privilege of rank is not much different from the selfish pilfering of Quartermaster-Sergeant Hughes or CSM Tyler, 'who knows how to thrust his flesh-hook and to fill his kettle, cauldron or pot, to make himself fat with the chief offerings' (73). When the routine five days of rest in reserves for front-line fighters is cut short, an infantryman grouses, 'Would you be-bloody-lieve it, chastised wiv / effin scorpiongs' (104). He speaks on behalf of modern Israelites driven almost to rebellion by contemporary Rehoboams (1 Kings 12) whose ease is paid for by the labour of the foot soldier and by his peril.

Officers of higher rank than those who live in the trenches with their men are privileged because they are not often in physical danger. 'That cissy from Brigade,' for example, whose knowledge of the front trenches is outdated by a week (40), is essentially a tourist here. He lives 'where once a day, perhaps, the pickled pilchards jostle the Gentleman's Relish on the top shelf, with the vibration' caused by a long-range heavy shell (92).

Within the lowest ranks the tension between human solidarity and class underlies a double change of heart in Corporal Quilter. Early in the poem, when privates complain of blistered feet, Quilter intones his litany of commands mixed with sarcasm. Then he 'retreats within himself' to his 'private thoughts' (6). When he speaks again, he volunteers to carry Private Saunders' rifle ('thet gas-pipe') and the rifle of another private he calls 'little Benjamin.' This is very uncorporal-like of Quilter. But later the habit of rank again eclipses his charitable humanity when, on fatigue duty, he gives Saunders, who has been sick, 'a dredging-ladle and the heavier pick,' taking the lighter pick himself (91).

Within the lowest rank, class distinctions repeat themselves in miniature as privilege attends specialization. 'Chosen fire-eaters ... co-opted runners ... flank bombers ... born leaders / the top boys ... the hero's grave squad / the Elect / the wooden-cross Dicks ... the White-men with Emergency Archie [the anti-aircraft gun]: all these types are catered for, but they must know exactly how to behave' (125). In contrast to them are the rifle strength

> the essential foot-mob, the platoon wallahs, the small men who permanently are with their sections, who have no qualifications, who look out surprisedly from a confusion of gear, who endure all things.

Essentially servants, they are qualified only for 'bringing up the Toffee Apples [trench-mortar shells] / or to fetch and carry for / the *Sturm Abteilung*' (126).

If Private David Jones felt social inequities during the war, so does the poet in the meditative present. As a member of the middle class, he considers himself 'neither flesh, fowl, or red herring, socially' attached 'to the upper classes' through friends and patrons 'yet with my roots among the lower orders ... whose reactions I have but [sic] for whom I feel a deep understanding at the same time.' And he thinks that his neurosis 'resides a lot in complex maladjustments of the social order. I feel pretty certain of that,' he writes: 'there are a million gradations, but some of us are caught & transfixed in a more obvious fashion between the "ruled" and the "rulers"' (to B 14 September 1940). His own personal

75 Secular Mythos

poverty must have aggravated this social discomfort: 'I must say,' he writes, '"economics" are as important as Marx said – he merely truncated the hierarchy of Being...' (to B 28 August 1940).

In a physical sense, and socially as well if we discount class antagonism, infantrymen are able to accommodate themselves after a fashion, for a time. Where they train for three weeks in France, they 'crowd together in the evening' in a room 'humane with the paraphernalia of any place of common gathering, warm, within small walls' (14). But having made themselves at home here, they find leaving all the more difficult. The afternoon before departure, Bobby Saunders felt 'a certain wistfulness' and even the drill field 'called familiarly to him' (15). On the way into trenches, where they wait in billets for the safety of darkness, they again begin to accommodate themselves, by seeking 'nails and hooks on which to hang their gear' and by arranging, 'as best they might, their allotted flooring,' since 'they would make order, for however brief a time, and in whatever wilderness' (22). And when Ball's platoon arrives at its front-line dugout, they 'sense here near habitation, a folk-life, a people, a culture already developed, already venerated and rooted' into which 'you too are assimilated' (49). Their predecessors had told them this place would be 'cushy – cushy enough' (49), and it is – because deprived of static, spatial accommodation, infantrymen revert to the nomadic, social accommodation of tribal people. That partly explains the poem's Celtic allusions and the evocations of the wandering Israelites in Part 4. But still they sing 'o my, / I want-er go home' (104).

Among other things, Part 4 is an extended demonstration of the soldier's homelessness. It is Christmas day, when men most want to be home. But the only person who has managed to make himself thoroughly and permanently at home in this place is the warden of stores, to whom Ball's fatigue party goes for dredging tools. He is 'seemingly native to the place' (89). Literally, because his legs are 'one whole of trickling ochre' (90), and figuratively too, he is 'knit with the texture of this countryside' (91). Of his storage trove it is said, 'You must have a lumber room where you have habitation' (90). The useless (ie gratuitous) things collected there suggest a personality, and together with his pet dog, Belle, they mediate his humanity. But this sort of domesticity is not available to Ball and his fellows; it is an anachronism. The warden of stores is a relic of the earlier, '"Bairnsfather" war' (ix). His species has been left behind by an accelerating evolution towards an increasingly inhumane kind of warfare. That, presumably, is why he is seen as a 'mandrill' baboon with 'shiny ... hind-parts' and 'aboriginal mask' (91). (Jones plays earlier with Darwinian theory when rats are carrion birds that 'have naturally selected to be un-winged,' [54].) Near the end of Part 4 is a striking symbol of the impossibility of being at home in the generally accepted sense. Behind the lines the sun sets in back of the ruined but still standing family home which artillery will reduce to rubble in the night (96).

For nomads, continuity of fellowship takes over from permanence of place, though there must always be some spatial accommodation. During stints in reserve, men find it in a farmhouse-turned-estaminet. There the man from Rotherhithe misses his neighbourhood pub, called, significantly, *The Paradise* (112). With its makeshift decor and inferior French beer, the estaminet falls far short of his desire, though the montage of conversations here does imply camaraderie.

But even this last-remaining, social aspect of accommodation cannot survive battle. During the assault on the wood, men experience the full meaning of the term 'no-man's-land.' Casualties are so great on this morning that in the wood you can find 'not a soul of your own – which ever way. / No mess-mates at call ...' (171). It is during this battle, near the mid-point of the war, that 'the wholesale slaughter of the later years' begins, which 'knocked the bottom out of the intimate, continuing, domestic life of small contingents of men ...' (ix).

The theme of disaccommodation pervades the poem and involves a number of subordinate motifs. One of them might be called 'childhood's end.' It involves a series of allusions to works by Lewis Carroll, which underline the horror of war, partly by recalling the protected world of childhood. The motif is introduced when Corporal Quilter regards his charges as 'little children' (41; see also 6). It is emphasized when 'you go like a motherless child' (34), when Ball weeps 'like a child' (53), when Watcyn's expression resembles that of 'a small child caught at some bravado in a garden' (167). To quote the title of Part 1 in a late typescript, the infantrymen are 'All Men-children,' as if in conformity with the etymological link between the words 'infantry' and 'infant.' In the estaminet, Alice 'had wondered for these newer ones,' recent recruits who 'drank *citron* ... who would dangle their bonnets' (105). As quasi-children, infantrymen share the vulnerability of Lewis Carroll's child-heroine in stories of which the dominant characteristic is a sense of impending violence.

'She had wondered ...' (105): who can read this about a woman named Alice without thinking of *Alice in Wonderland*? Anonymous in

77 Secular Mythos

early drafts, the proprietress of the estaminet receives her name during a late stage of composition, when the allusions to the Alice books are also introduced.[10] Like Lewis Carroll's heroine, the poem's Alice is argumentative (105, 109). She is an aging matron – as Carroll's heroine would have been by this time if she could have grown old. This makes its own fanciful sense and does not rely for its meaning on the poet's private life, but Jones's reasons for such projection and for making the French woman so motherly probably involve his mother's being named Alice and her having been born, as he thought, in 1854, which makes her a close contemporary of Dodgson's young friend Alice Liddell, who was born in 1852.[11] (Jones's elder sister was also named Alice.) The objective, cultural reason for the maternal aspect of Alice in the poem is probably that the Welsh have traditionally thought of the English as descendants of Vortigern's wife and, therefore, as 'Alice's children.'[12] In any case, the matronly femininity of the proprietress makes her estaminet more homelike.

References in the poem to Lewis Carroll's works occur after the regiment has become acquainted with the French matron. It is as though her name jars loose, from the subconscious, memories from a late-Victorian childhood. On the eve of battle, Ball, Olivier, and Reggie meet to talk 'of ordinary things... of many things' (139). In Malory the words 'they talked of many things' generally indicate a pause in action for the sharing of fellowship (see 10.78, 12.16). So it is here, but the words also recall a famous bit of nonsense verse in *Through the Looking-Glass*:

> 'The time has come,' the Walrus said,
> 'To talk of many things:
> Of shoes – and ships – and sealing wax –
> Of cabbages – and kings –
> And why the sea is boiling hot –
> And whether pigs have wings.'

The evocation involves ominous connotations, since young men before battle have some affinity with the rhyme's young oysters, about to be devoured. On the western front, moreover, pigs do have wings, the 'very latest winged-pigs' discussed at Alice's estaminet, which are trench-mortar projectiles usually called 'Flying Pigs' (214 n20).

Olivier goes on to remark, about the unlikelihood of the cavalry taking part in the assault, 'might as well count on the White Knight or the Great Twin Brothers' (143). He refers to the animated chess piece who rescues Alice from the Red Knight in *Through the Looking-Glass* and to Castor and Pollux in Macaulay's 'The Battle of Lake Regillus.' In the next day's battle no cavalry will ride to the rescue. The allusions to the Alice books might be, for the poet, postwar in origin, but the references to Macaulay here and later (164) originate in his childhood. He first recited passages from *The Lays of Ancient Rome* at about the age of eight, during one of his aunt's Christmas parties 'in, I suppose, 1903' (to G 13 March 1942). And he recited in full armour. He remembers that his white-haired great-uncle Pethybridge, a wealthy mariner's engineer,

> made a shield & sword & helmet of wood covered with some silverish material so that I could recite bits of Macaulay's *Lays* – especially 'The Battle of Lake Regillus' & 'Horatius' – jolly touching to think of in retrospect. But the literary critic of *In Paren.* or *The Ana* would hardly be likely to guess how those carefully made toys played quite a part in forming my earliest affection for 'The great Asylum' ... It's all very odd, but it does show how some impression of childhood makes an indelible mark.   (to G 9 October 1971)

At one point during the composition of *In Parenthesis* he 'toyed with the idea of calling ... Part 7 ... "In Harness on the Right" for the bit about the Great Twin Brethren' who transform calamity into victory for Rome (to G 9 October 1971).

To return to the Alice books, the assault that concludes the poem is a passing through the looking-glass to a world where nothing is predictable. The image is not mine: there really is 'a cunning glass' (65) – 'the mirror' (67, 96) of the periscope through which Ball and every other day-sentry has looked towards the enemy for the past seven months. When they enter no-man's-land on their way to the wood, soldiers advance across an 'undulated board of verdure chequered / bright ...' (165). The place is torn by artillery to resemble the checkerboard plain which Alice traverses and which Tenniel illustrates in chapter 2 of *Through the Looking-Glass*. In itself, of course, the chess metaphor is appropriate for forces facing each other in mirror opposition. 'We lie checkmated,' says someone on fatigue duty, soon after leaving Alice's estaminet (115).

The assault on the wood involves an escalation of the fight between the lion and the unicorn in the nursery rhyme and in Carroll's looking-glass land, where the unicorn harmlessly pierces the lion. At the Somme the roster of weapons includes 'One thousand a hundred and one unicorn horns for a pride of lions' (125). And in the wood, snipers and makers of booby traps have prepared for 'this hour / when unicorns break cover' so that 'the whole woodland rocks where these break their horns' (168).

Farther into the woods and at night, a rising flare reveals to John Ball 'the severed head of '72 Morgan, / its visage grins like the Cheshire cat / and full grimly' (180). This, the only explicit allusion to the first of the Alice books, fulfils Wonderland's constant threat of beheading. After receiving his wound, Ball crawls past two more decapitated men: 'you would believe this flaxen head had for its broken pedestal these bent Silurian shoulders' (184), but Ball realizes that the German head is too fair for shoulders of South Wales. This sort of maiming recalls Tweedledee's asinine understatement to Alice, 'You know ... it's one of the most serious things that can possibly happen to one during a battle – to get one's head cut off.'

The Hunting of the Snark contributes to the description of battle's wonderland by providing as the title of Part 7 'the five unmistakable marks' by which to recognize a genuine Snark. In addition to suggesting the five wounds of Christ, the title implies the imminence of death. If you meet a Snark which is really a Boojum, 'You will softly and suddenly vanish away, / And never be met with again.' Except for *The Hunting of the Snark*, Lewis Carroll's works are frightening but ultimately safe. It is the conventional concession of romance to innocence and vulnerability. Like the Snark poem, *In Parenthesis* breaks the convention.

At a deeper, mythic level of association, war's disaccommodating wonderland is hell. This is established through various lines of allusion. We have already seen references to Celtic mythology and legendary tales that locate infantrymen in the otherworld as Ball stands night watch. The password that night is 'Prickly Pear' (49), which immediately calls to mind Eliot's 'The Hollow Men' and its setting in Acheron on the border of Hades. There, shades waiting to cross into 'death's other Kingdom' chant 'Here we go round the prickly pear / Prickly pear prickly pear.' On night watch Ball repeats in order to remember, 'Prickly Pear / Prickly Pear' (50). Earlier he had wondered whether he and his fellows 'trapse dementedly round phantom mulberry bush' (34). Although 'The Hollow Men' was published in 1925, the allusion does not come entirely from the postwar meditator, as I once suggested it did. David Jones protested that the countersign is not an anachronism since the cactus was known to two men of his battalion, one from Argentina, the other

80 The Shape of Meaning

from Rhodesia, and that one of them – a friend commemorated under the name Dynamite Dawes – used to talk about it. So the allusion is partly a memento for this friend, partly, as Jones says, a suggestion of 'the visual tangle of iron bush that happened to be fairly thick in the bit of front I had in mind,' and only partly an allusion to Eliot's poem.[13] Scriptural and other literary allusions contribute to the definition of the place. The La Bassée road recalls the biblical road to hell. It is 'the broad paved grey way' (16), it is 'wide' (17; cf Matthew 7:13), and it leads to 'the stranger-world... where no man goes' (30). Biez Copse recalls places where men go to 'seek a way separate and more strait' (66), an allusion to Dante's situation at the mouth of hell. And, as 'the dark wood' (165), the place of battle recalls the *selva oscura* through which Dante approaches the inferno and its literary antecedent, the *tenebris nemorum* at the beginning of the descent into Hades in the *Aeneid* (6.238). During the battle, men 'grope... through nether glooms concentrically' (179), recalling the circular movement of the damned in the inferno's first circle. And they move 'forward to the deeper shades,' a word used twice (168, 179) to connote the dead. The word 'shades' recalls the play on *umbrae* in the *Aeneid* (6.257ff) and is reminiscent of the initial entry of infantrymen into 'their prison-house of earth' (92) when they saw 'wraiths' (33, 41). Then the men came to 'a great fixed gulf' (66; cf Luke 16:26). Later they enter hell proper, each by virtue of his rifle's 'bright bough' (183) as Aeneas entered Hades because he bore the golden bough. They advance for the 'harrowing of the woods' (181). *In Parenthesis* contains and gives original expression to the motif of the descent into hell, which characterizes the *Odyssey* and all conventional 'secondary' or 'literary' epics. In the next chapter we will return to this motif, since it involves a pagan rite that informs the poem's underlying ritual pattern.

FRIENDSHIP

A last refuge for authentic human gratuity and the most deeply accommodating mode of social fellowship is friendship. Its importance to men in war is partly a measure of their desperation. In the poem, friendships become intense as men first come within range of enemy machine-gun fire:

> With his first traversing each newly scrutinised his neighbour; this voice of his Jubjub gains each David his Jonathan; his ordeal runs like acid to explore your fine feelings... (42)

81 Secular Mythos

In *The Hunting of the Snark*, when a Jubjub's 'scream, shrill and high, rent the shuddering sky,' the Beaver and the Butcher, who had disliked one another intensely, suddenly became fast friends for life. Empathy is automatic for men in common danger and for whom affection is the only antidote to terror.

There are varying degrees of affection in the poem. The Borderer is friendly who tips Ball to a supply of dry firewood. He evokes from the narrator a retrospective farewell, 'Good night kind comrade' (49) – words from Hopkins's 'The Bugler's First Communion,' a poem about affection for a young soldier which also gives Part 3 its title. Similar kindness is again shown to Ball by an unknown corporal who offers him tea ('Give the poor little sod some char' [75]). And Ball's platoon mates are repeatedly called 'his friends' (70), though he is closest to Olivier and Reggie. His going to these latter on the eve of battle in order to assuage anxiety has affinity with the first friend-making at 'the voice of the Jubjub.' Some relationships are transformed metaphorically by the sublimated erotic intensity of chaste adolescent passion: the

> lighterman with a Norway darling
> from Greenland Stairs
> and two lovers from Ebury Bridge,
> Bates and Coldpepper ... (160-1)

In whatever degree of intensity, during this period of the war 'Roland could find, and, for a reasonable while, enjoy, his Oliver' (ix). And when, as the men go over the top in the assault, 'Roland throws a kiss – they've nabbed his batty for the moppers-up' (160), the medieval epic's celebration of friendship leaps out through the narrative surface. The poem's primary Roland and Oliver types, however, are John Ball and Mr Jenkins.

After being wounded, Ball is thoroughly identified with the dying hero of the *Chanson*. The 'four bright stones' he passes, 'the brown stone' that will not break his rifle, the thought of hiding it beneath his body, the sight of someone 'not of our men' (184–5): all this alludes to Roland's death agony. These allusions are to the translation by his friend René Hague, which Jones saw for the first time in December 1935 (to H 14 December 1935) and on which he based his final reworking of the poem's concluding pages. The allusions here are intended to give romantic depth of feeling to Ball's predicament, which is worsened by his attachment to his rifle. With the 'long auxiliary steel' of its fixed bayonet (156), it is even physically reminiscent of Roland's sword.

More remotely, these allusions associate Ball with Mr Jenkins, who as he dies evokes Oliver in the *Chanson*. Dying, Oliver goes blind and falls first into a kneeling posture and then flat on the ground. Mr Jenkins is leading his men in the assault on the wood (the lanyard here is a cord worn around his neck and attached to his pistol):

> He sinks on one knee
> and now on the other,
> his upper body tilts in rigid inclination
> this way and back;
> weighted lanyard runs out to full tether,
>   swings like a pendulum
>   and the clock run down.
> Lurched over, jerked iron saucer over tilted brow,
> clampt unkindly over lip and chin
> nor no ventaille to this darkening
>   and masked face lifts to grope the air
> and so disconsolate;
> enfeebled fingering at a paltry strap –
> buckle holds,
> holds him blind against the morning.
>   Then stretch still where weeds pattern the chalk predella – where it rises to his wire – and Sergeant T. Quilter takes over. (166)

The deaths of Jenkins and Oliver exist here in a brilliant and original allusive double exposure triggered by Jones's use of the Old French word 'ventaille.' And as Oliver dies beside Roland, Jenkins dies beside Ball.

For the visualization of Oliver dying, Jones relies on the Scott Moncrieff translation, which he used, according to a holograph list of sources, prior to receiving the translation by Hague. The death of Mr Jenkins had gone through extensive revision – fourteen drafts of it survive – and Jones was not inclined to change it to suit Hague's translation, which differs substantially from that of Moncrieff and is less accurate, even though more beautiful and moving. The death of Oliver was a favourite passage of David Jones. About the Hague version of it, he writes in Taplowese, it 'makes you fair howl – slat tears orl right – no hokey pokey' (to H Easter 1936).

The correspondence of Ball and Jenkins to the archetypal friends of the *Chanson* is in various ways suggestive, but its poignancy has to do primarily with the two men not having been friends. They might have been. There has been a match-borrowing informality (23), a certain sympathy (4–5). As we have seen, Jenkins is kind and has an affective nature. His grief at the loss of Talbot Rhys indicates the depth to which he feels friendship. Ball seems attracted to Jenkins when he likens him to the squire in Uccello's 'Rout of San Romano' (2). Jones illuminates the attraction of Jenkins when he writes about the men of whom Jenkins is typic, 'there was often a "wistfulness" about them which was very moving in the best of them' and 'no doubt whatever but that in England in 1915 the young Infantry subaltern was the idol,' the equivalent 'I suppose' of 'the fighter pilot' in the Second World War.[14] In an early draft of the night watch in Part 3, Ball thinks of 'all his platoon mates whom he loved, Mr Jenkins whom he wished he knew better.' But he cannot know Jenkins better, and friendship between them is impossible because it would violate the army's 'convenient hierarchy' (42). The effects of this hierarchy are intimated early on in the upper ranks when

> The Major's horse rubs noses with the horse of the superior officer. Their docked manes brush each, as two friends would meet. The dark horse snorts a little for the pulling at her bridle rein. (5)

Officers of differing rank do fraternize, of course, but difference in rank prohibits intimacy even by their mounts.

During the assault, friends go over together, Bates and Coldpepper, for example, and 'Dynamite Dawes the ole 'un / and Diamond Phelps his batty' (161). They fight side by side, Dawes and Phelps behind the cover of some beech trees (172). But when men are withdrawn to dig in, 'they've left Diamond between the beech boles / and old Dawes blaspheming quietly' (173). Now 'Bates without Coldpepper / digs like a Bunyan muck-raker for his weight of woe' (174). That night the Cockney rhyming slang of china/china plate/mate, as in 'mind the wire, china' (47), informs a visual image in which the white faces of corpses lie blood-stained 'like china saucers tilted run soiling stains half dry, when the moon shines on a scullery-rack' (175). Friends are more fragile even than friendships. They break as easily as china plates. From this battle on, 'companion lives were at such short purchase,' writes the poet, that friendships seldom formed (ix). More than anything else, friendship counterbalances an ordered efficiency and lends some accommodation in the Waste Land, even if it does, in the end, come to grief.

SEX AND DEATH

Friendship also partly compensates for the absence of women, which is an important aspect of the infantryman's deprivation. In personal terms the absurdity of war is felt in the frustration of sexuality. In mythic terms it is expressed as a perversion of sexuality.

Deprived of female company, soldiers yearn for women. On Christmas morning Cockney privates daydream of buxom barrow girls in Southwark Park selling produce at an open-air market in the evening: 'their loves whose burgeoning is finery trickt-out, who go queenly in soiled velveteen, piled puce with the lights' glancing.' Their bosoms repeat curves of the fruit they sell:

> The stall-flares' play defines or shades: in the flecked shadow warm cast half lights trace an ample excellence, strings of penny pearls, and jostled grace:
> ... they're two-a-penny, they're orl ripe, they're fresh as daisies dearie ...
> (69)

Later in the poem the image recurs when, called to carry orders for the offensive, a napping runner dreaming of girls 'waked rosy-cheek / remembering those deep-bosomed – to worry eyes with screwed fists' (128).

In earlier drafts of the poem there was more of this sort of thing. On Christmas morning, Germans 'secret looked at glossy photographs of flaxen-girls hand-coloured, here & there, by Frenchmen, bought in La Bassée, three for half a franc.' This may have been deleted because it violates the poem's range of viewpoints. And near the start of the poem, in the deleted material about Bobby Saunders, is a reverie of underwear and bosom based on Saunders' memories of his older sister's girlfriend and sentimentalized in the manner of the softest of pornography:

> The two girls used to giggle together and only half open the packages when he was in the room – and say he was too young, but she would smile at him, when his sister wasn't looking – and stand so, slightly leaning, her flowered frock like a casement opening on her loveliness ['bosom,' in the earliest draft], about the midst some undulating shadow, across whose deeps and borne up on what precious tide, a strand of ribbon floated, rising, fluttering free, falling, intimately still. She'd got that at Miss Jobbins he's seen some in the window, at least the pink was – only this was blue .... she offered him a toffee.

The poet exercises sound critical judgment when he scrawls 'god!' in the margin and draws a line through this stuff. I quote it here because it

85 Secular Mythos

suggests the roots of the sexual motif and demonstrates a tendency to idealize sex, which manifests itself most powerfully at the end of the poem in the mythical Queen of the Woods.

In the finished poem Jones sometimes idealizes or depersonalizes sex to release its full symbolic potential. The Cockneys remembering their girlfriends on Christmas morning sit 'as men who consider the Nature of Being.' Here the adverbial preposition does not simply introduce a simile; these men do consider Being, in its feminine fullness, its capacity to comfort, to nourish, and to protect. Woman becomes Mother Earth when men cling to the ground and pray, '*Mam*, moder, mother of me ... reduce our dimensional vulnerability to the minimal – / cover the spines of us' (176–7). She is idealized in Dai's boast as Helen Camulodunum, who is 'clement and loving, she's Friday's child, she's loving and giving' (81). In realistic terms, she is remembered as 'Mrs. Curtis-Smythe' in India: upper-class young officers 'fall for her in Poona' (154). And on the level of collective, colloquial imagination, she is 'the Armentieres lady' (108) and lies behind 'Mrs. Thingumajig's patent gas-dispensing flappers' (90). Always, underlying projection of and devotion to the accommodating female, is the universal, private longing shouted out in the estaminet: 'I want Big Willie's luv-ly daughter' (104). Like the idealization of women, the projection of femininity is a means of sublimation which partly relieves sexual frustration and thereby partly discloses it – as when sailors regard ships as female or when musketry instructors commend rifles to the men they train: 'Marry it man! Marry it! / Cherish her, she's your very own' (183).

Conventionally, love's ultimate frustration is death. The antithesis between love and death is sounded throughout the poem in a medley of allusions to folk ballads, which include 'Barbara Allen' (33), 'The Low Low Lands of Holland' (33) and 'The Golden Vanity' (183) – all songs in which death frustrates love. Jones contemplated another allusion to this tradition, for in the spring of 1935 he and Prudence Pelham intended to call Part 7 of the poem 'Poor Jenny is a-weeping on a bright summer's day' (*DGC* 71). Prudence Pelham is the muse of *In Parenthesis*, the unnamed friend he mentions in his preface 'who helped me ... very especially' (xv).

In Part 3, the name Johnny recurs from three different folk songs to form a single leitmotif, which contributes as much to the form of this section as it does to its meaning. Aneirin Lewis and Old Adams sing the Welsh song *Sospan Fach*, about ominous minor calamities beginning with 'little Johnny' being scratched by a cat and concluding with Dai

86 The Shape of Meaning

going off to be a soldier (53 n44). Earlier, men hear someone singing the English folk song in which Johnny's absence worries his sweetheart:

> O dear what can the matter be
> O dear what can the matter be
> O dear what can the matter be
> Johnny's so long at the Fair. (48)

Johnny is missing all right, and not because he has discovered a prettier girl at the fair. The men of the battalion have already passed the unearthed 'bundle-thing' that is his shapeless corpse: 'They've served him barbarously – poor Johnny – you wouldn't desire him, you wouldn't know him for any other' (43). Here the allusion is to the Irish song in which a wife laments her soldier-husband's loss of eyes, arms, and legs: 'Och, Johnny, I hardly knew ye.' The composite ballad of Johnny accompanies the battalion's journey into the trenches. It is played backwards from the discovery of his corpse, to his being missed, to the ill omen he suffers as a child. The various national origins of the songs go a long way toward suggesting that Johnny is typical of the men who make up the British Expeditionary Force.

Later in the poem Harry of Ilkley is chosen for fatigue duty and leaves the estaminet 'without his hat' (114). In dialect he is 'baht'at' like the central figure in the Yorkshire song 'On Ilkley Moor baht'at,' who catches his death of cold. The poem's Harry Earnshaw returns for his service cap, but during his fatigue duty he finds evidence of another poor Johnny as he unearths 'some poor fellow's skull' (115). The allusion to the ballad here primarily identifies Henry (Harry) Earnshaw as a Yorkshireman, but as such he also evokes the Earnshaws of *Wuthering Heights*, a novel about love and death.

In his preface, the poet mentions that for 'old authors ... the embrace of battle seemed one with the embrace of lovers,' and he adds, 'for us it is different' (xv). Different, but still an embrace. The infantryman's full battle dress is called 'bridal clobber' (104). After the waiting, the moment of attack is in some respects like sexual consummation: 'As bridal arranged-paraphernalia gets tumbled – eventually / and the night empties of these relatives / if you wait long time enough' (159). Battle's consummation parodies sexual intercourse and seems a perversion even of death itself. The men of the battalion advance over open ground,

> But sweet sister death has gone debauched today and stalks on this high

ground with strumpet confidence, makes no coy veiling of her appetite but
leers from you to me with all her parts discovered.
 By one and one the line gaps, where her fancy will – howsoever they
may howl for their virginity
she holds them – who impinge less on space
sink limply to a heap ... (162–3)

In this epic personification, Francis of Assisi's 'Sister Bodily Death' has lost her natural chastity.[15] She lives up to ominous premonitions of a lewd, vampirish Geraldine in the poem's earlier allusions to Coleridge's 'Christabel' (120, 130–1). Sex is first inverted and becomes threatening in the opening lines of the poem, when '49 Wyatt is almost late for parade. Quoting Thomas Wyatt's poem about girls coming to his bed, a sergeant sneers at Private Wyatt, 'I'll stalk within yer chamber.'

'Sweet sister death' also incorporates the beloved in the Song of Songs, who is called 'sister' in the manner of ancient Egyptian love poetry. Tired of drill and on his way to the combat zone, John Ball feels that the old metaphor of battle's love-embrace is valid. 'He would hasten to his coal-black love: he would breathe more free for her grimly embrace, and the reality of her' (28). ('Grimly,' meaning 'fierce,' is from Malory.) Like 'old authors,' he anticipates something resembling the biblical archetype who is 'black' and longs for her lover's 'embrace,' but by the time of the battle, no one in the battalion is so naive. Then, instead of looking forward to a metaphorical rendezvous, minds turn elsewhere, to 'a little sister / whose breasts will be as towers' (157). In the Song of Songs someone refers to the beloved as 'a little sister' and she retorts that her 'breasts' are 'like towers' (8:8–10) – so the girl remembered before the assault is someone's sweetheart, an alternative to the metaphorical sexuality of battle and an image of peace and a future he may not live to share.

The sexual theme has its mythic dimension in association with fertility myth. The symbolic correspondence between man and vegetation comes out of Malory, Sir James Frazer, and Jessie Weston, but it also reflects the linked memory of 'wounded trees and wounded men,' which, the poet writes, is 'an abiding image in my mind as a hang-over from the War.'[16] Mediating the correspondence between man and vegetative nature is artillery fire. We first see this when the primal shell-burst spatters the sap of 'a great many mangolds' (24). The name of the vegetable puns on humanity.

In its symbolic relationship to human sexuality, vegetative fertility first takes on perverse cosmic dimensions on Christmas morning 'at the time of Saturnalia' (65), the ancient festival of Saturn, the god of sowing and husbandry. As the last night-sentries watch, the receding darkness uncovers the earth:

> Stealthly, imperceptibly stript back, thinning
> night wraps
> unshrouding, unsheafing –
> ...
>   The flux yields up a measurable body; bleached forms emerge and stand.
>   Where their faces turned, grey wealed earth bared almost of last clung weeds of night-weft –
> ...
>   Her fractured contours dun where soon his ray would show more clear her dereliction. (59)

Here the image of waking from sleep merges with that of death. Morning's uncovering is an 'unshrouding,' with 'brume' continuing to 'shroud' the earth's low places (62). (The word 'brume' for mist evokes the Saturnalia because it derives from the Latin *bruma*, meaning the year's shortest day at the winter solstice.) Here 'morning' evokes its homonym.

The earth's proper consort is the sun, which Milton in his Nativity hymn calls 'her lusty Paramour' and which rises on this morning as 'the bright healer' (62) identified, therefore, with the healer Apollo, whose Celtic counterpart is Mac Og. (We have seen the latter as a mythic counterpart to the infantrymen.) On this Saturnalia, Mother Earth has certainly received sexual attention, but not from the sun. She has been raped, continually and sadistically, for her body, uncovered, is 'wealed,' or marked with ridges raised on flesh by a striking lash or rod. No longer a beauty, she sleeps the sleep of death, 'the cratered earth, of all growing things bereaved' (97). In the evening her illicit and cruel oppressor returns, not Apollo and not Saturn but necrophiliac Mars – originally a god of vegetative fertility (see A 176 n2) but now a life-destroyer. With the intense antiphonal artillery exchange that concludes Part 4, he treats her body again to his grim and deadly intercourse.

The cosmic copulation of fertility myth is the paradigm of a ritual commemorated in a folk tale to which the poem also alludes on this morning. After the unshrouding of Mother Earth and as he awakens sleeping infantrymen, Sergeant Snell consciously mimics the hero of the tale, the title of which he obliquely alludes to when he calls the men 'slumberin' lovelies':

89 Secular Mythos

Prince Charming presents his compliments. Who's this John Moores in his
martial cloak – get off it, wontcher – come away counterfeiting death –
cantcher – hear the bird o' dawnin' – roll up – it's tomorrow alright.
  Sergeant Charming's through your thorny slumbers, who bends over
sweet Robin's rose cheek.
...
  Whose toe porrects the ritual instrument to
  break the spell to
  resurrect the traverses.   (60)

Spellbound sleepers wake to kicks, not kisses. One of them greets his waker in the spirit of the poet's joke: 'Morning sergeant – kiss me sergeant.' The words combine an evocation of the fairy tale with a no doubt conscious allusion, on the speaker's part, to Nelson's dying words, 'Kiss me, Hardy.' The sardonic greeting combines sex and death, but here sex is the metaphor and death the impending reality. The image of the fairy-tale prince making his way through the tale's thorny barrier is echoed later as the assault force penetrates the enemy's barbed-wire defences, and 'you stretch out hands to pluck at Jerry wire as if it were bramble mesh' (166) where, in fact, 'iron warp' is 'with bramble weft' and there is 'cork-screw stapled trip-wire / to snare among the briars' (165). In war's loveless fairy tale, 'secret princes' (185) perform a parody of fertility ritual's sexual disenchanting; instead of marriage, men enter battle, with death for coitus.

  Their awakening this Christmas morning has only accidental affinity with Sleeping Beauty's symbolic awakening from death. Sergeant Snell tells them to toss off the cloak in which John Moore is buried in Charles Wolfe's famous poem, and he proceeds to 'resurrect the traverses.' Snell knows, and the poet implies by referring to the 'dry bones' of Ezekiel 37, that sleep is an image of death. But in the passage quoted above, the death image is further associated with a lovelessness that precludes death's fairy-tale reversal. Twice this involves evocations of Shakespeare. The sergeant bending 'over sweet Robin's rose cheek' recalls Ophelia's song of love frustrated by death (*Hamlet* 4.6.189–94), and Snell urging them to 'come away counterfeiting death' recalls Feste's song about a young man dying of unrequited love (*Twelfth Night* 2.4.51–66). Connotations of death as love's frustration deepen the irony of the fairy-tale charade by introducing the Renaissance play on sleep and dying, dying and coitus. The special currency of these metaphors during the Renaissance partly accounts for the Shakespearean allusions here. Death's triple meaning also lies behind the conclusion of the account of the waking:

> With unfathomed passion – this stark stir and waking – contort the
> comic mask of these tragic japers. (60)

A more compact and highly charged sentence would be difficult to find. Here, complementing the allusions to drama, is the iconographic mask of comedy, but the truth is tragic. If 'passion' denotes sexual feeling, it also expresses extreme suffering, two meanings here not mutually exclusive. And if a japer is a joker ('Kiss me, sergeant'), he is also one who does, or would like to, copulate.

Instead of restoring the Waste Land, infantrymen come to personify it by conforming to the archetype of the Maimed King and to the underlying archetype of the vegetation god Adonis. The latter was gored by the war god Ares in the form of a boar and bled to death in Aphrodite's arms. One such Adonis bleeds to death in John Ball's arms. He 'gets it in the middle body' (174). (In an early draft, he 'screamed with one in the groin.') And before that, another man's name becomes a dreadful Bunyanesque pun evoking the Malorian myth:

> Wastebottom married a wife on his Draft-leave but the whinnying splinter razored diagonal and mess-tin fragments drove inward and toxined underwear. (157–8)

The words 'married a wife' are charged with connotation, for they evoke the scriptural excuse for absence (cf Luke 14:20), particularly for the absence of a husband from war 'lest he die in battle' (Deuteronomy 20:7). Even the realism of 'the little Jew,' wounded and crying 'for Deborah his bride,' evokes the mythic antithesis of sex and death (155). And Mr Jenkins's death deprives his 'precious' (35) – in an early draft, 'the lovely darling' – of his love. The unmaking of the foot-mob at the Somme is emasculation carried to its ultimate extent, 'a first clarst bollocks' (138) in which casualties experience 'dismembering, and deep-bowelled damage' (162). They must endure 'the Dolorous Stroke' (162), which maims the king and wastes the land. It is an archetypal calamity going back almost to the Fall, for it is as old as brotherhood. Dead infantrymen symbolically correspond to Abel,

> Who under the green tree
> had awareness of his dismembering, and deep-bowelled damage; for whom the green tree bore scarlet memorial, and herb and arborage waste. (162)

Malory writes that the tree under which Abel died 'lost the green colour and became red; and that was in tokening of blood' (17.5). The second man born is an Adonis whose blood reddens vegetation. This is the first death, the first undoing of sex.

NATURAL ORDER

Closely related to the poem's fertility imagery and in symbolic antithesis to war's chaos are various images of ordered nature. All of these presuppose a sensitivity to form, in soldiers or in the reader, that opens towards a transcendent order and thereby enlarges the context in which war is assessed. This context is a continuous natural and supernatural order which supplies models of a peaceful society and also, through allusions to *The Rime of the Ancient Mariner*, presents a paradigm of inward conversion.

Like fertility myth, natural order is most evident throughout the poem in its military perversions. Here too the focus is on artillery. Heavy cannon are imitation trees (35, 141) and produce metaphorical flowers (111) — as though artillery could replace what it destroys. Most often shellfire is associated with rain. Both fall from the sky, both are accompanied at night by 'summer lightnings' (120), and the noise of a barrage is thunder to its rain of shells. Throughout the poem, moreover, shells and rain very often fall together (see, for example, 85, 147). During the assault, the counterbarrage is called, simply, 'the storm' (177, 179). This is something-less-than-art imitating nature. Metaphorically, it is the cosmic sexual perversion we have been considering, since rain is the cosmic intercourse of Sky Father with Mother Earth.

Twice artillery fire is associated with bees, which, like rain, contribute to vegetable fertility. While the battalion is en route to the Richebourg trenches but still many miles away, 'there seemed in the whole air above ... a strong droning, as if a million bees were hiving to the stars' (20). Bees and the sound of artillery are juxtaposed again seven months later as Privates Ball and Thomas observe a French priest reciting his breviary in a presbytery garden 'where ... bees hived, between low plants' (118). With a change in the direction of the wind, the sound of distant artillery mingles 'with the drone of bees' (117). Nature's bees signify order and contribute to the fertility of beanstalks in their 'vegetable beds' (117), and they thereby contrast with the explosive bees of Mars that destroy vegetable life and the lives of men.

The mythic antithesis between artillery and nature acquires a Welsh dimension through allusions to 'Kulhwch and Olwen,' the Welsh rendition of the Waste-Land myth. In Jones's poem, artillery is identified with the Welsh tale's Twrch Trwyth or Great Boar (86, 155), which wastes the land and kills its inhabitants. Only when it is driven off can marriage take place between Kulhwch and Olwen, the latter a nature-figure, since 'trefoils' (155) spring up where she walks.[17] In the poem, the Twrch corresponds to the war god Ares, who takes the form of the boar to kill Adonis in classical myth. In the Welsh tale, Arthur's status as a redeemer is confirmed by his chasing away the Twrch, thereby restoring the land and making possible the marriage of the prince and princess.

We have seen that at the end of Part 3 Arthur as redeemer seems to be symbolized by the rat of no-man's-land. The rat keeps his own peace and saps his ordered 'paradise... by a rule of his nature' (54). This is an unappealing variation on a conventional image we have just considered, 'for so work the honey-bees, / Creatures that by a rule in nature teach / The act of order to a peopled kingdom' (*Henry* V 1.2.187–9). Like the presbytery bees, rats here are primarily an image of order. That is why they evoke Arthur, who is archetypally 'the Saviour, the Lord of Order carrying a raid into the place of Chaos' (201 n42). As an image of nature's essential harmony, furthermore, they involve John Ball in an important series of allusions to *The Rime of the Ancient Mariner*, through which all the animal images of *In Parenthesis* take on a larger symbolic importance than has heretofore been noticed.

David Jones writes that Coleridge's poem 'was much in my mind during the writing of Part 3' (199 n40). Coleridge's poem probably influenced the whole of *In Parenthesis* from the first year of its composition, when he executed ten copper engravings illustrating *The Rime of the Ancient Mariner*, engravings involving 'between 150 and 200' preliminary 'pencil drawings' (DG 188). In his Introduction to Coleridge's poem, David Jones repeatedly likens it to Arthur's seagoing raid on the otherworld in *Preiddeu Annwn* (DG 191, 205), a poem he evokes in the concluding pages of Part 3. The Welsh poem, attributed to Taliesin, and Coleridge's poem have in common disastrous voyages in which most men involved perish. Both voyages pass through hellish seascapes. That of Coleridge's poem is alluded to when it is said that Very flares 'for this fog-smoke wraith ... cast a dismal sheen' (52; see 199 n40). These phrases do more than evoke Coleridge's hellish antarctic setting, however: the Ancient Mariner's statement about 'fog smoke white' is his last before confessing, 'With my cross-bow / I shot the ALBATROSS' (lines 81–2). And in Jones's poem, too, a shot follows soon after. On the page facing the allusions to Coleridge, John Ball fires for the first time at the enemy. His rifle shot falls short, killing no one, but it is one with all the shooting

93 Secular Mythos

later, when a German sniper is compared to a ship's 'arbalestier' or crossbowman (168) and Ball's rifle hangs round his neck 'like the Mariner's white oblation' (184). The albatross's corpse is a symbol of indeterminate scope, encompassing the deaths of the Mariner's crewmates. In Jones's poem the killing of men is what sustains these Coleridgean associations. The title of Part 1 of *In Parenthesis*, 'The Many Men So Beautiful,' evokes the subsequent line in Coleridge, 'And they all dead did lie' (line 237).

The alternative to killing is implied by the rats of no-man's-land, which represent the whole of nature in something like the way Coleridge's water-snakes do. As Ball stands night watch, the poem's setting is reminiscent of that in which the Mariner's ship lies becalmed. Ball watches, 'and the deepened stillness as a calm, cast over us – a potent influence over us and him – dead-calm for this Sargasso dank, and for the creeping things' (53-4). Earlier, 'slime-glisten' is said to coat the ground of the forward zone (39). This and the image of the 'Sargasso dank' and 'creeping things' evoke the Mariner's words, 'The very deep did rot ... / Yea, slimy things did crawl with legs / Upon the slimy sea' (lines 123-6). The 'creeping things' in no-man's-land are the 'amphibious' rats. Like the water-snakes in Coleridge, they seem at first loathsome, but in their instinctive goodness – which is, of course, ontological, not moral – they partake in a natural order which is beautiful and which implies what Maritain calls 'the Creative Intelligence.' Like the image of water-snakes, the image of rats symbolically includes what it implies, the human response that it ought to elicit. Jones locates 'the crux' of Coleridge's poem – and everyone agrees – at 'the loosening of the spell by an interior act of love when the Mariner, observing the iridescent beauty of the water-snakes, "blessed them unaware"' (DG 193). John Ball may achieve such a gratuitous inward act. We do not know. But in a sense, the crux of *In Parenthesis* is outside the poem in the reader, who is free to respond – and in a way that would make a real difference to the world he lives in. As we shall see, that is the meaning of Dai Greatcoat's final admonition.

The imagery of natural order offsets a little the poem's predominant imagery of disordered nature. The rats are not alone in this lopsided contest. Birds sing to the same purpose on the morning of the assault (154), and as men wait face down in the assault trench for the signal to attack, 'if you look more intimately all manner of small creatures, created-dear things creep about quite comfortably / yet who travail until now / beneath your tin-hat shade' (157). These 'created-dear

94 The Shape of Meaning

things,' who recall Coleridge's 'happy living things,' are one with 'the whole of creation,' which St Paul says 'groaneth and travaileth in pain until now toward a glory as yet unrevealed' (Romans 8:22). They are on the side of Arthur as redeemer. They too *are* this Arthur-redeemer, and they call man to join them, to complement their nature with his supernature. If the ordered lives of insects, birds, bees, and rats is a composite paradigm for civilization as opposed to war's chaos, they are also complementary to aesthetic form in their intimations of metaphysical order. David Jones may resemble Wordsworth in his response to nature here, but he is well within a tradition far older than romanticism, one which includes Hopkins, Francis de Sales (whom Jones first read in the trenches), Francis of Assisi, and Bonaventure – all of whom searched creation for signs of the supernatural reality they believed in.[18]

THE TRADITION OF WAR

Helping unify the poem's allusive substrata in relation to the realistic narrative surface is what the poet calls 'a kind of racial myth expressed in war' (DGC 86). Many allusions to the wars of history, of scripture, and of literature have only local reference in the text, though they all imply a continuity between ancient and modern warfare. This continuity is complicated, however, by a reciprocity between past and present of the sort that T.S. Eliot describes in 'Tradition and the Individual Talent' as implying 'a judgment, a comparison, in which two things are measured by each other.'[19] In itself, the relationship between past wars and the war in the fictional present makes a worthwhile study of the transformation of received 'content' that occurs in any successful work of art. It is also a study which has acquired a certain critical urgency because of an important attack on the poem by Paul Fussell, who writes that

> for all the criticism of modern war which it implies, *In Parenthesis* at the same time can't keep its allusions from suggesting that the war, if ghastly, is firmly 'in the tradition' ... which ... holds ... suffering to be close to sacrifice and individual effort to end in heroism; it contains, unfortunately, no precedent for an understanding of war as a shambles and its participants as victims ... The effect of the poem, for all its horrors, is to rationalize and even to validate the war by implying that it somehow recovers many of the motifs and values of medieval chivalric romance.[20]

Fussell is concerned here with a basic issue that has shaped the evaluation of all literature on public themes – its relation to history, which here includes the reality of war. In disapproving of *In Parenthesis* on this score he makes a number of false assumptions, the most important of which is that the poem is passive before the tradition it invokes. He fails to see how the poet selects from and redefines tradition, and how tone controls the meaning of its evocation. But before meeting Fussell's objections point by point, we must consider how the poem does involve the military past in its depiction of modern warfare.

The manner in which the present gains from the past is exemplified within the poem's realistic narrative as Mr Jenkins reads the regimental battle honours: 'Albuhera, Oudenarde, Malplaquet, Minden' – names reaching back to the early years of the eighteenth century. On the level of narrative realism, these 'are potent words' (122). They align the present with a past that has been half-transformed by imagination. In the poem's allusive substrata a similar alignment involves battles that have been fully transformed in elegy and romance. Association with these battles effects a translation of the realistic present into imaginative timelessness and profound psychological (not moral) valuation. The evocations of past warfare throughout the poem differ in one important respect, however, from Mr Jenkins's reading of battle honours. Jenkins is naming victories in what is an official act of propaganda meant to prepare men for battle, whereas the battles to which the poem mostly alludes and which constitute its tradition of war are, for the most part, defeats.

By means of alignment with, and assimilation of, past warfare, the narrative present acquires the sense of suffering remembered and epoch-changing loss, and a sense of destiny which approximates the epic sense of fate. By association with archetypal events, the Somme offensive becomes archetypal. It consequently elicits from the reader a depth of feeling that realism by itself cannot arouse. In a sense, the Somme offensive contains all battles. In its scale of destruction, it is worse than previous battles since it produced over a million casualties. Although that is a quantitative, inessential difference, it is imaginatively important since, combined with essential congruity with prior warfare, the scale of modern war makes this battle capable of symbolizing all previous battles. At the centre of all the poem's allusions to war are the Celtic defeats representing 'the lost causes of Western Britain,' which, the poet claims, have 'given our national tradition its distinctive character' (xiii). For David Jones, all of these defeats are symbolically contained by the legendary battle of Camlan, with which the battle of the Somme is primarily associated. Camlan is the great battle of Arthurian romance, an archetypal calamity in which the world of Arthur collapses. It is a secular apocalypse, 'the undoing of all things' (xiii).

The chief historical correlative to Camlan in the poem is Catraeth, a battle in which a party of three hundred Celts was annihilated by Angles. Catraeth is a literary battle as well, for it is commemorated in the oldest Welsh poem, *Y Gododdin*. This ancient poem provides the epigraphs that appear at the beginning of Jones's poem and at the start of each of its seven sections. Seamus Heaney once remarked to me that Jones's poem 'is ghosted through *The Gododdin*,' but really it is the other way around. The Old Welsh poem is a fragmented, multiple elegy without narrative sequence. By juxtaposing bits of it to his own narrative, David Jones endows it with the ghost of narrative continuity. This is one way in which *In Parenthesis* affects our perception of prior literary works, and we shall see others. We shall also see how these epigraphs from *The Gododdin* help define the structure of Jones's poem. But the ancient work is not as important to *In Parenthesis* as it might seem. Although he had long known about the Celtic defeat at Catraeth and that there was a poem commemorating it, Jones had virtually completed the text of *In Parenthesis* before reading *The Gododdin* (DGC 174). The many correspondences between the two poems are unintended and serve only to indicate the underlying similarity of all military campaigns.[21] The influence of Catraeth on the assault that concludes *In Parenthesis* derives primarily from the value of the ancient battle as a historical symbol. Catraeth occurs at the start of the seven-centuries-long defeat of the British Celts.

The finish of this long calamity is the killing of Llywelyn by the English in Buellt Wood in 1282. With his death, Wales lost its last vestige of political autonomy, and 'the last remnant remaining of the pattern of a Britain ... known to Arthur ... and to the Caesars' disappeared (E&A 62). Llywelyn is an ill-fated redeemer-figure. About the anniversary of his death, the poet writes that he has had 'for many, many, many years now a feeling about this day as though it were a kind of Dydd Gwener y Croglith [Good Friday] of the Welsh people' (to Saunders Lewis 11 December 1955). Llywelyn is chief among the 'sweet princes by malignant interests deprived,' whose followers, 'the broken men, nest with badger and marten-cat' in wooded areas (66). In Aneirin Lewis's imagination, Llywelyn's 'wounds they do bleed by day and by night ...' (89), a quotation from 'The *Corpus Christi* Carol' identifying Llywelyn as a Maimed King of a wasted land. In his thirteenth-century elegy, Llywelyn's

97 Secular Mythos

death is said to cause 'the trees of the forest furiously [to] rush against each other' (212 n42). After the death of 'secret princes' in the assault on the wood at the Somme,

> The trees are very high in the wan signal-beam, for whose slow gyration their wounded boughs seem as malignant limbs, manoeuvring for advantage.
> The trees of the wood beware each other ... (184)

This is enough to suggest that the poem's wood contains Buellt Wood.

Partly as a consequence of this symbolic assimilation, the battle also recalls, though at a further remove, the fall of Troy. This ur-catastrophe of western culture is evoked partly because Llywelyn's death was the end of a world (E&A 42, 61) and because he and all the Welsh claim legendary descent from the Trojans, which they inherit legitimately from the Romans. (As Jones knows, the Teutonic peoples referred to the Romans as *Waelisc* or Welsh [to G 27 November 1970].) For Aneirin Lewis 'Troy still burned' (89) and in death he is 'more blistered ... than painted Troy towers' (155). But the evocation of Llywelyn's death and the deaths of other Welshmen only partly account for the broad, if faint, correspondence between the battle and the fall of Troy. We have seen that for the poet the Somme offensive is a precipitous moment in the decline of the West. This too is a world ending, and it helps account for runners on the eve of the assault resembling 'fleet-foot messengers ... / on windy plains' (128), an echo of Tennyson's 'ringing plains of windy Troy.'

Symbolically, for David Jones, the fall of Celtic Britain occurs all at once at Camlan. Because it is the symbolic condensation of seven centuries of disastrous battle, the poet can say that Llywelyn belonged, already, before they pierced him, to the dead at Camlann' (212 n42). The battle of the Somme succeeds in evoking the fall of Celtic Britain (along with its Trojan evocation) largely because it evokes Camlan.

The correspondence between the events of the poem and those in Malory leading to that battle begins during the night-time march to the trenches in Part 3 and culminates in Part 6 before the assault. The last and least obtrusive of these correspondences occurs as infantrymen assemble for the offensive and see in darkness 'where by day there seemed nothing other than a stretched tarpaulin and branches artfully spread, eight bright tongues licked, swift as adder-fangs darted' (135–6). At Camlan, Arthur and Modred advance to negotiate peace after warning their assembled armies to attack at the first sight of a drawn sword. When an adder from a heath-bush bites a knight who, with automatic reflex, draws his sword to slay it, the opposing hosts, seeing the sword, attack, 'and never was there seen a more doleful battle in no Christian land.' At the Somme, Malory's fateful adder strikes from bushy camouflage.

Tangentially related to the defeat of the Celts as symbolized by Camlan is the defeat of Roland. In a sense, he is one of Arthur's knights, because his lord, Charlemagne, was the chief historical model for Arthur in the French romances that were Malory's sources. Roland dies at Roncesvalles, but, as Jones might have put it, he belongs to the dead at Camlan. As he dies, furthermore, with his horn and sword beneath him, Roland is evocative of the ancient statue of the Dying Gaul and so conforms to its archetype, which for Jones epitomizes the centuries-long decline of the Celts. *The Song of Roland* probably lies close to the imaginative source of the poem. David Jones began writing in 1928, soon after returning from his second trip to France, during which he stayed with Eric Gill's family at Salies-de-Béarn. From there he could see a mountain pass which Mary Gill identified for him as Roncesvalles (221–2 n15) and which, Philip Hagreen tells me, Jones visited. As the major European epic-romance before the breakup of medieval Christendom, *The Song of Roland* joins the Trojan allusions in evoking a tradition that is more than merely national.

Because events leading to the battle of Camlan underlie the narrative movement of *In Parenthesis* and because Camlan symbolically absorbs the other Celtic defeats alluded to, it dominates all allusions to past warfare and turns even historic victories – at Crécy, for example (79) – into losses. They are moral losses because they represent what Dai Greatcoat calls 'expeditionary war' (83) and because victory has little meaning for the ordinary foot soldier whose point of view governs the narrative. Moreover, the negative effects of war are also subjectively felt because of the intense individualism borrowed from literary romance, which increases the poignancy of the deaths of Jenkins, Lewis, and to a lesser degree other men. In this poem the fate of the individual person eclipses national self-interest.

A touchstone for interpreting the meaning of war is the remark of Private Henry Earnshaw when, after references to some minor British successes at the front, he makes his discovery: ''Tis some poor fellow's skull says he' (115). The poem's meditative voice is quoting a line from the anti-war poem of Robert Southey in which a boy finds a skull on the site of the battle of Blenheim, a British victory in 1704. The boy's grandfather cannot tell him why the battle was fought or 'what good came of it.' The boy's sister thinks '"twas a very wicked thing,' but the grandfather insists repeatedly and with increasing, unintended irony, ''twas a famous victory.'

It is in the context of the political wickedness of most wars that the poem's recurring references to Shakespeare's *Henry v* must be understood. As Jones suggests in his preface, the men of his battalion identified with the men of Henry v's army as Shakespeare depicts it (xi). Like their predecessors, they are a mixture of Englishmen and Welshmen. And like Henry's army exactly five hundred years before, they embarked from Southampton, arrived in the area of Harfleur, and subsequently fought at the Somme. The association was inevitable and is part of the poem's documentary realism. But by the manner in which he alludes to it, Jones controls the meaning of the history play as it bears on his narrative.

The allusions focus on the common soldiers and their low-ranking officers. '45 Williams (153) evokes the Williams whose arguments against war drive King Harry to equivocation. Private Bates (174) recalls the play's Bates. Fluellen lives again, though not at all comically, in Aneirin Lewis, who sings low 'because of the Disciplines of the Wars' (42), and in Captain Cadwaladr, who 'restores / the Excellent Disciplines of the Wars' (181) exactly as Captain Fluellen does in act 3, scene 2. 'Captain Gower' (14) bears the name and rank of Fluellen's boon companion.

Henry is present too but not as the royal patriot-nationalist. His momentary physical anamnesis is based on Vernon's description of him in *1 Henry IV*:

> I saw young Harry with his beaver on,
> ...
> Rise from the ground like feathered Mercury,
> And vaulted with such ease into his seat
> As if an angel dropp'd down from the clouds
> To turn and wind a fiery Pegasus,
> And witch the world with noble horsemanship. (4.1.104-10)

In Jones's poem this royal Harry is demoted and deflated in the person of 'hairy Herne,' a private lying on the ground 'like Romany kral' or gipsy king (128). His 'beaver' is his helmet. He rises from the ground when he is called to carry battle orders (ie he is a servant), and as he springs into the saddle of his bicycle, his friends call him 'Mr. Mercury Mystagogue' (130). Not only is the king demoted but, in a manner recalling the poem's change of battle-birds to rats, his 'fiery Pegasus' has become a bicycle. Accompanying these metamorphoses are expressions of a sentiment altogether foreign to Shakespeare's king. Herne announces the coming battle by telling his friends to prepare for death by making out wills ('T. Atkins hereby declares'; see 217 n40), and as he pedals off 'nimbly perched,' they sing '*O my I dont wantter die*' – till a sergeant stops them.

There is also an echo of King Harry's famous oration outside Harfleur, which, since it is the play's set-piece, is probably one of the passages fifteen-year-old David Jones knew by heart in 1910. The speech has troubled critics who wonder how far its emphasis on pretence absolves the king from its incitement of animal passions. He encourages men to 'imitate the actions of the tiger,'

> Disguise fair nature with hard-favoured rage.
> Then lend the eye a terrible aspect,
> Let it pry through the portage of the head
> Like a brass cannon ... (3.1.8–10)

The poem's infantrymen anticipate the coming battle by imagining the dreadful actualities of combat with nothing pretended:

> in one another you will hate your own flesh. Your fair natures will be so disguised that the aspect of his eyes will pry like deep-sea horrors divers see, from the portage of his rigid type of gas-bag ... (121)

All that remains of Harry's rousing oration is the hateful inhumanity to which he incites his soldiers and which makes us wonder about him.

By selective evocation, by parody of the sort we are familiar with in other, more thoroughly ironic modernist texts, and by virtue of an allusive substratum predominantly evocative of historic and legendary catastrophes, *In Parenthesis* alters Shakespeare's play in our perception of it. In itself, *Henry v* is an incipient problem play, retaining elements of an unresolved debate. *In Parenthesis* joins in the argument on the side of the common soldiers against the king. In this way the poet uncovers new dimensions to the play's meaning, and not only within the context of the poem. *In Parenthesis* has inspired an important critical revaluation of *Henry v* by John Bernard, who demonstrates that by repeatedly alluding to it, David Jones reveals the play's 'unachieved greatness' as originally intending to place more emphasis on the common soldier and to argue much more forcefully against war.²²

An important aspect of Jones's redefinition of military tradition is his reassessment of the soldier's role in modern war vis-à-vis traditional notions of heroism. Here the poet eschews modernist irony and parts company with most critics of modern technological war, who adopt the antiheroic convention. But the continuity with traditional heroism which David Jones discovers involves a certain amount of qualification and redefinition. The main aspect of this redefinition is the implication throughout the poem that heroism is not now peculiar to a few but is a general condition. The first indication of this is the battalion's marching to 'Of Hector and Lysander and such great names as these – the march proper to them' (6). Obviously none of them can be heroes as Hector and Lysander are, but tone here implies that the song is 'proper to them' not merely because all fusilier regiments march to it. A general heroism may seem a contradiction in terms, but heroism is not qualitatively diminished in any essential sense by being widespread. And variations in tone do suggest that it is widespread, though perhaps not universal. Irony is heavy when select assault-troops are called 'the hero's grave squad' (125), but mild with reference to a resting place in reserves for 'war-weary heroes' (111). And irony vanishes altogether when, during battle, stretcher bearers come 'to spread worshipful beds for heroes' (178). Certainly there is no irony in the bawdy medical officer's 'heroism and humanity' (13). In this poem, clearly, heroism has nothing to do with the glorified egomania of classical epic, of Norse saga, and of much medieval romance. That is the sort of thing which partly validates Falstaff's famous mocking of honour; but there is a moral side to honour which is not egocentric and which partly invalidates that mockery. The continuity in the poem between modern and traditional heroism is an aspect of the larger continuity between modern and ancient warfare, and it too is a discriminating continuity involving a certain amount of disparity.

The imagery of the poem implies that its definition of heroism is somehow consonant with chivalry. There are obvious differences between modern infantrymen and knights, differences in social class, physical circumstances and styles of combat. These incongruities can be felt in the poem's initial clue to continuity – the resemblance of Mr Jenkins to the squire in 'The Rout of San Romano' (2) – one of Uccello's paintings which, Jones writes, 'illustrate the later "chivalry"' (DG 137).

This was a chivalry that, under the influence of the Church, included among the criteria of knighthood the virtues of honesty, justice, and even charity. Another hint of continuity that initially suggests disparity is the location of the office of Ball's father in 'Knightryder Street' (23). We seem as far from the world evoked by the street-name as Ball feels from the streets of home. But death focuses the imagination on essentials, and no sense of incongruity informs the identification of dead infantrymen with dead knights in 'the crypt of the wood' (182). On the level of narrative realism infantrymen are not knights, but beneath the level of appearance the poem's allusive substrata reveal that if war is essentially what it always was, so are soldiers.

The apparent contrast and the underlying continuity would probably have been heightened if the poet had been able to include in the poem the illustrations he 'had intended to engrave' (xiii), which might have included depictions of knights in armour. This is indicated by drawings of knights on the backs of two sheets of the poem's first continuous foliation of drafts. When the poem was virtually finished, moreover, Jones intended to reproduce in it a photograph of the tomb effigy of a 'marvelous dead knight' he and Prudence Pelham had discovered 'in Ottery St Mary Church ... it's Our Lord & King Arthur dead & Lancelot & Roland & Jonathan & all Xtn men dead' (to H Shrove Tuesday 1935). Such illuminations would have stressed the poem's associations with medieval romance, with knights, and with chivalry.

Associations with knights in particular may be construed as idealizing war, but only by a reader who forgets about the rest of the poem, pays no attention to how knights are evoked, and has a naive notion of medieval romance. Through its allusions to romance, *In Parenthesis* primarily borrows the subjective intensity that makes romance the most revolutionary of fictional modes.[23] Although the characters of romance are aristocrats, they insist on the primacy of the individual by existing more as psychological archetypes than as extensions of society. Symbolically they make special and help interiorize the figures in the poem with whom they are associated. We saw this with Mr Jenkins, in his well-deserved identification with the *Chanson*'s secondary chivalric archetype. Another example is John Ball advancing through the wood at night, who becomes a Lancelot in the terrifying burial yard of Chapel Perilous (180). The allusion conveys an intensity of personal feeling peculiar to romance.

The most prodigal example of this sort of borrowing takes place in an elegiac catalogue that is formally congruent with a corresponding

103 Secular Mythos

catalogue of infantrymen listed by name two pages earlier. The names from the past evoke many of the motifs we have been considering, including sexual love, friendship, and gratuitous making – which, in addition to courageous fighting, make the lives of these men significant. Infantrymen die

> like those other who fructify the land
> like Tristram
> Lamorak de Galis
> Alisand le Orphelin
> Beaumains who was youngest
> or all of them in shaft-shade
> at strait Thermopylae
> or the sweet brothers Balin and Balan
> embraced beneath their single monument
>   Jonathan my lovely one
> on Gelboe mountain
> and the young man Absalom.
> White Hart transfixed in his dark lodge.
> Peredur of steel arms
> and he who with intention took grass of that field to be for
> him the Species of Bread.
>   Taillefer the maker,
> and on the same day,
> thirty thousand other ranks.
> And in the country of Béarn–Oliver
> and all the rest–so many without memento
> beneath the tumuli on the high hills
> and under the harvest places.   (163)

Very few of those listed are heroic in an active, successful sense, and even they are invoked here only in their dying. They 'fructify the land' because their humanity, which has become symbolic in death, humanizes culture. The significance of many of these names will be lost on most readers, and that is part of the meaning of the catalogue, for the reader resides in the Waste Land, which is nearly devoid of humanizing culture. The list of 'heroes' consequently requires extensive annotation, and the poet provides leads in his notes for the reader willing to follow them up. The only reference I will elucidate here is the 'White Hart transfixed' – an allusion to Richard II, whose crest bore a white hart.

104 The Shape of Meaning

(Philip Hagreen writes, 'In 1924 David's historical worry was the fall of Richard II' [to H 27 February 1978].) The reference is also to Jesus appearing briefly in Malory as a 'white hart' to signify the imminent restoration of the Maimed King and of the Waste Land (17.9).

Infantrymen are 'like' these 'other.' The preposition and the indefinite pronoun make a distinction, but ambiguously, so that infantrymen may be 'like' these 'other' not only in death but in fructifying 'the land.' They too are part of tradition now, and by joining it renew it, because their deaths are evoked whenever men recall 'the Somme' and because they are memorialized in this poem.

The humanity that becomes symbolic in death is that of living men. In death, the poem's infantrymen appear heroic because they retained their humanity in dehumanizing circumstances – by appreciating beautiful and rational form, by loving friends, by longing for girlfriends, by daydreaming gratuitously – and because they lived lives of fortitude, patience and humility.[24] These virtues especially ennoble men, and while suffering has no value in itself, virtue does ennoble it and differentiate it from the merely pathetic suffering of animals (see 111, 149).

Awareness of simple goodness as heroic began for the poet while he was in the trenches. After recovering from his leg-wound and returning to his battalion in October 1916 in the area north of Ypres, he met the Catholic chaplain who is the prototype of the poem's Fr Martin Larkin and who lent him a book by St Francis de Sales.[25] This was probably *An Introduction to the Devout Life*, which, like his other books, teaches that the daily practice of humility, patience, and fortitude is more important than occasional acts of great sacrifice and that patience is second only to charity in a life of heroic virtue.

In the poem courage too receives its due. It is a virtue so common that it might go unnoticed were it not conspicuous in Old Adams having masqueraded as a young man so he could enlist (53) and in the young captured German officer who, though dead-tired, 'comes to the salute for Mr. Trevor with more smartness than anything Mr. Trevor had imagined possible' (170). The regimental cook has also acted courageously and has been decorated for it, though his ribbon is indistinguishable 'on the fouled khaki, for spattered-up kitchen greases' (118). He is important in the poem, for he establishes a type. He is 'like / the worshipful Beaumains' who appears in the heroic catalogue above – Gawaine's innocent younger brother, the humblest of knights, who is usually 'bawdy of grease and tallow' from working in Arthur's kitchen

(17.5). He corresponds to the type of the *bel inconnu*, the fair unknown whose true character is disguised by outward appearance. In addition to the regimental cook, the infantrymen who are patient and humble but not conspicuously courageous conform especially to this type.

These latter also correspond to the correlative type of the Suffering Servant of Isaiah, which will be considered more fully in the next chapter. The non-specialists who belong to the army's lowest class, 'who endure all things,' are among them. They are the poem's most 'secret princes,' its 'undiademed princes' (184), a designation reflecting the widespread claim to princely pedigree among certain strata of Welshmen and evoking the prescriptive chivalric correlation of true nobility with virtue. Underlying the metaphor may also be Melville's idea of 'God's true princes,' who are 'hidden,' who 'do not seek outward world honours or power' (*Moby-Dick*, chapter 33) but who are God's 'selectest champions from the kingly commons' (chapter 26, entitled 'Knights and Squires').[26] The true, inner distinction of the poem's 'princes' is revealed by the floral wreaths of the Queen of the Woods, after 'Life the Leveller' has left them for 'less discriminating zones' (185).

Heroism can be 'upper-class' too, as evinced in the courage and honesty of the GSO at the meeting at divisional headquarters who speaks against the 'so-called frontal-attack' on the wood and says he will quit rather than be a party to it (138). He is called 'a man of great worship,' Malory's word for honour, which distinguishes him from the others at the meeting; they are 'honourable men' (137) in something like the sense Mark Antony intended during the funeral oration in *Julius Caesar*.

In *War and Peace* Tolstoy shows up the notion of active, battle-winning heroism as false in comparison to a true heroism of simplicity and honesty. Although David Jones never read *War and Peace*, for him too, heroism is a matter of personal virtue – in which he includes (while Tolstoy does not) active courage as a good thing regardless of its effects. Tolstoy's notion of true heroism derives from a Russian Orthodox vision of sanctity. Authentic heroism for Jones is likewise essentially Christian, and opens the poem towards transcendent, religious values. He writes that, even narrowly understood, 'the "heroic"' implies

> other-world values, because courage [i.e. fortitude] is one of the Four Cardinal Moral Virtues and those who evoke it cannot logically do so without an admission of the other three [justice, prudence, temperance]. And behind those again stand the three theological ones (Faith, Hope, and Charity). (DG 155)

Once you allow for virtue as good in itself, regardless of practical effects, you do admit an economy of meaning that is not entirely of this world. In the Christian epics of Dante and Milton, heroism was redefined as a matter of moral, not physical, virtue. Tolstoy and David Jones are within this tradition, but each in his own way transforms it by internalizing virtue within the context of war and thereby effecting a *rapprochement* with the earlier epic tradition.

By way of partial summary, we can now return to Paul Fussell and meet his objections to the poem one at a time. He says the tradition evoked in the poem holds suffering to be 'close to sacrifice.' His expression here is almost too fuzzy to object to; it certainly blurs distinctions. David Jones does not equate suffering with sacrifice, and neither does any part of the tradition he evokes. Sacrifice is a matter of ritual and theology for Jones, and while there are many evocations of ritual slaughter, as we shall see in the next chapter, none implies – as war propaganda does – that death in battle is sacrificial. There is nothing in the poem, furthermore, to suggest that suffering is a virtue, though suffering is a condition that may call forth certain virtues. These virtues may be heroic and courage may be among them. But nowhere is heroism an expression of what Fussell calls 'individual effort.' If, as he says, the poem contains no precedent for understanding war 'as a shambles,' it certainly goes far beyond that in its allusions to Catraeth and Camlan (and to the fall of Troy) in suggesting that war is utterly catastrophic. In saying there is no precedent either for seeing 'its participants as victims,' he overlooks the figures of the Maimed King, the Suffering Servant, and, among other victim-types that we shall consider later, the biblical scapegoat. He blames the poem for recovering 'many of the motifs and values of medieval chivalric romance.' Well, chivalry is one thing, romance another. While soldiers are heroic in ways continuous with medieval chivalry, their heroism in no way 'rationalizes or validates the war.' The major evocations of romance we have so far considered are the deaths of Oliver and Roland, the terror of Lancelot, and the battle of Camlan. Instead of validating war, they magnify its horror and intensify the grief it causes.

Fussell's objections are interesting because intelligent, and they exemplify the difficulty anyone might have with the poem's methods of selective evocation, its shifting between irony and positive symbolism, and its metaphysical, partly incongruous juxtaposition – what one critic calls Jones's use of 'the symbol as riddle.'[27] Fussell's is an honourable misreading, if you like, but it fails to allow interpretive reciprocity between the poem's narrative surface and allusive subsurface. Underlying this failure is the desire, evident throughout his book, to see modern war as radically discontinuous from previous warfare and from the rest of human experience. Seeing war as an exception diminishes the need for critical scrutiny of the rest of life, of history, and of human nature. War becomes a scapegoat. David Jones, on the other hand, is making modern warfare a test case for the whole of life, of which it is an undeniable part. 'I did not intend this as a "War Book,"' he writes in the preface; 'it happens to be concerned with war' (xii). If the horrors of war negate all meaning within war's parenthesis, as Fussell seems to believe they do, then the rest of life is likewise, in a fundamental sense, meaningless.

The tradition of war was more ambiguous before the First World War radically diminished any notion of battle as a positive experience. This change in perception is recorded in the poem. On his way into the trenches for the first time, Ball is eager for combat, but experience makes all the difference. There is a correlative paradigm for this change of perception in the poem's lunar imagery. While men first walk toward the trenches, the moon is beautiful and a source of beauty; the next morning, men see no-man's-land, which is a desolate, lunar landscape. In a sense, their journey to war is a journey to the moon, from distant admiration to near awareness. The tradition of war is full of distortions and lies. The truth about war must be rooted in lived, narrated experience, but it is also to be found in 'the tradition,' and in 'the racial myth of war.' *In Parenthesis* returns to and feeds on the tradition, but selectively. The poem gains from the tradition a broad, symbolic resonance, and in return endows it with the life of its own narrative realism – much as the ghosts of the past receive vitality when Odysseus pours out fresh blood. And, like Odysseus, David Jones is selective about the ghosts to whom he gives the power of speech. Because *In Parenthesis* is an important work of literature and because it denies some aspects of the tradition of war while reinforcing others, to use Eliot's words, it modifies 'the existing monuments' of war literature. And this is because it is a poem which occupies 'not merely the present, but the present moment of the past,' and expresses a consciousness 'not of what is dead but of what is already living.'[28]

DAI GREATCOAT

Although an extension of the war motif, Dai Greatcoat is also a special subject involving the Welsh imaginative synthesis of past and present. We hear him as he boasts, in what is structurally, spatially, and thematically the centre of *In Parenthesis*. A sort of poem-within-the-poem, his boast brings into focus most of its host poem's motifs. Because it comes close to being the entire work in microcosm, Dai's boast anticipates the *composition en abîme* of Robbe-Grillet's *nouveau roman*. But it is more than that, for if it partly summarizes the poem it also analytically and symbolically extends it. The boast is a catalogue of military service extending back through history and quasi-historical legend to mythological time immemorial. It is a rhetorical approximation of the central event of epic, the descent to the underworld, which is really a visit to the past in order to learn the future. The poet notes that Dai boasts after the fashion of the Welsh bard Taliesin, the English bard Widsith, and Arthur's porter, Glewlwyd, in 'Kulhwch and Olwen' (207 n37). They are bards, not warriors. And Dai's boast is not, as John H. Johnston claims, an epic-heroic boast by a warrior before battle but a bardic boast with elegiac overtones.[29] Dai recounts a largely military tradition that broadens as it deepens, very quickly becoming that of the entire West. As the personification of this tradition and as its speaking symbol, Dai himself telescopes backward in time and inward through legend and myth to iconic loss of personality and national character. His boast is an extended definition of Everyman as a soldier.

Dai and his time-synthesizing imagination originate in the 'reported conversation' alluded to early in the boast and described in a note:

> He was carrying two full latrine-buckets. I said: 'Hallo, Evan, you've got a pretty bloody job.' He said: 'Bloody job, what do you mean?' I said it wasn't the kind of work I was particularly keen on myself. He said: 'Bloody job – bloody job indeed, the army of Artaxerxes was utterly destroyed for lack of sanitation.' (207 n37A)

The poet apparently wants to avoid any impression that the conversation was important merely because he himself took part in it. In 1963, however, he confides that

> actually the 'reported conversation' was between a very rural Welsh-speaking Welshman and myself in a communication trench in the Ypres sector in 1917, two years after the events covered in *In Parenthesis*. I remember the man's name was Evan (I think Evan Evans). I did not know him well but met him with his latrine buckets ... I offered him a cigarette

109 Secular Mythos

and remarked as stated in the note. I can't imagine an English soldier (at least he would have to be somewhat exceptional) to immediately respond (and with quite natural indignation) as did this Welshman ... in writing the 'Boast of Dai' in Part 4 ... I employed the motif remembered from that 1917 conversation.[30]

The Welshman whose instantaneous historical memory is a model for that of Dai Greatcoat is probably the Evans who is the partial prototype for Aneirin Lewis.

And just as the poet has affinity with Lewis, he has affinity with Dai Greatcoat. Jones was known as Dai to his closest friends, and while writing *In Parenthesis* (and for long after) he habitually wore a greatcoat against the cold (see DGC 11). In life as in art, moreover, David Jones sometimes achieved the sort of anamnesis that characterizes Dai's monologue. Once in 1966, for example, a cheque that he dated 1066 had to be returned to him for restoration of the missing nine centuries (to B 2 July 1971). But the poet does not project himself in this figure as he does in John Ball or Private Walter Map. Dai begins as a typical full-blooded Welshman and very soon becomes an archetype. The poet never recorded a reading of Dai's boast – probably because Dylan Thomas read it for the 1955 radio broadcast scripted from the poem, and if ever there were an archetypal voice it is the high-thrown near-monotone of Dylan Thomas. After hearing his reading rebroadcast in the 1964 production, Jones wrote, 'Dylan was perfect' (to G 6 July 1964).

The context of Dai's boast adds to the adversarial character of Part 4, which opens with opposing armies facing each other at stand-to, includes the pastoral song contest we have considered, and closes with a prolonged exchange of artillery fire. Here at the centre of Part 4 is a boasting contest. It consists of three boasts which establish the aboriginal Celtic triad pattern that will be echoed within Dai's boast. (A triad is a mnemonic form briefly listing three related figures, objects, or events from bardic tradition.) First a soldier trying to discuss strategy is irritated by mockery into boasting, 'knew these parts back in '14 – before yer milked yer mother' (78). Someone counters with a boast on behalf of Nobby Clark, whose battle experience metaphorically extends back to the seventeenth century – the truth behind the metaphor being the collective military experience of Clark's family:

They're a milintary house the Clarks – '14,
'14, be buggered –

110 The Shape of Meaning

>   Pe-kin
>   Lady-smith
>   Ashan-tee
>   In-ker-man
>   Bad-er-jos
> Vittoria Ramillies Namur,
> thet's the Nobby type o'
> battle-honour.   (79)

This second boast passes from realism to metaphor. Dai completes the triad by passing into symbolism. Historically, the second boast extends back to the Renaissance and therefore encompasses the typically English, Churchillian notion of history. Dai picks up long before that and goes, in a sense, all the way back.

He begins, as might any ordinary Welsh soldier with a strong sense of tradition, by recalling the battle of Crécy:

> My fathers were with the Black Prince of Wales
> at the passion of
> the blind Bohemian king.
> They served in these fields.   (79)

In 1346 several thousand Welsh infantry fought under the nominal command of Edward III's sixteen-year-old son. (The s in 'Prinse' is to make the sound Welsh; Jones said he wished he had written it 'Priss.') The English and Welsh defeated a large French army because of the tactical advantage of the longbow, which allowed English archers to outfire the French army's mercenary Genoese crossbowmen by three to one. Dai recalls this battle because his fathers, 'boys Gower they were,' fought 'in these fields.' Actually they fought further south, at the Somme. There Crécy has its English commemoration in John Ball's Lee-Enfield rifle being celebrated as 'the tensioned yew for a Genoese jammed arbalest' (183). From the start of Dai's boast, we know there will be nothing partisan in it, because of his evident sympathy for Charles of Luxemburg, the King of Bohemia who, though blind, asked to be led into battle so he could strike with his sword at least once against the invading British army. His dead body was found the next morning, surrounded by those of his attendant lords.

From this point on, Dai speaks as an archetype no longer distinct from his predecessors. He recalls the distant past in the first person singular, which he subsequently combines with the present tense to transform identification into anamnesis. 'I am' Socrates serving in Potidaea during the Peloponnesian War. 'I am' the Roman-British legions serving under Helen, who is the Welsh Britannia and soldier's muse whose 'ample bosom holds' the officials and defenders of Britain. Then he reverts till the end of the boast to the past tense, his tone consequently becoming slightly elegiac. After saying he helped construct defences at Troy Novaunt, as Geoffrey of Monmouth calls early London, he comes to the centre of his boast, which is also the centre of the poem.

This central section is a late insertion into the boast. Originally, in the first continuous foliation of drafts, 'I served Longinus ...' (83) followed immediately after the words 'Troy Novaunt' (81). The insertion mostly concerns the exhuming of Bran's head by Arthur and the disastrous expeditionary wars that were a consequence of that exhumation.

In this insertion, Dai recites the great triad that is the heart of his boast, a triad which is based on information from the Welsh Triads.[31] It consists of the three emigrant hosts that left Britain as a result of the exhumation of Bran's head, which had been buried to ensure the island's defence. Dai claims to have accompanied 'the first emigrant host.' Under Caswallawn it invaded France to recapture Fflur, who had been abducted for her beauty by a Gaulish prince. According to the Triads, this army, though victorious, did not return. Dai then claims to have accompanied the second host, which invaded the continent to reinstate Helen's husband Maxen, deprived of his imperium by rivals in Rome. That army never returned. Then Dai says he experienced 'the turbulence in Ireland' (83), having crossed with Bran to avenge an insult to his sister Branwen, whose face had been slapped once a day for three years. This is 'the smart on Branwen's cheek ... the third grievous blow' (83) – actually the first grievous blow according to Triad 53, but its rank is changed to suit the sequence of Dai's triad. Bran's army, which was technically victorious but annihilated, may seem to be the third emigrant host since, like the previous two, it depleted the male population of Britain and left the land uncultivated and bare. Strictly speaking, however, and although he does list three hosts, Dai's triad is incomplete. The expedition under Bran precedes 'the first emigrant host' and obviously cannot be among those that left on account of Bran's head being exhumed. But the triad form demands completion, if only by implication. And the implication is that the British Expeditionary Force in which Dai now serves is the third emigrant host – it too is depleting a generation of the male population of Britain, by one third. In this respect, Dai's boast opens up to contain its context. And concurrently, the poem's narrative-allusive Gestalt undergoes an inversion.

After completing his triad (by leaving it incomplete) Dai describes Christ's crucifixion – mostly in imagery derived from medieval English sources. And finally he claims to have fought against Lucifer in heaven. There is much more than this to Dai's boast, which merits closer reading, but an exhaustive consideration of it would nearly amount to a thorough interpretation of the entire poem.

Called 'Dai de la Cote male taile' (70), Dai bears the nickname of Malory's Breune le Noyre, who is obsessed with the murder of his father. Because Breune's death is never reported in Malory – the figure merely fails to reappear – he may be imagined as conforming to the type of old soldiers who, in the song concluding Dai's boast, 'never die they / Simply fade away' (84). To infantrymen in the poem and to soldiers of every time and place, Dai is what Eliot unconvincingly claims Tiresias to be in *The Waste Land*, a 'spectator and not indeed a "character" ... yet the most important personage in the poem, uniting all the rest.' Tiresias too is a boaster, in Eliot's poem, and like him Dai has 'foresuffered all.' This may account for his first name being a pun, since, as the universal soldier, he is always dying. But because soldiers never stop fighting and dying, in another sense Dai lives forever, a Welsh Wandering Jew. One of his listeners, apparently alluding to the mark of Cain, asks him, 'where's that birth-mark, young 'un' (84).

In his boast Dai bears witness, but he also illuminates by implication the moral status of combatants, which is by no means as clear-cut as Cain's. Vincent B. Sherry Jr considers the boast primarily a riddle in which Dai tests the reader, 'and, as in most riddles, the speaker is the subject.'[32] This is quite right, though we know from the start what Dai is, of course – a soldier; what we wonder about, and what the best minds of our century have questioned, is the morality of being a soldier. In his many pre-existences, Dai the soldier is seldom, if ever, a personal aggressor, even though he is a member of invading armies. Once, as David, he collects stones for weapons. When he actually strikes, however, he does so without malice, even without intention, having been metamorphosed, like Taliesin, into an animal or inanimate object. He is 'the spear in Balin's hand' (79), he is 'the fox-run fire' (80) carried into Philistine fields. He is the innocent 'adder in the little bush' who causes the knight to draw the sword that starts the battle of Camlan. Dai is the innocent air that carries the horn-blast of Roland. (The invasion of Spain by Charlemagne and Roland is not approved, but felt from the

Saracen point of view as Dai repeats the words of Blancandrin about the French, 'it is much better that they should lose their heads ... than that we should lose *clere espaigne la bele*' [80].) In these symbolic manifestations, Dai is guiltless – a tool, an occasion, a medium, never a homicidal agent. Sherry acutely points out that this 'active passivity' is significantly different from the now conventional notion of the soldier as passive victim.[33] But when Dai suffers 'the smart on Branwen's cheek,' he is a victim. And his being 'with Abel' instead of with 'his brother' (79) suggests some identification with the victim, although he is primarily a witness, even here where there were no witnesses.

During the battle in heaven, Dai fights on the right side, 'in Michael's trench' (84). But his action at the crucifixion suggests an ambiguity in the soldier's role. With his spear he defended the body of Jesus from crow and raven. 'But,' he says, 'I held the tunics of these' – the executioners whose nailing worked a 'terrible embroidery.' The 'But' is pivotal, and suggests a passivity no more innocent than that of Saul, who looked after the garments of the men martyring Stephen, 'and Saul was consenting unto his death' (Acts 8:1). Yet, as a Roman legionary Dai acts under orders and this mitigates what personal guilt there may be. When all the evidence is in, he seems a figure approaching moral neutrality.

He is certainly no war-counselling 'Lord Agravaine' (83), nor a proud Arthur digging up Bran's sacred, peace-keeping head. Rather, he prays to Bran's head to prevent expeditionary war. Dai himself was one of 'the beneficent artisans' who sealed the head under for the land's security and fertility, in an act symbolic of the essential antipathy between Ars and Mars, which we have already considered. Because, as an artisan, he 'trowelled' the mortar (81), moreover, Dai is associated with the benign rat of no-man's-land that did 'trowel his cunning paw' (54). Through affinity with the rat, Dai as artisan resembles Arthur as the redeemer-figure evoked at the end of Part 3. As an artisan, however, Dai acted more as a man than as a soldier. The distinction seems valid, especially for an enlisted man. And it seems to be Dai's essential humanity that finds expression in his final claim, to be 'the Single Horn thrusting' into Helyon's stream, neutralizing its poison so that 'the good animals can drink there' (84, 210 nN). The poison he neutralizes would then symbolize his military circumstance. So the man counteracts the soldier. He brings metaphysical order to the bankruptcy of his profession by an interior, perhaps unconscious participation in an order of values we have so far glimpsed with respect to gratuity, symbolic form, and heroic virtue.

It might be argued that as the Horn, not the Unicorn, Dai is no more responsible for the good he does than for the evil he commits as the sword in Balin's hand. In a sense this is true. As soldier and sword, Dai is the instrument of Mars. As man and symbolic Unicorn Horn, he may be the instrument of a benign deity, for in medieval iconography the unicorn symbolizes Christ. But in Catholic theology a man concurring with God's will, consciously or not, is no mere instrument; he is incorporated into God, becomes a member of Christ's body – as the Horn is part of the Unicorn in a way that a sword cannot be part of Balin. This making of distinctions may be hair splitting and if so it is potentially endless, but at least it makes clear that the morality of being a soldier is a difficult question about a delicate balance. I would hazard to say that if we can allow the distinction between man and soldier, then as a soldier Dai is neutral at best, and as a man he is positively good.

The implied antithesis, from which this benign neutrality emerges as an implied synthesis, receives more explicit expression in a balance of contraries during Ball's conversation with his friends before battle. Reggie castigates the conscientious objectors of Mecklenburgh Square (Bloomsbury), Jewish Golders Green, and 'half the B.E.F.' (the British Expeditionary Force, 143). Olivier replies by satirizing warmongers like Fr Vaughan and the sergeant instructors who 'foster the offensive spirit.' The antithesis corresponds to what David Jones writes elsewhere, that society consists of 'pacifists and ... killers-by-proxy' who are united in 'their common moral indignation directed to opposing ends.' Distinct from these factions, though the instrument of one of them, is the soldier. He is free, as Jones goes on to say, 'to keep his charity ... to nose out the abstract "goods" and "beauties" behind the detestable accidents' (*DG* 147).

In his active life, however, he is dehumanized because reduced to the status of an instrument. Like the worker who 'knows little of the unity for which his hours are docketed,' he is deprived of personal motivation. Because soldiers act and suffer for the 'killers-by-proxy,' they are 'appointed scape-beasts come to the waste-lands' (70; see also 226 and the final drawing of the ram which closes early editions). As universal soldier, Dai is a scapegoat who talks back. He articulates the unspoken question that every soldier represents. He does not answer it. That is the task of the noncombatant reader, who is implicated by Dai at the end of the boast when he says, 'You ought to ask: Why, / what is this, / what's the meaning of this' (84). In other words, the reader has the power to ask the question that would lead to the restoration of the Waste Land (see 210

NM). And calling us back to the motif of disaccommodation, Dai concludes by chastising, 'Because you don't ask, / although the spear-shaft / drips, / there's neither steading [as in homesteading] – not a roof-tree.'

A wounded man named Dai is blown to bits while being carried on a stretcher during the assault on the wood. He seems to be Dai Greatcoat. The poem's economy of characters suggests it and so does Dai Greatcoat's nickname. 'La Cote male taile,' which Malory translates 'The Evyll-Shapyn Cote,' can be read as a bilingual pun on 'evil-shaped slope' (côte). Dai dies on 'the slope' (176) of a steep incline halfway between the wood and the assault trench. In his dying he recalls Roland, that other Dying Gaul, who also dies on a steep slope (un pui agut).[34]

Because Dai is the poem's central symbol, his is a significant death. The shell-blast that kills him leaves no corpse behind – only 'clots and a twisted clout' spattering the back of a soldier fifty yards away (177). Dai cannot be declared dead, therefore, but only 'missing in action.' His death is an explosive version of the fading away of old soldiers and the vanishing of anyone who meets a Boojum. Because he is not certifiably dead, he achieves imaginative permanence as an archetype.

Dai's fleeting evocation of dying Roland may be too slight or subtle to suggest a correspondence with John Ball, who is explicitly identified with Roland a few pages later, but they are counterparts. Welsh Dai is profoundly aware of tradition; English Ball is aware only of his physical circumstances and immediate emotions. Dai is mostly present in his speaking; Ball, though present throughout the poem, rarely speaks. We have seen that John Ball corresponds to the Ancient Mariner as the main character within Coleridge's narrative. Dai Greatcoat, who, we have seen, is a Wandering-Jew figure, corresponds to the Ancient Mariner as Coleridge's secondary narrator. This aspect of the relationship between Dai and Ball correlates with the poem's anatomical centre containing its narrative context. As this suggests, there is generic significance in the complementary relationship of the two men. Within the poem's conventional fiction Dai is the primary focus of the poem's allusive mode, and Ball the primary reflector of its narrative mode. In their mutual association with the Ancient Mariner, their respective modalities acquire a symbolic equivalence which corresponds to the actual equivalence of these modalities in the eruption of the poem's substrata through the narrative surface during the battle.

Dai Greatcoat's contribution to *In Parenthesis* is very great but essentially and deliberately problematic. He aggravates the antithetical character of the poem by introducing, at the centre of his boast, a negative counterpart to Arthur as the redeemer-figure alluded to at the end of Part 3. The contrasting Arthur-figure heightens the poem's dialogical tension, which is between the actual and the desirable. It is a tension first clearly felt in the pastoral song contest on Christmas morning, and, because debate is characteristic of such poetry, it reveals *In Parenthesis* to be at its core conventionally pastoral. The benign Arthur is a mythic demigod; the other a legendary figure, more human in scale. 'In his huge pride, and over-reach of his imperium' the latter breaks the primitive sacrament of the buried 'guardian head' (82). In this act, the two Arthur-figures are in direct symbolic conflict, for the buried head of Bran is correlative to sleeping Arthur as potential redeemer. One Arthur inadvertently wastes the land which the other Arthur would restore. The proud 'War Duke' at the heart of Dai's boast is an iconoclast who breaks the pagan sacrament. Symbolically, he is autonomous secular man whose pragmatism leaves no room for religious symbolism. If he is proud, the other Arthur is humble, and synonymous with the order visible throughout the poem in nature's meekest animal manifestations. Archetypally, one Arthur is a proud Lucifer; the other, Jesus. Their fundamental antithesis emphasizes the choice Dai presents to the reader at the end of his boast. The choice is whether to ask a question, but it is also, in the most profound of spiritual senses, the choice of which side to take in the first of all wars, which began in heaven and is not over yet.

These then are the motifs defining the outward and inward conditions that infantrymen must endure. In their archetypal dimensions, they comprise a myth of the actual largely symbolized by Dai Greatcoat.
I have indicated that the motifs comprising this mythos have formal implications. To paraphrase Jones's words about Malory and *Moby-Dick*, these motifs contribute to the accumulation of depth and drive in the poem as it proceeds to the final disaster. The poet's consciousness of the affinity of his work in this respect with Melville's plotless masterpiece underlies the allusion during the assault on the wood to the explosions caused by the German counterbarrage: 'There she breaches black perpendiculars' (164; see *Moby-Dick*, chapter 134).[35] The archetypal meaning of the poem's cumulative temporal movement is apocalypse. We considered the Celtic-British apocalypse that informs this mythos, and in the next chapter we shall see the extension of this apocalyptic movement beyond time.

Looked at spatially instead of temporally, the motifs of the poem contribute to its form in another way. Both on the narrative surface and in the allusive substrata, motifs tend to dovetail with one another, partly because of shared allusive matrices. I compared their interrelationship with weaving, which is an image that recurs throughout the poem.[36] Weaving suggests movement and, as I said, involves disappearances and reappearances – an elusiveness which, in the poem, acquires a metamorphic quality, particularly in the allusive substrata. This elusiveness seems also to correspond to the landscape over which John Ball stands watch at the end of Part 3 and the beginning of Part 4. This watery landscape, which elicits many of the references to the sea and ships within the English range of allusion, also suggests formal affinity with a broad range of material within the Welsh range of allusion. Jones writes that 'the folk tradition of the insular Celts seems to present to the mind a half-aquatic world' involving

> a feeling of transparency and interpenetration of one element with another, of transposition and metamorphosis. The hedges of mist vanish or come again under the application of magic ... just as the actual mists over peat-bog and tarn and *traeth* disclose or lose before our eyes drifting stumps and tussocks. It is unstable, the isles float, where was a *caer* or a *llys* now is a glassy expanse. (E&A 238–9)

Corresponding to this metamorphic setting is a metamorphic aesthetic. In 1935, while putting finishing touches on *In Parenthesis*, the poet remarks on this with reference to a number of the poem's literary matrices. It is

> a quality which I rather associate with the folk-tales of Welsh or other Celtic derivation, a quality congenial and significant to me which in some oblique way has some connection with what I want in painting. I find it impossible to define, but it has to do with a certain affection for the intimate creatureliness of things – a care for, appreciation of, the particular genius of places, men, trees, animals and yet withal a pervading sense of metamorphosis and mutability. The trees are men walking. That words 'bind and loose material things.' I think Carroll's Alice Books and *The Hunting of the Snark* inherit through what channel I do not know, something akin to this particular quality of the Celtic tales. The Snark is always a Boojum in Celtic legend, and tragically so in much Celtic history. *The Hunting of the Snark* has for me an affinity to *The Gododdin*

of Aneirin and the Hunting of the boar Trwyth in the Olwen tale, and the Grael Quest also.[37]

Jones realizes that his own writing also has 'that metamorphic quality' (to E 15 April 1943). In another description of the tradition that includes Welsh folk tales and the works of Lewis Carroll, he adds to it *The Rime of the Ancient Mariner*, and what he writes about that poem may be taken as applying also to *In Parenthesis*:

> I have referred to the elusive quality of this poem and also to its deep allusions. These allusions are themselves elusively presented, for its imagery has a metamorphic quality. With swift artistry, with something akin to the conjuror's sleight of hand, the images seem now this, now that, a little like the shape-shifting figures in Celtic mythology. (DG 190)

He was led to his appreciation of this aspect of Coleridge's poem by Livingstone Lowes' *The Road to Xanadu*. And he composed *In Parenthesis* within this deeply and elusively allusive tradition. The metamorphic character of the substrata of the poem is an important aspect of its form, but of its texture, not its structure. As we have begun to see, part of the impetus of the poem to undergo transformation is that, in their allusive roots, several of the motifs lead the imagination from the actuality or probability of realism toward the metaphysically desirable and hypothetically possible.

4

Sacred Mythos

THE SACRED MYTHOS of *In Parenthesis* concerns ultimate, metafictional meaning. It extends the assessment of realistic content beyond merely emotional and imaginative categories to those of morality and metaphysics. We have begun to see this mythos in the motifs of gratuitous form, natural order, and heroism and in the challenge to the reader of Dai Greatcoat's boast. But in a real sense the sacred mythos picks up where the secular mythos leaves off. If this is true in relation to meaning, it is also true in relation to form. Like the secular motifs, sacred motifs contribute to the movement and texture of the poem, but they also play a major part in delineating structure.

As the title of the poem implies, its structure is parenthetical. The primary constituent of this parenthesis is the broad rhythm of the narrative movement. The first three parts of the poem comprise a journey and an arrival, and the last three parts involve another journey and arrival. The epigraphs from *The Gododdin* emphasize this repetition by doubling what was, in Aneirin's Old Welsh poem, a single journey to battle. The two journeys are divided by Part 4, the still centre of the poem, which interrupts its forward momentum. Part 4 concerns the cycle of a single day, beginning in the darkness before dawn and ending after nightfall. And it contains the circular journey by John Ball's section to a nonexistent fatigue duty. Their destination is the place where on the previous night they had passed men recovering corpses (41). Now as then the smell makes Bobby Saunders sick (93). It is a symbolic journey to death, a macabre image of meaninglessness reminiscent of the circular journeying in Dante's hell. It is the spatial corollary of Dai Greatcoat's endless temporal *ricorso*, which has affinity with the suffering of Sisyphus and likewise threatens meaninglessness.

The poem's secular mythos and sacred mythos both have archetypal summary symbols. At the centre of the parenthetical structure and bracketed by accounts of the fatigue party's circular journey out and back is Dai Greatcoat. His monologue represents perennial realistic knowledge and mythologizes historical continuity. The poem's contrasting, teleological movement concludes at the end of the poem with the Queen of the Woods. If Dai represents knowledge, she represents love – he speaks; she acts. If he symbolizes the actual in its historical and archetypal dimensions, she symbolizes the fulfilment of metaphysical desire, whose only dimensions (for us) are hope and hypothesis. He and she complement one another, but they also represent the dilemma which has always divided the mind of western man and which Keats memorialized in his 'Ode on a Grecian Urn.' In Jones's poem the implied antithesis generates a tension felt in the whole of the poem through its duality of form.

The parenthetical structure is largely delineated by ritual motifs, which, more than the motifs we have so far considered, evoke metaphysical values. Because ritual motifs help delineate the structure of the poem while evoking these values, they render its structure symbolic. The structural parenthesis emerges through pagan initiation and fertility rites, Hebrew ritual, and Christian worship. The last is the dominant matrix of the three, consisting primarily of the Mass, the seasons of the liturgical year, and allusions to scripture intended, for the most part, to be understood in their liturgical contexts.

For David Jones, the ritual intentions of pagans and Jews harmonize with the Christian liturgy because Christianity does not, for him, eclipse the permanent validity of the other ritual traditions as signifying the authentic metaphysical values and the deepest longings of mankind. Furthermore, he considers pagan religion, as well as Old Testament Judaism, to be continuous with Christianity. That is why, without intending any disrespect, he can refer to the Easter Vigil as 'the vegetation rites of the Redeemer' (to H Holy Saturday 1932). In so far as the Christian matrix is distinctly Catholic, it originates in the postwar meditation of the poet, for although he 'was "inside" a Catholic in the trenches in 1917,' he had no extensive experience of Catholic worship until after the war.[1]

Religious ritual exists in symbolic relation to life. It endows life with meaning by uniting in a dramatized hypothesis the ordinary experiences of life with the fullness of belief and desire. The effect of associating such symbolic drama with the horrendous events of modern war is sometimes contradictory, sometimes paradoxical, and sometimes, in a straightforward way, symbolic. As with allusions to war literature and romance, the meaning of a liturgical allusion is largely determined by tone and the context in which it is made.

Liturgical associations emphasize the ritual character of military life, which, as Jeremy Hooker rightly points out, does not always exclude religious significance.[2] Because military and religious rituals sometimes order life in analogous ways, military life sometimes implicitly recalls aspects of the eternal economy of meaning to which religious liturgy explicitly testifies. But ritual analogues are double edged. If they stress the essential goodness of soldiers, they also generate ironies that disclose combat's physical destruction and spiritual outrage.

The power of this disclosure in *In Parenthesis* is unsurpassed in the literature of war. This is largely because ritual associations involve the greatest hopes of man. To the extent that war dehumanizes, it denies these hopes and generates an incongruity more intense than the conventional antithesis with secular peace. The incongruity persists throughout the poem, moreover, because what war evokes and opposes it cannot effectively negate. Suffering and death, however horrible, do not cancel the possibility of eternal life and infinite love. The wartime of our uncharity is consequently redeemable, even if it is damnable uncharity. In partaking of this moral ambiguity, war is of a piece with the rest of life. We have seen that the poem is ultimately about the whole of human life. The ritual analogues that war evokes in the poem signify that life need not be meaningless, because in war the apparent absurdity of life is magnified to become its own sign of contradiction.

Ritual associations contribute importantly, moreover, to the poem's epic dimension. They contradict the opinion of Bernard Bergonzi and David Blamires that *In Parenthesis* cannot be a 'true epic' because it does not reach 'out beyond the personal to a system of public and communal values which are ultimately collective, national, and even cosmic.'[3] The religious values informing the ritual mythos of the poem are broadly and deeply rooted in our culture and are certainly 'cosmic.'

RITUAL MOTIFS

Like the secular motifs, those involving religious ritual begin early in the narrative. For the most part, they are unobtrusive and arise as much from connotation as from explicit allusion. Because there are so many liturgical evocations and because I have discussed them elsewhere in some detail, I will not attempt a thorough explication of them here.⁴ Instead, I will concentrate on ritual motifs as they delineate structure. But to establish the broad allusive contexts in which these motifs operate, I will first consider how, in two distinct but interrelated aspects, the life of soldiers is liturgical.

All human interaction involves routine acts and signs. In this poem these acquire symbolic liturgical status. Jones notes in his preface, for example, that certain 'impolite words' acquire by their repetition a liturgical quality (xii). One of these eases the pain in John Ball's knuckle and is likened, by way of the half-hidden pun we considered earlier, to the 'efficacious' word of sacramental formula (53). Likewise on this basic level but more explicitly symbolic are the poem's two meals. Both are eucharistic. The first is the issuing of rations on Christmas morning, which is charged by allusions to Old Testament foretypes of the Eucharist taken from Lenten Epistles. Among these foretypes is the dispensing by Moses of quail and manna during the Exodus. Depleted and diluted by dishonest quartermasters, the rations are not much, but in the circumstances they are worthy of *eucharistia*; in the words of the poem, 'this is thank-worthy' (73). And shortly after receiving 'his own daily bread,' John Ball drinks from an 'enamelled cup' (74). He receives, as it were, under both species. In military vernacular, the meal on this morning is 'the mess' (73), a pun on the Mass. We will consider the poem's second eucharistic meal later.

The other aspect of liturgical allusion is distinctly martial. Officers preside over ceremonies and intone antiphons that initiate the 'liturgy of a regiment departing' – which is sung, for the most part, by sergeants (4). Those in authority pronounce 'ritual words' resembling sacramental formulae in that 'the spoken word effected what it signified' (3). (According to Maurice de la Taille, sacraments accomplish something 'by signifying it.') The intended 'effect' occurs when the proper person 'makes the conventional sign' (166) and the strength of the troops is 'sufficient body for the forming of efficient act' (42). In this peculiarly military range of experience, a liturgical allusion may be symbolic or ironic. It may also be ambiguous, as when the 'armed bishopric' of Mr Jenkins is called 'his little flock' (31) – an allusion to the 'little flock' that will be given the kingdom of heaven (Luke 12:13) but also recalling lambs led to slaughter (see Isaiah 53:7). Underlying the negative connotation is an implied perversion of the sacred mythos in which men serve 'Mars armipotente' (44), a less than omnipotent god of death and destruction.

Within a ritual motif, ambiguity varies in degree as emphasis shifts between the soldiers' humanity and their military purpose. The monastic motif involves an example of this. Veterans at the front are 'long professed' (44); new arrivals receive the 'habit' of hessian cloth and commence 'serving their harsh novitiate' (70). They eat 'in common' (71), and Ball on guard duty has 'a parapet for a [choir] stall' and buries his hands in his sleeves 'habit-wise,' like a monk (50). This monastic imagery originates in the postwar meditation of the poet. In '1923 or thereabouts,' he spent three weeks in a Carthusian monastery and was deeply moved by its liturgical life and the beauty of the chant. It 'made all other forms of life & art forms pretty contemptible by any standard' and was, for him, 'like recognizing a stupendous thing as in a love affair or an art work of overpowering significance' (to G 13 October 1964). Five years later he spent three months with the Benedictine monks on Caldey Island. The poem's monastic imagery may imply that military monasticism is especially 'contemptible' in comparison with the real thing. Nevertheless, it does retain positive symbolic value partly because the poem's metaphorical monks meditate 'as men who consider the Nature of Being' (69) and share the accommodating fellowship we considered in the previous chapter.

The motif becomes entirely ironic only when emphasis shifts to the primary duty of monks, the chanting of the Divine Office. The military counterpart to monastic chanting of psalms is the exchange of artillery fire. At the daily ritual of evening stand-to, a sort of Vespers, the opposing armies stand like two large choirs of monks 'in stalls' prepared for the antiphonal chanting of psalms. Soon after, the malign Office of Mars commences:

> Bursts in groups of four jarred the frosted air with ringing sound.
> Brittle discord waft back from the neighbourhood of the Richebourg truckway.
> Guns of swift response opened on his back areas. In turn his howitzers coal-boxed the Supports.
> So gathered with uneven pulse the night-antiphonal.   (99)

The recitation of the Divine Office and artillery exchange are further connected in a way that involves the antithetical significance of artillery within the motifs of fertility and symbolic gratuity. In the previous chapter, we considered the sound of artillery mixing 'with the drone of bees' in the presbytery garden where a priest recites his breviary. We saw that bees are the antithesis of artillery. Aligned with the bees against artillery in this scene is the priest's recitation of psalms 'where a canonical wiseness conserved in an old man's mumbling, the validity of material things, and the resurrection of this flesh.' This brief episode (117–8), and in particular this reference to the rubric obliging the praying priest to move his lips, contains the answer to a question arising later (173): 'why is Father Larkin talking to the dead?'

Artillery fire does not preclude resurrection, of course. But it does contravene the principal sign of hope in resurrection, the burial of the dead. A body in the forward zone, buried or unburied, is

> Each night freshly degraded like traitor-corpse, where his heavies flog and violate; each day unfathoms yesterday unkindness; dung-making Holy Ghost temples. (43; cf 1 Corinthians 6:19)

The expression of human dignity inherent in the burial of the dead is nullified by corpse-mutilation – exploding shells unfathoming that which, if left full-fathomed, would anticipate a change 'into something rich and strange' (*Tempest* 1.2.397). In the imagery of vegetation ritual, war allows

> ... no decent nor appropriate sowing of this seed
> nor remembrance of the harvesting
> of the renascent cycle
> and return ... (174)

Destructive of life, artillery further impoverishes by abrogating a natural order of signs.

In contrast to liturgical prayer, which complements the natural order, the martial Office effects an epiphany of disorder and de-creation. In the poem's first shell-burst, which concludes Part 2,

> ... pent violence released a consummation of all burstings out; all sudden up-rendings and rivings-through – all taking-out of vents – all barrier-breaking – all unmaking. Pernitric begetting – ... (24)

This description seems to echo the Latin of Virgil's account of the generation of bees from the carcass of an entombed bullock (*Georgics* 4.291–313). There bees with buzzing wings, *pennis*, burst suddenly through windows facing the winds, *ventis*. For the Church fathers,

Virgil's description of the generation of bees from a mouldering corpse is prophetic of the resurrection.⁵ In the forward zone the process is reversed; martial bees produce carcasses and then disinter and multilate them, as if in mockery of man's hope for rising again.

But even in combat liturgical analogues are sometimes not ironic. A single analogue can be symbolic in a positive sense and then turn to irony. And irony can vary in degree and then turn again to positive symbolism. This modulated ambiguity is characteristic of most of the liturgical motifs that help delineate the structure of the poem.

Aside from quality of meaning, what ultimately differentiates these motifs from their secular counterparts is the sense of formal pattern they bring to the poem. *In Parenthesis* opens in the weeks before Christmas and closes in the summer's battle. On this opening and closing, ritual analogues impose patterns of inception and completion, promise and fulfillment. Ritual initiation begun early in the poem is completed in the final battle. Evocations of the Nativity at Christmas are answered during the battle by allusions to Good Friday. Advent anticipates apocalypse in the first half of the poem: battle metaphorically fulfils that anticipation. And, as we have already begun to see, evocations of fertility myth at the winter solstice are answered at midsummer by perverse ritual enactments of fertility myth. Each ritual matrix alluded to involves the same temporal rhythm but with its own distinct significance, which contributes to this rich composite mythos.

With respect to the military *ecclesia*, the approach to the war zone is a kind of baptism. In fact, Part 1 of the poem seems informed by an underlying initiation pattern of mimetic death to an old way of life and a resurrection or rebirth to a new life. Conforming in part to pagan sacramental typology, the rite of passage begins with the channel crossing as the end of an old way of life. Like dying in classical mythology and pagan rites of initiation, this is a descent into Hades with the channel passage corresponding to the crossing of the Styx.⁶ Strengthening this suggestion is an officer who, in ordering the disembarking infantrymen to 'move left and right' (8), evokes Minos, the judge of Hades, who separates all who cross the Styx into those going right, toward Elysium and those going left, toward Tartarus (see *Aeneid* 6.432). The poem's subsequent imagery indicates that the men of the battalion journey toward Tartarus, for they 'moved left in fours' (17), 'took the way left' (22), 'turn sharp left' (49). Hades' turn for the worse may be echoed as well in references to the British traffic pattern maintained in the trenches: 'Keep well to left' (34), 'keep left, left' (36).

Furthermore, the trenches, when they enter them for the first time, evoke the Temple of Mars in Chaucer's 'The Knight's Tale,' which is based on classical descriptions of Hades.

All this is suggestive of the ancient pattern of initiation into a chthonian mystery, as at Eleusis where initiates, seeking identification with Kore Persephone and her mother Demeter, had to wander for a period underground in Hades, a place of 'darkness and mud,' according to Aristophanes (*Frogs* line 276). There, says Plutarch, they partook in 'abortive and wearisome wandering about, a number of dangerous journeys into the dark that lead nowhere' (*Florilegium* 4.107). The battalion's first uncertain wandering in the trench system – soon after an allusion to 'the cleft of the rock' at Eleusis (39) – takes place in darkness and mud, and we saw that the next morning's circular journey leads nowhere. The initiation at Eleusis took place over the course of at least one year. Its analogue here lasts the length of the poem. On the eve of battle, John Ball and his companions eat a 'seed-cake' which recalls the sesame cakes consumed by Eleusinian initiates. The following evening the initiation reaches completion in the thick of battle, Ball finding himself involved in what the poem calls 'the mysteries' (182). It is then that 'the gentleman must be mowed' (182), a metaphor evocative of the reaping of the ear of corn which concludes the Eleusinian rite.

But there is in the poem a less prolonged aspect of initiation. Its inception coincides with that of the poem's Eleusinian rite but it ends sooner, in the night-time arrival in the combat zone. This is a sort of baptism. As martial catechumens preparing for the sacrament, foot soldiers have received instructions – on military tactics, hygiene, the history of the regiment, and the Mills Mk IV grenade. Now 'their catechumen feet' are finally led toward the line (44) where they 'are assimilated' and receive 'an indelible characterisation' (49).

Complementing the motif of ritual initiation, to which we shall return, is imagery of the liturgical seasons. The events of the first three parts of the poem take place in the weeks before Christmas, and aspects of the season of Advent are established there as important motifs for the poem as a whole. Advent anticipates Christmas, of course, but it derives much of its character from the apocalyptic vision of the last Sunday of Pentecost, and its major concern is with the second coming of Christ and the Last Judgment. There are many evocations of this theme in the poem before Christmas but also after, and these increase with proximity to battle. They include a reference to the mounted officers of 'B' Company as 'the four horsemen' (124; cf Revelation 6:2–8), and the traditional tableau of the Judgment, which lies behind what appear to be the last words of Mr Jenkins: 'don't bunch on the left / for Christ's sake' (160).

The predominant image of Advent, one that occurs throughout the season, also recurs throughout *In Parenthesis*. Suggestive of the wide road to hell, 'the firm, straight-thrust, plumb-forward way,' also evokes the metaphorical way of which John the Baptist speaks daily at Lauds during Advent and in the Gospels of the third and fourth Sundays of the season:

> Prepare ye the way of the Lord! Make his paths straight. Every valley shall be filled, and every mountain and hill shall be brought low, and the crooked shall be made straight, and the rough ways shall be made smooth, and all flesh shall see the salvation of God. (Luke 3:4–6)

La Bassée road, visible on the map included in the poem's notes in early editions, is straight. In the poem, it is several times called straight, and as foot soldiers travel it in what one of them calls 'our advent' (49), work crews are observed making rough ways smooth by shovelling rubble into great torn upheavals in the paving (20–1). The straight way, as a metaphor, supersedes the presence of the physical road. The effect of artillery fire is such that, in a direct paraphrase of the words quoted above, 'small gulleys filled, and high projections' are 'made low' (86). During the assault, before enemy barbed wire, 'you seek a place made straight / you unreasonably blame the artillery' whose job it is to prepare the way for the foot-mob (166).

The 'prearranged hour of apocalypse' (135) arrives shortly after dawn on July tenth at the Somme. Here liturgical and scriptural allusions proliferate to define further what we have already seen as apocalyptic by association with the battle of Camlan. And here the motif of disaccommodation becomes intensely mythic. When the infantry scramble out of the assault trench to stand in no-man's-land, it is said there are 'riders on pale horses loosed / and vials irreparably broken' (160). The riders are a multiplication of the figure of Death riding 'a pale horse,' to whom, at time's end, will be given 'power over the fourth part of the earth, to kill' (Revelation 6:8). The broken vials are those containing plagues, bringing pain, stench, fire, blood, noise, and shaking of earth (Revelation 16). As the battalion passes through the German barrage falling along the centre of no-man's-land, it is 'red horses now – blare every trump without economy' (163). The red horses multiply the apocalyptic 'horse that was red,' who appears 'that they should kill one another' (Revelation 6:4). The blaring trumpets are those of Revelation 8:2–7, which invoke grievous plagues. The spectacular description of these plagues in scripture goes a long way toward expressing what it must have been like in the midst of the falling barrage. But the trumpets of Revelation are sounded in ordered sequence, one at a time. In the poem, they are blown 'without economy.' The scriptural hail, fire, blood, smashing, smoke, plunging from heights, darkness, scorpion-stingers flying through the air like bullets and shell-casing fragments: these occur at random, all at once or overlapping – wounding, and killing the third part of men. In immediate impact, if not in universal scale and import, the martial apocalypse surpasses its scriptural counterpart, so that the scriptural imagery must be intensified in the poem to match the havoc of modern battle. In an obvious sense the barrage parodies the apocalypse. Yet it also symbolizes the world's end, and for the men killed it is the end of time, involving 'their particular judgment' (162), whereby 'those happy who had borne the yoke / who kept their peace' are separated from those who had not (154; cf Matthew 11:29–30).

While Advent culminates thematically in apocalypse, the season of Advent ends at Christmas. Christmas has its liturgical antithesis in Good Friday and its liturgical complement in Easter. The complex symbolism of this far-reaching seasonal interrelationship informs the poem.

The battalion arrives in the trenches at Christmas, a day whose significance is emphasized by a number of allusions. On Christmas Eve the journeying infantrymen are 'star-gazing' magi (39) with 'apprentice wisdom' (40). On Christmas morning they become the shepherds of Luke's infancy narrative, bearing rifles instead of staves, and flockless. Their seasonal transformation is underlined with a reference to Milton's Nativity hymn, where the shepherds are unaware of the importance of the dawning day: 'Perhaps their loves, or els their sheep, / Was all that did their silly thoughts so busie keep.' The perspective of infantrymen separated from Cockney girlfriends in the second millennium since the birth of Jesus may differ only slightly:

> Perhaps they found this front-line trench at break of day as fully charged as any chorus-end with hopes and fears; or els their silly thoughts for their fond loves took wing to Southwark Park. (69)

We have already seen that these modern shepherds engage with enemy counterparts in an updated version of the conventional pastoral song contest.

The Germans sing of the winter rose symbolizing the newborn Christ, 'since Boniface once walked in Odin's wood' (67). The reference to the conversion of the German tribes by Boniface and his English monks ironically anticipates the incursion of the English (and Welsh) into the wood for a bloody parody of that conversion of Germans. Even now the English reply in a spirit out of sympathy with that of their missionary predecessors. They sing 'Casey Jones,'

> Which nearer,
> which so rarely insular,
> unmade his harmonies,
> honouring
> this rare and indivisible
> New Light
> for us,
> over the still morning honouring.
> This concertina'd
> Good news
> of these
> barbarians,
> them
> bastard square-heads.   (68)

(The words 'New Light' appear in two of the three Christmas Collects.) And someone urges the man from Rotherhithe to 'drown the bastards' with harmonica playing, for after all, 'wot type's this of universall Peace / through Sea and Land' (68). The speaker, who quotes Milton's Nativity hymn, seems unkind, but he and his disgruntled mates have a point: overt expressions of piety are embarrassing, not to say hypocritical, in the circumstances. Something of the same violation of sensibility is registered later when an Anglican parson preaches 'from the Matthew text, of how He cares for us above the sparrows. The medical officer undid, and did up again, the fastener of his left glove, behind his back, throughout the whole discourse.' And the irony intensifies when 'They sang *Onward Christian Soldiers* for the closing hymn' (107).

The elaborately described dawn witnessed by the battalion's shepherds signifies the birth of the messiah who sets his tabernacle in the sun. The presence of metaphorical shepherds may recall that the sun god was first worshipped in pastoral societies. At any rate, the rising sun's being called 'the bright healer' puns on the Greek *helios* and evokes the pastoral sun god Apollo. As we saw earlier, the adjective 'bright' is especially indicative of divinity. The sun as image of the Son of God occurs in the second stanza of 'O Come, O Come, Emmanuel' and in Advent antiphons from which the hymn derives the image. It also occurs daily in Lauds, at sunrise.

Discord between the feast of Christmas and the present occasion underlies the specifically Lenten character of the sun's description. The account of the sunrise evokes the Passion by allusion to the figure of Joseph, who is 'beautiful,' wears a coat of many colours, and has a prophetic dream in which all the stars make obeisance to him. Here is the Christmas sun rising:

> ... the last stars paled and twinkled fitfully, then faded altogether; knowing the mastery and their visitation; this beautiful one, his cloud garments dyed, ruddy-flecked, fleecy stoled; the bright healer, climbing certainly the exact degrees to his meridian. (62)

In the Lenten liturgy the story of Joseph's dream, his brother's envy, and his betrayal prefigures the betrayal of Jesus. Moreover, the sun's 'cloud garments dyed' recall Isaiah's vision, in the lesson for the Mass of Wednesday in Holy Week, of the messiah wearing 'dyed garments from Bozra' and prophesying that the blood of the people who have deserted him 'shall be sprinkled upon my garment' (63:1–3). This Lenten vision is echoed again during the assault, in the description of the German trench where 'dark gobbets stiffen skewered to revetment-hurdles and dyed garments strung-up for a sign' (167). Isaiah's association of bloodshed with religious infidelity is evoked in the poem to suggest that war is, as it were, a sacrament of religious infidelity, a sign effecting what it signifies.

The day that starts with the significant sunrise concludes with Easter imagery. In a reversal of dawn's stars fading, at dusk 'the first star tremored: her fragile ray as borne on quivering exsultet-reed' (98) – the reed that during the Easter Vigil bears to the paschal candle the flame signifying 'the Light of Christ.' But, as in the morning when the sun's 'New Light' was not well received, here the stellar *lumen Christi* is obliterated by flares sent up 'in hurrying challenge, to stand against that admirable bright' star (98). Other stars emerge, as if reflecting the spreading of paschal fire during the Vigil to the candles of the congregation in the darkened church. But 'high signal-flares shot up to agitate the starred serenity' (99). Instead of signalling the resurrection, this night's vigil ends in artillery fire which, as we have seen, is symbolically antithetical to resurrection. The antiphonal artillery exchange is a magnification of the morning's unseasonal song contest.

131 Sacred Mythos

The liturgical calendar of Mars displaces the two great feasts of Christmas and Easter and allows only for a recollection of Good Friday. The rubrics from the Good Friday Office that begin Part 3 of *In Parenthesis* suggest this. They specify that the celebrant sing 'in a low voice' – a regulation that we have seen Aneirin Lewis observe as he marches. The Advent 'liturgy of their going-up' to the line (28) corresponds partly to the journey described in Matthew 20:17–18:

> And Jesus going up to Jerusalem took the twelve disciples apart in the way, and said unto them, Behold, we go up to Jerusalem; and the Son of man shall be betrayed unto the chief priests and unto the scribes and they shall condemn him to death.

The 'going up' of the battalion continues in 'their anabasis' (114) to the Somme. A soldier's cry, 'We all want the Man Hanged' (104), is ambiguous in this context. Made with immediate reference to 'Big Willie' (the Kaiser), it nevertheless evokes Christ, the 'Hanged Man' of *The Waste Land* whose pagan counterpart, Odin, is recalled earlier in Jones's poem as 'the hanged, the offerant: / himself to himself / on the tree' (67). Symbolically, the cry in the crowded estaminet calls for the renewal brought about by Christ's death and signified by Odin and the hanging gods of vegetation. But it also resembles the cry of the crowd before Pilate, 'Let him be crucified,' and this suggests that Christ's Passion will be metaphorically re-enacted in battle.

Christ's death is unique and cannot be repeated. But if it is memorialized in the Mass and dramatized in the liturgy of Holy Week, it can also be, though only metaphorically, evoked in battle. Such evocation corresponds, also metaphorically, to liturgical anamnesis or re-presentation, and not merely by way of parody. In recalling the crucifixion, combat hints at a mystery capable of redeeming its own apparent absurdity. In this metaphorical repetition, the suffering of soldiers finds its archetype in the suffering humanity of Christ. And because of the spiritual communion initiated by the redemption, archetype here gives way to anagogue, or mystical assimilation. As David Jones puts it, 'I think that all our miseries and sufferings can be seen as in some way part of the whole anabasis and passion of the figure without whom our Western "culture" could not have been.'[7]

On the eve of the offensive 'the noise of carpenters' is apprehended by John Ball 'as though they builded some scaffold for a hanging' (138). The sound is frightening primarily in a vague and unspecified way. (In fact, the poet told me, they were building coffins, though 'Ball didn't know what was being made.') But the image of the gallows evokes the cross – in this poem partly through association with Christ-typifying Odin, the gallows god, but also because the gallows is traditionally equivalent to the cross.

On the morning of the assault, allusions to the Passion are more intensely focused. The battalion assembles as ordered in the Nullah, each soldier inclining his body to the slope, waiting, all 'in a like condemnation / to the place of a skull' (154) – a reference to Calvary or Golgotha, words originally meaning 'skull.' Here a distinction is implied between the suffering of soldiers and that of Christ, for it is the thieves crucified with him who are 'in the same condemnation' (Luke 23:40). But the predicament of infantrymen is similar to that of Jesus in the garden of his agony. The poem's narrative voice becomes frantic:

> ... you read it again many times to see if it will come different:
> you can't believe the Cup wont pass from
> or they wont make a better show
> in the Garden.
> Won't someone forbid the banns
> or God himself will stay their hands.
> It just can't happen in our family
> even though a thousand
> and ten thousand at thy right hand.   (158)

The last two lines are from Psalm 91, which expresses the hope against all odds that though a 'thousand shall fall at thy side, and ten thousand at thy right hand ... it shall not come nigh thee.'[8] 'The Cup' is Jesus's metaphor for his Passion, as he endures his agony. The 'show / in the garden' refers to Peter's violent attempt at rescue. These allusions recall the first evocation of Gethsemane on Christmas Eve as Ball gazes toward the enemy: 'Does he watch – / the Watcher. / Does he stir his Cup' (52). The Watcher is one of a class of angels (see Daniel 4) here associated with the angel strengthening Jesus for crucifixion. The suffering of the infantry is inevitable from the time of their arrival at Christmas, just as the Passion of Jesus is implicit in his Nativity. Further allusions to the commemoration of the Passion in Holy Week occur throughout the account of the assault.

All through the poem, furthermore, infantrymen are identified with the suffering Christ by reference to the Suffering Servant of Holy Week, who 'hath no form nor comeliness; and when we shall see him, there is no beauty that we should desire him' (Isaiah 53:2). 'Poor Johnny,' the British infantryman disinterred at Christmas in the Richebourg sector, is such a one – 'you wouldn't desire him' (43). Of a living infantryman it is said, 'they cant abide the sight of you' (119), and of another, 'hair on upper lip invests him with little charm' (27). And if some have no charm, others are 'small men... who have no qualifications' (126). As we saw in the previous chapter, they are literally servants.

The violent recalling of Good Friday in battle is complemented by a variety of liturgical allusions to various religious traditions. Most of the rites alluded to are in some sense sacrificial. All of them ascribe meaning to life and dramatize hope in life's increase or renewal; all are evoked here to be inverted in the conglomerate sacrilege of battle. While combat recalls sacrificial forms, it does so only to establish a contrast with sacrificial intentions. The poet does not imply, as Johnston and others contend, that war is in any real sense sacrificial or that it incoporates values of 'Christian sacrifice and expiation.'[9] Not that battle merely parodies sacrifice; battle's ritual evocations are positive in that combat involves extreme conditions which most urgently require religious restoration of meaning. One of these restorative rites is the Eucharist, which has metaphorical affinity with the battle in that it too recalls Christ's Passion.

We saw that the poem's first symbolic Eucharist, which takes place on Christmas morning, evokes the Exodus. So does the second symbolic Eucharist, which occurs on the eve of battle. Those partaking in it participate in anamnesis by becoming part of the rite's archetypal substrata. Ball and his friends eat unleavened seed-cake. 'In haste they ate it' (146), as the Passover meal was eaten before the coming of the angel of death. Ball and the others eat 'trussed-up in battle-order with two extra bandoliers slung, and rifles in their hands' (146), recalling the Israelites who were told to eat 'with your loins girded, your shoes on your feet, and your staff in your hands' (Exodus 12:11). Through the Passover allusion to the Seder's imaginative anamnesis, this last meal before battle is associated with the Last Supper and with the evocations of the Passion that proliferate as the battle draws near.

In addition to combining metaphorically with battle's evocation of the Passion, the Eucharist may have some bearing on the structure of the poem. David Jones admired 'the terrific shape' of the Mass (*DGC* 168), which is climactic like the forward movement of the poem and which tends to separate into two distinct movements, the first climaxing at the Offertory, the second attaining the greater climax of the Consecration.

134 The Shape of Meaning

This double movement closely resembles the double movement of the poem, with its minor climax at the end of Part 3 and its major climax in Part 7.

While there is no thoroughgoing parallel, the poem does evoke parts of the Mass in a way that suggests a correspondence between the Somme offensive and the Canon of the Mass, in which the Consecration occurs. The approach to the front line may be considered an extended Introit to the altar of sacrifice. Corporal Quilter, whose part it is 'to succour the lambs of the flock' is addressed early in the march by a limping private saying, 'I'm a bleedin' cripple already Corporal.' Quilter's reply, in its cadence and alliteration, echoes the Kyrie:

> Kipt' that step there.
> Keep that proper distance.
> Keept' y'r siction o' four – can't fall out me little darlin'. (6)

The poet assured me that the evocation of the Kyrie here is deliberate.[10] The Offertory, at which the bread and wine to be consecrated are presented at the altar, has its analogue in the arrival of the new recruits at Christmas. This is the arrival concluding the baptismal approach, in which soldiers cease being catechumens. Its parallel significance is appropriate, for the Offertory terminates what is called 'the Mass of the catechumens' and initiates the part of the Mass to be attended originally only by the baptized faithful. So the poem's first, minor climax thematically corresponds to the first, minor climax of the Mass. The parallel underlines the discrepancy between the bloody manner of immolation on the battlefield and the unbloody sacrifice of the Mass, what Maurice de la Taille calls its symbolic or mystical immolation.

The bloodshed distinguishing battle from the Mass provides some resemblance to the ritual immolation of the Old Testament. Mars, like David in the old dispensation, finds his place of sacrifice *in campis silvae* (153). Here, however, the fire of Hebrew sacrifice is replaced by gunfire. And no atonement is intended in this 'place of separation' (70). Combat's deviation from the intentions of Hebrew sacrifice is underlined by its association with one particularly appalling Old Testament immolation. At the end of *In Parenthesis*, in a surrealistic passage possibly representing the delirium of the wounded John Ball, the aftermath of battle is imagined with the wounded recovering on the south lawns of England:

> Mrs. Willy Hartington has learned to draw sheets and so has
> Miss Melpomené; and on the south lawns,
> men walk in red white and blue
> under the cedars
> and by every green tree
> and beside comfortable waters.   (186)

In this heavenly vision of peace, recuperating men in the colours of the Union Jack stroll through a landscape ironically evocative of Psalm 23, in which one is led 'beside still waters.' Making beds with Mrs Willy Hartington is Melpomene, the unmarried muse of tragedy. She is a reminder that, because of the toll of the war, one-third of this generation's young women would never marry. She has learned to adjust, however, and everything is bright, cheerful, quite nice. The words 'under the cedars / and by every green tree' add to the pastoral setting. But they also echo the single unannotated line in the first paragraph of Part 7 – 'and under every green tree,' which refers to the greatest horror of the Old Testament – according to Jewish biblical interpretation, a cause of the Babylonian Captivity and the permanent dispersal of the Twelve Tribes. This outrage was the sacrifice of living children to Moloch and Baal, when the unfaithful Israelites

> set them up images and groves in every high hill, and under every green tree ... And they caused their sons and their daughters to pass through the fire. (2 Kings 17:10, 17)

The metaphorical sacrilege of battle closes the poem's liturgical parenthesis. It is for this holocaust that the latter-day chosen people endure the exodus seen in both of the poem's ritual meals. This is the Passion that finishes what was begun at the Nativity. This the bloody Consecration that fulfils the Christmas Offertory. Also involved in the pattern of completion is the chthonian initiation begun at Christmas in the entrance to the trench system.

Eleusinian imagery is reintroduced in the latter half of the poem with Runner Herne, who is more than an evocation of Henry v. We have seen that his friends call him 'Mr. Mercury Mystagogue.' His tin helmet is called a 'bright *petasos*' – the brimmed Thessalian hat worn by Hermes or Mercury, the 'mystagogue' or initiator called by Aristophanes the 'guide of the dead' for shade-personating novices at Eleusis. True to

136 The Shape of Meaning

form, this Hermes inaugurates a dying, though not that of mimetic ritual. The orders he carries start the battle of the Somme, completing an initiation that has conformed from the start to the pattern of the mysteries at Eleusis, in so far as they are known to us.

At Eleusis initiates imitate a dying and entering of Hades, as the soldiers seem to do at Christmas. The wandering underground at Eleusis ends, says Plutarch, in a rising preceded by 'all manner of fears, shuddering and trembling' – very like the feelings of the men about to go over the top. The initiates then emerge, as though from Hades, to a bright, 'wondrous light.' Assaulting infantrymen 'vivified from the Nullah' stand above ground blinking 'to the broad light' (162) in a morning 'intolerably bright' (163). Then, says Plutarch, initiates hear 'a glory of sacred song' and pass 'pleasant landscapes and meadowland' into what Aristophanes calls the groves where the blessed rest.[11] During the assault, sacred songs are sung: 'Glory / Glory Hallelujah' by the English and, by the Welsh, 'Jesu / lover of me soul' (160). Their passion, their courage, their fright, and their singing must approximate in some way the religious ecstasy that consummates the Eleusinian rites. But the infantry's is no vision of peace, and the grove they go to is no Elysium. Instead of being adopted by Demeter and undergoing spiritual renewal, the infantryman goes 'like a motherless child' to the antithesis of what the ancient mysteries intended.

The poem's Eleusinian rite is a fertility ritual focused on the mother goddess. It merges in its termination with other fertility rites that suggest the general pattern of dying and rising, in which initiation to manhood takes the form of a mock slaying and resuscitation. In the wood, half the metaphor is taken literally: the rite kills; there is no mimetic rising.

Most of the fertility rites evoked are universal in their effects and derive from folk customs performed for the invigoration of the spirit of vegetation, who, in turn, exercises a fertilizing influence on human sexuality. Here too inception finds parenthetical completion. We have seen that the arrival of the battalion on Christmas occurs, because of proximity to the winter solstice, 'at the time of Saturnalia.' In an early draft it is called 'the morning of Saturnalia' and the rising sun is referred to as 'he whose Festival it was.' As we have seen, this morning contains evocations of cosmic sexual intercourse and a related fertility ritual commemorated in a fairy tale. The battle takes place at the opposite pole of the year, the summer solstice. In fact, the long bombardment initiating the offensive commenced on June twenty-fourth, Midsummer

Day. And traditionally the season's bonfires sometimes burned through to the end of July (*The Golden Bough* II 73–4).

True to the spirit of the season, British infantrymen entering the wood enact the folk custom in which an adolescent personating the spirit of vegetation enters a woods to awaken vegetable life. 'Your mate moves like Jack o' the Green, for this season's fertility' (168). Like the folk figure, he is draped with branches and leaves. But his ritual promenade draws unkind retaliation:

> they could quite easily train dark muzzles
> to fiery circuit
> and run with flame stabs to and fro among
> ...
> stamen-twined and bruised pistilline
> steel-shorn of style and ovary
> leaf and blossoming
> with flora-spangled khaki pelvises
> ...
> where adolescence walks the shrieking wood.   (170–1)

Plants, their reproductive organs ominously ripped away, are tangled round human pelvises. Together and equally, plants and men are vulnerable to tearing castration by machine-gun and sniper bullets. 'Shin and fibula' shot, blood from broken legs mixes with red sap so that 'draggled bloodwort and the madder sorrel' are twice dyed 'with crimson moistening' (171).

Ritual promenade gives way to ritual sacrifice. In the previous chapter we saw that, in their bleeding, soldiers resemble Adonis, the barley god whose flowing blood reddened vegetation. Everywhere in the wood men re-enact his midsummer passion. Ball himself is subsequently 'mown' to resemble John Barleycorn (224 n39), a latter-day figure of the barley harvested in midsummer. Infantrymen also come to resemble personators of Attis, who are castrated by the goddess Cybele during midsummer nuptials. We have seen how such wounding identifies soldiers with the correlative archetype of the Maimed King.

As personators of the vegetation-spirit, infantrymen drop while trees and branches fall. A young German named Balder dies as if for the northern tree-spirit's vitality being riven from the oakwood (185): in broken tree-limbs, 'Balder falleth everywhere' (177). Once immolated ritually in midsummer fires, he falls now because of midsummer gunfire. The immolation of Balder is a northern counterpart to the midsummer sacrifice of Adonis. Even their names are the same – Balder, like Adon, meaning Lord.

Interwoven with the northern ritual of the tree-spirit is the southern rite centring on the tree-spirit Diana, goddess of nature and of fertility in particular. British Jacks o' the Green enter the wood as personators of her divine mate Jupiter seeking to renew sacred marriage for the fruitfulness of vegetation and the human race. In this respect, the wood at the Somme fulfills the prophetic intuition inspired by the sight of Biez Copse at Christmas: a place that 'might well be special to Diana's Jack, for none might attempt it, but by perilous bough-plucking' (66). The bough requisite to entering the grove is mistletoe, 'a Golden Bough for / Johnny and Jack' (178). The infantryman also courts by virtue of his rifle – 'it's the bright bough borne' (183) – but according to the rubrics of the priests of Nemi, each of whom courts the goddess by plucking the golden bough and advancing to kill his predecessor. Having violently succeeded to the position of priest and spouse, he kills his would-be successors till he himself is killed (*The Golden Bough* 1 1–23). At Nemi the tree and its divine dryad are spared, and symbolically at least, fertility is promoted in the grisly succession of marriages. At the wood in which the battalion fights, even this mitigating symbolism is nullified, where 'shrapnel' is 'the swift Jupiter for each expectant tree' (178).

The intensity with which war contradicts fertility ritual in this poem reflects the ambiguous career of the mythic figure Mars, who was once an agricultural god. As fertility figure metamorphosed, he maintains his shape, as it were, to become an infertility god, the anti-self of what he was. We have already seen his opposition to what he once fostered, in the contrasts between artillery fire and the Christmas sun and between artillery and the fertilizing bees of the presbytery garden. It can also be seen in the shell-burst's 'pernitric begetting' (24), in which the nitrogen used in fertilizer is a constituent part of gunpowder.[12] The ritualized expression of this opposition in the wood at the end of the poem completes the liturgical metaphor by which war is seen as antithetical to man's deepest desires and hopes.

The infantryman is the priest and victim of combat's manifold immolation. He and his fellows are Mars' 'ministrants' (44), but unwillingly and because of circumstances almost entirely beyond their control. They attack, therefore,

> each one bearing in his body the whole apprehension of that innocent, on

the day he saw his brother's votive smoke diffuse and hang to soot the fields of holocaust; neither approved nor ratified nor made acceptable but lighted to everlasting partition. (162)[13]

Caught up in sacrilege, they, like Abel, maintain their innocence, lying dead in the wood with 'pale cheeks turned' (171) in significant obedience to Christ's injunction to turn the other cheek. If the reference is ironic, the irony is gentle, pertaining more to their circumstance than to their personal moral condition. Each of them is 'little Benjamin' (6), guiltless of betraying his brother Joseph.

As we have seen, moreover, soldiers epitomize patience and humility. In addition to conforming typologically to the suffering Christ, therefore, they may conform morally to his teaching and example. This inward identification is suggested by the poem's original pictorial parentheses, for the infantryman of the frontispiece stands quasi-cruciform to correspond to the Christ-symbolizing ram of the end-piece. Such inward conformity is implied with respect to a dead German soldier described leaning 'against the White Stone' (185) – the symbol of the saint's victory in the Book of Revelation where Jesus says, 'To him that overcometh will I give to eat of the hidden manna, and will give him a white stone, and in the stone a new name written, which no man knoweth saving he that receiveth it' (2:17). This uncanonized German saint also resembles Wolfram's Parzival, who attains the Holy Grail and for whom the Grail is a luminous stone inscribed with the names of the knights destined to attain it. Any ordinary infantryman can be, may well be, as successful. David Jones implies as much in his preface, where he writes that 'the "Bugger! Bugger!" of a man detailed, had often about it the "Fiat! Fiat!" of the Saints' (xii).

THE QUEEN OF THE WOODS

The sanctity, which is also the heroism, of 'this July noblesse' (186) has been obscured by 'Life the leveller' (185), a corrective reversal of James Shirley's 'Death the Leveller.' At the end of the poem, death brings hierarchical revelation in the ceremonial crowning of soldiers by the Queen of the Woods (185–6). Criticism has tended to ignore this mythic figure, even though she is a lyrical high point in modern literature and crucial to the ultimate meaning of this poem, which is that human life has value even when it is lived and lost in the apparent absurdity of war.[14] She is the dryad of the forest, the Acorn-Sprite (178) of its flora-fall. She delivers true judgments by which the 'undiademed princes' (184) 'have diadems given them' (185) – the steel-shorn branches and filigree of the woods. Her ceremonial action is the poem's final ritual, in which she unites most of the poem's secular and sacred motifs that have to do with desire, by becoming their archetypal fulfilment:

> The Queen of the Woods has cut bright boughs of various flowering.
> These knew her influential eyes. Her awarding hands can pluck for each their fragile prize.
> She speaks to them according to precedence. She knows what's due to this elect society. She can choose twelve gentle-men. She knows who is most lord between the high trees and on the open down.
> Some she gives white berries
>   some she gives brown
> Emil has a curious crown it's
>   made of golden saxifrage.
> Fatty wears sweet-briar,
> he will reign with her for a thousand years.
> For Balder she reaches high to fetch his.
> Ulrich smiles for his myrtle wand.
> That swine Lillywhite has daisies to his chain – you'd hardly credit it.
> She plaits torques of equal splendour for Mr. Jenkins and Billy Crower.
> Hansel with Gronwy share dog-violets for a palm, where they lie in serious embrace beneath the twisted tripod.
> Siôn gets St. John's Wort – that's fair enough.
> Dai Great-coat, she can't find him anywhere – she calls both high and low, she had a very special one for him.
> Among this July noblesse she is mindful of December wood – when the trees of the forest beat against each other because of him.
> She carries to Aneirin-in-the-nullah a rowan sprig, for the glory of Guenedota. You couldn't hear what she said to him, because she was careful for the Disciplines of the Wars. (185–6)

Fatty Weavel's sweet-briar, the love-token growing from the grave of Barbara Allen in her ballad, suggests that he is the ballad's 'Jimmy Grove' mentioned early in the poem (33). His 'thousand years' is the biblical millennium symbolizing eternity. The German Balder doubtless receives mistletoe – the golden bough that kills and subsequently contains the life of his divine namesake in Norse mythology. Ulrich's myrtle wand is the bough worn by initiates at Eleusis. Cockney Billy

Crower is now the equal of Mr Jenkins, for differences of class, rank, and wealth have ceased to matter. So has the common judgment of men, for, although he seemed unkind (15), 'that swine Lillywhite' receives daisies, which symbolize love. German Hansel and Welsh Gronwy, who died fighting each other, lie together like Malory's Balin and Balan 'beneath their single monument' (163), here a machine gun's twisted tripod. Their dog-violets symbolize suffering and steadfastness. St John's Wort, for Siôn, is a plant gathered on Midsummer's Eve as protection from harm. Aneirin Lewis's rowan or mountain ash, a sign against evil, is indigenous to his native Gwynedd.

In the tender and multifaceted Queen of the Woods, the poem's associations fully emerge from the ironies by which they indict war. She takes the poem's motifs beyond mortality and morality to metaphysics. She is the feminine principle nullifying the masculine malice of battle. The antithesis of 'Life the leveller,' she is 'sweet sister Death' as St Francis would have recognized her. She is the girlfriend that young soldiers longed for, and more: the beloved of the Song of Songs, Diana for these Jacks o' the Green, the Kore of their initiation, Demeter to mother them. She is the Celtic triple goddess: the mother, the lover, the presider over the dead. Hers is the judgment they wanted, the accommodation they missed. No empty or ironic symbol, she is sustained by the theological implication of the poem's ritual associations. In her, nature and grace are one. To her the end of *In Parenthesis* belongs.

The visitation of the Queen of the Woods is an important literary event. Not only is it among the most moving passages in English literature, but it is an early appearance of the composite goddess Sir James Frazer had written about at the start of the century. In *Ulysses* Joyce compares Molly Bloom to Gea-Tellus but only in passing. He evokes the earth goddess more fully in *Anna Livia Plurabelle*, which may be counted as her first appearance in modern literature. Jones's Queen of the Woods would then be her second appearance, her first in a poem, though here she is less emotionally and comically personable, more numinous and therefore more authentically a goddess. Beginning in 1924 and increasingly around 1930, Ezra Pound refers to Aphrodite and Demeter in the *Cantos* but does not make them imaginatively fully present. The goddess becomes prominent in criticism and poetry when Robert Graves writes about the White Goddess in 1948. But David Jones, who knew the Celtic sources better than Graves did, had discovered her there earlier for himself – though Frazer and Joyce doubtless pointed the way.[15]

The goddess means more to Jones than she does to her other modern literary devotees. For Joyce she is an archetype of universal femininity. For Pound and Graves she is an aesthetic and psychological symbol. For Jones, too, she is these things, but she also retains something of her primordial stature. Her divinity is no longer innate, certainly, but it survives nevertheless, having been redeemed, as it were, and returned to her by Christianity, which, for Jones, fulfils rather than displaces its predecessor-religions. In contrast, the goddess for Joyce, Pound, and Graves is, theologically or ontologically, merely the ghost of a dead mythology.

Because the Queen of the Woods is so different from Joyce's Anna Livia and is therefore without precedent in modern literature, I will imitate Livingstone Lowes for a moment and investigate her imaginative genesis, which should help to explain her remarkable emotional and symbolic power. The elegiac fantasy in which she appears is a late addition to the poem, roughly contemporary with the inclusion of the centre of Dai's boast. But as we have seen she is present throughout the poem – in typical, not archetypal, form – as the object of sexual desire. She is also present as such in the penultimate, holograph version of the poem's conclusion, which concerns a sleepy corporal behind the lines on the morning after the assault. He hopes to dream of a girl named Susan or another named Philomel, or he will 'make a drowsied paradise of sweet F.A.' – an absence, with punning sexual connotations, colloquially personified as Fanny Adams. Then a French woman, who seems to be the poem's 'mademoiselle at Croix Barbée' with her mastiff-guard (35), asks a mess-cook the date. She expects the return of her lover today and, with her ancient dog, is clearly a Penelope-figure. As the present manifestation of the woman of desire and on a realistic level, she is, as it were, the Queen of the Woods in first draft. In some sense, furthermore, the Queen of the Woods is a distillation of sixteen sketches of women drawn by David Jones on sheets of the poem's handwritten drafts, seven of the drawings on the fronts of pages on which text is written. Reproduced here is one of six of these sketches on the final handwritten foliation of Part 7. This drawing, on the back of a page, is linked to the poem by the name Melpomene, which appears in the text soon after the visitation of the Queen of the Woods (186).

The Queen of the Woods was also present as an archetype in the early stages of the poem's composition and not only in the idealized and projected femininity we considered in the previous chapter. In the excluded material about Bobby Saunders it is said of the battle (still

143 Sacred Mythos

Melpomene

seven months in the future) and with reference to the girl to whom Saunders is attracted:

> on a day of many nuptials, he saw that
> Beauty whose proportioning informed her,
> her and Helen, and that Margaret who like
> him, found the compelling Lover in a wood.

The notion of meeting a lover in a wood comes from the thirteenth-century romance *Aucassin et Nicolette*, which David Jones had read before the war (to G 7 May 1964) and which he includes in his handwritten list of sources. In the medieval story, the woman hides deep in a wood, waiting for her knightly lover who searches for her. When he finally locates her bower, she appears to him.

There are other literary influences – among them, probably, goddesses who appear in epics. In 1956 the poet writes to Harman Grisewood that

> this intervention-of-the-gods thing which people say is so unconvincing & unreal and unlike anything we can be expected to feel is, on the contrary, *extraordinarily* like 'reality.' Also, I find that all the things Pallas Athene does & says in relation to Telemachus and Odysseus & Penelope very close indeed to our Xtian ideas about – well, the saints & guardians & Our Lady especially – not that *I* know anything about these things, but I refer to what spiritual writers say ... Do you remember the bit where Athene makes Penelope go to sleep and then washes the tears from her cheeks with a special cosmetic that Aphrodite herself used for special occasions & then she makes her taller & more shining & whiter than 'newly sawn ivory.' (DGC 168–9)

He goes on to say that, interwoven with epic tribal savagery, 'such tenderness and civility and sophistication ... makes one jump – and weep also.' The effect of the Queen of the Woods is very close to this. She belongs to this category of figures in works that *In Parenthesis* approximates in genre.

But she also has a prototype in more recent literature – Sabrina in Milton's *Comus*.[16] Jones hints at this when he writes in his preface that 'From Layamon to Blake "Sabrina" would call up spirits rather than "Ypwinesfloet"' (xiii). Another hint occurs four pages before the Queen of the Woods appears, when Ball reaches 'the ancient stillnesses' of 'the very core and navel of the wood' (181), an echo of 'the navel of this hideous Wood' in which Comus lives (line 520). Milton's wood is a place of 'enchantments,' of metamorphoses, of 'grim aspects,' and of 'barbarous dissonance.' Like the wood Ball has entered, it is quiet only at its centre. In Milton's wood, Comus casts a virtuous lady into a death-like sleep, from which she is awakened by the naiad Sabrina sprinkling Severn water on her. Sabrina,

> Made Goddess of the River; still she retains
> Her maid'n gentleness, and oft at Eve
> Visits the herds along the twilight meadows,
> Helping all urchin blasts, and ill-luck signs
> That the shrewd meddling Elf delights to make,
> Which she with precious vial'd liquors heals.
> For which the Shepherds at their festivals
> Carol her goodness loud in rustic lays,
> And throw sweet garland wreaths into her stream
> Of pansies, pinks, and gaudy Daffodils.
> And, as the old Swain said, she can unlock
> The clasping charm and thaw the numbing spell ... (lines 842–53)

Milton's naiad receives wreaths; Jones's dryad dispenses them. The latter is the former's counterpart and literary descendent. In her the pastoral element, which is parodied by Christmas morning's song contest and with reference to Milton's Nativity hymn, is here, at the end of *In Parenthesis*, set right with the muted assistance of a second poem by Milton. Jones's goddess is, however, a much more powerfully imagined figure than Milton's Sabrina. The Queen of the Woods personifies a confluence of divinities and fulfils desires for more than pastoral recovery and protection.

Underlying all the literary influences is a protosource in Private David Jones's experience in a field hospital on the day after he was wounded in Mametz Wood:

> I remember the hot tent & (not unnaturally) the voice, the very English, very upper-class 'decurion' voice of a nurse of some sort. I remember I thought it was the nicest sound in the world. *Voices are extraordinary, I think.* They have almost limitless power to deject, repell, bore or elevate, enchant, console, attract and all the rest ... that particular voice was special for me, for I'd not heard an English woman's voice then since the previous December (1915), so I suppose that having come straight out of

> the 'bloody wood where Agamemnon cried aloud' and gone to sleep (& I expect injected with some opiate) and coming-to in the hot marquee, & being asked, in cultivated English, how I felt, left an indelible mark on me. & indeed it may be, it may *well* be that that is why, in subsequent years, I've felt, to a rather exaggerated extent, the potency of hearing a certain sort of voice as if it were a *physical touch* – a healing thing it is almost, in a sense, anyway jolly nice.   (DGC 175)

While the written word can convey intonation, it cannot convey the timbre of a voice. So the Queen of the Woods is unheard, but quietly, in her ritualized intimacy, she approximates and symbolically recaptures what a wounded soldier heard in a nurse's voice.

In the Queen of the Woods, different levels of experience converge in a rare moment in literature which, in its context, is a transcendent and exceptionally moving piece of writing. It brings together in a single complex of images most of the threads of the poem's thematic interweave and takes them to their furthest degree of archetypal intensity.

DIALOGIC TENSION

The absence of Dai Greatcoat is the sole disquieting factor in the poem's concluding idyllic distribution of wreaths. The Queen of the Woods 'calls both high and low' for Dai, as a true lover calls in *Twelfth Night* (2.3.42). 'She can't find him anywhere ... she had a very special one for him.' He is absent on different levels of imagination. Realistically he is missing because he has been blown to bits; as archetypal soldier, he cannot be found among soldiers who have symbolically reverted in death to their elemental humanity; and he is absent from the conclusion of the poem (as the concluding reference to his absence emphasizes) because his place is at its centre.

The poem is a complex of many forms, which vary in allusive texture and depth and exist in varying relationships to one another. We have seen, for example, that there are complementary catalogues – one of infantrymen, the other of 'heroes' – and that the German dugout is juxtaposed with the cemetery chapel. There are also entire days which correspond to one another in their wholeness of presentation: the day beginning in Part 2 and ending at the end of Part 3, the day in Part 4, and the final day in Part 7. And we have seen how human figures, who are also symbols, correspond to one another in ways that have formal as well as thematic implications.

From the poem's multiplicity of interrelated shapes emerge the two overall forms I mentioned earlier: the climactic movement and the parenthetical, centered structure. Because it is temporal, climactic movement belongs to music and literature. Here it culminates in battle and in the mythic time beyond battle in which the goddess visits the dead. In contrast, centric form is spatial and visual. It typifies pictorial art.[17] In the poem its focus is Dai Greatcoat's boast. He is the centre, she the countercentre. Symbolically they complement one another, for he focuses the themes of the known real and she the themes of the desired possible. Together they constitute a dynamic structure, not only because they are symbolic complements but also because the aspects of form to which they belong exist in dynamic tension.

Because the goddess occupies the conclusion and because literary form is weighted at the end, she dominates the reader's initial experience. She occupies the foreground of memory, but her rhetorical advantage over Dai's centricity is counteracted by the reference to his absence during her visitation and by a pattern of allusions and images that emphasizes the poem's spatial structure. The pattern balances on the focal point of Dai's boast (79–84). The following is a partial list of the elements of this pattern with the numbers of the pages on which they appear:

Ball and hunting 2–169
blistered feet 6–119
'gas-pipe' 6–184
artillery and bees 20–118
Malory 6.15 31–180
the Brave Old Duke of York 32–124
obstacles in the night 32–179
wraiths, shades 33, 41–168, 179
Barbara Allen 33–185
motherlessness 34–176
Christabel 35–120, 130
Pauline 'shod feet' 36–159
muck raking 43–174
whited sepulchre 43–148
stretcher bearing 46–176
iron briary 50–166
chthonoi sleeping 51–163
Gethsemane's cup 52–158

the Ancient Mariner 52–184
rats, insects 54–157
wealed earth, cratered earth 59–97
Birnam Wood 60–179
Sleeping-Beauty thorns 60–165
Ezekiel's bones 60–175
Twelfth Night quoted 60–186
brumous morning 62–154
Isaiah's 'dyed garments' 62–167
opening lines of the *Inferno* 66–165
the golden bough 66–178, 183
Christmas, Easter light 68–98
dreaming of buxom women 69–128
loose tea and sugar 72–97
symbolic Eucharists 73–146
Ball speaks 75–142
Lewis-gunners at loophole 77–99
the boar Trwyth 86–155
Llywelyn 89–184

Add to these the repeated references to broken trees throughout Part 3 and Part 7 and the eruptions of archetypes through the narrative surface at the end of Part 3 and in Part 7. The configuration is roughly symmetrical and, as a whole, has the geometrical implications of a parenthesis. This composite spatial shape complements the poem's ritual pattern of inception and completion and focuses the centrality of Part 4 within the poem's broken momentum and the position of Dai's boast within the circular journey there. The parenthetical configuration of allusions and images is not obvious, because there are a great many images and allusions that are not part of it. But the pattern probably does influence the perception even of a reader not consciously aware of it, since the paired images do call to one another across the length of the work. Once the pattern is consciously perceived, it energizes the poem's spatially imagined, centric structure, which actively contends with the poem's temporal, climactic movement.

This elaborate parenthetical aspect of structure gives the poem striking architectural affinity with the *Iliad*, in which similar scenes are placed in balancing positions to echo each other – for example, the famous quarrel in Book 1 and the reconciliation scene in Book 24. Just as David Jones was influenced by the emphasis on geometric form in post-impressionist art theory, Homeric composition was influenced by the dominant contemporary visual style known as 'Attic high geometric.' And, of course, Jones may be influenced by the *Iliad* – about which he must have learned a good deal from René Hague (see DGC 259) – though, as we have seen, Jones achieves something more subtle and complex than Homeric form.

In *In Parenthesis* the spatialization of form is completed, in a sense, by the parenthetical configuration. It begins in allusions to romance and to liturgy, both of which transform the contemporary, plastic time of the poem's fictional realism into the fixed, structured time of epic, in which destiny displaces possibility. This is archetypal or mythic time, in which the outcome is known at the inception. It is paradigmatic time, realized all at once, as space is.

Making the poem's form spatial initiates a contest. The Queen of the Woods tends to unbalance the spatial equilibrium of knowledge, to go beyond it, but Dai Greatcoat refuses to submit to her attraction. The result is a dialogical tension between them and between the two dominant aspects of form which they represent. Not that there is any essential contradiction between knowledge and desire – but redemption, which is the object of desire, does not absolve society and the reader of the moral outrage of war. The secular mythos does not give way to the sacred mythos, since, if 'all manner of thing shall be well,' things are nevertheless not well now.

Although the poem's temporal movement and spatial structure inform literature here, the tension between them probably originates in the poet's experience as a visual artist. In the introductory chapter I mentioned his affinity with mannerism as a movement characterized by the use of visual distortion. Mannerist painters are also known for generating formal tension that makes the viewer vacillate between two equally significant and plausible but mutually contradictory visual interpretations. The most famous examples are the composite, multistable portraits of Guiseppe Arcimboldo, though such tension may be seen on a lesser scale in the movement toward and away from centricity in Rembrandt's 'Self-Portrait' (1600) and El Greco's 'Agony in the Garden' (c 1500). The same tension characterizes most of Jones's paintings, including 'The Garden Enclosed' and 'Petra im Rosenhag.' The affinity between the dialogic tension informing *In Parenthesis* and the tension characteristic of mannerism is suggested by Rudolf Arnheim's description of the latter: 'The Renaissance cherished the circle as the shape of cosmic perfection, whereas the Mannerist phase of the Baroque took to the high-strung ellipse, which plays on the ambivalence of roundness versus extension.'

Arnheim also says that 'the complexity of the Mannerist composition' sometimes involves the viewer in 'a tug of war that may offer no definitive outcome.'[18] David Jones writes about our attitudes to war, 'it is the business of a poet ... to express the dilemma, not to comment upon it, or pretend to a solution' (DG 130). The greatness of *In Parenthesis* is partly its Keatsian 'negative capability,' this fidelity to the dilemma of knowledge and desire. Its greatness also partly resides in the original expression of this dilemma by combining antithetical forms that are conceptually proper to different arts. Never before, in this century at least, had this been done.

The Anathemata

5

Form

The Anathemata is an anatomy of western culture from its prehistoric beginnings to the present. The tendencies distinctive of this genre are to catalogue, to enumerate, to digress, and to illuminate through encyclopaedic erudition. The initial indications of the poem's genre are the presence of notes on the pages of primary text and the quantitative near-equivalence of notes to text. *In Parenthesis* has fewer notes, and they are gathered at the back. In *The Anathemata*, notes and text are generically congruent, the difference being that the notes are prose, the text usually poetry. Seamus Heaney says that '*The Anathemata* ... is pedantry worked to the point of art – a very high art.'[1] 'Pedantry' is not quite the right word. For David Jones, knowledge is a corollary of love, not a means of ostentation. Moreover, the justification of its public display is its meaning and, as Heaney implies, the artistic shape to which it contributes. Jones knew a great deal more than he put into his poetry.

The Anathemata is, however, an anatomy unlike any other, except Pound's *Cantos*, and, with the *Cantos*, it constitutes a genre which I would call 'displaced epic.' *The Anathemata* is not, like *In Parenthesis*, a narrative poem and therefore cannot be an epic, but it repeatedly identifies itself as epical. Its opening words – 'We already and first of all discern him making this thing other' – launch the poem *in medias res*. Its long central monologue, which largely recounts sexual liaisons and a voyage, has some affinity with Odysseus's central narrative monologue to the Phaeacians. The poem alludes to Calypso (74) and at its conclusion explicitly evokes the conclusion of the *Odyssey*. Jones's poem implies a narrative, but as Harman Grisewood points out, 'the "imitable action" is outside the book.'[2] The action implied but excluded is that of

God the creator who becomes Jesus the redeemer. That is the mythos whose spirit – its meaning but not its form – pervades *The Anathemata* and makes possible the poem's anatomical approximation of the kind of epic Virgil invented in the *Aeneid*, a search through the remote and recent past for the meaning and destiny of a people. Anatomy can approximate and imply epic in this way because, as we saw with *In Parenthesis*, it is a subgenre of epic.

While *The Anathemata* is primarily anatomy, it contains all other genres. Its language and imagery are usually lyrical and often richly symbolic, so that the poem's movement in fictional time, if it is often rhetorical, is also governed by symbolic associations. The 'quasi-free association' (31) of the work's primary meditator and of the personae who think or speak within his imagining involves the psycho-logic of monologue and interior monologue. Narrative too is present: realistic and suspenseful in the dramatic account of an ancient ship approaching the dangerous Cornish coast, dramatic and allegorical in the account of the voyage of a medieval ship called the *Mary*. Imagined figures, speaking or silent, differ from one another in fictional modality, and a single figure may occupy the full modal range from realism to myth. As the poet suggests in his preface, this is poetry that abhors 'any lessening of the totality of connotation, any loss of recession and thickness through' (24). Certainly Elizabeth Ward, in her unsympathetic and reductionist reading of the poem, is wrong to say that it 'displays the one-dimensional quality of fantasy.'[3] In subgeneric interplay and modulation of modality this poem is at least as rich as *In Parenthesis* and employs, as *In Parenthesis* does not, the mode of allegory, the generic first cousin of anatomy.

The chief difference between the poems is that *The Anathemata* is free of the controlling gravity of a realistic narrative ground. As a consequence, its form is much less conventionally determined than that of *In Parenthesis* and therefore its shape is less easily perceived. The free form of *The Anathemata* resembles the fragmentation and juxtaposition of *The Waste Land* and other modernist works. But to say that is only to identify its method of sequential organization and fails to convey the impression made by its fragmentation in combination with the progression of its meditative consciousness.

The Anathemata comprises a multitude of images and personae moving like electrons in the four dimensions of space and time, a literary galaxy of moving parts in which the meaning of each part involves its symbolic resonance with the other parts. The poem's meditative awareness moves inward, often in the interrogative mood, towards the nucleus of these orbiting images. That nucleus is the Eucharist – for David Jones and other Christians committed to a traditional sacramental theology, the great Symbol, synonymous with time's central, redemptive event. The poem's meditative movement often loses direction in daydream digressions and loses impetus – while gaining in depth – in contemplation of figures who rise and then subside within the primary meditative consciousness. The images and personae in the poem's galactic orbits appear and disappear by means of a time-shifting more radical and far-reaching than anything Joseph Conrad and Ford Madox Ford (or Alain Robbe-Grillet in the 1970s) ever imagined. Always, however, and sometimes after many digressions, the original progression resumes. It is the ordered disappearance and reappearance of certain images and snatches of narrative that suggest orbits – as though the meditator moves straight through them, past the centre and out through the same orbits on the other side. This is an impressionistic description and needs qualifying. If, moreover, we shift our primary attention from the meditator's consciousness, as determining point of view, to the imagined temporal and spatial content of his meditative dream, our impression becomes that of a radical, mazy zigzagging up and down what Jones calls 'the history-paths.' Jeremy Hooker describes the poem this way, as a 'circular maze' involving 'the ritual pattern of initiation.'[4] His impression is valid, though I think the image of intragalactic (or subatomic) travel is truer to the poem's combination of rhetorically defined viewpoint and imaginative progression.

Criticism has barely begun to analyse the shape of the poem. That *The Anathemata* is thematically unified no responsible reader would question, but arguments for its formal unity have been vague and inadequate. The poet is partly to blame. In his preface he writes of 'the meanderings that comprise this book' and the 'sprawl of the pattern, if pattern there is' (33, 31). This I take to be David Jones's characteristic reluctance to make claims for his own work. The poem's subtitle, *fragments of an attempted writing*, also suggests disunity, though the poet explains his subtitle as referring to the genesis of the work, sections of it having originated in fragments of earlier manuscript material (14–15). The poem does consist of eight numbered 'fragments,' of course, each with its own title and, to a degree, its own unity. This raises the question of the work possibly being a sequence rather than a unified poem – a possibility which need not be entertained indefinitely if the poem is, as we shall see it is, structurally and thematically whole.[5]

There is a tendency towards sequence because two of its sections, 'Angle-Land' and 'Redriff,' stand as detachable units within the poem's structure. They are, however, contained by that structure and contribute to the meaning of the poem and to what I call the 'form of its content,' which we shall consider later in this chapter. When the poet regards the poem 'as a series of fragments, fragmented bits, chance scraps,' he refers to its content – to which, he says, he 'would give a related form, just as one does in painting a picture' (34). And in painting, as we have seen, David Jones does more than convey a sense of motion and variety: 'the ultimate problem,' he says, is 'to make a whole, a unity, out of varying parts. This is all I try to do.'[6] He implies that the poem has formal, structured unity, moreover, when he writes in his preface that 'ars is concerned with the shape of a finished article' (29).

The critics who argue for the poem's unity of form include Gwyn Williams, who claims that the poem conforms to the interlace pattern of Celtic art.[7] No doubt the abstract Celtic aural and visual aesthetic does influence the form of the poem. In his preface, the poet alludes to 'the "Battersea shield", and that ... other abstract art of the La Tène Celts in the British Museum' (32). But the image of Celtic interlace is of a kind of form rather than of a specific unifying pattern. Jeremy Hooker's sense of the poem as a labyrinth is a variation of Gwyn Williams's impression of form, though a variation with interesting symbolic connotations. Hooker also sees the poem as unified by a thoroughgoing interrelationship of symbols.[8] Neil Corcoran develops this insight with reference to what he calls 'metamorphic form,' a new and descriptive term for the musical theme and variation that characterizes symbolic interrelationships in most important modernist poems – though Corcoran demonstrates how Jones transforms the technique into a new means of extended progression that achieves change while retaining continuity.[9]

Symbolism is unquestionably an important aspect of the poem's form, though it is also, and perhaps primarily, a manifestation of content. It has formal but not (as Corcoran claims) structural implications. If the shape of *The Anathemata* consisted only of its symbolic resonances, Elizabeth Ward would have some reason for her assertion that the poem is 'incremental or additive' in form 'rather than genuinely complex in structure.'[10] She is echoing John Holloway, who wrongly equates Jones's rich, often metaphysical symbolic technique with Pound's 'mode of super-position,' or juxtaposition, but if we can allow the substitution for the sake of argument, Holloway has a point when he says, with regard to *The Anathemata*, that 'unless it is the servant of a deeper architectonic ... baldest accretion is what the mode of super-position naturally and characteristically creates ...' There is, however, an architectonic, or structure, in *The Anathemata*, and it does invalidate Holloway's judgment of the poem, endorsed by Ward, as 'an array of not-plannedness.'[11]

In some long works – the *Cantos*, for example – symbolic motifs are the sole constituent of form (which largely amounts to saying that these works merely cohere thematically), but *The Anathemata* has several additional, interrelated formal dimensions. First, there are structures or patterns implied in subject matter. Through these the poet discerns in the current of prehistoric and historical time what Proust calls 'the form of time.' These patterns are the result of imaginative-philosophical interpretation; they are the form of the poem's content, not the form of the poem. But they are integral to the work's two strictly formal aspects: its progressive movement, which is diachronic or extended through time, and its structure, which is synchronic or simultaneously present. As with *In Parenthesis*, the temporal movement and the synchronous or spatial structure of *The Anathemata* are, to a degree, antithetical. In fact, the movement repeatedly breaks on what is meant eventually to be perceived as the poem's structure. But ultimately – and here *The Anathemata* differs from its predecessor – both aspects of form are circular and their circles partly coincide. This coincidence occurs in the work's fictional setting.

The poet hints at this framing context when he writes that the poem contains 'matters of all sorts which ... are apt to stir in my mind at any time and as often as not "in the time of the Mass"' (31). In deference to this hint, Jeremy Hooker tentatively considers the poem as 'the meditations of a man attending Mass' but finally shies away from the hypothesis because it confines the poem 'to a specific temporal or spatial dimension.'[12] In a similar, uncharacteristic lapse into *a priori* criticism, Neil Corcoran also rejects this contextual hypothesis because the poem would be 'damaged if ... thought narrowly restricted to a single perceiving vision' of a meditating persona.[13] Certainly the poem's primary consciousness does not belong to a persona like those within the poem, who are dramatically involved in more or less realistic social interaction. Even more than *In Parenthesis*, this poem is an expression of 'the mind of Europe,' but the European mind can only exist within the consciousness of individual people. And what loss occurs if the person behind the poem is a persona rather than the poet? Ultimately, the distinction need not be made, but whoever is thinking the poem has a point of view rhetorically defined by the frequent questions he asks. He also defines himself by the selection of subject matter, though that is fairly comprehensive within the history of western civilization, since what is not explicitly included – the fate of the European Jews in this century, for instance – is often implied by symbolism or analogy. What to make explicit and what to imply is as much an expression of 'personality' as it is a decision required by poetic economy. The manner of exposition, what we call tone, likewise implies personality. And in this poem, even when that personality belongs to a projected persona, he or she is often, to some degree, transparent and mediates the awareness and convictions of the primary meditator. Moreover, the meditator refers to himself in the first person (115) and in autobiographical prose ('when I was a young man in France... And this I know...' 216). Regardless of setting, therefore, the poem is the expression of 'a single perceiving vision,' however broad and penetrating. And regardless of what the reader may prefer, the poem does have a realistic context, one even more 'narrowly restrictive' than 'the time of the Mass' – though, as if to demonstrate that 'less is more,' it is a context infinite in its symbolic implications. The context is not the Mass merely but the Consecration of the Mass. *The Anathemata* begins with the elevation of the consecrated Bread, the 'efficacious sign' (49), and closes seconds later with the elevation of 'the stemmed dish' (242). The fictional premise is as daring and original as it is suggestive. As if anticipating objections to so much meditation and daydreaming taking place in so short a time, the poet states in his preface:

> The speed of light, they say, is very rapid – but it is nothing to the agility of thought and its ability to twist and double on its tracks, penetrate recesses and generally nose about. You can go around the world and back again, in and out the meanders, down the history-paths, survey *religio* and *superstitio*, call back many yesterdays, but yesterday week ago, or long, long ago, note Miss Weston's last year's Lutetian trimmings and the Roman laticlave on the deacon's Dalmatian tunic, and a lot besides, during those few seconds taken by the presbyter to move from the Epistle to the Gospel side, or while he leans to kiss the board or stone (where are the tokens of the departed) or when he turns to incite the living *plebs* to assist him. (32)

However long the work takes to read, its meditative daydream occurs instantaneously, occupying only those few seconds during the latter part of the consecration. In this respect the poet speaks literally and with precision when he says that the work 'returns to its beginning' (33). One of Jones's metaphors for the poem is a traveller's 'song or story about a journey ... from his home through far places and back' (42). It may be that for the meditator and the reader, the end of all this exploring will be to arrive where he started 'and know the place' as if 'for the first time.'[14]

I will chart this journey, the work's sequential movement through meditated time. The difficulty of the work calls for a map, which, by briefly indicating the poem's content, should dispel certain critical misapprehensions, including that of M.L. Rosenthal and S. Gall, who consider the poem 'a mythical history of England.'[15] Moreover, no commentator – not even René Hague, who had the poet's help in writing his *Commentary on The Anathemata* – has accurately charted the poem's movement. A description of this movement will provide a context for subsequent discussion and a reminder that the initial experience of the poem is of the broken rhythms of its forward or inward progress. We shall see that the movement of the poem establishes patterns, sometimes parallel patterns, which attain the status of symbolism. It is during the initial sequential experience of the poem, moreover, that memory begins to spatialize literary time so that an overall structural pattern begins to reveal itself. This pattern consists of a number of closing circles, each involving a return to a beginning. The outer circles contain the inner ones in ordered succession and create a structure resembling the circles of a target, which diminish in radius with proximity to the centre. The following account of the poem becomes abbreviated as it progresses because the poem moves more often in the opening sections and later rests more often and longer in dramatic or descriptive vignettes and in reverie.

MOVEMENT

Part 1, entitled 'Rite and Fore-Time,' opens with the priest consecrating the bread and then elevating the sacramental body of Christ. This is done 'for *them*' (49) – the dead to whom the poem is dedicated in the Latin inscription facing the page and who are the special concern of Part 1. For them the Eucharist is efficacious by explicit 'pre-application' during the Last Supper and at the Offertory of the Mass. 'These' (49, 50), the priests who celebrate Mass in buildings crudely imitative of the architecture of earlier, healthier phases of western culture, are anachronisms in a technological civilization in which utilitarianism has habituated man to neglect significant, gratuitous expression. On the Roman Catholic priest is momentarily superimposed an ancient Roman *pontifex* who cares for ritual objects during an analogous phase of an earlier epoch (50). This is one of the poem's deliberate 'ambivalences' (31): it may be a metaphor; it may be a literary equivalent of photographic double exposure. The ambiguity clears as the Christian priest 'within the railed tumulus' (51; see n1) sings, as rubrics direct him, in 'a low voice,' like Jesus at the Last Supper as he institutes the Eucharist.

With this simile, the perspective of the poem shifts from the time and place of meditation to the setting of the Last Supper as the apostles Peter and John arrange seats and clean the room.

There follows a bracketed excursus (55–8) concerning the earliest geophysical processes that formed Jerusalem's height during Precambrian orogenesis (mountain making) and the Permocarboniferous glaciation. These begin the preparation that the apostles will complete on Holy Thursday afternoon. The account of these processes purposely conflates orogenesis and glaciation, which belong to adjoining Precambrian and Primary Palaeozoic geological ages. In doing this the poet reverses the ratio of climate to land elevation during orogenesis, when the land rose during cold periods and sank during warm periods.[16]

The place of the paschal events having been established, their historic, temporal setting becomes the centre of perspective for the ensuing search into the past, toward the time of the first men who died.

The Supper and Passion occur about two millennia since Abraham entered Canaan, and four millennia since man began to cultivate grain – events that precondition the form and meaning of the Eucharist. Its institution at the Supper, partly a work of *ars*, occurs twenty millennia after man's first symbolic artefacture. This is the cultural springtime of the race, associated with the springtime of modern western culture by reference to Gregorian chant. The meditative consciousness wonders how long ago on some other Palaeolithic springtime night, fire was first kindled. From that 'Easter of Technics' (61) all subsequent fires have been lit (as the fire spreads during the Easter Vigil from the paschal candle to all other candles in the church). The paschal events take place a hundred thousand springs since Neanderthal men buried their dead with tokens signifying hope in life after death.

The meditator wonders whether Neanderthal ritual derived from an older tradition originating during the Pleistocene glaciation. The climatic alternations of this glaciation (62–4), as distinct from those accompanying orogenesis (55), belong to the most recent ice age. It is during these oscillations and the consequent shifting of climatic zones in Europe that the human 'type' evolved most rapidly. This is the biological springtime of the race, aligned by reference to plainsong with the cultural spring earlier associated with chant. The Pleistocene shifting of climates is a metaphorical chanting of Lauds – this is the morning, as well as the springtime, of the race – chanted partly in German and Spanish to bracket linguistically the regions most affected by the fluctuating temperatures. What chiefly distinguishes this glacial age from its Permocarboniferous predecessor is that now men, not mountains, dance to climatic music.

These ritual dancers may have had human or humanoid ancestors in the preglacial, Tertiary warmth, and possibly before that. The temporal range of the poem reaches to the most remote point at which men may first have evolved. The prayer for these first among the human dead (65–6) marks the outer limit of those included among '*them*' (49) whom the Mass benefits. At this point the temporal perspective of the poem shifts from the paschal events to these earliest men, and its rhetorical movement rebounds, with special reference to geological changes, through ensuing Pleistocene and Recent times.

The first men lived and died before the receding Pleistocene ice packs formed basins for Welsh lakes, before the ice of that glaciation covered the mountains of North Wales, before ice moved south from Scotland, its floes carving river courses that would be migration routes. The earliest men lived before glaciers gouged out the Irish Sea.

'For them,' for these first among the dead, 'the New Light beams' from before time and through the epochs prior to human evolution (73). The Light is the Logos of John's Gospel, shining through every category and classification of being, penetrating each geological and biological layer including the stages of human evolution whereby we are and with us, eventually, the Light incarnate.

Having gone back as far as human existence allows and having traced the Light's beaming from before that, the poem's imaginative-rhetorical movement joins the Light moving in time's direction down the ages of man. Because man is mortal, the Light is now the funerary *lux perpetua*, penetrating the graves of an Aurignacian woman and nobleman (77), searching the remains of the neolithic kitchen-midden culture, penetrating to where the dead of the Bronze Age lie, searching the raised, sacrificial platforms within the trapezoidal enclosures of Terramare, which are the historic prototypes of the Roman quadrilateral plan. The destiny of all dead men, and our lot too, is illuminated by the Logos, whose protosign is water, which makes fertile the earth so that 'his barlies grow / who,' like Osiris, 'said / I am your Bread' (82) at the Last Supper. From page 73, the poem's consciousness and the penetrating divine Light have been moving gradually up through geological and archaeological strata to the earth's top layer of 'dark humus' (82). They finally break the surface with the growing barley.

Part 2, 'Middle-Sea and Lear-Sea,' resumes the temporal perspective and line of questioning seen earlier (61) but now dating the paschal events with reference to the historic past in a sort of countdown. The questions will break off and resume again, reaching conclusion in 'Mabinog's Liturgy' on page 189. It is nearly twelve hundred years since the fall of Troy, and fewer years since the prehistoric beginnings of Rome, which an anonymous Roman persona briefly contemplates. But how many years since Clio, the muse of history, subsequently found Ilia pregnant and in labour with 'the Roman people' (86)? A parenthetical flashback records Ilia's memory of intercourse with Mars on the site of the city's foundation. The paschal events take place about 500 years since the liberation of Rome from the Etruscans, 167 years since Tiberius Gracchus attempted unsuccessfully to bring about land reform, 61 years since the principate was established in 27 BC.[17]

The line of questioning returns to 1200 BC, not now to Troy but to Greece, when invading Dorians 'fractured the archaic pattern' of Mycenaean culture. The forms of the succeeding Greek culture are derivative of the declining Cretan civilization, but six centuries later 'kouroi' (young men) and the 'Korê' (Maiden) appear in sculpture not again equalled until the twelfth century AD, and perhaps not equalled since. A century later come 'the skill years' of classical sculpture. The paschal events occur 'one hundred and seventeen olympiads,' or 468 years, after Phidias sculpted the statue of Athena Parthenos, seated in the Parthenon or 'Maiden's chamber' (94). And outside, towering above, is the bronze figure of Athena Promachos, the 'champion' or 'foremost fighter' – visible as far away as Sunium.

The countdown breaks off as the poem focuses on a Greek ship heading for Phaleron, the ancient port of Athens, sometime after 450 BC.[18] Coming from the eastern Mediterranean, the vessel has rounded Sunium and is within the Saronic Gulf. The sky is overcast, the sea grey. Suddenly, at the exact month, day, and hour of Christ's death, though centuries before, the sun emerges from behind clouds, blueing the Aegean. In the bright light – evocative of the Light shining through fore-time – the colossal statue of Athena Promachos atop the Acropolis becomes visible, delighting the Attic top-tree boy, who is coming home, and the sea-hardened old captain, who is supposed by the crew to be of ancient Phoenician origin and to have sailed to mythic Thule.

From this point (97, line 20), a ship is imagined approaching Cornwall, not the Greek ship nearing Athens but one manned by Phoenicians and Phocaeans sometime earlier, possibly in the second millennium BC (see 105 n2).[19] It sails 'from Phaléron' (103) and so extends the previous ship's voyage, but only symbolically. The more ancient vessel's destination is Ictis Insula (St Michael's Mount), a port of the tin trade in Mount's Bay between Bolerion (Land's End) and Ocrinum (The Lizard). Because of obscuring fog, the bay is not sighted, and the ship continues up the channel until the top-tree boy sights Dodman Point. His crying the landfall is postponed (98, line 22) by an account of the voyage thus far, which leads back to him calling out 'Cassitérides!' (102) or Tin Islands, thinking he sights one of the Scillies. In his premature enthusiasm he invites his mates to consider the effect of their imminent fortunes on sweethearts back home. But the brume clears and it becomes apparent that they have passed their port and so must reverse course. Sailing south, they are driven by wind toward the rocky Cornish coast and are in danger of being wrecked. But they manage to skirt The Lizard, steer towards Land's End, turn into Mount's Bay and then toward the 'hoar rock' of Ictis Insula. Whether they finally arrive safely remains uncertain.

The reversal of course at Dodman's Point parallels the poem's movement so far: first into the past and then, from the 'sighting' of the first prehistoric dead man (66), towards the future in which the paschal events take place. The correspondence of the two movements is stressed when it is asked of the Dodman, 'and did he call it / the Deadman' (98)? The meaning of the parallel is, at least partially, an equation between the paschal events, towards which time and the poem are sailing, and wealth, which facilitates sexual coupling or marriage.

In several respects, furthermore, the entrance into Mount's Bay corresponds to the Greek ship's entrance to the Saronic Gulf earlier in the poem but centuries later. The two haven-findings are juxtaposed to emphasize the correspondence. The account of each entrance is incomplete. The gulfs entered by the ships resemble one another in physical topology because each is located in the southern end of a peninsula and opens toward the southeast. Moreover, the course of the Phoenician-Phocaean ship returning around the Lizard exactly parallels the course of the Greek vessel that has rounded Sunium. In some sense these two comings into harbour – and perhaps every other ship's arrival – are archetypally simultaneous.[20]

In Part 3, 'Angle-Land,' topological references continue up the east coast of Britain from beyond Dodman Point, so that the voyaging symbolically continues the course broken off at page 102. But the temporal reference has shifted forward to after the fifth century AD, when the Anglo-Saxon settlement is already well under way. Moving up the coastline, the poem's consciousness wonders whether a ship, any ship, sailed safely past the sandbars, shoals, rocks, and fogs south of the Thames. It might have gone down there or beyond, past Kent, whose Angle settlements bear '*ingas*-names' (111), past Essex, once the land of Boudicca's British Iceni, or past *Venta Icenorum* near modern Norwich, where Saxons bury their dead. The ship's wreck might be past the fens and, farther, past towns ending in 'ham,' 'ton,' and 'thorp' – like Burnham Thorpe where Nelson was born.

And it might have entered waters where the flow of the island's eastern watershed is 'confluent with' and 'tributary to' the 'fathering' Rhine (114). This image of Britain's essential unity with continental Europe is anticipated when, in Pleistocene times, 'Thames falls into Rhine' (64), a reference inserted into 'Rite and Fore-Time' after 'Angle-Land' was added to the poem. This confluence of rivers occurred before glaciation gouged the place of their confluence for the North Sea to fill. Still the waters mix, making a '*Brudersee*' (115), which is symbolic here of the kinship then being established by the racial mix on land. But brotherhood will turn to fratricide during the modern world wars, when German submarines will operate 'from Orcades to the fiord-havens,' violently complementing the supposition in 'Angle-Land' that a ship may have been sunk.

Part 4, 'Redriff,' opens with the meditative voice wondering whether the ship, any ship, entered the Thames and ordered replacements and repairs of Eb Bradshaw, master mast and block maker. The time now is the mid-nineteenth century. And the incident actually took place, between a ship's captain from Palermo and the poet's maternal grandfather, whose name really was Ebenezer Bradshaw. Most of this section is his monologue. He is imagined listening to a messenger from the ship requesting quick, unprofessional service that would allow the vessel to avoid prolonged payment of heavy harbour fees. Bradshaw refuses. He has evidently been offered extra money to procure wood, for he refuses to relax his standards even for the sorts of wood that he proceeds to catalogue. An attempt may have been made to intimidate him, for he says he will not bend, not even for the 'port's authorities' or 'the Trinity Brethren' (who, in 1909, would be renamed 'The Port of London Authority') or for the pope of Rome. His monologue is an extended dramatic pun on his Protestantism.[21]

Bradshaw is portrayed as Cockney in the 1955 BBC radio production based on the poem, and one critic identifies his speech as Cockney.²² But I remember Jones protesting, 'The accent is not Cockney. The right accent is home-county – well, Churchill had a bit of it, and George V. The "g"s were dropped at the ends of words and it was "gels" instead of "girls." These Rotherhithe work-supervisors wore top hats.' By the mid-Victorian period, Cockney was the speech of London's lower class; Bradshaw was middle-class. A photograph survives in which he sits – bearded, handsome, physically powerful, and wearing a formal black Sunday suit – obviously no mere workman.

Part 5, 'The Lady Of The Pool,' consists mostly of the monologue of Elen Monica, who peddles lavender in the dock area of London in September sometime between 1451 and 1465, the years of John Whethamstede's second term as abbot of St Albans (see 153). In her youth, Elen had been intellectually and sexually appetitive. That she is no longer young is indicated by her wondering whether one of her former lovers died 'young' of the 'black deth' (128-9). Her age and the section's autumnal setting symbolize cultural decline in the late Middle Ages.

The section begins with the meditator wondering whether the captain of the ship (any ship) came to London, which is, in the Middle Ages, upstream from Bradshaw's Rotherhithe.²³ If he did, he might have met Elen. She is heard calling her wares and stops to warn a Mediterranean captain of the coming cold, which is heralded by the feast of the Exaltation of the Cross (14 September) soon to be celebrated in London's churches. She intends to urge him to ship out before winter catches his Mediterranean craft in the North Atlantic, but deviates from her purpose to catalogue certain of the churches in which Crouchmasses will be said. She will return to her original purpose after a mazy discourse which is the spoken counterpart of 'the troia'd lanes of the city' she represents. In fact most of her monologue consists of this long parenthetical excursion, within which further excursions open up, each within its predecessor. The first excursion, the catalogue of churches, is interrupted by another concerning the possible success of a former lover, a 'cock-clerk' she knew just after his graduation from Oxford (128-9). A subsequent and very long digression from her listing of churches concerns two meetings with another lover, who was a veteran of the Hundred Years War (133), a 'freestone mason,' an ardent Romanophil, and a habitual daydreamer. To interrupt one of his Roman reveries, Elen once protested her own lack of learning. But she was quick to qualify her self-deprecation by relating what she had learned from various sailors.

165 Form

Ebenezer Bradshaw

One of these was 'the master o' the *Mary*' (137), whose voyage she describes, including its crew's temptation by mermaids. In the face of her listener's skepticism, she impersonates a mermaid-siren (143–6). After recounting other of the ship's ordeals, she characterizes certain of its crew, paraphrasing its Welsh boatswain's antique comparisons and his elaborate boast and oath as they were related to her by one of the crew (149–54). Her account of the voyage also incorporates material learned from a sailor of Syro-Phoenician and Pelasgian parentage, who had also described to her two ancient voyages, one around the coast of the Red Sea, the other from Egypt around Africa and back. Reminded by Egypt of the childhood of Jesus, she mentions certain events of his life.

Elen's consideration here of the Passion and its relationship to the Eucharist (157–8) is the furthest excursion from the original intention of warning her listener about the imminence of winter and occurs at the fifth level of remove, occupying the focal point of a recession of four excursions within her monologue. The first is the catalogue of churches, the second concerns the mason, the third concerns the captains of ships that include the *Mary*, the fourth is the Syro-Phoenician's tale of ancient voyages. These excursions are the innermost of the poem's circles. From here on they begin to close, one after another in order of increasing measure of radii from the inner circles to the outer. Elen returns to the Syro-Phoenician's stories, refers once more to her having learned from captains, then to her mason-lover, whom she never saw again. She finishes listing the churches, concludes her warning about winter, and resumes calling her wares.

Part 6, 'Keel, Ram, Stauros,' opens with a continuation of the questions about the typical captain that introduce the poem's previous three parts. The questions fade back into those of the Greek crewmen about their particular captain (171), an inquiry begun in 'Middle-Sea' (97) and interrupted by the more ancient voyage to Cornwall. The Greek ship is now within Phaleron harbour. Its crew members remark on the captain's excessive drinking and complain about their proletarian condition.

Then the poem's consciousness focuses attention on the ship's keel. Whether of rowboat (with 'capping and thole,' 174) or sailing ship, the keel is the basic beam on which every other constituent of the vessel rides. A catalogue follows of the structural wood extending upward and outward from the keel to the above-deck paraphernalia and finally to the crew who are 'over-all' (175). This movement from the keel up recalls the movement of the Light (another kind of 'beam') in 'Fore-Time' up through geological and archaeological layers. The parallel implies equivalence between the earth and the ship so that, like the Light, the Keel is the divine Logos underlying and sustaining cosmic order.

After contrasting war engines, which the world-ship carries, with wooden cult objects, and after a parting consideration of the keel, attention returns to the Greek captain as he pours a libation toward Athena Promachos. His ship draws in towards its berth, finally ending the voyage already nearly complete at page 96 in 'Middle-Sea.'[24] This haven-finding is the first and last voyage of the poem. Structurally it contains, and symbolically it unifies, all intervening voyages as constituent of the single great voyage of mankind. With this voyage's end, one of the poem's outer circles closes, containing within it the closed circles of Elen Monica's monologue.

Another outer circle begins to close at the opening of Part 7, 'Mabinog's Liturgy,' with a resumption of the temporal perspective and questions last seen on page 94 of 'Middle-Sea.' This countdown to the paschal events reaches the imagined present, when Sejanus runs the empire for Tiberius, then dissolves in mythic reverie about the cross as maypole (190–2). The reverie is followed by the numinous sight of Gwenhwyfar (Guinevere) standing for the Offertory of a midnight Christmas Mass (195–205). The description of her, which may be the lyrical high point of the poem, is followed by the conversation of three Welsh witches. While speaking of Mary they make esoteric references which give way to boasting about erudition but, as if in imitation of the humility of the Virgin, they are led by one of them named Marged to kneel 'if only on this, HER NIGHT OF ALL' (215). Psychologically, the piety of the witch Marged is unconvincing, but the poet immediately peeks from behind her persona to admit all this has been 'allegory' and 'fancy-fed.' The reader does not have to believe it. After this admission, the poet recalls Christmas fraternization of soldiers with the enemy in 1915, a realistic and historical collective change of heart which may be equally incredible and is, like that of the witches (and perhaps of Gwenhwyfar), temporary – but still significant.

The poem returns to midnight Mass in early-medieval Britain, though not necessarily the one Gwenhwyfar attends, and then to Rome where the pope is celebrating Christmas Mass. 'Mabinog's Liturgy,' the theme of which is metamorphosis, concludes with this final metamorphosis: Christian Rome from what had been the imperial city of Tiberius and Sejanus at the opening of the section. So far the poem has moved thematically from geophysical and biological through racial and cultural metamorphoses to spiritual metamorphosis.

168 The Shape of Meaning

In Part 8, 'Sherthursdaye and Venus Day,' meditation returns to Jerusalem and concentrates on Jesus at the Supper and on the cross. The section nears completion as the sacrifice of Christ simultaneously takes place at the Last Supper, on Calvary, and at Mass. These three are momentarily synchronous in triple exposure (from 241, line 7, to 242, line 10) to suggest their theological identification, for Christ's sacrifice is pre-enacted at the Supper's oblation, enacted in Calvary's immolation, and re-enacted in the Mass.[25] As far as the crucifixion is concerned, the triple exposure relies on the evocation of the cross by 'the *upper* cave of bread' and of the two crucified thieves by the statement 'between his creatures again his body shows' (242). ('His creatures' are also the apostles in the upper room.) The poem ends as the triple exposure resolves first into the double exposure of the Last Supper and the Mass (242, lines 11–17), then into the single image of the modern Mass, the priest elevating the chalice and completing the action of consecration already under way moments before on page 49. The final elevation, which closes the poem's outermost circle, might be read as being performed only by Christ at the Supper instead of, finally, only by the priest at Mass were it not for the repeated references to Masses 'in many places' (242, 243) and the footnote referring to 'the rubric which has already directed him – when he handled the bread to consecrate it' (242 n5). This rubric is echoed in the prayer quoted in Latin in note 2 on page 49.

STRUCTURE

While teleological for the most part, the movement of the poem is ultimately circular by virtue of its return to meditative setting. This circular closing is the outermost of a recession of circles that constitutes the poem's structure and may be visualized as follows:

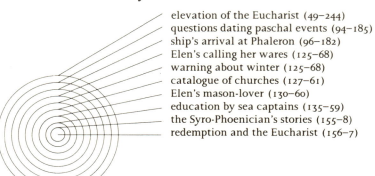

elevation of the Eucharist (49–244)
questions dating paschal events (94–185)
ship's arrival at Phaleron (96–182)
Elen's calling her wares (125–68)
warning about winter (125–68)
catalogue of churches (127–61)
Elen's mason-lover (130–60)
education by sea captains (135–59)
the Syro-Phoenician's stories (155–8)
redemption and the Eucharist (156–7)

Some might prefer to diagram the narrative structure as a linear recession of parentheses. But a parenthesis implies an extended interval between the opening and closing of brackets, whereas the poem's start and finish are virtually simultaneous, coinciding as they do with the priest's brief continuous act of consecration. Conceptually, then, what might appear to be a parenthesis is really a circle, for which there is no hiatus between opening and close. If this is true for the poem's outermost circle, it is true as well for the circles contained within it. They are all figures of simultaneity, as is the entire recession of circles, for the poem's outer circumference coincides with its central point: sacramentally, the Eucharist and the paschal events it makes present are identical.

The poet himself seems to have visualized the structure in this manner. He writes that 'The Lady of the Pool' concludes by returning to earlier themes in a movement 'back, by a wide circle' (*IN* 80). In an introduction for his 1967 recorded reading from the poem, he writes that '*The Anathemata* is cyclic in character and however wide the circles the action of the Mass is central to it and insofar as a circle can be said to have a "beginning" or an "end", it begins and ends with the Mass.'[26] So the Mass is at the work's centre and, since circles 'begin' and 'end' on their outer curve, the Mass is its circumference. It is interesting, if only in an anticipatory and subliminal sense, that while working on the material which would ultimately become *The Anathemata*, David Jones sometimes uses the expression 'wheels within wheels' (to G 21 May 1940). Certainly his awareness of the structure of the finished work influences his remark that the poem 'has not a "plot" in the English sense of the term, but it is, I suppose, a kind of "dance round the maypole" of the *stauros* – I suppose' (*IN* 75).[27]

There are certainly hints of structural circularity in the poem. Elen introduces her brief, central recalling of the Passion with reference to Jerusalem as the 'navel of the world' (156). And the innermost circle enclosing the central passage is associated with the Syro-Phoenician's account of a 'periplous' (155 n3) and a 'circumnavigation' (156 n3), terms for voyages whose courses are circular.

Any doubts the reader may have about the structure diagrammed above would be dispelled by an examination of the extensive early manuscript drafts of the poem, which clearly reveal the major steps in its composition. You do not have to see these drafts to perceive the poem's structure – I first noticed it six years before seeing them – but the drafts do show that David Jones discovered the structure of his poem early in its composition.[28] He began by selecting a short fragment containing the beginning and end of the finished work. Influenced probably by having inserted new material into the middle of Dai's boast at the centre of *In Parenthesis*, Jones split *The Anathemata*'s ur-fragment in half for the insertion of additional material. The result was a text about five times as long, which he halved again to insert more material, including 'The Lady of the Pool.' In composing that section, he initially wrote to the end of the brief celebration of the redemption and the Eucharist, which is the centre of Elen's monologue and of the poem. He subsequently added the closing of the monologue's circles, the closing of the outer circles already being achieved by the previous splitting of the text. Jones writes, 'What I have written has no plan, or at least is not planned' (33). The qualification is important, for it suggests that there is a structure and that it was discovered during the composition of the work.

It is incorrect to assume, as Neil Corcoran does, that the poem's 'structural possibilities were discovered only long after the actual composition of individual sections of the poem' and that Jones practised 'composition by the juxtaposition and patterning of pre-existent fragments.'[29] Premature assumptions about the work's 'fragmentary' nature imply that it is a sequence, whereas structurally it is a single work. True, it is based on material the poet began to write in 1939, but he performed a radical deconstruction of that material before using parts of it in *The Anathemata*. Moreover, the poem is largely made of entirely new material written between 1946 and 1952: Jones attests that in reworking the earlier 'wodges of stuff' he made 'a quite different form... with wholly new & long passages added, e.g., most of the "geological" theme in Section I & all "The Lady of the Pool" & "Mabinog's Liturgy," most of "Sherthursdaye & Venus Day," all of "Redriff" & large parts of "Middle Sea & Lear Sea." Yet none the less a lot of stuff was here & there drawn upon from the material written in Sheffield Terrace [during the war], but a lot more either eliminated or wholly recast & entirely rearranged' (to G 9 October 1971).

The Anathemata seems, in fact, to be a sequence inside out. In 1939 Jones began writing a number of Mass-poems, some set in London, one in Dublin. Four of these survive. In one of them (*RQ* 113ff), the attention of a daydreaming meditator moves from the Mass he is attending to the Last Supper and then to the Passion. This is exactly the movement of *The Anathemata*'s ur-fragment. All these Mass-poems involve a tendency to move mentally away from the Mass in progress. Jones seems to have had in mind a sequence of poems with different meditating personae and different settings. The sequence was apparently to be entitled *The Mass*.³⁰ He abandoned this sequence and at some point in 1946 decided to write a long poem with a single celebration of the Mass for its setting. At that point he selected his ur-fragment, which is one of these Mass-poems or a section of a longer Mass-poem, and split it. In its creative potential and imaginative results, it was, for David Jones, an act as momentous as splitting the atom.

Perhaps the passage of twenty-nine lines that I say is the poem's centre (156–8) has not previously been perceived as such because, except for the formality of its regular half-line lengths, it does not call much attention to itself. About this I may be wrong. Corcoran, who has been especially sensitive to the poem's language, calls it 'one of the great set-pieces of *The Anathemata*.'³¹ But the passage is nevertheless nothing like as lyrically powerful or as memorable as other episodes, the description of Gwenhwyfar, for example. There seems to me a teasing paradox between the restraint with which the central passage is written (or the quiet inwardness with which it is imagined as spoken) and its central, structural importance to the poem. It is a paradox reminiscent of mannerist technique in the visual arts. In fact, the understatement involved in the paradox resembles that in Brueghel's painting of the fall of Icarus, a catastrophe seen only by a small shepherd who, though he occupies the centre of the painting, is the last figure in it to be noticed by the viewer. In any event, the poem's structural symmetry defines the centre of the poem, and its subject justifies this centricity, for the paschal events and the sacrament with which they are synonymous are the principal focus of the poem. And, as Rudolf Arnheim puts it, 'elementary visual logic dictates that the principal subject be placed in the middle.'³²

Because of its centred structure, *The Anathemata* comes to a final stop inwardly but is capable of infinite expansion. This may account for the poet's initial sense of the work as fragmentary, possibly unfinished, or incapable of completion. The poem's proof copies bore the title *Part of The Anathemata*.³³ After all, anything else he might publish would also have to be centred in the Eucharist, and it is true that thematically all his subsequent poetry is an extension or elaboration of *The Anathemata*. But that poetry is excluded from this poem by structural closure. By the return to setting, Jones made *The Anathemata* whole and complete; it is not an open structure in the sense of being capable of continuation.

In its paradoxical equation of centre and circumference, the poem's structure symbolically corresponds to the sacrament with which it is coextensive. In the Eucharist, divinity, the infinite Sphere containing all being, becomes contained by the finite physical sphere. According to Gregory the Great, it is characteristic of God to be 'penetrating in encompassing, encompassing in penetrating' (*Morals* 2.20), but in the sacrament, divine immanence answers in a special way to divine transcendence.

The poem's structure may derive from the ancient figure of the divine circle, symbolizing perfection and fulfillment. The image has been used paradoxically since the twelfth century when it first received its most familiar expression: 'God is a sphere of which the centre is everywhere and the circumference is nowhere.' This paradoxical image has been invoked as illustrative of the form of *The Anathemata*, but, while it may suggest thematic homogeneity, the image is of a circle that is not a circle and therefore can have no bearing on form.[34]

The image of the circle has been applied to the Incarnation, however, in ways that do resemble the poem's structure. The seventeenth-century German poet Johann Scheffler writes, 'When God lay hidden in the womb of the virgin / Then the Point contained the Circle.'[35] And Richard Crashaw describes the infant Christ as the 'All circling point, All centring sphear.'[36] Such images for the Incarnation apply equally to the Eucharist, which extends, and is the sacramental counterpart of, the Incarnation. We shall see that the correspondence between the Incarnation and The Eucharist is one of the themes of *The Anathemata*.

Whatever its source or analogues, the image of circles whose centre is also their outermost circumference symbolizes the poem's major theme of the Eucharist being implicit in, and containing, everything. The structure, involving intermediate spheres, is not static but diffusive: the centre radiates through the spheres towards their outermost circumference, which itself radiates inward. The intermediate spheres mediate this intraradiation partly by means of the poem's symbolic correspondences, through which all suffering and every joyous consummation has its centre of meaning in the paschal mystery. Because the poem is not only multicyclic but also encyclopaedic its spheres involve virtually every aspect of material and human existence. In a letter to Saunders Lewis in 1971 David Jones writes that 'the action of the Mass was meant to be the central theme of the work for as you once said to me, "The Mass makes sense of everything."'[37] The poem's structure of circles within circles is a symbolic corollary of that statement.

Defined as it is by its setting in time, the structure of *The Anathemata* implies a simultaneity that has its analogue in the sacrament, for by the theological principle of anamnesis, the consecration of the Mass annihilates time. In the Eucharist, Christ is, in a real sense, made present and his Last Supper and Passion are re-enacted. The poet quotes a passage of Gregory Dix explaining that sacramental anamnesis is not merely a mental recollection of something absent, but has the sense of '"recalling" or "re-presenting" before God an event in the past so that it becomes *here and now operative by its effects*' (205 n1). Temporal and spatial distances are lost in a reality greater than time or space. Because of its context in time, the poem is timeless in the sense that it should finally be apprehended all at once. Only then, moreover, can its inner structure be clearly perceived.

This is the only extended work of literature that corresponds in its conceptional fiction to Ezra Pound's definition of an image as 'an intellectual and emotional complex in an instant in time.' Most extended narratives involve a variation between action and exposition – Proust's *Combray* is a famous example. Much less common is variation between dramatized and undramatized or subjective time. It occurs in *In Parenthesis* when the 'real' time of the primal shell-burst slows to allow the full significance of the event to register. It occurs more spectacularly in the 'Circe' episode of *Ulysses* where five minutes of dramatized time expand, because of semiconscious reveries, to fill 123 pages of text. Relative to brevity of 'real' time, expansion of subjective time is even more extreme in Ambrose Bierce's story 'An Occurrence at Owl Creek Bridge,' in its clone 'The Secret Miracle' by Jorge Luis Borges, and possibly in William Golding's *Pincher Martin*. But *The Anathemata* is the most radical and symbolically powerful expansion of undramatized, subjective time in literature.

At the source of the poem's disparity between chronological time and subjective time may be Einstein's theory of relativity. David Jones writes that relativity theory 'was much in the air' in the 1920s (to H 24 September 1974), and we know that he read Arthur Eddington's *Space, Time and Gravitation* (1920) and met and conversed with Eddington.[38] That relativity theory was on his mind during the composition of *The Anathemata* is suggested by his reference in the preface to 'the speed of light' (32) and in the poem to 'the bent flanks of space' (68). In 1938 in *The Book of Balaam's Ass* manuscript he writes that 'space itself, they say, leans, is kindly, with ourselves, who make wide deviations to meet ourselves' (*RQ* 188). The image equating curved space with a circular temporal journey has implications for the form of *The Anathemata* if we consider the broad thematic organization of its content as a sort of spatial curve.

PHYSICAL AND SEMIOTIC CONTINUINGS

We have been considering form abstractly, almost as though it existed apart from content, but there is another dimension of form which is virtually indistinguishable from content or statement – the thematic disposition of material. This dimension of form establishes a special complementary relationship between the opening section of the poem and its two concluding sections. The conceptual basis of this formal relationship is the rhyming of the Incarnation and the Eucharist, a correspondence implied in the poem when the Supper-room in which Jesus institutes the Eucharist is called 'the high cave' (52), 'his second Ephrata,' (the ancient name for Bethlehem), 'the *upper* cave of bread' – an evocation of the Hebrew *beth lehem*, 'house of bread' (242). The correspondence is further implied by the juxtaposition of Christmas and Holy Thursday in the last two parts of the poem.[39] Of the Last Supper it is said, 'there's continuity here' (51), and that can also be said, obviously, of the Nativity.

For the Supper, continuity consists of the related traditions of human artefacture and ritual; for the birth, continuity is geophysical and biological. These continuities are linked by a remarkable synthetic combination of geophysics, biology, theology, and semiotics in a vision of cosmic harmony which exceeds even that of Teilhard de Chardin. At the end of 'Fore-Time,' the poet alludes to Milton and Darwin in his reference to the worm from whom 'is exacted the night-labour' that makes the earth fertile (82). Jones thought it a 'pity old Darwin did not have a glimpse of what even Milton, in his blindness, had a glimpse of' (to H 24 September 1974). By 'blind' instinct, animals cooperate with the rest of nature for a purpose that Jones, like Teilhard, sees as revealed in Christianity. But the geophysical-biological theology of Teilhard, whom Jones first read a decade after completing *The Anathemata*, is incomplete. I remember Jones regretting that Teilhard knew nothing about the arts.[40] To whatever in the poem has affinity with the broad vision of Teilhard, David Jones adds an implied analysis of primitive art and ritual signs. The latter involve conventions of meaning that derive from prior and similar forms and are continuously grounded in human psychology, in which the primary realities are sex, food, and death.

Consideration of these linked physical and cultural continuities begins near the start of the poem in prehistory and culminates at the end of the poem in the birth of Jesus and in the institution of the Eucharist. In a handwritten note found in one of the poet's copies of *The Anathemata*, David Jones cryptically describes this aspect of the poem's organization and discloses its paradigm:

> The liturgy, cycle comes full circle:
> from the cosmic Advent to the
> Xmas & Paschal nts.
>   W. A's Gwenhewyvarr we
> assist at
>   In the last – we are back.

The poem's 'cosmic Advent' is its opening part, 'Rite and Fore-Time.' The themes of this section culminate on the night of Christmas Eve in the penultimate part, 'Mabinog's Liturgy,' and on the night of the Last Supper in the final part, 'Sherthursdaye and Venus Day.'

Like the liturgical season of Advent, 'Rite and Fore-Time' anticipates Christ's birth and his second coming. Its liturgical text is the earth itself. Orogenesis and glaciation pre-enact the Baptist's prophecy recurring throughout Advent, 'the mountains and hills shall be made low' (cf 68 n2), when during the Precambrian Era mountains 'for one Great Summer / lifted up' are 'by next Great Winter / down' (55). Certain stages of geological formation also recall the messianic assertion that the 'first shall be last and the last shall be first': seven-hilled Rome lies under low 'terra-marl' of the earlier Po Valley culture from which Rome's quadrilateral plan is derived. And 'it's Ossa on Pelion now' (55). This is a reversal of a mythic reordering with its own apocalyptic overtones, for in an attempt to reach heaven two giants piled Ossa on Olympus and then Pelion on Ossa (*Odyssey* 2.315ff).[41] Biological forms too are prophetic, for in the earth's Mesozoic life-strata 'Tyrannosaurus' lies 'down with herbivores' (74), like the lion and lamb of Isaiah's text.

Prophecy here is a metaphor for physical preparation, in which the geological formation of the earth as place of the Incarnation is joined in its latter stages by the evolution of biological life. These processes are implicitly acknowledged in the Mass of Christmas mentioned at the conclusion of 'Mabinog's Liturgy,' which, Jones notes, emphasizes 'the physical birth of a child in time at a specified site' (220 n4). And, if the liturgy also emphasizes the 'radiance which the birth sheds on the world-darkness' (221 n3, n2), the same radiance shines already, though less brightly, throughout prehistory. This is emphasized in 'Fore-Time's' coda or partial recapitulation:

> From before all time
>   the New Light beams for them
> and with eternal clarities
>   *infulsit* and athwart
> the fore-times:
>   era, period, epoch, hemera.
> Through all orogeny:
>   group, system, series, zone.
> Brighting at the five life-layers
>   species, species, genera, families, order. (73–4)[42]

Throughout every category and classification of being shines the 'New Light' – words taken from the Collect of the second Mass of Christmas. The words 'clarities / *infulsit*' evoke the Christmas Preface, which reads, *nova mentis nostrae oculis lux tuae claritatis infulsit*.[43] These liturgical allusions imply that the Incarnation is the destiny of the earth and of life from their earliest stages of formation and development.

Later in the coda of 'Fore-Time' the divine Light illuminates specific earth-layers that record the principal stages of evolution down through mammalian sexuality, which makes the Light shine 'Brighter,'

>   for these continuings
> certainly must praise him:
>   How else, in his good time
> should the amorous Silvy
>   to her sweetest dear
> her fairest bosom have shown?
>
>   How else we?
>   or he, himself?
> whose name is called He-with-us
> because he did not abhor the uterus. (74–5)

Christ, the prophesied Emmanuel or 'God-with-us,' is human because, in the words of the *Te Deum*, 'he did not abhor the Virgin's womb.'

Linked with the prehistoric themes anticipating the Incarnation are those that culminate in the Eucharist, which also has to do with sex.

The coda of 'Fore-Time' moves from the uterus to the 'uberal forms' of female breasts, and then to the question, 'How other his liturgy?' The breast is the first source of nourishment and therefore the prototype of the sacrament whose sign is food. This is further implied in 'Fore-Time' by a reference to the Venus of Willendorf, a prehistoric sculpture of the earth goddess:

> Chthonic? why yes
> but mother of us.
> Then it is these abundant *ubera*, here, under the species of worked lime-rock, that gave suck to the lord?   (60)

The earth mother represented here prefigures Mary and implies the mode of her son's chief sacrament. Breasts 'under the species of worked lime-rock' recall the theological formula whereby Christ is said to be present 'under the species of bread.' Partly because of this 'continuing,' then, the prehistoric Light shines also at the institution of the sacrament on 'Sher [ie bright] Thursdaye.'[44]

Bread too comes from the mother, Mother Earth, and partly by the same prehistoric geophysics that anticipates Incarnation. Grain for bread grows only after the Pleistocene glacier recedes. Metaphorically, its recession is liturgical: 'This is how Cronos reads the rubric, *frangit per medium*, when he breaks his ice like morsels, for the therapy and fertility of the land-masses' (69). By way of the ancient conflation of Cronos and chronos, Father Cronos is geological time personified (and preordained). His action conforms to the rubric directing the priest to break the host during Mass and echoes on a grand scale 'the fracture sound' referred to in 'Sherthursdaye and Venus Day' (227). The land freed by the breaking of ice is subsequently readied by water and 'the essential and labouring worm' (82). Only then do 'barlies grow' so that in the fifth millennium BC 'the first barley mow' can take place (58).

Grapes and barley, the gifts of the earth, have yet to be transformed by art and technology. Bread, for example, requires the fire which first 'wormed / at the Easter of Technics' early in fore-time (61). It 'wormed' instead of 'warmed' to suggest the first curl of smoke but also to recall its biological counterpart, the 'labouring worm' essential to the growth of grain. As important as the first lighting of fire is the forming of the first cup during the neolithic kitchen-midden culture. This 'rudimentary bowl' is the technological prototype of 'the *calix* / without which / how the re-calling?' (78–9).

Technology is necessary to the sacrament, but not sufficient; ritual or symbolic making is also essential. The neolithic cup, for example, would have no liturgical future without the world of signs evinced by the palaeolithic 'cup-marks' of Neanderthal funeral rites (61 n2, 65), and later by the rite of sacrificial libation performed by the Greek sea captain (182). In 'Rite and Fore-Time,' the relation of the sacrament to such signs parallels the dependency of Christ's physical body on prior biological mutation. Symbolic forms, like biological forms, are 'co-lateral' and 'cognate' (63, 65), but they do not, strictly speaking, evolve. They are 'things ... laid up from other things' (28), and passed on in traditions, often parallel traditions, of causal or typological recession from which form and significance are partly derived. And this is as true for the Passion as it is for its sacramental recalling. 'Men can but proceed from what they know' (79).

Christ's death has its prehistoric prototype in the hunt, which for primitive man was sacrificial, and the hunt has its own proto-Eucharistic anamnesis. In 'Sherthursdaye and Venus Day,' the place of crucifixion is called 'the hill of the out-cry' as he 'by whom all oreogenesis is /... cries from his own *oros*' (233). (Here the Greek for 'hill' puns on the Latin for 'mouth.') Christ's 'hill-cry' echoes the scream in 'Fore-Time' of an animal victim immolated for the life of the family or tribe when, during an ice-age hunt, Cronos 'might see how his lemmings run and hear the cry of his tailless hare' (62). The allusion to the nursery rhyme about the hunting of 'three blind mice' implies that the human race is in its infancy. (It is, writes the poet, 'the earliest "nursery rhyme" told to me by my mother' [to H 24 September 1974].) Words from this rhyme recur, significantly, in a passage concerning the ritual enactment of the hunt's violent immolation:

> And see how they run, the juxtaposed forms, brighting the vaults of Lascaux; how the linear is wedded to volume, how they do, within, in an unbloody manner, under the forms of brown haematite and black manganese on the graved lime-face, what is done, without,
> far on the windy tundra
> at the kill
> that the kindred may have life.   (60)

The stone's 'lime-face' and its 'brightening,' which evokes the Logos-light, recur during the crucifixion in 'Sherthursdaye And Venus Day' when 'the dark cloud brights the trembling lime-rock' (237). (The earth is quaking, the limestone of Calvary appears bright against the dark cloud.) But the cave-painting, like the Eucharist, is an 'unbloody' enactment of sacrifice, 'under the forms of' haematite and manganese instead of bread and wine. The correspondence here of what is done 'within' to 'what is done, without,' is echoed later in references to the Last Supper taking place 'within' (227, 228). The words 'they do,' in their syntactical isolation here, take on special ritual weight, as they would in Greek, Latin, or Hebrew.

The specialized use of the verb 'to do' associates the ritual art of Lascaux with the earliest rite of fore-time, 'the *Vorzeit*-masque' performed by generations of 'antlered mummers':

> The mimes deploy:
> > anthropoid
> > anthropoi.
> Who knows at what precise phase, or from what floriate green-room, the Master of Harlequinade, himself not made, maker of sequence and permutation in all things made, called us from our co-laterals out, to dance the Funeral Games of the Great Mammalia, as long, long, long before, these danced out the Dinosaur? (63)

The 'green room,' where actors wait before coming on stage, exists in the tropical Tertiary period when man first evolved. The creative Logos is here a theatrical director, calling actors out of 'co-laterals,' an anthropological pun on stage-wings. The elaborate dramatic metaphor is significant. The primal dancing of the race is literally *dromenon*, the origin of the word 'drama' and also the Greek for 'rite.' It means 'a thing done,' specifically a thing ritually pre-done or re-done.[45] The funerary aspect of fore-time's masque suggests the tragic mode, which, in turn, may recall the earliest known form of Greek *dromenon* and the origin of tragedy – the dithyramb enacting the death of Dionysus, who is remembered at the end of the poem under the epithet 'Liknites' (232). His *dromenon* and that of the immolated mammoths are liturgical doings. As such, each anticipates Christ's command at the Last Supper to 'DO THIS / for my Anamnesis' (205) and exemplifies the sense in which the Eucharist at the Supper is a predoing of Christ's sacrifice and, subsequently, has been a redoing of it.

Diverse traditions or cultural orders have their own interrelated rites and symbols, but all together, and irrespective of historical relationships, they form a 'scale or Jacob's ladder or song of degrees' (30) with the Eucharist at the top, incomprehensible but for the subordinate

180 The Shape of Meaning

symbols that sensitize man to 'significance.' Because it conforms to 'the *disciplina* / of this peculiar people' (241), as the Jews are called in Deuteronomy 14:2, the Eucharist is directly linked to prior signs. But the meaning of the sacrament also resonates with historically unrelated rites and signs. The use of bread and wine, for example, is symbolically evocative of the dying gods Dionysus and Tammuz, who are evoked at the end of the poem with reference to the route from Bethlehem to Jerusalem (232-3) and are ritually symbolized by wine and bread respectively. The ahistorical, inward continuity of the sign-world also justifies the Roman analogues to the Last Supper late in the poem. One of these is augury (226), a rite in which a battle's outcome takes place in advance of the fighting. This and other Roman metaphors imply, furthermore, that the distinction between other-worldly and this-worldly symbols is not fundamental and that the acts of Jesus fulfil and transform the meaning even of ritual forms that have become subordinate to utilitarian considerations. In every historic instance of ritual action, there is inward continuity with what Jesus does, who institutes his sacrament

> in accord with the intentions
>   of all peoples
> and kindreds
> *et gentium, cenhedloedd, und Völker*
> that dance
>   by garnished *Baum*
> or anointed stone.   (241-2)

As the poet puts it elsewhere, 'what was accomplished on the Tree of the Cross presupposes the sign-world and looks back to foreshadowing rites and arts of mediation and conjugation stretching back for tens of thousands of years in actual pre-history' (*E&A* 168). The poem's geological, biological, artistic, and ritual motifs generate a broad relationship of development and fulfilment between 'Fore-Time' and the poem's final sections. We saw that a similar parenthetical curving informs the motifs of promise and fulfilment in *In Parenthesis* and that there too the allusive basis of form is liturgical. In *The Anathemata* the more than merely thematic correspondence between the opening section and the two closing sections receives special symbolic focus in the figure of Gwenhwyfar in 'Mabinog's Liturgy.' The poet suggests this by his cryptic reference to Gwenhwyfar in the handwritten note quoted earlier. The

181 Form

Christmas Mass she attends in sixth-century Britain involves a thematic convergence of the Nativity and the Eucharist, in which all the themes of 'Fore-Time' find a single, symbolic consummation. In the next chapter, we shall see that Gwenhwyfar herself personifies these themes and becomes a typological equivalent of the earth – the heroine, as it were, of prehistory.

TIMESCAPE

The form of a literary work is related to, but not the same as, the shape of its content. Works of literature must generate their own form, and they must also discover shape or pattern in their subject matter. Coherent structure does interpret the content of *The Anathemata* by giving it aesthetic form, and we have seen that content is also interpreted by a cumulative thematic placement by which the birth and paschal acts of Jesus in the final sections fulfil the human and prehuman metamorphoses of its opening section. But there is much more to the content of the poem than this, for *The Anathemata* also concerns historic culture in the West. We shall now examine how the poet comprehensively interprets ancient and modern western history by a theory of culture that delineates the changing status through time of spiritual values within phases of civilization. In doing this he implies that history has a distinctive inscape.

By impressionistic time-shifting, the poem's meditative consciousness zigzags back and forth through western history. The result of this fracturing of chronology is a temporal structure more significant than mere diachronic sequence. Similarities between various culture-phases gradually emerge which initially suggest Spengler's morphology of cultural life-cycles. Here David Jones is indebted to *The Decline of the West*, which he reread in the 1940s while working on *The Anathemata*.[46] According to Spengler, parallel phases are contemporary. They occupy identical sections of time's morphological curve. But Spengler's conceptualization of time is modelled on the biological cycle, whereas David Jones's conceptualization is modelled on the seasonal and mythic cycle of birth, maturity, death, and rebirth, which he probably derives from *The Golden Bough*. In *The Anathemata*, declining civilizations become matrices for cultural vitality that eventually transforms collapse into renewal. This schema extenuates the cultural mortality of Spengler's closed circles, therefore, by breaking them, connecting them to each other in sequence, and extending them into a spiral.[47] In this way, the poet retains the conventional continuity of ancient, medieval, and modern culture-phases, which Spengler intends to do away with by separating 'classical' culture from 'modern' culture. The spiral of time and the formal affinity of that spiral with what we saw to be the poem's structure are initially suggested by the poem's epigraph, a folk fragment suggestive of an infinite regression of circles connected by narrative continuity so that they form a spiral:

> IT WAS A DARK AND STORMY NIGHT, WE SAT BY THE
> CALCINED WALL; IT WAS SAID TO THE TALE-TELLER,
> TELL US A TALE, AND THE TALE RAN THUS: IT WAS A
> DARK AND STORMY NIGHT ...

By assimilating the audience, moreover, this aural fragment implies the transfictional aspect of the poem as concerning the historico-cultural reality '*WE*' inhabit.

The meaning of time's continuous helix is not merely progression – as, for example, with the Hegelian dialectic; the spiral remains Spenglerian to the extent that it retains morphological repetition.[48] In this respect Jones's temporal schema resembles that of Yeats. For both poets, morphological repetition makes possible, through significant similarities and differences, the psychological illumination of historically separate culture-phases. But Yeats's long view of time is limited to meaningless movement back and forth within interpenetrating gyres. The centre of Jones's spiral is, by contrast, a continuous forward movement which is teleological and, as we have already begun to see, gives time a cosmic meaning. This movement initially coincides with that of the Light shining through fore-time, and will end in the ultimate disclosures of apocalypse. But the initial difference between the morphologies of Yeats and Jones is in the psychological principle by which each discriminates between culture-phases.

For David Jones, the principle of discrimination is the balance between utility and gratuity – utility being the technological motive, gratuity the quality essential to religion and art. Derived originally, as we have seen, from Aristotle, the distinction between utility and gratuity 'is the only rubicon' Jones acknowledges as 'dividing the activities of man' (E&A 275). A culture-phase predominantly on one side or the other of this rubicon produces anathemata, or special things, by which its character may be distinguished. Jones's idea of anathemata is influenced by Spengler's conception of symptoms of 'the physiognomic of world happening':

Poems and battles, Isis and Cybele, festivals and Roman Catholic masses, blast furnaces and gladiatorial games, dervishes and Darwinians, railways and Roman roads, 'Progress' and Nirvana, newspapers, mass-slavery, money, machinery – all these are equally signs and symbols in the world-picture of the past that the soul presents to itself and would interpret. (I 160)

David Jones brackets this passage in the copy of *The Decline of the West* that he was reading in the 1940s. For the poet, the physiognomic symbols or anathemata on one side of the rubicon contrast with those on the other side. Jones intends the title of his poem to connote this contrast: he writes in his preface that the word 'anathemata,' which originally means 'holy things,' means just the opposite in the New Testament, and, he continues, 'this duality exactly fitted my requirements,' serving 'my double purpose, even if it did so only by means of a pun' on the English 'anathema' (28). The duality of Jones's title deserves stressing, since critics habitually interpret the word 'anathemata' only in its positive sense.[49] Positive anathemata symbolically express positive spiritual values; negative anathemata imply the displacement of such values by pragmatism and expediency. Positive anathemata are primarily symbolic; negative anathemata are only secondarily and inadvertently symbolic. Between these two extremes are anathemata that combine the gratuitous with the utile in equal or inverse proportions. The proportion or disproportion of this combination is the primary indicator of the spiritual and cultural condition of a historical phase. Another, parallel indicator in this poem is the presence or absence of imperialism.

The exploration of time in *The Anathemata* extends back into prehistoric fore-time, but only during the three millennia of western history does a spiralling shape clearly emerge. This shape is that of a continual metamorphosis which formally evokes and extends through history the geological and evolutionary mutations of fore-time. During the historical millennia, culture-phases rhyme to form a pattern centring at the time of Christ. In this respect David Jones shapes his synthesis of Spengler and Frazer to traditional patristic historiography. With Christ at its temporal centre, it is a schema with striking affinity to what we have seen to be the poem's centric, conceptually spatial structure.

In *The Anathemata*, the phases preceding the Incarnation rhyme with corresponding phases that follow it. The aftermath of the Dorian invasion rhymes with the medieval Dark Ages, sixth-century Greece rhymes with the high Middle Ages, fifth-century Greece rhymes with the late Middle Ages, and the period of Roman world dominance rhymes with the modern commercial and industrial age extending from the Renaissance to the present. While consistent in sequence, these chronological parallels involve no relative correspondence between dates or durations of phases. There are, furthermore, internal rhymes cutting across the regular rhyme-pattern which preclude simplistic schematization and which have, till now, obscured the poem's cultured *cynghanedd* of historical phases.

The Dark Ages that follow the fall of Rome rhyme with the wake of Mycenaean civilization, which is destroyed by Dorian 'storm-groups' (90). As the evocation of Nazi blitzkriegs suggests, David Jones believes we are now entering a new Dark Age.[50] But the correspondence is primarily between the Dorian invasion and the barbarian destruction of classical Roman civilization.

The Dorian warriors 'fractured the archaic pattern,' and their rule from the end of the Bronze Age into the Iron Age is distinguished by no enduring cultural achievement. The voice of the poem asks, however,

> Within the hoop
> of the iron years
>   the age is obscure –
> and is the age dark? (90)

Darkness, as distinct from obscurity, may be no more applicable here than it is to the period glibly called the Dark Ages by historians of the Enlightenment. If Greek artisans under Dorian rule 'beat out utile spares,' they also shape 'amulets' to signify the 'new-god-fears' of raiding Dorian captains. Here, as in the recent Dark Ages, gratuity is eventually restored to balance utilty, and this makes possible a renewal of cultural vitality: 'From the tomb of the strife-years the new-born shapes begin already to look uncommonly like the brats of mother Europa' (91). The tomb of Mycenae is the womb of the ancient West – at parturition, 'the West-wind on our cheek-bones.' If this age is dark, it is the darkness of dawn, 'very grey and early in our morning' (91).

The corresponding gestation of the modern West during the more recent Dark Age is the subject of 'Angle-Land' and is touched on during the description of Gwenhwyfar in 'Mabinog's Liturgy.' In the latter, in Britain at the start of the Dark Age, 'the situation is obscure' (204) and so recalls that of post-Mycenaean Greece. A century or more later, in what is now Angle-land, barbarian invaders have fractured the archaic pattern of Roman city-life. Once-civilized Roman Britons are forced to flee

> from the *fora*
>   to the forests
> Out from *gens Romulum*
>   into the *Weal*-kin
> *dinas*-man gone *aethwlad*
> *cives* gone wold-men ... (113)

The cultural mix-up of Latin, Celtic, and Teutonic elements is figured in the language – fractured and fused, halting, broken (though musically assonant), Babel-like. Concerning the start of the current Dark Age when post-Roman Britons fight a guerilla war, it is asked,

> has toga'd Rhufon
>   (gone Actaéon)
> come away to the Wake ...? (112)

'The Wake' is the funeral watch and eddying aftermath of Roman Britain, and it also recalls the Saxon outlaw Hereward the Wake, or 'the alert,' who, centuries later, will resist the Norman invaders and so re-enact the present resistance. 'The Wake' evokes *Finnegans Wake*, furthermore, which is concerned like 'Angle-Land' with metamorphoses of language and culture and, like *The Anathemata* as a whole, with cyclic time.[51] The evocation of Joyce's *Wake* implies imminent cultural revival.

The nature of this revival is hinted at by reference to Irish 'Nials gathering hostages' (204), who include St Patrick. He is one of the Celtic saints, many of whom will enter England and appeal to the 'god-fears' of the barbarians who dread the apparition of a Roman-British ghost announcing 'IAM REDIT ROMA' (112). The Latin of Virgil's Fourth Eclogue, interpreted in the early Church as prophesying the coming of Christ, here also recalls the prophecy about Arthur, who led the Roman-British resistance, a prophecy which has affinity with the words of MacArthur, 'I shall return.'[52] Christian culture will return, and it will be Roman. Cultural renewal is the primary difference between Jones's historical schema and that of Spengler, for whom a culture dies and remains dead at the end of its life-cycle. Because Elizabeth Ward thinks Jones merely borrows Spengler's morphology without transforming it into something new, she insists repeatedly and at length on the poet's 'historical pessimism' and 'private cultural despair.'⁵³ Neither pessimistic nor optimistic, unless by turns, Jones's spiralling schema anticipates more than a new Dark Age, which in any event is not dark with the darkness of despair but with the obscurity of gestation, which will issue in rebirth.

Jones's 'despair,' which is only for our particular phase of culture, can hardly be considered private when it is shared by many of the great writers and thinkers since the inception of the Industrial Revolution and by the most important modern writers, including Joyce – if Earwicker's impotence means anything in *Finnegans Wake* – and Beckett. In his preface to *The Anathemata*, Jones writes that cultural decline has 'been evident in various ways to various people for perhaps a century; it is now, I suppose, apparent to most' (15).

In historical sequence, the next correspondence between culture-phases is between Greece in the sixth century BC and Europe in the thirteenth century AD.

In Hellas it is now, since the Dorian takeover,

> Six centuries
>   and the second Spring
> and a new wonder under heaven:
>   man-limb stirs
>   in the god-stones... (91)

This wonder, which contradicts the cynicism of Ecclesiastes, is both aesthetic and spiritual. Greece experiences a 'second Spring' – words that combine Spengler's term for cultural vitality with Newman's term for a general renewal of religious life. Before this, cult statues are almost entirely chthonic, 'god-handled' like the Venus of Willendorf (59), but now for the first time sculpted kouroi capture human nature in balance with the divinity they symbolize. This balance is analogous to the hypostatic union of humanity and divinity in Jesus. The analogy is underlined by the statue of the 'Delectable Korê,' which seems 'all parthenai made stone' (92), and is therefore an aesthetic approximation to the Incarnation, in which 'the Word was made flesh.'⁵⁴

This Kore also evokes famous women – one who helps shape the ancient culture-phase which the Kore represents and two at least who help shape the modern culture-phase to which the ancient phase corresponds:

> by the radial flutes for her chiton, the lineal, chiselled hair
> the contained rhythm of her
>   is she Elenê Argive
> or is she transalpine Eleanore
> or our Gwenhwyfar
>   the Selenê of Thulê
>   West-Helen? (92)

The career of 'transalpine Eleanore' of Aquitaine (transalpine from the Greek point of view) has marked affinities with the story of Helen Argive. Moreover, Eleanore commissioned the Arthurian romances. As the heroine of these romances Gwenhwyfar is 'West-Helen' – the counterpart to the heroine of the Homeric epics, which, at this time in Greece, are about a hundred years old in written form. The ancient epics and the modern romances are anathemata with a great deal in common: they are concerned with love, war, and the end of civilizations, and are redactions of centuries-old oral traditions. Regarding this correspondence, the poet writes in an early, pre-foliation draft of the description of Gwenhwyfar in 'Mabinog's Liturgy' that she is as

> Helenê too, for some bitter
> tides flooded & neaped to
> her lunulations, and over our
> New Hissarlik the fires
>   because of her
> & neo-Hectors dead
>   because of her
> and over all the West a New Song
>   to this day
> because of her.

For 'transalpine Eleanore,' Jones may also have in mind the Eleanore who married Llywelyn, the last Welsh prince, whose death in 1282 is the final reverberation of Arthur's fall and therefore a near-contemporary historical enactment of the written romances. Jones calls Llywelyn 'the living "Arthur"' (to G 11 December 1970).

The numinous Kore of sixth-century Greece radiates the profound paradox of feminine humanity. She is 'Agelastos Petra,' the chthonic Laughless Rock of Eleusis, but as the poem says, addressing her, 'you smile from your stone' (92). The paradox has to do with Kore Persephone being a dying and rising goddess. Sculpture approximating the Kore in quality, and such a smile, will occur 'not again, not now again' until a nameless queen smiles from the *Portail Royal* of Chartres Cathedral, one of the 'west-portals / in Gallia Lugdunensis' or central France (92), which David Jones visited in 1933 with Eric Gill. (Together, in fact, they visited Chartres Cathedral.) At Chartres the lady's smile represents a new, post-Romanesque humanism, and it expresses the belief that she, like the smiling Kore, will rise from the dead. Near the medieval smiler, at the centre of the west *portail*, is a statue of Christ in which 'the Word is made stone' (93) — words that echo the description of the sculpted Kore of the earlier, parallel phase.

Now, as then, personal resurrection has its analogue in cultural renewal:

... West-wood springs new
           (and Christ the thrust of it!)
and loud sings West-cuckoo
           (Polymnia, how shrill!)   (92)

In the spirit of the smile, men of the Middle ages are singing,

   Sumer is i-cumen in –
    Lhude sing, cuccu!
   Groweth sed and bloweth med
    And springth the wode nu.
      Sing, cuccu!

From Polymnia, the veiled and solemn muse of stately hymns, this eleventh-century song is surprising. Especially shrill is the word 'cuccu,' the highest part of the madrigal, sung by the highest voice. It is the high Gothic period, and the high proportion of gratuity and symbolism in its anathemata make this, like sixth-century Greece, a 'second Spring.'

The spiral of time next turns to the late classical culture of fifth-century Athens, which corresponds in spirit to the late Middle Ages:

Down we come
      quick, but far
   to the splendours
      to the skill-years
and the signed and fine grandeurs.

189 Form

> O yes, technique – but much more:
> the god still is balanced
>   in the man-stones
>   but it's a nice thing
> as near a thing as ever you saw. (93–4)

Sculptured figures, now no longer predominantly 'god stones,' still symbolize divinity, although the balance between god and man is precarious. Examples of such sculpture in this period are the colossal statue of Athena the Champion towering beside the Parthenon and, within, the chryselephantine statue of the Parthenos by Phidias. She symbolizes wisdom but she is also a warrior goddess. Later we shall see that historically, in Greece at this time, Athena is a morally ambiguous figure, but for now we will concentrate on the archetypal purity with which she personifies classical wisdom and evokes the Hellenic devotion to the arts that informs western culture. The 'grandeurs' of Athena are 'enough and to snare: / West-academic / West-hearts' (94). As everyone knows, the Renaissance seeks to be and to some extent is a rebirth of the spirit and ideals of classical Greece. But the correspondence here is to the Middle Ages, which is when this rebirth really begins – with the monastic preservation of classical texts, with the practice of rhetoric and the other classical arts, and with the influence of Aristotle and Plato on scholastic philosophy and theology.

Elen Monica, 'the Lady of the Pool' of London in the late fifteenth century, imagines a theological dispute consisting of the interplay of the liberal arts inherited from classical Greece:

> ... does the Trivium curtsy and does each take
> hand and to the Quadrivium call: Music! for a saraband?
>   And does serene Astronomy carry the tonic *Ave* to the
> created spheres, does old Averroes show a leg? (129)

If the music of the spheres accompanies an *Ave Maria*, it is because the debate concerns the dignity and theological status of the Virgin Mary, the Christian counterpart of Athena. The Greek goddess in her fifth-century 'Maiden's chamber' is a 'tower of ivory' and 'house of gold' and, towering above the Acropolis outside, a 'Virgo Potens' (94) – all titles of Mary in her litany. Like Athena, who personifies wisdom, Mary is liturgically identified with wisdom (see 234 n1), and 'the budged owls' or scholars of Oriel College who argue about her recall the totemic

190 The Shape of Meaning

night-birds of Athena-Minerva. On a medieval Christmas Eve in 'Mabinog's Liturgy,' the witch Marged says of academics in their ornate universities, 'more surely on this night the white owls of Britain, seeking their Lady Wisdom where the columned Purbeck gleams, would find her under Pales' thack, *ad praesepem*' – at the stable (215–16). The classical allusion to Pales and the Latin of the medieval nativity hymn concisely evoke the Spenglerian contemporaneity of the late classical and late medieval cultures.

Moreover, medieval disputation corresponds aesthetically to classical sculpture by maintaining (but only barely) a balance between technique and gratuity – because the elaborate technique of disputation serves the gratuitous purpose implied by the root meaning of the word 'philosophy,' love of wisdom. The ultimate 'uselessness' of medieval disputation is underlined by the chaplain of the medieval ship *Mary* posing the question, 'Sirs, consider nautics, is it in itself a good?' and by the vehement cursing this elicits from the Redriff mate (149).

The balance between 'technique' and utility reflects a cultural harmony between what Augustine calls the earthly city and the city of God – 'the twin-*urbes*' (50) that all men inhabit. Elen Monica indicates this balance in the late Middle Ages when, at the start of 'The Lady of the Pool,' she marks time 'by tax-chandler's Black Exchecky Book' and also by 'Archie's piscopal *Ordo*' (127). The imagery here recalls Christ's remark about taxes: 'Render to Caesar the things that are Caesar's and to God the things that are God's' (Mark 12:17). Late classical Greece and late medieval Europe have in common, then, this exact cultural balance, 'as near a thing as ever you saw.'

Time's spiral turns, finally, to the period of Roman world dominance, which corresponds to the military and commercial imperialism that begins in the Renaissance and reaches its height in the mid-twentieth century. Of all the poem's temporal parallels, this one receives by far the greatest emphasis, and it demands, therefore, special attention. One of the criticisms of *The Anathemata* that irked David Jones is the complaint that the poem is not contemporary in its content, that it 'draws mainly on the last few millenniums *exclusive of the last few decades*' (*E&A* 138). Recent decades are not absent from the poem but present by implication through analogues in Roman history which presume the reader's knowledge of contemporary history. This is a reversal of what Eliot calls 'the mythic method,' for the implied parallel works not from the present to the past but from the past to the present. In this poem, moreover, the twentieth century is an extension of the previous century, which receives a great deal of explicit attention.

The correspondence between imperial Rome and the present age is established at the start of the poem by the 'Cult-man' who is at once, metaphorically or by double exposure, an ancient Roman pontifex and a modern Catholic priest (50). Both priests live in phases of civilization in which aesthetic and spiritual balance has been lost, though neither priest may realize 'that dead symbols litter to the base of the cult-stone, that the stem by the palled stone is thirsty, that the stream is very low' (50). (The stone table, the tree, and the pool of the Roman *Atrium* are also the altar, the cross, and the font of a modern church.) The images here evoke those of Eliot's *The Waste Land*, in which

> ... you know only
> A heap of broken images, where the sun beats,
> And the dead tree gives no shelter, ...
> And the dry stone no sound of water.   (lines 21–4)

As the surviving cult implies, for early Rome there were once 'wonder years' (85). But numinous myth was soon displaced by imperialism and pragmatism. This change is captured in the metamorphosis of the god Mars implied in the recollection of him by the earth-figure Ilia, on whom he fathered Romulus and Remus. In words evocative of the coming of the Holy Spirit at Pentecost, she remembers 'how his glory filled the whole place where we were together' (85; see Acts 2:1–2). He is 'of the Clarissimi' – a member of the highest social rank but also, as one of 'the bright ones' of heaven, a god and a planet. But he approaches Mother Earth like a technocrat. First he surveys the site, locating the position of the market place on the Palatine where the 'sacred commerce' is to take place. Then he proceeds, without gratuitous foreplay, 'nor had he gratitude to unlace the mired greaves of surly iron' (87). In retrospect Ilia realizes that 'his aquila over me was robbery,' in contrast to the banner of love in the Song of Songs (2:4). Their intercourse typifies its fruition. Ilia is the first to know: ''T's a great robbery / – is empire' (88).

For Ilia and for the earth, 'departed myth / left ravished fact' (86), but the diminution occurs first of all in the god Mars. Just as pre-Mycenaean Athena was a goddess of fertility and subsequently became a war goddess, Mars is originally an agricultural deity – as Ilia can still tell 'b' the clod smell on him.' She calls him a 'Georgie,' punning on Virgil's agricultural *Georgics* and on 'Geordie,' which is slang for a Newcastle pitman, who in pre-industrial times would have been a farmer and who remains as a miner the farmer's industrial counterpart, reaping even if he does not sow. Like the modern Geordie, Mars has left the farm and has undergone metamorphosis. No longer a fertility god, he wears a Bronze-Age Greek helmet, which associates him with imperialist Athena, and body-armour to signify his recent identification with Ares, the god of war. His ancient liturgical text – which originally may have meant 'Be thou sower, Sower Mars, sow the soil' – is now interpreted, as Jones notes, 'Be satiated fierce Mars, leap the threshold' (176). He retains his elemental sexuality, but in brutalized form.

The modern transformation of vital culture to imperialistic civilization is projected in the siren whom Elen Monica imagines as tempting the late-medieval ship *Mary* to its doom. As with Mars and with all mermaids, her approach is sexual. But she promises another kind of commerce as well, for she asks of sailors 'a trident,' a shield ('Ægis'), a helmet, and somewhere to sit (145–6). In short, she – the siren, that is, not Elen Monica who impersonates her – wants to be Britannia, symbol of the British empire. And, from the Renaissance on, she *will* be Britannia – a debased Athena, goddess not of wisdom but of pragmatic greed. She plagiarizes Athena's iconography but is basically the female counterpart to imperial Mars, with whom she is linked symbolically by her deadly sexuality. He is her true archetype, and that suggests a trans-sexual dimension to her perverse, aggressive femininity. Britannia is Mars in drag.

The brutal sexuality of Roman Mars is expressed in a series of ancient weapons with sexually suggestive nicknames. These include 'Bumping Hecate,' 'Long Doris,' and 'Lysistrata No. 2,' which recalls the play by Aristophanes that has as its dominant image the erect phallus. By operating such siege engines, a British recruit in the Roman army earns his reputation as 'the layer, from Londinium' (177). In one of the twenty-three prefoliation drafts of the passage about siege engines, they are called 'piercers of the echelon'd veils of cities.' Later we shall see that cities in this poem are feminine.

Roman war-machines symbolize dehumanization in imperial Rome and evoke the same condition in the modern world. They are offensive weapons and therefore essentially imperialistic. Their chief significance is not their use, however, but the restriction of their meaning to their usefulness. In an essay published in 1947, David Jones writes that weapons are quintessentially utile, owing 'their existence and meaning to what they *effect* rather than what they *are*.' If they are beautiful, that is an accidental by-product of function and without intentional significance. Theirs is what the poet calls 'the beauty of a mathematical formula "made flesh," given material projection.' He adds, 'the gods of

193 Form

the power-age are best symbolized by those objects which are themselves power-devices. In the weapons, pure function stands naked' (*E&A* 104 n2). This is true of the battering rams in the poem. One of them emerges in typographical blue-print on the page:

Off the secret list?
                maximum impact
                penetrative power
                bias, rebound
                    effect of 'X' releases
on propulsion-gear, deficiencies
serious defects
listed in detail for the coded files
summarized for circulation to affected departments
metamorphosed for general release? (178)

The bare technological language suits its subject. Weapons of this sort are anathemata in the negative sense of the word.

Republican Rome has experienced a decline of cultural vitality by the time 'Tiberius Gracchus / wept for the waste-land / and the end of the beginnings' (89). In 133 BC, the senatorial capitalists murder Tiberius Gracchus for promoting land-reform legislation. In a passage Jones marks in his copy of *The Decline of the West*, Spengler sees this murder as an indication of the end of classical culture (II 50). There are a number of modern parallels, perhaps the most striking being the murder by Italian Fascists in 1924 of the socialist Giacomo Matteotti, a man of extraordinary integrity and vision. The parallel, or one very like it, does not go unnoticed at the time, for Filippo Turati, delivering Matteotti's eulogy, alludes to the last stand on the Aventine by the brother of Tiberius, Gaius Gracchus, who is likewise murdered by opponents of reform.

There are further evocations of the politics of the twentieth century. A hundred years after Tiberius's murder, Augustus builds the Ara Pacis or Altar of Peace to commemorate a senatorial decree of 'Peace in Our Time' (186). The words are those of Neville Chamberlain's famous reassurance after meeting with Hitler at Munich in 1938. Concerning the Ara Pacis David Jones notes, 'there have been Temples of Peace built in our time also.' He has in mind the Peace Palace at the Hague and the Assembly Hall of the League of Nations at Geneva, with its large wall-sculpture by Eric Gill.

Like Augustus before him and in the manner of the modern dictators, the emperor Tiberius makes republican forms a vehicle for dictatorial power. Under Tiberius for a while, moreover, Sejanus exercises power as 'co-ordinator of groupings' (186), a phrase evocative of the Nazi policy of *Gleichschaltung* or co-ordination, whereby every aspect of social and cultural life is brought under the control of the party. Sejanus has 'his weather-eye on the Diaspora' (187), furthermore; like the Nazis, he is ill disposed to the Jews, and is probably responsible for the senatorial decree of 19 AD deporting four thousand of them from Rome to Sardinia and for the ultimatum to the remaining four thousand that they repudiate 'their unholy practices by a given date' or likewise be banished from Italy.[55]

But Sejanus does not last long. Tiberius has him killed for plotting against the imperial line of descent, and 'Tiber, by way of the Mamertine, has his broken body' (187). A striking modern parallel is the murder of Ernst Röhm by Hitler in 1934. Just as the political power of Sejanus rests on his leadership of the Praetorian Guard, the power of Röhm rests on his leadership of the Nazi SA. To get at Sejanus, Tiberius circumvents the Praetorian Guard by using the City Watch. To get at Röhm, Hitler circumvents the SA by using the SS. Sejanus is executed in Mamertine Prison; Röhm is murdered in Stadelheim Prison. Each man dies, ostensibly, for plotting a coup. Sejanus's death may also recall the numerous murders by Stalin of his political colleagues and generals, but here as in *The Sleeping Lord* the chief contemporary manifestation of imperialism is fascism, particularly in Germany.[56]

For ancient Rome, 'the waxing of the megalopolis and the acute coarsening of the forms' (90) becomes generally symptomatic of cultural decline from about the time Augustus establishes the principate. The corresponding phase in the modern era is the nineteenth century, when 'Western Man moved across a rubicon' (15) to an exaggerated emphasis on utility at the expense of gratuity and symbolism. In 'Redriff,' the Victorian shipwright Eb Bradshaw holds to the integrity of his craft and resists utilitarian pressures from potential clients, but he fights a losing battle. His own work may transcend expediency – certainly his language is elaborately symbolic – but he exemplifies the isolation of the artist in the modern world. For David Jones, a contemporary type of the alienated artist was Eric Gill, who, as a passionate arguer on behalf of good craftsmanship, probably underlies the characterization of Eb Bradshaw. (Bradshaw is named for the poet's maternal grandfather; Eric Gill was also a father figure for the poet, and very nearly his father-in-law.) Shortly after Eric Gill's death in 1940 David Jones writes about the isolation of the artist that 'we are all very like men forced into guerrilla tactics – we operate in a terrain over-run by the enemy' (E&A 106), or, putting it a little less metaphorically: 'Today we live in a world where the symbolic life (the life of the true cultures, of "institutional" religion, and of *all artists*, in the last resort – however much we may disavow the association) is progressively eliminated – the technician is master. In a manner of speaking the priest and the artist are already in the catacombs, but *separate* catacombs – for the technician divides to rule' (E&A 103). Cultural fragmentation, with priest and artist in separate catacombs, accounts for the Mass at the opening of the poem being celebrated in a neo-Gothic church, bastardized with elements of classical and baroque styles:

> between the sterile ornaments
> under the pasteboard baldachins
> as, in the young-time, in the sap-years:
> between the living floriations
> under the leaping arches
>
> (Ossific, trussed with ferric rods, the failing numina of column and entablature, the genii of spire and triforium, like great rivals met when all is done, nod recognition across the cramped repeats of their dead selves.) (49)

In contrast to the Gothic architecture of the Middle Ages, when 'Westwood springs new,' this product of the nineteenth-century Gothic Revival signifies cultural decline. The passage reflects Spengler's contention that cultural decline in our own age, and in every modern period, is characterized by eclectic revival of archaic, 'dead forms ... put into the pot anyhow, and recast into wholly inorganic forms. Every modern age ... puts revivals and fusions of old styles in the place of real becoming' (I 207, 294).[57]

While Eb Bradshaw resists expediency in Victorian London, Austrian ladies and gentlemen dance to Strauss's *Die blaue Donau*. They 'maze the waltz-forms' in gay Vienna (59) in unconscious imitation of the Roman troia or maze-dance which, according to the poet's friend Jackson Knight, was 'intended to create a magical field of exclusive force, and abstract defensive entanglement.'[58] But the bourgeois culture of these dancers cannot stave off the decline of the West. Strauss's lovely waltz lacks explicit transcendent significance, in contrast to its musical predecessor 'in the young-time,' when in Gregorian chant monks 'god-shape the modal rhythms for nocturns in Melk' near Vienna (59). The waltz's evocation of the Troia has its primary meaning, therefore, in the troia's funerary association: the troia was danced at funerals and is part of the funeral games of Anchises in the *Aeneid* (5.545–603). Viennese waltzers 'in the ramshackle last phases' of the Austro-Hungarian empire dance at the funeral games of the West. Imperialism, along with utilitarianism, waxes at the waning of vital culture. The Austro-Hungarian empire will be torn apart only to be swallowed, eventually, by the Third Reich. And the British empire enjoys a dominion whose range is implied by Eb Bradshaw's catalogue of wood, which includes West Indies lignum vitae and 'cis- or trans-Gangem-land teak' (118, 120). The Latin for Ganges, and the echo of 'cis- and trans- alpine Gaul' suggests the correspondence with Roman imperialism. This correspondence also underlies a reference in 'Sherthursdaye and Venus Day' to Pontius Pilate as 'the fact-man, Europa's vicar,' taking his nap 'under the tiffany' (mosquito-netting) 'after tiffin,' which is British Indian-army for 'lunch' (239). The poet derives the term 'fact-man' from Spengler's 'civilization-man' or 'pure man of fact' who is 'strong minded, completely non-metaphysical man, and in the hands of this type lies the intellectual and material destiny of each and every "late" period' (I 38, 32).⁵⁹

The poem's earliest and most striking representative of British imperialism is Sir Clowdisley Shovell, commander of several warships sunk off the Scillies in 1707. The voice of the poem asks, 'what Caliban's Lamia / rung him for his Hand of Glory' (100)? His drowned body is robbed, but Sir Clowdisley too is a thief. A 'hand of glory' is the greased hand of a corpse used as a candle by a thief to render himself invisible and to keep his victims asleep.⁶⁰ The phrase 'Hand of Glory' refers as well to Shovell's expensive rings, and is capitalized to evoke the nationalistic song of imperial England, 'Land of Hope and Glory.' Such songs, and the propaganda they comprise, are likewise used to render robbery, or imperialism, invisible.

Imperialism always wraps itself in ideological myth, which usually involves bogus eschatology. Goebbels is a modern master of this ultimate debasement of art, and there are others whose political myths are less malign than his, though no less futile. The ancient counterpart to such modern political propagandists is Augustus, who promoted 'the conscious revivals, the eclectic grandeur / ... the grand years / since we began our / Good Time Coming' (90). Not now the valid myth and mystery of the 'wonder-years'; instead, Augustus announces a bright secular future to the tune of Stephen Foster's 'There's a Good Time Coming,' which was written, ironically, shortly before the start of the American Civil War. Augustus's good time turns out to be the materialism and general corruption of the empire. Despite his programmes and propaganda, 'the branded numerals: *sexcenti sexaginta sex*' already appear 'on every commodity and on the souls of men' (90). The failure of secular eschatology becomes the target of authentic prophecy in the Book of Revelation (13:16–18), where the number of the Beast is the sum of the numerical equivalents of the Greek letters spelling 'Caesar God' and also of the Hebrew letters spelling 'Caesar Nero.'

Augustus's political myth fails to bring about the society it advertises, but it does give prophetic expression to a fulfilment greater than, and altogether different from, anything expected by Roman propagandists. It is Virgil, the greatest of these latter, who, to please Augustus, foretells the passing of the iron age and the commencement of a new circuit of time when 'IAM REDIT .. VIRGO / .... IAM REGNAT APOLLO' (219).[61] We saw that for the early Church Christ fulfils the prophecy of the Fourth Eclogue. He infuses the Roman world with spiritual vitality and benign gratuity enough to balance and outlast imperial utility.

This then is the diachronic rhyme-scheme of *The Anathemata*, culminating in the rhyming of the Roman empire and modern civilization. The Incarnation is the hinge and centre of the spiralling historical schema, uniting the ancient West with the modern West. The coming of Christ during the cultural decline of Rome suggests either that the current decline of western culture will coincide with a revival of Christianity like that which began during the Dark Ages, or that the current decline will end in Christ's second coming. In any event, time's poem is not complete within the bounds of history. Fore-time must yet find its rhyme in the end-time, when the spiral of chronology collapses into the eschatological circle.

In 'Rite and Fore-Time,' this circle is implied by the coincidence of the actual beginning of the world with its symbolic ending, but the cataclysm symbolized is one of ice, not fire (see 58 n1). Just as once, in fore-time, the world is covered with the great, Permocarboniferous glacial sea, so, in the future, it is possible that 'there shall be yet *more /* storm-dark sea' (58). The image recalls and reverses that of the Book of Revelation, where 'there was no more sea' (21:1). The end may not be far off: 'Already Arcturus deploys his reconnoitring chills in greater strength: soon his last *Putsch* on any scale' (68). The northern constella-

198 The Shape of Meaning

tion here evokes Arthur, who will come again to set things right, but whom Elen Monica consigns, with other Celtic warriors, to the earth 'till the Sejunction Day' (164). In a symbolic sense, the approaching eschatological chill is the winter that Elen, in 'The Lady of the Pool,' warns her listener about.

The first forecast of time's end occurs in brackets during the telescoped account of orogenesis and the Permocarboniferous glaciation, which is also an elaborate catalogue of place-names (55–8). Early in the poem this poetically powerful catalogue establishes civilizational catastrophe as a general counterpart to individual mortality, which together, but in different ways, express the human need for the renewal or resurrection that can only come through religion. Although it is too long to quote, the catalogue deserves thorough explication. We have already touched on its apocalyptic connotations with regard to the words 'it's Ossa on Pelion now.' The reference may also evoke mortality because Hamlet and Laertes mention these mountains as they argue at Ophelia's grave (6.1.253, 283). Most of the catalogue's other apocalyptic images acquire rich historical associations by evoking the endings of the 'worlds' constitutive of the West, present here before the West began. These worlds are evoked by the names of heights listed in an abbreviated, catastrophic history of the past five millennia. All the famous West-sites lie with 'Ark-hill' under a world-ending flood of ice, including Parnassus, which is the Mt Ararat of the classical flood-story. The major, central portion of the catalogue is devoted to Troy's Hissarlik, the site of ur-catastrophe which, as we saw in *In Parenthesis*, resonates in subsequent catastrophies. Also under ice are the Cyclades. Together with Troy's hill, they recall the great mercantile powers formative of Aegean culture from the third millennium to the first millennium BC. Mentioned too is Mycenae, which will fall to invading Dorians despite the defensive magic of its famous 'Leo-Gate' (57).[62] Thebes is also under ice, and a name to conjure with, especially when evoked in association with its tutelar love-goddess. It is the site of the Oedipal tragedies which history seems almost to imitate on a larger scale when the city, previously the possessor of a Boeotian empire, is utterly destroyed in 336 BC under Alexander for rebelling against Macedonian rule. Rome's 'montes' and Mount Sinai lie under, along with '*hautes* eagle-heights,' which evoke the death of Roland by way of the *Chanson*'s '*hautes montagnes*.' Low lies Bredon hill where the Belgae, expanding under Cunobelin (Cymbeline) in the first century AD, will massacre defenders of the hill's fortress, though Rome, before the end of the century, will snatch their 'British empire' from them. Low too lies Lambourn Down, site of 'The Seven Barrows' or mass graves and one of the 'West horse-hills' associated with the last victory of Arthur and the battles of Alfred. And where, asks the poem, are the hills of Wales, 'all the efficacious asylums / *in Wallia vel in Marchia Walliae?*' The word 'asylums' recalls the first Asylum on the Capitoline that will have fallen long before these outermost extensions of Rome cease to give aid. The fall of Wales, which completes the fall of Rome, also re-enacts the fall of Troy because '*Terra Walliae*' is the 'Enclosure of the Children of Troy' (55). All these high places lie under,

> obedient to the fiery stress
> *und* icy counter-drag
>   down ... (57)

This is the geological equivalent to German *Sturm und Drang*, the pre-romantic political and literary movement to sweep away all established institutions and conventions. The symbolically charged catalogue of heights implies the violent fall of empires as a repeated image and reminder of the ultimate world-ending.

Among the catalogue's depressed heights are 'crag-*carneddau*,' which include Carnarvon's mountains and, chief among them though not specified here, Snowdon. The highest peak in Wales has special apocalyptic connotations (see 68 n2). Elsewhere in 'Fore-Time' it is called 'the gestatorial couch of Camber the eponym' (67), whose bed of Precambrian bedrock 'the muses' keep for as long as time lasts (68). (One of Snowdon's Welsh names means 'Hill of the Muse,' which establishes it as the Welsh equivalent to Parnassus in the bracketed list.) Sleeping Camber will dream the dream of history

> ... till the thick rotundities give, and the bent flanks of space
> itself give way
>   and the whitest of the Wanderers
> falters in her transit
>   at the Sibyl's *in favilla*-day. (68)

Then Camber will be rudely awakened by the collapse of Einstein's curved space and by the 'shaking thunder' that will 'smite flat the thick rotundity o' the world' in answer to Lear's call for an end to things. This will be the *Dies Irae's* 'day of ashes.' 'Lord! what a morning,' writes David Jones at the conclusion of his catalogue of submerged heights

(58). The words belong to the Negro spiritual that anticipates the day 'when the stars begin to fall.'

Because of its eschatological boundary, which is beyond the inscape of time, the spiralling diachronic content of *The Anathemata* symbolically collapses into circular synchronism. This is suggested by the symbolic presence of the world's end in the world's beginning, and it is insisted upon by the poem's narrative context being the Consecration of the Mass, which establishes the meditative time of the poem as nearly instantaneous. Because the birth of Christ marks the midpoint of history's spiralling duration and because the sacrament is correlative to and theologically includes the Incarnation, the poem's diachronic spiral has the Incarnation as its meditative circumference as well as its centre of meditated duration. Without losing its extension in time, history is consequently, and paradoxically, coextensive with the synchronic circle of the Christian eschaton, which is also the circle of the Eucharist. Without this coincidence of time's spiral and eternity's circle, the helix of history would have only the aesthetic sense of its own repeated pattern. But since the spiral and the circle do coincide, aesthesis passes beyond itself to metaphysics, and relative form symbolizes ultimate meaning.

In *The Anathemata*, meditative time is instantaneous and meditated time forms a circle that opens in prehistory and rounds to completion at the birth of Jesus, on Holy Thursday, on Good Friday, and in every celebration of the Mass. Time ends in eternity even before the end of time. In this way diachronic movement implies synchronic structure, but it is also true that the latter contains the former. As we have seen, this is implied by the broad cycle and the historic spiral of meditated time occurring within the contextual fiction of an instantaneous daydream.

Simultaneity together with the all-inclusiveness of the structure's circles within circles corresponds to the hypothesis of the sacrament which is the poem's context and correlative. The Eucharist makes present Christ, who as man symbolically embodies the earth and humanity. And because Christ is also God, present to all space and contemporary with all time, the symbol is literalized and expanded. His anamnesis is the real presence of everything and this is largely what the poem means. In his preface David Jones writes that 'poetry ... evokes and recalls, is a kind of *anamnesis* of, i.e. is an effective recalling of, something loved' (21). If this is true in varying degrees of all poetry, it is true in a special sense of *The Anathemata* by virtue of its manifold form.

6

Typology

Devoid of controlling narrative, *The Anathemata* initially discloses its meaning through symbolic interaction. Jones writes that, in contrast to *In Parenthesis*, this poem is 'more evocative and recalling – with more overtones and undertones, – but making the facts speak for themselves as *signa*, no less extensive in their content, but rather more.'¹ Without explicit connection, subordination, or co-ordination, these 'facts' or '*signa*' – and these range from place-names to dramatic personae – unify the poem by generating typological correspondences and thematic continuity which counteract the diffusive tendency of anatomy. We have begun to see how this happens in our consideration of the work's biological and ritual 'continuings' and in correspondences between figures such as Mary and Athena. Symbolic interrelationships of this sort presuppose the poem's spatialization in the reader's memory for, Jones writes, 'what goes before conditions what comes after and *vice versa*' (33). This symbolic interaction is an elaboration of what he calls, in a loose manuscript note, 'the first rule' of visual art:

> Tell the child that once he has put two marks on the drawing paper – he has made, not two marks, but three & it is by that third invisible 'mark' that we know whether the other two have significance.

Only when the reading of the poem moves from sequential progression into the literary equivalent of pictorial space does unity of meaning emerge from the poem's galaxy of symbols.

Our concentration in the previous chapter on form and in this chapter on symbolism largely as contributing to form might convey the impression that the poem is more abstractly schematic than it is. Its subject is not as dramatic, not nearly as physical as that of *In Parenthesis*, and for that reason *The Anathemata* is not as accessible to readers. But it does have personal and dramatic dimensions – by virtue of its primary meditative voice and also because of its cast of characters. These personae serve as nodal centres which symbolically focus themes and in various ways humanize them, in a personal sense and in a more universal sense.

An important function of symbolism in the poem is to trace the human inscape, which is archetypal. In varying degrees of emphasis, all the genuine archetypes are present in the poem: apocalypse, cosmic marriage, cosmic conflict, the journey (here the voyage), renewal or resurrection, the male guardian or saviour, the female to be saved, the female guardian and the villain. Listed in this manner, archetypes are of little interest and serve to indicate how unfair would be the reduction of the poem, or any complex literary work, to its archetypes.

The Anathemata concerns not archetypes merely but their interrelationships within shifting medial contexts. Usually archetypes are hidden in the particular real or half-hidden in the general type, so that archetypal relationships occur at various degrees of psychofictional displacement. In this respect, the poem moves between the primacy of archetypes in the mythic mode and the displacement of archetypes by the realism and quasi-realism of the descriptive and dramatic modes. It is a difference in kinds of meaning.

For example, in 'Redriff,' Eb Bradshaw speaks as a realistically dramatized middle-class Victorian Protestant. His monologue even approaches the quasi-documentary character of *In Parenthesis*. Jones said that although 'I never knew my grandfather... my mother told me all about him. Whole sections of the poem are practically direct quotations from her, rounded off. And I had heard his contemporaries, my uncles, talk.'[2] The dramatic realism of his impassioned speech recalls monologues by Browning – and Jones may intend to evoke that other Victorian craftsman. But underlying the dramatized personality of the historically real shipwright is the artist type and, beneath that, the archetype of the father and male guardian. In the subsequent section Elen Monica commemorates such 'fathering figures' as buried under the earth, defending and fructifying it in a radical reworking of the metaphor of sex and death (163). Typologically, Elen equates with Mother Earth. If Eb and Elen were reducible to their archetypes, therefore, he would be married to her, and because his archetype is buried in hers awaiting rebirth, he would also be her foetal son. On the level of archetypes this makes sense, but it sounds more than a little absurd because these personae exist more as realistic characters and as intermediate types than as archetypes, and what is archetypally valid is not always valid on the other psychofictional levels. Yet even in their realistic contexts there are suggestions of correspondence, since Elen was 'reared up by Redriff mast-pond' (135) and both of them – Bradshaw through a messenger – talk to, or rather at, Mediterranean captains who cannot, or can barely, squeeze in a word of reply. This sort of modal interplay and the metaphysical tension it generates make the poem extraordinarily vital and complex.

Even where expression is weighted towards them, archetypes are present here with most of their psychobiological roots and cultural branches. Sexuality, psychology, anthropology, history, and theology continually determine the meaning of archetypes and influence their relationships. I say influence, not control, for sometimes these relationships are startlingly original precisely because they contradict conventional expectation. The conflation of husband and foetus in the typology of Eb Bradshaw relative to that of Elen Monica is an example, though even here, that which is physically impossible and may seem culturally unprecedented is psychologically valid – if Freud's Oedipal theory has any validity, and the poet certainly thinks it has. It is a mistake to assume with Elizabeth Ward, who tries to reduce the poem to its archetypes, that *The Anathemata* is 'a self-referring world in which internal relationships ... are merely established by fiat.'[3] In this poem, David Jones relinquishes narrative and dramatic continuity, but he does not desert the world Aristotle and most of the rest of us perceive as real for a Platonic or Frygean (after Northrop Frye) heterocosm. An important concern of the poem is, after all, to renew the symbols of traditional western culture, and to do that the poet must remain within the tradition.

The archetypes of the human inscape are fundamentally sexual. The poet was able to appreciate this with special clarity after undergoing intensive psychotherapy in 1947 immediately prior to beginning work on *The Anathemata*. Throughout the composition of the poem and into the mid-1960s, he visited and was visited by Dr Bill Stevenson, a trained Freudian who had been his therapist and became a friend. I remember Jones saying that while Jung was more intelligent than Freud, he was also esoteric and 'got carried away.' Jones preferred Freud for his 'basicness.' It may be enough to realize that psychotherapy deepened the awareness already evident in *In Parenthesis* that human experience and, consequently, human desire bear <u>an indelible sexual imprint</u>. But to appreciate thoroughly the typology of this poem we must consider more fully the poet's neurosis as it pertains to his work, even though this will involve an excursion into biography and a certain amount of psychological conjecture.

David Jones was deeply in love in the mid-1920s with Petra Gill, later with Prudence Pelham, and later still with Valerie Price. Yet he never married. This is partly a consequence of his commitment to his art, which never provided enough income to support a wife and family. (As a Catholic, he believed that marriage meant raising a family.) For much of his life he had to live on the charity of friends. And according to the testimony of those who knew him well, he was celibate. This may reflect moral convictions bound up with his religious faith. As his close friend René Hague once put it, 'He wouldn't have gone to bed with a woman he wasn't going to marry.' Jones writes, 'I've always always as long as I can *ever* remember felt my business (however blindly) to be my work, and always knew that everything had to go for that' (to G 20 July 1935). But there is probably more than morality and artistic dedication behind his avoidance of sex and marriage.

David Jones suffered from neurasthenia and experienced two emotional breakdowns. His first, in 1932–3, was precipitated by an increasing inability to paint, which led a neurologist to advise him to stop painting. He followed that advice and began to concentrate on writing poetry. At the onset of his second breakdown he writes, 'It wasn't trying to paint this time that "caused" it ... I've ... been struggling hard with my book' (to E 15 January 1945). When the neurologist he had consulted before told him this time to quit writing, he sought help elsewhere and found it at Dr Crichton Miller's clinic at Bowden House where, in 1947, he underwent six months of Freudian therapy. There he began to understand the causes of his neurosis and to counteract its effects. While undergoing therapy and probably at the suggestion of Dr Stevenson, he read and reread *Totem and Taboo*, in which Freud regards 'the "Oedipus complex" ... as the nuclear complex of neuroses.'[4] David Jones came to believe that 'Freud really had it right, this father/mother relationship' (*DGC* 131) and, as he says, he began to see 'the ramifications of the sexual impulse and how the fear of assuming the "father figure" position works in the most unexpected conjunctions, and ... how all my life I've avoided such a position in innumerable and subtle ways' (*DGC* 140).

Like all boys, young David Jones had Oedipal feelings. These may have outlived their natural course as a result of an increase in his mother's affection for fifteen-year-old David when his only brother, Harold, died at the age of twenty-one in 1910. Naturally David's love for his mother entailed the repression of sexual feelings. Probably these feelings were so strong and their repression so intense that sexual repression became a generalized characteristic of his relationships with women. He must have come to understand all this in 1947. From reading *Totem and Taboo* and doubtless from conversation with Dr Stevenson he would have realized how the repression of the libido becomes automatic and shifts to other areas of subconscious release, such as artistic creation, which it attempts to block. Dr Stevenson advised him to combat repression where it manifested itself, in painting and writing. Nicolete Gray remembers that Jones asked her to bring him his manuscript, portions of which would eventually be included in *The Anathemata*, about a week after he entered the clinic (to H 24 November 1978). His treatment, which continued in weekly visits with Dr Stevenson through the next twenty years, was successful and made possible all Jones's later poetry and painting and his lettered inscriptions.

The nature of his neurosis helps account for the power with which David Jones imagines the Queen of the Woods, Elen Monica, Gwenhwyfar, and the female figures of *The Sleeping Lord*. If the inhibition of artistic creation originates in sexuality, his uninhibited artistic creation is, especially when he creates females, a form of subliminal lovemaking. It is much the same for all muse poets, and Jones himself believed that subliminal enactment 'is the inner secret and nodal point of *all* the arts' (DGC 190). Jones says of a man writing a poem about his sweetheart,

> Heaven knows what his poem will really be 'about'; for then the 'sacramental' will pile up by a positively geometric progression. So that what was Miss Flora Smith may turn out to be Flora Dea and Venus too and the First Eve and the Second also and other and darker figures, among them no doubt, Jocasta. One thing at least the psychologists make plain: there is always a recalling, a re-presenting again, anaphora, anamnesis. (E&A 167)

Jocasta is, of course, the mother of Oedipus.

I do not mean to imply that Jones's poetry can be explained in terms of an Oedipal fixation. I mean only what he himself says, that '*everything* one does is conditioned by one's psychopathology' (DGC 139). Nor can the man be reduced to his neurosis. As he himself protests to his psychiatrist, his dedication to art is not merely 'a "rationalization" of my inhibitions and fears of sex' (*DGC* 137). Nevertheless, the frustration of sexual desire intensifies sexual desire. And the intensity of his desire conditions the art by which it is only partly sublimated.

For David Jones, then, Freud complements Frazer, Spengler, de la Taille, and post-impressionist critics by providing a myth or 'morphology' by which he can discern shape in an aspect of personal experience that he had never before understood. Jones writes about psychotherapy that in his 'own case the experience was indeed like pouring acid on an etching plate – there was the pattern quite clear ...' (*DGC* 139). We have seen several allusions to Oedipal mother-love in *The Anathemata* and we shall see others. In making such allusions, the poet is not being merely subjective or private. Freudian theory universalizes such love, which, as we shall see, acquires objective expression in the widespread conflation of mother and consort in primitive myth. At some level, moreover, Oedipal typology conditions the loves and desires of all males. If, more than any other work of literature, *The Anathemata* returns to the roots of western culture, it may also be, in a psychological sense, among the most radical of modern poems.

The underlying subject, which governs all the poem's typological and symbolic interaction, is the relationship between God and man. It is a mutual relationship succinctly expressed in words by St Athanasius that meant a great deal to the poet: 'God became man that man might become God.'[5] Man is the focus of this reciprocity, which must be shaped to the human inscape to have any meaning. Comparing Jesus to Odin, the poet writes: 'Who made the runes would read them' (225). In this poem, the runes are the psychological-imaginative archetypes that Jesus reads with his body in his birth and in his Passion. His reading is anticipated in primitive religion and expanded through subsequent centuries in liturgy, in theology, and in art. It is because the Incarnation conforms to the human inscape that the Freudian mythos conditions the poem's eschatological intimations of what Hopkins calls 'the heaven of desire.' This heaven is cosmic marriage, the poem's unifying archetype. It involves subordinate archetypal couples and a special emphasis on the woman, who emerges through particular women (divine and human) to represent the earth, the ship, the city, and mankind as the bride of God.

COUPLING

'There is only one tale to tell,' writes the poet (35), and in his preface to Richard Barber's *Arthur of Albion* he expands: 'There is, after all, but one tale to tell: *Dilectus meus mihi, et ego illi* as *The Canticle of Canticles* puts it.'⁶ This is so, he says, even for the person for whom there is 'no *Dilectus meus*, or should I say *et ego illi*.' Elen Monica, long past her prime and nostalgic for departed lovers, is such a person. Sexuality is the source of her monologue's melancholy undercurrent while being also the source of its positive spiritual resonances. As Jones implies by quoting from the Song of Songs, this ambiguity reflects the fact that sex is spiritual as well as physical, which is to say that it is primarily psychological. Ever since 'the amorous Silvy / to her sweetest dear / her fairest bosom' bared (74–5), directly or indirectly sex informs all modes of giving and receiving love. That is true also of divine love, at least in so far as man is concerned, which explains why Jones thinks physical and spiritual love are complementary aspects of a single mystery. In a letter to Grisewood dated Whitsunday 1946, he writes:

> I've been trying to read dear old D'Arcy's new book *The Mind & Heart of Love* (Faber) ... It's about Eros & Agape & animus & anima & Co, de Rougemont, the Tristan theme etc & is roughly speaking an attempt to let Eros & Agape kiss each other, as it were – a laudable objective (which of course they must in any case as I see it, whatever anyone says).

Sex is love's metaphor.

In exploring the typological aspects of redemption, the poet interprets the poetics of sex largely as it derives from two sources: fertility ritual and Judaeo-Christian spirituality. The first concerns life's renewal and increase; the second, the eschatological union of God and man. These sources, which have common psychological roots, are mediated and refracted throughout the poem primarily by western love-conventions as found in pastoral poetry, folk songs, Homeric epic, and medieval romance.

The Anathemata has a number of sexual couples who in varying ways combine the archetypes of cosmic marriage and cosmic battle. This combination, which involves the conventional association of love and death, has its prototype in the early Indo-European fertility myth in which the god fights for his consort to make possible the marriage that renews the land.⁷ Especially evocative of such archetypal sexual pairing are two couples situated, like parentheses, at opposite ends of the poem's spiralling history of the West. The male of each couple dies, in one instance for a city, in the other for a ship – these being the poem's important symbolic microcosms.

The first couple defines the significance of Troy, a 'little' place yet

>   high as Hector the Wall
>   high as Helen the Moon
>   who, being lifted up
>   draw the West to them.   (56)

Together this man and woman conflate the themes of love and war that characterize the subsequent literature of the West (see 57 n1). Here they recall, furthermore, the boast of Jesus, 'And I, if I be lifted up from the earth, will draw all men to me' (John 12: 32). The evocation of Jesus has typological significance: Hector is killed by being dragged

>   widdershins
>   without the wall.
>   When they regarded him:
>   his beauties made squalid, his combed gilt
>   a matted mop
>   his bruised feet thonged
>   under his own wall.
>   Why did they regard him
>   the decorous leader, *neque decor ...*
>   *vulneraque illa gerens* ... many of them
>   under his dear walls?   (84)

A good question. The answer is partly that the dying hero represents with tragic intensity the common fate of man and so strikes a chord deep in the human psyche. But Hector's death is also a ritual immolation – his bruised feet show he is alive as he is dragged 'widdershins' to unwind the city's defences, which were ritually established at the city's foundation by the troia or maze-dance (see *Vergil's Troy* 123; *Cumaean Gates* 90). The reversed ritual of his dying implies his role as saviour or defender of the city by recognizing his mystical identification with the defensive wall of Troy – 'his own wall' because his name means 'city-holder.'[8] 'They regard him' because in a mystical sense his death is Troy's fall. In the passage quoted, the Latin from Isaiah (53:2) identifies him as a Suffering Servant like Jesus who also dies 'without the wall,' on Calvary outside Jerusalem.

What Hector guards within the city is Helen. Because of her, the hall of Priam is 'the laughless Megaron' evocative of the Laughless Rock at Eleusis, which contains the vaginal cult object of essential femininity representative also of the Kore (Persephone) whom we have seen as a counterpart of Helen. Within the megaron Helen is 'the margaron,' the

209 Typology

pearl of *Troilus and Cressida* 2.2.87 and the biblical 'pearl of great price' which a man sells everything to obtain (Matthew 13:46). The incongruity between typology and realism (Helen's union with Paris) precludes simple allegory, but on the level of archetype, on this 'Crux-mound' (56), and in conjunction with the Passion of Hector, Helen typifies the eschatological bride whom Jesus dies for, himself a 'suitor, margarongainer' (225). Here, of course, death is real, not sexual, but the hard reality of violent death is among the human runes Jesus must read.

At the other end of Western history and corresponding to Hector and the city containing Helen are Nelson and his ship. Like Hector, Nelson is a dying saviour, though a successful one since his victory at Trafalgar prevents Napoleon's planned invasion of England. Nelson's fall 'outside the Pillars' rhymes with the deaths of Hector and Jesus outside the walls. Moreover, the same care taken to establish the exact month, day, and hour of Jesus's death (52, 239) is taken to mark the time of Nelson's fall. Nelson is 'him whom Nike did bear / her tears at flood' (114). The goddess is identical with his ship, HMS *Victory*, so that the image evoked is of the *pietà*.

At the centre of the poem's timescape and bracketed, as it were, by the ancient couple and the modern couple are Jesus and Mary. The death of Jesus has for its primary metaphor sexual death with his mother. In the springtime of the year, Mary is 'this year's Mab o' the Green' (188) whom Jack Christ embraces for the spiritual renewal of the human race.

>   White and ruddy her
>   beautiful in his shirt
>   errant for her now
>   his limbs like pillars.   (224)

A knight-errant, Jesus is also the beloved of the Song of Songs, 'white and ruddy' with legs 'like pillars' (5:10, 15). 'Sherthursdaye and Venus Day' begins with the statement 'He that was her son / is now her lover' (224). We have had a hint of such transformation in the underlying typology of Eb Bradshaw and Elen Monica. The discomforting change of relationship recalls the incest of gods in fertility myths, but here it is made possible by a change in emphasis from Mary's physical maternity at the Nativity to her being the archetypal bride at the Passion:

>   Not *Lalla, lalla, lalla*
>   not rockings now

nor clovered breath for the health of him as under the straw'd crucks that baldachin'd in star-lit town where he was born, the maid's fair cave his dwelling. (194)

Now it is *crux* instead of 'crucks.' And the infant is a lover – as is implied in this passage by the echo of the opening of 'Barbara Allen': 'In scarlet town where I was born, / There was a fair maid dwelling.' The association of sex and death is intensified by Barbara and her lover being united in the ballad only after death.

Christ's conformity to the types of the dying saviour and the cosmic bridegroom is begun on Calvary and elaborated in the centuries of imagining that shaped the liturgy. In the liturgy, the Church is seen as both maternal and bridal, and Mary as both a mother and the paradigm of bridal mankind. Widespread Oedipal feelings doubtless inform this historical imagining, but the incest of mythology is sublimated. What was sex is now love, even though it must remain sexual at some level. Cosmic marriage has two main effects: spiritual renewal and, potentially at least, cultural renewal. Both are symbolized by the modulation of the sexual motif into that of the renewal of the Waste Land when, by his death on the cross, Jesus 'frees the waters' (225). Typologically this is a sexual melting, for by dying he is the 'loosener of the naiad-girdles' (235) and naiads, like women of old, loosen their girdles to accept intercourse or to give birth. A prototypic analogy takes place when

> ... they unbound the last glaciation
> for the Uhland Father to be-ribbon *die blaue Donau*
> with his Vanabride blue. (59)

In Norse myth, the sky god lives in Uhland, and Vanabride or Frey is a Venus-figure, here cognate with the Venus of Willendorf, the earth mother. Her river, the Danube, symbolizes her warming coitus with the sky father. The receding of the glacier had left Mother Earth a 'new founded Oberland' (58) – an evocation of Donne's metaphor for his mistress in Elegy 19, 'O my America! my new-found land' (line 27). Cultural fertility as a result of symbolic spiritual sex is implied by a series of cult objects which are juxtaposed, by way of contrast, to the brutally phallic seige engines considered earlier as the negative anathemata of a bankrupt civilization. These cult objects are fertility symbols:

> *dendron*
> for a torch-goddess?

> *ashera*
>   to vermilion and incise?
> Erect?
>   for the wheat-waves to be high?
>   for the sea wattles to be full?
> for the byres to be warm with breath, for the watering by
> precedence to be clamorous?
>   for the lover's lass?
> For the dedicated men in skirts to cense
> before, behind, above, below
>   on the glad invention morning? (178–9)

The *dendron* is a tree in the grove sacred to Demeter and Persephone – both goddesses of fertility, the latter depicted carrying a torch (see 231). The *ashera* is a wooden pole or cross symbolizing the Canaanite goddess of love and fecundity. A third, implied object is the cross of Christ, which is incensed by priests 'in skirts' on the feast of its 'invention' or discovery. The cross, too, symbolizes fertility here and expresses the vital intention of which sex is the original sign. The sexual metaphor is emphasized by the cross being incensed 'before, behind, above, below' – another echo of Donne's Elegy 19, in which the poet beseeches his mistress, 'License my roving hands, and let them go / Before, behind, between, above, below.'

The intercourse of Jesus with mankind begins in his death; it presupposes human mortality but issues in a rebirth that is physically personal as well as spiritual and cultural. This conforms to mythic typology, which presumes that if by sex we live then by sex we live again – a primitive belief attested by the foetal position of 'the hidden lords in the West-tumuli' buried with their 'members in-folded' (225). It is with this hope that the Neanderthal dead were buried with phallic 'votive horn' and covering stone 'cupped' with womb-shapes (61). These signs and the same hope inform the prayer of the poem's meditator:

>   By the uteral marks
> that make the covering stone an artefact.
>   By the penile ivory
> and by the viatic meats.
>   *Dona ei requiem.* (65)

The sexual shapes of the primitive life-symbols are visible in the Grail and spear of the Waste-Land myth, which are depicted in Jones's wood-engraving reproduced facing page 213 of the poem.[9]

In a universal sense, the wasting of the land is death because, as we saw in *In Parenthesis*, death is the ultimate castration. It is in restoring the waste land of death that Jesus attains 'his twelve-month-and-a-day' (226), which is the projected length of the Grail-quest (Malory 13.7). But to transform the meaning of death he must first endure it, joining the maimed and 'sleeping' heroes in a universal tradition of mortality that contains Nelson and Hector and also their prehistoric analogue:

> Himself at the cave-mouth
>   the last of the father-figures
> to take the diriment stroke
>   of the last gigantic leader of
> thick-felled cave-fauna.   (66)

In one of the preliminary drafts of this passage, the poet writes 'Salvific' in the margin. The cave man probably dies defending his family. 'The diriment stroke' recalls the Dolorous Stroke that maims the king in Malory. 'Diriment' is a legal term for an impediment, such as castration, that nullifies marriage. The reflexive pronoun 'himself' recalls Odin immolated 'himself to himself' (225). This is the terminus of purely biological typology for the cave-bear's victim, for Hector, for Trystan and Iseault (see 97–8), for Eb Bradshaw and Elen Monica (now dead), for Nelson, for Tiberius Gracchus who 'wept for the waste-land' (89), for all the poem's sleeping lords, ladies, and commoners, named and unnamed, all the way back to the Aurignacian lord and lady (77) and beyond. Jesus is true to type in his dying – though his humanity leaves him no choice, of course – and in his rising he also conforms to typology, not of universal experience but of universal myth and desire.

The dying of God for man is sexual, but only as a metaphor for love. That it is only a metaphor is stressed by a complementary, canine metaphor for the same love between God and man which is elaborately expressed in the poem's second long anatomical list. The list occurs near the end of the poem, when Jesus is seen as Odysseus come to claim his Penelope and it is asked whether the dog Argos lifts its aged head in recognition (243).

Like the initial catalogue of heights, the list of dogs may appear diffuse and merely categorical but is symbolically cohesive and merits close analysis. After referring to the neolithic kitchen-midden culture, in which 'the guardian and friend' was first domesticated, the poet asks:

> How else Argos
> the friend of Odysseus?
> Or who should tend
> the sores of lazars?
> (For anthropos is not always kind.)
> How Ranter or True, Ringwood
> or the pseudo-Gelert?
> How Spot, how Cerberus?
> (For men can but proceed from what they know, nor is it for the mind of this flesh to practise poiesis, *ex nihilo*.)
> How the hound-bitches
> of the stone kennels of Arthur
> that quested the hog and the brood of the hog
> from Pebidiog to Aber Gwy?
> How the dog Toby? How the flew'd sweet thunder for dewy Ida? (79–80)

The rhetorical meaning of this brief catalogue is that fictional dogs are projections of real ones, but as canine names evoke their fictional contexts, the faithful dog – the word is the anagram of 'God' – alternatively connotes divine fidelity to man and human fidelity to God. In the puppet show, the dog Toby demonstrates his loyalty by relentlessly biting the nose of Punch who tries to steal him from his master, Mr Jones. Gelert, buried at the foot of Snowdon, was commanded, in legend, to guard his master's sleeping infant and, in defence of the child, killed a wolf. Seeing blood on the dog's mouth and no child, the returning master plunged a spear through the dog's chest, discovering too late that his baby was safe and the dog its saviour.[10] The dog is typologically identical to Odin and Jesus, 'wounded with *our* spears' (225; the possessive pronoun evokes the Suffering Servant in Isaiah 53:4–5). Gelert is a Christ-type but also a model Christian, for the real occupant of the grave is Celert, a sixth-century saint. When we discuss 'The Hunt' in the next chapter, we shall see that, in their quest for the hog, the hounds of Arthur are co-redeemers. Here, like Gelert, they are also men, for 'the stone kennels of Arthur' are actually the megalithic tombs of South Wales (see 80 n1). The hunting dogs of Theseus in *A Midsummer Night's Dream* are the ones who 'flew'd sweet thunder for / dewy Ida' (4.1.124, 122) and while Theseus may not seem a Jesus-type, he is a bridegroom in the play and its *deus ex machina* as well as a saviour in the myth of the minotaur. The dogs Ranter, True, and Ringwood also hunt. They belong to John Peel, who is a Jesus-figure in his song, for his cry 'would awaken the dead,' and he is celebrated in a way that might be called eucharistic:

> Then here's to John Peel from my heart and soul,
> Let's drink to his health, let's finish the bowl,
> We'll follow John Peel through fair and thro' foul,
> If we want a good hunt in the morning.

The imagery of questing and hunting resonates with themes to be considered later: the Grail-quest in 'Sherthursdaye And Venus Day' and the voyaging quest for wealth by Phoenician-Phocaean sailors. These sailors call themselves 'sea-dogs' of a goddess (105). And the chaplain of the *Mary* is called 'God's dumb hound' (148) because he is a Dominican, *Dominicanus*, homonymous with *Domini canis*, 'the Lord's hound.' It is a homonym that must often have occurred to the poet, who became a Dominican tertiary in 1923 although he effectively ceased being one in 1925 (Hagreen to H 5 March 1978). If Argos recognizes a divine Odysseus at the end of the poem, the Homeric hound is certainly a *Domini canis*. And because he is 'a sleeping dog' (242), this recognition, while remaining only a possibility, has affinity with the general resurrection, for Elen Monica says that 'till the Sejunction Day' the dead are 'sleepers... slumberers' (164). The list involves, then, a remarkable symbolic conflation of God, man, and dog. Its implied contention that man's relationship to God should resemble that of a dog to its master might be unacceptable were it not for the correlative implication that God is dog-like in his unconditional devotion to man. God is man's best friend, and vice versa. Like the more prominent sexual metaphor, it is an image of mutual love.

The tendency in many instances to emphasize the metaphorical status of sex is owing, I think, to the poet's having trouble warming to the symbolism of western religion in which the soul is female to God. Most males have the same difficulty. How can a man love God as a woman loves a man? The difficulty certainly accounts for the uneasiness of males, even Christian males, with John of the Cross, whose poetry David Jones once told me he 'could never get into.' The sexual connotation of his remark was doubtless unintended but may nevertheless be significant, for only with some difficulty can most males sustain the imaginative sex-change required to identify with the female soul and the female Church in love with a masculine God. David Jones attempts to solve in this poem the hermeneutical problem which the sexual image involves for men and which has troubled the religious consciousness of the West.

The primary way he does this is by removing the focus of attention from God to the female lover of God, with whom the female reader can still identify and to whom the male reader can respond without imaginatively straining his sexual identity. That is why women dominate the poem: Venus, Helen, Demeter, Persephone, Athena, the Virgin Mary, Elen Monica, the three girls named Themis, Phoebe, and Telphousa, Gwenhwyfar, and the witch Marged. We saw that several of these figures are explicitly regarded within the poem from a male point of view and some of them are idealized, though less so than the Queen of the Woods in *In Parenthesis*. In a realistic sense, their presence here is true to the male psychology of the poem's meditator. In a letter to Tom Burns, after drinking 'a Haig,' the poet writes, 'A great flight of pigeons have gone across the window – like the sacred doves of Aphrodite at the temple at Askalon,' and he adds in the margin, 'I think a lot about girls' (28 August 1940).

Poetically, in *The Anathemata*, the greatest of the female figures are Elen Monica and Gwenhwyfar. As is indicated by their association with sea-captains who capture narwhal ivory (136, 199), Elen and Gwenhwyfar are counterparts. Each represents western civilization in decline and each is primarily a lover. As Helen-figures, both women are archetypally the earth goddess and the bride of Christ. In this last respect they complement one another because Elen's monologue focuses on the Passion as made present in the Eucharist, while the description of Gwenhwyfar focuses on the Incarnation in relation to the Eucharist. Dramatically, too, these women counterbalance each other: Elen is not described but talks nonstop for forty-three pages; Gwenhwyfar stands silently as the poet describes her. In themselves, these women are important symbolic constellations which merit detailed exploration.

THE LADY OF THE POOL

Late middle-aged and corpulent, Elen Monica walks London's riverfront in the late Middle Ages. The traditions of the West live in her memory and imagination and symbolically in the topology of the city she describes. She is London's consciousness and, as though body were reciprocal to mind, London is iconographically female – a 'twin-hilled Urbs' (127), more conventionally feminine than 'seven-breasted Roma' (75). Through the city's centre, moreover, flows the Walbrook, underground since the fourteenth century, 'the seeding under-stream' (127) – a menstrual flow emptying at Downgate, the ancient Roman port, now the site of the Steelyard (the western head office of the pan-European trade monopoly called the Hanseatic League) and still, therefore, the primary locus of commercial intercourse. Partly through her identification with the microcosmic city, Elen's symbolic girth expands to encompass all the world. In a symbolic correspondence of dramatized personality to archetype, her magnanimity and pathos reflect nature's largesse but also its finitude and need of completion by grace.

Soon after the poem's publication, David Jones writes that Elen 'is herself an amalgam of *many* figures – from a waterside tart of sorts to the tutelary figure of London, as, say, was Aphrodite of the city of Thebes or Athena of Athens.' The setting is late-medieval because

> she had to represent to some extent the British sea thing which rose only after the end of the 15th Cent., so that the figure had to combine Hogarthian, Turneresque, even Dickensian worlds with the Catholic world of 'Dick Whittington', Chaucer, Langland, Geoffrey of Monmouth's Trojan-London myth, as so on & so on. Consequently the interpenetration backwards & forwards & up & down of all the images historical, legendary *and* mythological (both the Xtian Mythos & the non-Xtian) must be taken as the main *subject* of the section. (*IN* 69–70)

Hers is the mind of Europe because it is first of all the mind of London, whose traditions she personifies by articulating them. Like the spatial existence of her city, moreover, she transcends the fleeting ontology of time and embodies the city's historic and prehistoric past and, through deliberate anachronism, its historic future.

She discloses the future, for example, when she refers to April as the month 'the poet will call cruel' (157), alluding to the opening of Eliot's London poem much as Lear's fool, in the epigraph of *The Anathemata*, alludes to Merlin's future prophesying. Her Shakespearean allusions are often ambiguously anachronistic, referring to plays yet to be written while placing her historically in her own time, as when she refers to a 'skimble-skamble tale' (161), recalling *1 Henry IV* (2.1.154), and mentions guards who 'do the small beer play at dice,' recalling *Henry V* (4.Prologue.19). Anachronism is entirely future-oriented when she evokes the 'budged owls' (129) of Milton's *Comus* (line 707) and songs of the eighteenth century, like 'Yankee Doodle' (157) and 'Amo amas I love a lass' (132). Her reference to a rainfall during which runnels flow 'down stream with dogs and garbage an' such poor Tibs as had come to the ninth death b' water' (130) combines a strong evocation of Swift's 'A Description of a City Shower' with an echo of *The Waste Land*. Her phrase 'England home-land beauties' (149) evokes the London of Dickens's Micawber, who toasts 'England, Home and Beauty.' These and other references to the future are moments of transparency in which the meditator imagining her is visible through her – as Elen puts it, 'What's under works up' (164) – but this is done not so much to dramatize the presence of the poem's primary monologuist as to establish Elen as a special symbol. She is London, England, Mother Earth. (She is England when she remembers the clerk she loved calling her 'after the name of' Mary's 'dower,' 144). References to the future endow Elen with the permanence of place in time.

More commonly, place evokes the past, and so does Elen. She especially refers to the city in terms evocative of its Roman history. Above Billingsgate is 'Romeland.' The Roman 'Vicinal' Way runs under Aldgate (127). She is also herself evocative of Roman London – at least she is for the lover who is a rhapsodic Romanophil 'freestone-mason.' Inspired by the Roman brickwork in the city wall and by Elen, he equates London with Rome by identifying Elen first with *Flora*, a manifestation of the mother goddess whose name was sometimes used as a mystical synonym for Rome, then with *Bona Dea*, the guardian deity of the city. Both goddesses are versions of Mother Earth. The associations are made during two rhapsodies of which the muse is Elen and the mode and occasion is sexual.

The first of these rhapsodies occurs after the mason and Elen have made love while sheltering from a rain-storm in a 'cranny of the wall' beside Ludgate (132). The place is significant since a city's gate was associated in antiquity with the sexual organ of its tutelary goddess (see *Vergil's Troy* 137). The rain symbolizes the intercourse of the Sky with Mother Earth. The clear glow of the ensuing twilight corresponds to Elen's own sexual afterglow. In a vividly evocative passage, she remembers:

> In this wild eve's thunder-rain, at the batement of it, the night-shades now much more come on: when's the cool, even, after-light. When lime-dressed walls, petals on stalks, a kerchief, a shift's hem or such like, and the Eve's white of us ... looms up curiously exact and clear, more real by half than in the busy light as noses everywhere at stare-faced noon – more real ... but more of Faëry by a long chalk.
> An' in this transfiguring after-clarity he seemed to call me his ... Fl - ora ...

> *Flora Dea* he says ... whether to me or into the darks of the old ragstone courses? (130-1)

Elen herself has been a 'wild eve,' and, in sexual excitement and release, she has become the goddess Flora. Her transformation seems especially influenced by Botticelli's *Primavera*, which depicts the metamorphosis of a quite ordinary nymph into the goddess Flora through the sexual attentions of Zephyr – the change being achieved in a 'gale of passion.'[11] In Botticelli's painting, Zephyr blows passionately on the nymph Chloris, from whose mouth come flowers that fall onto the dress of Flora depicted beside her. The flowers from Chloris's mouth join the floral-print pattern of Flora's dress. It is a visual metaphor for metamorphosis, pivoting, I think, on a pun on the *ora* (a form of the Latin for 'mouth') out of which Flora comes. Jones verbalizes Botticelli's visual pun in Elen's tentative articulation which ideogramically depicts the metamorphosis: 'Fl - ora ... *Flora Dea*.'

Here we pass through the city's Roman foundation to Elen's underlying archetypes. Flora Dea is a Roman goddess of spring and fertility. Elen's amorous nature symbolically justifies the association by giving it realistic extension. Her amorous nature and, obliquely, the Flora-association further identify her with Aphrodite or Venus, whose birth from the sea is mentioned early in the poem where 'florid she breached,' a phrase which is homonymous with 'Flora Dea' – as Hague notes in his *Commentary* – and echoes the familiar whaler's cry, 'Thar she breaches.' Corpulent Elen associates herself with Aphrodite through the whale image when she says 'I'ld make a whale of a mere-maid' (166). Moreover, one of the epithets of Aphrodite is *Antheia*, 'Flower-goddess,' and Venus is, like Flora, originally a Latin goddess of spring. As the English incarnation of Flora, Elen is tutelar and personification of her city, which is referred to earlier in the poem, in an allusion to Dunbar, as the 'flower of towns' (170).

The encounter during the storm, in which Elen becomes Flora, occurs in July. On the evening of Friday August eighteenth, the lovers meet again in the same trysting place,

> ... but this time it's *Bona Dea* he cries ... Hills o' the Mother he says, an' y'r lavender, the purple, he says, an' then he says, but more slow:
> Roma aurea Roma
> Roma ... amor, amor ... Roma. Roma, wot's in the feminine gender, he says. (132)

219 Typology

The words 'aurea Roma' are from an epigraph on Rome's wall, which the mason may know about from the preface of William Fitzstephen's twelfth-century *Life of Becket*, translated by John Stow in his *Survey of London* (1598). Fitzstephen asserts that London is Rome's twin. The rhapsody begins in an appreciation of Elen's 'Hills o' the Mother,' which evoke those of Rome, and 'y'r lavender, the purple' (132). Later her 'livid flower' (166) or 'living flower' (168) suggests the genital hue during arousal. For the mason, Roma and amor are inextricably joined in a way that implies the necessary role of a female muse in any important cultural creation. It is the role Elen plays in his dreamy evocation of Roman London.

Her role in his imaginative recreation evokes the foundation of Rome. As she and her mason embrace 'between the heats and the cool' on this August evening, Venus, 'the whitest of the Wanderers,' shines over Bride's Well (132) as she had shone, 'West-star' (87), at the mating of Mars and Ilia. For Elen and her mason, however, sexual commerce under the auspices of Venus does not leave fact 'ravished' of 'myth.'

The medieval lovers correspond to another Roman couple, who redeem the loss of myth that occurred in the foundation of the secular city by Mars on Ilia. Before Elen and the mason make love, he, 'a-fondleing the wall' with its Roman brick, remembers and seems to see Constantius Chlorus entering the city in 296 AD and he sings out the Latin words of a medallion struck to commemorate the occasion: REDDITOR LVCIS ÆTERNÆ ('restorer of eternal light'). Depicted on the medal, which Jones describes in a note, is Constantius landing 'where the keels tie up below Fleet Bridge' (134) and being welcomed by a kneeling woman designated as London.[12] Constantius is literally her saviour. Having helped to defeat a tyrannical secessionist British emperor in the field, he and his fleet arrive to save the city's inhabitants from marauding German mercenaries.

Because Constantius was the consort of Flavia Julia Helena, of legendary British birth, the medallion's crowned female figure with arms outstretched in welcome evokes 'the British Elen' (131) who is Elen Monica's patron saint and one of her corresponding types. In an elaborate note on Helena, the poet writes that as consort of Constantius she helped restore and order the realm, and that 'she is indeed almost Britannia herself.' Constantius' nickname, Chlorus, is the masculine form of Chloris (Greek for 'green') and by a sort of mirroring, emphasizes Helena's affinity with Roman Flora, whose name had once been Chloris. As the Christian mother of Constantine, moreover, Helena helped

220 The Shape of Meaning

prepare for the momentous *pax* between empire and Church which allowed Christianity to become the religion of the West. In this she may be seen as the sociopolitical counterpart of Mary, by whom the Incarnation was. Jones notes that Helena too is 'envisaged as Holy Wisdom' in her Mass, and he goes on to say that she may have been identified with primordial 'matriarchal figures' (131–2 n3). He has especially in mind 'a cult-figure "Elen" in Celtic prehistory' (to G January 1966). Elen Monica, who assimilates all these mythological, legendary, and historical females, first suggests the linkage between Rome and Christianity in her initial topological references. She evokes the Roman surveyor's north-south and east-west bearings, the *decumanus* and *kardo* – first referred to and described with reference to the rape of Ilia (87 n3) – by suggesting intersecting lines running the length and breadth of the city: from St Mary Whitechapel outside the west wall to St Bride's outside the east wall and 'from Hallows-on-Wall [the north wall] to the keel-haws' on the river (127). The intersecting lines implied by these references evoke the cross as well as the lines of the Roman survey and imply what is historically true, that London is signed with the cross because she was first marked by the Roman surveyor at her foundation.

When the mason calls out 'REDDITOR LVCIS ÆTERNÆ,' Elen silently responds, 'Let's to terrestial flesh, or / bid good-night' (134). Apparently she interprets his Latin as liturgical, thinking perhaps of the *lux aeterna* that symbolizes Christ in requiem Masses. In view of St Helen's role and the destiny of Roman Europe, Elen is more correct than her more learned mason might surmise.

Because he brings *lux aeterna* and is a saviour-figure, Constantius corresponds to Jesus, with London (which is Helena) as mankind. This parallel joins those discussed earlier in which Christ and mankind correspond to Hector and Helen (or Troy) and to Nelson and Nike (or England). Typologically, the male figures save, or attempt to save, the same woman.

London is symbolically equivalent to the city Hector defends. It is 'Lud's town of megara' (165), the plural of megaron here meaning churches and recalling the megaron of Priam that houses Helen Argive. Moreover, London is Troy Novaunt according to the legend evoked by Elen's reference to founding fathers 'from Old Troy' (164). And it is partly because of its identification with Troy that London is a universal symbol. For the poet at least, this reflects Jackson Knight's claim that 'Troy is an ideal equivalent of the earth because it is ideally a labyrinth' (*Cumaean Gates* 132). At the opening of the monologue, London's

221 Typology

labyrinthine, Trojan character is encapsulated in the single image of its 'troia'd lanes' (124).

Near the conclusion of her monologue, Elen remarks that in one of London's megara a Cockney priest will soon celebrate Crouchmass, with affection, 'twisting his cock's egg tongue round / the Vulgar *lingua* like any Trojan licentious of divinity' (165). Double meanings and malapropisms obscure and enhance meaning here. The priest is Trojan in the colloquial sense of 'plucky' and also by legendary descent from Aeneas. He pronounces the Vulgate's Latin as though he has an academic licentiate in divinity. But the adjective 'licentious' also recalls the lust of Trojan Anchises for divine Aphrodite, by whom Aeneas was born and could claim a degree of divinity, as can his descendants, therefore, including the medieval priest. But such a claim has a better, theological foundation in the Mass he celebrates, whereby men in communion with Christ partake of divine life. In Catholic theology, the purpose of redemption is that men might share divine life. This, ultimately, is the meaning of the transformation of the nymph Chloris into the goddess Flora as re-enacted in the experience of Elen with her mason.

Elen and her lover correspond to Jesus and mankind in eschatological marriage. This is suggested when, as Elen recounts her embrace with the mason, she compares rain water 'from the *right* side of the gate' (130) to the saving water of Paschaltide's *Vidi aquam*, which evokes the water flowing from the wound Jesus received during his nuptials with mankind on Calvary. Eschatological coupling is further suggested when Elen confesses that during the mason's second rhapsody, 'I for love languished' (133). She quotes the beloved of the Song of Songs (2:5), who goes on to say of her lover, 'His left hand is under my head, and his right hand doth embrace me' (2:6). The mason plays this lover's part in a way that identifies the woman with the city, for he fondles both at once: Elen remembers, 'his left hand was under my head ... and with his right that did embrace me, he touched, his palm open, the courses of the wall, the back of his hand to the freestone face' (133). (She speaks as though she is the stone and can feel the back of his hand touching her.) The city as bride of God is also suggested by the Walbrook, under Walbrook Street, that waters the city 'from the midst of the street of it' (127), a reference to the river of life in the New Jerusalem (Revelation 22:2), a city 'prepared as a bride adorned for her husband' (21:2).

Between the love of the embracing couple and eschatological consummation there is, of course, a great difference owing partly to time's impermanence and party to the nature of the lovers' relationship. The image is, in the poetic sense, elaborately metaphysical. Elen's account of their August meeting begins, 'And again, once in especial,' which evokes Thomas Wyatt's powerful lines:

> ... but once especial –
> In thin array: after a pleasant guise
> When her loose gown did from her shoulders fall,
> And she me caught in her arms long and small,
> And therewithal so sweetly did me kiss,
> And softly said, 'Dear heart, how like you this?'

For Wyatt's persona as for Elen, this is memory of past happiness, which emphasizes subsequent loss. Wyatt's poem begins, 'They flee from me that sometime did me seek,' and Elen finally says of her mason, 'from that / most august eve I saw him no more' (160). Then she repeats what she had said concerning another departed lover: 'They come and they go' (129) – a refrain at once sexually suggestive and pathetic in its understatement. She immediately covers her feelings, rebounding into the flow of her monologue, but the pathos at the centre of her life has been revealed. She is a bride with no groom. The suffering of her muted passion can be heard in her street-cry, 'come buy, good for between the sheets' (166). Sex may symbolize heaven, but the looked-for consummation does not take place in time. Even for those luckier (or more prudent) than Elen, life is a matter of contingency and finitude.

Mortality and an end to human loving are implied from the beginning of her monologue when Elen cries her *introit in a* Dirige-*time*,' and her lavender, an autumnal flower, is said to be 'threnodic,' in mourning. Elen's monologue is an elegy for her lost youth, but it has larger implications. She may mourn for her times, saddened by a great economic depression and the ineffectual rule of Henry VI. For the poet, at least, a further cause for sadness is the decline of medieval culture, since the 'loud ... West-cuckoo' of its springtime (92) has now 'flown' (125). Near the end of the monologue, finitude is implied, at the conclusion of her list of churches at which Crouchmass will be said, by a topological zeroing in on the Tower: 'that's where they keep the chopper bright, captain / and no candle / to light you to bed' (162).

It is this dark inevitability that psychologically requires a hero, a saviour, a redeemer. From the beginning, the catalogue of churches has evoked the nursery rhyme 'Oranges and Lemons,' which ends, in the modern version, 'Here comes a candle to light you to bed, / Here comes a chopper to chop off your head.' Folklorists maintain that the rhyme contains intimations of primitive human sacrifice in which a victim is buried within or beneath a fortification so that his spirit will defend the city. Elen mentions several guardian figures and, though none were sacrificially killed, she refers to them as 'immolated kings' (164). Among them are Bran, whose 'blessèd guardian head, cisted under... keeps Lud's town' (130) and

> ... Belins, 'Wallons an' Wortipors
> agèd viriles buried under that from Lud's clay have ward of us that be his townies – and certain THIS BOROUGH WERE NEVER FORCED, cap-tin!! (163)

The emphasis on defence here and also in the reference to Constantius Chlorus saving London from Germans undoubtedly expresses the feelings of the poet writing this section of his poem in London shortly after the Second World War. It also corresponds to Elen's character and perhaps her corpulence being partly modelled on Winston Churchill. David Jones writes to his friend Grisewood about the sort of person suited to reading Elen's monologue aloud:

> I thought, with considerable amusement... that Winston, in a certain mood, would be ideal for the job!! It certainly is a pleasant thought, nor is it a totally idle thought, conceptually. The fact that the Old Man should occur to one at all in this connection indicates how damned complicated the requirements are. Actually while writing [Elen's monologue] I found myself thinking more than once of the Old Man. (Also of Queen Elizabeth I and Richard II and of course of various women of the days of my childhood, those Dickensian figures, some relatives, others who worked for my mother – along with much else, the Guardian Goddesses &...) Do you remember us listening to his ''Ome Guard' speech? (16 October 1952)

Once the suggestion is made that Elen owes something to Churchill, she does acquire an extra, incongruous vividness, especially as a personification of England.

But of course she is profoundly female both psychologically and in her chthonic typology, to which the nickname her mother gave her adds a Celtic resonance. 'The Lady of the Pool' is an urban variation on 'the Lady of the Lake' – a figure whose origin in Celtic folklore is a fay associated with water and triple in aspect. Her mythic original is the triple goddess: the mother, the lover, the presider over the dead.

Elen accommodates the dead in her memory as she prays for them, especially near the end of her monologue. Some of them she recalls as guardian figures – though for her they are primarily 'fathering figures' underground promoting fertility,

> ... making to bear
> bean-stalks, cherry-gardens, tended 'lotments, conservatories and stews of fish, pent fowl, moo-cows and all manner o' living stock, such as, like us women, be quickened of kind: so God will. (163)

The fruitful coition of these fathers with Mother Earth has its psychological and imaginative corollary in Elen, in whom they contribute to a living tradition that does invigorate the city by preserving vital culture, which is the life of the *civitas* and of civilization. Mythically and symbolically her accommodation of the dead combines with her other roles, that of lover and that of mother.

Elen is also a guardian of the living. In this role she warns the Mediterranean captain to ship out before winter sets in, and she warns another captain not to abuse 'a pretty boatswain's boy' (167). 'Here,' writes the poet, 'the L. of P. is a "mother-figure" in the ordinary sense of having compassion on the little boy' (*IN* 72). She is also a nature-figure forbidding buggery. 'Spare him the rope's end' suggests more than whipping, and this is even clearer in an early draft: '... or may the Loathly worm shivver y'r joy-stick – I know y'r fund of amusements once the land tips astern ...' Not that she is a prude, for she says to him, 'I wish no harm to y'r lawful occasions' (167). Like all aquatic fays, she is primarily a lover or a would-be lover. But she would like to adopt the African ship's boy and baptize him 'Austin Gregorians in Thameswater.' If as Elen (Helen) she is a lover, as Monica she is a mother. This psychological and archetypal ambiguity may partly account for the Oedipal confusion of the 'aurioled clerk,' one of her lovers, who sometimes 'did meddle me with' his mother 'that nourished him bodily' (144).

Elen's association through the fays of folklore with the triple goddess is secured by her juxtaposed references to two sculptures of the Gallo-Roman *Matronae* that will be found under churches. Beneath Holy Trinity 'the three created fays do play,' and under Crutched Friars 'the Three Mothers' (162).

225 Typology

Like the *fays du lac*, the Mothers are aquatic. Their sanctuaries were the river-sources of western Europe, where the earth mother's womb was thought to open. Throughout the poem, water is her feminine manifestation, but the 'fluvial doings of the mother' are especially characteristic of London (164). As the poet notes, 'the early accounts of the city suggest that the wells, rills, shares, bourns, streamlets, ponds, apart from the great tidal river, impressed the imagination of the writers' (126 n7). Particularly striking is the 'long bourn of sweet water' flowing beside Mary Woolnoth or 'Mary of the Birth' (127). The suggestive combination of water, Mary, and the Nativity may reflect the residual paganism of medieval Christians who built churches near or over running water, which they thought to be a direct means of communication with the womb of the world in the depth of the earth.[13]

Because of contemporary archeological discoveries, Elen is fully conscious of continuity between pagan and Christian mysteries. The bearing of a buck's head into the cathedral on the feast of St Paul was thought in the late Middle Ages to derive from Roman sacrifice on the spot, under one of the south chapels, where excavations in 1316 had uncovered animal remains, which seemed to indicate that the site was that of a temple of Diana.[14] Elen alludes to the bearing of the buck's head and then to its pagan prototype when she refers to 'faiths under Paul' (127). (She is also making a topological pun since, as Stow's *Survey* records, 'under the choir of Paul's ... was a parish church of St Faith, commonly called St Faith under Paul.') Elen explicitly professes her earth-motherly faith in the continuity of religions when she says,

>   Chthonic *matres* under the croft:
> springan a Maye's *Aves* to clerestories.
>   Delphi in sub-crypt:
> luce flowers to steeple.   (127)

In a real sense, it is only because 'the Three Mothers ... sit, / crofted under' (162) that *Aves* spring to where stained glass narrates the 'clear stories' of the New Testament. Delphi is the shrine of a fertility goddess who engenders flowers such as luce, the lily of the Virgin, represented by the *fleur-de-lis* of Gothic ornamentation. This is grace built on nature but, because human nature has always been religious and receptive to grace, this is also grace built on grace.

Water, the earth, the city, mankind and its primeval goddesses: Elen contains them all. In her, moreover, archetype is balanced by type and by realistic personality. Her monologue may be too long and too often transparent to be credible in realistic terms, but it does reflect realism, which is why its immediate effect is to obscure the geometric structural pattern it contains. Initially her monologue seems chaotically organic, 'open,' or formless. In 1953, the poet writes that

> the jumble is in part deliberate, because conversations of that sort tend to be very jumbled and consist almost entirely of 'asides'. At least that is my experience of simple persons. They begin by telling you about their own aunts & that reminds them of food & that of farming & that of a tradition current in Summerset when they went to stay with Uncle Sid who said that King Arthur lived at Tauton and that George III was a good farmer & so on. My job in this section was rather to use this sort of conversation for my own ends – for the ends of *The Anathemata*. (*IN* 71)

In its initial impression of chaos but also in its underlying form, Elen's monologue also resembles the conversation of David Jones. As Stanley Honeyman remembers, 'He had this extraordinary gift ... of constructing a conversation and if you didn't know him terribly well, you'd think he was just rambling ... but there in his mind the whole time was the shape of this conversation and this is why if you started to go he would become very distressed because he hadn't brought the conversation full circle. And he'd say, "Well, I must rush this bit then just to tell you ..."'[15] This is an illuminating observation because it suggests a relationship between the poet's habit of mind and the shape not only of Elen's monologue but of the poem as a whole.

Co-redemption is the theme of her monologue. This is because the allegorical subject of her tale of the voyage of the *Mary* is, as we shall see, the co-redemptive role of Mary, whose archetypes, the bride of God and the mother, Elen shares. Elen's obvious charity indicates that she gives these archetypes realistic moral extension. In this regard, her unchaste sexuality is a metaphysical inconsistency which emphasizes that it is 'compliancy of ... will,' not virginity, that makes Mary (and Elen) typic of co-redemptive humanity.

If Elen is not entirely credible as a realistic character, that does not fault her wonderful monologue, for this is not realistic fiction, and whatever Elen loses in realistic credibility she more than makes up for in richness of symbolic meaning. And that meaning does include a compelling personal energy and warmth which is convincingly feminine and an emotional range that runs nearly the entire gamut of human possibility.

She contains a real woman but she is bigger than any real woman. If, as I suggested, she resembles Molly Bloom, she also has affinity with Anna Livia – as the poet acknowledges when he has Elen answer the question one of Joyce's washerwomen asks about the Findhorn's name (145 and n1). Elen is unique in literature because she contains so much from so many literary figures, among them Chaucer's Wife of Bath and Sheridan's Mrs Malaprop. Yet she retains her own strong, dramatically convincing personality.

As a character, she has some affinity with the subject of Pound's 'Portrait d'une Femme.' Elen's social standing is much lower, but of her too it might be said:

> Your mind and you are our Sargasso Sea,
> London has swept about you this score years
> And bright ships left you this or that in fee:
> Ideas, old gossip, oddments of all things,
> Strange spars of knowledge ...

For Elen as for the woman of Pound's poem, knowledge is largely a by-product of carnal knowledge. 'Yes, you richly pay,' writes Pound, 'You are a person of some interest' – compound interest, certainly, in Elen's case, for she is a kind of poet. Her rendering of a Welsh boatswain's boast, and possibly of the entire voyage of the *Mary*, is 'pieced in parts with and descanted upon of' a sailor's tales of other, ancient voyages (155). She corresponds, therefore, to her dreamy mason-lover who is in more than one sense a romantic poet. But that was long ago, and Elen herself is essentially a modernist poet of the sort – like Pound, Williams, and MacDiarmid – that makes collages combining imaginative creation with the reproduction of documents – though all Elen's documents are hearsay.

Because hers is a synthetic and creative imagination, our initial association of Elen with Eb Bradshaw can be enlarged upon. We saw these two Londoners as archetypal counterparts; now we see typological affinity. If the shipwright is an artist-type, so is Elen – as a poet-figure and as an actress in her secondary monologues, especially her 'try-out' as a siren (146). Eb and Elen are both orators, of course, and we have seen that to some extent (and with Bradshaw more noticeably in his style) both are Churchillian. He personifies Protestantism; she, Catholicism. As Eb is archetypally Elen's child, Protestantism is the offspring of Catholicism. The two belong together, which is why the monologues of Eb and Elen are adjacent.

Without becoming an outright myth, Elen Monica occupies the centre of her poem in symbolically so powerful a way that she seems almost to contain every other female figure in the poem and to enwomb all its male figures, including the meditator whose imagination contains her. But this symbolic absorption is merely implied, not explicit as with Dai Greatcoat. In the same way her implied temporal ubiquity, ranging from prehistory to the present, is restrained by the realistic dimension in which she is convincingly conditioned by her historical setting. Psychologically, symbolically, verbally, she is a remarkable example of unified diversity. In her, fictional and generic modes modulate in an active complexity which almost defies analysis and which contributes greatly to the reader's sense of the poem as a galaxy in motion. In human microcosm, Elen is what a city is, and what a civilization is, when invigorated by a living sense of its own history and literature and by a depth of imagination which is religious and mythic.

Elen's monologue is important in English literary history because it alters the imaginative topology of London. After Joyce defined the Dublin of the imagination, Eliot redefined London, which had been, before the publication of *The Waste Land*, imaginatively Dickensian. Before Dickens it had been Blakean (for the few who read *Jerusalem*), before that it was defined by Pope, Johnson, and Defoe, and before that by Ben Jonson and, especially, Shakespeare. In 'The Lady of the Pool,' David Jones retrieves medieval London, which had never before received extended literary definition, and he gives it a human personality. The breadth of this definition and the warmth of her personality begin in her speaking Cockney. If this makes her seem, more than Eb Bradshaw, our contemporary, it is nevertheless no anachronism – since Cockney was the language of all native Londoners, except members of the court, from the Middle Ages till the nineteenth century. Elen's London is a remarkable literary achievement and the most positive depiction of a city in English literature since the Renaissance. Partly because cities do symbolically preserve their past and partly because Elen's account of her home town is so vivid and multilayered, David Jones's late-medieval city will haunt modern London and permanently alter it as a city of the imagination.

GWENHWYFAR

A full millennium before Elen walks London's river-front, Gwenhwyfar stands during the Offertory of Christmas midnight Mass. She is numinous. The description of her is as close as poetry can come to painting, though figure-painting only, for 'we are not concerned with portrait' (202). And because language here matches pictorial vividness, this is the most intensely lyrical part of the poem. She is rendered in the full range of modality, from realism to myth, and in a way that gives personal focus to the motif of metamorphosis that characterizes 'Mabinog's Liturgy.' The setting derives from a reference in *The Mabinogion* to 'Gwenhwyvar, the wife of Arthur, when she has appeared loveliest at the Offering, on the day of the Nativity ...'[16] Although the description of her is remarkable in its length – seven pages, if we discount the interlude concerning Manawydan's voyage – it is conventional in that it moves in its first stage 'from top to toe' (202) in accordance with the *amplificatio per descriptionem* of medieval *artes poeticae*. The description is also influenced by modern journalistic convention. In letters to friends, the poet paraphrases 'The First Court of the Season' in *The London Times* of 28 March 1935 which, he says, reads

> like Joyce, with a very small alteration here & there. I mean as – For Mrs Loftus a gown of crystal & silver, hand embroidered entirely of a heavy white net over close-fitting foundation of silver tissue with a train of silver widely-bordered with embroidery of crystal & diamond. For Miss Rosemary Pretyman a draped gown of lavender & for Viscountess Ratedone a train of satin, pearl necklace, pearl earrings, pearl & diamond tiara. & for Mrs Napper-Tandy .... however, her name is joy enough.   (to G 30 March 1935; cf *DGC* 67)

The description of Gwenhwyfar reads like an expanded entry in such a list and is evocative of the superficial luxuriance of social-column journalism. It is also a variation on the anatomical catalogues we saw earlier. Unlike them, however, this catalogue is unified by the person wearing the objects described, so that she is the focus of its manifold significance.

Symbolically, Gwenhwyfar represents Roman-Celtic Britain and recalls that its cultural and political unity will end partly because of her adultery. This ending has its analogue in her mortality, which is emphasized with reference to the 'cere-cloth of thirty-fold' that will be her shroud (196). Even now she may be, like Elen Monica, no longer young. Of her blond hair it is asked,

> ... was there already silver to the gilt?
> For if the judgmatic smokes of autumn seemed remote, John's Fires were lit and dead, and, as for gathering knots of may – why not talk of maidenheads?   (197)

Bound up with mortality is morality. Repeated three times in her description, the word 'gilt' evokes its homonym and suggests that her conscience causes 'the toil within' (197), so that her sexual passion has its own agonizing 'in-cries.' Her neck is now perfectly still

> yet, as limber to turn
> as the poised neck at the forest-fence
> between find and view
> too quick, even for the eyes of the gillies of Arthur, but seen of the forest-ancraman (he had but one eye)
> between decade and *Gloria*. (198)

The simile evokes the medieval theme of the amatory hunt, in which the hart is an allegorical figure for the lady loved. To whom but Lancelot would Gwenhwyfar look? The perceptive ancraman, who conforms to Christ's admonition to be 'single' eyed (Matthew 6:22), resembles Malory's forest-hermit, who knows that repentant Lancelot 'by hys thoughts... ys lyckly to turne agayne' (15.5).

Gwenhwyfar's role in the approaching catastrophe is suggested in the description of her hair and corona in what may be the most beautifully evocative passage in the poem:

> If her gilt, unbound
> (for she was consort of a *regulus*) and falling to below her sacral bone, was pale as standing North-Humber barley-corn, here, held back in the lunula of Doleucothi gold, it was paler than under-stalks of barley, held in the sickle's lunula. So that the pale gilt where it was by nature palest, together with the pale river-gold where it most received the pallid candle-sheen, rimmed the crescent whiteness where it was whitest. (196–7)

Since Gwenhwyfar's name means 'white spirit,' this passage captures the essence of her. And the resemblance of her hair to 'North-Humber barley-corn' – while it suggests her mortality, as an allusion to John Barleycorn later suggests the mortality of Jesus (228) – also recalls the location, in Northumberland, of Lancelot's castle.[17] In the pallor of her hair and complexion shines 'the inconstant moon.' Her crown a lunula; her forehead a 'crescent whiteness' and, as the description goes on to say, 'puckered a little, because of the extreme altitude of her station'; her temples gleaming like 'Luna's rim': she is virtually identical with the perennial symbol of love and mutability.

231 Typology

Gwenhwyfar is 'high as Helen the Moon,' for it is said of her

> If as Selenê in highness so in influence, then as Helenê too: by her lunations the neapings and floodings, because of her the stress and drag. (197)

Allusion to German *Sturm und Drang* anticipates the completion of conquest by Teutonic invaders and recalls the 'stress / *und* icy counter-drag' in the pre-enactment of world-endings in 'Fore-Time' (57). The resemblance between the Greek names Selenê and Helenê is noted in *Vergil's Troy*, in a passage Jones marks, as possibly explaining Helen's traditional identification with the moon (92). We saw that in 'Middle-Sea and Lear-Sea' Gwenhwyfar is 'West-Helen' (92), and we noted the resemblance between Homeric epic and medieval romance and suggested that the women correspond to each other primarily because of the calamitous results of their adulterous passions. The calamities they help cause are linked, furthermore, by the legendary descent of Britons and Romans from Trojans.

Despite the moral dilemma that distresses her, Gwenhwyfar is, like Helen Argive and Elen Monica, typologically God's bride. Her adultery does not negate the sincerity of her devotion any more than professional obligations undo the worship of courtesans like Phryne and Lais in 'Keel, Ram, Stauros' (180). Gwenhwyfar's guilt is greater, of course, but to her credit, she feels it. Her golden hair may therefore be 'Maudlin gilt' (146) and symbolize guilt which is ultimately regenerative like that of Mary Magdalene. According to Malory, the adulterous queen, still 'limber to turn,' dies repentant in a cloister.

What remains problematic on a realistic level is transparently clear on the level of archetype. This woman is the earth in a way that has important structural implications for the poem as a whole. She is the earth because her description corresponds in many respects to that of the earth in 'Rite and Fore-Time.' The manuscript drafts show that after the late addition of Gwenhwyfar to the poem, Jones inserted into the complete 1949 holograph text for the typist pages 61-74 of 'Rite and Fore-Time,' which includes material with which Gwenhwyfar's description resonates. After inserting this material, Jones adjusted her description to heighten the resonance. In 'Fore-Time,' the earth is clothed in geological strata and 'life-layers.' The queen actually wears what might be called rock strata: her 'spun Iberian asbestos' (196) or 'shining fire-stone' (202), verbally redolent of the earth's 'fire-wrought cold rock' (74); and her 'Dalmatian tunic of gold stuff' which is 'mantling' (202) reminiscent of the earth's 'mantle-rock' (82). The queen's clothing also represents a wide variety of biological life. Over her skin she wears flax. On her feet, buckskin of deer and ivory of narwhal. Her *lacerna* or chasuble is edged and lined with fur 'of marten and pale kinds of wild-cat,' and embroidered with forms 'as *apis*-like as may be' (203). Complementing these bee-forms, the laticlaves of her tunic are coloured with dye from real kermes insects (202). And her barley-pale hair (196–7) recalls the 'barlies' (82) at the end of 'Fore-Time' which crown the processes formative of the earth. Her barley-hair identifies her, furthermore, with the earth goddess Demeter, who is evoked throughout the poem by name and by her ritual and mythic associations. Demeter, too, is blonde, her particular symbol is barley, and her name – deriving partly from the Cretan *deai* for 'barley' – means 'Barley Mother.'

Gwenhwyfar is also the earth because metaphorically she herself is made of rock, and this makes her the focus of the poem's pervasive motif of stone. She is called 'the breathing marble' (202), her neck is 'of full entasis, as though of Parian [marble] that never ages' (198), and her veins are said to 'vein the hidden marbles' (203) – an image identifying her with the white island of Britain seen from off Cornwall, in which 'the tin-veins maculate the fire-rocks' (106). She is called a 'column' (204), but she is more accurately a statue. As such she evokes the other female statues in the poem, which are literally made of Mother Earth. These are the Venus of Willendorf; the Kore, which recalls Helen Argive and Demeter, as does this Celtic queen (92); and the Athena Parthenos, which is 'chryselephantine' like the queen with her pale skin and golden hair (203, 94). Marble is hardened limestone, moreover, and the Venus of Willendorf is 'worked lime-rock' (60). For Lascaux cave-art, the earth itself is 'graved lime-face' (60). The wall circumscribing Elen's London is made of 'ragstone' (131), a synonym for coarse limestone. And at the end of the poem, Calvary is 'lime-rock' (237). Limestone suits 'grave Demeter' (230) because of the high proportion of fossils in it. In this respect, furthermore, it makes Calvary a fitting prototype of Christian altars, which contain 'relics of the dead' (51 n1).

When Gwenhwyfar bows at the end of her description, the inanimate symbolism of which she partakes passes by imaginative transference to the altar and chalice she bows toward. Like her, the altar represents the earth and is clothed: 'over the stone the spread board-cloths.' Like her too, the chalice (its metal a refinement of rock) is clothed and, like her, it stands upright: 'the up-standing calix that the drawn-over laundered folds drape white' (203). Chalices are, of course, symbolically female.

During her description, then, Gwenhwyfar represents the earth before the altar holding the gifts of the earth, which include bread 'of Ceres,' the Latin for Demeter. As earth-figure and personally from 'the reserve-*granaria*' (203), Gwenhwyfar herself has provided the bread. But Demeter is 'germ of all: / of the dear arts as well as bread' (230) and so the queen, in her elaborately ornamented regalia, also represents the tradition of human artefacture. Symbolically and thematically she revives the themes of 'Rite and Fore-Time,' which will pass on to their culmination in 'Sherthursdaye and Venus Day,' but she is their preliminary, symbolic culmination. Throughout her description she stands as still as a statue. In her bowing, she is a cosmic Galatea responding to a divine Pygmalion. Her gesture is a fiat, in which she spiritually and symbolically approximates the Virgin, who said yes to God. Gwenhwyfar is the earth of fore-time; in her bow the primordial earth gives human assent, acknowledging its purpose and fulfilment. By providing the elements for transubstantiation, she returns as far as man can the favour of creation. With Gwenhwyfar 'cycle comes full circle,' as Jones puts it in the holograph note that he placed in one of his copies of the poem, 'W. A's Gwenhewyvarr we / assist at / In the last – we are back.'

The poet writes that it is a good thing she 'faced the one way' with the rest of the congregation 'or else when the lifted Signa shone they had mistaken the object of their worship' (205). He is careful to preserve the theological distinction because, typologically, he does imply an equivalence. The earth goddess and God join in the sacrament, moreover, because their marriage takes place there but also because, if Jesus is present there under the species of bread and wine, so is Demeter. It is appropriate that Gwenhwyfar's colours, white and gold, are iconographically eucharistic. But symbolism aside, there is correspondence to divinity even in her realistic flesh, for her body is

> ... the defeasible and defected image of him who alone imagined and ornated us, made fast of flesh her favours, braced bright, sternal and vertibral, to the graced bones bound. (196)

The passage echoes words addressed to God at the opening of 'The Wreck of the Deutschland' – 'Thou hast bound bones and veins in me, fastened me flesh.' The allusion partly acknowledges Hopkins as the first to work English to the chiming intensity of Welsh *cynghanedd*, which David Jones also approximates in the language of Gwenhwyfar's description. He does it to give her a rich and beautiful verbal setting which is also an extended aural allusion to her historical setting. It is a language almost as appropriate to the Celtic queen and early-medieval Britain as Cockney is to Elen Monica and late-medieval London.

Verbally and symbolically, the description of Gwenhwyfar is beautiful and powerful to depths of reverberation which poetry seldom reaches. If she is numinous, so is the language that depicts her.[18]

VOYAGING

The motif of voyaging complements that of eschatological marriage. What the poet says about life as a love story, he says also of voyaging: 'there is but one voyager's yarn to tell' (*DG* 215). Even though the poem's voyages are distinct in realistic terms and occur in different historical periods, voyaging constitutes a single continuous symbol which contributes importantly to the unity of the poem. As a symbol, the archetypal voyage has a variety of aspects, including the movement of commerce which effects cultural change, the journey through life of the individual soul, the quest of God for mankind, and the experience of the Church in the world. Each theme has its moments of priority, so that the voyage is a metamorphic symbol, but the themes are all subsumed in the cosmic voyage, which has its clearest exposition in the anatomy of the world-ship in 'Keel, Ram, Stauros.' Essentially, the voyage is an image of movement in time. As such it extends through historic time the teleological movement of the divine Light through geological and biological fore-time. Like that movement, the voyage implies direction, destination, purpose. Its course corresponds to the line that centres the spiral of western history and to the interrupted but continued movement of meditative consciousness inward through imagined time and space to the Eucharist and forward through subjective, meditative time to the paschal events. Jones's own metaphor for the poem is, after all, 'a song or story about a journey' (42), and the symbolic voyage comprising many voyages gives the poem its nearest approximation to narrative continuity.

More than anything else, what transforms the poem's voyages into a single symbol is their continuity of direction. In a sense, there is a single course, westward and then northward. As many commentators have noted, this course symbolizes the ancient movement of Mediterranean culture and civilization. But deeper than this lies a combination of classical and Celtic archetypal voyages to the land of the dead, Thule for the Greeks (97), identified in the poem with Britain (92). This is the voyage's end for Phoenician-Phocaean sailors and for the captains who

235 Typology

deal with Eb Bradshaw and meet Elen Monica. It is a destination symbolized at the end of all the poem's voyaging by Gwenhwyfar, to whom ships bring symbolic merchandise. With reference to Odysseus's voyage to the underworld, Jackson Knight writes that 'this western land of the dead, reached by Odysseus, has lately been identified as Britain, which is famous as the land of the dead to Celts, unless it is more exact to say that that was the Scillies' (*Cumaean Gates* 29). No wonder Dodman Point is called 'the Deadman' (98). The region of the Scillies is particularly suggestive of the land of the dead partly because of the many 'menhirs' and megalithic burial sites there which spell 'DIS MANIBUS' (100), the classical equivalent to RIP. And there 'the sea-Lamia' devours mariners (102). Since her name originally means 'cave,' this Lamia combines the realism of shipwreck with the two mythical ways of entering the otherworld, by voyaging and by going into a cave. For the Phoenician-Phocaean crew, Britain is 'where the tin-veins maculate the fire-rocks' (106), words which, as we have seen, identify Gwenhwyfar with Britain, but which also, primarily, evoke 'the elements of flame concealed in the veins of flint' at the place where Aeneas begins his descent into Hades (*Aeneid* 6.7).

Much of the imagery related to ships identifies the archetypal voyage as religious and cosmic. At the opening of the poem, the Supper room is a metaphorical ship, furnished with 'thwart-boards' for apostle-oarsmen, one 'at the right-board' or chief mate's place for Peter. As fishermen, Peter and John are reflectors justifying the meditator's use of nautical terms. They 'make all shipshape' and 'Bristol-fashion' for the launching of the Church (53). In the margin here beside the word 'shipshape,' the poet writes in one of his copies of the poem, 'pivot for the Argosy / II p. 95–IV [sic] 182.' The first arabic number indicates the page on which the Greek vessel begins its approach to the harbour of Athens; the second indicates the page on which that vessel completes its entry. All the poem's narrated and dramatized voyaging takes place in the pages between. We saw that the preparation of the Supper room is juxtaposed to the geophysical preparation of the earth. The planet too is a metaphorical ship for, during the formation of the earth, the divine Light 'beams ... athwart the fore-times' (73) – 'athwart' being a nautical term for the direction perpendicular to the length or course of a ship.

Conversely, in 'Keel, Ram, Stauros,' a ship becomes the earth in symbolism which entirely eclipses the dramatic realism of the Greek vessel entering the harbour of Athens. As 'prime measure' (173), this ship's keel evokes the prime meridian. It also evokes the Prime Mover, for the keel is the 'beam' symbolizing the Logos sustaining all created being. Personified, the keel also symbolizes the Logos incarnate, who is for man what the pre-incarnate Logos is for all creation:

> Recumbent for us
> the dark of her bilges
> for fouled canopy
> the reek of her for an odour of sweetness.
> Sluiced with the seep of us
> knowing the dregs of us. (180)

This evocation of Jesus through Isaiah's Suffering Servant combines with the keel's evocation of the creative Logos to identify the Church with the earth.

Jesus-as-keel is a nautical counterpart to the scriptural cornerstone (see Ephesians 2:20-2). According to Jackson Knight, the scriptural metaphor derives from the 'foundation stone of the temple at Jerusalem' which 'separated the temple from the waters of the abyss below the earth' and was 'in a sense divine.' Since the poet marks these words in his copy of *Cumaean Gates* (37), they probably lie behind the image of the keel riding 'the waters of the abyss.' In the Greek of the New Testament, the word for 'cornerstone' also means 'key-stone.' The scriptural ambiguity is lost in translation but restored in the poem by the keel being the apex of the ship's 'inverted vaults' (173), an image anticipated in the cenacle's 'high nave' (52), which is echoed by the ship's 'leaning nave' (181). Because the nave of a church is originally so called for its resemblance to a ship or *navis* turned bottom up, the high 'roof-beam' of the Supper room (229) is symbolically equivalent to the underriding 'chose beam' of the cosmic ship. The equivalence of topmost and bottom-most beams has affinity with what we saw to be the symbolic equivalence of the poem's structural centre and outermost circumference.

The image of the institutional Church as a ship partly derives from a patristic perception of the shape of the cross in the intersecting mast and yard of ancient vessels. The poet discusses the image in his 'Introduction to *The Rime of the Ancient Mariner*' (DG 215-6), which, more than any other of his essays, illuminates imagery of ships and voyaging in *The Anathemata*. In the poem, the cross is evoked when the mast of the Greek ship is called 'the trembling tree' (173), an allusion to the cross in 'The Dream of the Rood' (line 42). But any of the ship's wood may evoke the wood of the cross. Eb Bradshaw refers to 'best Indies lignum vitae'

237 Typology

(118), which may evoke Good Friday's *lignum crucis* and certainly recalls the patristic *lignum vitae cunctis credentibus*.[19] The keel too is *lignum vitae* – 'lignum for the life of us' (181). The association originates in the identification of the cross with the tree of life, at the base of which flow the four rivers of paradise (Genesis 2:8–10), an image alluded to in the poem when Jesus on the cross is said to be 'Of all the clamant waters / firthing forth from the Four Avons / himself the *afon*-head' (236–7). These interrelated images symbolically conflate the Church and the world to imply the immanence of metaphysical meaning in physical existence.

But because the cosmic ship is put to other uses, voyaging in the poem involves symbolic contradictions and ambiguities which, in certain instances, preclude straightforward allegorical significance. The world-ship of 'Keel, Ram, Stauros' transports cult objects (176) but it also carries war-machines (177–8). A similar antithetical tension informs the approach to Athens in late-classical times. The Greek ship passes 'Cleruchy' (95) – the isle of Aegina renamed for the *klerouchoi* (settlers) from Athens who replaced the native islanders massacred for their resistance to Athenian imperialism. While Athena does typify wisdom, therefore, she also represents the Athenian maritime empire, which amassed the wealth that made possible the construction of her Parthenon. The antithesis here between wisdom and greed may be symbolized by Athena's two statues: 'maiden' within, 'champion' without. In this phase of Greek culture the balance between gratuity and utility is also a moral contradiction.

A similar ambivalence pertains to the ship destined for Cornwall. It is manned by a combination of Phoenicians and Phocaeans partly to suggest maritime monopoly. They sail 'all for thalassocracy' (104), a word for sea empire originally used for Athenian maritime dominance over the Greek world. The internal disposition of crew members is not, however, thalassocratic. In danger of shipwreck on the Cornish coast, they chant,

> Wot'ld you do with the bleedin' owners?
>   What would you do with 'em?
> put 'em in the long boat
> put 'em in the long boat
>   put them in the wrong boat
> and let them sail her
>   over the seas to Dis. (104)

They can go to hell, the capitalists who do no work, run no risks, and for whom shipwreck would mean 'a proper siren's cruise' financed by insurance 'coverage' (172). What better place than Hades for those who promote and benefit from 'Pluto's Thalassocracies' – Pluto, the lord of the dead, being popularly confused with Plutus, the Roman god of riches, so that 'plutocracy' means the rule of the wealthy.[20]

During their dangerous passage round The Lizard, the ancient crewmen disclose their fundamental loyalties in a frantic litany to the sea-goddess who is patroness of their ship. Her shrine below deck would be in the bow, where ordinary crewmen bunk down (138 n1), which is partly why they are 'matlos of the Maiden' and can cry, 'Maiden help y'r own' (104). The goddess is invoked by the names she has in various ports but she is usually Aphrodite or an equivalent, for these sailors conform to stereotype. As notorious lovers, they dread drowning because it means a permanent 'adieu to y'r / Miletus Ladies' (prostitutes; see *RQ* 8 n12), and a final

>   ... farewell to you
>   Lady of Thebes
> when we founder
>   when we embrace the sea-stript dead ... (172)

The Lady of Thebes is Aphrodite, and death here is a parody of sexual embracing.

Upon sighting Cornwall, the top-tree boy calls,

>   we shall be rich men
> you shall have y'r warm-dugged Themis
> and you, white Phoebe's lune
>   ... and laughless little Telphousa
> what shipman's boy could ask another?
> said she'd smile
>   for tin!   (102)

Tin, of the Cornish trade but also 1920s slang for money, is not really their goal but only a means to securing relationships with women – relationships which may or may not mean marriage. The attraction of these girls is unabashedly sexual. Phoebe's lune, something crescent, may have genital connotations. 'Telphousa,' cognate with 'Delphi,' is synonymous with the female genital organ.²¹ Here too sex has religious connotations. The goddess Telphousa is identified with Demeter and, a few pages later, 'laughless little Telphousa,' is associated with the 'Agelastos Petra / cleft for us' (104) – the Laughless Rock at Eleusis, redemptive for man and consequently having affinity with the evangelical 'Rock of ages cleft for me.'

The names of these young women derive from a passage which Jones marks in his copy of *Cumaean Gates* about the patronage of Delphi belonging to a series of figures, among them, 'Themis, who is near to identity with Earth, and ... Phoebe, who ... may be already the moon ... all these forms of the earth goddess at Delphi are the female partners in the cosmic sacral marriage. Another of them ... was Telphousa ...' (57). Longing for cosmic marriage is implicit in sexual longing, particularly when the girl involved is named Themis, Phoebe, or Telphousa.

As cosmic brides, they all have affinity with 'Helen the Moon,' Phoebe most of all because of her 'lune,' though, in the poem's second draft foliation, Helen (56) is called 'Telphousa our margaron.' The sailors voyaging to Cornwall in quest of these women disclose the archetype that underlies the Trojan story, but which is also partly disguised by it. Grumbling against thalassocracy, the crewmen complain,

>   Where 'ld be their bleedin' miracle
>   that is Graecia
>   but for us ones
>   as cargoes-up
>   the thousand ships?   (172)²²

As this ship approaches the Cornish coast, it rides waves that are said to be 'echeloned' (108) and therefore recall Troy's 'echeloned Skaian' Gate, beyond which lies symbolic Helen, 'the margaron' of great price (56). When the top-tree boy first sights land, hope for union with his own Helen shines in his smile, who 'grins, like the kouroi' (96) – the sculpted male counterparts of the smiling Kore, earlier identified with Helen (91–2). The kouroi are 'stanced solemn' (91), a posture resonant with Mars 'checking his holy stance' immediately before copulating with Ilia (87) and subsequently echoed in the 'stanced feet' of the helmsman steering the Greek ship into its berth (181).

If the top-tree boy grins for a sexual consummation, the ship's captain 'grins too' (96).

> Who else should they choose
> to handle the bitch
> (and what a crew!)
> if not the cod's-eye man?   (173)

The metaphorical femininity of the ship is mated to the masculinity of its captain. In the margin of these lines in one of his copies of the poem, Jones writes, 'Cf. USA folksong: "she wants the cods eye man,"' a reference to the sea shanty correctly known as 'The Hog's-Eye Man,' in which the hog's eye is euphemistic for the vulva.

Archetypally, the ship's captain is 'the eternal skipper' (*IN* 61), but his symbolic associations are various. In an undated note addressed to Hague, the poet describes him as 'the tough, *eld*, experienced "strong one" – seeming to be Mannan mac Lir himself or the gladius-bearing Fisherman, the Vicar of *Sees* & Seas, a type of our Xtus-Ulysses.' These associations are interrelated but, strictly speaking, mutually exclusive – so that, like the symbolic ship, the image of its captain involves constant imaginative metamorphosis and ambiguity. But whether as hardened seaman, St Peter, Celtic sea god, or Christ, one of his dominant characteristics is sexual. While coitus awaits crewmen at their voyage's end, for the captain, sailing itself is a continuing intercourse, so that the lusty captain suggests an immanent eschatology to complement the future eschatology implied by the longing of the crew. If not a Christ-figure, he is nevertheless a Christ-type and, as such, is in communion with his ship. 'O how he cons her!' (107). The verb 'to con' means 'to steer' and 'to know' – in its latter sense having biblical sexual connotations. The ambiguity resembles that implied by the erudition Elen Monica has gleaned from her lovers.

The significance of the captain is further defined by his being called Iacchos (97) after Dionysus as the god of journeying. It is a name deriving from the ritual call of pilgrims en route to Eleusis, where the god presides over the mysteries. In combination with the commercial imperialism that obscures inherent spiritual hope, this association confers allegorical significance on the direction of the Greek ship moving in the Saronic Gulf 'straight ahead' toward 'obscured Eleusis' (95). Symbolically as well as literally, Eleusis lies in the same direction as that considered above apropos of voyaging to the underworld.

Iacchos-Dionysus is also the wine god whose drinking devotees become intoxicated with divine life. The Greek captain does his utmost to assimilate the god in this way. He is 'pickled' (96), 'the ancient staggerer /

241 Typology

the vine-juice skipper' (182). The latter epithet identifies him with Jesus by way of the 'lime-juice skipper' of 'Shallow Brown,' a sea-shanty in which it is asked about a ship, 'Who d'you think was master of her,' a question asked at the opening of the poem about the cenacle-ship Jesus captains (53). The association of the captain as drunkard with Jesus is less tenuous than it may seem, for the Pharisees were scandalized by Jesus the 'winebibber' who came 'eating and drinking' (Matthew 11:19). And Captain Christ is foretypified by Noah, a skipper who 'drank... wine' and 'was... drunken' (Genesis 9:21). St Augustine saw Noah's intoxication as foreshadowing the Passion (*De civitate Dei* 16.2). It is also typologically eucharistic.[23]

Both of these connotations are operative when, as the ship leans to port, the captain 'inclines himself outboard' on the starboard side and pours a libation in the direction of Athena Promachos atop the Acropolis:

What little's left
                    in the heel of his calix
asperging the free-board
               to mingle the dead of the wake. (182)

This is sacrifice in the colloquial sense – 'In the deeps of the drink / his precious dregs' (182) – but also in a technical sense, for 'when a libation of wine was poured out the wine was immolated' (E&A 40). And since the captain has assimilated the wine god, this libation is self-immolation. In his manuscript the poet sketches a ship with the wine 'asperging the free-board,' flowing down its right side – *a latere dextro*, in the words of the *Vidi aquam* of Paschaltide, which refers to the temple (here the ship) as symbol of the body of Christ. In Christ's sacrifice, blood and water mingle as they run down his right side, a mixture evoked by the eucharistic commingling of wine and water (see 204) and here by the flowing of wine into the sea. The 'dead of the wake' recalls, furthermore, dead sailors in their vast watery grave and the practice of pouring libations at graves to revitalize the dead with the immortal life of Dionysus.

The Greek ship sails home; the Phoenician-Phocaean ship approaches a foreign port for treasure. In the correspondence between their courses relative to similar topologies, we saw that although they sail as much as a millennium apart, these ships are symbolically identical. They suggest, therefore, that treasure seeking and homecoming are complementary aspects of the conclusion of life's voyage. This voyage to and through death becomes synonymous with that of 'our Xtus-Ulysses' when it is asked with regard to the Greek ship, 'What bells is that / when the overcast clears on a Mars' Venus-Day / Selene waxed, the sun in the Ram' (96)? The answer comes near the end of the poem with reference to the precise moment of Christ's death: 'On the keels-roads ... they would be sounding six bells' (239; see n2). For the Greek ship, but centuries before the crucifixion, this is the moment when home is first sighted. Suddenly 'the sea-hues / suffer change,' grey to blue. (In retrospect the word 'suffer' takes on new meaning.) And, as the sun's rays reach the ship, 'the build of us / patterns dark the blueing waters' (95). Symbolically at least, the more ancient Phoenician-Phocaean ship enters Cornwall's Ictian Bay also on Good Friday, for a similarly evocative change takes place as 'the lead dark sea' and 'iron dark shore' (106) are illuminated (and, remember, the poet later uses the unusual form 'brights' in his account of the crucifixion [237]):

> a sky-shaft brights the whited mole
> wind-hauled the grinders
>   white the darked bay's wide bowl ... (108)

The ship heads in to Albion, the white island, which is also the western land of the dead, now brightened gloriously by the sun, homonym of the Son. Like the sunrise on Christmas morning in *In Parenthesis*, this poem's symbolically simultaneous sunbursts should be read in the context of liturgical and patristic application to Christ of the imagery of pagan Helios worship. 'Now,' as one of the Greek fathers says, 'the sunlight of the cross surrounds man with its rays and he is illuminated.'[24]

Sustaining the symbolic conflation of these voyages with the passage of Jesus through death is a theology in which redemption is retroactive. For the poem's primary meditative consciousness, the praying of ancient sailors in danger amounts to their saying to priests at Mass:

> make *memento* of us
> and where the gloss reads *jungit manus* count us among his argonauts
> whose argosy you plead, under the sign of the things you offer. (106)

In his essay on *The Ancient Mariner*, the poet provides what may be taken as a gloss on this passage:

> What is pleaded in the Mass is precisely the argosy or voyage of the Redeemer, his entire sufferings, death, resurrection and ascension. It is

243 Typology

this that is offered on behalf of us argonauts and the whole argosy of mankind and indeed in some sense of all earthly creation, which, as Paul says, suffers a common travail. (*DG* 190)

The typological continuity of the poem's various voyages is emphasized by repeated allusions to *The Rime of the Ancient Mariner*. With reference to 'Keel, Ram, Stauros,' the poet acknowledged to Desmond Chute in 1953 that Coleridge's poem 'is behind a number of forms used in this section & elsewhere in *Ana*,' and he adds, '*The An. Mariner* is one of the clues to *Ana* (*IN* 62). The cosmic ship is identified with the Mariner's vessel by its bearing [of ancient egypt]

>   ... the thewed bodies
> the true-hearted men so beautiful
>   between perpendiculars
> and over-all. (175)

The position 'over-all' allegorizes the meta-physical value of those whom Coleridge calls 'the many men so beautiful' (line 236). Because the ship is a microcosm, the bride in Coleridge's poem ('red as a rose is she,' line 34) is also aboard, where the cross is venerated by girls 'red, and as / roses-on-a-stalk' (179).

Such allusions strengthen the mythic world-ship's assimilation of the other ships, whose voyages are realistic for the most part. The Phoenician-Phocaean ship arrives at Cornwall after 'a weary time a weary time' (98; cf *Rime*, line 145). The *Mary* endures meeting 'wraith-barques' and 'vengeance of white great birds' (142), and very like a wraith-barque herself she enters port with spars mended, main sail patched and, exclaims Elen,

>   her cordage!!
> how does it stand
>   to stay?
> how does it run
>   to brace or lift or hale?
> can the wraith of a laniard extend the ghost of a shroud? (138)

The *Mary* resembles the Mariner's vessel returning to port as Jones describes it in his essay on Coleridge's poem: 'Her shrunken timbers, her canvas, shrouds and all her cordage are a sad spectacle' (*DG* 194; cf *Rime*, lines 529–34).

What primarily identifies all the ships in Jones's poem with the ship of the Ancient Mariner is the affinity of the poem's sailors with the Mariner. The initial basis for affinity is age. The Phoenician (or Phocaean) captain is an 'old Pelasgian' (107), the Greek captain an 'old triton' (96), an 'ancient staggerer... eld, bright-eyed / *marinus*' (182) recalling Coleridge's 'bright-eyed mariner' (lines 20, 40). Captain Manawydan, in a Welsh-Norse retelling of the parable of the pearl, is very old and has a tale to tell. As old as any of these is the Milford boatswain aboard the *Mary*. He claimed 'he were with them in the ships' destined for Troy and that he had taken part in the voyages of Jonah and Noah (149–50). ''T were *too* much,' as Elen comments, 'Yet, you could not choose but hear' (154), her words recalling the wedding guest who 'cannot choose but hear' (line 18). Elen was not this Welsh mariner's spellbound listener – she has the story third-hand – but she has her own spellbinding eloquence, and in a sense reverses roles by delivering her relentless monologue to a sea captain she calls an 'ancient man' (166; cf *Rime*, line 39), who apparently cannot choose but hear. Like Dai Greatcoat and like their common archetype, the Wandering Jew, the Mariner-figure has a future to match his immeasurable past. Eb Bradshaw says 'he's got / till the Day o' Doom / to sail the bitter seas o' the world' (121). But the sailors who evoke him retain their realistic separate identities and so deprive him of full mythic force. At most he is a symbolic wraith, haunting the poem.

The Coleridgean typology is essentially pre-Christian but nevertheless harmonious with the Christian mythos. After all, Coleridge's poem is a parable of sin and expiation. Iconographically, the pierced albatross resembles Jesus – as David Jones emphasizes in his copper engraving in which the bird is pinned by the arrow to the cross-shaped mast. It must have been shot while perching 'for vespers nine' (line 75) – words Jones underlines and marks in the copy of Coleridge's poems he acquired, according to his inscription, in August 1952 and which he echoes, without any distortion of scriptural data, in the 'ninth hour out-cry' of Jesus, soon to be pierced with a spear (238; cf Mark 15:34). If the bird has perched for nine consecutive days at Vespers, moreover, it has striking affinity with the Christ-type Odin, 'nine nights on the windy tree' (225), an affinity which may derive initially from Coleridge's reading of Norse mythology. (By making this association *The Anathemata* suggests an original addition to Coleridge criticism.) As he makes expiation for his crime, the Mariner seems to take over the bird's Christ-signification. In any case, Jones writes that Coleridge's poem 'is evocative of the argosy of mankind and hence cannot avoid evoking the Redeemer, our Odysseus, who in Homer is, at his own command, made fast to the stepped mast' (*DG* 214). But the motif of the Ancient Mariner is essentially neutral, theologically. And in Jones's poem it loses its original strong moral emphasis to suggest, at most, the continuity of the human condition as fallen yet caught up in a destiny in which the fall is being overcome. The motif supplies an archetypal breadth which unifies the poem's voyages without reducing them to Christian allegory.

The symbolic meaning of pre-Christian voyages emerges with allegorical clarity only in Elen Monica's narration of the voyage of the *Mary*. The story of the *Mary* interprets the poem's other voyages partly because the course of the *Mary* recapitulates all their courses. Like the Greek ship, she sails from the eastern Mediterranean.[25] Like the Phoenician-Phocaean ship, she sails westward through 'the Pillars' (148; cf 97) and toward the land of 'those caliban Corn-Welsh' (148; cf 100). Like the ships in 'Angle-Land,' she sails up the English coast, and like the ships of the captains whom Eb Bradshaw and Elen Monica talk to, she enters the port of London.

Allegorically, the *Mary* is 'the pilgrim city' of God (*De civitate Dei* 1.35) – not the Church as recognizable social institution but the body of redeemed mankind whose members articulate in their lives, if not always in their conscious minds, an affirmative response to grace. Mary is the model of such affirmative articulation. As the witch Marged puts it:

> It all hangs on the fiat. If her fiat was the Great Fiat, nevertheless, seeing the solidarity, we participate in the fiat – or can indeed, by our fiats – it stands to reason. (214)

Throughout this poem, Mary represents mankind as subject, medium, and co-agent of redemption. Elen boasts on her behalf,

> She's as she of Aulis, master:
> not a puff of wind without her!
> her fiat is our fortune, sir: like Helen's face
> 'twas that as launched the ship. (128)

That is, her *fiat* launched it. As its material cause, she is the start of the voyage – like virgin Artemis at Aulis, against whose will the Greek fleet could not sail for Troy. As formal cause, she is also the finish of the voyage – like Helen for whom the Greeks sail, a type of the eschatological bride. In one of his copies of the poem, David Jones heavily marks the four lines above and gives them the abbreviated gloss '1st subj,' meaning that the significance of Mary as *fiat*-giver and type of bridal mankind is the chief concern of 'The Lady of the Pool' and therefore one of the major themes of the poem.

As we have begun to see in our consideration of Elen Monica, Jones redefines Mary within her liturgical tradition by shifting emphasis away from sexual purity towards magnanimity. In a note to the lines quoted above, he writes that in the gospel, 'Jesus leaves no doubt that the blessedness of his mother resides firstly in the compliancy of her will' (128 n5, see Luke 11:27–8). And in another note he interprets the title *Mater amabilis* from her litany as implying 'buxomness of spirit' (217 n4). In her responsive moral beauty, she conforms to the figure of Prudentia as the poet describes her, 'the tutelary genius who presides over the whole realm of faith, moral, religion, ethic; she is thought of as Holy Wisdom' (E&A 145). It is in her capacity as Prudentia personified that Mary is the new Athena, the Christian Aphrodite and, as such, the tutelar of the ship, which is the city of God, and the patroness and prototype of every soul in that sailing city.

Before launching into the allegorical dimension of the *Mary*'s voyage, we should remember that the voyage also has dramatic and mythic aspects and that the element of allegory exists primarily in the imagination of its medieval narrator. Although foreign to the realistic bias of modern sensibilities, the extended metaphor is therefore realistic in its context. It is historically feasible that a medieval woman – or one or both of the medieval sailors through whom the story comes to her – would interpret a real voyage as an allegory of the perils and ultimate triumph of the Church. And, of course, it is entirely probable that a late-medieval ship should be named for Mary, although in fact this ship may partly derive its name from the *Mary Rose*.[26]

The main theme of the allegory is the spiritual danger to mankind of imperialism, especially when in league with institutional religion. An example of such imperialism is a nominally Christian ship that attacks the *Mary* – 'the most Christian Doge's dago latins amiral'd of a vandal of a baptised Cypriot Jew from Damietta that was a camouflaged alcalif's marmeluke' (147). The Doge's vessel is sunk by a cannon-shot fired by the 'mum and praying clerk' who calls, 'To prayers, all is won, all is won. / To prayers.' The *Mary*'s gunner-sergeant echoes, 'To prayers all is won' (147), deleting the comma to underline the allegory.

The danger of empire is internalized and greatly increased, however,

247 Typology

when present in the form of temptation by one 'of y'r genuine rock-sirens' (142). The figure of the siren, deriving from the *Odyssey*, was used in patristic writing as a metaphor for lust, primarily, and for the lure of the devil and the secular world. True to classical and patristic form, the Siren that confronts the *Mary* is

> twice as natural as the Mother of All Living, foam-white as a Friday Venus, wetter nor Soo-zanna, clear gilt-tressed enough to hang a dozen Absolons. (142-3)

For sailors she is what bathing Susanna was to lecherous elders (Daniel 13), a tempting foam-born Venus. The mother of all living is Eve (Genesis 3:20), Adam's temptress and the liturgical antithesis of the *Mary*'s namesake.[27] The Siren makes 'music to the tune of Greensleeves' (143), whose lyrics concern a harlot. To the sailors she tosses flowers to the tune of 'Maiden in the mor lay,' which is about a water sprite who appears briefly in villages to fascinate and ultimately to frustrate those who fall for her. She also smells of Chloris transformed by sexual passion into the goddess Flora. We saw Elen Monica re-enacting this metamorphosis herself, but here it is the Siren, who like Chloris in Ovid (*Fasti* 5.1) and in Botticelli's *Primavera*, exhales 'distillations of the entire flora / and of WOMANKIND / to the man at the wheel' (144).

But the Siren's allure is only superficially sexual. What she really wants is to arouse lust for power. She asks to be serenaded in the heroic musical mode called 'Dorian' (146), which recalls the poem's earliest historical instance of imperialist conquest by 'Dorian jarls' (90). We saw in the previous chapter that she wants to be Britannia, the latter-day debasement of Athena Promachos. Earlier in time (but later in the poem) a siren is associated with Athenean capitalists 'on a proper siren's cruise' (172). In Elen's tale, the maritime imperialism of Athens is directly evoked by the Siren desiring to be acclaimed 'Jack Neptune's latest espoused Jill and Last Thalassocrat' (146) – an image which also evokes intercourse akin to that of Mars with Ilia, which results in empire. The Siren wants to personify the British empire, a term thought to have been coined, as Jones knows, by the Elizabethan court physician and astrologer, John Dee (to H 4 May 1974). Dee, says Elen, is

> A very John-on-Patmos for uncoverings and all rombuses, vaticinations an' anagrams; as see the apotheosis of imperium in a cloud of his own bottled smoke, under the form of a woman clothed with the sea, head-

armoured like a Troian-Greek and in her fist the tree of a fish-spear. (136)

In conjunction with 'apotheosis,' the word 'imperium' homophonically echoes 'empyrean,' suggesting the fundamental antithesis between worldly empire and heaven. An imitation Athena, here Britannia is partly demythologized, partly remythologized, for the famous spear is 'in her fist,' a word significantly harsh, and the shaft of the spear is a 'tree' to evoke Satan's spear in *Paradise Lost* (1.292), an image Jones refers to in his essay on Coleridge (DG 222). John Dee conjures 'a woman clothed with the sea' in contrast to St John's 'woman clothed with the sun' (Revelation 12:1) – a personification of the Church and a figure liturgically equated with Mary.[28]

Throughout her impersonation, Elen dramatizes the Siren's antithesis to Mary. The Virgin is synonymous with humility, is chaste, and delivers a responsive *fiat*. The Siren is pushy, proffers sexual intercourse, speaks pompously in the royal plural, primps, and preens. Enthroned, she would be the sort of 'pretty sitter' Mary opposes in 'Luke's lay,' where she praises God for putting 'down the mighty from their thrones' and exalting 'the lowly' (see 153).

But there is more here than mere opposition. 'Foam-white' (like Aphrodite) and 'gilt-tressed' (142), the Siren is a tower of ivory and house of gold like Athena Parthenos (94) and Mary in her litany. The Siren is a counterfeit. If Mary is the world-ship's Prudentia, the Siren who would replace her is the bogus Prudentia about whom the poet writes: 'those who reject the postulates of supernatural religion are no less bound than are the men of religion by the allurements of *a* Prudentia.' And he goes on to say that when the true Prudentia is abandoned, a false alternative is necessarily embraced:

> Her charms are substantial and unelusive. Her get-up is woven of the immediate and the contingent. She assures us that she is unconcerned with moral, yet there is about her a familiar tang, and no wonder, for she uses Black Market products, concocted of crude ethic and raw moral, certain important ingredients, suspending agents and solvents being omitted from the stolen prescriptions. She induces us to do this rather than that. She is full of does and don'ts. She is on intimate terms with a number of party-leaders. (E&A 146)

As a spurious Flora-Aphrodite-Athena-Maria singing traditional airs, the Siren is just such a motley of ingredients lacking integrity. She implies as much herself when she comments on the wind-blown tresses of her 'Maudlin gilt' hair, 'a tangled order / and ... how it do become us' (146). Not, of course, that she is a Magdalene either, for all her golden hair.

Like Athena but less happily, the Siren is 'enough and to snare: ... West-hearts' (94). Her unwisdom will characterize the polity of Europe from the Renaissance through modern times. In a sense, she is the answer to the question asked earlier about Sir Clowdisley Shovell: 'what Caliban's Lamia / rung him for his Hand of Glory?' (100). 'Caliban' is originally an anagram for 'canibal,' and, like Lamia, sirens eat human flesh. If this Siren consumes Sir Clowdisley, she does it primarily by having convinced England (and most of Europe) to build empires.

The Siren's pernicious charm is not, however, directed solely to the world of secular affairs. The institutional Church is also her target. This is suggested by the ring she wears: 'it were gave us long since by a' ancient fisher; 'tis indulgenced till there be no more sea' (145). It seems to be an ecclesiastical ring representing an office to which men are appointed by the papal successors of St Peter, 'the Fisher with the ring' (160). But the Siren's 'ancient fisher' is more probably the devil, the first fisher of men – though that hardly precludes her symbolically incorporating any number of bishops and cardinals, who wear ecclesiastical rings.

In fact, she has a marked affinity with Dostoevsky's Grand Inquisitor, a cardinal who reprimands Jesus, come again to earth in the fifteenth century, for having refused the devil's temptations, which, he says, the Church has since adopted as standard policy.[29] In his own monologue, the Inquisitor rephrases two of the devil's three temptations and puts them again to Jesus. The Siren implicitly addresses the same two temptations to the men of the *Mary*. The devil, says the Inquisitor, had offered world domination to Jesus if he would fall down and worship him. The Siren, sitting 'where keels tie, come from all quarters of a boisterous world' and showing her ring, says to sailors, 'Here is our regnant hand: ... kiss it. / No, no, ... you shall kneel' (145). And the aegis she would like to have is a symbol of divinity. The devil, recalls the Inquisitor, had challenged Jesus to change stones into bread. The Siren asks for a halliard-hemp necklace

                        for 'tis to garnish paps
that nourish such as must strike soundings in the gannet's bath.
                                If we furnish to the part
maybe we'll play it – as Saint Aristotle would 'a' said.   (146)

We have already seen the relationship of breasts to eucharistic bread. She offers to nurse and mother men who sail 'the gannet's bath' – an Anglo-Saxon kenning for the desolate sea. To such men, a rock-siren's teat might appeal as the devil thought bread out of stones would to Jesus half-starved in the desert. Such an offer by the Siren is also sexual, of course, and represents an Oedipal conflation of the sort we have seen before.

To the extent that she is an Inquisitor-figure, the Siren symbolizes the institutional Church won over to the world. This moral perversion is underlined by her exclamation 'sweet Loy!' (146), which associates her with Chaucer's Prioress, whose 'grettest ooth was but by seinte Loy,' the patron saint of goldsmiths. In every respect, Chaucer implies, the Prioress conforms to the values of the secular world while retaining the outward forms of institutional religious life.

An important function of the Siren in the poem is to imply a distinction between two superficially similar but fundamentally antithetical kinds of anathemata: sacramental religion and magic. While sacraments are gratuitous, magic is pragmatic. It is the original technology for procuring and exercising power. Tossing flowers concocted of 'transaccidentated spindrift' (143), the Siren is a magician like John Dee, whose dream-child she is, under the guise of Britannia. 'Transaccidentation,' a spurious approximation of transubstantiation, suggests the difference between magic and sacrament. The poet's own consciousness of the distinction was probably focused by his reading of Thomas Gilby's 'The Genesis of Guilt,' in which he brackets the following sentences: 'The theory of the sacraments is diametrically opposite to the theory of magic. There is no question of capturing the god and forcing him to serve our purpose.' Jones also marks a passage that illuminates the psychological appeal of what the Siren and Dostoevsky's Inquisitor offer men:

> The temptation is to hug the formula by which safety may be bought, to tinker with magic instead of waiting ready for the gift, and we fall for it whenever conventional security replaces the generosity of love and a label is preferred to life. This danger is particularly evident in all official faiths, from Catholicism to Marxism.[30]

The temptress can infiltrate the forms and counterfeit the values she seeks to undermine. In a note added in 1959 to an essay originally published in 1941, the poet writes about the products of modern technology:

251 Typology

> The *numina* which preside over these forms are masters of illusion – this is a magician's world – the living God, the life-giver is not, after all, projected from the machine. (E&A 104 n2)

The Siren is one of these *numina*.

The Siren's foil in the poem is the witch Marged, in 'Mabinog's Liturgy.' Marged and the Siren are contemporaries in the process of the poem's composition: according to a manuscript note, the Siren-episode was written in 1949; Marged too arrived in the poem at about that time, in the fifth-draft foliation. Both women practise 'transaccidentation' (207). Both mistakenly literalize the philosophical concept of formal causality: we heard the Siren say, 'If we furnish to the part / maybe we'll play it' (146); Marged says apropos of her Graymalkin (an 'ape'), 'if he but take the posture / the old grey ass may bray a *Gloria*' (215). The Siren and Marged each speak in an occult code which obscures what it communicates. But the witch chooses to sail, as it were, aboard the *Mary*, while the Siren tries to sink it.

For the men of the *Mary* the brush with the Siren is 'the crux of the voyage / and a near thing' (143). By resisting her temptation they imitate Odysseus as Christ-figure, but also Jesus in the desert. And there are other respects in which they parallel the life of Jesus. When the ship is 'Veronica'd of marrying falls of foam' in a tempest, it re-enacts Christ's Passion in a perilous metaphorical eucharist:

> white as the Housel of spume.
>   The tilted heavers
> her oblation-stone
> imménser hovers dark-ápse her. (140)

She herself is the housel or bread, whitened by spume. Her altar is the churning waves. Her church, the lowering clouds. The latter are 'immenser,' punning on solecistic Latin for 'non-altar.' Beneath them the watery altar is conventional only in its containing relics of the dead:

> unfathomed under her
>   in the under-stills
> the washed-white margaron'd relics lie, where the pearl is,
> as was the weather-eye of Ben Backstay ... (140–1)

'The late Ben Backstay,' that is (155), one of 'the dead of the wake' who are, in an obvious allusion to *The Tempest* (1.2.399), pearl-precious to Christ.

During the storm, the sea extends the church-symbolism of the ship. The *Mary* is pregnant with living members of Christ's mystical body. This is suggested by her being 'overdue a nine month' (137), which doubles the term of pregnancy and implies the imminence of rebirth. As Christ's mother 'ark'd him' (225), her ship now arks his followers – like the Ark of the Covenant and like Noah's Ark, a traditional symbol of the Church.[31] Analogously, the sea is pregnant with the dead (cf Revelation 20:13). The correspondence this implies between Mary, the *Mary*, and the sea is echoed in the poem's verbal chiming of 'Mary,' MAIR, and *mare*. As we have seen, the correspondence is further extended to the earth as a grave personified by a goddess.

During the storm, the fire of Castor and Pollux appears on the ship, indicating 'that she *cannot* be lost' (142). The corposant 'exhalations' shine 'FIVE on 'em,' recalling Christ's wounds (141). Because they shine at the ends of the main yard, the bowsprit, the mizzen-mast, and the rear mizzen-yard and therefore form the sign of the cross on the ship seen from above, they recall the five wound-signifying incense grains in the shape of the cross on the paschal candle. Lit to symbolize the risen Christ, 'the fair-garnished percher,' as Elen calls it (161), is the Easter symbol of victory over death and is used to bless baptismal water. The Christian symbolism here interprets an earlier reference to Castor and Pollux as washing their 'celestial arms ... fouled in terrestrial war' (86). In a stanza from which Jones quotes (142 n1), Macaulay links this washing with their ability to save ships:

> Safe comes the ship to haven,
> Through billows and through gales,
> If once the Great Twin Brethren
> Sit shining on the sails.
> Wherefore they washed their horses
> In Vesta's holy well,
> Wherefore they rode to Vesta's door,
> I know, but may not tell.[32]

The importance of Vesta at childbirth and the procreative significance of her ritual fire suggest that washing in her spring restores the Dioscori, or god-men, in an act analogous to Christ's 'rebirth.' The analogy is strengthened by the washing being 'a thing seen of many' (86) words

253 Typology

echoing Paul's reference to those who saw the risen Christ (1 Corinthians 15:6–8). The appearance on the *Mary* of the fire of the Twins is, then, a pagan symbol of the post-resurrection divine life that men share through baptismal incorporation into the body of Christ. This sharing lies behind the *theosis* or divinization of the mother of Jesus, which the clerk whom Elen loved is imagined arguing for. Elen explains, 'He were a one for what's due her, captain. / Being ever a one for what's due *us*, captain' (129) – a reference to the statement of Athanasius about men becoming gods.

The *Mary*'s final entry into the pool of London, which is the first part of her voyage described, multiplies allegorical signs. The ship is 'hulled, SEVEN TIMES' (139) for the Sorrows of Mary in Catholic liturgical tradition. Water comes 'from the *right* side, about midships' to represent the spear-wound in Jesus's side and the water from the temple in the *Vidi aquam*. (In one of his own copies, Jones inscribes in the margin here the words *a latere dextro* from the hymn.) The image further recalls the Greek captain's libation, but what was then a chalice is now the ship. Behind the symbolic transference is a basic formal analogy, for the poet once said, 'I'm very interested in the bowl-like character of ships.'[33] So this is a continuation of the ship's metaphorical eucharist. The date of her arrival is the feast of the Annunciation, which celebrates Mary's *fiat mihi*. By virtue of an interweaving of phrases from the gospel accounts – 'Making it: / one morning, very early, on the second day of the week at the rising, the dawn began but whiles it were yet but darkish …' (137) – it is also symbolically the morning of Christ's resurrection.[34]

The allegorical combinations here have symbolic import. The arrival of the ship coincides both with the beginning of the redemption at the annunciation and with its conclusion in the resurrection. Symbolically this is correlative to the ship's eucharist. And the symbolic collapsing of time by the conflation of his conception and his rising recalls the symbolic simultaneity of the poem's structure. Here as there it suggests the abolition of time in eternity – an event apocalyptic or revelatory but preceding the end of time. Blake calls such moments 'Last Judgments.' Eliot says of them, 'To be conscious is not to be in time.' For David Jones or for Elen Monica the ship's wounds imply that at such moments Jesus and Mary (God-man and man) attain anagogical singleness of identity.

Jones writes that he especially likes 'the ship passages' in the poem: 'all the ship bits are the best bits – the "poetry" seems to get going most in those' (to G 18 February 1960). Certainly the transformation of the voyaging motif into a variegated eschatological symbol is an impressive achievement. It helps unify the poem and channels its movement in a rich continuity of imagery which modulates in fictional modality between drama, narrative, extended metaphor, and symbolism, and through psychological modality from realism to myth.

The significance of the motif extends even to the shape of the poem, which incorporates, as it were, the structures of the *Odyssey* and *The Rime of the Ancient Mariner*. The similarity between the central monologue of Elen and that of Odysseus is part of a larger resemblance between the structure of Jones's poem and what classical scholars call the 'ring composition' of the *Odyssey* – by which the story of Telemachus frames the story of Odysseus's journey home, which, in turn, frames the long central narrative monologue of Odysseus. A simpler but similar shape – with narrative frame and central monologue – informs Coleridge's poem. These works may have influenced Jones's composition, though perhaps not consciously. Certainly he had read them repeatedly, so that he possessed them at a level deeper than consciousness. The structure of *The Anathemata* cannot, of course, be 'accounted for' by possibilities of influence. It is far more complex than Homeric structure and symbolically much more powerful. But part of the significance of the shape of Jones's poem is that it achieves a contextual, structural affinity between the voyages of Odysseus and the Ancient Mariner and the voyage of the Logos-Redeemer, which symbolically subsumes all previous and subsequent voyages.

Because typology provides continuity in the voyages of the poem and unity of reference for its human figures, it focuses the work's internal allusive and symbolic reverberations. Typologically mankind, the ship, the city (Troy, Rome, London), the Church, Athena, Aphrodite, Helen, Flora Dea, Mary, Elen Monica, Gwenhwyfar, Marged, and the Siren are all versions of, and variations on, one another. So are the male heroes who have God for their primary archetype. And language sounds these reverberations in ways we have only begun to see. The result is a multiple, internal anamnesis by which, it might almost be said, the whole of the poem is present in all of its parts. It could be demonstrated that the final section, 'Sherthursdaye and Venus Day,' evokes most of the motifs of the preceding sections. And we have seen the elaborate echoing of the first section, 'Rite and Fore-Time,' in the figure of Gwenhwyfar. Like the Supper room, then, the poem is 'gaudeous' (53), a word which puns on 'gorgeous' and denotes a gaudy or feast for 'old boys' returning to college. The expansive inclusiveness of the poem is achieved by its vast vocabulary and the richness of its connotations, by its metaphysical juxtapositions, in which the differences expand the significance of the points of similarity, and by the vast breadth of its analogical reach. Conceptually, all prior and subsequent rites, all acts of artefacture, and all mythic archetypes are 'old boys' attending the 'gaudeous' institution of the Eucharist. It is the same for every Mass, including that which the primary meditator attends. Because at the Last Supper, on the cross, and in the Mass Jesus makes history of myth, he renews all this amassed tradition so that the cumulative maypole of human culture is no longer the barren 'mortised stake' of merely remembered or imagined form (190). Spiritually and therefore ontologically, it blooms. If this is always true within the Mass and especially at the moment of sacramental transformation, which is the poem's fictional context, it is also potentially true for the reader, for groups of people, and for our civilization. That is why the primary meditator concludes his final reference to Jesus by paraphrasing the questions of the Grail myth:

> What did he do other
> > recumbent at the garnished supper?
> What did he do yet other
> > riding the Axile Tree?   (243)

Since to ask the questions is to renew the land, the meditator's instantaneous daydream is a miniature, personal (but not merely subjective) revitalization of the cultural waste land.

And so, aesthetically, is the poem that communicates his daydream. This is a work of art of immense breadth and depth of resonance and great richness of fictional and psychological modality. Its combination of structural and organic forms with interpretive ordering of content is original and symbolically powerful. Consequently, this poem really does approximate the theological hypothesis by which all times and places, all things and all dimensions of being are sacramentally present because God, who is present to them all, is made present in the sacrament. For readers capable of appreciating *The Anathemata* – and these include those who do not share the religious belief that inspires it – the poem is a sacrament of vital culture, containing what it signifies.

In every respect *The Anathemata* is less accessible than *In Parenthesis*, but it is not inferior to it, only different in kind. Because mythos is displaced in *The Anathemata*, it has less immediate dramatic appeal.

We care more easily for a half-dozen infantrymen than for something as large and abstract as western culture, although human figures and monologuists do give *The Anathemata* personal warmth and a dramatic dimension. The allusions in *The Anathemata*, which are dense and not subordinate to narrative, serve as an alienation technique to prolong the act of reading and to postpone response. But what they delay they also bring to pass, and the effect is worth waiting (and working) for. It is less a mixture of fear and desire, as with *In Parenthesis*; more an extended revelation through symbolic interrelationships, and a meditation on culture which goes beyond aesthetic response to illuminate the historic context of the reader.

The Anathemata is a great work. In originality, unity, and scope it belongs to a range of achievement that includes the *Aeneid, The Divine Comedy, Paradise Lost,* and, if we may mix genres, *Ulysses.* Because Jones's poem has never been subjected to close analysis, we have read it, as it were, from the inside. In the brief conclusion to this book, we will view the poem from a broader perspective.

The Sleeping Lord

7

Sequence

THE SLEEPING LORD is not the 'continuation, or Part II of *The Anathemata*' that David Jones, in 1952, anticipated publishing (*A* 15 n1). That work would have been another long poem, divided, like its predecessor, into sections. When Vernon Watkins asked him in 1955 to contribute a poem to the Dylan Thomas memorial issue of *Poetry* (Chicago), Jones at first declined: 'I never write separate poems ... I mean it's awfully hard to take a bit out of the kind of stuff I write & publish it as a separate piece' (*LVW* 22). He eventually did send something which, he said, had been 'part of a "work in progress" in c. 1944' and had subsequently 'belonged to *The Anathemata* in one of its various stages' (*LVW* 24).[1] The piece he chose is 'The Wall,' which was to be the opening section of the proposed continuation of *The Anathemata*.[2] 'The Wall' was published in *Poetry* 87 (November 1955) and in 1956 won that publication's Harriet Monroe Prize. This success encouraged him to continue mining his manuscript material for bits that already had or could be given integrity of form. He revised them, sometimes substantially rewrote them, or, in the cases of 'The Tutelar of the Place' and the 'Sleeping Lord' fragment, wrote new poems that incorporated pieces of the old manuscript. Between 1958 and 1973 he published eight of these 'fragments.' Seven of them – all but 'The Narrows' – are collected together with 'The Wall' in *The Sleeping Lord*. After being extracted and reworked for separate publication, these poems had become – in various, often quite complicated ways – structurally complete and consequently independent of one another. In this respect they differ from most of the numbered sections of *The Anathemata*. By the middle sixties, therefore, Jones's 'work in progress' had become a poetic sequence rather than a single long poem.

Sequence

In 1971 David Jones intended to include in his new book 'a part of a dialogue between Judas & Caiaphas & a monologue by Judas arguing with himself & also a complicated longish passage about Romans in Wales, but all requiring recasting' (to G 9 October 1971). None of these is included in the finished collection. The monologue of Judas (RQ 132–9) and the dialogue of Judas and Caiaphas – actually their adjoining monologues (RQ 140–51) – are certainly publishable. The monologue of Caiaphas, with his clerical cosmopolitanism and prophetic vision, approaches in quality the best of the work Jones published in his lifetime. It is a monologue reminiscent of 'Bishop Bloughram's Apology' and resembles 'The Tribune's Visitation' in the ambiguity of the motivation of its persona. Jones may have excluded the Judas-Caiaphas material partly because it conflicts dramatically with the Roman poems. These latter are also set in Jerusalem and (all but one) at the time of the Passion, but their narrative personae are not consciously involved in the events of the Passion as Judas and Caiaphas are. The passage about Romans in Wales (RQ 64–83) is excluded at least partly because in manuscript it remains shapeless and, in its premonitions of Arthur, forced and merely rhetorical.

The exclusion of the passage about Romans in Wales has important consequences for the form of the book. The Roman poems are 'interrelated fragments' (SL 24), largely because of a common setting, tone, and type of persona. These poems clearly form a sequence. And the subsequent pair of Arthurian poems form a minisequence. The material about Romans in Wales would have bridged between these groups of poems, making of the whole a single, chronologically linked sequence – one to which the 'Balaam's Ass' fragment probably would not have been added. 'Balaam's Ass' and 'A, a, a, Domine Deus' originate in an earlier manuscript than that from which the other poems derive. In the absence of the bridging material, the relationship between the Roman and Arthurian poems is only suggested in the Roman poems, though strongly suggested, by the presence of Celtic recruits in the Roman army and by references to Britain. This is achieved most forcefully in 'The Dream of Private Clitus,' in which Celtic material is a late insertion precisely for the purpose of suggesting the relationship between the two groups of poems. In a retroactive attempt further to suggest this relationship, a short passage about the British military service of a Roman soldier, which originates in the excluded material about Romans in Wales, is inserted into the 'Balaam's Ass' fragment (98–9), as is a reference to 'Celestial Arcturus' (98), made apparently when Jones was correcting proofs. In its final form the book is still informed by chronological sequence, though historically ordered periods are now discontinuous and juxtaposed. This discontinuity allows for the addition of the 'Balaam's Ass' fragment, which extends into modern times the temporal momentum generated by the preceding groups of poems.

The discontinuity also emphasizes that the book is dialectical as well as chronological in arrangement. The dialectic begins as dialogue, of which the basis is Spengler's morphology of culture-phases. The Roman poems are set in the late-imperial phase, what Spengler calls the autumn of a culture. They contrast with 'The Hunt,' which concerns a cultural springtime. 'The Tutelar of the Place,' the Roman poem preceding 'The Hunt,' concerns the collision of Celtic culture with imperial Roman civilization, a collision of spring and fall without intervening summer. In this poem, at the heart of the book, the opposing culture-phases are not separated by time, so that what would otherwise remain mere contrast becomes dramatized conflict. In this conflict, synthesis seems no more possible than it was in the English imperialist war with Zulu tribesmen or in Italy's invasion of Ethiopia, both of which Jones saw as analogous to the opposition of culture-phases in 'The Tutelar of the Place.' And as the second Arthurian poem, the 'Sleeping Lord' fragment, subsequently implies, the turning of the Spenglerian culture-cycle is no substitute for synthesis. The poem evokes fifteen centuries of Celtic cultural decline to be a metaphor for and eventually to symbolize the modern decline of the West. This modern decline rhymes with that which underlies the Roman poems, and has its grim epiphany in the mechanized warfare of the 'Balaam's Ass' fragment.

If 'The Hunt' were the only poem to represent a positive phase, the collection's cultural dialogue (between hope and despair) would be one-sided, but, like 'The Tutelar of the Place,' most of the Roman poems are themselves dialogical. In the imaginations of their narrative personae, present cultural poverty is juxtaposed with past cultural vitality and sometimes, by implication, with future cultural vitality. In most cases, furthermore, the persona's sympathies are with the alternative, spiritually vital culture-phase. So the debate that arises from this colloquium of monologuists is fairly even. It reaches its greatest intensity in the implied argument between the persona of 'The Tribune's Visitation' and that of 'The Tutelar of the Place.' Together these poems form the centre – a divided, antithetical centre – of the book's eight major fragments.

On the level of historical phases in conflict and on the level of the interpersonal debate, there is no agreement. But on an intrapersonal

261 Sequence

level, the book does finally achieve a reconciliation of physical and cultural catastrophe with spiritual affirmation. This paradoxical agreement is made possible by variations between realistic, mythic, and anatomical fictional modalities.

The poems are written in mimetic modes appropriate to their place in the book's dialogical arrangement. Individual poems themselves involve shifting modes, but the Roman poems are basically realistic and rhetorical, though containing within them symbols as the seeds of myth. And the two Arthurian poems are primarily symbolic and mythic in mode, though evocative of real, historical contexts which generate and sustain the Arthurian myth. Thus far, the shifting of modes emphasizes antithesis. In the first half of 'Balaam's Ass,' the primary mode is again rhetorical and historical, with symbolism relegated to a secondary level, but this relationship reverses itself halfway through the poem. Its modal structure consequently repeats and summarizes that of the entire book. But the genre of this last poem is the modally near-neutral form of anatomy, which allows an easy merging of history and myth (or realism and symbolism) and therefore makes possible a synthesis of modalities. It is this final synthesis that transforms the dialogical structure of *The Sleeping Lord* into a dialectical one.

On various levels, then, the poems in this book are arranged in a significant progression. The full title, *The Sleeping Lord and Other Fragments*, lays no claim to the loose unity of a sequence and, in his correspondence, David Jones refers to the book as a 'collection.' But it is not simply a collection like Browning's *Men and Women*, for example; at the very least, *The Sleeping Lord* is nearer to being a sequence than a collection. This will become more evident as we begin to notice motifs that recur and sometimes undergo metamorphosis as the poems or groups of poems progress through chronological time and shifting mimetic modes. Nevertheless, the book is unified primarily in its parts, not as a whole, and with a view to shape we must consider it poem by poem.

'A, A, A, DOMINE DEUS'

'A, a, a, Domine Deus' is the book's extended epigraph.[3] It conditions all that follows by defining the cultural poverty of the historical present. Its voice is that of the poet, whose formal complaint expresses personal frustration with material that cannot, without disconcerting ambiguity, be made to symbolize the God of Christian belief. Unlike most poets since the romantics, David Jones searches for God not in nature but in the products that typify his age:

> I have looked for a long while
>   at the textures and contours.
> I have run a hand over the trivial intersections.
> I have journeyed among the dead forms
> causation projects from pillar to pylon.
> I have tired the eyes of the mind
>   regarding the colours and lights.
> I have felt for His Wounds
>   in nozzles and containers.
> I have wondered for the automatic devices.
> I have tested the inane patterns
>   without prejudice. (9)

The poet may notice in 'trivial intersections' a shape like the cross. Openings certainly remind him of Christ's wounds. But formal analogy is not enough to constitute a symbol. When products are exclusively utile or made solely to turn a profit they refuse to be positive signs; instead, they are negative anathemata signifying only the absence of vital culture. 'I have watched the wheels go round,' the poet writes, 'in case I might see the living creatures like the appearance of lamps.' He alludes to Ezekiel seeing 'in the middle of a wheel ... the living creatures' who have come to be identified with the four evangelists and who appeared 'like the appearance of lamps' (1:13, 16).[4] In his search, the poet has 'tired the eyes of the mind' – a reference to the Preface for Christmas and Corpus Christi, which maintains that 'by the mystery of the Word made flesh' God's glory shines 'upon the eyes of the mind.' But where there is no aesthetic life, there can be no revelation of 'the Living God'; where there is no reflection of personality, there can be no symbol of a personal God; and where there is no expression of a complete humanity, there can be no symbol of the incarnate God.

    The products of a late, technological civilization are 'dead forms.' Steel cannot respond to the plea 'be my sister' as had natural things, including 'Sister Bodily Death' for Francis of Assisi in an earlier culture-phase. These products likewise resist the sort of imaginative integration achieved by the sixth-century Welsh bard Taliesin, who claims to have been freed from speechlessness by a hag who boasted of fleeing pursuit through a long series of transformations:

263 Sequence

> I have fled with vigour, I have fled as a frog,
> I have fled in the semblance of a crow, scarcely finding rest;
> I have fled vehemently, I have fled as a chain,
> I have fled as a roe into an entangled thicket;
> I have fled as a wolf-cub ...[5]

David Jones syntactically evokes Taliesin by beginning ten of the sentences in his short poem with the words 'I have,' and he seeks a symbolic equivalence to Taliesin's literal mediation and preservation of humanity. Frustrated, he echoes the cry of Jeremiah (1:6) in the title and first line of the poem. Jeremiah is convinced he cannot prophesy, but goes on to foretell disaster and, beyond that, a new covenant. For David Jones too, the cry which is also a prayer is a beginning. If he cannot project the fullness of his humanity and discover the object of his spiritual desire in the products of his age, he can at least imitate Taliesin's hag by 'becoming' the narrative personae of the following monologues, who suffer a similar alienation in an age paralleling our own. The Roman poems that follow are, however, an approach to, not an escape from, the modern cultural and spiritual impoverishment that torments the poet.

In this short poem, David Jones invokes oracles who imply the triple heritage or 'trivial intersection' of western culture as he perceives it. We saw that one oracle is the Welsh bard and two others are Hebrew prophets. A fourth seems to be invoked when the poet writes, 'I have journeyed among dead forms.' In *The Waste Land*, the Greek prophet Tiresias says, 'I have walked among the lowest of the dead' (line 246). This evocation suggests, furthermore, that the setting of this poem is symbolically equivalent to the classical Hades, which T.E. Hulme describes aptly, because negatively, as 'a place of no happiness.'

'THE WALL'

The first of the Roman poems is a five-page interior monologue by a soldier on guard duty somewhere on the periphery of the empire during the middle night watch. His attention shifts from perturbation over the politics he helps enforce to an imagined triumphal march winding through the city of Rome. The parade's main attraction is a captured Celtic chieftain. The soldier then wonders whether the imperial present is the fulfillment of the Roman past, which Virgil has interpreted as teleological. He recalls the events that led to Rome's prehistoric foundation as a sacred city, and contrasts that city with the current 'megalopolis that wills death' (13). He remarks that while soldiers once marched for Rome and the war god Mars, they now, apparently, enforce a peace which is necessary for healthy commerce – so that, ostensibly,

> now all can face the dying god
> the dying Gaul
> without regret. (14)

But he cannot reconcile himself to this armed peace.

Dislocation is the theme of 'The Wall' and the principle that governs its form. Jones calls the poem 'a soliloquy or interrogation addressed' by a Roman soldier 'to himself as far as he represents the Roman thing' (LF 36).[6] The soldier engaged in this interior monologue is morally and spiritually alienated from imperial Rome, and because he is at once an agent and a victim of empire, he is alienated from himself. His psychological and moral dislocation results from awareness of contrast between the partly mythologized past and the political present – a contrast which begins in ambivalent topological imagery as he recreates the triumph and which has its ultimate expression in the structure of the poem. It is a contrast sustained by sexual imagery and by the poem's primary motif, the troia or maze-dance, to which all its other images are related, often in contradictory ways.

Sequentially the poem has four movements. The anonymous soldier-persona considers his job of patrolling the walls of the empire, he imagines the triumph, he recalls the prehistoric past of Rome, and he returns his attention to the imperial present. These movements disclose an abstract, quasi-geometrical structure, which is the basic primitive form of a labyrinth, a maze within a circle. The circle is the departure from and return to meditative setting. Narrative tone adapts itself to this circular movement as the personal pronoun used by the soldier shifts from 'we' at the start to the more intimate 'you' of self-address and back again to the first person plural of public discourse.

Time and space are synchronized on the circumference of meditative setting. Within the circle, time and space are separated so that the maze within the circle is really two mazes – one in space, the other in time – but they are identical in pattern. The spatial maze of the Roman triumph exactly traces the winding route of the triumph during the Augustan period. The temporal maze, the rhetorical question about the meaning of the past for the present, is imagined as being asked during the triumph but picks up where the account of the triumph leaves off.

This question is a maze because, in tracing the genesis of Rome, it fractures chronology. Like the Book of Genesis, which is itself labyrinthine in its interweaving of the various literary and theological traditions of Israel, the narrator's account of Rome's foundation mixes myth and legend with archaeological fact. The account begins with two mythic-legendary loops or zigzags as time moves from Aeneas's 'hard journeyings' (11) to the mating of Mars with Ilia and her conception of the Twins, then back to Aeneas's 'troia'd wandering,' forward again to the wolf nursing the Twins, and then back furthest of all to Troy's fall when the star fell from the Pleiades. The account then becomes archaeological and historical in what amounts to a single large loop starting at the survey of the city's site and the ritual plowing of its perimeter, then moving back to the second-millennium Terramare culture, then far forward to the seventh century BC in the alliance of hill-site tribes and forward again to the sixth-century wall of Tullus.

Dramatically and psychologically the fragmentation of time by memory is entirely realistic. But here the resulting shape also closely approximates the route of the triumph as the narrator describes it, with its two initial curves or zigzags and its final large loop round the Palatine. This pattern may be seen by tracing the route of march on any sufficiently detailed map of ancient Rome. Structurally, then, the temporal maze duplicates the spatial maze. The duplication emphasizes the separation of space and time and also the contrast between the present (in space) and the past. As we shall see, however, the single pattern of these separate mazes implies a paradoxical correspondence that transcends contrast.

The dislocation of time from space, and of the past from the present, begins during the narrator's imagining the triumph when two brief parenthetical questions intrude into his consciousness. Each question, simultaneously evokes the past and the present so that a double exposure implying a moral contradiction results. Each question has for its focus the Capitoline Hill, which is the conclusion of the route of march. In a sense, the triumph is Rome returning to its centre and source, but what returns is the opposite of what it was in the beginning.

The first of these questions interrupts the narrative as the triumph is imagined moving 'by where Aventine flanks The Circus / (from Arx the birds deploy?)' (11). 'The birds' are the eagles on the standards of the legions now marching in column, but they are also the vultures that long ago augured well for city-founding Romulus (Livy *Ab urbe condita* 1.6.4). A contrast is implied by the difference in species of birds. Plutarch explains that for Romans vultures 'are the least harmful of all creatures' since they do not kill, in contrast to eagles, which slay even 'their own kind' (*Romulus* 9.6). In proximity to the Arx, the implied contrast recalls that the centre and source of oppression and homicide was once the saving Citadel, providing protection for Romans and all others who sought it.

The second ambiguous question interrupts the narrative as the triumph heads towards the bronze wolf that 'brights Capitoline for ever.' (It is still there, in the Capitoline Museum.) The wolf is the legionary's 'totem mother,' but does her ghost 'erect her throat to welcome the lupine gens' (11)? The posture of the neck, as portrayed by the statue, is essentially and unambiguously defensive because she guards the nursing Twins.[7] Not without profound incongruity, therefore, can she be welcoming legions home from imperialist aggression.

The incongruities of these brief parenthetical questions initiate and are carried over into the long rhetorical question about whether Rome's past was meant to culminate in the sprawling empire 'that wills death.' This elaborate question climaxes in an extended image of the ancient pre-imperial city, which sacramentally makes present 'the *civitas* of God' (13). Though it belongs to the past and was Rome, in an important sense the sacred city exists outside time and space. In contrast to the present 'world city' (14), its small circumference paradoxically contained 'a world' (12) and more. About the sacred cosmic city, the narrator asks:

> did they project the rectilineal plane upwards
> to the floor of heaven
> had all
>   within that reaching prism
>   one patria:
> rooted clod or drifted star
> dog or dryad or
> man born of woman
>
> did the sacred equation square the mundane site ...? (12–13)

In this place, earth and sky, animals and plants joined man in an anthropomorphic community in which everything was valued apart from its usefulness and nothing existed solely to be exploited. Founded according to astrological observations, furthermore, the city symbolically united earth and heaven. It was the earth in microcosm as the image of heaven – 'mundane' because worldly but also because it was heavenly since its centre was the *mundus*, a word which means 'the earth and the heavens.'[8] For David Jones and the reader, though not for the poem's persona, the *mundus* is further significant as a place of sacrifice centred at 'the median intersection' (12) of a city-wide cross – where the survey's *decumanus* and *kardo* cross (see A 87), which is where the *via praetoria* and the '*via quintana*' (10) subsequently intersect.

Although the image of the sacred city does not occupy the middle of the text, as the furthest point of the narrator's imaginative temporal maze-journey it is the centre of a labyrinth and therefore corresponds to the *mundus* at the centre of the maze that is the city of Rome. As the centre once sanctified the city, the vision of the ancient city now graces the narrator's imagination, but a shrinkage and reversal have occurred. What once sustained man is now sustained by him and only inwardly as a mixture of memory and desire – not now a hope even, but only a measure of disaccommodation and suffering. This is partly the significance of the *mundus* being the centre of a topological cross. Moreover, the imagining of the triumph concludes with the captive Celtic chief being led at the end of the parade, so that he, as a victim of imperialism, is the centre of the spatial maze – a suffering figure consonant with the topological cross and apparently, initially at least, cancelling the benign city at the centre of the temporal maze.

The temporal image of the maze within a circle suggests, furthermore, antithetical valuations of experience. Though time past is fragmented to form a maze, it is conceptually linear and implies purpose and direction. The implication of value in linear time is strengthened by obvious parallels with salvation history, such as between the wandering of Aeneas and the wandering of the Israelites in the Book of Exodus. This is teleological time as it informs both the Bible and the *Aeneid*. But the present denies the promise of the past because, for the foot soldier, contemporary time is circular and therefore meaningless. This is emphasized by the narrator's continuous walking 'round and round and back & fro' (10), which recalls the meaningless circular walk at the centre of *In Parenthesis* but is far worse. For twenty years of military service, his endlessly repetitive 'walk of life' resembles the punishment of Sisyphus and the endless circling of the damned in the first circle of the *Inferno*. When the narrator thinks of going 'round and round the cornucopia' (14), moreover, he verbally situates himself in Acheron, the vestibule of Hades in Eliot's 'The Hollow Men,' a poem I once heard Jones recite from memory. Structurally, 'The Wall' sustains these associations with Hades because a maze within a circle can be one of only two kinds of labyrinth – a prison, like the Cretan labyrinth, or a tomb.[9] Here it seems both.

By analogy the narrated past, which contrasts with the narrative present, also contrasts with the reader's present, particularly in the capitalistic West. 'The Boarium' through which the triumph passes (11) is the stock market – it was once literally that – which Jones calls 'the Roman equivalent to Wall St. or Throgmorton St' (*LF* 35). But the main emphasis is on the state capitalism of Italy and Germany in the first half of the century. The 'flat palm' on legionary standards recalls the fascist salute; the standards themselves, complete with eagles, recall the fascist standards copied from them; the triumph recalls the fascist parades and Nürnberg rallies; and the marchers' 'extra fancy step' (10) recalls the Italian 'Roman step' and its German counterpart, the goose step. There is a dark continuity too with the past, for in the sixth century BC 'the hostile strong-points' on the Roman hills are 'one by one, made co-ordinate' (12), a word that evokes *Gleichschaltung*, the Nazi term for the ordering of all aspects of life by party policy. Then the conquering Etruscans were the co-ordinators and the Romans their victims; now the Romans do the co-ordinating.

The image of 'walls that contain the world' (10) may recall 'the iron curtain' of Soviet imperialism. The soldier does refer to a fellow soldier as 'comrade' (14), although this was a military term before it became a political one. For the most part, however, David Jones saves communism for 'The Narrows,' a less interesting poem but thematically a companion piece to 'The Wall.' There a Roman soldier complains to 'comrade Porrex' about the endless enlistment of men for which 'the Dialectic' and the rest of 'the Party Line' are merely camouflage (*RQ* 59, 63).

The tutelar deity of 'The Wall' and the real force behind the archetypally feminine *Pax Romana* – which Irene, the goddess of peace, supposedly represents – is 'Plutus, the gold-getter' (14). The god of commerce identifies Roman ideology as 'plutocratic imperialism,' which according to Christopher Dawson also typifies the modern West. Plutus is another of the poem's double images, since he was regularly confused with Pluto. As a consequence, he indicates the socio-economic character of the Hades the soldier-persona inhabits.

Thematically related to the tension in 'The Wall' between past and present is a conflict between masculinity and femininity. Like all ancient cities 'Roma,' with her hills and 'creviced Palatine,' is female.

The earth mother makes the stones marking the ancient *pomerium* blossom (13) because this is her city, she its tutelar deity. And, as only the female can, she fully accommodates man. But from very early on, the feminine principle has been denied, and all that survives is the masculinized state, which we saw symbolized in *The Anathemata* by phallic siege-engines. In 'The Wall' the standards stand 'Erect... erect for Ilia' (11).

The soldier-persona himself suspects that such exaggeration of the masculine violates the feminine. With reference to the vestal fire that bakes ritual bread, he asks himself whether the original mating of Mars with Ilia was annunciation or rape: 'What was it happened by the fire-flame eating the griddle-cake... or by the white porch where our sister sang the Sabine dirge' (14)? The first half of the question has its answer in the second half, which implies, moreover, the continuing suffering of women. Punning on the name of the earth mother Tellus, the soldier wonders about this suffering, which amounts to a tradition:

> What did our mothers tell us? What did their mothers tell them? What the earth-mother told to them? But what did the queen of heaven tell *her*? (14)[10]

The queen of heaven is Juno, the source of a tradition of complaint which includes 'the Sabine dirge,' but her title also evokes Mary, the heart-pierced Queen of Sorrows (see A 215), and therefore suggests that women suffer also because of what happens to their sons.

Tradition itself is feminine, since it is transmitted by women – Juno to Tellus to grandmothers to mothers to us – and Juno's characteristic sense of ill-usage may stem from Rome's disinterest in a tradition that comprises what Juno has to say. In 1942 David Jones writes that the rejection of Juno constitutes 'the deprivation of the Romans,' which 'may be ours also,' and he then quotes Jackson Knight:

> There is a difficulty in seeing what the personality of Juno means, and why a goddess, honoured in Rome, should be so hostile. The answer is that Juno is fiercely feminine. She was not among the principal early deities of Rome, and was never one of the greatest. Rome worshipped male gods first. Rome began, because Juno acknowledged defeat.
>
> Virgil knew the cost of Empire; the cost in suffering, and the cost to conscience and to so many graceful things... The male principle, which is seen in Fascism now, is always fighting the female principle, which has

found its way into Communism, and lost much of itself as it went ... To such things poets will return. T.S. Eliot has returned to them, in 'stone, bronze, stone, steel, oakleaves, stone, horses' heels.' (E&A 241)

When writing 'The Wall' David Jones must have had in mind this passage from *Cumaean Gates* (170) and Eliot's 'The Triumphal March.'

The Roman standards erect for Ilia suggest an imperial rape of the world. But the suppression of traditionally female values in imperial Rome is now so complete that it requires a transformation of the rape metaphor. When the goddess of peace 'crooks her rounded elbow for little Plutus,' she cradles the infant god in her arms as she does in statues, but the language also connotes the giving of one's arm to an escort. Plutus popularly evokes Pluto, who in addition to being the god of Hades is also classical mythology's prototypical rapist. Rape is passé, however, when you have the cash and Persephone has lost her virtue. Because Irene has lost hers in the Roman *Pax*, her name may imply an obscene bilingual pun on the word 'peace.' (Later in *The Sleeping Lord* Private Clitus wonders whether *Dea Roma* isn't really a 'meretrix,' a prostitute, 23.) The sexual metaphor changes, but not entirely. It undergoes refraction or dislocation: mythic whoring remains realistic rape. The rape metaphor survives when, with reference to the nursery rhyme about the spider's seduction of the fly, the Celtic prisoner led in triumph is described as 'well webbed in our marbled parlour' (11).

The motif of the ritual maze-dance also involves contradictions that suggest the contrast between past and present. The troia-dance, to which the soldier alludes with reference to Aeneas's 'troia'd wandering' (12), is symbolically enacted both in the soldier walking his rounds on 'the labyrinth of the wall' and in his imagined triumphal march. Originally the troia magically strengthens the Roman wall, first at the city's foundation and subsequently each March as the priests of Mars dance the troia throughout the city. The dance sacramentalizes the wall, so that breaching it is sacrilege. But the current reversal of the wall's primordially defensive purpose is likewise sacrilegious. Instead of excluding, walls now forcibly contain, so that the city, once a cosmic 'prism,' is now a prison. The current symbolic enactments of the troia ritualize this perversion. The soldier's patrolling is a travesty of guard duty, and the triumph he imagines is a celebration of robbery, not defense. The troia is therefore a demonic liturgy – a black troia. It more than merits the judgment implied by the triumph's passing through the Carmental Gate's 'dexter arch' (11), which, as Jones knows, is the evil arch of what is consequently considered Rome's 'Wicked Gate.'[11]

We saw that the imagining of the triumphal march ends with a captured Celtic chief. As the march draws near the Capitoline Hill, he will be diverted to the Mamertine prison for execution. His death has ritual connotations because it is timed to occur immediately before the sacrifice that concludes the triumph at the temple of Jove. The triumph's enactment of the troia consequently recalls the human sacrifice once performed at the foundation of a city. This dying Gaul has some affinity, therefore, with the figure of the dying god. The soldier-persona suggests as much when he remembers that Roman soldiers have 'helped a lot of Gauls and gods to die' (14). The correspondence with the dying god is certainly implied by the further affinity of the captive Gaul, whom the soldier calls a 'king' (11), with the 'King of the Bean' (13). The soldier refers to the Mock King of Saturnalia merely to suggest that the Roman imperium is actually a misrule, but the Mock King originally personates the god Saturn and is put to death to promote fertility. Frazer cites records of the grisly rite being enacted by Roman soldiers as late as the fourth century AD (*The Golden Bough* II 310). The resemblance between the Celt and the dying god might by itself be enough to evoke Jesus, but the evocation becomes stronger – and the perspective of the reader diverges further from that of the soldier – as the city through which the Celt is being led begins to evoke the city of Jerusalem.

This happens when the narrator refers to Rome as 'the Omphalos' (10). Traditionally for the reader, certainly for David Jones, Jerusalem too is the world's omphalos (*LF* 36). The evocation of Jerusalem increases in strength when the reader subsequently learns that the specific narrative setting of the poem is Palestine (24) and probably, as with 'The Fatigue,' the wall of Jerusalem. With increasing retrospective definition, therefore, Jerusalem becomes superimposed on Rome in symbolic double exposure. For the poet at least, the doubling of vision involves the labyrinthine route of the triumph through Rome, because, while all cities are mazes, he regards the old city of Jerusalem as especially so. He writes of his 1934 visit there that from his window in the Austrian Hospice near the ancient eastern wall, 'I ... used to watch ... the tangle of meandering streets from immediately below and stretching away to the west; and I used also to meander about the densely crowded and incredibly noisy streets.'[12]

The correspondence between the two cities confirms the typological affinity between the Celt and Christ. Both are led to execution by Roman soldiers through a maze of streets. The *via dolorosa* of Jesus winds from the Fortress Antonia not far from the eastern wall, just south of where Jones stayed in 1934, to Calvary just beyond the western wall.

Both victims are wounded. And like the Saturnalian Mock King who is the Celt's symbolic foil, Jesus wears 'the rejected fillet' (13). He is the dying God whom the Celt and the Mock King evoke. Because setting is not precisely specified within 'The Wall,' however, the evocation of Jesus and his Passion is initially faint. Yet it is operative, as Jones certainly intended it to be – for while writing 'The Wall' he conceived of its setting as 'the wall of Jerusalem ... on the night of the Last Supper' (*LVW* 24). This means, furthermore, that while the soldier-persona is suffering the anxiety of his meditation, Jesus is undergoing his agony in the garden.

The soldier's affinity with Jesus is largely established by his primary typological correspondence to the suffering Celt. The soldier and the Celt are both fighters, both physically maimed: the Celt's clothing is 'tinctured' with blood, and the soldier bears in his body 'the marks' of Mars (14; cf Galatians 6:17). Both men are spiritually wounded. The Celt is 'bitched and bewildered and far from his dappled patria' (11), and the soldier on the perimeter of empire is also, in the original words of the formula used by veterans of the Great War, 'fed up, fucked up and far from fucking home.' Home is Rome, but in the fullest sense the modern city is not a home; as the soldier daydreams of being back there, he experiences moral and spiritual disaffection. If as 'the maimed king' (11) the Celtic chief correlates with 'the wasted *landa*' of a Gaulic war zone, then the analogous maiming of the soldier correlates with his inhabiting an imperial waste land. Each man walks a troia which is symbolically perverse except with respect to its funerary connotations. The troia of the Celt is that of his own funeral; the troia of the soldier establishes the walls of the world-tomb. In the Celt, the Roman symbolically slays himself.

While the soldier's troia is his endless patrolling, it is also the wandering to and fro in the 'inner labyrinth' (14) of his mind. For the reader, this movement through the maze is an initiation to the soldier's underworld, a hollow classical Hades that symbolizes his civilization, and therefore to the Roman poems that follow. This appears to be a demonic initiation to match the black troia, since from the soldier's point of view there seems no emergence from Hades. But the meaning of the poem is larger than the despair of its narrator. Even maze symbolism suggest this, for, as Jackson Knight writes, 'a maze represents the state of doubt and confusion that frequently precedes a revelation of divine truth' (*Vergil's Troy* 96). The soldier evokes this sort of ambiguity when he thinks of all those 'who walk in darkness, in the shadow of the *onager*, in the shadow of the labyrinth of the wall...' (13–14). He alludes to Isaiah 9:2, 'The people that walked in darkness have seen a great light. They have dwelt in the land of the shadow of death, upon them hath a light shined.' Like the middle night watch to which he is assigned, the soldier's inward journey begins and ends in the dark. And although he does catch a glimpse of light in the image of the heavenly city, it is for him a ghostly light shining only in memory and soon extinguished. Yet owing to evocations the soldier-persona cannot appreciate, the light shines a little brighter for the reader and does not go out. Structure, too, adds brightness to the light, by implying a significant image-ratio. We have seen that within the circle, the delineation of the poem's spatial maze culminates with the suffering Celt, and the delineation of its temporal maze culminates with the heavenly city. We saw that each image occupies the same place in geometrically identical patterns. Though the Celtic chief and the city seem to be antithetical images, their parallel contexts imply an equivalence which makes sense once the Celt is seen as a Christ-type. The images remain antithetical and the triumph remains a perversion – but, for the reader, the motif of the troia danced at the foundation of a city paradoxically assumes new meaning because, in an original elaboration of St Augustine's metaphor, the painful troia of Jesus through Jerusalem's maze founds the city of God. (In an early draft-foliation of *The Anathemata*, Jesus is said to found 'the new Urbs.') And so for the reader, at least by implication, antithesis becomes synthesis, and in a way that anticipates the ultimate transformation of the entire sequence from debate to dialectic.

'THE DREAM OF PRIVATE CLITUS'

The second of the Roman poems resembles the first in that it too constitutes a circular journey in space and time, with a heavenly vision at its centre. But the resemblance mostly highlights differences. While the persona of 'The Wall' reflects the general moral and spiritual perturbation of men in imperial society, the narrator of 'The Dream of Private Clitus' represents a personal alternative to that condition.[13] The first poem conveys dislocation; the second conveys a personal inner harmony that spills over into the social microcosm of friendship. Even the language of this poem expresses integration as tone modulates gracefully between the colloquialism and characteristic rhythms of a soldier's waking speech and the lyrical language and rhythms of his dream-account. The persona of the first poem is anonymous, his experience historical, universal, and, within the poem's conventional fiction, uncommunicated. In contrast, Private Clitus is someone in particular, and his experience is autobiographical and communicated. Generically, the first poem belongs to the twentieth century, since it is an interior monologue of the sort developed by Eliot. In a generic sense, 'The Dream of Private Clitus' belongs to earlier times. More than any other of the poems in *The Sleeping Lord*, it resembles the spoken monologues Jones admired in Browning's *Men and Women*. In a way that parallels the narrator's return to psychological and mythic beginnings, furthermore, the poem contains its generic beginnings – for this monologue includes one of the earliest forms of monologue, the narrated dream-vision. In itself, therefore, the poem's dream-vision is symbolic, but it also interacts symbolically with the rest of the monologue to establish significant relationships between the personality of its speaker and certain widely separated phases of western history. The dream and its contexts – that of the dreaming and that of the narration of the dream – comprise two overlapping figure-ground relationships. These combine with the character of Clitus to make 'The Dream of Private Clitus,' which is one of Jones's shortest and simplest poems, unusually rich in emotional and intellectual texture.

As Jones discloses in his prologue to the poem, the setting is 'Jerusalem at the time of the Passion.' Private Clitus, a fifteen-year veteran of the Roman army, is speaking to a young Greek recruit named Oenomaus. Clitus recalls a dream he had during his first year of service when he and a Celtic battle mate named Lugo were fighting Germans in Teutoburg Forest. (The name Lugo and related Celtic references are among the final emendations to the poem. Initially Lugo was a Roman nicknamed Panthero and in subsequent drafts, Tarcho.) After a nightmare about gigantic Germans, Clitus, still dreaming, finds himself and Lugo bivouacked beneath the Ara Pacis – the Altar of Peace, a small temple within Rome's Flaminial Gate. Sculpted in mid-relief on the temple's east wall is the earth mother Tellus holding the Twins. She is the antithesis of Irene in 'The Wall,' the goddess of peace who in statues crooks her arm to cradle Plutus (14). Tellus is enlarged in scale by the dream moon, which recreates in Clitus the perspective of childhood. 'The marble goddess' leans from the relief-work and lifts to her lap the two infantrymen. As if by etymological regression, they become her infants. Then she changes from stone to flesh, and Clitus finds himself back on the family farm as a young boy. In a sense, the dream continues the thrust of the sculpted marble, in which the human shape of the *mater* emerges from the

275 Sequence

Tellus Mater on the Ara Pacis

materia of stone. Because of the sculpture's medium (earth) and its subject (Mother Earth), the sculpture's relief-form is itself a metaphor that becomes a sacrament of the subconscious, effecting in Clitus's dream what it signifies in stone.

To a large degree 'The Dream of Private Clitus' is a conventional poetic dream-vision in the tradition of 'The Dream of the Rood,' 'The Dream of Macsen Wledig,' 'The Dream of Rhonabwy' (these latter in *The Mabinogion*), *Piers Plowman*, and *Pearl* – each of which David Jones quotes from or alludes to in his earlier writing. Jones's poem has special affinity with two of these dream-poems.

The close repetitions of the word 'dream' at the start of the third and fifth paragraphs on page 17 seem to echo the beginning of 'The Dream of the Rood.' In the Anglo-Saxon dream-poem, a narrator also sees a standing piece of architecture that undergoes visual metamorphoses, enraptures him, and briefly transports him out of time to the realm of archetypes. The correspondence between the Ara Pacis and the cross is confirmed by the affinity between Rome and Jerusalem first hinted at in 'The Wall.' Just outside the northwest portion of the old wall of Rome, the location of the Ara Pacis corresponds very closely to Calvary beyond the northwest wall of Jerusalem. We saw similar, symbolically charged topological rhyming, of Greece and Cornwall, in *The Anathemata*.

Clitus's dream also has special affinity with the medieval dream-poem *Pearl*, which, like 'The Dream of the Rood,' Jones greatly admired. *Pearl* and 'The Dream of Private Clitus' are both set in 'the fall of the year' (18). In each poem the dreamer comes to understand the meaning of death and experiences a foretaste of heaven. *Pearl* is partly an elegy, and so is Clitus's recollection. Both include the late-classical and early-medieval motif of *consolatio*: the *Pearl* dreamer is consoled for the death of his infant daughter; Clitus is consoled for the death of his friend in the infantry. The lamb to be sacrificed in Clitus's dream evokes the sacrificial Lamb of the Book of Revelation, an important influence on the medieval dream-vision and an image continually alluded to in *Pearl*.

In form though not in spirit Clitus's dream also resembles a classical Roman literary dream-vision, which we will consider after examining the monologue in more detail.

What distinguishes Private Clitus's narrative from conventional dream-narratives is the attention given to the waking context of his dream and to the context of its subsequent recounting. These contexts interpret the dream and extend its meaning beyond the awareness of Clitus, so that the poem forecasts ends and new beginnings for man and for civilizations.

The context of his dreaming is charged with reminders of personal mortality, to which the dream brings a pagan-theological matrix of hope and belief. Teutoburg Forest in 15 AD contains the unburied dead of the three legions under Varus massacred six years earlier in one of the worst military calamities to befall Rome in a single battle. Clitus would have been among those detailed to gather and bury the bones of the eighteen thousand dead. These dead he does not mention, because his listener, Oenomaus – and any reader of Tacitus – would already know the macabre details of the campaign. Moreover, the deaths of the eighteen thousand are less important to Clitus personally than the death of his bivvy mate Lugo. References to Lugo's death bracket Clitus's account of the dream. Furthermore, Lugo's being asleep within the dream prefigures his death. But in the dream, the lap of Tellus is for both men the entrance to an otherworld at once older and newer than the bleak Hades of classical mythology. For Clitus, death involves the renewal hoped for in primordial fertility rites like the dream's springtime feasts of Fordicidia and Matronalia – the latter honouring Juno Lucina as patroness of childbirth. Renewal in the dream takes the form of becoming children again, partly in symbolic fulfillment of the biblical prerequisite for entering the kingdom of heaven (Matthew 18:3; cf *Pearl* 61, line 3). The Christian theological vindication of this aboriginal hope is implicit in the monologue's implied contextual instance of death. While Clitus is narrating his dream, Jesus is being put to death, and the corollary of that death is resurrection. The significance of this temporal coincidence is secured and expanded by Clitus's echoing the language of St Paul's teaching about men transformed at the general resurrection 'in the twinkling of an eye' (20; cf 1 Corinthians 15:51–2). Clitus himself has had a foretaste of heaven – like the 'man in Christ' whom St Paul mentions as having been 'caught up into paradise.' Clitus was 'caught up into that peace, whether in a marble body I cannot tell ... the genius of the dream knows' (20). St Paul's acquaintance 'was caught up ... whether in the body, or out of the body, I cannot tell, God knoweth.' Paul says this happened, as it did with Clitus, 'above fourteen years ago' (2 Corinthians 12:2–4).

Clitus's monologue evokes, furthermore, the festival at Eleusis, in which pagan initiates experience a foretaste of life after death. Like Clitus's dream, the Eleusinian festival takes place in autumn. During the festival, initiates ritually descend to Hades and emerge with assurance of immortality. In terms of the myth, they descend to join Demeter in quest of Persephone, whom Clitus and the Romans call 'Proserpine' (20). The Greek origin of Oenomaus gives an added resonance to the Eleusinian association.

As in 'The Wall,' the allusive correspondence is primarily structural. Like the soldier's meditation in that poem, Clitus's narrative proceeds through shifts in time and place. The place-shifting from Jerusalem to Teutoburg Forest to Rome to the family farm coincides exactly with the time-shifting from the narrative present to the dream's setting fifteen years earlier and then further back to Clitus's childhood. Then the narrative returns to the time and place of the dream and then to the narrative present. This temporal descent and return combines with connotations of Hades in 'the shadowy labyrinth' of Teutoburg Forest (16) to evoke the Eleusinian ritual of descent and return. The monologue itself, therefore, is a literary counterpart of the Eleusinian ritual, with Clitus as Hermes initiating Oenomaus and the reader.

In broad outline the initiation pattern resembles that of 'The Wall,' and Clitus's dream of Tellus resembles and is symbolically related to the femininized heavenly city at the centre of 'The Wall.' But the central dream-vision of Clitus expands to occupy the major portion of his poem, textually displacing its waking contexts. In the previous poem the vision of the heavenly city is brief. It confirms the anonymous soldier in his desolation, whereas the dream of Clitus has so conditioned his imagination that now, fifteen years later, he is still able to escape desolation by recalling his dream.

Bound up with personal mortality and life after death in 'The Dream of Private Clitus' is the death and rebirth of culture. Clitus foresees the fall of Rome (23), which has its precedent for him in the destruction of the three legions. Though Clitus does not know it, the death of Lugo on the imperial frontier prefigures the final reverberation of that fall. Lugo's full name, Lugobelinos, is the old Celtic form of Llywelyn, the name of the Welsh prince whose death in 1282 finally breaks the last living political symbol of the Roman-Celtic hegemony begun in Lugo's time. Already Lugo, like the early medieval Welsh, considers himself Roman. Clitus says 'a stray got him' (16) – echoing Jones's account of Llywelyn's death, also in a wood (E&A 47). The forest in which Lugo is soon to die is partly characterized by 'contesting boughs' where 'each swaying limb of each tree struggles for the mastery' (16), recalling the thirteenth-century eulogy of Llywelyn, in which 'the trees of the forest furiously rush against each other' (IP 212 n42). By the century of

Llywelyn's death, however, the vacuum left by Rome's fall has been filled by medieval Christian culture. Llywelyn dies bearing on his person a relic of the cross.

Because Clitus is not, in his values and attitudes, a man of the imperial present but is of the mythic past, he also belongs, in a sense, to the future. This symbolically justifies Clitus's anticipation of the medieval dream-convention and his presaging the great physical achievement and enduring symbol of medieval culture, the High Gothic cathedral. He foresees the cathedral when he compares, as Spengler does (1 396), the shapes of the German forest to architectural columns and 'pointed arches' (16). The Gothic cathedral shares with the sculpted relief on the Ara Pacis a common inspiration, moreover, since the panel Clitus admires depicts the archetypal mother who as 'Gate of Elysium' (20) recalls Mary's epithet 'Gate of Heaven.' It is to this Christian Tellus under the title of Notre Dame that so many of the great cathedrals are dedicated: those, for example, of Chartres, Rheims, Amiens, Rouen, and Paris.

The influence of the feminine principle is essential to cultural vitality, and because it is absent from the imperial state Clitus serves, his is already a dying civilization. In a special sense, then, 'Proserpine' has withdrawn and will stay away, as Clitus says, 'from fall till crocus-time' (20). Her absence and its effect on culture is signalled by the dream's taking place at evening in the autumn 'of a dying year' (16).

Clitus is not reconciled to his condition. 'Fed up and far from sweetest home' (18), he longs for his native Rome but also and more deeply for cultural and psychological accommodation — and for freedom too. He has been in the army for fifteen years. The Teutoburg campaign in which he fought necessarily recalls the widespread mutiny of troops in Pannonia the year before, which was caused by Augustus extending the twenty-year term of military service to twenty-five years and beyond. The Teutoburg campaign was undertaken as a direct consequence of the mutiny, solely to busy the infantry in order to prevent further uprisings. The suffering of men under imposed servitude is further recalled by the name of Oenomaus, to whom Clitus is talking. On the back of a page of the first foliation of *The Anathemata* manuscript, Jones notes that 'Oenomaus & Crixus were the names of two lieutenants of Spartacus in the slaves' revolt of 73 BC.' Like that rebellion, the recent mutiny was not successful: the yoke of *imperium* is not easy nor is it easily tossed off. The memory of his dream consoles Clitus for his continuing slavery, therefore, as well as for Lugo's death.

Until the final redrafting of the poem the allusion to the slave revolt was stronger, for Clitus was named Crixus and the poem was entitled 'The Dream of Private Crixus.' In their earliest stages of development, the first three Roman poems were continuous – with Oenomaus, who was then a six-year veteran, delivering the monologue of 'The Wall' to a drowsy Crixus, who responded by narrating his dream. Their conversation broke off after Crixus noticed the disturbance beyond the Water Gate that is mentioned in 'The Fatigue.' In that poem, as we shall see, Crixus retains his original, suggestive name.

In their enforced military service, Roman infantrymen correspond to Isaiah's figure of the Suffering Servant in the liturgy of Good Friday and, therefore, to the suffering Christ. This resemblance is implied by Clitus's being Christ's contemporary. Romans begin military service at the age of sixteen. Clitus is that age in 15 AD, which puts his birth in the year 1 BC. The affinity between Jesus and soldiers like Clitus and Lugo is further strengthened by the resemblance of Tellus and her *infantes* to medieval carvings of the Madonna and Child, and, because of the presence of an ox and a sheep on the sculpted frieze, to the Christian nativity scene. The humanity of these soldiers, which God takes for his own in the Incarnation, symbolically resides in their being mothers' sons.

Clitus's only alternative to waking reality is to recall his dream, which is, in more than one sense, to return to the womb. The city of his dream is female; its tutelar goddess is Roma, who is typologically synonymous with Tellus and is depicted on another panel of the Ara. As we saw earlier, moreover, according to primitive symbolism city gates are vaginal. 'Within the gate' (20) and on the lap of Tellus 'all the world seemed at peace' (19), and Clitus is 'caught up into that peace' (20). He experiences the paradisal 'Arcady' of classical mythology, which he associates at the start of his monologue with the femininity of nymphs.

His sense of universal well-being results at least partly from a profound psychological communion with nature, which is personified and iconographically depicted in the relief. His is a preterrational sensibility, which is traditionally associated with femininity, not because it especially characterizes women, though it may, but because for everyone it originates in prenatal communion with one's mother. It survives in psychologically balanced adults as a capacity to know by connaturality, a sharing of being that integrates the inner person and therefore precludes alienation from self.[14] This kind of awareness may be approximated by the experience of dreaming, which entails the surrender of aggressive, analytical consciousness to the subconscious, here symbolized by Oceanus (20) – for subconscious 'dream tides,' like those of the ocean, swell for the moon's femininity.

The feminine, prerational faculty survives in Clitus and contributes to his being the most appealing of Jones's Roman narrators. Clitus enjoys friendship. And his prophetic intuitions about the future are tempered by what Jones calls 'the saving scepticism of the female mind' (E&A 240) – for Clitus doubts that pointed arches will ever be seen in stone, and refuses to endorse Lugo's interpretation of 'homing eagles' as an auspicious sign (17). In the second instance, as in the first, he is mistaken; two of the lost legionary standards are eventually recovered. But the sign Lugo heralds as auspicious is not lucky for him, and this dignifies Clitus's scepticism as corresponding to the valuation of personal life over the collective enterprise.

The foil and antithesis of Clitus as a dreamer is the NCO called Brasso who wakes Clitus from his dream. Brasso is an organization man and, as a perennial Roman type, may, Clitus fancies, have been one of the original Twins. The metaphor emphasizes Brasso's contrast with Clitus, who on Tellus's lap takes the place of one of the Twins. Brasso's 'hallucinations' are spurious myths like the one historically represented by the Ara Pacis, built to commemorate a political pretence that Lugo and the three legions die defending. (It is by a reversal of irony that the dream of Clitus redeems this sham, transforming it into an experience of the peace that surpasses understanding.) Brasso's 'delusions' also include an egocentric pragmatism that narrows the scope of reality and of human expression.

In this regard and in his relationship to Clitus, Brasso counterbalances Lugo, the friend. Brasso's pragmatism determines his human relationships in a way that renders him unloving and unlovable. Aggressively ambitious, Brasso is sycophantic to superiors: his 'face is purple ... to match the Legate's plume' (23). And he is demanding of subordinates: his nickname derives from an obsession with the shine on his men's brass breastplates and helmets. The fates of Brasso and Lugo are symbolically linked, furthermore, in an inverse ratio implied by Clitus when he says about Brasso's rising through the ranks: 'the higher the casualties, the higher the climber ... and his main leg up was the packet we got in that show' in Teutoburg Forest (21). Ambition is the antithesis of friendship. As one increases, the other dies.

The structure of the poem figuratively weighs Brasso against Lugo. Lugo occupies the introductory part, before the account of the dream, and Brasso occupies the concluding part. This structural weighing-scale, with Clitus as fulcrum, is abbreviated, or reflected *en abîme*, in the metamorphosis of the image that concludes the dream. Clitus as a boy bellows for a lamb being taken for sacrifice. The lamb corresponds to Lugo, soon to die, whom Clitus also grieves for. As Clitus wakes, his crying for the sacrificial lamb becomes Brasso's calling men for the watch. Lugo is Clitus's friend; Brasso merely his boss.

For 'a fact-man' like Brasso, love, intuition, and even dreams are subject to calculation. It is as though Brasso had never been humanized by a warm relationship with his mother, and in his case regimental fantasy reverses the dream-transformation of a stone mother to one of flesh. The men say Brasso's mother was a metal wolf with womb of bronze and teats of iron who nursed him 'by numbers' (22). Men like Brasso are psychologically incomplete, and consequently break the 'unities and blessed conjugations' of dreams and vital cultures (21). Brasso is now chief centurion of the first cohort. Clitus after fifteen years is still a private, probably because as a dreamer and a recounter of dreams he is out of sympathy with the exigencies of empire.

If Clitus has his Roman foil, so does his dream. It is Cicero's 'The Dream of Scipio' (*De republica* 6.9–26), in which the dead Africanus appears to his grandson Scipio when he is 'little more than a private' (*miles*, 11; actually Scipio is a military tribune).[15] Like Jones's poem, Cicero's work is a monologue. Like Clitus, Scipio dreams while on the periphery of the empire, in his case in Africa. Just as Tellus appears to Clitus under a form familiar to him through a sculpted image, Africanus appears, says Scipio, in 'that shape which was familiar to me from his bust' (6.10). Like Clitus's dream, that of Scipio concerns human mortality and what lies beyond death, but in Scipio's dream heavenly glory is the reward for preserving and expanding the empire. And unlike the dream of Clitus, that of Scipio is typically Roman in its exclusive masculinity: Scipio converses with his dead grandfather and father, and renews his dedication to the fatherland (*patria*). Since 'The Dream of Scipio' is largely imperial propaganda, Jones may have Scipio (and Cicero) in mind when he writes, 'there's calculation in the very dreams of a Brasso' (22).

The contrast between the dreams of Scipio and Clitus implies another metamorphosis – that of the poetic dream-vision. Because of its immense influence throughout the Middle Ages, 'The Dream of Scipio' is the prototype of all medieval dream-poems. Those to which Jones alludes in this poem, and on which he partly models the poem, exemplify the mystical vision and metaphysical hope that transform the genre and fill the great emptiness of classical civilization. The generic transformation reflects the larger cultural transformation, of which Clitus has prophetic intimations.

'The Dream of Private Clitus' must have had special, personal meaning for David Jones, because the experience of Private Clitus in Teutoburg Forest seems to reflect the experience of Private David Jones in Mametz Wood as *In Parenthesis* records it. Like Teutoburg Forest, the wood in that poem recalls the mysteries at Eleusis, resembles a cathedral, and evokes Llywelyn's elegy (*IP* 182, 186). If you walk in Mametz Wood today, furthermore, you will see that the first stretch of woods resembles Teutoburg's 'smooth, straight boles... and no low growth with the sward between each as it were like a pavement' (16). It was basically the same in 1916.[16] And like the diminutive Welshmen in Mametz Wood, these Romans are dwarfed by the big-bodied Germans they fight.[17] Tellus, who appears to Clitus dreaming in Teutoburg Forest, is essentially the same Queen who appears to the dead in the woods at the Somme, although for Clitus she is Roman, initially urbanized, and exclusively maternal.

The correspondence between the assault on Mametz Wood and the Teutoburg campaign is a special aspect of the parallel with modern times implied in all Jones's Roman poems. In this poem the parallel is also established by colloquial military language, by an allusion, in the words 'lancer-whiskered bloody bucinators' (22), to the waxed-moustached bandsmen of World War I, and by the allusion in the nickname Brasso to the trade name of the modern metal polish.[18] Brasso himself recalls, for Jones at least, the sergeant majors of the First World War, who, he said, 'were almost all bastards.'[19] In this instance the poem's parallel with modern times also constitutes the furthest dimension of the future inherent in Clitus's visionary meditation on his past. Clitus himself has some affinity with Mr Jenkins, 'the Mercian dreamer' of *In Parenthesis*, but Clitus is a private, and I think anyone who knew David Jones will agree that of all the personae in his poetry, Private Clitus comes the closest to being a self-portrait.[20]

The kind of man Clitus exemplifies is ill at ease in the pragmatic late phases of civilizations. He can be accommodated only by a historical phase like the High Middle Ages in which man's spiritual aspirations receive full cultural expression. But such a man is never entirely at home in any historical phase, for in imagination he inhabits the boundary between time and eternity. Although he conflates and reverses the

284 The Shape of Meaning

biblical sequence, Clitus is, in this sense, a living symbol of 'the last days' in which 'your young men shall see visions and your old men shall dream dreams' (Joel 2:28, Acts 2:17).

'THE FATIGUE'

'The Fatigue' opens in the darkness of Good Friday morning.[21] A non-commissioned officer interrogates and harangues two Celtic recruits being relieved from the middle night watch on the southwest corner of the wall of Jerusalem's Fortress Antonia.[22] Both of the recruits report seeing beyond the Water Gate what must be the party leaving for Gethsemane to arrest Jesus. As punishment for looking in a direction other than the one assigned, they are detailed for immediate fatigue duty there, probably to supply extra security when the arrest party returns. The Jews who have gone after Jesus act on their own but not without informing the Romans, certainly not when security is tight, as now 'in this city / pending the Passage / of their god' (30). There follows a meditation on another fatigue, the execution party for which a soldier will carry the implements of crucifixion or guard the cross. This being the crucifixion of Jesus, theological considerations emerge to displace the Roman, historical point of view. Finally attention shifts to imperial Rome, where policy, accidents, and superstition influence 'the ball' of command as it rolls through the maze of bureaucracy and military hierarchy to determine, at the lowest local level, that 'you will furnish / that Fatigue' (41).

In the previous Roman poems, tone is subjective and point of view is primarily that of the speaking personae. Now the voice of the poet abstracts itself, trading emotional immediacy for objectivity and scope. In time, in place, in social context, 'The Fatigue' puts in perspective the Roman poems that precede and follow it. More distinctly than 'The Dream of Private Clitus,' its structure is tripartite and implies a threefold comparison. The first part of the poem concerns ordinary man; the second part, Christ's crucifixion; the third part, the political world. Each part is written in a fictional mode appropriate to its subject: the first part, dramatic dialogue; the second, description; the third, anatomy. Unifying the work are images and symbols resonating across these sections. But the threefold division delineates the poem's subject, which is the reciprocal relationship each to the other of ordinary man, Jesus, and the world. In the poem's narrated time this multiple interrelationship is undergoing a revolutionary transformation which implies a Christian dialectic.

Point of view in the poem also undergoes transformation. In the first section it is, for the most part, that of the NCO. In the central section it attaches itself to the Celtic recruits, who become narrative reflectors, and moves by means of the ambiguous second-person pronoun from intimate self-address to objective direct address. In effect, an omniscient narrator emerges from the interior of the soldiers' consciousness. He then alternates between their perspective and his own Christian point of view, though his metaphors for the crucifixion derive mostly from the Roman soldiers' world. Employing direct address, he moves forward in time from 'you' who are assigned to the immediate fatigue, to 'you' who will be assigned to the midday execution party, to 'you' who will be assigned to guard the place of execution throughout the early afternoon.

In the final section (38-41), the momentum of this temporal progression carries over into movement through space and through the collective mind of Roman bureaucracy. The entire section consists of two periodic sentences hinging on two prepositions. 'From' the desk of Sejanus through the corridors of power, authority moves. 'By' accidental influences on civil servants, policy is shaped and implemented on its way east and down the ranks from a legate's executives to a tribune to an orderly officer to a sergeant to a corporal to 'you.' This narrated movement goes one way, from the centre of power to the ordinary man. But concurrent with narrated movement is narrative movement, which goes in and then comes out. Point of view moves like a movie camera first inward through the buildings of the central administration in Rome to the desk of Sejanus and then back again through mazy architectural space. Jones said that this physical movement reflects his memories of frequent visits to Bernard Wall, head of the Italian section of the Foreign Office Research Division in London during the Second World War.[23] The outward movement continues and becomes internalized, without becoming personal, as it passes through the surface of the bureaucratic mind. Because the overall movement in and out is labyrinthine, it symbolizes initiation.

The knowledge gained during this initiation is about the political world. The movement inward through physical space builds anticipation, which is met by emptiness. A sentry's cloak lies in its niche, and in the 'most interior room' documents lie on Sejanus's table awaiting his signature, but though we are told that this is where functionaries 'sit the regulated hours' (from nine to five), we meet no one. The absence of people is eerie. It suggests dehumanization and recalls the troia's tomb-connotations. With its centre just beyond 'check-point Minotaur'

(39), this place is death-haunted. The countersign for the day is 'Capri,' moreover, which reminds us (as Jones does in the poem's preface) that Sejanus, now running the empire in the absence of Tiberius, is soon to be liquidated on orders sent by Tiberius from Capri.

On the way out of this maze our knowledge is completed by the trivialization of the maze's horrible central vacuity. The influences shaping policy in the bureaucratic mind are accidental or delusory. They include the time of meetings (before or after lunch), the working condition of a steam bath, the chill or lukewarmness of a drink, the effect of weather on the garden or the kidneys, and divination by astrology or with 'a shuffled pack' of cards (40). Superstition had become common by the end of the Republic, as it has in the first half of the twentieth century, most notably with Mussolini and Goebbels. This passage resembles and may have been influenced by Part 5 of Eliot's 'Dry Salvages,' in which superstition and other 'distractions' are seen as characterizing the lives of secularized men.

The main distraction here is taken for granted and looms almost too large to be seen. The ground against which all the accidental and delusory influences figure is power. The bureaucratic maze is a channel of power, its purpose the preservation of power. But power is not an end; it is only a means masquerading as an end. Consequently, nothing in this maze is ethically or metaphysically real.

The antithesis of the hollow 'Urbs, throughout *orbis*' (39) is the 'defined orbis' centred by the cross (37). Separated by time in 'The Wall,' the city of the world and the city of God are now contemporary and spatially tangential. Calvary on the perimeter of Jerusalem is also, in a sense, on the circumference of Rome because Jerusalem is on the perimeter of the empire and because the two cities continue to be identified with one another. Like Rome, Jerusalem has an 'Arx' (28; cf 11), and in the place just outside Jerusalem corresponding to that of the Ara Pacis on the edge of Rome stands the cross – referred to in the poem as the '*ara crucis*' (35). The antithesis of imperial Rome, the *orbis* of Calvary is correlative to the ancient heavenly city in 'The Wall.' Calvary has stone '*termini*' (37) like those marking the ancient *pomerium*, and a 'flowering transom' (34) recalling the city's blossoming 'stone lintels' (13; a transom is a lintel). The sacred city unites 'rooted clod' and 'drifted star' (13). And so does Calvary, whose 'Yggdrasill' (35) is rooted in earth with its boughs in the heavens. Born of another Ilia, Jesus is the new Romulus, founding once more and forever the heavenly city.

The opposition between Christ's tiny cosmic city and the imperial megalopolis is emphasized by superficial similarities. Like the imperial maze, Christ's circle is death-haunted. Its location is 'Skull Hill' (28), called 'The Tumulus' (38), a place of killing and of burial. It is also called 'the marked-out *adytum*' (36), a word Jones defines as 'the inner sanctuary from which issued oracles' (37 n1); it is therefore analogous to 'the most interior room' of Sejanus, from which issues policy (39).

At the centres of their respective circles, moreover, Jesus and Sejanus ironically resemble each other. Each determines policy that kills. This aspect of their resemblance underlies the poet's long footnote describing de la Taille's theology of the Passion. 'At the lighted and festal board in the Supper-Room,' Jesus makes an 'oblative act' that commits him 'to his actual immolation on the morrow ...' (36). As a place where dying begins, the Supper-table has its secular counterpart in 'the wide-bevelled marbled table' of Sejanus (39).[24] The action begun at one table converges, moreover, with the action begun at the other, so that both tables correspond to 'the stripped *mensa*,' or table of the cross (36). Although the politics of Sejanus kills others, it also and very soon now will bring about his own death, which thereby corresponds, obliquely and negatively, to the death of Jesus.

At Passover, with the population of Jerusalem swelled by a hundred thousand pilgrims, imperial Rome is apprehensive. The NCO asks the sentries, 'Not seen the ghost / of Judas Machabee / b' any chance' (28)? But Rome cannot even conceive of, much less anticipate, the revolution currently under way. In fact, Rome unintentionally co-instigates this revolution. 'The ball' of command (39) rolls through the maze of the world for the purpose of ensuring the status quo, but paradoxically it becomes an Ariadne's ball of twine by which a new Theseus saves mankind from being sacrificed, like the youth of Athens, to the Minotaur. The maze remains, the Minotaur is unslain, but the ball rolls to a new centre occupied, as in the mazes of medieval Christian iconography, by Jesus.

The relationship of the circle of Christ to the world-city is dialectical, with the world as thesis, Christ as antithesis, and the implied transformation of the former by the latter as synthesis. The small circle on the edge of the empire will expand to contain the imperial circle. This absorption has its secular analogue in the small circle of Tiberius (officially a god), shrunk to the isle of Capri, expanding to swallow Sejanus, whose circle has grown to encompass all the world.

The spiritual and cultural character of the Christian synthesis is conveyed in fertility imagery that is more broadly rooted in the text than may at first appear. The opening dialogue contains for example an allegory of the land's renewal. The sentries have seen movement 'by the Water Gate' near 'Virgin Post' (28). The gate is named for being used to fetch water from the Well of the Virgin. Now it is being used to fetch Jesus, born of a virgin and the one who 'Frees the Waters' (35). The allegory implied by the reference to 'Virgin Post' is emphasized five lines later when the NCO, exclaiming 'O admirable collaboration!' (30) unconsciously echoes the antiphon of the Octave of Christmas that begins *O admirabile commercium* and continues, in translation, 'the creator of man, having assumed a living body, deigned to be born of a virgin ...' As 'the Man Hanged' (34), furthermore, Jesus is the dying vegetation god and the Hanged Man of the Tarot pack, here evoked in its original association with water and fertility in contrast to the superstitious use of the 'shuffled pack' in modern Rome.[25] A similar contrast is implied in *The Waste Land* where Madame Sosostris divides the Tarot pack and cannot find the Hanged Man.

Redemption and its effect on culture have in common the metaphor of photosynthesis. This is established in the poem's beautiful prefatory lyric – which concludes early drafts of the poem and is therefore, from very early on, conceptually integral to it:

ARBOR AXED FROM ARBOUR-SIDE
    THAT NOW STRIPT
IS MORE ARRAYED
MORE THAN IN THE SILVAN RIDE
    WHEN TO PIERCE THE GREEN
AND TANGLED TENEBRAE
    COMES APOLLO'S RAY
SEE WHAT SHEEN THE LOPPED BOUGHS
NOW LIFT HIGH
    ... FRONDE, FLORE, GERMINE
O CRUX AVE
    AVE VEXILLUM. (27)

Here the cross is compared to what it was as a tree when the sun's rays did 'PIERCE' its foliage (27). The sun's piercing corresponds to that of 'the long *lancea* / obliquely thrust' (36) when, in words quoted from the Good Friday hymn *Crux fidelis*, Jesus on the cross is 'FRONDE, FLORE, GERMINE' (leaf, flower, bud). Each piercing is life-giving, and because the sun is 'APOLLO' – Christ's classical counterpart in early Christian art, in *In Parenthesis* (62), and in *The Anathemata* (219) – the sun that pierces is also the foliage pierced, 'himself to himself' (32).

In the main body of the poem the image shifts emphasis from foliage to the sun and changes from a metaphor to an implied symbol. The transformation begins in the parallel movement of Jesus and the sun, which is the poem's unifying motif. Although the sentries have been ordered to look west into the darkness, they look eastward in anticipation of the dawn. The sky must already be lighter there, where Jesus too is beginning his journey westward. At noon ('the sixth hour,' 31) the sun will be at its height, and so will Jesus on the cross. Then the sentry will stand 'alone under the meridian eye' (34), his back to Jesus and 'beneath the implacable ray / that beats / where y'r scorching backplates rivet' (35). The discomfort is disturbing beyond realism. The Romans have crucified the Sun. As a symbol, this is only implied, yet it is awesome and communicates what is nearly inaccessible to the imagination, the divinity of Christ. It is an original symbol but derives from pagan Helios worship, from the patristic metaphor that underlines the English homonym of the Sun/Son, and from a biblical image to which the poem's concluding imagery alludes. By the end of the poem, narrative time has moved from the darkness at the end of the middle night watch to dawn:

>   and look! the red-dyed sky-drape
> from over Bosra way
>   to-morrow is already
> putting on to-day.   (40–1)

In Isaiah 63:1 it is the messiah, 'mighty to save,' who comes 'with dyed garments from Bozra.'

The third thematic element in the poem's dialectic is ordinary man represented by the sentries. He is the medium within which the Christian dialectic will reach its synthesis – because he lives *in* the city of the world but, to the degree that he remains fully human, is not *of* it. By his nature he is at home only in 'the twin-*urbes*' (A 50), the city of the world culturally twinned with the city of God. In the current imperial world-city, therefore – and by analogy in the modern world of the reader – ordinary man is either dehumanized or disaffected.

The tendency of the secular world to dehumanize is suggested by the emptiness of the administrative maze, and exemplified by the ambitious, Brasso-like NCO ('on his way to promotion,' 29) whose nagging, however necessary to the poem dramatically, impoverishes the language of its opening pages. He gives dehumanization its symbolic focus in a prescriptive simile that echoes the more awkward, paradoxical image of 1 Peter 2:5, in which men are 'lively stones' of 'a spiritual house':

>   each man as mans the wall
> is as each squared, dressed stone
>   fronting the wall but one way
>   according to the run of the wall.   (28)

Because soldiers are 'the instruments' (31) that implement 'necessities and accidents' (39) that have nothing to do with soldiers as persons, they are in danger of becoming unspiritual stones. Those who remain human suffer a disaffection which is symbolized by the 'root of Saturn's Loathing' that the makers of policy are said to 'enclose with each directing chit ... for every jack man ...' (39). The meaning of the image is more horrible than malice, however, which is here merely a metaphorical projection disclosing the still-human imagination of men at the receiving end of the line of command. Nothing personal, not even spite, influences the directives issuing from the central administration. Soldiers who remain human suffer what seems a combination of existential and Marxist alienations.

As we saw in 'The Wall,' imperialism also involves moral alienation. The empire, like the Cretan maze, is a prison. On the ramparts of the Antonia on Jerusalem's east side, sentries are directed to face west, into the city. But as if by primordial defensive habit or to express their disaffection with the policy of containment, the two guards whom the NCO questions have been looking the opposite way, outside the city wall. To have done this, furthermore, they must have left their posts.[26] Probably they have gone off together. Because he suspects this, the NCO calls for Crixus as soon as he hears what the first sentry has seen. We are not permitted to eavesdrop on the sentries' private thoughts, as in 'The Wall,' but their disregard for standing orders symbolizes disaffection with their role and, like dereliction of duty in *In Parenthesis* (eg 15), demonstrates gratuitous independence, which is a sign of undiminished humanity.

It is primarily to enjoy each other's company, of course, that the anonymous sentry and his 'Gallic buddy' Crixus (29) have gone off together. Underlying the symbolism of their departure, therefore, is a moral opposition between friendship and the servile state. As Simone Weil writes, 'relationship breaks its way out of the social' and 'is the monopoly of the individual.'[27] It also precludes the absolutizing of power. Thematically, friendship takes us back to 'The Dream of Private Clitus,' in which the structure of the poem weighs Clitus's friend Lugo against Brasso. The structure of 'The Fatigue' works similarly to weigh Crixus and his friend against the poem's other pair, Tiberius and his one-time protégé Sejanus, who plot against one another, for whom power is more important than love. The annihilation of Sejanus by Tiberius merely redistributes power without affecting the *realpolitik* of the secular world. In contrast, Crixus and his friend are metaphysical dissenters. The NCO is quite right to tell them, 'It's whoresons like you ... as are diriment to our unific and expanding order. / A few like you can undo / and properly bitch / all the world plan ...' (28–9). And he calls Crixus 'insubordinate' (29). The adjective fits the name for, as we have seen, Crixus, like Private Clitus's friend Oenomaus, is named after one of the ringleaders of the previous century's slave rebellion. But because they choose love over power, Crixus and his friend are more profoundly in sympathy with the cosmic revolution of Jesus. And the name Crixus may suggest such agreement if, when the NCO repeats it five times in quick succession (29–30), the reader hears it as a near homonym for Christ or Christus.

The sentries participate in the robbery that is empire, but a moral distinction may be made between thieves. As we have seen, such a distinction is implied by the weighing-scale aspect of the poem's form. But here structure suggests more. The shape of the poem, with the crucifixion at the centre, parallels the familiar triple-imaged crucifixion scene of European painting, especially in triptychs. The good thief on the right, the bad thief on the left, and Jesus in the middle. 'The Fatigue' reads like such a painting if we conceive of the poem as structurally spatial and facing the reader, with the good thieves on the right (at the opening of the poem), Jesus in the centre, and the bad thieves, Sejanus and Tiberius, on the left. The pictorial allusion presupposes an analogy between sequential and visual forms that would be beyond the imaginative reach of most poets. The schema is not simple, with the NCO on the right and the enlisted man who is 'you' in the middle and on the left, but the correspondence does seem likely, because the emphasis is on the sentries, Jesus, and the arch-technocrats respectively, and because Jones is himself a painter and thoroughly familiar with European art history.

In his own painting *Vexilla regis* (1947), moreover, the three dominant trees evoke the traditional motif. Jones says so in a letter to the woman who bought the picture, and he specifies that the tree on the left is 'partly imperial standard – a power symbol... St. Augustine's remark that "empire is great robbery" influenced me here' (*DGC* 150). Apropos of the crucifixion at the poem's centre, furthermore, Jones has long been interested in the image of the cross as 'steelyard,' a kind of *libra* or scales that weighs right against left.[28]

By the end of the poem, two important terms have expanded in meaning to become symbols. Because of ambiguity of reference, which includes self-reference, the 'you' who begins as a Roman soldier now includes the reader and the poet. And the fatigue to which 'you' are assigned now refers partly to the eucharistic re-enactment of the offering whose immolation occurs 'once and for all on the dark Hill.' To this, Jones notes, the *milites Christi* are committed at the Supper-table by Christ's 'command "Do this"' (36n). For the poet and for every reader, furthermore, the fatigue is also life itself, the labour involved in living in a world largely governed by chance and dehumanizing necessities. Marxist and neo-Freudian hopes notwithstanding, alienation we have always with us, and within us. Though the poem's Latin epigraph from the *Dies irae* refers primarily to the Passion, it is also, in this context, a prayer on behalf of the human condition: 'that such great labour be not in vain.' The city of God founded by Jesus does not replace the city of the world, and in a late phase of civilization it does not eliminate alienation. But it does ensure that human life and human labour need not be meaningless.

In the middle-length poems of *The Sleeping Lord*, David Jones rarely steps from behind a narrative persona to speak with 'the voice of the poet,' but he does so in this poem, which therefore implicitly concerns the role of the poet. In 'The Fatigue' the poet is aligned with the ordinary soldiers, for like them, but in a special sense, he is the cultural medium of Christian synthesis. Jones demonstrates how the poet achieves this synthesis when he adopts Roman military awards as metaphors for Jesus's wounds (32). In his preface to the poem he quotes similar metaphors, '*milites Christi* and *militia coelestis*' (26). Each of these images is a paradoxical union of the worldly city and the city of God. The meaning of such an image is greater than the sum of the meanings of its constituent parts because of the contrast implied and the conversion effected by their combination.

In the poem and in cultural history, the greatest example of such semiotic conversion is the image of the cross, which once scandalized the ancient world. The cross is 'the Anathema' (35) changed to the most powerful of positive anathemata. Partly to evoke the imaginative synthesis that completes the poem's dialectic, Jones alludes to two works that are for him the greatest literary expressions of the symbol of the cross – the sixth-century Latin hymn *Vexilla regis* and the Anglo-Saxon poem 'The Dream of the Rood.'

The latter he repeatedly alludes to. 'The Dreaming Tree' is the Rood (32); the tree 'AXED FROM ARBOUR-SIDE' (27) resembles the Rood 'cut down at the edge of the woods' (line 29); and reference to equipment 'of lift, of haul / of stay / against a Fall' (33) refers not only to the reversal of Original Sin but also to the Rood's saying 'Fast I stood / who falling could have felled them all' (lines 42–3).

The *Vexilla regis* is evoked by imitation. The hymn makes the Roman triumph a metaphor for the Passion as re-enacted in Good Friday's liturgy of the cross. One half of this *symbalein* or joining together is seen in 'The Wall' where the triumph is strictly a secular ritual, though for the reader it does evoke the Passion. In 'The Fatigue' the symbol is complete, with Calvary replacing the Capitoline at the conclusion of the triumph. In language evocative of the biblical epithet 'King of Kings,' which recalls the 'maimed king' of 'The Wall,' the cross is

> Where the Spoil of Spoils
> hangs to Iuppiter
> and the trophies
> are the Conqueror... (32)

The *Vexilla regis* is also alluded to at the conclusion of the poem's prefatory lyric, in the words 'O CRUX AVE / AVE VEXILLUM.'

The sixth-century hymn's fusing of the cross with the Roman military standard carried in triumph does not imply that the city of the world is synonymous with the city of God. This never happens. But if a celebration of robbery can be made to celebrate salvation, then some of the worst aspects of the city of the world can be turned into signs pointing the way to the city of God. Jones writes in 1958 about the *Vexilla regis* as an example of such sign making: 'It is the sort of thing that poets are for; to redeem is part of their job' (E&A 261).

Because 'The Fatigue' is the middle poem of the Roman poems, its central section (31–8) is their centre. The section is exceptional within these poems because it places Christ's Passion in the narrative foreground and gives full expression to the Christian perspective, which is elsewhere displaced. Structurally and symbolically, therefore, this section centres 'The Fatigue' and all the Roman poems, as *The Anathemata* is centred, in the Passion of Christ. As with the longer poem, the centre of 'The Fatigue' (which begins with material from an old draft of *The Anathemata*) was inserted into an early continuous draft which was split to accommodate it at what now corresponds to pages 31/40.

'THE TRIBUNE'S VISITATION'

In September 1972 after we listened to his recorded reading of 'The Tribune's Visitation,' David Jones told me, 'I feel inside that it is the best thing I've done.'[29] No comparison with *In Parenthesis* or *The Anathemata* was intended, for it is in reference to his shorter works that he writes, 'of all the separate pieces,' this is 'the best thing I've managed to make' (to G 14 July 1971). 'It states quite simply the situation of today,' he adds, and 'it's the "whole works" in brief space' (to G 15 August 1971). His estimation of the poem may seem surprising, since 'The Tribune's Visitation' lacks the intense lyricism of many of the other middle-length poems published in *The Sleeping Lord*. But 'The Tribune's Visitation' is an act of historical ventriloquism and, owing to dramatic decorum, its language must be, though not impoverished, at least restrained. The speaker of the monologue represents Roman pragmatism and is a self-declared enemy of poetry. Because his monologue is an argument, furthermore, rhetoric tends necessarily to displace lyricism. The restraint imposed upon language here symbolically correlates with the dehumanization that results from the speaker's rejection of traditional, gratuitous values. About this dehumanization David Jones said after listening to his recording of the poem, 'Chaps can't see that it is happening today.' No doubt his own estimation of the poem partly expresses a sense of prophetic urgency, but, as he fully realized, 'The Tribune's Visitation' is also a remarkable work of art. It is probably the most subtle and ambiguous of the poems in *The Sleeping Lord*. Certainly it is the darkest poem David Jones ever wrote. Its speaker is a Roman military tribune who, because of his iconoclasm and apparent honesty, resembles the existentialist spokesmen of the postwar French novel. But few figures in modern fiction are so complex and elusive. The fascinating complexity of this dramatic persona involves the relationship of his personality and his motives to his ideology, to the imagery he generates, and to the larger hermeneutical context of David Jones's modern literary and historical consciousness.

Throughout his monologue the Tribune's tone changes so that his personality seems in constant motion. First he is the imperious general officer, then the nagging noncommissioned officer, and then the fervent ideologue. For fleeting moments he is fussily human, briefly he is the genuine man with a personal history, and finally, at a level deeper than personality, he is the man who suffers. He seems progressively to shed layers of social and personal identity.

As his voice shifts, the viewpoint of his implied audience undergoes corresponding changes. Initially the Tribune addresses his audience as those who are apart from and in disagreement with him, then he empathizes with them, and occasionally he soliloquizes, allowing them to eavesdrop – as when, in parting, he addresses his words to Juno Lucina. When he speaks like this to himself or to the empty air, his monologue becomes interior monologue, which implies that he has absorbed his audience. And maybe he has. The effect of his shifting in tone and point of view is to disorient you from your own relatively fixed perspective. You are not sure where, vis-à-vis the Tribune, you stand. You are drawn into a radical experience of rhetorical relativity in which the Tribune's pragmatic reductionism comes to seem the only reality. This imaginative reorientation is not complete, however, largely because certain images, especially towards the end of his monologue, recall an alternative, Christian hypothesis. And, in retrospect, the reader's sense of disorientation may diminish as an apparent strategy emerges in the Tribune's rhetorical metamorphoses.

The voices of the Tribune correspond to levels of sensibility that are dissociated and mutually contradictory. He disparages poets but is himself a kind of poet, he attacks myth but seems credulous of a political myth, and he ridicules ritual but concludes his monologue by enacting a ritual. In short, the content of his monologue disagrees with the form of his monologue. This is a symbolic inconsistency, for he is a man opposing his own nature. His philosophy attacks the gratuitous life of imagination from which he cannot (or will not) entirely extricate himself. He seems, moreover, to suffer from the conflict, for, while he renounces personal and cultural values, he says he regrets their loss. And he advocates a dehumanization which his own personal warmth seems to contradict. Though he is the arch-technocrat of *The Sleeping Lord* and of all Jones's poetry, the Tribune is no stage villain.

The poem comprises four movements, the first of which is prefatory and lacks rhetorical direction. Its unity consists of its liturgical references, which establish a symbolic resonance that reaches to the end of the poem. The sergeant, to whom the Tribune first speaks, mentions

'October Games,' the Roman festival at which a horse is sacrificed by means of a spear. (From the reader's point of view, the reference to this festival implies an evocation of the *'lancea* / obliquely thrust' into Christ's body in 'The Fatigue.') The horse personates a vegetation god whose death ensures a full harvest. The Tribune himself then alludes to the Roman Hilaria, a festival which takes place at the vernal equinox. According to Sir James Frazer, this feast commemorates the resurrection of the vegetation god Attis and involves secret mysteries that 'seem to include a sacramental meal and a baptism of blood' (*The Golden Bough* IV 273–4). Then the Tribune refers to the Jewish Passover as comprising 'equinoctial runes / and full-moon incantations' (47). Because of its animal sacrifice and ritual meal, the Jewish Passover typologically subsumes the Roman feasts already mentioned and strengthens their Christian connotations. The Tribune sees prescribed military routine as liturgical too, and his monologue itself has liturgical analogues. What he says of the sergeant's belated attempt to call men to attention could serve as a text for the sermon he is about to deliver: 'A liturgy too late / is best not sung' (47).

The brief second movement twice involves 'a routine word' (47) such as an NCO might speak. He tells infantrymen they should be polishing weapons and armour instead of talking and singing round the fire. In passing he mentions Saturnalia, the fertility festival that is winter's counterpart to autumn's October Games and spring's Hilaria. As we shall see, the seasonal cycle and the cyclic momentum implied by this cumulative evocation of fertility rituals have a corollary in the overall form of the poem.

Out of the second movement's seminal antithesis between duty and fun comes the third movement, 'a more necessary word' (49). Here the Tribune attacks myth, ritual, folklore, and domestic attachments. They belong to the past, he says, adding that as modern men and better to serve the state his listeners must become pragmatic. Beginning with a reference to the Jordan falling into the Dead Sea, he spins a conceit for this need and for such a transformation. Just as familiar local streams and rivers leave home and cease being themselves when they empty into the world-sea, so we who have left home must cease being human, in the old sense. The image of the rain cycle is here broken and rendered teleological, ending in a universal, imperial dead sea. But since a part implies the whole, the fragment implies the entire rain cycle, which involves renewal as well as death, and contributes to the symbolic resonance already established by seasonal and ritual cycles.

In the fourth and final movement, the ritual motif evoked by allusions in the first two movements issues in symbolic form. The Tribune institutes a ritual meal to commemorate utilitarian purgation and the passage from myth to fact. In this he initially recalls, for the reader, Jesus at the Last Supper. The Tribune-persona becomes transparent here in this respect, but the poet preserves the Tribune's fictional integrity. As Jesus gives new meaning to the old forms of the Passover meal, the Tribune here gives new meaning, as far as he is concerned, to the sacramental meal of the Roman Hilaria, one of the festivals to which he alludes at the start of the poem. The Hilaria involves a ritual of initiation, furthermore, and this too he has in mind as he imparts to his men 'the gnosis of necessity' (58) and leads them through symbolic death to a metaphorical rebirth. The cycle of initiation is the poem's penultimate cyclic image. The final one is the diurnal cycle implied by the dawn.

This is not, however, the dawn of Good Friday with which 'The Fatigue' concludes. The Tribune's statement that the name Pontius is synonymous with trouble (47) suggests that probably, at the earliest, he is speaking late in Pontius Pilate's ten-year procuratorship, which ends in 36 AD, six years after the probable date of the execution of Jesus. As we shall see, the Tribune is quite capable of making his unguarded remark during Pilate's time as procurator, but he may well be speaking after the removal of Pilate from office on account of his intractably provocative attitude toward the Jews. Jones's prefatory reference to the *Cohors Italica* (45) suggests, moreover, a later date, around the year 40.

Unannounced, the Tribune enters a guardhouse on Jerusalem's wall in the early hours before dawn on the morning after Passover. For Romans it is the season of Hilaria, and as if in the spirit of that festival, men of the middle night watch, recently relieved, are mocking parade-ground discipline instead of attending to duties. The Tribune catches them at it and appreciates the humour, but is compelled to take the fun seriously. Part of what compels him is memory of those events in the not too distant past that impinge on Private Clitus's monologue. When the sergeant tells the Tribune he won his battle honours on 'the German *limes*' (46), he probably refers to the Teutoburg campaign in 15 AD, which was fought to occupy troops in order to forestall a repetition of the previous year's mutiny of soldiers in Pannonia. The Tribune refers directly to this mutiny when he mentions Vibulenus, its leader, and Lucilius, its most famous victim. Partly with this rebellion in mind, the Tribune attempts to reconcile his men to the world-order, which for them entails prolonged military servitude. The Passover, which celebrates the liberation of a people from slavery, is an ironic context for a speech such as this.

To reconcile his men to their condition, he must reshape their imaginations. He attempts to do this first of all by removing his listeners from a web of attachments that form a personal, cultural, and ritual continuity. For the Tribune, myth is 'fantasy' and ritual is foolishness. Metaphysically life is empty, however much its cultural husk retains emotional appeal. Even though traditional emotional attachments are regularly invoked for purposes of propaganda, they are dangerous, he says, because private loyalty 'by a subconscious trick / softens the edge of our world-intention' (52), and makes 'our bowels turn when we are commanded to storm the palisades of others' (55). A soldier must forget home, family, native drink, drinking songs, and native religious and folk festivals. He must cultivate detachment, become objective. To further this, these familiar things must be dissociated from their present military analogues. The 'chitty's fire' must not recall the family hearth, the ration of wine must not recall the wine of home.

Such detachment is attained only at great cost, as the Tribune testifies, perhaps sincerely, but also perhaps by way of a deliberate emotional appeal to his audience. As he counts the costs, he stirs the feelings he denies, and risks undercutting his position, though the risk may be worth taking to engage his audience.

For the reader, however, he unintentionally stresses in another way the moral incongruity he wants to avoid. He says that as he drinks 'the sour issue tot' he, like his listeners, remembers a 'fuller cup / from Luna vats' (53). David Jones said that these are the 'vats of Luna' in Macaulay's *Lays of Ancient Rome*. The allusion is to 'The Lay of Horatius,' whose hero dies defending early Rome from Etruscan aggression. The Tribune goes on to say that he too remembers home – the 'little porch below Albanus' which he sees in his mind's eye (53). This also evokes Horatius who, during his heroic struggle against aggression, sees 'on Palatinus the white porch of his home.'[30] What Romans suffered then and successfully resisted, they inflict on others now. This moral reversal is stressed when the Tribune refers to 'our world-Maristuran' (54) – *Maristuran* being Etruscan for 'Mars the Lord.' Rome long ago conquered Tuscany, so that its armies now contain many a soldier like the poem's Elbius 'with the Etruscan look' (47), but in the process the Etruscan spirit of conquest conquered Rome.

The Tribune and his listeners may share something like the modern reader's awareness of the ironic allusions to Macaulay, even though the *Lays of Ancient Rome* contains recreations, not translations, of ancient ballads. By the time in which Jones's poem is set, the Latin ballads have been lost for well over a century, and all that remains is the memory that they once existed.³¹ But Jones has anachronistically delayed the loss of these ballads so that legionaries from rural regions still remember and sing together the 'old rhyme' (50) of 'antique song ... Latin song' (51). We shall see that the Tribune prefers, or at least alludes to, the newer, Hellenized poetry of Virgil, which is, partly at least, imperialist propaganda. The Tribune opposes the old songs because they are, in a profound sense, anti-imperialistic propaganda. As Jones writes elsewhere, 'There is a sense in which *Barbara Allen* is many times more "propagandist" than *Rule Britannia*. The more real the thing, the more it will confound their politics' (A 22). The old Latin songs are 'Barbara Allen' to Virgil's 'Rule Britannia,' but the Tribune's listeners are being cut off – as, historically, they would already have been cut off – from elements in their heritage which celebrate pre-imperial virtues. The Tribune wants to complete the severance.

When David Jones has his Tribune call this 'a specific but recurring moment in *urbs*-time' (50), he has in mind Spengler's morphology of recurring phases of civilization. Because for Spengler and for Jones recurring phases are symbolically contemporary, the Tribune is a modern man for whom politics is autonomous, having lost 'connection not only with religion or metaphysics but also with all the other forms of man's ethical and cultural life. It stands alone – in an empty space.'³² Because the state is autonomous, it can be totalitarian. Although this has long been the underlying truth of state policy, it is not acknowledged by the official party line. Augustus re-established cults and priesthoods which the state continues to subsidize. This is precisely what the Tribune has in mind when he asks, 'does Caesar mime?' and answers, 'That seems about the shape of it' (56). All such pretence aside, 'now,' he says, 'we serve contemporary fact' (50). An exclusive emphasis on 'fact' is the essence of what Spengler calls 'Caesarism.' In a passage in *The Decline of the West* which Jones marked and which greatly influenced him, Spengler defines 'Caesarism' as 'the "will to power" which ignored traditions and reckoned only with forces. Alexander and Napoleon were romantics; though they stood on the threshold of Civilization [as distinct from Culture] and in its cold clear air, the one fancied himself an Achilles and the other read Werther. Caesar, on the contrary, was a pure man of fact gifted with immense understanding' (I 38).

Philosophically, the Tribune's 'Caesarism' resembles the positivism of the modern Hegelian philosopher Edward Caird, whom Jones saw as typical of our age. He writes in 1964 that Caird urged men to 'take particular facts for no more than they are,' and that 'with serene assurance he envisaged a world in which the notion of the sacral would not exist, where the whole idea of this or that material thing being the sign and figure of something other than itself would be excluded, except by artists and the like' (*DG* 201 n9). The Tribune makes basically the same exception: 'poets ... must need weave dreams and yet more dreams, saleable dreams, to keep the duns from doorstep,' and poets who are not pragmatists in this sense are fools with 'hearts as doting as those elder ministers who think the race of gods wear togas' (54). Not that poets, or priests for that matter, have any real social importance in the modern world of the first century or of now.

For the Tribune 'contemporary fact' is primarily 'the fact of empire' (51), but empires are never merely facts. All his demythologizing is for the sake of a political myth implied in Caesar's divine personification of the state. The modern version of the myth is Hegel's idealization of the state as the 'Divine Mind' as it exists on earth, a doctrine that encouraged the rise of fascist and Soviet totalitarianisms. The Tribune is an ur-Hegelian. For him, the personification of the state by *Divus Caesar* (43) involves a transferred epithet: the state, not Caesar, is god. This is what Jones calls 'the situation of today' because, as Simone Weil contends, nowadays 'the collective is the object of all idolatry' since it alone 'can be taken as an end, for in relation to the human person it possesses a kind of transcendence.'[33]

Roman deification of the state gives focus to the Jewish stricture against idolatry, which the Tribune evokes by reference to 'shorn' legionary standards (57). These aniconic standards, which lack the usual medallions bearing the image of the emperor, are the only ones used in Jerusalem because the Jews will not allow in the city the graven images on regular standards. For the Tribune, Pilate's name means 'trouble' partly because, by bringing standards with such images into Jerusalem, Pilate twice caused massive protest demonstrations.

What makes the Tribune's otherwise commonplace worship of society intriguing is that, while he absolutizes the state, he does not idealize it. He withholds his love, and seems actually to prefer certain things that are now lost and, he thinks, should therefore be forgotten. The 'older fantasies' are 'beautiful,' 'remembered demarcations' are 'sweet' (50), pieties are 'dear' (51), and differences are 'blessed' (54). It is not that these things should have been lost; they *had* to be lost. For the Tribune as for Marxists in modern times, the myth of the state is sustained by belief in historical determinism. This 'necessity,' which is also Spenglerian, has gravity as its metaphor in the Tribune's geographical conceit of streams and rivers – symbolizing all that man loves – falling to 'the indifferent sea' of world-wide empire (53). Because the state is all-important, all other things, men included, have value only to the degree that they are, as the modern cliché has it, 'useful to society.' This is 'the gnosis of necessity' (58) in which the Tribune as mystagogue initiates his listeners.

Their rite of passage is through death to a new life of sorts. Though he couches his remarks in the interrogative mood, he is honest about the reality of the death required:

> Are we the ministers of death?
> of life-in-death?
> do we but supervise the world-death
> being dead ourselves
> long since?
>
> Do we but organize the extension of death whose organisms withered with the old economies behind the living fences of the small localities? (56)

We are, or should be, 'dead to nature.' 'Yet,' he adds, 'we live / to Caesar / from Caesar's womb we issue / by a second birth' (58). The Pauline echoes underline, by contrast, the absence in this transformation of any benefit to man (see Romans 6:2, 8–10). But because his listeners cannot catch the allusions, for them the Tribune's baptismal image connotes a new vitality. The connotation is false, but the Tribune may not intend to coat the bitter pill or pretend that rebirth is anything but a metaphor for the cultural and spiritual abolition of man. As he notices the dawn, he asks, 'What light brights this deliverance? / From darkness / to a greater dark / the issue is' (58). Despair is the meaning of the 'greater darkness.' It intensifies the moral darkness in 'The Wall,' where enlisted men 'walk in darkness' (13) 'for twenty years of nights' (10), 'trapesing the macrocosmic night' that corresponds to 'the night within' (14). The Tribune does not hide from his listeners their proximity to the heart of darkness. 'Listen! be silent!' he insists, 'you *shall* understand / the horror of this thing' (54). In his recorded reading, David Jones emphasizes the words 'the horror' so that they cannot but recall the famous last words of Conrad's latter-day imperialist Kurtz

The language of the Tribune repeatedly implies continuity between ancient and modern forms of imperialism. When he says that 'Rome's back is never turned' upon its neighbours (48), he recalls the British empire upon which, according to the Victorian slogan, 'the sun never sets.' He also evokes George Orwell's fictional conflation of Nazi and Soviet states when he says, 'I am your elder brother' (57). Big Brother gives 'a human face' to the servile state he personifies, just as Caesar now does to the empire.

A consequence of the metaphorical humanization of the state is the dehumanization of its citizens. Human gratuity is diminished to the degree that it is projected onto the personified state. Now Caesar can mime, and Private Elbius cannot. The abomination of such personification is emphasized by the reigning Caesar probably being Caligula. But regardless of who the dictator is or whether he personifies society, the servile state always confiscates the freedom of its citizens.

Rhetorically, the Tribune's monologue is persuasion; its topic is dehumanization and so is its intended effect. Philosophically the Tribune corresponds to O'Brien in *Nineteen Eighty-four*, who tells his victim, 'If you are a man, Winston, you are the last man. Your kind is extinct; we are the inheritors.'[34] Man, as he has been traditionally understood, must make way for the technocrat. In a sense truer than metaphor, this is homicide. If the Tribune's assertion that he is his audience's 'elder brother' evokes Big Brother, it may also suggest that he is Cain to their Abel. The action of the Tribune as he speaks, therefore, repeats the action of the primitive Hilaria and Saturnalia. Both festivals originally culminate in human sacrifice. In this regard, at least, the Tribune resembles Pilate, the 'fact-man' of *The Anathemata* (239). When the Tribune says he 'would speak as Caesar's friend' (52), he unintentionally evokes Pilate who, to prove himself 'Caesar's friend' (John 19:12), has put Jesus to death.

The Tribune can commit metaphysical homicide because he has almost succeeded in killing himself. His inner conflict is not so much alive as remembered and, for rhetorical purposes, imaginatively resurrected. 'Reality' and 'necessity' do seem to have triumphed over his emotional and imaginative attachments.

The Tribune's rhetoric is nevertheless compelling largely because he is, for the most part, 'forthright Roman' (48). He avoids propaganda and may seem to offer no false consolation. But in the final pages of the poem, as his rhetoric comes full circle, he appears to restore in altered form all that he has said his listeners must do without. He has said that we must forget our homes (51–4), but now he says 'these guard-house walls ... enclose our home' (57). He has said we must deny 'the Lares of a remembered hearth' (50), but now he says 'this chitty's fire' is 'our paternal hearth' and 'these standards' are the household *penates* (57). He has said we must forget 'our sister's song' (52); now he says 'these fatigue-men ... busy with the pots' are 'our sisters' (57). He has said we must forget our native brew and old companions; now he says we are joined together as comrades, drinking the same 'issue cup' (58).

The Tribune, who disparages poets, has himself spoken poetically before this, but now he poeticizes with a vengeance. He may do so consciously, for he earlier boasts, 'I could analogise to the end of time ... and out-poet ovates ...' (48). Jones emphasizes the Tribune's poetic role by allowing him to quote from Wordsworth's definition of a poet in the Preface to *Lyrical Ballads*: the Tribune claims to speak 'as a man speaking to men.'[35] 'But,' he adds, 'as a special sort of man speaking to a special sort of men' (50). In other words, he is not an ordinary poet. What makes him peculiar as a poet is that his images tend to be metaphors. For a poet like Wordsworth and for most of us, home is a symbol – a real place, but also the embodiment of our most cherished values and associations. When the Tribune says the guardhouse is now home, he invokes two fixed and separate meanings, one eclipsing the other in a kind of ontological translation. The word survives as a homonym of its former self; the guardhouse can be home only because the word 'home' has lost its meaning. The translation from symbol to metaphor reduces human life to an allegory of what it was. In *The Decline of the West*, Spengler writes that 'the world-city means cosmopolitanism in place of "home"' and goes on to say, in a passage Jones marks, that 'home' is 'a profound word which obtains its significance as soon as the barbarian becomes a culture-man and loses it again as soon as the civilization-man takes up the motto "*Ubi bene, ibi patria*"' (133). The Tribune does not explicitly deny the loss involved in the transition from local culture to imperial civilization, but because his now figurative language has not entirely lost its meaning, the Tribune's metaphorical hearth, home, and family do suggest a continuity or restoration that is not in fact real. The connotations of these images resist the denotative meaning of his statements. They console for and make palatable the horror he says he wants men fully to feel. He may well have set about to resolve the doublethink or dissociated sensibility that propaganda feeds on and contributes to, but deliberately or not, he merely succeeds in refining that mental duplicity. Perhaps the Tribune cannot himself fully bear his own reality.

About such a man, the words of Private Clitus may serve as a warning:

> these fact-men, Oenomaus, have their hallucinations, don't forget that, indeed their delusions would beat a garret poet – only there's calculation in the very dreams of a Brasso. (22)

The Tribune establishes his affinity with Brasso of 'The Dream of Private Clitus' when he adopts the role of an NCO and orders his listeners to 'get on to ... those brasses' (47). (In fact, the Tribune-persona originates in the Brasso-like NCO of 'The Fatigue,' who in an early version of that poem dismisses the watch with the same command, 'get on those brasses.') The Tribune's sincerity does not preclude calculation. He takes us once again into the deceptive realm of what David Jones calls 'pseudo-Prudentia,' whose admonitions are made of 'Black Market products' and 'stolen prescriptions' from which 'certain important ingredients, suspending agents and solvents' have been omitted (E&A 146–7). Not much is missing. The Tribune's integrity is impressive, but finally he is one of 'the technicians' complained about in 'The Tutelar of the Place' who 'manipulate the dead limbs of our culture as though it yet had life' (64).

He is no mere pragmatist, however, at least not in his tone, for he speaks with the ardour of a committed ideologue. In his commitment to the truth as he sees it, there seems a large degree of philosophical gratuity. And because the truth is unappealing, he seems existentially heroic in his adherence to it.

Moreover, his central philosophical insight – the distinction between utility and gratuity – is sound. In a note concluding an early draft of the poem, Jones comments that the Tribune 'was in fact delineating a dichotomy inseparable from the human condition. His "Sergeant, that will serve for now" [58] is still serving – for we cannot resolve the dichotomy any more than could the tribune.' And he adds, irrespective of external, civilizational conditions, that this dichotomy is 'no less, *mutatis mutandis*, within the brain-pan of a tribal chief or that of Dr Nodens' calm, efficient & elegant stenographist.'

What seems especially genuine about the Tribune, moreover, and so further complicates our reaction to him, is his love of the 'sweet men'

(54). When he rejects the wine cup and companions of home for 'this issue cup' and the fellowship of his men, he exchanges a symbol not for a metaphor but for what is, at some level, another symbol. The new communion is real in so far as it is based on shared suffering. These men do have in common the 'red scar' of combat (57) and the inner wound of spiritual deprivation. To suffer is human, even though men cannot fully retain their humanity while renouncing it, and shared dispair is no basis for authentic communion. Their final fellowship is partly illusory, therefore, but the compassion of the Tribune makes it also partly real. The concluding rite that symbolizes this fellowship is consequently highly ambiguous.

Without realizing it, when he breaks 'this barrack bread' and drinks with his men 'this issue cup' (58), the Tribune mimics the words and actions of Jesus. The Tribune does not so much simulate the Last Supper, however, as he does its re-enactment in the Mass. For one thing, he salutes the standards, which contain the basic shape of the crucifix the priest salutes (by bowing) at Mass. The Tribune's final words are, furthermore, technically a *missa* – the term for the dismissal of soldiers which, by the year 400, designates an act of public worship and is the origin, therefore, of the word 'Mass.' The Mass of the Tribune moves from the Liturgy of the Word to 'the Offering proper' (cf A 195). The gifts offered up for desubstantiation are the human selves of the Tribune and his congregation.

This metaphorical Mass is an extension of the yearly public renewal of the legionary oath, which must recently have occurred, perhaps with the speaker presiding, since it takes place in March and before a tribune. The oath, *Idem in me*, is the *sacramentum*, from which the word 'sacrament' derives. Because the Tribune reaffirms this initiation oath during his ritual meal (58), the meal particularly resembles the Mass of the Easter Vigil, at which the faithful, likewise in the early hours before dawn, renew their baptismal vows. The correspondence to the Vigil suggests that the precise time of the Tribune's monologue is early Easter morning, though probably not the first Easter morning. His reference to Passover strengthens the suggestion. So does his parodying the Hilaria, for the feast of the rising of Attis is the pagan Roman counterpart of Easter. The Easter Vigil is, furthermore, an occasion not only for renewing baptismal vows but also for performing baptism. This secures the monologue's correspondence to the Vigil since, as we have seen, the Tribune is presiding over a rite of passage in which men are reborn to a new life, albeit that of spiritual humanoids.

The Mass of the Tribune and the dreadful baptism he administers deliberately exclude 'the leaven of illusion' which he thinks religion provides. The phrase conflates the New Testament's image of the kingdom of heaven with an evocation of Freud's positivist attack on religion as childish and neurotic in *The Future of an Illusion*. The phrase also recalls Marx's 'opium of the people,' but, unlike Marx, the Tribune resists the equally compelling illusion of modern political mythology, that human fulfilment comes entirely in and through society. His eucharist is thankless because he is honest about this.

His honesty establishes him as the latest in a line of literary technocrats who indulge in partly confessional monologues. Orwell's O'Brien speaks candidly to Winston Smith, as does Huxley's Mustapha Mond to John Savage. A variation on the type is Camus' philosophical reductionist Jean-Baptiste Clamence in *The Fall*. The prototype and greatest fictional character in this tradition is the Grand Inquisitor in Dostoevsky's *The Brothers Karamazov*. (When I asked the poet whether he thought the Tribune resembled the Grand Inquisitor, he answered enigmatically, 'They all make a lot of that.') The Tribune resembles the Inquisitor in his approval of Caesar and in his dedication to the idea of 'a world state,' but also in his apparent selflessness and spiritual desolation. Because he suffers, the Tribune may typologically conform — like the speaker of 'The Wall' — to the victim of sacrifice. His ritual meal, while it parodies the Mass, is not therefore without some element of straightforward symbolism. The physical and spiritual wounds upon which his new fellowship is based are symbolically continuous with the sufferings of Christ. Jones seems to indicate this when the Tribune says of men dozing in the guardhouse, 'let these sleep on and take their rest' (47), which echoes the words of Jesus to his sleeping disciples in Gethsemane (Matthew 26:45).[36] The Tribune and his ritual of despair are consequently more than mere objects of literary irony. If out of compassion Dostoevsky's Jesus kisses the Inquisitor, he would certainly kiss the Tribune. The Inquisitor rejects the kiss. We do not know whether the Tribune would reject it, though I suspect he would.

As he announces to his men the Bad News, the Tribune repeatedly echoes St Paul, his contemporary and fellow orator.[37] Paul too may now be engaged in the conversion of men. The allusions to him and the unintended miming of the Mass call to mind the growth of Christianity taking place probably even as the Tribune speaks. For the reader, therefore, his monologue recalls the spiritual renewal that is alleviating the despair the Tribune feels and revitalizing the civilization he sees as a living death. Although mixed with dark ironies, this benign evocation may be the ultimate significance of Jones's allusion to April Fool's Day as a modern counterpart of the Hilaria (46 n1). Historically and in the light of eternity, the joke is on the Tribune, though not necessarily at his expense.

In any case, there is an irony at once deeper and lighter than that which the Tribune intends in his parting reference to Juno Lucina. He asks her, present in the dawning, 'what irradiance / can you bring / to this parturition?' He alludes, perhaps intentionally, to Virgil's Eclogue 4, concerning the imminent return of the Golden Age. Virgil writes, 'Only do thou, pure Lucina, smile on the birth of the child, under whom the iron brood shall first cease and a golden race spring up throughout the world' (lines 8–10). For men who 'issue / by a second birth' 'from Caesar's womb' (58), the Tribune anticipates only a continuation of the dark age of iron. Underlying Virgil's apocalyptic political propaganda, which the Tribune dispenses with, is a pragmatism the Tribune would appreciate, for Virgil imputes great significance to the birth of a child to his patron, the consul Pollio, in what seems a sycophantic accommodation of political 'fact.' This eclogue represents the poetry that exists, as I suggested, in implied antithesis to 'antique ... Latin songs.' But poetry may mean more than its authors intend, and may alter in meaning with changing hermeneutical contexts. Owing to the spiritual and cultural transformation now taking place, this eclogue will acquire an authenticity that endows it, in retrospect, with the mythic power of the early Latin ballads. In the cultural darkness of which the Tribune is so painfully aware, the Easter light shines, and amid widespread and extreme dehumanization men are being born again in the Easter sacrament of baptism, so that while the Tribune speaks, the eclogue's prophecy, as the Church fathers interpret it, is being fulfilled, and the cultural synthesis that the eclogue will typify is becoming possible.

We have seen the Tribune's affinities with St Paul, Jesus, the Grand Inquisitor, Big Brother, Kurtz, Hegel, Freud, and Marx – but, for the poet at least, there is one more analogue. The monologue and its setting partly originate in a memory from his years of military service. Jones once played his recording of the poem to

> a chap who ... said of course it would be quite impossible for a *tribunus militum* to suddenly burst out in such a manner before a few N.C.O.s & men. But he supposed that was a, so-to-say, 'poetic licence' to convey what I wanted to say. But as a matter of fact, I once heard a fairly highly

placed officer make a speech not far removed from this [in] nature. He may have regretted it after, but it was to a few trusted 'other ranks' and apart from someone saying, in the fashion of the time, 'He's gone Bolshie,' I heard of no repercussions.   (to G 14 July 1971)

The officer's criticism, presumably of the High Command, here becomes the Tribune's revelation about the pretences of Caesar. What was in actual fact simple, benign, and entirely human is now altogether more complex.

The Tribune is the most elusive and disturbing of David Jones's personae. His monologue resembles Jones's later watercolour paintings, with their overlapping, semitransparent tones and multiple vanishing points. The overlapping tones invite the eye to various levels of penetration, and the vanishing points demand of the viewer a continuous shifting of point of view. As a viewer, you feel your consideration of the painting can never reach conclusion. Because the Tribune so often and so subtly changes his viewpoint and reveals various and conflicting levels of personality, you cannot be sure you have him figured out. You may feel he is being utterly candid, but his rhetorical skill is so great that you cannot be certain he is not, at times and maybe all the time, deliberately manipulating his audience. If you choose to trust him for the most part, as I do, you feel yourself caught up in the grip of his direct address, torn between the man, who attracts, and his message and intent, which repel. His human depth and sincerity compensate, to a degree, for his message, but they also underline the deprivation he urges in the total submission of man to the state.

As his passing resemblance to Brasso of the earlier poem suggests, the Tribune, like Brasso, is a negative foil to Private Clitus. Clitus is Roman Cockney; the Tribune speaks with patrician sophistication. One is warmly human; the other is warmly inhuman. The contrast between the two is emphasized by their extensive echoing of St Paul and by their each conducting an initiatory descent into Hades. For Clitus it is a mystical descent; for the Tribune, a ritual descent.

David Jones – who, as we have seen, resembles Private Clitus – seems to hint at his own relationship to the Tribune when the Tribune claims a 'Transpadane grandma' (48). For the Italian Tribune, a grandmother from 'beyond the Po' would be a Gaul. In the opposite direction, David Jones too has a transpadane grandma, since his maternal grandmother was (on her mother's side) of Italian descent. The inverse parallel suggests what is in any case true, that philosophically the Tribune is

David Jones inside out. Not that Jones's response to the Tribune would be one of simple opposition. The Tribune cannot be reduced to his philosophy. In that respect, his monologue contains its own rebuttal.

'THE TUTELAR OF THE PLACE'

'The Tutelar of the Place' is the hinge-poem in *The Sleeping Lord* between the Roman poems and the later, Arthurian poems. It is something of a coda, bringing together themes and images from the preceding poems. And it anticipates the Arthurian poems partly in its language and images and partly because its monologist is 'a Celt serving in the Roman army who is thinking of his homeland' (*LF* 37).[38] As a first-century Gallic recruit, he prays to the earth mother, whose cult is widespread among the Celts in the early centuries AD. But in its final form the monologue is unfixed in time. Jones writes that the poem expresses 'a state of mind which must have belonged to countless communities of people in various situations in history' and 'carries far forward' from Roman times 'into a *much* later period,' that of 'the Doomsday [survey], Charlemagne, missi [despatches]... early Wales, etc.' (*LF* 37). Facilitating this historical ubiquity is a lack of information about the monologist's occupation and setting and an archetypal universality in his terms of reference. In this poem, for example, the central government is identified merely as 'the Ram.'

Thematically, the poem concerns the relationships of child and adult, man and woman, place and person, heaven and earth, religion and poetry. Encompassing these themes is the perennial antithesis between humanity and technocracy, an antithesis symbolized by the opposition between the Tutelar and the Ram. The tutelary goddess promotes fertility and protects hearth and home. The Ram is named for the beast symbolizing empire in Daniel 8:4 and evokes the siege engine that levels homes. In a real sense, the Ram's spokesman is the Tribune of the previous poem, which Jones designates as this monologue's 'companion piece' (45). Within 'The Tutelar of the Place,' the opposition between the Ram and the Tutelar implies an argument between the Tribune and the thinking persona who reveres the Tutelar and whose consciousness is the main subject, as well as the vehicle, of the poem.

Like 'The Tribune's Visitation,' this poem consists of four principal rhetorical movements, but here they establish a significant parallel. First we read that the tutelary goddess 'bends her head from far fair-height' when her name is spoken 'as between sister and brother at the time of beginnings' (59). Next we read that 'she inclines with attention from far fair-height' as when adults enact religious rituals (60). The first statement ends in a reverie of children at play; the second, in a meditation on folk ritual. Then the monologist leads imagined children in childish prayer and finally he prays his own adult prayer, which occupies the latter half of the poem. Child's play and worship, each a quasi-dramatic miming, balance one another, as do the prayers of the children and the adult. The double parallel implies a psychological and spiritual correspondence between children and the sort of adult who can still play house in his imagination and who exercises religious faith. The correspondence is important to the relationship of this poem to 'The Tribune's Visitation.'

The Tribune's narrowly objective consciousness contrasts with the broad, integral awareness of the persona who reveres the Tutelar. The Tribune is little more than half a man: objective in his knowledge, subjective only in his regret. The persona of 'The Tutelar' also knows objectively. He is easily the equal of the Tribune in intellectual sophistication, but, as a man of religious faith, he knows subjectively as well. Psychologically he is whole because he lives in what Merleau-Ponty calls 'one intersubjective world.' To a degree then, and only as a mature adult in a late phase of civilization can, he enjoys the primitive awareness or *participation mystique* that Karl Stern attributes to children. In the previous poem, the Tribune, by debunking religion as fit only 'for the young time' and 'for child-man' (50), endorses this affinity between the primitive and the child and their further affinity with the believing adult.

The veneration of the goddess by the meditating persona in 'The Tutelar' symbolically preserves the matrix of his preterrational knowledge. Stern writes that 'All *knowledge* by *union*; all knowledge by incorporation (incorporating or being incorporated); and all knowledge through love has its natural fundament in the primary bond with the mother.'[39]

The origin of such knowledge in the relationship with the mother seems to underlie the correspondence between the absence or presence of such knowledge and the opposing attitudes towards women held by the Tribune and the meditating persona in 'The Tutelar.' The Tribune typifies the exclusively masculine, Roman sensibility glimpsed earlier in 'The Wall.' According to conventional imagery of sexual polarity, his characteristic objectivity and logic are masculine traits, and he is antifeminine. He insists that men forget the streams and rivers associated in memory with sisters and mothers (53). For him, fatigue men replace sisters, metaphorical rebirth is 'from Caesar's womb' (58), and 'Saturn's Tellus' (52) becomes 'the Italic fatherland' (51). In contrast, the persona in 'The Tutelar' is psychologically androgynous. His character combines the symbolically masculine and feminine qualities of objectivity and subjectivity, of analysis and intuition. Even his voice is androgynous, for he mimes an old woman putting children to bed. This imagined 'gammer' is symbolically important, furthermore, as the speaking counterpart to the Tribune's merely remembered 'Transpadane grandma.' Through the gammer-persona, the poem's primary persona imaginatively contains and preserves the femininity that theologically and psychologically sustains him. Throughout his monologue he celebrates the feminine, though never to the exclusion of its masculine counterpart. Sister plays with brother. The divine 'donabelle' evokes Anna Livia Plurabelle, and like Joyce's archetype, this 'Jill' has her 'Jac' (64). Dominance by the male is here not corrected by female dominance or even by female autonomy. Instead, antithesis calls for synthesis, and this is no mere restoration of balance or equality: it is wedding.

Psychologically this union may take place in a male, as it does in the poem's persona and in Private Clitus, and it may fail to take place in a female. 'The Ram's wife,' for example, chooses power over love (63). It is possible, therefore, for the male Lamb to be 'the spoiler' of the masculinized Ram (64). But, as the Lamb's mother, the Tutelar typifies half the qualities of mind and heart which humanize him and which he derives from his early communion with her.

The conflict between the Ram and the Lamb implies a contrast between the adult and the child, and between different types of males. It correlates, furthermore, with an implied contrast between the phallic battering ram, which is the Ram's homonym, and the equally phallic maypole. These latter resemble the contrasting horizontal and vertical wood on the world-ship in *The Anathemata*. The battering ram epitomizes power; the maypole, love. Where the Ram dominates, there is no vaginal 'crevice,' nor a living flower's phallic 'stamen' (63). Where the vertical maypole rises, marriage is celebrated between the king and queen of heaven, the latter being a 'queen *im Rosenhage*' (61) and 'Mother of Flowers' (63).

The heavenly royal couple correspond to the deities of fertility cult and, for the poet, to Christ and his bride, but the language by which they are evoked first of all recalls the king and queen of 'Sing a Song of Sixpence' and, repeatedly, Jack and Jill. The nursery rhymes strengthen the continuity between childhood and folk liturgy, and remind us that as children we first learn to distinguish between male and female and discover that they belong together. This dual awareness is expressed by the childhood play of sister and brother – she holding her doll, he holding at bay the family cat. 'Man-travail and woman-war here we / see enacted are' (59). The transferred epithets stress the psychological androgyny or marriage within the male and within the female as prerequisites to a healthy union of man and woman.

The Tutelar is 'of the place' partly because place is the next thing, after mother, that a person knows. Home is an extension of the womb; it encloses and accommodates. It is known, moreover, as the mother is known, subjectively. In *The Poetics of Space*, Gaston Bachelard describes how home becomes a potent personal symbol, imaginatively charged by hours of creative daydreaming during childhood. Such is the activity of brother and sister who 'prefigure and puppet on narrow floor-stone the world-masque on wide world-floor.' The home's 'door-stone and fire-stane,' 'childer-crock' and 'curd-cup,' 'settle' and 'trestle-struts' (59–60): all of these constitute a memory-map of the psyche which is presided over, in its genesis, by the mother. Because home and mother are continuous, the childhood home is felt as feminine. We see this when Private Clitus's dream of the earth mother takes him back to the family farm of his childhood. Primitive man sees a further dimension of the analogy, by which 'one earth brings us all forth, one womb receives us all' (59). But this is only a mythic extrapolation of the personalization of space which every child experiences. Because native place is personalized, it is necessarily distinct and special for all people, regardless of how 'neighbouring' they may be 'by nigh field or near crannog upstream' (59). The Tutelar of place is the divine 'belle of the mound' only for the human 'Jac o' the mound' who knows the place as no other can, because he loves it and because, in a sense, it loves him.

Such a man cannot but feel his relationship to place violated by the mathematical 'grids' with which the 'assessors bearing the writs of the Ram ... square the world-floor' (63). Mere measurement depersonalizes space by asserting equivalence between places. This occurs in *The Anathemata* when, during the world wars, 'they strictly grid / quadrate and number' the map of the sea (115). The Cartesian grid – from Descartes' analytical geometry – quantifies space for practical purposes. Personally significant space is circular; the decentring of space, which occurs when the Ram 'squares the world-circle' (64), is a violation of the person.

A symbolically related transformation occurs in the Tribune's geographical conceit in which all rivers and streams of individuation are lost in the liquid entropy of the tideless Mediterranean. Here a natural image illustrates an unnatural concept, but the metaphor is forced. A stream's water lost in the sea is not the stream, and time does not, as the Tribune implies, eradicate space. To this egalitarian conceit the persona of 'The Tutelar' implicitly objects when he asks, 'What co-tidal line can plot if nigrin or flax-head marching their wattles be cognate or german of common totem' (59)? No line of tidal equivalency can indicate kinship between the dark-haired man and the blond, or between their cult objects.

The poem's persona senses in the objectification of place an implicit threat to his humanity. As a prelude to exploitation, utilitarian detachment easily becomes a mental habit which may begin with nature but eventually extends to people. This is essentially why Blake, Goethe, and Kierkegaard objected to the Industrial Revolution. The Ram's technocrats are being psychologically consistent, after all, when they quantify space with grids, 'number the tribes' (63) and, like advertisers and pollsters, 'number the souls of men' (62). (Biblical evocations are operative here: in 1 Chronicles 21:1–3 Satan provokes David 'to number Israel ... from Beersheba even to Dan'; in Revelation those marked by the beast [13:16–17] sell the 'souls of men' [18:13].) The reification of man is already under way when 'the forked rod' divines water or 'the dark outcrop / tells on the hidden seam' of coal in 'the green valley' (63). These last words evoke the title of Richard Llewellyn's popular novel *How Green Was My Valley* (1939), but already the possessive pronoun is missing, together with the personal attachment it signifies. The loss is more sharply felt as a violation of the person when bureaucrats compute personal possessions for taxation: each 'hide and rod ... *pentan* and pent ... beast-head / and roof-tree' (62). These things 'counter, parti, pied, several / ... known and handled' (62) evoke Hopkins's 'Pied Beauty,' in which particular things are appreciated as beautiful in themselves and as redolent of God's glory. To enumerate such things as a measure of exploitability is 'to audit what is shameful to tell' (62), as the Anglo-Saxons knew who suffered the Norman survey of the Conqueror (cf A 212 n2).

The poem's persona affirms the human attachments the Tribune denies. He remains faithful to the awareness of the primitive and the child, but without pretending that for an adult in a late phase of civilization these are, in themselves, philosophically valid. In this respect he concurs with the Tribune. Both men demythologize place by asserting that the mother does not inhabit the earth. But their reasons differ. One man thinks she does not exist, while the other believes she resides in heaven. As a positivist, the Tribune is constrained by intellectual consistency to deny the part of his humanity that originates in, and is preserved by, the feminine personalization of place. The persona in 'The Tutelar' affirms this personalization as permanently, symbolically valid because he believes in the reality of the mother in her celestial sphere, which while distinct from earth is continuous with it.

He is at one, therefore, with the men and women who look for, assert and celebrate this continuity in folk ritual. The 'beating feet' (60) of the poem's ritual dancers evoke the 'Feet / rising and falling' in T.S. Eliot's 'East Coker' during a midsummer night's dance, 'signifying matrimonie' (1, line 30). In 'The Tutelar,' however, the marriage celebrated is between the male and the female principles, which is also a marriage between heaven and earth. For primitive man, the marriage of heaven and earth would be implied by the union of sky father and earth mother – a notion which may influence the poem's persona though, for him, the divine male and female both inhabit heaven.

It is largely in another sense, then, that the marriage of heaven and earth takes place in this poem's ritual dancing. The maypole of the cosmic marriage-dance is 'the sawn lode-stake on the hill where the hidden stillness is at the core of struggle' (61). The stillness recalls 'the still point' of the dance in Eliot's 'Burnt Norton' (2, line 62), which gives the earthly dance its meaning and allows it, in Jones's poem, to partake of the heavenly dance round a living, 'green lode-tree' where struggle is transformed,

> Where the marauder leaps the wall and the wall dances to the marauder's leaping, where the plunging wolf-spear and the wolf's pierced diaphragm sing the same song ... (61)

Again 'Burnt Norton' is evoked, for in Eliot's poem, below 'the bedded axle-tree / ... the boarhound and the boar / Pursue their pattern as before / But reconciled among the stars' (2, lines 2, 59–61).

In dancing, correspondence becomes continuity, and earth and heaven symbolically unite to accommodate man fully. 'There is only one dance,' as Eliot says. And this dance is, for the Celtic persona, what the sacred city is for the Roman persona of 'The Wall.' As sacramental media of eternity, moreover, the primitive dance and the ancient city are symbolically cognate because of the relationship of each to the troia. Although the Celtic maypole-dance is chiefly concerned with fertility, it does, in a sense, establish and preserve home 'within our labyrinth' (61). And like the city with its prismatic extension and astronomical foundation in the heavens, the dance has its heavenly extension in

> far fair-height outside all boundaries, beyond the known and kindly nomenclatures, where all names are one name, where all stones of demarcation dance and interchange, troia the skipping mountains, nod recognitions. (60)

The imagery seems as much to distinguish earth from heaven as to relate them, and so it may seem to reduce continuity to correspondence. But here the heavens, the traditional symbol of eternity, evoke the entire material universe as conceived of in modern physics. This is home indeed – our universe, of which Galileo supposedly said *eppur si muove* (*DG* 198). The stones dancing troias round the skipping mountains (an allusion to Psalm 114:4) mime planets orbiting their suns as they, in turn, move in their moving galaxies. The moving structure of the celestial macrocosm also informs the mini-microcosm of the atom, as the poet implies when his persona refers to inhabited places as 'nucleated holdings' (61). Orbiting planets, human dancers, and whirling electrons give special meaning, furthermore, to 'the exorbitance of the Ram' (63), whose operations do not comply with the economy of heaven since they violate the moving structure of material and psychological ontology.

The poem's primary symbol, the centre within multiple circumferences, recalls the structure of *The Anathemata*. Here, however, the image is not reflected in narrative structure but is echoed throughout the poem in analogical images. Its shape resonates in the circle-dance round the maypole, in the troia which the persona prays will encircle 'the holy mound' (64), and in the womb of the Tutelar which encloses the Lamb.

The most powerfully evocative of these analogous images is itself enwombed by parentheses: '(within the curtained wood the canister / within the canister the budding rod)' (64). The curtained outer container is the Holy of Holies; the inner container is the Ark of the Covenant (see Exodus 26:33). The latter has affinity with the Tutelar as 'arc of differences' (63; from the Latin *arx, arcis*, 'fortress or refuge') and with Mary, one of whose epithets in her litany is 'Ark of the Covenant.' These associations symbolically dovetail with the affinity between the poem's

Lamb and Jesus and between these and the Ark's 'budding rod,' which is 'Aaron's rod that budded' (Hebrews 9:4). Its budding correlates with fertility ritual and signifies hope for a cultural-religious springtime. As a rod it is phallic, furthermore, and its containment within a female symbol suggests sexual intercourse. Although they seem mutually exclusive as concepts, the rod's gestation and intercourse here symbolically coincide because generation and fruition are spiritually simultaneous.

The encircled centres of 'The Tutelar' evoke and therefore partly symbolize tradition, but the poem's chief symbol of tradition is the hearth-flame, the living nucleus of the home and therefore of the troia. The hearth is the locus of physical and imaginative nourishment, and the symbol of continuity by which 'our *disciplina*' is 'given to us' (61). The origin of the hearth-fire is so far in the past that it is uncertain: 'the seed of far-gaffer? fair gammer's wer-gifts' (60)? In other words, an ancient progenitor may have carried a smoldering coal – an act evocative of pregnancy, though masculine in its sexual image – or the fire may have been kindled by a grandmother's manlike labour (*wer* is Old English for 'man'). In the generation of fire, then, as in the poem's imagined child's play, there is intrapersonal sexual wedding – which seems to correspond to the bonding of the proton and the neutron in the atom. Matter itself, the human person, the married couple, the home, and now the home-fire live because of sexual wedding. Like the Vestal flame, whose origin is the hearth-fire, the hearth-flame is never intentionally allowed to go out. Physically and metaphysically it warms 'kith of the kin' as, under the form of 'the chitty's fire' in 'The Tribune's Visitation,' it warms legionaries and draws from them 'that chatter and that witch-wife song' of their native hearths (49). The persona of 'The Tutelar' prays for the survival of the hearth-fire and its attendant traditions when he asks the goddess to 'pile the dun ash for the bright seed' (64), which is the 'seed of fire' (90). It is symbolically cognate with 'the secret seed' of vegetation which is to be hidden, the persona hopes, 'under the mountain ... between the grids of the Ram's survey' (64). Both seeds contain the integrity of spiritual culture and true humanity. For the Celtic meditator, furthermore, fire may have a special, symbolic equivalence with man, since the Welsh word for man is cognate with the Welsh for heat and for spark – which suggests, as George Borrow puts it in *Wild Wales*, that 'the ancient Cumry entertained the idea that man and fire were one and the same.'[40]

Hiding vital seed 'under the mountain' evokes biblical end-time, in which men cry 'to the mountains ... Fall on us, and hide us' (Revelation

6:16). But the apocalypse that now threatens hearth and home is in accordance with 'the Ram's book of Death' (63) instead of 'the Lamb's book of life' (Revelation 21:27). Throughout 'The Tutelar,' heights, hills, mounds, tumps, and mountains are identified with home because in primitive cultures they are places of safe habitation. And because they are also sacred places, heights symbolize heaven and help secure the imaginative wedding of heaven and earth. Instead of 'twin-*urbes*,' primitive man inhabits twin heights. When the Tribune urges men to forget the hills of home – Apennine, Palatine, and Mons Albanus where his own home is – he is breaking the ancient symbol of heaven as man's essential home and of its continuity with his earthly home. For the advent of secular man, heights must psychologically be made low. The apocalyptic image is not mine; the Tribune says that the 'Ordovician hills' of Britain are 'shortly to be levelled to the world-plain' (55; see Isaiah 40:4, Luke 3:5).

Home and tradition are synonymous. To eliminate both, the Ram has only to eliminate one, but he batters at each. His economic-industrial strategy compels men to go 'from this mountain' to 'the rectangular tenements' of the city, and there to spend their days working 'in the houses of the engines' (63). Imperial Rome, the 'great city' of Revelation (17:18), here merges with its modern counterparts. It becomes even more transparent to modern cities 'in the bland megapolitan light' of nineteenth-century gas and more recent electricity, which eliminate even the elemental diversity of day and night. But social co-ordination, or *Gleichschaltung* (63), is not limited to cities, for the Ram's commissioners travel, and his 'decree concerning the utility of the hidden things' applies universally (64). Everywhere 'the rootless uniformities' replace 'the holy diversities' of traditional culture (62). Home gradually disappears, therefore, even for the person who refuses to leave his native mountain.

The influence of the Ram is counteracted in the poem by the persona's concluding prayer, which is the positive counterpart of the Tribune's concluding ritual in the preceding poem. Here as there the conclusion of the poem is dramatic as well as rhetorical. By praying, the persona in 'The Tutelar' is himself keeping alive the hearth-flame of tradition and enwombing in his consciousness the secret seeds and budding rod of cultural vitality. The poem's title consequently applies to him as much as to the goddess, for he too is the guardian of place, and in a real sense she lives in and acts through him. This may be implied when he asks the feminine archetype, under the Welsh name for Mary, to dance a troia for the defence of home and tradition, since in rhythm and sound he enacts the very dance he prays for:

> Sweet Mair devise a mazy-guard
> in and out and round about
> double-dance defences
> countermure and echelon meanders round
> the holy mound
>   fence within the fence ... (64)

If the troia dance is a prayer, his prayer is a verbal troia.

The relationship of language to liturgical dance suggests that in this poem, as in 'The Fatigue' and 'The Tribune's Visitation,' poetry is itself an important theme. This may be implied by the poem's allusions to *Four Quartets*, which has poetry as its secondary theme. It is certainly implied by the linguistic conceit in the persona's opening description of ritual dancing:

> As when on known-site ritual frolics keep bucolic interval at eves and divisions when they mark the inflexions of the year and conjugate with trope and turn the season's syntax, with beating feet, with wands and pentagons to spell out the Trisagion. (60)

'Spell' here has two meanings, for to spell is to read or write, and by casting spells primitive men discern and profess belief in the Trisagion – the Thrice Holy God who is for the Celtic persona the triple goddess. If dancing cult-men 'laud and magnify ... with halting sequences and unresolved rhythms, searchingly ...' (60), so do poets like Hopkins and Eliot, to whom we have seen Jones allude in this poem. The author of *The Anathemata* suggests his own affinity with dancing cult-men when his persona describes them here as seeking 'hidden grammar to give back anathema its first benignity' (61). Hopkins, Eliot, David Jones: these are pre-eminent among modern poets who celebrate what the Christian liturgy celebrates. They work at 'gathering all things in, twining each bruised stem to the swaying trellis of the dance' (61). This is the business of the liturgy and, in an analogous sense, of the arts, for if the language here echoes St Paul on gathering 'together all things in Christ,' it also echoes Stanley Spencer's statement, which Jones considers an 'apt expression of the artist's business': 'All must be safely gathered in' (E&A 243). The alternative to the utilitarian civilization of the Ram may initially be to retreat into the private imagination, but even in an age of almost complete secular pragmatism, such personal enwombing may issue in poetic birth, which begins, at least, to restore to man his full humanity. The persona is himself an incipient poet, and by giving independent life to the gammer, he establishes a correspondence between himself and David Jones, who creates all the speaking personae of these poems.

In the privacy of his imagination, the persona's concluding prayer is a poem. And outside of the dramatic fiction of the work, it concludes exactly the sort of poem that attempts to preserve important human values. The relationship between the private, poetic prayer and the published poem is underlined by an allusion to one modern poem in particular with which 'The Tutelar of the Place' has a marked affinity. When the persona asks the Tutelar to remember those gone off to the secular city, even 'though they shall not come again' (63), he echoes the persona of Eliot's 'Ash Wednesday,' who prays for himself 'Although,' as he says, 'I do not hope to turn again' (6, line 1). Eliot's poem is also a prayer to the female Tutelar of place, referred to as 'Blessèd sister, holy mother, spirit of the fountain, spirit of the garden' (6, line 9). Eliot's poem concludes with the words, 'Suffer me not to be separated / And let my cry come unto thee' (6, lines 34–5). Jones's persona opens his prayer with the same liturgical response (62), suggesting that the one poem-prayer begins where the other leaves off.

As we have seen, within the poem the adult's prayer parallels the child's prayer. The parallel is emphasized by the correspondence between Lupa in the child's prayer and the Ram in the adult's prayer. The two animals are symbolic cognates, furthermore, because the wolf is the totem of Mars and, in the zodiac the Ram is Aries, corresponding to the month of Mars and a homonym for Ares, the Greek counterpart of Mars. The child is made to pray about the wolf, 'Make her bark keep children good' (61) – in other words, let children be afraid of the wolf who 'sniffs the lode-damps for stragglers late to byre' (60). The threat of wolves to children helps to locate narrated setting in Gaul and links imagined ancient children to their real modern counterparts. The origin of the best-known English lullaby, 'Hush a by baby,' is thought to be a corruption of what French nurses used to sing to their obstreperous charges, '*Hé! bas, là le loup*' (Hush, here comes the wolf).[41] And when modern children sing 'Who's afraid of the big bad wolf,' they express a residual fear of wolves. The correspondence between the Ram and the wolf establishes an archetypal continuity of healthy fear, and the correspondence between the prayers of the child and the adult suggests the childlikeness that underlies the transformation of soldiers into children in 'The Dream of Private Clitus' and is essential to true religion.

This fear and the desire for a renewal of this childlikeness are what motivate the persona's final plea to return to the womb:

> Open unto us, let us enter a second time within your stola-folds in those days – ventricle and refuge both, *hendref* for world-winter, asylum from world-storm. (64)

As with the desire to return to the womb in 'The Dream of Private Clitus,' Freudian connotations apply here. The persona desires the protection that he himself offers to children in their grandmother's voice: 'here's a rush to light you to bed / here's a fleece to cover your head / against the world-storm' (60). The allusion to 'Oranges and Lemons' adds to the poem's nursery associations, but it also implies that the world-storm involves 'the chopper to chop off your head.' The allusion may also evoke the world of *Nineteen Eighty-four*, in which this nursery rhyme is a dominant motif. That would balance the allusion in 'The Tribune's Visitation' to Big Brother. The reality of the danger to man posed by the Ram justifies the persona's yearning for protection. There is also a death-wish here but, as in 'The Dream of Private Clitus,' death is heaven's entrance. So Freudian metaphor combines, at the conclusion of the poem, with the physiological literalness of Nicodemus, who thinks that to be 'born again' a man would have to 'enter the second time into his mother's womb' (John 3:4).

The spiritual and psychological balance and the resulting imaginative vitality of this poem's persona seem, in 'the December' of his culture (64), to be a thing of the past. But they are of the future too, as are the same characteristics in Private Clitus, who, though Roman and obviously less sophisticated, resembles this Celt. That the persona in 'The Tutelar' belongs to the future is suggested by the poem's extensive use of Anglo-Saxon vocabulary, compound nouns, and kennings, and the rich alliteration characteristic of Old English and Middle Welsh poetry. The phrase 'mistress of asymmetry' is, for example, a perfect equivalent of Welsh *cynghanedd*. One effect of all this aural medievalism is to make 'The Tutelar' the most richly lyrical of the poems so far considered. Its lyricism is enhanced, moreover, by proximity to the crisp but relatively bare language of the utilitarian Tribune. In texture of language 'The Tutelar' resembles the Arthurian poems that follow it more than the

Roman poems it brings to conclusion. This richness of language is related, of course, to its theme of poetry as a means of preserving and restoring authentic spiritual culture. Even more richly lyrical is the language of 'The Hunt,' the following poem, which is set at the end of the 'world-winter' in the beginning of the cultural spring that the persona in 'The Tutelar' longs for.

'THE HUNT'

At four and a half pages, 'The Hunt' is the shortest of David Jones's middle-length works. The lyrical appeal of its language is immediate, strong, and continuous. Its allusions are unobtrusive, their meanings not essential to initial comprehension or emotional response. And the force with which it conveys the intense and galvanizing stress that transforms a body of men in the moments before combat is remarkable. In his own recorded reading, David Jones provides easy access to the poem's depth of feeling and auditory richness. This richness consists of interpenetrating alliterative patterns which approximate the *cynghanedd* of Middle Welsh verse and so constitute a continuous historical allusion. But you do not have to catch the allusion to enjoy the sound; before beginning to comprehend in any depth the meaning of 'The Hunt,' the reader is caught up in the rich texture of its sounds and images. But 'The Hunt' also has depths of meaning that expand the poem's initial appeal to the full aesthetic resonance of an important literary work.

In 'The Hunt' Arthur leads mounted men against the monstrous boar Trwyth, which symbolically incorporates the historical reality of foreign invasion, recalled by 'the defences of the hill' (67), and also the internal divisiveness that so often undermined Celtic political autonomy (cf E&A 237). We know from the original story in 'Kulhwch and Olwen' that before coming to Britain the boar has laid waste nearly half of Ireland. Because of its destructive power, the boar is, in physical terms, the early-medieval, legendary equivalent of an atomic holocaust. A variation of the previous poem's Ram-archetype, this is the beast of the Celtic, Dark-Age apocalypse. In the introductory notes for his reading of the poem, Jones writes that 'the great boar is the personification of destructive potency, so that the tale is largely one of the immemorial struggle between what is salvific and what is inimical – "cosmos" against "chaos."'[42] But while the boar is the primary concern of the original Welsh story, it is merely the occasion for Jones's poem. On the level of narrative, moreover, almost nothing happens in 'The Hunt.' Its theme is delineated not in action but by structure, point of view, allusion, and imagery – which combine to exemplify what has come to be called 'technique as discovery.'[43]

The subject of 'The Hunt' is basically twofold. The first two pages concern the men of Arthur's war-bands; the second two pages concern Arthur. Coinciding with this division of subject is duality of genre. The first half of the poem is anatomy; the second half is primarily symbolism. The two halves work in opposite imaginative directions: anatomy discriminates, proceeds by analytical division; symbolism assimilates, creates synthesis. So an initial tendency toward scattering is countered, in the poem's second part, by a symbolic gathering. There is, furthermore, a brief coda of less than half a page, which concerns the entire body of men as a whole. This coda suggests that Arthur has resolved the initial, analytical diversities, so that the second part of the poem transfigures the first part. But structurally the poem remains double in focus.

In the first half, the anatomy comprises social, psychological, and moral antinomies. Because there are three principles of division, the categories of division overlap. A given rider may be, for example, highborn, passionate, and cowardly. But another man of equal social rank may be even tempered and brave. Since no gradations between extremes are mentioned, there are nine possible combinations. In specific ways, therefore, each man resembles or differs from each of the others. Riding in unison, they constitute a social Celtic interlace, for which Jones provides a corresponding image in the word 'wattle' (65). Analytical discriminations give this riding society an ambiguous relationship to time. Social distinctions of class and privilege fix men in specific historical time, whereas distinctions according to temperament and moral inclination establish each man as a sort of Anyman inhabiting every time.

The various tensions generated by analytical antitheses and subsequently by structural division anticipate metamorphosis, which is the poem's recurring motif. One aspect of metamorphosis is cultural. Historically 'The Hunt' is set in a period of transition. Britain at this time is, as Jones writes in 1961, 'rather like the Congo today' (to G 23 March) – post-imperial, experiencing a resurgence of tribalism. While the riding of mounted war-bands recalls the dominant strategy of the late empire and forecasts the chivalry of the High Middle Ages, these riders are no longer cavalry and not yet knights: they are warriors. The Celtic tribalism of the distant past now characterizes the present, replacing the Roman civilization of the recent past and foreshadowing the feudalism yet to come. *Civitas* gives way to *comitatus*. As a time between times, this is primarily a beginning. Arthur and the war-bands move in 'the lateral light' (67) of symbolic 'morning' (69). In his essay 'The Myth of Arthur,' the poet writes that the age of Arthur is 'a bright birth-time' after 'the long toil and dark winter of the West' (E&A 256). The impetus of this unfinished cultural metamorphosis is a spiritual transformation whose effect on society is the main theme of the poem. The interrelated spiritual and cultural metamorphoses symbolically merge in a common archetype: Arthur and his men ride for the renewal of the Waste Land.

In its spiritual aspect, metamorphosis is reflected in the work's form. The structural and generic transition from anatomy to symbolism involves a transformation in the perspective of the poem's implied narrator. During the anatomy of the war-bands, the narrator's consciousness remains apart from what he considers and immersed in its own abstract categories, so that the reader actually experiences the speaker's mind as much as the society he analyses. When the speaker shifts his attention to Arthur, however, analysis gives way to contemplation and consciousness becomes nearly transparent. Description moves, temporarily at least, from the past tense into the present tense. And now instead of abstract discriminations there are contrasting emotions: the speaker says of Arthur that 'if his eyes are narrowed from the stress of the hunt and because of the hog they are moist for the ruin and for love of the recumbent bodies that strew the ruin' (67). Narrative point of view nearly merges with its object in a new, lyrical immediacy that culminates in the almost microscopic detail of the cock-thrush simile:

> Like the breast of the cock-thrush that is torn in the hedge-war when bright on the native mottle the deeper mottling is and brighting the diversity of textures and crystal-bright on the delicate fret the clear dew-drops gleam: so was his dappling and his dreadful variety ... (68)

The epic formality of the simile highlights by contrast the breathless accretion of detail. Description here tends to go its own way and borders on ecstasy. As though regarding an icon, the speaker (and therefore the reader) views the figure of Arthur without awareness of his own fixed position in space and time. Consequently, Arthur, unlike the war-bands he leads, seems not to inhabit time. The description of Arthur here complements the powerful, numinous picture of his wife, Gwenhwyfar, in *The Anathemata*. Like her, Arthur is silent throughout. Like her he is doomed in time by 'calamitous jealousy' (65). And like her, he becomes a numinous figure of anagogical proportions.

The transformation in narrative point of view corresponds to a change in range of allusion. In the first part of 'The Hunt,' references are mostly to the ancient Welsh Triads and to distinctions codified in the tenth-century Laws of Hwyel Dda. Such documents are solely historical in importance and help to root the poem in the past. In the second part of the poem, allusions are mostly literary, mythic, and biblical. They tend to liberate Arthur from time and – because they identify him with figures who are, in various ways, divine – they suggest that Arthur is, symbolically at least, a god.

Arthur's liberation from time and his identification with gods owe a lot to the resurgence of Celtic tribalism, which fills the void left by the collapse of Roman civilization. As 'the speckled lord of Prydain' (68), Arthur himself evokes this resurgence of the past. In an early draft of 'The Hunt' the word Prydain, spelled Priten, is glossed by Jones:

> from the fourth century B.C. until the time of the Caesars geographers called these islands the Pretanic Isles, implying Pretani for the inhabitants. This word can be identified with the early native form, i.e. Priten, and it is supposed that later writers, in using the word Picti of the northern inhabitants, were only translating into late Latin this native word for painted or speckled by which originally the men of the whole island were known. (*RQ* 25–6 n55).

Because of his 'dappling' (68) 'the speckled lord of Prydain' is a visual flashback to the pre-Roman, pre-Christian past in which Arthur has his mythic origins.

One of the gods with whom Arthur has affinity through his continuity with the past is Arawn, prince of Annwvyn, the Celtic Otherworld. Jones calls him 'the Prince of Hunters' in the 'Sleeping Lord' fragment (91). In 'Pwyll Prince of Dyfed,' the first branch of *The Mabinogion*, the hunting dogs of Arawn are described in these words: 'and as the whiteness of their bodies shone, so did the redness of their ears glisten.'[44] In 'The Hunt' it is said of Arthur that

> ... if through the trellis of green
>   and between the rents of the needlework

>   the whiteness of his body shone
>   so did his dark wounds glisten.   (68)

The evocation of the dogs of Annwvyn implies that Arthur too is from the Otherworld and suggests an affinity with Arawn. The suggestion is a likely one because in the history of folk tradition Arthur displaces Arawn. Arthur leading the hunt evokes, for example, the pan-European folk motif of *die wilde Jagd*, in which the leader of the Wild Hunt is generally identified as Arthur but is thought originally to have been Arawn.[45]

Arawn may, in turn, subsume or merge with older cult figures. As the poet writes in a manuscript note closely associated with an early draft of 'The Hunt,'

> it seems likely that the Arthur-motif, in some form or other, may have been present from very remote times. There is, for instance, the suggestion that the Gaulish inscriptions commemorating an agricultural deity, Artaius (later a war-god) and the female deity Artio (associated with a bear-symbol) may connect with a bear-totem of a still earlier society; that many centuries later the name of an historical leader, Artorius ... became associated with the immemorial, primeval cult-figure or figures – at least with regard to the protector and saviour motifs, to the dying-and-living-deity concept.[46]

The 'Ar' root common to the names of the figures mentioned in this passage strengthens the likelihood of Arawn's assimilating the earlier gods and being himself assimilated by Artorius-Arthur.

Jones implies that, for his followers, Arthur tends to personify a 'sky-god' (67n), who would be 'the hero of a Solar Myth' (E&A 240). This gives an extra, mythic dimension to the hunt's taking place in the morning, and extends the remarkable solar motif we saw in 'The Fatigue.' It also associates Arthur with the widespread folk motif of seasonal battle between the fertility god and his antithesis. A glimpse of such warfare appears in a passage in *The Mabinogion* that Matthew Arnold, in a book Jones read, links to 'the great feast of the Sun among Celtic peoples.'[47] The passage, in 'Kulchwch and Olwen,' concerns Gwythyr and Gywnn, who fight for the maiden Creiddylad (the prototype of Cordelia) 'each May calends till the day of doom.'[48] In the first branch of *The Mabinogion*, Pwyll breaks this cyclic pattern when, standing in for Arawn, he kills the figure who has been coming annually to fight Arawn for his kingdom – so that, through his human counterpart, the god finally triumphs. The cyclic character of the original pattern probably informs the traditional belief that Arthur, dead or asleep, will come again. But because of immediacy of narrative perspective, in 'The Hunt' there is no sense of cyclic repetition. The present contest is everything. It has the urgency of a Last Battle, a Celtic Armageddon.

Arthur's correspondence to a god of fertility is further suggested when he is called the 'man in the green' (68), words which evoke folklore's Jack o' the Green. The phrase also alludes to *Sir Gawain and the Green Knight*, in which the marvel-figure who survives decapitation and, like Arthur, leads a boar hunt, is twice called 'the man in the green' (lines 2227, 2259). Some scholars identify this figure with Arawn, others with a vegetation god.[49] Symbolically, in any case, Arthur combines gods of both animal and vegetable fertility. The vegetation god seems dominant, since Arthur rides 'for the healing of the woods' (68), but animal life is also important. Dogs and horses partake in the hunt, and when all the hunters pause at the check, their hard breathing, in addition to shaking 'the silent flora,' wakes the forest's 'fauna-cry' (68–9).

Nevertheless, the poem's imagery does emphasize Arthur's association with vegetation. His face is several times compared to the surface of the earth (67), and he is verbally equated with the forest:

> ... by reason of the excessive fury of his riding when he rode the close thicket as though it were an open launde
>   (indeed, was it he riding the forest-ride or was the tangled forest riding?)   (67)

The second line of the question in parentheses may take the viewpoint of Arthur, relative to whom the forest seems to be rushing past, but the line also suggests that Arthur himself is the 'riding' forest. This meaning becomes primary when, as the passage continues, Arthur is seen to represent the forest in all its manifold diversity:

> for the thorns and flowers of the forest and the bright elm-shoots and the twisted tanglewood of stamen and stem clung and meshed him and starred him with variety
>   and the green tendrils gartered him and briary-loops galloon him with splinter-spike and broken blossom twining his royal needlework
>   and ruby petal-points counter
> the countless points of his wounds ...   (67)

The red petals that counterpoint Arthur's wounds are probably those of the wood anemone (cf 74) — the flower of the vegetation god Adonis, who receives his fatal wound from a boar during a hunt.

In the passage quoted above, the fertility quest underlying cosmic battle resonates in the mode of romance typology with the thirteenth-century tale *Aucassin et Nicolette*. In the medieval tale the knight Aucassin frantically rides through a forest

> in search of Nicolette, and the charger went right speedily. Do not think that the spines and thorns were pitiful to him. Truly it was not so; for his raiment was so torn that the least tattered of his garments could scarcely hold to his body, and the blood ran from his arms and legs and flanks in forty places, or at least thirty, so that you could have followed after him by the blood which he left upon the grass.[50]

In 'The Hunt' the imagery is less grotesque and the language immensely richer.

In fact, the language of the poem here is itself symbolic. Not only do its striking alliterative patterns approximate *cynghanedd*, they also aurally trace the variety and visual interlace of the tangled vegetation. The visual tangle, in turn, approximates the multivariant interweaving of society's wattle. The affinity suggested by this correspondence between society and forest is supported by the symbolic union of humanity and forest in the riding figure of Arthur.

His divinity, or his symbolically becoming divine, is revealed in the fury of his riding. The account of his riding — which is visual, emotional, and kinaesthetic — is also allusive in its evocation, for example, of Botticelli's *Primavera* in which, during sexual arousal, Chloris becomes the goddess Flora. Although Arthur's passion is not sexual passion but anger, it is metamorphic, and transforms him into Flora's counterpart, the male fertility god who is folklore's May King and consort to the female Tutelar of the previous poem. Because Arthur is 'caparison'd in the flora' (68), his coat matches Flora's dress, which in Botticelli's painting is embroidered with real flowers.

As his wounds and the thorns that cling to him suggest, Arthur also symbolically assimilates Christ: Arthur is scourged as he rides; 'the numbered bones' of his feet (68) allude to the Good Friday psalm (22:17). Moreover, the imaginative history of Arthur in early folklore and his typology in 'The Hunt' evoke the hypostatic union — for Arthur is a man-god, human in his wounds and emotions, divine in his assimilation of pagan gods. In this respect, Arthur's correspondence to Jesus is further implied by Arthur's assimiliation of Arawn – for in *The Mabinogion* the god Arawn exchanges identities with the man Pwyll. Pwyll is married to Rhiannon, who, as the Great Mother Ragantona of Celtic religion, is more properly the consort of the fertility god Arawn. After harrowing the Celtic Hades for him, moreover, Pwyll takes Arawn's title, 'Prince of the Otherworld.' The man and the god are interchangeable, in short, and if not completely synonymous at least confused in legend to an extent that metaphorically approximates the union of man and God in Jesus. In a sense, Pwyll becomes Arawn as Chloris becomes Flora. To paraphrase T.S. Eliot, the gift half understood in the figure of Arthur is Incarnation. And this, in addition to the motif of metamorphosis, gives narrated time affinity with the moment of Incarnation, which is designated in 'The Hunt' as 'the Change Date and the Turn of time' (66).

In the light of Arthur's symbolic assimilation of gods (and God), the moral distinctions of the first part of 'The Hunt' imply a test of virtue which has apocalyptic implications. The very word 'hunt' is sometimes, in Malory at least, synonymous with 'juridical inquiry.' And the allusions to the first branch of *The Mabinogion* and to *Sir Gawain and the Green Knight* stress the connotation of judgment, for Arawn and the Green Man each test the integrity of men. In *Sir Gawain* the test involves the motif of sexual temptation, which derives from Celtic legend and makes one of its earliest literary appearances in the story of Arawn and Pwyll. The motif is alluded to in 'The Hunt' when the war-bands are said to include 'those who would stay for the dung-bailiff's daughter and those who would ride though the shining *matres* three by three sought to stay them' (66). But if Arthur's hunt does imply the Last Judgment (the Day of Sejunction or division), that implication is moved to the background by the near abolition of narrative viewpoint in the poem's second part and by the final unanimity, however temporary, of riders so inherently diverse from one another.

If Arthur's theophany is as apparent to the riders as it is to the poem's narrator, they may experience something like the near abolition of point of view which the narrator experiences as he contemplates Arthur. In the poem's coda, the riders in the war-bands are seen as sharing Arthur's determination. They hunt the hog 'life for life' (69) – a phrase to which Jones gives great emphasis as he reads the poem and which appears twice during the account of the hunt in 'Kulhwych and Olwen' and several times in Malory to indicate extreme peril. Underlying shared risk is, furthermore, unanimity of emotion:

>   And the extremity of anger
> alternating with sorrow
>   on the furrowed faces
> of the Arya
>   transmogrified the calm face
> of the morning
>   as when the change-wind stirs
> and the colours change in the boding thunder-calm ... (69)

The imagery of metamorphosis suggests that the riders have themselves undergone a transformation. And the measure of this change is that the feelings earlier attributed solely to Arthur now belong to the entire body of men. The duality of shared emotion recalls the earlier divisions, in the poem's opening analytical section, but now differences in social status cease to matter, and divergent temperaments and moral inclinations converge in a single dedication.

If the riders do undergo an interior change in response to Arthur's divinity, that change, which corresponds to the change in the poem's narrative point of view, is conversion. The common action of the riders does not guarantee their motives, but their final, emotional communion with Arthur does suggest that spiritual metamorphosis has occurred. Consequently, this moving body of men symbolizes not the *civitas Dei* – for that metaphor must temporarily disappear with Roman civilization – but the war-band of God. The action of the poem is not merely transfiguration, therefore, but also redemption.

In 'The Myth of Arthur,' the poet writes that because Arthur is 'the conveyer of order, even to the confines of chaos,' he is a 'redeemer' (*E&A* 237) – which is his role especially in the early poem attributed to Taliesin, *Preiddeu Annwn*, 'The Harrowing of the Otherworld' (see *IP* 200). Now Arthur is harrowing the earth, whose antithetical vegetation ('thorns and flowers') symbolically equates with his followers. If this harrowing is effective, therefore, and 'the men of mean spirit' and those present from 'the Three Faithless War-Bands' actually experience true, inward conversion, their transformation is largely in response to the almost indescribable love of the Christ-figure they follow:

> And if his eyes, from their scrutiny of the hog-track and from considering the hog, turned to consider the men of the host (so that the eyes of the men of the host met his eyes) it would be difficult to speak of so extreme a metamorphosis. (68)

To the degree that the men of the host reciprocate this love, the hunt, like the Passion, involves a harrowing of the sort described in *Piers Plowman*, where the redemptive character of the harrowing of hell is expressed by the phrase 'lyf for lyf.'[51]

This is 'the Passion' not only of Arthur, however, but also 'of the Men of Britain' (69) whose riding, if it symbolizes redemption, also symbolizes co-redemption. After all, they ride with Arthur for a single purpose, which is illuminated near the end of the poem by the image of the sweat of the men and the horses, which 'salted the dew of the forest floor' (68). The men of the host are now synonymous with those to whom Jesus says, 'You are the salt of the earth.'

Because of the poem's shift in perspective, its temporal setting is at once the early sixth century and the universal present. In one sense, the full effect of co-redemptive riding on society and culture lies in the narrative future. In another sense, it lies in eternity, and the passion that sustains metamorphosis will find release not in cosmic nuptials but in cosmic battle. The poem conveys the tension of this unresolved passion in its overall syntax – which is that of an autonomous adverbial clause moving toward a grammatical culmination that never comes, perhaps because it occurs on the other side of time.

'THE SLEEPING LORD'

Like 'The Hunt,' the title poem of *The Sleeping Lord* has Arthur as its primary symbol, and as in 'The Hunt,' Arthur is synonymous at one level with Christ. This is implied in the title, which refers to Arthur but alludes to Milton's *Hymn on the Morning of Christ's Nativity* where Jesus is the 'sleeping lord' (line 242). And there are other indications here that Arthur is a Christ-figure, including his resting from the hunt on the night of the 'Ides of Quintilis' (75), which is the date the Romans sacrificed their equivalents of the biblical scapegoat.[52] The 'Sleeping Lord' fragment and 'The Hunt' grew to their present forms in close proximity to one another. 'The Hunt' was originally composed as an insertion to a series of questions at a point immediately preceding the questions that constitute the rhetorical frame of the 'Sleeping Lord' fragment. Moreover, the setting of 'The Hunt' was originally specified as 'the ford of Ammon flow,' which is, like the setting of 'The Sleeping Lord,' in the Black Mountains. Despite similarity of subject and proximity of setting and textual matrix, however, 'The Sleeping Lord' is a very different poem from 'The Hunt' – longer, more complex in form, and remote in viewpoint from Arthur, who is, for the most part, personally absent and dormant. Because the speaker's disposition is interrogative and approaches, without being absorbed by, the anagogical figure of Arthur, the speaker is free, like the meditator of *The Anathemata*, to wander imaginatively in time and to create secondary narrative personae. Here the legendary setting of 'The Hunt' is only one of three narrative contexts. It contains the setting of the historic sixth century and is contained by the twentieth-century narrative present. Each setting differently conditions our perception of Arthur. In the context of the boar-hunt he is legendary, in the sixth century he is realistically human, and in the modern century he is mythic. In contrast to 'The Hunt,' in which time and place cease to matter, Arthur's absence here, alternating with his marginal presence, allows setting to emerge as an important feature of the poem. While 'The Hunt' is compact and its imagery layered in a way that makes Arthur a symbolic palimpsest, 'The Sleeping Lord' is spread out, its imagery scattered and requiring an imaginative expansion to see how Arthur gathers all within himself. This expansion is the dramatic movement of the poem, which culminates with Arthur as a mythic giant on the scale of Finn MacCool in *Finnegans Wake*.[53] Since the poem is also about the meaning of its own imaginative expansion, it is, without being obviously self-referential, a poem about poetry. In this respect, the full significance of 'The Sleeping Lord' involves the complex symbolic interrelationship of the poet, the poem's ancient bard, its candle-bearer, Arthur's hall-priest and foot-holder, two Norman sentries, Arthur himself, a Norman castellan, and other types and archetypes, divine and human. The resonance between these figures is part of a larger relationship between imagery and structure that renders the shape of the poem symbolic.

In so far as it is specified, the spatial setting of the poem is the *Mynedd Du* or Black Mountains of Breconshire. Here tradition gives a specific location for Gwely Arthur, or Arthur's Bed, though in the poem it might be anywhere in the heights above the immense South Wales coalfield. The poem and in some respects its power to move the reader originate in the poet's love for this landscape. Between 1924 and 1926, during his engagement to Petra Gill, Jones stayed here for about a year with the Gill family at Capel-y-ffin. Alone or with friends he wandered among the powerfully beautiful bare hills and forested valleys with their foxgloves, ferns, and rushing streams. Sometimes when he was alone he would shout psalms in Welsh into the hills.[54] Several times he went south to Caldey Island, which is the poem's 'Pirus' rock' joined to the mainland by 'Giltar shoal' (93). Once at least – in the company of Eric Gill and Canon John Gray – he walked to Hay-on-Wye, eight miles north of Capel, where he saw the ruins of the twelfth-century Norman Castle on whose southern ramparts Anglo-Norman sentries converse near the end of the poem. Completed in 1966, then, 'The Sleeping Lord' evokes landscape (and weather) which for over forty years conditioned the poet's sense of his own Welshness and gave remembered shape to his imagination.[55]

Textually the poem originates in a fairly short sequence of questions written in about 1939 (see RQ 27–9) that take their terms of reference from the landscape. As with the seminal text of *The Anathemata*, this sequence is broken in half to accommodate later material. The large central insertion consists of a series of additional questions, about Arthur's foot-holder and candle-bearer, which is divided in its turn to accommodate the silent prayer of Arthur's hall-priest. Additional minor insertions into the original sequence are the early parenthesis concerning the palaeolithic *nobilis* (71) and, near the end, the imagined conversation of the Anglo-Norman sentries (94–6).

The form that finally emerges from this process of insertion still consists mainly of questions – one replacing the other in a steady, fluid undercurrent that moves the reader into the final westward going of the poem's conclusion. The original questions have been thoroughly reworked, however, to clarify the speaker's imaginative progression through history and legend to myth, with his final questions implying Arthur's gigantic identification with the landscape of South Wales. The main, central interruption of these questions is an inward, rather than a forward, movement. And because this central section equals in length what goes before and what comes after, the poem is divided into thirds, so that its structure resembles the spatial triptych of 'The Fatigue.'

We may identify the speaker of the first and last parts of the poem with the poet. During his opening series of questions, allusions to scripture, legend, and folklore accumulate and provide the terms in which Arthur can be understood. In the last part of the poem, the mood of the speaker becomes increasingly elegiac as his questions concentrate on the boar's devastation of the land and the corresponding ecological ravaging of South Wales in modern times.

The central third of the poem is largely the silent prayer of Arthur's hall-priest. Here as in *The Anathemata* narrated chronological time is slowed by an acceleration of consciousness. The priest's interior monologue at the conclusion of grace before supper is 'brief and momentary'

(79) but 'swift' (86) and so fills seven pages.[56] In contrast to Jones's poetic imagining, which is informed by legend and tends towards myth, the fictional priest's view is entirely historical and realistic. To him Arthur is merely the leader of British resistance against foreign invasion. While the poet creates sensory images and speaks a lyric language that sometimes approaches the alliterative richness of *cynghanedd*, the priest thinks in prose rhythms and with a harsher, less assonant music. Mainly he remembers the dead men and women of Britain in what amounts to a catalogue of names, many of them from 'Kulhwch and Olwen.' And like that work's long name-lists, the priest's catalogue evokes a tradition destined for the most part to be lost. His *memento* is therefore doubly elegiac.

The first and last thirds of the poem share with the middle third a continuity of movement from present to past and back again, which implies a correspondence between Jones-as-poet and the priest. Initially, the poet imaginatively moves from the present (identified as such by his geological terminology and archaeological knowledge) to the sixth century and the imagined presence of the historical Arthur. Then Arthur's hall-priest extends this temporal movement from his own present to the Last Supper, the Passion, and the person of Christ (83-4). This is the central point of the priest's interior monologue and therefore the spatial centre of the poem. It is also the end of the poem's continuous and gradual recession into the past. From here, narrated time rebounds at the end of the priest's prayer to the sixth century and eventually, as the poet resumes his questions, back to modern times. This movement in narrated or meditated time has clear formal affinities with the structure of *The Anathemata*.

The continuity between poet and priest suggested by this movement in time is accounted for by the priest's existing within the poet's imagination. This imaginative accommodation is mutual, in a sense, because the priest contemplates 'the Bard of the Household,' about whose legendary subject matter the priest is dubious. The bard is the modern poet's counterpart; he and the poet are both, by the priest's standards, 'weavers ... of the fabulous' (82). By a sort of symbolic ontology, then, the interior monologue of the priest contains the poet and, consequently, the poem which the priest is contained by. Perhaps this suggests that the realism of the priest contains the legend and myth of poets – though in another sense, as the structure of the poem emphasizes, myth and legend contain factual reality. The relationship is reciprocal, as in *The Anathemata*, where 'Verity' and 'Poesy' are 'wed' (129).

The continuity (and the distinction) between poet and priest also emphasizes the affinity between Arthur and Christ. Arthur is the object of the poet's questioning and occupies the historical past to which his questions eventually reach. Jesus is the object (as distinct from the subject) of the priest's praying, and occupies the furthest recession of the past that his prayerful imagination reaches.

The poem's movement in time is not as schematically simple as I make it sound. The final part of the poem, before it loses all sense of time in its concluding mythic expansion, concentrates on the sentries in the twelfth-century Norman castle. But the sentries who make the largest break in the overall pattern do so only to affirm the pattern by re-enacting a significant inversion of it – not in time but through the chain of command. They hear something in the Welsh night and consider telling the sergeant who would then tell the captain of the watch who would then wake the Norman castellan to tell him. As John Terpstra remarks in a fine essay on the poem, the castellan is their 'sleeping lord.'[57] He is the furthest point of their mental progression, which quickly returns back down the ranks in their dread of 'his temper' the next morning. In their subjection to the movement of authority through the ranks, the sentries resemble their Roman counterparts in 'The Fatigue.' The sentries in the present poem are the secular foils of the poet and the priest who imaginatively accommodate and serve the Norman lord's sleeping, mythic antithesis.

The main effect of the poem's structural division into modern and early-medieval perspectives is to juxtapose the different but analogous culture-phases. As we have seen, this juxtaposition is a recurring motif in David Jones's poetry, but its effect here is different and darker than ever before. This is because sixth-century Britain is here seen not so much as a prelude to medieval cultural revival but as the beginning of a decline which in varying ways continues for the Celts to the present day. Here Jones is qualifying the historical schema that informs *The Anathemata* and some of the earlier poems in *The Sleeping Lord*. The juxtaposed culture-phases are now regarded no longer with Spenglerian detachment but from within, and with specific cultural attachment. As a consequence, history now appears as what Jones elsewhere calls it, 'a rake's progress ... a criminal dissipation of noble things' (*DG* 154). In this poem, therefore, he counteracts what he sees as 'an attempt made in the minds of most of us to pretend that the loss of some admitted "good" in any epoch is "worth it" because of some quite other "good" in the following epoch' (*DG* 153). For the British Celts of the Dark Ages, the later medieval renewal is not, after all, a renewal of *their* culture. If cultural rebirth follows cultural death, the fatality is nevertheless real and in some important respects final.

In other respects it is not final, of course, and the poem's motif of paradoxes emphasizes this; but a paradox works both ways. In the poem's epic simile, which turns on the zodiac, the date is established as mid-July and the movement through the calendar implies cyclic renewal, but the stress is on the weather's wintry chill. The conceit concludes, moreover, with the 'steelcold stones of hail' in the month of Mars (76) – an image that corresponds to the early-medieval British experience 'on three fronts' (78) of 'devastation-waves of the war-bands' (80). The residually Roman, increasingly Celtic world of Arthur is coming to an end. Terpstra points out that the aging hall-priest with his failing memory typifies the aging towards death of the culture he commemorates.[58] Even more so does the aging Arthur with 'his thinning tawny hair of lost lustre streaked whitish' (77–8). The decline of Celtic Britain continues through the ninth century, marked by the Welsh lament from that period which the poet quotes (88). The decline continues through the Anglo-Norman occupation of Wales and beyond to the thirteenth-century death of Llywelyn. (The latter is recalled in the allusion to the place of his death [71] and in the reference to 'these broken dregs of Troea' [95], an echo of the words of Edward I's clerks upon hearing of Llywelyn's death. In a sense, moreover, it is Llywelyn's coming that the Anglo-Norman sentries hear in the night, for he is the last of several Welsh princes to attack and burn the castle at the Hay.) Medieval cultural rebirth does not entirely reverse or mitigate this decline. In fact, as the poem suggests, the dying of the Gaul continues in various ways through the Renaissance into modern times.

When the Twrch Trwyth is imagined stoving in 'the wattled walls of the white dwellings' (90), he gives allegorical expression to the British defeat throughout the Dark Ages. But the legendary beast also evokes the nineteenth-century depopulation of rural Wales. In an act reminiscent of the Ram's destruction of the symbolic hearth in 'The Tutelar,' the hog stamps 'out the seed of fire,' and shatters 'the *pentan*-stone within the dwellings' (90). He breaks the continuity of hearth, which should extend even beyond the life of its fire. According to Welsh rural tradition, which antedates the Laws of Hywel Dda, the *pentanfaen* or fireback-stone of a deserted household must never be moved or destroyed, for it is the enduring sign of a habitable site which may always be reclaimed. Because the hog breaks the symbolic stone, a return to the land is no more possible here than it is for the imperial population of whom the persona of 'The Tutelar of the Place' thinks, 'they shall not come again because of the requirements of the Ram...' (63). It was partly in protest against this disruption of Welsh rural tradition that Saunders Lewis, later a friend of David Jones, burned the Caernarvonshire bombing school in 1936. And as Saunders Lewis stressed during his trial, for him this rural cultural tradition – the matrix of Welsh national culture – had as its symbol the ancient and historically important Penyberth farmhouse, which had been destroyed to make way for the bombing range.

The devastation of the land by the Twrch particularly involves the destruction of trees. His tusks tear down the high trees (*arbusta ... alta*) and sacred oaks (*sacras quercus*). They shatter the ash (*fraxinus*).

> It is the Boar Trwyth
>   that has pierced through
> the stout-fibred living wood
>   that bears the sacral bough of gold.
>   It is the hog that has ravaged the fair *onnen* and the hornbeam and the Queen of the Woods. It is the hog that has tusk-riven the tendoned roots of the trees of the *llwyn* whereby are the tallest with the least levelled low and lie up-so-down. (89–90)

Such wasting of the land, while first of all symbolizing the suffering of the early-medieval Britons, also and in almost literal terms indicates what Wales subsequently suffers. From the sixteenth century through the eighteenth century, the great forests of South Wales are cut down to supply charcoal for smelting. This ecological rape of the land begins with the Tudor demand for metal, but its political connotations are suggested earlier by the site the poem's Anglo-Normans occupy being called, in the Anglo-French from which the modern 'Hay' derives, 'a cutting or glade through a woodland.'[59] In Welsh the place is called 'the Shattered Grove.'

At the end of the eighteenth century, when coal replaced charcoal for smelting, the deforestation of Wales ceased, and a new form of exploitation began. The Norman lord at the Hay symbolically anticipates it as he sleeps 'with his Dean-coal fire / nicely blazing' (95). (This is not, however, an anachronism: from earliest times coal was taken from surface deposits for fuel.) In the last third of the poem and in recent centuries, 'the black pall' covering coal-mining towns (92) indicates a continuity with 'the darking pall' which early in the poem symbolizes the deepening of the Dark Age (75). And 'the mountain-ash,' once the hog's victim, now 'droops her bright head' in the polluted air (92).

Arthur continues to sleep and to suffer in his sleep throughout this continuing decline. No longer that of post-Roman Britain, and not only of Wales, this is the decline of the West. The poet wonders whether streams and rivers bear Arthur's 'broken-heart flow' (92) to the sea where his tears mingle with 'the mullocked slag-wash' of iron works, whether his royal balm mixes with 'flotsomed sewage and the seaped valley-waste,' and whether his jetsamed 'golden collar' is distinguishable beside the 'dole-tally' that entitles the unemployed to welfare (93). Now 'the dying gull' caught in an oil slick on the Atlantic is a pun on the dying Gaul of the earlier period of decline. The ecological imagery is contemporary, but we remain in the Waste Land, though now the devastation extends even to the fouled sea.

The catastrophic dimension of the continuing decline is sounded by allusions to the fall of Troy. Because of Welsh legendary genealogy, Troy's fall reverberates in Wales ceasing to be itself. But the Trojan motif resonates more broadly than that, since Troy's fall is the aboriginal catastrophe of the West, which is now culturally ceasing to be.

All this loss is redolent of human mortality, and that contributes to its poignancy. The hall-priest recalls the living, many of whom will die fighting for the lost Celtic cause, and he remembers the dead. These latter sleep, as Mistress Quickly would put it, 'in Arthur's bosom.' As 'maimed king' (93), furthermore, Arthur typologically subsumes 'the Lord Llywelyn' (71 n1) and the palaeolithic prince buried in Gower. Arthur is the Lame King with 'wounded ankles' (90), and so incorporates Hector, dragged 'widdershin' by the ankles (75), and Achilles pierced in the heel (72). Here as in scripture, feet have genital connotations. The Maimed King's wound renders him impotent, and, as in *In Parenthesis*, the extremity of impotence is death. In a real sense, of course, the historic British resistance-leader is dead too. The reference four times in quick succession at the start of the poem to Arthur's 'bed' must recall its orthographic twin, the Welsh word *bedd*, which means 'grave.'[60]

Funerary imagery appears with increasing frequency towards the conclusion of the poem. It begins with the priest's whispered *requiem*-versicle and continues through the candle-bearer's sung response and a Latin passage Jones adapts to express the violence with which the hog breaks trees (89) – a passage which gathers funeral connotations from

Homer, Ennius, and Virgil.[61] (It is a text evocative of the beginnings of western literary tradition, and appropriate, therefore, to the funeral of both the early-medieval and modern West.) 'West-world glory / in transit is' (94). (The syntax is Latin, and the words evoke the medieval motif *sic transit gloria mundi*.) In the Isles of the Blessed, 'they sing / their west In Paradisums' of the burial service. And the slowly 'dying gull' sings her own dirge in Latin of the Office of the Dead as she drifts on the polluted water, literally going west.

Arthur's identification with gods who suffer extends the negative aspect of his sleeping, which comprises the deaths of men and cultures. But because they are gods, they either do not die or do not die for long, so that they imply as well the positive aspect of Arthur's sleeping, which is the inevitability of his waking. One of these gods is Math, the old Celtic high god, pre-eminent for his compassion towards the suffering. His feet, like Arthur's, are wounded. Another of Arthur's divine counterparts is evoked by the 'fragile *blodyn-y-gwynt*' (74) – the wood-anemone whose Welsh name echoes the word 'blood.' This is the flower of the god Adonis, who dies of a hog-wound and is alluded to here as Arthur rests from hunting the hog. The allusion is subtle but undeniable because the anemone is located in a hollow along with 'the spume-born maiden's hair' (73) – a fern which is also called Venus-hair and is here, therefore, doubly evocative of the 'spume-born' goddess. She it is to whom the poet refers when he says that foxgloves and other flowers 'are ... made over to her' (73).[62] The entire forest bows in the wind towards the lowly anemone, as though the living green knows its vital source in sacrificial red. (The anemone's covering 'briar-tangle' gives it connotations of Christ, moreover.) Bowing to the flower, the forest corresponds symbolically to Arthur's foot-holder leaning 'low to his high office' (73). The divinity of Math and of Adonis, who rises annually from the dead, balances the mortal humanity of Arthur's other counterparts. And as we saw in 'The Hunt,' this balance approximates the union of divinity and humanity in Jesus, who with his 'eternally pierced feet' (73) is therefore Arthur's primary counterpart and, for David Jones, the theological vindication of the myth of Arthur.

With regard to the Dark Ages, the paradoxical balance between Arthur's humanity and divinity has its historical corollary in the Celtic heroic age of doomed military resistance coinciding with the Age of the Celtic Saints. Arthur's hall-priest emphasizes the dual aspect of the age when he remembers in close proximity to her military leaders Britain's priests, monks, and hermits. He also recalls *émigrés* now coming 'by thalassic routes from southern Gaul bringing with them a valuable leaven' (80). These words refer to the immediate future when Christianity, having been largely swept aside on the continent and in Britain, still flourishes in Wales largely because the western sea routes remain open to the isle of Lerins off the south coast of Gaul. On this island is a monastery at which visiting Celtic Christians like St David absorb a strong ascetic spirituality that originates with the desert fathers. From bases in Wales, this ascetic and monastic Christianity spreads to Ireland, largely in the person of a Welsh Briton who takes the name of Patrick. And from Ireland in the seventh and eighth centuries, Christianity spreads back through what has become Angle-Land and across northern Europe. All this lies behind the poet's question near the conclusion of 'The Sleeping Lord':

> does the vestal flame in virid-hilled Kildare
>   renew from secret embers
> the undying fire
>   that sinks on the Hill Capitoline? (93)

In 'The Myth of Arthur,' Jones writes that the traditional association of Arthur with the Celtic saints is historically dubious but conceptually valid (E&A 259). These saints are the *milites Christi* who, at one level of meaning, ride behind Arthur in 'The Hunt.' And because of them the chaos wrought by the Twrch Trwyth is truly apocalyptic, for when because of him the trees are 'the tallest with the least levelled low' (90), the hog unintentionally prepares 'the way of the Lord' (Isaiah 40:3; Luke 3:4).

For now, the Lord sleeps and is the Maimed King, but the image is meant to give impetus. Standing beside Arthur is his candle-bearer, the flame of whose candle is shaped 'like the leaf-shaped war-heads / that gleam from the long-hafted spears / of the lord's body-guard' (77). The leaf-shape gives focus to the poem's vegetation imagery. The tableau – that of a youth holding a metaphorical spear beside a Maimed King – evokes the crucial scene in Malory and in the Welsh Percivale story, in which Peredur 'in the Court of the Lame King' sees 'the youth bearing the streaming spear' (IP 210 nM). To restore the king and his wasted land, Peredur must enquire the meaning of what he sees. We saw that at the end of Dai Greatcoat's boast in *In Parenthesis*, the reader is urged to ask the restorative questions. At the conclusion of *The Anathemata*, the poet himself asks them. He seems to be doing the same thing in the broken series of questions that largely comprise the 'Sleeping Lord' fragment.⁶³ But, although the poet asks questions, the land is not, as far as he can tell, renewing itself.

In 'Art in Relation to War,' David Jones describes the present era as

> the hour of the daemons of power that take possession of the Waste Land when true cultural life is at its lowest ebb and the 'young hero' has not yet restored 'the maimed king' and the time of resuscitation is not yet. When all is 'doing' and there is no 'making'. When the end is all, and the means nothing. When there is no organic growth, but only organization and extension of dead forms.
>
> The artist, however, in whatever age, and whatever the determined destiny, has both to believe and to tremble and somehow or other, to affirm delight. (DG 129)

While the land lies waste, the artist – in this poem, the poet – has a special role, which seems to involve the inspiring of questions.

Here the poet is not only present as the primary narrator but may also correspond to the bearer of the candle, 'a true artefact' (76), whose flame is an image of delight. The candle-bearer even verbally declares this light. We will consider further the meaning of light in the poem. For now, it is enough to suggest the poet's affinity with the candle-bearer.

As the poet and the priest are 'continuous,' the candle-bearer seems symbolically continuous with the foot-bearer, who may therefore be the priest's counterpart. The poet and priest who have negative foils in the sentries would then have positive counterparts in Arthur's attendants. Like the attendants, they too sustain Arthur. The poet imaginatively perpetuates the tradition of Arthur, and the priest renews in prayer the religion of Christ, Arthur's principal counterpart.

This sustaining is most clearly elaborated in the service of the foot-holder, and with water-associations to balance those of fire belonging to the candle-bearer. The poet remembers that in *The Mabinogion* Math will die unless 'the daughter of Pebin of the Water-Meadow' holds his feet in her lap (72). Her water-connotations resurface when the wounded ankles of gigantic Arthur are imagined as 'lapped with the ferric waters' of South Wales (90) – waters which recall as well the 'oxide of iron' lovingly buried with the palaeolithic lord. Mary Magdalene's tears wash Jesus's feet (73). 'The patient creature of water' has helped to make Arthur's geological bed (72). All this protective, preserving feminine care correlates with the enwombing imagery at the end of

'The Tutelar.' In a sense, then, the poetic attendants of Arthur (and the priestly attendants of Christ) renew for themselves life-giving tradition, which they thereby preserve for the future. They stay awake and render service, in the words of the Welsh hymn, 'all through the night' (90).

Now darkness reigns – in the age, in the polluted air, and in failure of perception, as when the 'blind & unchoosing creature of sea' cannot distinguish sacred balm (93). At its greatest intensity, darkness blazes in the 'dark fires of the hog's eye' (92), an allusion to the hellish 'darkness visible' of *Paradise Lost*. Darkness is an absence of culture related to an absence of cult, which is owing to the widespread loss of faith during the Dark Ages and today. I remember David Jones saying once, with deep regret, that the closest most modern Welshmen come to religious belief 'is membership in the Labour Party.' That, or something like it, can be said for most of us.

The darkness is deep and the fire is almost out. The hearth-fire 'smoulders' (78), the candle gutters (74). But if the candle is actually going out, far at sea 'the corposants toss / for the dying flax-flame' (94). The poet refuses to be as pessimistic as he seems inclined to be. It is almost as though David Jones is heeding the advice of a local priest who once visited him in his room at Harrow-on-the-Hill and saw on his wall the inscription he had made that reads: HORA NOVISSIMA / TEMPORA PESSIMA / VIGILEMUS. The last word, in red, had faded, and the priest told him, 'Best not lose sight of that last bit.' The 'Sleeping Lord' fragment is almost an expanded commentary on the Latin inscription, with the darkness receiving by far the greater emphasis. But in a real sense, darkness does not diminish light; it enhances it. And if there is any sentence in which the poem crystallizes its meaning, it is this: '... cold is wind / grey is rain, but / BRIGHT IS CANDELA' (90).[64]

The light that burns weakly but brightly on the candle, in the hearth, and in the corposant is the Light of the risen Christ. Light is Christ's chief liturgical symbol at Easter, and throughout the poem fire is defined as 'One of the Three Primary Signa' of Jesus (77) who is the Credo's '*lumen de lumine*' (77) and the 'LUX PERPETUA' (87) that shines for the sleeping dead – sleeping because this Light guarantees their rising. The guarantee is implied in the poem's first fire image, at the geomorphic rising of the Welsh mountains when 'There's no resisting here: / the Word is made Fire' (72).[65]

Having seen the Christological connotations of fire, we are in a position to resume our consideration of the poem's three-part structure, which we can now appreciate as an important aspect of the work's symbolism.

We have seen that the second of the poem's three parts – the priest's interior monologue – occupies considerable meditative or subjective time but very little narrated, chronological time. In objective time it is condensed so that the conceptual geometry of the poem's overall structure resembles the floor plan of Arthur's hall, which Jones takes some trouble to describe (78 n2). The hall or *neuadd* is a rectangle divided in half by a screen. The halves correspond to the first and last parts of the poem. The screen, dividing rather than occupying space, corresponds to the momentary prayer of the priest, chronologically considered. This structural correspondence between narrated time and architectural space suggests, first of all, that the poem is the literary equivalent of the *neuadd*. The equivalence is corroborated by the attention paid to the centre of the hall. Its dividing screen is itself divided midway by 'the centred hearth-stone' where the fire burns which is 'the life of the household' (78). The narrow screen corresponds to the priest's brief prayer, and we saw that the centre of the prayer is spatially (and theologically) Jesus – one of whose primary signs is fire. Jesus at the middle of the prayer; the hearth at the middle of the screen. Jesus, the centre of the poem; the hearth, the centre of the hall. Symbolically, the poem and the hall have the same centre.

The correspondence between Christ and the hearth-fire is strengthened by the hall's architectural affinity with, and possible origin in, the Roman 'quadrilateral plan.' The priest remembers it with reference to 'the *limes transversus*' (79) delimiting the Roman rectangle, which is divided exactly as the screen divides the hall. At the midpoint of the line of division is 'the auspicious area' (79), the *mundus* referred to in 'The Wall' (13), where the altar is enclosed, as the hall-priest recalls, by walls of 'squared stone' (79).[66] So Jesus is the Fire, the Hearth and the *Mundus* of sacrifice.

While the hall has the poem as its literary equivalent, its quadrilateral prototype has its own literary equivalent – structurally to begin with, but also symbolically – in 'the four-fold account... of the *quattuor evangelia*' (84). The hall-priest stresses the number of the gospels by considering them the sacred counterpart to the four branches of *The Mabinogion*. (The resemblance is more suggestive than the priest realizes, for the four *mabinogi* originally relate the story of a Celtic god, now the man Pryderi.) The quadrilateral plan of the gospels contains Jesus and so, symbolically, does the structure of Arthur's hall. And so does the poem, where Jesus is not only the centre, but like the warmth and light of the fire, expands to fill the whole poem in his symbolic identification with Arthur.

343 Sequence

As the noise of the screen reverberates through the hall when the silentiary strikes its post (78), the priest's *memento* resonates throughout the poem. His prayer is to the 'Sleeping Lord' fragment what Dai Greatcoat's boast is to *In Parenthesis* and what Elen Monica's monologue is to *The Anathemata* – not only the work's spatial centre but also its primary focus of meaning, which radically conditions our experience of the poem as a whole. In conjunction with the poem's imagery, moreover, the prayer of the priest, conceived and structured as it is, establishes the shape of 'The Sleeping Lord' as its ultimate and all-encompassing symbol. It is in his essay entitled 'The Myth of Arthur' that David Jones endorses Stanley Spencer's contention that in a work of art 'all must be safely gathered in' (E&A 243; cf Ephesians 1:10). In its comprehensiveness, 'The Sleeping Lord' is such a work of art, for symbolically it includes even itself.

Together with the Arthurian elements in the two long poems and the important Arthurian essays in *Epoch and Artist* and *The Dying Gaul*, 'The Sleeping Lord' and its companion poem, 'The Hunt,' are a greater authentic (ie not merely fanciful) contribution to the tradition we call 'the Matter of Britain' than has been made by any writer since Malory.

'BALAAM'S ASS'

The full manuscript of *The Book of Balaam's Ass* (RQ 187–211) was written after Jones's 1932 breakdown, before he put what he calls 'the finishing touches' on *In Parenthesis*.[67] Initially he abandoned it because, he told me, 'it would not come together' as a work of art. The fragment he subsequently extracted from the manuscript for publication might have been discussed earlier, as an addendum to *In Parenthesis*. It complements that work because its subject is the more mechanized mass slaughter of the last two years of the war. In his introductory note to the fragment, moreover, Jones says he includes it here partly because it is a bridge between *In Parenthesis* and *The Anathemata*. In subject matter and tone, 'Balaam's Ass' seems to have little in common with the other poems of *The Sleeping Lord*, and perhaps that prompted Henry Summerfield to omit the poem from his *Introductory Guide* to the collection. But the 'Balaam's Ass' fragment was reshaped, as we have seen, to contribute to the unity of the book. It secures the temporal progression of its major fragments from past to present, and it gives significant structure to the book as a whole. Since 'A, a, a, Domine Deus' is originally part of *The Book of Balaam's Ass* manuscript, *The Sleeping*

Lord returns in the end to its text of departure, which is also a return to the twentieth century. Because of historic analogy and transparency of voice, the Roman and Arthurian past have almost always contained the historic present. Now this containment is reversed and becomes structural in a way reminiscent of the circular return in *The Anathemata*. More important, the poem is a sort of coda, which in various ways contains and adds to the contexts of the preceding poems. So there are good reasons for considering this work in its context of publication.

Unlike *In Parenthesis*, 'Balaam's Ass' is not based on direct experience. David Jones had been at the front for eleven months after recovering from the leg-wound he had received in Mametz Wood when his regiment was moved from the northwest area of the Ypres salient to south of Armentiers to take part in the first phase of the Passchendaele offensive. His battalion's objective was Pilken Ridge. Jones himself saw only the first few days of action 'and even then,' he writes, was 'hardly in the thick of it for I was posted to a reserve group ... but I saw enough to guess something of the assaults over a terrain of churned-up mud, water-brimming shell-craters, not a yard of "dead ground" not a fold of earth the length of y'r body and sighted with his usual accuracy his sweep of fire from narrow slits of concrete pill-boxes covering all the approaches, & heavy mortars operating from behind each stark ridge' (*DGC* 252). The poet did not participate in the assault on the pillbox that is narrated in the poem. That may help to account for the peculiar force of feeling that infuses the beginning of the poem and the distanced perspective throughout. After a few days in a reserve group, Jones was sent behind the lines to Battalion Nuclear Reserve – for the continuity of regimental identity should the rest of his battalion be wiped out. He disliked being separated in this way from the fighting and suffering of men he felt he belonged with (see *DGC* 27). Because he knew of the catastrophic assault on the Mill only from report, it must have had an unusual impact on his imagination. T.S. Eliot writes that agony acquires unique permanence when it is 'nearly experienced, / Involving ourselves,' but is not 'our own.' Jones bears witness to such agony here, but with imaginative force derived partly from combat he had experienced himself on other battlefields. By his own account, the poem's clumsy and cowardly Pick-em-up Shenkin is based on himself. Shenkin must be the narrator, moreover, for it is he who overhears the cries of the dying, and he alone knows and can report his own inward response to those cries.

The continuity of this poem with the preceding Arthurian poems is chiefly in its form, which is Celtic. Its greater part consists of nominal allusions, which together with an uncharacteristic abundance of puns gives 'Balaam's Ass' more than any other work by Jones affinity with *Finnegans Wake*. But Jones's principal model is 'Kulhwch and Olwen,' with its listing of 478 personal names. And here as there (as also in the priest's *memento* in the 'Sleeping Lord' fragment), the catalogue of names evokes a tradition threatened with extinction – though here the tradition is a familiar one, that of England and the modern West.

Encyclopaedic in range though not in comprehensiveness, the names evocative of western culture have symbolic focus in the Mill being called Aachen Haus on German maps. Aachen is Aix-la-Chapelle, the capital of Charlemagne's Frankish kingdom and so the first political and cultural capital of the modern West. Charlemagne is called 'father of Europe' because his conquests brought back into political and religious unity most of the lands once united within the 'locked shields' of Rome 'that determined the boundaries of western man' (104). Spengler's measurement of modern history is 'from Charlemagne to the World War' (II 50).[68]

Through its directory of names, the poem summons European culture to judgment in the face of an atrocity for which it is partly responsible. At the conclusion of Part 4 of 'Hugh Selwyn Mauberley' (a passage Jones liked very much), an embittered Ezra Pound condemns 'a botched civilization,' 'an old bitch gone in the teeth.'[69] This is an emotional resolution, which elevates the poet above his culture. In contrast, Jones's speaker does not stand outside what he judges. 'The mind of Europe,' as Eliot calls it, is the mind of the speaker as well as of his audience. The trial implied by this crisis is also for the speaker, therefore, a test of himself.

Partly because of its compilation of names, the form of the poem is anatomy, with an inclination towards satire, caricature, and humour. In 1972 Jones said of the poem, 'No one else thinks so but I think it's funny.' I have since found that most readers do appreciate its humour, but it is a humour alternating with pathos. The resulting ambivalence gives the work an unusual tone, which keeps the reader emotionally off balance. Combined with this ambivalence of tone is a thematic tension between the physical and spiritual conditions of dying men. This tension is rhetorical and comprises an implied dialogue, which is also characteristic of anatomy and which makes this, like *In Parenthesis*, essentially a pastoral poem. Instead of having spatial structure, the work is loosely informed by its dialogical movements. Broadly speaking, it consists of two parallel dialogues, one explicit, the other implied.

The first dialogue is literally an argument. It occurs in the introductory section, before the account of the assault. Talking to civilians soon after the war, the speaker defines his audience (by paraphrasing Romans 1:28–31) as being blinded to the horrors of war by their own virtues.[70] He then defines himself by analogy with other military Ancient Mariners whose tales 'you couldn't choose but hear' (98). Finally he defines his subject, the soldier as scapegoat who must die to ensure the ignorant virtue of the general population. Here the dialogue commences. As he speaks he creates an ancient Roman persona analogous to himself and alludes to Shakespeare's history plays. The rhetorical countermovement begins when Lavinia, one of his listeners, protests. Her objection is identical to that of Paul Fussell to the romance allusions of *In Parenthesis*. As we have seen, Fussell contends that such allusions glorify war by equating it with literary romance. Lavinia, mockingly employing sixteenth-century vocabulary and allusions, protests,

> Tilly-vally Mr Pistol that's a petty tale of y'r Gallia wars. Gauffer it well and troupe it fine, pad it out to impressive proportions, grace it from the ancients. Gee! I do like a bloody lie turned gallantly romantical, fantastical, glossed by the old gang from the foundations of the world. (99)

To this the poem's primary narrator replies partly by admitting that she has a point:

> To adopt the initial formula, 'Ladies and gentlemen, I will remove the hat.' You will observe the golden lily-flowers powdered to drape a million and a half disembowelled yeanlings.
> There's a sight for you that is in our genuine European tradition. (100)

The sight within the tradition is twofold: a vision of corpses and of their denial by whited-sepulchral lily-gilding. (The irony is intensified by the allusion to gilding the lily, a metaphor for adding unnecessary ornament to something already perfectly beautiful.) But the narrator suggests that the modern experience of battle redefines tradition by stripping it of whitewash. Romance may cosmetically disguise atrocity, but the narrator's allusions to romance hide nothing. Since the speaker is, in a sense, counting corpses, the relationship between real horror and literary romance cannot be the denial of truth. Romance has its horrors too, and may serve to communicate the intense, subjective dimension of actual horror. 'The salient is Broceliande,' says the narrator, referring to the forest in Brittany where Merlin is imprisoned forever (100). Here the narrator implies, furthermore, that in addition to being an Ancient Mariner fated endlessly to retell his story, he is, as a metaphorical magician, a Merlin imaginatively inhabiting the Ypres salient for the rest of his life.

In the narrative proper, the parallel to the initial argument is suggested by the tension between the two main rhetorical units, which are lists. The first compiles the names of the dead who correspond to figures in western cultural tradition. The second records and interprets their death-cries in what amounts to a religious litany. The spiritual value implied by the litany transfigures the calamity of their dying in a way that many readers will find intolerable, if not incomprehensible. But a close parallel in more recent history may clarify the transformation: walking in file to the gas chamber at Auschwitz, one group of Jewish children sang psalms. Their singing transfigured the atrocity because, in all but physical terms, it defeated the Third Reich – although, as in the poem, transfiguration remains problematical because man is physical as well as spiritual. The poem's implied dialogue between matter and spirit cannot easily reach objective intellectual resolution, therefore, though its speaker attains subjective equanimity as a consequence of his faith.

The range and modulation of tone in this work is extraordinary. In the introductory section, the speaker's voice is bitterly insistent, neurotic, and therefore reminiscent of the poetry of Wilfred Owen. In fact the narrative impetus seems very like that of Owen, who when on leave used to carry photographs of maimed soldiers to show civilians. But during the actual narration of the assault the bitterness recedes and tone begins to modulate between humour and pathos. The comedy consists of puns and of occasional mock-epic formality reminiscent of Flann O'Brien's *At Swim-Two-Birds*. As the narration moves into the litany, the formal elevation of tone ceases to be comic, and emotionally at least the dialogue reaches a synthesis that sustains the concluding movement from comedy in the description of Shenkin to equanimity in the account of Austin and his praying mother. The alternation between humour and prayer relieves point of view from an intense focus on agony, which would be, for the reader, either paralysing or voyeuristic.

The allegorical list invokes western culture from an English perspective in the manner of the nominal invocation of national tradition throughout *In Parenthesis*. Here, as there, not all names are significant in this sense, but most are. And since the poem has never been annotated or explicated, I will take a few pages to indicate historical and literary correspondences, though what follows is by no means an exhaustive account.[71]

Among the names listed are those of poets, musical composers, and painters. The poets' names are Lovelace (102) and (two in one) Vaughan-Herbert (98) after metaphysical poets Jones considered in some respects Welsh. The composers are Purcell (103) and Byrd (104).[72] The painters are Varley (97), Altdorfer (105), and Bosch. The latter is indirectly evoked by Hieronymus Högemann (104) since this Hieronymus is a Bosch, French slang for a German – as Hieronymus (Jerome) is Jerry, which is English slang for German. Like his prototype in the sixteenth century, this Bosch creates a hellish landscape, though his medium is the large trench-mortar.

Other historical characters answering to the roll call are Terentius Varro, defeated by Hannibal at Cannae – or is this Varro the Roman satirist? (100); Cadwaladr of the British struggle against Saxons (99); and Hygca the Saxon who settled in what is now Buckinghamshire (102). From Shakespeare's history plays: Aumerle (100); Herefert, not named but like the 'ex-clerk ... armed at all points' (99); Brackenbury, Clarence's keeper (101); Warwick, and Talbot (99). '22 Hilton and '55 Rolle evoke Walter Hilton the monk and Richard Rolle the hermit, fourteenth-century religious writers and contemplatives. Their modern counterparts march 'without talking' (101).

The Celtic warrior-poet of the ninth-century Juvencus *englynion* is indirectly present in Lieutenant Fairy who cannot find 'cover for himself nor all his franks' (100). Because the syntax is ambiguous, the franks, which may be chits with orders written on them, also evoke the Frank who, with the Briton he fights for in the Old Welsh poem, cannot find cover the night after a disastrous battle. Because the word 'franks' is plural, furthermore, it recalls the armies of Charlemagne, whose longest and bloodiest struggle was against the Germans.

From the nursery come Jack Horner (107); Winken, Blinken and Nod, rhythmically recalled by the Hampshire names 'Grover / Bunker and / Cobb' (102); the sparrow who shot Cock Robin with his 'little bow and arrow,' evoked by Balder Helige and his 'little gun' (102). And 'the house that Jack built' resonates in the fire, the wood, and the byre door used to cook the Picardy gander which, we may assume, is a mother goose (101).

Guy of Gisbourne (from the Robin Hood ballad), Clym of the Clough, and a Robin surnamed Goodfellow are the three who steal, cook, and consume the goose. They leave only their fire's 'cinder ring,' which is fairy ring enough for Goodfellow, whose alias is Puck. Also from ballads come Lamkin (99) and Thomas Rhymer (104). '66 Adam and '66 Bell are numerically equivalent in the rosters of their battalions and so, in a sense, equal Adam Bell of the ballad (101). Willy Cawdor comes from a Yorkshire folksong (102). Lieutenant Fairy destined for 'a soldier's fall' (100) recalls Vincent Wallace's patriotic opera *Maritana*. And Punic Trelawny (103) evokes R.S. Hawker's rewriting of an old Cornish ballad, 'The Song of Western Men,' whose refrain is, 'And shall Trelawny die?' (This poem's Trelawny dies.)

Much of the tradition evoked is literary. Because these men attack a pillbox named the Mill after the many windmills in the Ypres area, they are so many Don Quixotes: 'Here we have the windmill. There you see the advancing hero' (100). Also related to the name of the place are '16 Nicholay with 'branded arse' and '02 Absolon 'who laughed' and took for himself Sergeant Carpenter's girl (102) in a re-enactment of Chaucer's 'The Miller's Tale.' Other medieval names are synonymous with friendship and brotherhood. There is no cover, says the narrator, for

> Corporal Oliver of No. 1 nor for
> Corporal Amis and
> Lance Corporal Amile of No. 2, nor for signaller Balin and his incompatible mess-mate linesman Balan ... (101)

The only names here we have not met before in Jones' poetry are from the Anglo-Norman romance of friendship *Amis and Amiloun*, adopted from the French *Li amitiez de Ami et Amile*. By conflating English and French titles, Jones evokes the steadfastness of the two friends and alludes to Ciceronian equality between friends (through the cliché 'A miss is as good as a mile'). *Piers Plowman* is evoked as is its author (104). *Gammer Gurton's Needle* ('Back and side go bare') dovetails with *A Sentimental Journey* ('God tempers the wind to the shorn lamb') when the narrator asks 'where is His tempering for our bare back and sides' (104)? '02 Snug recalls Snug the Joiner in *A Midsummer Night's Dream* (104). Harry Gill evokes the poem by Wordsworth (103 n2). Bullcalf, whose prototype was recruited by Falstaff in *2 Henry IV*, also recalls Oliver Twist when he naively asks 'for two dinners on one plate' (101).

Many allusions that invoke western tradition recall motifs in the previous poems of *The Sleeping Lord*. The imagined persona Nodens is a Roman soldier (98), and there are many incidental references to the Roman army – its siege engines ('wounding towers'), earthen rampart (agger), square shield (scutum), and the joining of shields to form the tortoise. Nodens refers to 'Clitus so bored and Crixus so tight' (99). This is a change Jones made in the final typescript of the poem in order to unify his sequence with a specific reference to the early, Roman poems. I said that in another late inclusion, Nodens also refers to Arthur in the constellation Arcturus. Högemann recalls the hog that Arthur hunts, for the German's name means hog-man and, as Jones says in his spoken introduction to his recording of 'The Hunt,' the Twrch is a man changed into a hog. Like the hog, Högemann and his colleagues annihilate first the men of Ireland, in spring and autumn 1915, and then the men of Britain. Because 'Högemann feeds his Big Willie [mortar] in Aachen Alley' (104), furthermore, his gun recalls the Minotaur of the earlier, Roman poems — the half-bull, half-man to whom Athenian youth were fed. The triple-belted and trip-wired defences in Aachen Alley comprise the maze that completes the evocation of the Cretan labyrinth.

The cultural catalogue gives its concluding emphasis to the three survivors of the assault: 'Private Lucifer / Private Shenkin / Private Austin' (105). Together they evoke the three survivors of the battle of Camlan as described in the Welsh Triads and in 'Kulhwch and Olwen.'[73] The allusion to Camlan complements the poem's other Arthurian associations and suggests the apocalyptic aspect of this battle for, as we have seen in our discussion of *In Parenthesis*, at Camlan the world ends, the same world that is partly reconstituted two centuries later with its centre at Aachen. Here and now, the later manifestation of that world re-enacts its earlier destruction in the symbolic suicide of a civilization.

The three survivors have further traditional associations. When David Jones was preparing 'Balaam's Ass' for publication, he said about Private Lucifer, 'the stuff they throw at the Tommy goes right through him and he keeps firing.' Then he paused, looked at me, and when I said, 'Milton's war in heaven,' he smiled and nodded. (On a previous occasion he had said that Book 6 of *Paradise Lost* contains the best description in literature of battle as he had experienced it on the western front.) The second survivor, Pick-em-up Shenkin, who receives his nickname from a drillmaster's shout, takes his surname from the eighteenth-century song 'Of Noble Race Was Shenkin' — about a comical Welshman whose name is a corruption of Jenkins. After nightfall, hiding in his shell-hole, Shenkin remembered 'the Rocky Mountain goat' and 'leapt from shell-hole to shell-hole (and no one could tell whether he leapt because he feared or feared because he leapt) until he regained the security of the assembly trench' (110). This is wonderful writing, which captures fear compounding itself within an epic formality that intensifies the humour. It echoes a colloquial expression about farting and leaping and may also recall Kulhwch mentioning in his list of names a man who 'would clear three hundred acres at one bound.' The third survivor, Austin the Dodger, whose mother prays for him, recalls St Augustine. The poet writes in a letter that this figure 'has certain characteristics of that Great African' (to H 4 May 1974). One of them is a devoted mother. (St Ambrose is supposed to have told Augustine's mother that 'the son of so many tears' could not be lost.) Another characteristic may be Neoplatonism, for Private Austin's surviving the devastating gunfire suggests an essence that is immaterial.

In addition to evoking a rich complex of cultural associations at the conclusion of the poem's list, the three survivors of the battle constitute an extended metaphor for the futility of natural prowess in the fire before the Mill. The metaphor extends the principle by which, in Malory, knights who do 'marvellously' in battle are considered 'sent from heaven as angels, or devils from hell' (2.10). Whether from below as with Lucifer (but facetiously) or from above as with Austin, only supernatural intervention can explain survival in such a place. In his own way, moreover, Shenkin demonstrates that soldierly virtues are ineffectual here. He survives precisely because he lacks courage and skill, though also because he possesses low cunning.

If this poem has a Balaam's ass, it is Shenkin, who, 'because he had no effective interest in the G.O.C. in C.'s diversion before the Mill' (106) and like the ass before the forbidding angel (Numbers 22), falls down and refuses to move forward to what is certainly a violation of God's will. Supporting Shenkin's affinity with Balaam's ass is the Roman designation of soldiers as 'mules of Marius.'[74] There should be, in any future editions of *The Sleeping Lord*, an image to corroborate this suggestion, for Jones writes that where Emeritus Nodens discourses on camels, 'I actually *meant* to write, "O! Cripes he's commenced on the *mules* – their hostility to man, their peculiar aversions and perfections"' (to H 4 May 1974).

The account of the three survivors at the conclusion of the poem's cultural compilation is clearly a distinct narrative unit, but it is a unit broken and opened up to give expression to the religious litany which rhetorically balances the culture-list. After Lucifer is described and before we come to Austin, Shenkin lies in a shallow shell-hole listening to the cries of the dying. Structurally, then, the anaphora of their cries rises from within the cultural compilation and represents the cult within the culture. Although the culture at first seems utterly ineffectual in the face of this calamity, its cult transforms the calamity and thereby redeems the culture.

To a degree, the meaning of the litany is located in the imagination of Shenkin, who reports not simply what he hears but also what it begins to mean to him at the time and what it has subsequently come to mean. Here too, then, we are as removed from the immediate action as we have been all along. The cries of agony are initially cries for water and for mothers, sweethearts, relatives, and friends, and they extend the cultural compilation. But gradually there emerges the distinctive shape of a religious litany progressing, as Christian litanies do, through the Trinity to Mary and the saints. Some of the names cried (Mary, Peter, John) are doubtless not intended as saints' names, and many cries of 'Christ' and 'God' are not prayers. But some are, and these for Shenkin convert most of the rest, which he hears as prayers. (This conversion is a generic restoration, since cursing has its origin in prayer.) The litany and the theological perspective it brings transform the poem by giving death an enlarged context.

This is the culmination of the motif of transformation in a poem in which everything changes. With reference to the legend and the painting of King Cophetua and the Beggar Maid, and then to the dance of the seven veils, the narrator says of the landscape,

> We have seen transfigurations on a plain, swiftly and slowing, unsheafing slow like beggar-shifts king's hands make fall from secret queens.
> ...
> at night the veils were drawn slowly for you to see the limbs there; it was at night they spangled the clods with stars and lit torches for the humble and meek. (99)

These latter inherit the earth all right. Death plays on sex here, but the limbs you can see are real enough and belong to the carcasses of the Irish and the Scots who attacked the Mill two years before, then as now at the express command of the GOC in C.

The main physical transformation in the poem is that of men on fire. They are killed by 'incomings to transmute the whole dun envelope of this flesh.' These men show 'how the leaden clay' can 'flame' (99). They die in the image of Guy Fawkes, the burning of whose effigy – lest 'gun powder treason should ere be forgot' – is alluded to at the opening of the poem where the narrator wants to make his listeners 'laugh on the other side of their faces at gunpowdered reason' (97). Guy Fawkes here symbolizes the foot soldier as immolated scapegoat. The image of burning is literal but also puns on the more general, less spectacular effects of gunfire. Without losing its horror, the motif of fiery transfiguration subtly and paradoxically acquires positive biblical connotations, since God has his theophanies in flame, accepts sacrifice in flame, and descends as the Holy Spirit in flame. That catching fire on the battlefield can have a benign connotation seems obliquely suggested by the emphasis near the end of the litany on the eucharistic act of transformation. The suggestion is clearer in the litany's invocation of the Holy Spirit:

> The Sanctifier and bright Lord who is glorious in operation, the dispositioner, the effector of all transubstantiations, who sets the traverse wall according to the measure of the angel with the reed, who knows best how to gather his epiklesis from that open plain, who transmutes their cheerless blasphemy into a lover's word, who spoke by Balaam and by Balaam's ass, who spoke also by Sgt. Bullcock. (107)

The name Bullcock implies that even a 'cock and bull story' may be a medium for the Holy Spirit. And when the Spirit sets the traverse wall by the measure of the angel with the reed, the trench belongs to the New Jerusalem (see Revelation 21:15–16). War, then, does not take place beyond the perimeters of the city of God. The passage just quoted is crucial to the poem's meaning; while working on the poem in 1938, Jones writes that

> It is about how everything turns into something else & how you can never tell when a bonza is cropping up or the Holy Ghost is going to turn something inside out & how everything is a balls-up & a kind of 'Praise' at the same time. (DGC 86)

Because the slaughter, without ceasing to be physically appalling and tactically stupid, is transformed by God into an occasion for good, 'by Him even the G.O.C. in C.'s diversion before the Mill can shine with the splendour of order' (107). This is the dreadful order of physical causality, but a higher order too, since, because of her prayers, 'it was urged by some that Mrs Austin conditioned and made acceptable in some roundabout way the tomfoolery of the G.O.C. in C.' (111–12). At this level the poem's dramatic conflict is between God and the GOC in C. But what is, on the dramatic level, dialogical conflict becomes, on an anagogical level, dialectical by virtue of a synthesis resembling that of the negative dialectic of Dionysius the Pseudo-Areopagite. It is the Christian synthesis implied in 'The Wall' and 'The Tribune's Visitation' and made explicit, in its cultural dimensions, in 'The Fatigue.'

The duality of circumstances in 'Balaam's Ass' seems, in a special way, to resonate in the poem's concluding name, that of Austin the Dodger. The Artful Dodger of *Oliver Twist* is incorrigible, but Augustine is a model of self-reform. The movement from one connotation to the other involves imaginative transformation and is itself an image of conversion. The notion of conversion is first obliquely introduced apropos of St Augustine when Lavinia calls the narrator's talk 'Ambrosian racket' (99), for the eloquence of St Ambrose is the primary impetus of Augustine's conversion. (In its context, the allusion is also to magical metamorphosis, for Merlin's second name was Ambrosius.) While the narrator's declared intention, moreover, is to convert his audience, he actually transforms himself as he ceases bitterly to regard his listeners and loses himself first in reminiscence and subsequently in prayer. Even in narrated time, Shenkin is 'not ... ungraced because of the diverse cries' of the dying, and undergoes 'the baptism by cowardice which is more terrible than that of water or blood' (110).

The horror of this assault forces Shenkin/Jones (and consequently his listeners/readers) to the edge to which the postwar existentialists pushed and which Jones's Tribune passes, where life is either absurd or has meaning that can only be religious. The horror that forces the question is at the basis of all thoughtful atheism. The poem's narrator asks, about God and about his own experience,

> And what of His sure mercies that He swore in the ancient days – where is His tempering for our bare back and sides – where is provided the escape on that open plain? (104)

In physical terms the question has no satisfactory answer. Only when the terms of the poem become metaphysical, in the litany, is it possible that God's mercies may yet be sure and that there may be escape on that open plain, though not necessarily an escape from death.

The cries of the dying mediate the transition from a material to a spiritual frame of reference. The transition is not, therefore, merely rhetorical. But it does require a leap from longing to faith that will leave many readers behind on the field of slaughter. Never before – certainly not in *In Parenthesis* – has David Jones been forced to make so radical a change without sustaining it imaginatively and mythically. In the Queen of the Woods, all readers have an imaginative experience of redemption, though it is an extremely poignant experience because she is a pagan figure in whom no reader really believes. But even the salvation you really may hope for is only a hypothesis, whereas death and suffering are not, so that the experience of readers in this regard may not vary all that much according to degrees of belief. But here the Christian hypothesis, as distinct from the longing that partly gives rise to it, is imaginatively unsustained. As Jones writes in a letter, this is owing to the conditions imposed upon him by the subject of the poem:

> for bare earth & mud, rusted barbed wire hedges, concrete 'pill boxes' – you would be put to it to find the material required for the sacramental signa of daisy chains & floral crowns of any sort and the Queen of the Groves, no less than any other sacral award-giver, cannot function without what the earth yields – such offerands can do no more than make petition 'spiritually,' 'mentally,' with words maybe, as *essential* protestant belief maintains – in direct contradiction to what is crucial & central to the Catholic faith and which does but ratify & set the seal to what 'man' *qua* man consciously or unconsciously holds. (DGC 256)[75]

This then is a Catholic's Protestant poem. The dehumanizing context with its absence of lyrical and symbolic possibility forces a retreat to the Protestantism of his youth and to the dualistic Marcianism that he told me was once the form his Christianity took. The poverty of the occasion is as great a poetic challenge for Jones as his subject is a philosophical challenge for all men. And, both poetically and philosophically, Jones comes closer here than anywhere else in his work to leaving behind the material world.

But he does not leave it, and we are not removed from human experience, for the agony of the dying is the primary symbol of its positive spiritual antithesis. A man on fire is no theophany, but psychologically requires the revelation of God which the image evokes. Through allusion to the gospels, the dead ex-clerk recalls the Passion as he stands 'upright between two ... crowned with iron and bearing the weight of it' (99). He is not so much a Christ-figure, however, as an image that appeals to the Passion. Even the symbolism in this poem is dialogical. The litany, which transfigures dying, remains rooted in suffering. The dying call upon Christ 'because He was familiar with the wounding iron ... because He could not carry the cross-beam ...' (107). Aside from purely theological considerations, salvation that does not match the agony of those longing for it is imaginatively unacceptable. Unless God pays for human suffering with his own, his salvation insults its beneficiaries. This imaginative logic partly accounts for the poem's success. The Passion is the work's underlying concept as well as one of its motifs. Its influence on the poem derives largely from the name of the poem's setting. About the Passchendaele war Jones writes, 'I suppose it is the site-name that made it as famed & held in the memory of soldiers & civies alike in post-war years' (to H 14 December 1973). The Passion also belongs integrally to this poem because it is rhetorically dual in meaning, corresponding to the work's antithetical aspects of death-agony and redemption.

The assault on the Mill is a crisis that forces a refraction of the poet's consciousness. This refraction may be seen in the poem's form and images, but it is most immediately evident in its language. In addition to keeping point of view at a distance, puns and hybrid compounds extend the motif of transformation. Here are some examples we have not yet touched upon. The surname of Skinny Bowditch (103) combines Bow Bells and Shoreditch. CQMS Snook speaks with a 'wry look' (103), which is part of what it means to 'cock a snook.' The name Spud Bullen (98) puns on an Irish Bull, an illogical absurdity, which is what his 'unwearied and graphic account of an assegai's [an African spear's] accurate trajectory and penetrating down drive' resembles to men in a trench being rocked by an artillary barrage.[76] The upright 'ex-clerk' mentioned above is no longer a civilian, but he is also an ex-clerk because he is dead. Corporal Holt and Private Heath evoke Chaucer's Prologue to the *Canterbury Tales*, in which April winds blow 'in every holt and heathe' (101). And 'Ober-Leutnant Bebba's parabellum' (101) is Latin for 'prepare for war' and so evokes the proverb 'If you want peace, prepare for war,' but it is also the parabola of his machine gun's sweep of fire. And Bebba echoes the German verb *beben*, to shake – for Bebba shakes while firing his gun. In a real sense, the reader comprehends the structure and viewpoint of the poem once he realizes that its prevailing and characteristic figure of speech is the play on words. The pun encapsulates the poem's refracted consciousness and manifests its form in microcosm.

This is a remarkable poem – because its emotional and intellectual impact is very strong and its humour disconcerting, but also because it lacks definite structure without lacking form. The absence of structure may have troubled David Jones, for I remember him wondering aloud whether the poem is 'good artistically.' When he chose finally to publish it, and to do so as the conclusion of *The Sleeping Lord*, he was taking a risk. But 'Balaam's Ass' is wonderful, a daring and original work in which structure is sacrificed for movement, the element he prized in art above all others except form itself. And form does survive structure. In fact, the form is everywhere and the same throughout – the dialogical movement of its introduction, of its narrative proper, of its analogical list, of its agonized litany, of its symbols, and of its language. This is not an easy poem critically to evaluate, and perhaps for that reason it has been the most neglected of Jones's important poems. In many ways, the wild and unconventional finale of his last major published work characterizes the imagination of the poet.

Structurally the middle-length poems of *The Sleeping Lord* are divided into halves, thirds, and quarters. The bipartite poems generate contrast. In 'The Hunt' (if we discount the coda) the contrast is between ways of thinking which are appropriate to society and to Arthur. In 'Balaam's Ass' the contrast is between the material and spiritual dimensions of culture, which achieve a paradoxical synthesis. Of the four-part poems, 'The Tribune's Visitation' doubles the bipartite contrast in alternating rhetorical movements of affirmation and denial, and 'The Tutelar of the Place' matches a correspondence (between child and cult-man) with a contrast (between nurturing culture and destructive civilization). The tripartite poems are essentially parenthetical, enclosing centres that reveal or transform their contexts. 'The Wall' contains a dual centre – the dark troia and the bright city – which implies a dark contrast but with positive connotations. 'The Dream of Private Clitus' has a bright dream-centre that compensates for its waking contexts. The centre of 'The Fatigue' redeems the personal and cultural dimensions of its context and indicts the dehumanizing political dimension. 'The Hunt' (which is tripartite if we include the coda) has a bright personal centre that redeems and unifies society by uniting it to himself. The same centre in the 'Sleeping Lord' fragment is dormant, only peripherally or symbolically present; it is sustained by its context, which it thereby endows with meaning. The tripartite structure of these poems is repeated in the ordering of the entire sequence according to setting, with the Arthurian poems as its centre. In each of the poems and in the sequence as a whole, structure contributes to dialectical meaning by emphasizing antithesis or implying synthesis.

Although there is structural affinity within groups of these poems, they do not repeat one another. Within and between poems, language modulates in various ways between poetry and prose, and genres range between soliloquy and spoken monologue to prayer, which is a mixture of both. There are also variations in mimetic mode. And there are variations in tone which express differences between personae in their relationships to themselves, to the objects of their thought or speech, and in dramatic monologues, to their auditors.

In fact, these poems are so different from one another that critical comparisons are dangerous. The most lyrical in language is 'The Hunt,' the most lyrical in imagery is 'The Dream of Private Clitus,' but neither of these is as psychologically interesting as 'The Tribune's Visitation.' Close to 'The Hunt' in lyrical language is 'The Tutelar,' but in some respects 'The Tutelar' is the only weak piece in the collection. It is rhetorically insistent at the expense of psychological complexity and dramatic interest. That its persona should address imaginary children as he does is not, to me, believable, and neither is his adopting the voice of an imagined or remembered grandmother, even though she is symbolically important to the poem. In other respects, however, the poem is powerful. Structurally it is fairly simple, but its form is enriched by a complex interplay of complementary images and allusions. And functionally it may be the most important poem in the collection, because it refutes the Tribune and registers a collision of antithetical culture-phases. By doing so it focuses the debate, which gives to the book as a whole a thoroughgoing pastoral aspect culminating in the dark pastoral of 'Balaam's Ass.' 'The Tutelar' also initiates or strengthens motifs that are important in the later poems.

The book's symbolic motifs make it either a sequence, as I think it is, or very nearly one. The motif of initiation is present in the first four Roman poems and in 'Balaam's Ass.' The contiguous image of the troia pervades the Roman poems and seems syntactically echoed in the questions of the 'Sleeping Lord' fragment. The image of the Maimed King appears in all the poems except 'The Dream of Private Clitus' and 'The Tutelar,' where it may be present by implication. The related image of the scapegoat emerges in 'The Fatigue' and again in 'The Sleeping Lord' and 'Balaam's Ass.' Vegetation imagery is a minor motif in the Roman poems and a major motif in the Arthurian poems. Pervading all the poems except 'The Wall' is the theme of art, which combines with the vegetation motif in 'The Dream of Private Clitus,' where the forest evokes Gothic architecture, and in 'The Hunt,' where the forest evokes Celtic verbal and visual interlace. In both poems, the living growth symbolizes the living art of a vital culture-phase.

Motifs not only unify the sequence, they also give impetus to its progression by undergoing metamorphoses. In the Roman poems, darkness contrasts with the dawn. The light of dawn becomes the sun (and the Son), which shines in the cultural morning of 'The Hunt' and is at one level a Celtic sun god. Beginning in 'The Tutelar' and continuing in the 'Sleeping Lord' fragment, sunlight changes to the hearth-fire, candle flame, corposant, and finally, in 'Balaam's Ass,' fire's fearful, transfiguring theophany. Along the way, light and fire acquire connotations of art and culture. The heavenly city and New Jerusalem of the Roman poems become the tribe of God and then that tribe's few faithful remnants. Tension between the sexes becomes marriage. The classical Hades becomes the medieval Waste Land and finally the modern battlefield. The Minotaur becomes the Ram who becomes the hog who, partly because of Högemann's mortar, becomes the Mill. All the poems share the motif of the Passion, though it changes from a contemporary fact to a universal paradigm and from an event to a theological hope for transcendent meaning in the worst of circumstances. In this sense, 'Balaam's Ass' concludes the quest of the poet in 'A, a, a, Domine Deus,' since if man cannot find a symbol of Christ in the products of his civilization, he can nevertheless be such a symbol by virtue of his suffering. The paradoxical union in 'Balaam's Ass' of physical catastrophe and spiritual affirmation may recall, furthermore, the scandalous paradox of the cross in the first half-millennium of our epoch, which is implied in the Roman poems. The legions that bend and break the world to totalitarian rule are making straight the *viae* for the gospel as the primary impetus of our civilization's authentic cultural vitality. Underlying the changing motifs and the dialogical shifting of modalities, of intensities of language, and of differing personalities in all of these poems is the tension between the antithetical principles of power and love.

8

Conclusion

THE POETRY of David Jones is intellectually important because it is informed by an original, penetrating, and widely applicable analysis of culture. It is aesthetically remarkable because it conveys its meaning thoroughly, in its language, its imagery, its allusions, its intermediate forms, and its unifying structures.

Although much can be said for the poetry of Basil Bunting and Hugh MacDiarmid, David Jones is the native British poet who has made by far the most important contribution to literary modernism. The first generation of modernists – Joyce, Pound, and Eliot – occupy a special place in history as the first to develop a new kind of literary form. But David Jones deserves to be placed near them, because his writing, like theirs, is a major achievement involving important formal innovations and because in it he importantly extends and develops the dialogue they began between the past and the present. He broadens that dialogue by giving new life in his poetry to scripture, to the liturgy, to the Welsh deposits, to Malory, and to other literary works. Because Jones is less ironic and more positively symbolic than the other modernists, he discerns new dimensions of coherence and continuity in western culture. One of these dimensions is the implied conception of poetry as *dromenon* or enactment continuous with a historical tradition of gratuitous sign making, so that a poem extends the life of the culture.[1]

Jones also makes an important contribution to the mythic sense of history that characterizes modernism, and he has been influential in passing on this timeless sense of historical time to the poets who have read him. Bunting's *Briggflatts* would probably not be as suffused with it if not for the example of Jones's two long poems. (Bunting has long been an advocate of David Jones, who he thinks 'must be placed close to ... Yeats, Pound, Eliot, Carlos Williams ...')² Mythic simultaneity also characterizes the historic dimension of *Mercian Hymns* and gives it, as Geoffrey Hill readily admits, an affinity with *The Anathemata*.³ Seamus Heaney's mixture of archaeology, history, and myth owes something to Jones's sense of time. Heaney writes that the poetry of David Jones has been, for him, 'a confirmation of proceeding by mythic indirection' and an affirmation that 'the political role of the writer can be fulfilled by maintaining the efficacy of his *mythos*.'⁴

In developing the modernist mythic sense of time, David Jones is not merely passing on the influence of Joyce. By making the historic past his narrative present in so much of *The Anathemata* and *The Sleeping Lord*, he reverses the mythic method. Now the present does not evoke the past but the past evokes the present. This inversion may have its roots in the ambiguities of *The Waste Land*, but it is in Jones's later poetry, for the first time, that – to quote *Briggflatts* – 'Then is suffused with Now.'

More than any native British poet since Hopkins, David Jones is an innovator in poetic form. Among his innovations are the catalogue that has symbolic and often structural significance (unlike the merely cumulative catalogues of Rabelais, Burton, and Joyce); the allusive reflector whose presence in narrative triggers and justifies allusions; topological rhyming, in which separate places or objects are seen as symbolically synonymous; symbolic transference, by which the meaning of one image is passed on to another or to others; 'metamorphic form,' as Corcoran calls it, which is a progression by means of analogical images; multiple exposure, in which two or more images are simultaneously evoked; the miming of narrative movement by narrated movement; the correspondence between poetic structure and a thematically relevant structure or structures from religious ritual, visual art, and architecture. Jones develops the monologue form in new ways by placing one or more monologues within another monologue, and he creates transparent monologists who nevertheless retain their fictional psychological integrity. His greatest innovation is, of course, his conception of structure as spatial and symbolic. Because, in literature written in English, his works are our principal models of the transmutation of literary experience when structure is also symbolism, they are likely to have an important influence on the poets and possibly the novelists of the future.

He also has helped to develop a new, dark pastoralism. In traditional pastoral poetry, the city is a distant threat to the idealized countryside. In the twentieth century, the city dominates the country – whether through the machines of war or, more subtly, through technological civilization. This is the setting of *In Parenthesis* and *The Sleeping Lord*, which is rendered pastoral or darkly pastoral by being made the context of thematic debate. Debate in Jones's poems differs importantly from its near antecedents, complaint in the poetry of Matthew Arnold and the First World War poets, irony in Hardy's works and in Eliot's *The Waste Land*. An authentic dark pastoralism does appear in *Women in Love*, where landscape and debate are symbolically combined. D.H. Lawrence did not, however, go on to develop this subgenre. (*Lady Chatterley's Lover*, for example, is a conventional pastoral idyll.) Aside from Lawrence, who was not apparently an influence for Jones, the nearest approximations to Jones's dark pastoral are found in the Renaissance, in sections of *Orlando Furioso*, *The Faerie Queene*, and in *Comus* – where debate becomes conflict, and the forest, as place of moral or rational disorder, symbolizes the dark side of pastoral. Certainly this symbolism bears on the conclusion of *In Parenthesis*, which takes place in 'the dark wood.' But in Jones's poetry the crisis, limited in earlier works to the forest, has spilled over onto the plain. And conflict retains the nature of debate, although it has broadened to a debate between civilization and culture, between the past (or future) and the present. If Lawrence invented this version of pastoral, Jones was the first significantly to develop it.

The poems of David Jones deserve a special place in modern literary history primarily because, while they are structurally whole, they remain 'open' in immediate and intermediate form. In other words, they mediate between the traditional prescription of formal unity and the discursive, organic, 'open form' which originates in modernism and continues in postmodern literature. Jones is not alone in this respect. Eliot's *Four Quartets* has unifying formal elements. The same may be said of *Briggflatts* and of *Mercian Hymns* and Hill's subsequent sequences. But these are not structurally unified poems; they are sequences. And they are 'long' only in comparison to the conventional short lyric. Only David Jones has written middle-length and epic-length poems that are at once thoroughly whole and free of the constraints of narrative and prosody. This is an achievement of special significance because criticism in the twentieth century has been characterized by debate over literary form, a debate that focuses most intensely on the contrast between the traditional long poem (from Homer through Milton) and the modern American long poem. The poetry of David Jones has brought this debate into dialectical synthesis.

In all his poems the diffusive tendency of anatomy and allusion is counteracted by symbolic and archetypal synthesis. In this respect Jones resembles Shelley, for whom all myths reflect a true ur-myth. Jones is not, like Shelley, a myth-maker, however. He has no deep affinity with the syncretic mythology of the eighteenth century that influenced Blake and Shelley and survives chiefly in the writings of Jung. Myths are not interconvertible for David Jones since, for him, history determines that one myth takes precedence over and absorbs the others. Because the Christian Word was made flesh, it assimilates the pagan 'words,' which otherwise remain mere fantasies – as they do, I think, in Pound's *Cantos* and the poetry of Robert Graves. Whatever the reader's personal beliefs, in our culture – even in an unbelieving age – the Christian assimilation is imaginatively possible and, in Jones's poetry, it provides a unifying thematic synthesis which is a major imaginative achievement. It resembles that of *Finnegans Wake*, where mythic types, historical figures, and fictional characters assimilate one another in turns in the neutral, egalitarian ontology of Joyce's fictional dream. But it also differs importantly from the Joycean synthesis. Jones never loosens connections with historical reality to the extent that Joyce does.

The formal importance of Jones's mythic or thematic synthesis is apparent if we compare *The Anathemata* with the *Cantos*. Although Pound invented the genre of displaced epic, his long poem actually consists, in its archetypal underlayers, of several displaced epics that are never successfully unified by symbolic assimilation. The relationship of the *Odyssey* and *The Divine Comedy* to Pound's life experience (which is his unifying subject) remains merely metaphorical. Pound could not find a single archetype powerful enough to assimilate all the others and to unite myth with history. In this respect, Jones had the imaginative advantage over Pound of being a believing Christian and a Catholic.

Jones's religion is no mere ideology, but it does involve a system of ideas which renders it ideological and, as such, capable of sustaining epic-length composition. From the *paideia* of Homer to the Puritanism of Milton, epics have required, and communicated, ideology – which provides a pre-aesthetic shape that lies under and complements aesthetic form. It also provides intellectual coherence that helps sustain extended expression. We have seen how it supplies the metaphysical values which help interpret the experience of war in *In Parenthesis* and which, in the later poems, give meaning to culture and poignancy to its decline.

For literary purposes, a religious ideology is probably the best kind of ideology since it involves depth of feeling which requires archetypal and anagogical expression. That is why the poets with the greatest range of psychological modality in their work have always been in some sense religious. In our time, the best of these are Hopkins, Eliot, and if we allow that his eclectic Neoplatonism is a religion, Yeats.

A writer may concoct his own religion, but a traditional religion has its advantages. One of these is a historical dimension which objectifies the writer's thoughts and emotions by uniting them to a collective moral wisdom and a generalized expression of feeling that has been refined over centuries. Jones himself seems aware of this advantage when he wishes 'Dickens ... had had a religion and a philosophy instead of a filthy tenth-rate emotional "morality" ...' (*DGC* 65).

If Jones's religion is a poetic asset, however, it can also be a liability. In some of the later poetry it sometimes contributes to a dogmatic hardening that removes poetry from sensation. It also produces poetry which some readers may feel has 'a palpable design on us,' though I find Jones's direct expression of Christian belief unobjectionable and, in parts of 'Mabinog's Liturgy' (eg 214–15) and in much of 'Sherthursdaye and Venus Day,' very moving. Occasionally in the later poems, however, language collapses into allegorical code in order to convey Christian doctrine (see *A* 85, 207–9; *SL* 108–9) or to retell biblical stories. The worst example of this is the seven pages of conversation in 'Mabinog's Liturgy' (209–14) in which witches recapitulate Christ's life in a Welshified, Latinate language that does not repay the difficulty of reading it – even though there is some dramatic justification for witches speaking in obscure code. This is an instance of bad judgment very like that which, in *Ulysses*, lies behind Joyce's dreary accumulation of parodies in 'The Oxen of the Sun.'[5] Clearly, Jones's motive is to avoid clichéd religious language and thereby to make Christianity imaginatively more accessible. He achieves this with remarkable success in the symbolic and archetypal dimensions of his poetry, though not always in his use of language.

But the language of his later poems is seldom deficient in sound or in the relation of sound to meaning. There is nothing in *The Anathemata* like the banality that mars the middle books of *Paterson* or the stretches of unmusical prose in so much of the middle and late *Cantos*. At its best, Jones's language is gravel to the fine sand of Yeats or Pound at his best. Jones does not have a lyrical gift equal to theirs, and that may explain why he does not write concentrated lyrics – although we have seen lyrical passages throughout his work that any poet might envy. Even the unspectacular stretches in his poems are generally alive and subtly beautiful – handsome, as it were, rather than lovely. His is a masculine language in the way that Dryden's language is masculine, incorporating a certain roughness. See, for example, the catalogue of dogs (A 79–80), quoted in its entirety on page 213 above. The rhythm is basically continuous but varies, is interrupted and resumed. The passage flows through a changing consonance of *r*, *s*, *h*, *g*, *w* and *y* sounds, and is enlivened at its opening and close by internal rhymes. Another example, chosen at random, is a fairly representative sentence:

> But it's early – very grey and early in our morning and most irradiance is yet reflected from far-side Our Sea, the Nile moon still shines on the Hittite creatures and Crete still shows the Argives how.   (A 91)

The long *i*'s, the *s*'s, the *t*'s, the *l*'s and the *sh*'s modulate on a middle ground of short vowels, *r*'s and *m*'s, and the rhythm is charged by a repetition of strongly stressed iambs and of the word 'early' near the start and 'still' near the end. More demonstration of this sort might be of help to some readers, but to most it would be tedious. Either you hear this particular kind of music or you do not. Some do not. Donald Davie has nothing good to say about the language of *The Anathemata*, and Elizabeth Ward is nearly as negative, but they are in the minority. Auden, MacDiarmid, Bunting, Heaney, Michael Alexander, and Jeremy Hooker – to mention only poets – praise the language of *The Anathemata*. The difficulty for some readers may have to do with comprehension. Although Eliot claims that you can appreciate the sound of poetry before understanding it, you cannot finally evaluate poetic language until you understand its connotative, allusive, and dramatic aspects. I find that when a critic quotes Jones to illustrate dissonance, the passage quoted usually refutes the critic.[6]

An important factor in appreciating the language of Jones's poetry is his vocabulary, which is among the richest to be found in English literature. Compare it, for example, with the middle range of vocabulary used by Eliot and the extremely narrow range of Yeats. Range of vocabulary is not merely a quantitative criterion; it has implications for variety of sound and rhythm, for texture of connotation, and for range of reference. We have seen something of the remarkable extent to which Jones's language is charged with allusion and connotation.

The place of David Jones among the modernists and his stature among British poets is clarified if we return to our comparison of *The Anathemata* with the *Cantos*. Both poems are displaced epics. They are alike in their macaronic mixture of languages, their procedure by juxtaposition, their quick shifting between fictional modes, and their subject, which is human culture. But as Monroe K. Spears has suggested, the differences are more striking than the similarities. All but the committed Poundians will agree, I think, with Spears's observation that

> the *Cantos* become, after the first few [and with the exception of the *Pisan Cantos*], increasingly uneven, eccentric and idiosyncratic; to an increasing extent, they seem lacking in awareness of the present and irresponsible intellectually and morally ... Jones, in contrast, never seems capricious or self-indulgent; he is personal chiefly in that he regards himself as an intersection of channels whose archetypal significance he explores as he traces them to their confluence with central streams of myth and history. Pound laboriously discovers (if he does not invent) meanings for his Sigismundo and his minor American and Chinese statesmen; Jones remembers well-loved places, people, poems, stories.[7]

To continue the comparison, Pound's use of sources is sometimes superficial and his historical references arbitrary. His collages of quotations in the Jefferson Cantos seem to be the product of quick secondary historical research that has not been imaginatively and emotionally assimilated. Even his intentions are rendered suspect by what have been shown to be strictly subjective, private references and by the sheer invention of figures which are ostensibly mythic, as in Canto 17 where he invents three goddesses. Jones, on the other hand, has thoroughly assimilated his sources. His poetry conforms to his conviction that the artist 'must only deal with what he loves, and therefore knows.'[8] And most of what he writes about he has loved and known for much of his life. That is why, as Basil Bunting says, Jones's knowledge is 'more accurate than that of ... Pound,' and it helps explain why *The Anathemata* is five hundred pages shorter than the *Cantos*.[9]

The chief difference between the *Cantos* and *The Anathemata* has to do with form. Pound himself never ceased regarding the *Cantos* as a single poem – the word 'canto' in poetry equates with the word 'chapter' in prose fiction – and near the conclusion of the *Cantos* Pound laments that he 'cannot make it cohere.' Critics have recently attempted to come to his rescue by redefining the work's genre as a sequence or 'sequence of sequences.'[10] Maybe they do know better than Pound what he was doing. We can call his work a sequence of poems, a constellation of poems, a serial poem. In some respects it is a verse journal like William Carlos Williams's *Paterson*, Olson's *The Maximus Poems*,

Berryman's *Dream Songs*, and Lowell's *Notebook 1967–68* – all of which are indebted to the example of the *Cantos*. Like Pound's long work they are capable of indefinite continuation, and like it *Paterson* and *The Maximus Poems* were ended only by the deaths of their authors. In any event, a sequence or collection or continuity of poems is less of an artistic achievement than it would be if it were a single unified long poem. One might argue that the *Cantos* is greater as a sequence (or whatever you choose to call it) than *The Anathemata* is as a long poem. But Jones's work is a structural unit; Pound's is not. In this century only David Jones has succeeded in writing poems that are both epic in length and scope and formally whole.

I have pursued this comparison at some length because the affinity between the *Cantos* and *The Anathemata* is one of the reasons David Jones has been neglected. In England since the 1950s there has been a widespread reaction against modernism, which resulted in David Jones's being excluded by Anthony Thwaite (who was Philip Larkin's 'ghost-editor') from *The Oxford Book of Twentieth-Century Verse*. The reaction is primarily against Pound as an epitome of modernism and, in the opinion of some, a failed poet. It is the reaction of readers whose patience the *Cantos* has exhausted and who are unwilling to make a similar investment of time and energy in another long modernist poem which they think might be equally disappointing. Consequently, *The Anathemata* has not been widely read and read repeatedly and carefully as it must be if it is to be understood. It is important to realize, therefore, that *The Anathemata*, on which Jones's reputation largely stands or falls, is not merely an Englishman's version of the *Cantos*.

Although a few poets have been influenced by, or feel affinity with David Jones, his impact on their work has been minimal. Certainly no poet has discerned or used a fraction of the strategies or techniques Jones has invented in the making of his poems. And those who have imitated his style – Auden in his later verse, for instance, and John Montague – have not benefited by doing so. But the question of influence has only a tangential bearing on the value of literary works. Blake's middle-length prophecies, for example, have had virtually no influence on succeeding generations of poems and therefore remain literary anomalies, yet they are among the great imaginative achievements of the romantic movement. Jones's poetry may well change the way we respond to and write works of literature, but whether it does or not, it will remain among the great achievements of modern literature.

In Parenthesis is original, powerfully moving, and beautiful. It is the most complex and profound literary work in any language to emerge from the experience of the First World War and is unsurpassed by subsequent works on war. It is certainly the greatest literary treatment of war in English. And it is the only authentic and successful epic poem in the language since *Paradise Lost*.[11] (Although critics have called the *Cantos* an epic, it is not a narrative and so cannot, strictly speaking, be considered an epic.)[12] We have seen how *In Parenthesis* expands the genre, as all important epics do. If Jones had written nothing else, he would deserve to be considered an important poet.

The Anathemata develops and perfects the new genre of anatomical displaced epic. It is the only epic-length work in any language, as far as I know, in which structure successfully replaces narrative as the primary principle of order. And more than merely ordering content, the structure of *The Anathemata* gives it powerful symbolic focus.

The Sleeping Lord is among the best poetic sequences published in recent decades. It is exceptional in that its poems are middle-length, several of them longer than entire sequences by other poets. And these middle-length poems have a high degree of structural unity. Considered as separable entities, many of them are comparable in achievement to Eliot's 'Quartets' and the more successful of Pound's 'Cantos.' As a sequence, the poems of *The Sleeping Lord* have remarkable breadth and inclusiveness. Moreover, they have special significance for contemporary poetic theory and practice because they bridge the gap between the short lyric and the long poem. We have seen how such middle-length units became long poems when placed in narrative sequence in *In Parenthesis* and when inserted one within another in *The Anathemata*.

The long poems of David Jones and his sequence of poems are major works, and David Jones is certainly a major poet. He is, I think, the most important native British poet of the twentieth century.[13] More than that, he deserves to be recognized, after decades of critical neglect, as one of the pre-eminent writers of our time.

Notes

Chapter 1 Introduction

1 The opening anecdote, this remark, and all subsequent information about and quotations of David Jones for which I cite no references are taken from twenty-four hours of conversation with the poet during four visits by William Blissett and me in 1971 and 1972. Blissett's accounts of those visits, published in *The Long Conversation* (Oxford: Oxford University Press 1981), provide some corroboration. I quote not from his accounts, however, but from my own recollection with the help of notes made after each visit. Additional information about Yeats's praising *In Parenthesis* was given to me by Stanley Honeyman, who recalls Jones speaking about it, and by E.C. Hodgkin, who was present when Jones and Yeats met.
2 *Speculations* (London: Routledge & Kegan Paul 1924) 34. David Jones discusses at length the prolonged defeat of the Celts in two important essays, 'The Myth of Arthur' (*E&A*) and 'The Dying Gaul' (*DG*).
3 Letter to the author, 18 April 1979
4 Jones is clear about the nature of his religious faith in a letter to Harman Grisewood of 9 October 1971, in which he considers 'the Churches of the Eastern Orthodox as well as the Catholic Church of the West' as doctrinally constituting the original Christian Church.
5 In Jones's library are the following books by Dawson, listed here in order of publication – all of them acquired by Jones in the year of publication or in the subsequent year: *The Age of the Gods* (1929); *Progress and Religion* (1929); *Christianity and Sex* (1930); *Beyond Politics* (1932); *Enquiries into Religion and Culture* (1933); *Edward Gibbon* (1934); *Religion and Culture* (1948); *Religion and the Rise of Western Culture* (1950); *The Formation of Christendom* (1967); *The Dividing of Christendom* (1971).

6 Jones acquired von Hügel's *The Mystical Element of Religion* in 1931.
7 Jones read *The Road to Xanadu* before or during the composition of *In Parenthesis* and includes it in a manuscript list of sources for the poem.
8 See also *The Long Conversation* 44.
9 Letter of 15-19 July 1973, quoted by René Hague *David Jones* (Cardiff: University of Wales 1975) 9
10 Roger Fry 'Preface to the Catalogue of the Second Post-Impressionist Exhibition' (Grafton Galleries 1912), in *Vision and Design* (London: Chatto and Windus 1924) 158
11 *The Philosophy of Art* tr Rev John O'Connor (Ditchling, Sussex: St Dominic's Press 1923) 87, 84. This is the only translation of Maritain's *Art et scholastique* that Jones read.
12 Fry *Vision and Design* 157, 8, 192
13 *Speculations* 101, 84, 94
14 *David Jones* (London: Tate Gallery 1981) 25
15 See Joseph Frank *The Widening Gyre* (New Brunswick, NJ: Rutgers 1963), 10ff.
16 *The Long Conversation* 45-6
17 'The Visual Art of David Jones' *Agenda* 5 (Spring-Summer 1967) 153
18 'David Jones: Artist and Writer,' an unpublished typescript of a recorded interview, ed Peter Orr (British Council 1973) 9
19 'Some Recent Paintings by David Jones' *Agenda* 5 (Spring-Summer 1967) 98
20 'David Jones' *Essays* (London: Alden 1947) 152
21 *The Long Conversation* 19
22 Alfred Daniell 'Some Remarks on Certain Vocal Traditions in Wales' *Transactions of the Honourable Society of Cymmrodorion* (Session 1910-11) 11, part of a longer passage 'with some pains transcribed' in a letter to Hague, 22 December 1933, in which Jones adds ironically that when the lecture was being delivered he was 'at Camberwell Art School ... drawing stuffed rabbits and Voltaire's death mask'
23 'David Jones: Artist and Writer' 7
24 Jones had begun teaching himself Welsh by the age of sixteen. He could never speak it, but he could make his way through written Welsh. He once said that soon after the publication of Hopkins's poems he mentioned to an Oxford don that he thought he could detect in them the influence of ancient Welsh metrical patterns. The don thought it an 'impertinent' suggestion.
25 Letter to the author (n3 above)
26 Hopkins, quoted by Herbert Read in a book Jones owned and inscribed with the date 1932, *Form in Modern Poetry* (London: Sheed and Ward 1932) 48
27 'Letters to Jim Ede' ed John Matthias *PN Review* 8 (1981) 15

28 Douglas Lochhead *Word Index of In Parenthesis by David Jones* (Sackville, New Brunswick: Harrier 1983) iv
29 'Ulysses, Order and Myth' *The Dial* 75 (November 1923) 483
30 Jones indicates where and approximately when he met Eliot in a preliminary draft of a letter of condolence to Valerie Eliot.
31 Northrop Frye introduces the concept of 'anatomy' into the language of literary criticism in *Anatomy of Criticism* (Princeton: Princeton University Press 1957). Anatomy is non-narrative, excursive, enumerative, and tends towards encyclopaedic inclusiveness. For Frye's extended definition of the term, see 311–14.
32 James Frazer *The Golden Bough* II (London: Macmillan 1915) 381. Because this work is one of the poet's important sources, all subsequent references, which are to the twelve volumes of the third edition, appear in the text. Jones owned two copies of the abridged version (London: Macmillan 1923 and 1925) as well as *The Scapegoat* (London: Macmillan 1914), *The Dying God* (London: Macmillan 1912), *Adonis* (London: Watts 1932), which he acquired in 1932, and *Adonis Attis Osiris* (London: Macmillan 1906), which he acquired in 1951.
33 The phrase is originally Desmond Chute's. See *IN* 23.
34 'Two Letters from David Jones' *Agenda* 11 (Autumn–Winter 1973/4) 23
35 I remember Jones saying, in 1972, 'I am interested in an American poet, contemporary with Hopkins, but can't remember his name.' In one of many drafts of a never-completed essay on Hopkins written in 1968 and intended for publication in *The Month*, Jones writes that it was in 1919 or 1920 that 'I first heard the name of Hopkins, but it was no more than a name, mentioned by a fellow art-student, I *think* in connection with the poetry of Walt Whitman.'
36 Conversation with the author
37 *The Long Conversation* 6
38 Jones worked out for himself a literal line-by-line translation of almost all the texts in Henry Sweet *An Anglo-Saxon Reader* (Oxford: Clarendon Press 1898). Jones's copy is inscribed with the date 21 February 1950.
39 *The Celestial and Ecclesiastical Hierarchy* tr Rev John Parker (London: Skeffington & Son 1844) 18, 19
40 In a marginal note in his copy of Wyn Griffith *The Welsh* (London: Penguin 1950) 103, Jones writes of Hopkins, 'I should have thought there was something Welsh in "his turn of mind." Cf. Vaughan, Traherne, Donne, Herbert, all of Welsh affinities.'
41 See Kathleen Henderson Staudt's remarks on Jones's refusal 'to empty the signifier' in 'The Poem As Sacramental Act in *The Anathemata* of David Jones' *Contemporary Literature* 26 (Spring 1985) 8.

42 See especially these essays: 'Art and Sacrament' (E&A), 'Use and Sign,' and 'Art in Relation to War' (DG).
43 'In Love with All Things Made' *New York Times Book Review* (17 October 1982) 9

Chapter 2 Genre and Technique

1 Jones began work on *In Parenthesis* 'in 1928 at Portslade in Sussex'; he finished the first continuous draft 'at Pigotts, Aug. 18, 1932,' and after recovering from his first breakdown, resumed work in 1934, writing the preface, revising and adding to the text, and completing the notes (to H 27 September 1963; to Miss [Mary E.] Jones 27 April 1962).
2 The 'sweet princes' primarily include Llywelyn and his brother David, the last native princes of Wales, but Jones quotes the phrase as showing 'that though I.P. was virtually finished by 1934, I completed it after Nov. 1936. It also shows how upset I was at the time. It would take a hell of a lot of detective work to get that one' (to H 18 September 1974). The association of Edward with Llywelyn is not entirely private, however, for Edward left England on the date of Llywelyn's death. Like most front-line fighters, the poet had a great affection for Edward and thought he should not have been forced, as Jones then thought he was, to relinquish his claims.
3 The extent to which *In Parenthesis* underwent revision is suggested in a draft of the preface in which Jones writes that the title is 'as first conceived and comprises the only words of the poem not altered at least twelve times.'
4 For his sixteenth birthday he received from his father John Rhys and David Brynmor-Jones *The Welsh People* (London: Unwin 1909) and a copy of Geoffrey of Monmouth [*Historia regum Britanniae*] tr Sebastian Evans (London: Dent 1904) inscribed, significantly, to 'Walter David Jones, Champion of the Ancient Welsh from a converted Saxon, T.P.' The donor was probably one of his Pethybridge cousins, who in earlier years used to infuriate him by chanting, 'Taffy was a Welshman, Taffy was a thief.' Also in 1911 Jones bought or received W.J. Griffith *A Short Analysis of Welsh History* and *A Pocket Dictionary, Welsh-English*.
5 One of twelve incomplete, undated drafts of a letter to Bernard Bergonzi probably written in 1965
6 See my article 'A Book to Remember By: David Jones's Glosses on a History of the Great War' *Publication of the Bibliographical Society of America* 74 (1980) 221-34.
7 Hague *David Jones* 47
8 Draft of the letter to Bergonzi

9 Ibid
10 Jones quoted by Hague in *David Jones* 36. René Hague, the poem's typesetter, remembers having printed a few sheets: 'it was just like columns out of a newspaper, and the idea was that you could fold the [book] in half [lengthwise] ... and slip it into your pocket ... it would have to have been in a paper cover ... We must have been awfully young and optimistic because the idea of any publisher doing that is absolutely ridiculous ... and de la Mare [at Faber and Faber] thought we were completely round the bend' (recorded conversation with William Blissett in 1975). Jones wanted his book 'foolscap size with a limp greyish cover stiffened at back with red buckram' like the 1936 'Tablet Publishing Company's Memorandum & Articles of Association printed by "Electric Law Press"' (to H 23 March 1936).
11 Manchester: David Jones Society 1979
12 Elizabeth Ward *David Jones Mythmaker* (Manchester: University of Manchester Press 1983) 88. Neither Hughes nor Ward reduces the poem to mere chronicle, but the poet's treatment of chronology and factual detail is more creative and unhistorical than either of them allows.
13 Draft of the letter to Bergonzi
14 Apropos of the assault on Mametz Wood, the authors of *A History of the 38th (Welsh) Division* record that 'one of the most magnificent sights of the war' was 'wave after wave of men ... advancing without hesitation and without a break,' and Jones notes in the margin of his copy of this book, 'I saw something of this myself and it was an impressive sight.'
15 Hague *David Jones* 46
16 Letter quoted by Colin Hughes *In Parenthesis As Straight Reporting* 12
17 Ibid 20
18 DGC 249; *The Long Conversation* 82; Colin Hughes *In Parenthesis As Straight Reporting* 6
19 *The Long Conversation* 133. See *IP* 109.
20 See David Blamires 'The Medieval Inspiration of David Jones,' in *David Jones: Eight Essays on his Work* ed R. Matthias (Llandysul: Gower Press 1976) 18.
21 These stories, which I heard Jones relate in some cases more than once, are recorded more or less as I heard them in *The Long Conversation*.
22 The poet owned a photograph of this valley with troops encamped there, on the back of which he had written, 'Bivouacking in Happy Valley before attack on Mametz Wood.'
23 See Blissett 'The Efficacious Word,' in *David Jones: Eight Essays on his Work* 26-7.
24 *The Poetry of the First World War* (Princeton: Princeton University Press

1964) 284ff. Jones considered Johnston's chapter on *In Parenthesis* 'very good & perceptive' (to H 9–15 July 1973), 'a remarkable and accurate account of what I was trying to do' (to G 7 March 1962), in which Johnston 'understood my whole intention and the way in which I tried to work it out' (to Johnston 23 March 1962).

25 George Lukacs *The Theory of the Novel* (Cambridge, Mass: Harvard 1971) 56
26 Pound *ABC of Reading* (London: Routledge 1934) 46; Bowra *From Virgil to Milton* (London: Macmillan 1948) 1ff; Tillyard *The English Epic* (London: Chatto and Windus 1954) 4–14; Frye *Anatomy of Criticism* 318; Merchant *The Epic* (London: Methuen 1971) ii
27 Draft of the letter to Bergonzi
28 Wilde borrowed the surname of Dorian Gray from his friend the minor poet John Gray, who became a Catholic, then a priest, and after the war an acquaintance of David Jones. See *The Long Conversation* 10–11, 90. Mr Jenkins's elegance may owe something to that of Canon Gray.

Chapter 3 Secular Mythos

1 This drawing, which was not reproduced in earlier reprints, appears on the cover of the most recent Faber paperback edition. The end-piece drawing, which was also dropped in earlier reprints, has not reappeared.
2 *Vision and Design* 24
3 *Transformations* (London: Chatto and Windus 1926; repr Garden City: Doubleday 1956) 8
4 See *Art* (London: Chatto and Windus 1914; repr New York: Putnam 1958) 45.
5 *The Philosophy of Art* 49
6 Bell *Art* 54; Maritain *The Philosophy of Art* 35
7 *The Decline of the West* tr C.F. Atkinson (London: Allen & Unwin 1934) I 47, 40, 37. Jones first read Spengler 'quite early' (*The Long Conversation* 65), probably in the early 1920s. References in the text are to this edition, which Jones acquired in 1941.
8 108, 117
9 Draft of the letter to Bernard Bergonzi
10 While Jones may have read them earlier, we know he read the Alice books while writing *In Parenthesis*. He received *Alice's Adventures in Wonderland* for 'Xmas 1930' and *Alice through the Looking-Glass*, from Prudence Pelham, probably the following year. In 1935 he says he has been reading *Alice in Wonderland* (DGC 70) and by that title he seems also to have meant *Through the Looking-Glass* (see DGC 83).
11 According to her marriage certificate, his mother was born in 1856. Whether

or not this is an error, David Jones thought she was born in 1854. He said so to William Blissett and me, mentioning that it was 'the first year of the Crimean War.' He gives the same year for her birth in a letter to Hague (4 September 1974).

12 See Dafydd Llwyd 'Cywydd I Harri Seithfed,' where Englishmen are 'cywion Alis'; and Tudur Penllyn 'I Reinallt ap Gryffudd ap Bleddyn o'r Twr,' where they are 'egin Alis.'
13 See David Jones's long note on 'Prickly Pear' in *The Long Conversation* 62–3.
14 Draft of a letter to J.H. Johnston 27 April 1962
15 The first to identify 'sweet sister death' as deriving from 'The Canticle of the Sun' is William Blissett '*In Parenthesis* among the War Books' *University of Toronto Quarterly* 42 (Spring 1973) 275.
16 A letter quoted by David Blamires in *David Jones, Artist and Writer* (Manchester: University of Manchester Press 1971) 3
17 In the preface to *The Works of Gildas and Nennius* tr J.A. Giles (London: James Bohn 1847), Jones marks the following words about Olwen: 'She is a personification of nature, and is only to be won by exploring her mysteries.' Jones bought this book 'in Oxford, 1937.'
18 If he had read *The Brothers Karamazov* by the time he wove this motif into his poem, Jones may also have been influenced by Dostoevsky's Zossima, who teaches: 'Every blade of grass, every insect, ant, and golden bee, all so amazingly know their path, though they have not intelligence. They bear witness to the mystery of God and continually accomplish it themselves ... It's touching to know that there's no sin in them, for all, all except man, is sinless, and Christ has been with them before us ... It cannot but be so ... since the Word is for all. All creation and all creatures, every leaf is striving to the Word, singing glory to God, weeping to Christ, unconsciously accomplishing this by the mystery of their sinless life' (tr Constance Garnett, rev Ralph Matlaw [New York: Norton 1976] 273–4).
19 *Selected Essays* (London: Faber and Faber 1937) 15
20 *The Great War and Modern Memory* (New York and London: Oxford University Press 1975) 146–7
21 Johnston enumerates some of these correspondences in *The Poetry of The First World War* 309–11, but there are many more, including the wounding in the leg of the poet-combatant who survives to commemorate the action.
22 'The Murder of Falstaff, David Jones and the "Disciplines of War,"' in *Evidence in Literary Scholarship* ed René Wellek and Alvaro Ribeiro (Oxford: Clarendon Press 1979) 27
23 See Northrop Frye *Anatomy of Criticism* 304–5.
24 Heroic humanity is discussed by Mary E. Jones 'Heroism in Unheroic

Warfare' *Poetry Wales* 8 (Winter 1972) 15. She and Johnston (334) rightly see the practice of ordinary virtue as heroic.
25 Dilworth 'A Book to Remember By' 230 (chapter 2 n6 above)
26 In his holograph list of sources for the poem, Jones includes *Moby-Dick*.
27 Vincent B. Sherry Jr '"Unmistakable Marks": Symbols and Voices in David Jones's *In Parenthesis*' *Critical Quarterly* 25 (Winter 1983) 64. In 'David Jones's *In Parenthesis*: New Measure' *Twentieth Century Literature* 28 (Winter 1982) 375–80, Sherry indicates a weakness in Fussell's argument by pointing out fertility imagery which Fussell ignores and which I have not dealt with here. Elizabeth Ward attempts to refute Fussell more directly, though in doing so she mistakenly claims that Jones evokes heroism only ironically and expresses 'the suppression of individual dignity' (*David Jones Mythmaker* 103–6, 110). Because her argument is limited to the imagery of the poem's realistic surface, it is not very strong, and if he chose to, Fussell could rebut it.
28 'Tradition and the Individual Talent' 15, 22
29 *English Poetry of the First World War* 306
30 Draft of the letter to Bernard Bergonzi
31 The poet read the Triads in *The Ancient Laws of Cambria* tr William Probert (London: E. Williams 1823). Jones inscribed his copy with his name and the year 1929.
32 'A New Boast for *In Parenthesis*: the Dramatic Monologue of David Jones' *Notre Dame English Journal* 14 (Spring 1982) 115
33 Ibid 116
34 For noticing the pun on 'cote' and *côte* and for acutely observing that Roland and Dai both die on hills, I am indebted to Patricia Emond.
35 These are not the upright trees of the woods, as Sherry claims in '"Unmistakable Marks"' 70. Compare the 'black perpendiculars' with the description of an earlier barrage in which 'black columns rise – spread acrid nightmare capitals' (86).
36 Ball sees 'spread before him on the blue warp above as though by a dexterous, rapid shuttling, unseen, from the nether-side, a patterning of intense white ...' (20), and later his 'night phantasm ... weaves with stored-up very other tangled threads' (32). On their way to the woods, infantrymen must penetrate 'the iron warp with bramble weft' (165). For further, incidental instances, see 35, 59, 72.
37 'Letters to H.S. Ede' ed John Matthias *PN Review* 22 (1981) 11. The quotation is taken from the conclusion of an autobiographical account written for Ede and dated 5 September 1935.

Chapter 4 Sacred Mythos

1 Jones to H 23 February 1972; quoted by Hague *David Jones* 56
2 *David Jones, an Exploratory Study* (London: Enitharmon 1975) 14. Hooker is the most daring of the pioneers of David Jones criticism and one whose work particularly interested David Jones.
3 Bernard Bergonzi *Heroes' Twilight* (London: Constable 1965) 308. David Blamires agrees with Bergonzi in *David Jones: Artist and Writer* 81. No one has differed with Johnston's contention that *In Parenthesis* is an epic except by inadequately reading the poem or, like John Silkin, by introducing irrelevancies as criteria of epic; see *Out of Battle* (London: Oxford University Press 1972) 319-20.
4 See *The Liturgical Parentheses of David Jones* (Ipswich: Golgonooza Press 1979).
5 Origen refers to the formation of 'a bee from an ox' as analogous to the qualitative transformation that takes place in the resurrection of the body (*Contra Celsum* 4.57). See St Jerome Ep 18.1 (*Patrologiae cursus completus ... series latina* 30 1820), on the significance of the bees of Virgil's *Georgic* for the paschal mystery and its liturgical celebration.
6 David Blamires is the first to suggest the motif of the Styx crossing (*David Jones: Artist and Writer* 102). See also remarks by Jeremy Hooker about an initiation motif informing the poem in *David Jones, an Exploratory Study* 18, 21-2.
7 Quoted by Hague in 'Myth and Mystery in the Poetry of David Jones' *Agenda* 15 (Summer-Autumn 1977) 64
8 These words also occur in an anthem sung by the Royal Welch Fusiliers at mess. See Robert Graves *Goodbye to All That* (London: Jonathan Cape 1929) 197.
9 *English Poetry of the First World War* 334. See also Mary E. Jones 'Heroism in Unheroic War' (chapter 3 n24 above) 15; and Paul Fussell *The Great War and Modern Memory* 147.
10 In his preface, furthermore, Jones writes that Cockney in the army has the status of a liturgical language and that the formula '"Kipt thet dressin cahncher" might well be ... what Kyrie Eleison is, breaking the Latin crust' (xii).
11 Plutarch quoted by Stobaeus *Florilegium* 4.107; Aristophanes *Frogs* 154-9
12 Sherry 'David Jones's *In Parenthesis*: New Measure' 377
13 The concluding words of the passage are a negative paraphrase of the *Quam oblationem*, the prayer of the Mass immediately preceding the Consecration.

14 Silkin, Bergonzi, and Fussell mention her briefly in passing; Elizabeth Ward fails even to mention her.
15 When I asked Jones what he thought of *The White Goddess*, he replied, 'Not much. There is no documentation and you can't check him out, and even I have noticed a few things that are just wrong. The sorts of connections he'll make are all right in poetry, but not in a book of this sort. For example, he might connect the god Baal with the Welsh figure Balin. Like me, he is an amateur; he would have been unerring had he written about the classical sources.'
16 Jones alludes to *Comus* in RQ 206 and refers to the Severn as Sabrina in IP 131, A 69, and SL 190.
17 On centric space as the primordial and predominant perceptual structure of pictorial art, see Rudolf Arnheim *The Power of the Center* (Berkeley: University of California 1982).
18 Ibid 135, 79

Chapter 5 Form

1 Conversation with the author in 1977. Heaney thinks that while *The Anathemata* is less 'organic' than *In Parenthesis* it is 'maybe more beautiful.'
2 *The Dublin Review* 226 (1952) 85
3 *David Jones Mythmaker* (chapter 2 n12 above) 152; by 'one-dimensional' I assume she means 'two-dimensional' or lacking depth, which would likewise be wrong.
4 *David Jones, an Exploratory Study* 49–50. Pages 32–52 of this book remain the best short introduction to *The Anathemata*.
5 *The Anathemata* is discussed as a sequence in a cursory manner by M.L. Rosenthal and Sally M. Gall *The Modern Poetic Sequence* (New York and Oxford: Oxford University Press 1983) 296–9, 273. They consider most of this century's long poetic works to be sequences in what is clearly, in part at least, a strategy to circumvent the problem of unity.
6 'David Jones: Artist and Writer' (chapter 1 n18 above) 9
7 *The Burning Tree* (London: Faber and Faber 1957) 15
8 *David Jones, an Exploratory Study* 40
9 Corcoran's *The Song of Deeds* (Cardiff: University of Wales Press 1982) is a good critical appreciation of the poem, which contains an excellent discussion of its symbolism, 75ff. For his consideration of 'metamorphic form,' see 87–8.
10 *David Jones Mythmaker* 141
11 *The Colours of Clarity* (Hamden, Conn: Archon 1964) 122

12 *David Jones, an Exploratory Study* 32
13 *The Song of Deeds* 83–4
14 In describing his circular journey, the poet alludes to the end of 'Little Gidding' by referring to 'the clarity of a waterfall here ... the note of a bird elsewhere' (42–3).
15 *The Modern Poetic Sequence* 298. On the basis of this misapprehension and assuming, apparently, that England is a region, they consider Jones a 'neo-regionalist' (306).
16 See Christopher Dawson *The Age of the Gods* (London: Sheed and Ward 1934) 4–5. This book is an important source for the whole of 'Rite and Fore-Time.'
17 The poet makes a mathematical error when he writes that it was 'sixty-eight years, since / in came the Principate' (90).
18 In *A Commentary on The Anathemata of David Jones* (Toronto: University of Toronto Press 1977), René Hague mistakes this ship for the 'Pelasgian' ghost ship (95) it passes in the mist, and he consequently thinks the voyage occurs centuries before and that the subsequent Greek references are anachronisms.
19 Before David Jones told Hague that there are two ships on separate voyages, all interpreters of the poem failed to distinguish between the Greek ship sailing for Athens and the more ancient ship sailing for Cornwall. Apparently the distinction needs to be emphasized, since critics continue mistakenly to conflate the two ships. Corcoran claims that a single voyage goes from the harbour of Athens to Cornwall and back (*The Song of Deeds* 64). Samuel Rees misinterprets these voyages as a single Roman voyage that discovers Britain (*David Jones* [Boston: Twayne 1978] 82).
20 For David Jones, there may be an influential precedent for this rhyming of route and topology in Welsh Fluellen's believing that Henry v and Alexander the Great are similar in stature and that this is indicated partly by the geographical resemblance between their birthplaces: 'if you look on the maps of the world, I warrant you sall find, in the comparisons between Macedon and Monmouth, that the situations, look you, is both alike' (*Henry* v 4.7.23–6). The same goes for the Saronic Gulf and Mount's Bay and for the routes of the ships entering them.
21 The poet records that his grandfather read from Milton and the Book of Common Prayer daily before breakfast, that although Church of England and a parish clerk, 'his proudest boast was that his name was the same as the first signature on the warrant that brought "the man Charles Stuart" to his decapitation,' and that he claimed 'to be descended from the family of Justice Bradshaw, the regicide.' See 'Fragments of an Attempted Autobiographical Writing' *Agenda* 12/13 (Winter–Spring 1975) 101.

22 Corcoran *The Song of Deeds* 102
23 Hague is mistaken in his *Commentary* about the setting of this section and about the location of the pool; see 155. Elen's reference to 'the Lower Pool' implies that she is not there (125). The Upper Pool, where she now is, reaches to London Bridge.
24 Hague and all other commentators fail to see this as a continuation of the Greek ship's approach to harbour earlier, though the poet emphasizes the continuity by his note on page 181.
25 This is the theology of Maurice de la Taille, whose book *The Mystery of Faith* the poet acknowledges in his preface as a 'crucial and great' work about 'the relationship of what was done in the Supper-room with what was done on the Hill and the further relationship of these doings with what is done in the Mass' (37).
26 Prose insert, 'David Jones reads *The Anathemata, In Parenthesis* and "The Hunt"' ed Peter Orr (London: Argo RG 520, PLP 1093, mono 1967)
27 He writes that the Carthusian motto, *Stat crux dum volvitur orbis*, 'is what I was trying to remember much of the time in writing *Ana*, but couldn't recall how it went' (*IN* 44).
28 I describe the structure of the poem in 'The Anagogical Form of *The Anathemata*' *Mosaic* 12 (Winter 1979) 183–95.
29 *The Song of Deeds* 27
30 On the radio script of a Mass-poem recorded by the BBC in 1958 but never broadcast is a paper cover on which Jones writes, 'The Mass. A fragment' and the words 'about 1945.'
31 *The Song of Deeds* 63. Chapter 5 of Corcoran's book contains an excellent discussion of the poem's language.
32 *The Power of the Center* (Chapter 4 n17) 72
33 Douglas Cleverdon 'David Jones and Broadcasting' *Poetry Wales* 8 (Winter 1972) 78
34 The image, which first appears in the pseudohermetic manuscript of *The Book of the Twenty-four Philosophers*, is invoked by David Blamires (*David Jones Artist and Writer* 119) and by Kathleen Raine *David Jones and the Actually Loved and Known* (Ipswich: Golgonooza Press 1978) 21.
35 Schleffer, who wrote under the name Angelus Silesius, is quoted by Georges Poulet *The Metamorphosis of the Circle* (Baltimore: Johns Hopkins Press 1966) xxiii.
36 'In the Glorious Epiphanie of Our Lord,' line 26
37 *Agenda* 11 (Autumn–Winter 1973/74) 20
38 Hague *A Commentary on The Anathemata* 63
39 For more on the relationship between the Eucharist and the Incarnation, see

DG 209 n16. The relationship is succinctly expressed in a Greek Orthodox saying Jones liked, which refers to 'Mary as "she who bore our Eucharist"' (to G 15 August 1971).
40 Here are Jones's remarks as I remember them: '*The Phenomenon of Man* was difficult for me because I know no science but I could see the thought was intelligent and difficult. I don't think much of his theory, the alpha-omega thing. Teilhard knew nothing about the arts. There is no improvement in the arts. Picasso is no improvement over Lascaux. The same is true in literature: the works are different but no better than each other in a temporal progression. *The Divine Milieu* was an excellent book – just as spiritual reading.'
41 On an early draft of the material on page 55, the poet draws and labels the mountains piled on one another in this earlier, mythic order, with Olympus on the bottom.
42 The second occurrence of 'species' in this line is not, as some have suggested, a misprint for 'subspecies' but, as in Jones's source, indicates the variety of mammalian species existing at contiguous stages of evolution. See 'David Jones's Use of a Geology Text for *The Anathemata*' *English Language Notes* 15 (December 1977) 115–19, in which I discuss Jones's coda in some detail. (The recent Faber reprint mistakenly corrects this line.)
43 'The new light of your brightness has poured into the eyes of our mind.'
44 Jones writes that '*Sher* in Thursdaye had some allusion to a brightness or a gleaming of some sort' (to B 17 October 1971). We have seen that, by translinguistic reverse etymology, brightness is redolent of divinity.
45 See Jane Ellen Harrison, *Themis* (Cambridge: Cambridge University Press 1912) 44ff. Jones lists the author among his sources for the poem (37).
46 According to his note on its front endpapers, Jones acquired his own copy of the book on 'Aug. 19th, 1941.' We know he was 'immersed in Spengler' in February 1942 (DGC 115).
47 In his copy of Patricia Hutchins *James Joyce's World* (London: Methuen 1957), David Jones underlines her contention that time is 'a spiral, not a straight line' and writes in the margin, 'concedo' (81).
48 In his copy of *The Decline of the West* Jones brackets the following passage in the translator's preface: 'after studying and mastering [this book], one finds it nearly if not quite impossible to approach any culture-problem – old or new, dogmatic or artistic, political or scientific – without conceiving of it primarily as "morphological"' (xi).
49 See most recently Corcoran *The Song of Deeds* 10; and Rosenthal and Gall *The Modern Poetic Sequence* 299. The only critics who explicitly recognize the antithetical meaning of 'anathemata' are William Noon SJ *Poetry and Prayer* (New Brunswick, NJ: Rutgers University Press 1966) 228–9 and Ann

Carson Daley 'The Amphibolic Title of *The Anathemata*' *Renascence* 35 (Autumn 1982) 49ff.
50 In a letter to Desmond Chute, Jones writes, 'we are in the 6th ... Cent' (*IN* 57).
51 On the same page as the lines quoted, Jones writes the words 'fiendish marsh,' which he could not have written without thinking of the 'Fiendish park' in the Anna Livia chapter of *Finnegans Wake*. All of this chapter is heavily marked in the copy of the *Wake* that he acquired in 1948. The allusion here to Joyce is doubtless intended partly as a tribute to the man whom Jones, in 1972, called 'the greatest poet, word-artist, that the West has produced.'
52 Arthur's epitaph, *Rex quondam rexque futurus*, is quoted on page 164. In 1952 Jones writes, '"Arthur" has become as historically feasible as MacArthur, and as congruent with a given situation' (*E&A* 201).
53 *David Jones Mythmaker* 153
54 Reproductions of the Kore and the other Greek statues mentioned in the poem can be seen where the poet may often have looked at them, in a book he owned: J.D. Beazley and B. Ashmole *Greek Sculpture and Painting* (Cambridge: Cambridge University Press 1932), figures 25, 29, 36, 36, 48, and 51.
55 Tacitus, *Annals* 2.85 and E. Schürer *The History of the Jewish People in the Times of Jesus Christ* (Edinburgh: T. & T. Clark 1886–90) II, ii, 236; I, ii, 86n. Hague is wrong in saying that the reference here to a 'Diaspora' is an anachronism (*Commentary* 182).
56 Elizabeth Ward argues fallaciously (in a technical, logical sense) that Jones's antitotalitarian 'bias' is irreconcilable with his criticism of the nontotalitarian West because, like the fascists, he dislikes western rationalism and materialism and idealizes the past (*David Jones Mythmaker* 190). The differences between his perceptions and fascist ideology are enormous, both in what he disapproves of (Jones was never a racist) and in what he proposes as a remedy, which is cultural and religious, not political (and this is why he idealizes the early Middle Ages and not, like the fascists, imperial Rome). Ward insinuates, furthermore, that in the thirties the poet himself was pro-fascist. Certainly he was sympathetic to Germany, but his sympathy was moral rather than ideological. As Harman Grisewood writes in a letter to me dated 10 August 1984, 'His sympathy was with the portrayal of injustice in *Mein Kampf*, not with the brutal means taken to correct it ...' His pre-war sympathies were with the Germans as 'a vanquished people ... oppressed by exultant and tyrannous conquerors.' The pre-war, pro-German sympathies of David Jones should not, I think, arouse scepticism about, or require qualification of, the clear evidence in his later poetry that when he wrote it he was profoundly unsympathetic to fascism. For more on this subject, see my essay 'David Jones and Fascism' *Journal of Modern Literature* 13 (March 1986)

149–62 or the expanded version in *David Jones: Man and Poet* ed John Matthias (Orono, Maine: National Poetry Foundation 1988). For a deft and convincing refutation of Ward's contention that Jones's poetry is ideologically protofascist, see Kathleen Henderson Staudt 'Recent Criticism on David Jones' *Contemporary Literature* 27 (Fall 1986) 416–20.

57 In his own copy of *The Decline of the West*, David Jones marks the paragraphs in which Spengler argues this point. The passage from *The Anathemata* quoted here also reflects Spengler's comparison of Gothic architecture with living vegetation (I 396), which in his copy Jones marks and glosses with the comment 'good.' See also the architectural criticism of Eric Gill, *Autobiography* (London: J. Cape 1940) 102.

58 *Cumaean Gates* (Oxford: Basil Blackwell 1936) 78; see also 76. David Jones acquired his copy of this book in 1940. References to this work appear hereafter in the text.

59 Jones marks these words in his copy of Spengler, and first uses his own expression, 'fact-man,' in a marginal comment in volume II 220. Ward accuses the poet of regarding 'Nazi and British imperialism' as 'indistinguishable' because he allows Roman imperialism to evoke them both, whereas he merely identifies them as the same species of vice (ie robbery) without specifying – as it hardly seems necessary to do – the degree to which mass murder and repression differentiate them (*David Jones Mythmaker* 190).

60 John A. MacCulloch 'Celtic Mythology,' in *The Mythology of All Races* (Boston: Marshall Jones 1919) 107

61 When the eclogue was written, Octavius was not yet Augustus and Virgil's patron was the consult Pollio, a supporter of Anthony; nevertheless, the poem seems to celebrate the policies of Octavius, who is favourably referred to throughout the *Eclogues* as a special devotee of Apollo.

62 Concerning the defensive intent of the Lion Gate, see Jackson Knight *Vergil's Troy* (Oxford: Basil Blackwell 1932) 131. According to a note on the flyleaf of his own copy, Jones had this book out of the library 'in 1949 or 1950.' References to this work appear hereafter in the text.

Chapter 6 Typology

1 'Two Letters from David Jones' (above, chapter 1 n34) 20

2 In a letter to Hague (18 September 1974), the poet elaborates in some detail: 'his "greatest oath" was, if really angry or determined – "No I will not, not for the Pope of Rome." That is verbatim from my mother. It was *I* in writing *The Ana* who changed for reasons inherent in the text, the Pope of Rome into "the Scarlet Pontiff of the West" ... the "in curial-cursive and leaded" was also of

my making ... I used the raw material of what my mother told. The figure of the "boosed Murphy" ... was straight from my mother ... "running-blocks, new dead-eyes to the standing shrouds,'" "not fer a gratis load of sound teak in Breaker's yard," "best float of Oregon" – all that or those terms, & site names such as "Dockhead" and "Princess Stair" were direct reportage of what my mother had mentioned – as also "dash m' buttons" & "bonded stuff" & even "Trinity Brethern"... "Not if the Holy Ghost made ready to blow on his mainsail" is *not* direct from my mother's reportage but indirect from such expressions as "if the heavens blew convenient." Eb B would I *think* refrain from saying "not if the Holy Ghost" etc as *somewhat* blasphemous.'
3 *David Jones Mythmaker* 151
4 Sigmund Freud *Totem and Taboo* tr J. Strachey (London: Routledge & Kegan Paul 1950) 129
5 David Jones heard this statement repeatedly in sermons by a French Augustinian at his parish in Brockley. About him Jones writes, 'Fr Bernardine was a marvellous man ... I had a special regard & affection for him – he had a great influence on me' (to H 9 September 1974). It is probably because he heard it from an Augustinian that he mistakenly ascribes the dictum to St Augustine (129 n4).
6 Richard Barber *Arthur of Albion* (London: Barrie and Rockliff 1961)
7 A key text for David Jones in this regard is the reference in *The Mabinogion* to the annual struggle each May first between Gwythyr and Gwyn for a maiden named Creiddylad (tr Guest 106). This conflict is reflected on a larger scale in the opening *mabinogi*'s account of Pwyll's fighting on behalf of Arawn, god of the otherworld. The lady there is Rhiannon or Ragantona, the Celtic earth mother. In books which Jones read, Matthew Arnold and John Rhys both discuss how the first text, in 'Kulhwch and Olwen,' reflects fertility myth. See *The Study of Celtic Literature, The Complete Prose Works of Matthew Arnold* III ed R.H. Super (Ann Arbor: University of Michigan 1962) 332; and Rhys *Studies in the Arthurian Legend* (Russel: London 1891) 36.
8 The poet marks the passage in which these words occur in his copy of *Vergil's Troy* (124) and writes in the flyleaf the meaning of Hector's name.
9 For the significance of these symbols, see Jessie L. Weston *From Ritual to Romance* (Cambridge: Cambridge University Press 1920) 75.
10 George Borrow tells the story in *Wild Wales* (London: John Murray 1901) chapter 46. Jones acquired a copy of this book in 1948.
11 See Edgar Wind *Pagan Mysteries in the Renaissance* (New Haven: Yale University Press 1958) 100–10. About 'the Botticelli *Primavera*' Jones writes, 'I remember enjoying it tremendously, as a picture, when it came to Burlington House before the last war' (to E 15 January 1951).

12 A photograph of the medal is reproduced in Gordon Home *Roman London* (London: Eyre and Spottiswoode 1948) 96.
13 Friedrich Heer *The Medieval World* (London: Weidenfeld and Nicolson 1962) 316
14 Hague errs in his *Commentary* in saying that the poet is 'transferring the old temple from Jupiter to the goddess of the chase.' Before the great fire, a place near the cathedral was called 'Diana's chambers,' and the cathedral itself is traditionally identified with the site of a temple of the goddess. See Sir Lawrence Gomme 'The Tradition of London in its Welsh Aspect' *Transactions of the Honourable Society of the Cymmrodorion* (Session 1912–13) 11–12.
15 Unpublished typescript by Peter Orr of an interview in 1978 with Stanley Honeyman
16 Tr Guest 152. The poet marks these words in his copy, which he bought in 1940, and also in the translation by Gwyn Jones and Thomas Jones (London: Dent 1949) 157.
17 Concerning the probable location of Joyous Gard, see *The Works of Thomas Malory* ed E. Vinaver (Oxford: Clarendon Press 1947) 1660 n1257, 27–8. Jones owned the three-volume first edition, which, according to his note on the flyleaf of the first volume, he purchased in 1947. See also Hague's *Commentary* 216.
18 This is one of the moments in *The Anathemata* that make me wonder how Rosenthal and Gall arrived at their judgment that the poem 'maintains its forward movement ... without quite reaching heights of intensity' (*The Modern Poetic Sequence* 296).
19 *Carmen de pascha vel de ligno vitae (Corpus scriptorum ecclesiasticorum latinorum* 3:3, 308)
20 The poet marks in his copy of Dawson's *Beyond Politics* (London: Sheed and Ward 1939) the words 'we cannot transform a plutocratic imperialism into a democratic community' (85).
21 In a passage in *Cumaean Gates* marked by Jones, Knight writes that 'Delphi means the female generative organ' (51).
22 These lines combine allusions to Marlowe's *Doctor Faustus* (14.93), Shakespeare's *Troilus and Cressida* (2.2.81–3), and Poe's 'To Helen' (line 9).
23 See Cyprian of Carthage in *The Mass, Ancient Liturgies and Patristic Texts* ed G.A. Hamman (New York: Alba House 1967) 187, 192.
24 Pseudo-Athanasius *De passione Domini (Patrologiae cursus completus ... series graeca* 28 1056B). For more elaborate examples, see St Ambrose *Expositio Psalmi 118* (*Corpus scriptorum ecclesiasticorum latinorum* 62 186. 15–17) and Clement of Alexandria *Protrepticus* 11.114.1–4 (*Die greichischen christlichen Schriftsteller* 1 80).

25 Elen refers to the *Mary*'s captain as 'him from Aleppo come' (137), but he is, of course, English; his ship has returned 'from Aleppo to England' (*IN* 79).
26 Jones writes 'Mary' in the margin beside a reference to the *Mary Rose* in a volume which his pencilled notes and diagrams indicate he used as a reference while writing 'The Lady of the Pool': Geoffrey Clowes *Sailing Ships: Their History and Development as Illustrated by the Collection of Ship Models in the Science Museum* Part 1, Historical Notes (London: HMSO 1932).
27 See the hymn *Ave maris stella*, in which Mary is addressed by the 'Ave which from Gabriel came ... reversing Eva's name.' Through Eve came the fall; through Mary the redemption.
28 See the Introit for the feast of the Assumption and the Office for the feast of the Queenship of Mary.
29 The poet told me that *The Brothers Karamazov* 'is the only one of those long Russian novels I've read.' He read it at the insistence of Leslie Poulter, the Olivier of *IP* (to H 9–15 July 1973). Jones probably read it during the Second World War, for in the margin beside a reference to Dostoevsky in his copy of *The Decline of the West* (II 211), he writes, 'at paw [ie at hand] in Sheffield Terrace' in London, which is where he lived from 1941 to 1945.
30 Pages 8, 17 of an undated offprint of a paper originally delivered at a conference on medical psychotherapy and later published with different pagination in *The Proceedings of the International Congress on Mental Health* 3 (London 1948) 10–18
31 In her litany Mary is called *foederis arca*, a phrase echoed on page 235. For examples of the Church as Noah's Ark see *De civitate Dei* 15.26; Aquinas *Exposition of the Apostles' Creed*; and *Piers Plowman* 16, line 144.
32 Thomas Babington Macaulay *Lays of Ancient Rome* (Oxford: Oxford University Press 1906) 59
33 'David Jones: Artist and Writer' 8 (Chapter 1 n18 above). He said this with reference to ship-paintings done in 1931 and 1962.
34 The scriptural passages interwoven here are from Mark 16:1–2, Matt 28:1, and John 20:1.

Chapter 7 Sequence

1 Extensive elements of the Roman poems in *The Sleeping Lord* are present at an early stage of composition of the manuscript material in which *The Anathemata* has its origin.
2 In a letter to Grisewood, Jones states that his 'new book' will begin with the trumpet-call 'Tarantantara!' (August 1952), the word with which 'The Wall' opens in a draft at this time (see *IN* 41).

3 The poem originates in *The Book of Balaam's Ass* (RQ 209–10). Its opening twenty-one lines first appear in print in 'Art and Sacrament,' in *Catholic Approaches* ed Elizabeth Pakenham (London: Weidenfeld and Nicolson 1955) and again in E&A. The complete poem appears for the first time in *Poems by W.H. Auden ... David Jones ... et al* ed Eric W. White (London: The Poetry Society 1966) and then in *Agenda* 5 (Spring–Summer 1967).
4 Elizabeth Ward *David Jones Mythmaker* 166
5 *The Mabinogion* tr Guest 266
6 After its publication in *Poetry*, 'The Wall' was published in *Landmarks and Voyages* ed Vernon Watkins (London: Poetry Book Society 1957); *An Anthology of Modern Verse: 1940–1960* ed Elizabeth Jennings (London: Methuen 1961); *Agenda* 5 (Spring–Summer 1967); *The Lilting House: An Anthology of Anglo-Welsh Poetry, 1917–67* ed John Stuart Williams and Meic Stephens (London: Dent 1969); *Twenty-Three Modern British Poets* ed John Matthias (Chicago: Swallow Press 1971) – all anthologies which also include Jones's 'The Tutelar of the Place'; and *The Poetry Anthology 1912–1977* ed Daryl Hine and Joseph Parisi (Boston: Houghton Mifflin 1978).
7 Frazer emphasizes the defensive significance of her posture in his edition of Ovid, *Fastorum libri sex* II (London: Macmillan 1929) 372. Jones acquired his copy of the five volumes of this edition in 1952.
8 If the city is a microcosm, it is because the *mundus* is a microcosm. It is the ritual pit Romulus dug when he founded the city, which was afterwards filled and topped with an altar (*Fastorum libri sex* IV 821ff). The word *mundus* equates with 'cosmos' and means the universe, the earth and the heavens – the world but especially the heavens (Lewis and Short, sv).
9 David Jones read in *Cumaean Gates* that the Cretan maze was actually a prison and that tombs were designed as labyrinths to keep in the dead. In this respect, tombs are prisons (47–58, 63).
10 'Tell *her*' evokes the plural of *tellus*, *tellura*. In his copy of *The Skeleton Key to Finnegans Wake*, which he acquired in 1954, Jones writes 'Tellus Mater & Alma Mater' in the margin beside Joyce's words, 'the cry goes up again for the little woman: "Tellus tellas allabouter"' (84).
11 Ovid, *Fastorum libri sex* II 321. On the flyleaf of his copy, Jones enters this page number and the words 'Carmental Gate.'
12 'Two Letters from David Jones' *Agenda* 11–12 (Autumn–Winter 1973/74) 23
13 'The Dream of Private Clitus' was written 'c. 1960, but based, in part, on a longer work begun c. 1940.' It was published first in *Art and Literature* 1 (March 1964), then in *Agenda* 5:1–3 (Spring–Summer 1967).
14 See Karl Stern *The Flight from Woman* (New York: Farrar, Strauss and Giroux 1965) 18–22.

15 Jones marks a reference to 'The Dream of Scipio' in his copy of *Cumaean Gates* 175. Another, possibly subconscious influence on Jones's poem may be the 'Queen Mab' chapter of *Moby-Dick*, in which Stubb tells Flask of dreaming of Ahab being transformed into a pyramid.
16 After seeing photographs of the interior of Mametz Wood taken by Colin Hughes in 1969, Jones writes to Hague: 'It looked almost exactly the same as it had when last I saw it in July 1916' (14 June 1970).
17 See Robert Graves *Good-Bye to All That* (New York: Blue Ribbon 1931) 252–3.
18 Jones writes in a letter to Hague that he wanted 'some way of suggesting that wax-moustached feeling' of 'bandsmen in my mob who retained the Regular Army fashion. Anyway in Liddell & Scott, I chanced upon "lancer-whiskered bucinators." It seemed too good to be true. It had the exact feeling I wanted – merely had to slip in "bloody" & the bottom line on page 22' was 'given me on a plate' (9–11 June 1974).
19 Jones writes to Grisewood, 'I was glad to read in your book *The Roman Army* ... that the centurion corresponds most of all to our Sergeant Majors, because that is what I've always *thought* of them as & have tried to express in my MS.' He goes on to say that while centurions were 'like Company Commanders "functionally,"' they were 'like Sergeant Majors "psychologically."' And of those who held the rank to which Brasso has risen, that of senior centurion, Jones writes, 'Christ! I bet they were bastards' (13 March 1942).
20 Clitus's remaining a private after all his years of service has special autobiographical resonance for David Jones, who in 1915 repeatedly refused promotion. He said that Colonel Dell (Bell of *In Parenthesis*), 'when he heard I was educated, wanted me to become an officer. I kept refusing. He said I was shirking my duty and that we needed new officers. Then I told him I had gone to *art* school, and he dropped the subject.' Two of Jones's reasons for refusing promotion were that he did not want to be cut off from friends by a difference in rank, and he did not want to take the extra risk involved owing to the distinctive uniforms that made officers easy targets.
21 'The Fatigue' was first published as a short book for subscribers in a limited edition of 298 copies (Cambridge: Rampant Lions Press 1965).
22 Approximate place is implied by the NCO's spatial references and by his saying that to have observed movement beyond the eastern wall the sentries would have had to 'see through stone' (30), and Jones specifies exact location in a manuscript note (*RQ* 44 n99).
23 *The Long Conversation* 141; see also Wall's obituary in *The Times* 4 May 1974.

24 Jeremy Hooker is the first to suggest a relationship between Jesus and Sejanus and between their tables; see *An Exploratory Study* 58.
25 See Jessie Weston *From Ritual to Romance* (New York: Doubleday 1957) 80.
26 In a manuscript note, Jones writes of the first of the sentries, 'He could not, without leaving his post, observe any movement in the area of the Porta Aquarum and the Mount of Olives – these would be round to his left beyond the roofs of the Temple buildings' (RQ 45 n99). The same is true for the second sentry, since the NCO says of both that to see what they report they would have to see through stone.
27 *Gravity and Grace* (London: Routledge and Keegan Paul 1952) 145. As markings and annotations show, David Jones read this book. His copy is inscribed 'David from Clare, June 1955.'
28 The image, alluded to in the central passage in *The Anathemata* (157), derives from the *Vexilla regis*, a hymn which is quoted in the prefatory lyric of 'The Fatigue' (27). See E&A 261; DG 221–2. The image of the cross as *libra* appears in the passage about Romans in Wales that was intended for, but finally excluded from, *The Sleeping Lord* (RQ 75).
29 'The Tribune's Visitation' first appeared in *The Listener* (22 May 1958). It was subsequently published as a book (London: Fulcrum Press 1969). The recording of David Jones reading the poem is *Poets of Wales: David Jones* (London: Decca Records, Argo Division, PLP 1180, mono 1972). An early version of my discussion of this fragment appeared in *Renascence* 28 (Winter 1986) 103–16.
30 Macaulay *Lays of Ancient Rome* (chapter 6 n32 above) 7, 22. Jones knew 'Horatius' by heart from about the age of eight.
31 See Macaulay's preface viii–xx, in which he describes how the ancient ballads mentioned by Ennius, Fabius, and Cato were lost in the transformation of Roman literary culture under the influence of Greek classicism, so that Cicero could only lament, 'Would that we still had the old ballads of which Cato speaks.'
32 Ernst Cassirer *The Myth of the State* (Oxford: Oxford University Press 1943) 140. The poet inscribes his copy with the date 1953. He does not mark this passage.
33 *Gravity and Grace* 144
34 George Orwell *Nineteen Eighty-four* (Penguin: Harmondsworth, Middlesex 1954) 217
35 Henry Summerfield spots this allusion in *An Introductory Guide to ... The Sleeping Lord Sequence of David Jones* (Victoria, BC: Sono Nis 1979) 161.
36 My thanks to William Blissett for spotting this allusion. It has ambiguous implications, of course. It identifies the Tribune with Jesus in his agony, but

Jesus had initially wanted his disciples awake to 'watch and pray that you may not enter into temptation.'

37 In addition to the allusions indicated earlier, the Tribune says, 'For me the time is now' (49; cf 2 Cor 6:2); 'all are members / of the Strider's body' (58; cf Eph 5:30); 'And if not of one hope / then of one necessity. / For we all are attested to one calling' (58; cf Eph 4:4).

38 Jones goes on to say that the poem is 'soliloqual in character' although, as he writes elsewhere, it originated as a dramatic monologue by a 'Gaulish soldier' on the wall of Jerusalem ('Two Letters from David Jones' 24). 'The Tutelar of the Place' was first published in *Poetry* (Chicago) 97 (January 1961) and won that publication's Levinson Prize for that year.

39 *Flight from Woman* 54

40 *Wild Wales* xv n1 (chapter 6 n10 above)

41 See *The Oxford Dictionary of Nursery Rhymes* 61.

42 Prose insert, 'David Jones reads ... "The Hunt"' (chapter 5 n26 above)

43 See Mark Schorer's famous essay, 'Technique as Discovery' *The Hudson Review* 1 (Spring 1948) 67-87. 'The Hunt' was written 'c. 1964 incorporating passages written c. 1950 or earlier' and was first published in *Agenda* 4 (April-May 1965) 3-6, subsequently in *Agenda* 5 (Spring-Summer 1967) 23-7, and then, with revisions, in *The Anglo-Welsh Review* 15 (Summer 1966) 7-10. My discussion of 'The Hunt' was first published in *The Anglo-Welsh Review* 85 (1987) 93-102.

44 Tr Guest 13

45 R.S. Loomis *Wales and the Arthurian Legend* (Cardiff: University of Wales Press 1956) 82. In *The Anathemata* a Roman Briton, having reverted to living in the wild, is called a '*wilde Jäger*' (113).

46 *RQ* 18 n36. This note is to a passage on a manuscript page prior to that on which a draft of 'The Hunt' begins. Cf E&A 233n.

47 *The Study of Celtic Literature* (chapter 6 n7 above) 322

48 The poet underlines these words and marks them with a marginal line in his copy of *The Mabinogion* tr Gwyn Jones and Thomas Jones (London: Dent 1949) 107.

49 The identification with Arawn was made by A.H. Krappe in 'Who *Was* the Green Knight?' *Speculum* 13 (1938) 206-15 and R.S. Loomis in *The Arthurian Tradition and Crétien de Troyes* (Columbia: New York and London 1948) 126, 420. The identification with a vegetation god was made by Robert G. Cook in 'The European Sky God' *Folklore* 17 (1906) 308-48, 427-57 and became prevalent in the myth criticism of the 1930s and 1940s. See William A. Nitze in 'Is the Green Knight a Vegetation Myth?' *Modern Philology* 23 (1936) 351-66 and Krappe in 'Who *Was* the Green Knight?' In 1972 Jones

called *Gawain and the Green Knight* 'the most magical of those early things' and said he read it in translation.
50 Tr Eugene Mason (London: Dent 1910) 23–4. We have already seen that this short romance influences the episode of the Queen of the Woods in *In Parenthesis*. The imagery of blood and grass from the description of Aucassin's riding obviously influences the following lines of an early draft of 'The Hunt':
Was the blood stay at his breast?
Was the stay at his fair loins?
or did the unbending grass for the
lightness of his horse-tread, stay
the flow? Was it to nourish
the furrow that he bled?
51 B Passus 17, line 341. Langland's poem was a favourite of David Jones, who writes that 'no work could be more belonging to this island' of Britain. Letter to *The Listener* 4 April 1957, page 564
52 This is 8 July, the feast of the *vituli*. See W. Warde Fowler *The Roman Festivals* (London: Macmillan 1933) 179. My discussion of the 'Sleeping Lord' fragment was first published in *The Anglo-Welsh Review* 76 (1984) 59–70.
53 Jones and Joyce are writing about the same Celtic archetype. On the flyleaf of his copy of Alwyn Rees and Brinley Rees *The Celtic Heritage* (London: Thames and Hudson 1961), Jones writes 'Finn like Arthur' and refers to the page that concludes a discussion of the parallels between Arthur and the hero of the Ossianic cycle. Both Arthur and Finn harrow the otherworld, hunt a hog, and repulse foreign invaders. Jones may also be influenced by Albion, the sleeping giant in Blake's *Jerusalem*, and possibly by Hopkins's 'Hurrahing in Harvest,' in which 'the azurous hung hills' of Wales are Christ's 'world-wielding shoulder / Majestic.'
54 This I heard from Fr Kevin Scannell, who heard it at Ditchling in the 1960s.
55 My special thanks to Diana and Huw Ceiriog Jones for introducing me to this remarkable landscape. Philip Hagreen, in 1985, recalled Jones walking to the Hay with Gill and Gray.
56 Samuel Rees mistakes grace before supper here for 'a *requiem* Mass'; see *David Jones* (chapter 5 n19 above) 113. Elizabeth Ward repeats his error (*David Jones Mythmaker* 199).
57 '"Bedad he revives! See how he raises!"': An Introduction to David Jones's "The Sleeping Lord"' *University of Toronto Quarterly* 52 (November 1982) 104
58 Ibid 101
59 This is David Jones's translation of 'La Haie Taillée' (94) in a letter to Hague, 10 October 1962.
60 As David Jones knows, the earliest mention of Arthur's resting place occurs

in 'The Stanzas of the Graves [Beddau].' See E&A 213, 228 and DG 39, 53.
61 The passage Jones adapts, which describes the felling of trees for the burning of the dead after the battle of Heraclea (Annals 6, fr 9), is modelled on Homer's funeral preparations for Patroclus (Iliad 23.114ff), and is subsequently echoed by Virgil's account of funeral preparations for Misenus (Aeneid 6.179ff).
62 Ffion (foxgloves) is a masculine noun, but in Welsh is used as a girl's name, as Jones notes in a letter to Hague, 9 September 1974.
63 See John Terpstra 'Bedad he revives!' 98–9.
64 In addition to their symbolic power, these words have a peculiarly Celtic connotation which the poet mentions in a note to an early draft of the poem: 'This is a borrowing from an early Irish tale, where it occurs as three separated exclamations & runs, I think, as follows: "Wave is rough," "Wind is cold," "Candle is bright." I regret that I have no further or precise recollection of the source.'
65 The 'if' in 'the Word if made fire' is a misprint.
66 Arthur's hall also evokes the archetypal Christian church. The *pared* across the width of the hall resembles the *cancelli* or 'screen' (78 n2) of the ancient Roman basilica, which is the prototype of the medieval churches that are divided, by screen, arch, or iconostasis, into nave and chancel.
67 Jones told William Blissett and me when he wrote the poem. Where he wrote it was 'partly at Sidmough & Hartland Point & in that "cottage" on the Stanmer estate where Prudence and Lady Chichester lived' (DGC 250).
68 The poet marks these words in his copy.
69 Jones marks this section in a copy of Pound's *Personae* which he acquired in 1965.
70 One of his listeners, 'Pamela-born-between-the-sirens,' is quite young, having been born during a Zeppelin raid. I mention this because René Hague, not realizing that there were air raids on London during the First World War, mistakenly judges the text to be written in the 1940s and in anticipation of 'a conversation that will take place some twenty years after' (RQ 275). *In Parenthesis* alludes to Zeppelin air raids on London when one of Ball's companions hopes 'Jerry puts one on Mecklenburgh Square – instead of fussing patriotic Croydon' (143).
71 My catalogue builds on a preliminary census William Blissett compiled in 1974. See *The Long Conversation* 138.
72 Jones mentions Byrd, the Catholic composer of Elizabeth I's court chapel, in a letter to H 13 December 1963.
73 *The Mabinogion* tr Guest 102. Jones marks the description of the three survivors in his copies of *The Mabinogion* and in his copy of *The Ancient*

Laws of Cambria tr William Probert (London: E. Williams 1823) 403, Triad 83. This last book he acquired in 1929.
74 See 'the marching mules of Marius' in 'The Narrows' (*RQ* 60). In the manuscript in which the Nodens-insert originates, because of his stubbornness Nodens is called a '"mule of Marius" in a sense not generally meant' (*RQ* 72).
75 Although Hague says that the letter in which this passage occurs is undated, it does bear the date 24 September 1974.
76 Spud Bullen's account originates in a conversation in the late 1930s or early 1940s with retired Colonel George Richey, who told Jones in a pub in Kensington Church Street 'that chaps who'd never seen the power and accurate aim of an assegai joked about opposing rattling-guns to bits of wood, but in fact the effect of well-aimed assegai was not at all funny & the wounds inflicted were nasty indeed' (to G 14 July 1971).

Chapter 8   Conclusion

1 See Kathleen Henderson Staudt on Jones's conception of the text as 'the index of an "act,"' 'The Poem As Sacramental Act' (chapter 1 n41 above) 8.
2 Letter to the author, 18 April 1979
3 Letter to the author, 13 June 1979
4 Letter quoted by Corcoran *The Song of Deeds* 109
5 Behind this episode of *Ulysses* is a huge strategic error for, while the episode apparently conforms in every respect to Joyce's intentions, its form is not in significant relationship to its content and the writing fails to repay with sufficient meaning or pleasure the labour of reading it.
6 See Donald Davie in *TLS* (22 August 1980) 935, in which he quotes the *Benedicite* passage in *A* 63–4, but seems not to take into account the differences between Church pronunciation of Latin and the usual learned pronunciation.
7 'Shapes and Surfaces: David Jones, with a Glance at Charles Tomlinson' *Contemporary Literature* 12 (Autumn 1971) 419
8 Typescript of a 1935 autobiographical account written in 1935 for Jim Ede
9 Letter to the author, 18 April 1979
10 Rosenthal and Gall *The Modern Poetic Sequence* 104
11 *The Dunciad, Milton, Jerusalem, Don Juan, The Prelude, Idylls of the King, The Dynasts*: all these are epical in various respects, including length, but they were not perceived, either by their authors or by their reading publics, as epics. I am, of course, using 'epic' not to connote value but only to denote genre.

12 Michael Bernstein argues that the *Cantos* is an epic, but his four epic criteria pertain only to subject matter. And even he admits that 'the foregrounding of [Pound's] private situation is attained only at the cost of compromising the *Cantos*' epic ambitions.' See *The Tale of the Tribe: Ezra Pound and the Modern Verse Epic* (Princeton: Princeton University Press 1980) 180.
13 Of Jones's British contemporaries the most highly regarded critically is W.H. Auden, a thinker in verse who is technically more versatile than Jones but less innovative and more restricted in mimetic scope. More widely read and passionately loved is Dylan Thomas, a daring neoromantic whose poetry is usually flawed by a disjunction between thought and feeling. Although poetry so different in kind may not yield fruitful comparison, it seems reasonable to say that David Jones is aesthetically more daring, emotionally more resonant, and technically more innovative than Auden; and like a great many poets, he is technically more successful than Dylan Thomas. Among more recent poets Ted Hughes and Geoffrey Hill have been much praised. The long sequences of Hughes, however, are technically out of control, and although Hill is a very fine poet, an obsessive perfectionism inhibits him technically and his imaginative scope is restricted in comparison with that of Jones. It is highly probable that no British poet of this century has produced work which equals that of David Jones in intellectual scope and importance, in depth of feeling, and in technical originality and mastery.

Index

Abel
- and Cain 90–1, 302
- as type of infantrymen 139
abstract form. *See* form
Achilles 337
Adam 247
'Adam Bell' 349
Adonis 137–8, 327, 338
- slain, correspondence with infantrymen of 90, 91, 92. *See also under* figures in *SL*, Arthur
Aeneas 221, 235, 265, 267, 270
Aeneid. See Virgil
Alexander the Great 198
Alexander, Michael 365
Alfred, King 199
Allen, Reggie 46
'All Through the Night' 341
allusions
- in Jones's poetry 4
   in *The Anathemata* 256
   in *In Parenthesis* 95: as positively symbolic 100
- Joyce's use of 4
- and reciprocal knowing 60, 94, 100, 106–7
- and visual transparency 18
Altdorfer, Albrecht 348
Ambrose, St 354

- *Expositio Psalmi* 385n24
Amis and Amiloun 349
Li amitiez de Ami et Amile. See Amis and Amiloun
'Amo amas I love a Lass' 216
anamnesis 10, 173
- as essence of art 10, 24
- and the structure of *The Anathemata* 200
'anathemata' (defined) 182–3
The Anathemata 152–257, 289, 334. *See also under* archetypes; fictional modes; figures; motifs; personae
- admired by contemporary writers 3
- and the *Aeneid* 153
- 'Angle-Land' 163, 184–5
- Anglo-Saxon settlement in 163
- archetypes in. *See under* archetypes
- Britain in
   geological formation of 160
   as land of the dead 234–5, 242
   and Rome 231
   and Troy 231
- Calvary in 232
- and the *Cantos* 363, 365–7, 368
- composition of 169–71, 368
   analogous to painting 9
- content, form of 156
- culture in, analysis of 183

- cyclic time in 181–5
- earth, geological formation of 159, 160, 163, 175, 177, 197–8, 231
- and *Finnegans Wake*. *See under* Joyce
- form of 254–5. *See also* A, movement in
    - atomic or galactic 153–4
    - catalogues in: dogs 212–3, 365; Gwenhwyfar's description 229; heights 198
    - and Celtic art 155
    - centric 183, 228
    - and Christ 200
    - circular 30, 156, 158, 166, 167, 168–75, 200
    - compared with that of *In Parenthesis* 152–3, 156, 180
    - and content 156, 174–200
    - double exposure 159, 191. *See also* A, form of, triple exposure
    - juxtaposition of Christmas with Holy Thursday 174
    - metamorphic 155, 232, 234, 240
    - and relativity theory 173
    - spatial 201
    - symbolic transference in 232. *See also* A, form of, metamorphic
    - topological rhyming in 162, 241: and *Henry V* 379n20
    - triple exposure 168. *See also* A, form of, double exposure
    - unity of 154–7, 367. *See also* A, structure of
- genre of 255–6. *See also* A, sub-genres in
    - anatomy 152–3, 201
    - epic, displaced 152–3
    - sequence (resemblance to) 154–5, 170–1
    - transfictional 182
- historic time in, 181–200, 361. *See also under* motifs in A, history
- importance of 256, 368
- and *In Parenthesis* 201, 202, 255–6
- Jones on 4, 201, 234, 243
- 'Keel, Ram, Stauros' 166–7, 234, 235, 237, 243
- 'The Lady of the Pool' 164–6, 169, 170, 189–90, 215–28, 343. *See also under* personae in A, Elen Monica
    - form of 226: galactic 228
    - structure of 226
    - theme of 226, 246
- 'Mabinog's Liturgy' 161, 167, 170, 175, 184, 228–34
    - manuscript drafts of 169–70, 251
- and the Mass 157. *See also* motifs in A, Eucharist
- as meditation 153–4, 157–8
- 'Middle-Sea and Lear-Sea' 161–2, 167, 170
- modes in. *See* fictional modes
- motifs in. *See* motifs in A
- movement in 153–4, 158–68, 234
    - circular 168–9
    - and Eucharist 154, 234
    - narrative movement miming narrated movement 162
    - and paschal events 159–62, 168, 234
    - relation to structure of 156, 200
    - and time-shifting 154
    - and voyaging 254
- narrative time in 157–8
- notes to 152
- personae in. *See* personae in A
- and symbolism 202
- points of view in 17
    - primary 156–8, 215
- radio broadcast of 164
- 'Redriff' 163–4, 170
- 'Rite and Fore-Time' 158–61, 163, 166, 170, 175, 176–7, 197
    - and Dawson's *Age of the Gods* 379n16
    - and Gwenhwyfar 231–3, 254
    - manuscript drafts of 231

relation to 'Mabinog's Liturgy'
and 'Sherthursdaye and Venus
Day' 180
- setting of 156-8, 168-70, 171, 172-3,
200. *See also under* A, historic time
in
Eucharistic 168, 169
- 'Sherthursdaye and Venus Day'
168, 170, 175, 214, 233, 254
- structure of 156-7, 158, 168-74, 226,
231-2, 253, 315, 333
and anamnesis 200
centric 171-2, 183, 236, 294
circular 168-75, 200
and Eucharist 171, 173, 200
and mannerism 171
and movement 156
symbolic 172
- subgenres in 153
allegory 167, 245, 246
drama 202. *See also* personae
in A
- symbolic correspondences in 20, 34,
35
- symbolism in 153-4, 155, 158, 201
mythic method 190, 361. *See also*
A, typology in; archetypes in
A; figures in A; motifs in A
- time as liturgical in 177, 178
- typology in 201-56
of artist 202
and form 254
and psychology 206
and realism 209. *See also* archetypes
- and *The Waste Land*. *See under*
Eliot
- western history in. *See also* motifs
in A, culture-phases
structure of 181-2
'anatomy' (definition) 371n31
Anchises 221
The Ancient Laws of Cambria, Jones's
reading of 376n31, 392-3n73

Ancient Mariner. *See* archetypes in
IP; motifs in A
Aneirin (author of *The Gododdin*)
57, 118, 119
Anglo-Saxon poetry, read by Jones 33,
371n38
Annunciation 253
Aphrodite 90, 215, 218, 221. *See also*
figures in A
Apollo 88, 129
Ara Pacis 193, 286. *See also under The
Anathemata; The Sleeping Lord*
Arawn. *See also* figures in SL
- and the Green Knight 390n49
- in *The Mabinogion* 384n7
- and vegetation deity 390n49
ARCHETYPES:
See also figures; motifs; personae
in *The Anathemata* 202-3, 255
- battle, cosmic, and cosmic
marriage 207
- bridegroom, cosmic 210
- bride of Christ 215
- bride of God 206, 215, 221, 226, 231,
245-6. *See also under* motifs in
A: city, earth, ships
- dying god 212
- earth mother 177, 181, 210, 216,
217, 224, 231, 232-3, 384n7. *See also
under* Demeter; figures in A:
Aphrodite, Gwenhwyfar, Helen,
Ilia, Mary; motifs in A: London,
sculpture, sex; personae in A, Elen
Monica
and Elen Monica 202-3
and water 223, 225
- father 212, 224
and Bradshaw 202-3
- fictional context of 203
- God. *See* archetypes in A: father,
guardian, saviour; figures in A,
Christ; motifs in A, divine Light
- Grail-quest 155, 211, 212, 214, 255, 339
- guardian 202, 223. *See also*

ARCHETYPES:
archetypes in A: father, saviour
- Maimed King 212
- marriage. *See also under* motifs in A: sex, voyaging
    cosmic 206: and cosmic battle 207
    eschatological, and voyaging 234, 240, 246
- mother 220, 226. *See also* Celts, myth, triple goddess in
- Mother Earth. *See* archetypes in A, earth mother
- and non-mythic modes 202–3
- Prudentia. *See* archetypes in A, Wisdom
- Satan 248, 249
- saviour 209, 210, 219, 220, 222. *See also* archetypes in A: father, guardian; figures in A: Christ, Hector, Nelson
- Wandering Jew 244
- Wisdom 220
    and Athena 237
    as Prudentia 248
in *In Parenthesis*
- Ancient Mariner 147
    and Dai Greatcoat 115
    relation to John Ball 115
- Arthur 102
- Dying Gaul
    and Dai Greatcoat 115
    and Roland 98
- earth mother 85, 88, 91
- Grail-quest 118, 139
- Hanged Man 131
- Maimed King 63, 66, 137, 104
    correspondence with infantrymen 90, 106
    and Llywelyn 96
    personification of Waste Land 90
- Wandering Jew 112, 244
in *The Sleeping Lord* 358
- Dying Gaul 271, 335, 337
- dying god 271, 272
- earth mother 269, 274, 309, 314. *See also* Celts, myth, triple goddess in; figures in SL: Tellus, Tutelar and Mary 279
- Hanged Man 288
- Maimed King 272
    and Arthur 337, 339
- Mock King 271, 272
- mother 266, 279, 280, 282, 312, 314, 328. *See also* archetypes in SL, earth mother
Arcimboldo, Giuseppe 149
Ares. *See also* Mars
- as boar 90, 92
Argos. *See* motifs in A, dogs
Ariadne 287
Ariosto *Orlando Furioso* 362
Aristophanes 135, 136
- *Frogs* 126
- *Lysistrata* 192
Aristotle 189, 203
- influence on Jones 9, 11, 53
- and mythos 62
- *Nichomachean Ethics* 65
- preferred by Jones to Plato 23
Ark of the Covenant 252, 315
Arnheim, Rudolf *The Power of the Centre* 149, 171, 378n17
Arnold, Matthew 5
- poetry of 362
- *The Study of Celtic Literature* 325, 384n7
art
- Celtic. *See* Celts
- metaphysical, significance of 65
- as sublimation 205
Artaxerxes 108
Artemis at Aulis 245
Arthur 187, 259, 391n60. *See also under* archetypes in IP; Celts, myth; Dying Gaul; figures in A, in SL; Matter of Britain; Motifs in IP, in SL; Romance; Wales

- and Camlan 96, 97, 98
- and Christ 57–8, 61
- Jones on 382n52
- significance in British and western mythos 5
Athanasius, St 206, 253
Athena 247, 248. *See also* figures in *A*
- as fertility goddess 191
Attis 137, 296, 305
Aucassin et Nicolette 327, 391n50
- as source of *In Parenthesis* 144
Auden, W.H. 365, 394n13
- on *The Anathemata* 3
- on *In Parenthesis* 3
Augustine, St 273, 351
- on Noah 241
Augustus 193, 194, 196–7, 279, 383n61
- and state cults 299
Ave maris stella 386n27

Baal 135
Bach, J.S. 24
Bachelard, Gaston *The Poetics of Space* 312
Balder 137–8, 140
'Barbara Allen' 210, 299. *See also* under *In Parenthesis*, songs in
Battersea shield 12. *See also* Celts, art
Beazley, J.D. and B. Ashmole *Greek Sculpture and Painting* 382n54
Beckett, Samuel 186
Bell, Clive 65
Bell, Colonel J.C. 50–1
- prototype for Colonel Dell 49
Benjamin (brother of Joseph) 139
Bergonzi, Bernard 121, 378n14
Bernard, John 100
Bernardine, Fr 384n5
Bernstein, Michael 394n12
Berryman, John *Dream Songs* 367
Best, Lieutenant 50
Bierce, Ambrose 'An Occurrence at Owl Creek Bridge' 173

Black, Lazarus 49, 51
Blake, William 24, 253, 367
- and Industrial Revolution 313
- *Jerusalem* 228, 391n53, 393n11
- *Milton* 393n11
- and mythology 363
Blamires, David
- on *The Anathemata* 380n34
- on *In Parenthesis* 121, 377n3, 377n6
Blissett, William 53, 369n1, 375n11, 389n36, 392n67, 392n71
- on *In Parenthesis* 375n15
- *The Long Conversation* 373n21
Blunden, Edmund 49
Bonaventure, St, response to nature 94
Boniface, St 129
Bonnard, Pierre 10, 18, 19, 24
The Book of Balaam's Ass manuscript 173, 387n3. *See also The Sleeping Lord*, 'Balaam's Ass'
- Jones on 32
Book of Revelation 127–8
The Book of the Twenty-four Philosophers 380n34
Borges, Jorge Luis 'The Secret Miracle' 173
Borrow, George *Wild Wales* 316
Bosch, Hieronymus 348
Botticelli, Sandro *Primavera* 21, 218, 327
- Jones on 384n11
Bowden House 204
Bowra, C.M. 54
Bradshaw, Ebenezer (the poet's grandfather) 165
- Jones on 379n21, 383–4n2
Branwen 111, 113
Braque, Georges 10, 14
'The Brave old Duke of York' 147
Britain. *See also* Matter of Britain; Wales
- Roman-Celtic, and Gwenhwyfar 229

Britannia 219, 247, 248
Bronte, Emily *Wuthering Heights*
 – alluded to 86
 – possible model for *In Parenthesis* 59
Brooke, Rupert 49, 55
Browning, Robert 202
 – 'Bishop Bloughram's Apology' 31, 259
 – 'The Bishop Orders his Tomb' 31
 – 'Cleon' 32
 – 'Epistle of Karshish' 32
 – 'The Grammarian's Funeral' 31
 – influence on Jones 31–2
 – *Men and Women* 261, 274
Brueghel 'The Fall of Icarus' 171
'Brunanburh' 60
Brunel, Isambard 57
Bunting, Basil 360, 365
 – on *The Anathemata* and Catholicism 5–6
 – *Briggflatts* 360, 362
 – on Jones 360–1, 366
   and Welsh poetry 26
Burns, Tom 6, 215
Burton, Robert, catalogues of 361
Byrd, William 348
Byron, George Gordon, Lord *Don Juan* 393n11

Cadwaladr 348
Cain. *See under* Abel
Caird, Edward, and Tribune of 'The Tribune's Visitation' 300
Caligula 302
Camberwell Art School 9, 47, 370n22
Camlan, battle of 350. *See also under* motifs in *IP*, apocalypse
 – as archetypal battle 95–8, 106
 – in Malory, alluded to 112
Campbell, Joseph and H.M. Robinson *Skeleton Key to Finnegans Wake* 387n10
Campbell, Roy 25

Camus, Albert *The Fall* 306
Capel-y-ffin 14, 16
Caractacus 55
Carroll, Lewis
 – allusions to his works in *In Parenthesis* 76–9
 – Alice books 117–18
   Jones's reading of 374n10
 – *Alice in Wonderland* 76–7, 79
 – *The Hunting of the Snark* 79, 81, 117
 – *Through the Looking Glass* 77–9
Cassirer, Ernst *The Myth of the State* 389n32
Castor and Pollux 78
Caswallawn 111
Catholicism. *See under* Jones; motifs in *A*: Eucharist, Incarnation; motifs in *IP*, liturgical, Mass
Catraeth, battle of 96, 106
Celts, Celtic
 – art 14–16, 327. *See also under* cynghanedd; motifs in *SL*, art; Wales, poetry of
   and form of *The Anathemata* 155
   as influence on Jones 12
   and *In Parenthesis* 64
   and Jones's use of language 34
 – decline of 260. *See also under* Matter of Britain; motifs in *SL*, Celts
 – myth 60–1
   landscape in 117
   triple goddess in 141, 224, 318, 328
centricity. *See under* form, abstract; individual titles: form of, structure of
Ceres. *See* Demeter
Cervantes *Don Quixote* 349
Cézanne, Paul 10, 14
Chamberlain, Neville 193
Chanson de Roland 81–3, 98, 198
Charlemagne 112, 309, 345, 348
 – as prototype of Arthur 98

Charles of Luxemburg 110
Chartres cathedral 188, 279
Chaucer, Geoffrey 216
- *Canterbury Tales* 356
- 'The Knight's Tale' 126
- 'The Miller's Tale' 349
- Prioress 250
- Wife of Bath 227
Cherbury, Herbert of 56
Chesterton, G.K., influence on Jones 6
chivalry 101-5, 106
Chloris 219, 221, 247, 327
Christ. *See also* figures in *A*; motifs in *SL*
- agony in the garden 60, 132, 147
- as archetype 102
- going up to Jerusalem 131
- as hanged man 131
- and human suffering 131
- identification of infantrymen with 139
- Last Supper of 133
- Passion of 131-3
- as unicorn in Dai's boast 114
- wounds of 79
Christmas Preface. *See* Corpus Christi Preface
Churchill, Winston 5, 223, 227
Chute, Fr Desmond 243
Cicero 'The Dream of Scipio' 282
circularity. *See* form, abstract; individual titles: form of, structure of
civilization. *See also* gratuity, and utility; motifs in *A*: culture-phases, gratuity and utility; motifs in *IP*, gratuity
- modern 64, 66
Claf Abercuawg 34
Clark, Kenneth 21
Clement of Alexandrea *Protrepticus* 385n24
Clowes, Geoffrey *Sailing Ships* as source for Jones 386n26

Clym of the Clough 348
Cockney. *See also In Parenthesis*, language in
- in army, affinity with liturgical language 377n10
- and 'Lady of the Pool' 228, 234
- rhyming slang as metaphor 83
Coleridge, Samuel Taylor
- 'Christabel' 87, 147
- influence on Jones 33
- 'The Rime of the Ancient Mariner' 60, 91, 92-4. *See also under* archetypes in *IP*; motifs in *A* evoked in *The Anathemata* 243-5
  illustrated by Jones 244
  Jones on 118
communism 268. *See also* motifs in *A*, imperialism; motifs, in *SL*: communism, imperialism (Soviet)
Comus. See Milton, John
Conrad, Joseph 154
- *Heart of Darkness* 301-2
Constantius Chlorus 219-20
Cook, Harry 47, 49
Corcoran, Neil, on *The Anathemata* 155, 156, 170, 171, 378n9, 379n19, 380n31, 381n49
Corpus Christi Preface 262
Crashaw, Richard 172
Crécy, battle of 98, 110
Creiddylad 325
Crux fidelis 288
cubism 14, 16, 19
culture. *See also* gratuity, and utility; motifs in *A*: culture-phases, gratuity and utility; motifs in *IP*, gratuity
- analysed by Jones 36, 62-74
Cunobelin (Cymbeline) 55, 198
Cybele 137
Cymbeline. *See* Cunobelin
cynghanedd 34, 320, 321, 327, 333. *See also* Wales, poetry of

– and the description of Gwenhwyfar 233

Daley, Ann Carson, on *The Anathemata* 381–2n49
Dante 106
– *The Divine Comedy*
   and *The Anathemata* 256
   and *The Cantos* 363
– *Inferno* 119, 147, 267
   alluded to 80
– Jones on 23
D'Arcy, Martin 6, 207
Darwin, Charles 174
– theory of evolution alluded to 76
Davenport, Guy 36
David (biblical) 134
– and Jonathan. See under motifs in *IP*, friendship
David, St 339
Davie, Donald, on *The Anathemata* 365, 393n6
Davies, Corporal 48
Dawson, Christopher 268
– *Age of the Gods* as source for *The Anathemata* 379n16
– *Beyond Politics* read by Jones 385n20
– influence on Jones 6, 369n5
de Chardin, Teilhard 174
– Jones on 381n40
Dee, John 247–8
Defoe, Daniel 228
de la Mare, Richard 373n10
– and *In Parenthesis* 3
de la Taille, Maurice 206, 287
– influence on Jones 6
– *The Mystery of Faith* 134
   importance for Jones 380n25
Delphi 225, 385n21
Demeter 126, 136, 211, 215, 232, 233, 278. See also under archetypes: earth mother (in *A*, *IP*, *SL*), mother (in *A*, *SL*)

de Rougemont, Denis 207
Descartes, René 312
Diana 138, 225
– and St Paul's Cathedral 385n14
Dickens, Charles 216, 217
– allusions to characters of
   the Artful Dodger 354
   Dick Swiveller 56
   Job Trotter 56
   Oliver Twist 349
– Jones on 364
'Dick Whittington' 216
Dies irae 199, 292
Dionysius (the god) 240, 241
Dionysius the Pseudo-Areopagite 354
– *The Divine Names* 35
– influence on Jones 35–6
Ditchling 17
The Divine Comedy. See Dante
Dolorous Stroke 212. See also archetypes (in *A*, *IP*, *SL*), Maimed King
Donne, John 35, 371n40
– *Elegy 19* 210, 211
Doomsday Book 309
Dostoevsky, Fyodor *The Brothers Karamazov* 306
– Grand Inquisitor 249–50, 306
– possible influence on *In Parenthesis* 375n18
– read by Jones 386n29
dramatic monologue. *See also* fictional modes in *IP*, dramatic
– Jones's use of 31–3
'The Dream of Macsen Wledig' 276
'The Dream of Rhonabwy' 276
'The Dream of the Rood' 236, 276, 293
Dryden, John 365
Dunbar, William 218
– 'Lament for the Makers' 72
Dying Gaul 5. *See also* archetypes in *IP*, in *SL*; Celts, myth; Matter of Britain; Wales
– and Roland 98

Easter Vigil 130, 159, 305
Eddington, Arthur *Space, Time and Gravitation* 173
Ede, H.S. 19
Edward VIII 40
- and Llywelyn. See Llywelyn (last Welsh prince)
Edwards, Jack 48
efficiency. See gratuity, and utility
Einstein, Albert 199
Eleanore of Aquitaine 187
Eleanore, wife of Llywelyn 187
Eleusis 240, 277–8, 283. See also Demeter; motifs in *A*, Agelastos Petra
El Greco 24
- 'Agony in the Garden' 149
Eliot, T.S. 253, 328, 364, 365
- on *The Anathemata* 3
- 'Ash Wednesday' 319
- 'Burnt Norton' 314
- and dramatic monologue 274
- 'Dry Salvages' 286
- 'East Coker' 314
- *Four Quartets* 318, 362, 368
- 'The Hollow Men' 79, 267–8
- influence on Jones 11, 17, 26, 33
- on *In Parenthesis* 3
- on Jones 25
- 'The Journey of the Magi' 33
- 'Little Gidding' 379n14
- 'The Metaphysical Poets' 34
- and modernism 360
- quoted 107, 156, 344, 345
- symbolism, his sense of 13
- 'Tradition and the Individual Talent' 94
- 'Triumphal March' 270
- *The Waste Land* 36, 131, 228, 288
    alluded to 191, 216, 217, 263
    and *The Anathemata* 150, 153
    as influence on Jones 27–9, 361
    and *In Parenthesis* 28–9, 59
    irony in 362
    Tiresias in 112, 263

Ellul, Jacques 66–7
Emond, Patricia 376n34
Ennius 338
- *Annals* 392n61
epic. See also individual titles, genre of
- Christian 106
- of war 106
Eucharist. See Mass. See also under motifs in *A*, in *IP*, in *SL*
Eve 217–8, 247
- and Mary 386n27
Ezekiel 262. See also motifs in *IP*, Ezekiel's bones
Exodus 122, 133, 135, 267

fall, the 63, 65. See also motifs in *IP*
Fawkes, Guy 352–3. See also motifs in *SL*, scapegoat
Fflur 111
FICTIONAL MODES:
movement between 8
and point of view 16
in *The Anathemata* 153, 202, 226–7, 228, 229, 254
- movement between 20
- and symbolism 24
in *In Parenthesis* 29
- allusions, use of 35
- associative 38–9, 40–1, 42, 48, 53, 54–5, 58, 59–60 115, 117. See also allusions; motifs in *IP*; *In Parenthesis*, Dai's boast in, form of (double exposure)
    'Prickly Pear' 80
    and romance 102
- dramatic 38, 41, 52–3. See also personae in *IP*
- lyrical 38, 41, 53
- meditative 39, 40, 41, 51, 74
- movement between 9
- narrative 38, 41, 59, 96, 119
    and archetypal symbolism 148
    and associative modes 107

FICTIONAL MODES:
    movements, influence on 59
    as plotless 59
- realism
    movement between myth and 20
    movement to symbolism from 9
- relation between 102
- shifting of 38–9, 40–1, 110
- and subgenres 54–6, 58
- symbolism 9. See also figures in *IP*; personae in *IP*
    archetypal 55
in *The Sleeping Lord* 261
- 'Balaam's Ass' 261
- and dialogical form 359
- 'The Fatigue' 284
- 'The Hunt' 322
- Roman poems 261
- 'The Sleeping Lord' fragment 330, 331, 333, 332

FIGURES:
    See also personae
in *The Anathemata*
- Abraham 159
- Aphrodite 254
- Arthur 198, 199
- Athena 189, 215, 254
    and imperialism 192
    and Mary 189–90, 201
    and wisdom 237
- Aurignacian lord and lady 212
- Bradshaw, Eb 244. See also Bradshaw, Ebenezer
- captain
    Greek 162, 167, 253: as Iacchos or Dionysus 240; and Ancient Mariner 244
    of the *Mary* 386n25
    medieval, listening to Elen Monica 164: and Ancient Mariner 244
- captains, Mediterranean 203
- Castor and Pollux 252
- Christ 153, 159, 161, 166, 176, 180, 197, 251
    as bridegroom 209–15
    his coming foretold 185
    his crucifixion as sacrifice 178
    and culture 210, 211
    and Hector 208–9
    as Logos and Redeemer 254
    and Mary 209–10, 253
    and Odysseus 212, 240
    Passion of 168, 251
    and structure of *The Anathemata* 200
    and sun 242
- clerk, lover of Elen 253
- Clio, muse of history 161
- Cockney priest 221
- Constantius Chlorus 219–20, 223
    and Christ 220
    as saviour 219
- Cronos 177
- Dee, John 247–8, 250
- Dionysus 180
- dogs. See under motifs in *A*
- father, prehistoric, at the cave-mouth 212
- Gwenhwyfar 21, 167, 171, 175, 180–1, 187, 205, 215, 228–34, 235, 254
    and abolition of point of view 18
    and altar 232
    and Britain 229
    and chalice 232
    and Demeter 232, 233
    and the earth 231–3
    and Elen Monica 215, 229, 231, 234
    and Eucharist 215, 233
    and form of *The Anathemata* 233
    and Galatea 233
    and Helen 231
    and Incarnation 215
    and Mary 233
    and Mary Magdalene 231
    and the Mass 228, 233
    and prehistory 231–2

Index

FIGURES:
  and 'Rite and Fore-Time' 231–3, 254
- Hector 208–9, 212, 220
- Helen Argive 208–9, 215, 220, 231, 232, 245, 254
    as bride of God 209, 215
- Helena, Flavia Julia, and London 219–20
- Ilia 161, 191, 219, 220
- Iseault 212
- Jesus. *See* Christ; *see also under* figures in A, Christ; motifs in A: Eucharist, Incarnation, individual Paschal events
- John, St 159, 235
- Lais 231
- Lamia 196, 235, 249
- Manawydan 229, 244
- Mannan mac Lir 240
- Marged 245, 254
    and Siren 251
- Mars 161, 191–2, 219, 247
    and Ares 192
- Mary 167, 215, 217, 220, 225, 254. *See also* motifs in A, voyaging, of the *Mary*
    and Aphrodite 246
    and archetypes 210, 226
    and Artemis 245
    and Athena 189–90, 201, 246
    and Christ 209–10, 253
    and earth mother 177
    and Gwenhwyfar 233
    and Siren 248, 249
    and Wisdom 246
- mason, lover of Elen 164, 168, 217–19, 220, 221, 227
- Milford boatswain. *See* figures in A, Welsh boatswain
- Nelson, Admiral Horatio 163, 209, 212, 220
- Odysseus and Christ 251
- Osiris and Christ 161
- Peter, St 159, 235, 240, 249
- Phoebe 215
- Phoenician or Phocaean captain and Ancient Mariner 244
- Phryne 231
- Pilate, Pontius 196
- Pollux. *See* figures in A, Castor and
- Sejanus 167, 194
- Siren 166, 227, 247–51, 254. *See also* figures in A, Lamia
    and Aphrodite 248, 249
    and Athena 192, 247, 248, 249
    and Britannia 247, 248, 250
    and Chloris 247
    and Eve 247
    and Flora 247, 248
    and Grand Inquisitor 249–50
    and Marged 251
    and Mars 192
    and Mary 248, 249
    and Mary Magdalene 249
    and the *Mary* 249
    as mother 250
    and Satan 248, 249
    and Susanna 247
    and Venus 247
- Telphousa 215
- Themis 215
- Tiberius 167, 193–4
- Welsh boatswain 166, 244
- Welsh witches 167, 364

in *In Parenthesis*
- Ball, John
    affection for rifle 70
    as allusive reflector 39–40
    and Ancient Mariner 92–3, 115
    as associative reflector 56
    attitude to battle 87, 107
    and Dai Greatcoat 115
    as flat character 58
    historic namesake 56, 73
    and Jones 45–8
    and Lancelot 102, 106
    his latch-key 72. *See also* motifs

FIGURES:
    in *IP*, scapegoat
    late for parade 66–7, 73
    narrative reflector 115
    on night watch 60–1, 79
    and Roland 81–3
– Bembridge, Aunty, prototype for 49
– Calthrop 47
– Cohen, Lazarus 49
– Dai Greatcoat. *See under* personae in *IP*; *In Parenthesis*, Dai's boast in
– Dell, Colonel, prototype for 49
– Donkin, Joe 49
– Elias, Captain 49
– Herne, Runner 99–100
    as mystagogue 135
– Jenkins, Mr
    as associative reflector 49, 56, 60
    and his beloved 90
    characterization of 53
    death of 82
    and Oliver 81–3, 102, 106
    sources of 48–9
    symbolic names of 56–7
    as type 83
– Larkin, Fr Martin, prototype for 49
– Lewis, Aneirin
    as associative reflector 48, 56
    as flat character 59
    and Fluellen 99
    and the Queen of the Woods 57, 141
    sources of 48
    symbolic names of 56–7
– Map, Private Walter 50
    disaccommodated 73
– Meotti, Runner 49
– Mulligan, Bomber 49
– Mulligan, Old Sweat 52
– Olivier, prototype for 46
– Queen of the Woods 29, 139–46, 149, 205, 215, 355
    and Aneirin Lewis 57, 141
    and *Aucassin et Nicolette* 391n50
    and Dai Greatcoat 120, 147, 148
    fictional anticipations of 142–3
    and idealization of sex 85
    literary prototypes of 144–5
    metaphysical significance of 141–2
    and motifs 141, 146
    and point of view 18
    as primary symbol of sacred mythos 120
    as revealer of true nobility 105
– Reggie, prototype for 46
– Rhys, Talbot 48
– Saunders, Bobby 58, 84
    disaccommodated 73
– Shallow, Corporal 56
– Snell, Sergeant 49, 53
– Sweet Sister Death 87
– warden of stores 75–6
in *The Sleeping Lord*
– Arawn 328
    Arthur and 324–6
– Arthur 321–46, 350, 357
    and Achilles 337
    and Adonis 327
    and Arawn 324–6
    and Artorius 325
    and the Celtic saints 338–9
    and Christ 327–8, 330, 340, 342
    and Finn MacCool 331, 391n53
    and Gwenhwyfar in *The Anathemata* 324
    and Hector 337
    Jones on 325
    and Llywelyn 337
    and May King 327
    and palaeolithic lord 337
    and South Wales 332
    and sun 325
    and Tutelar 327
    and vegetation god 326
– Arthur's bard 331
    and poet-persona of 'The Sleeping Lord' fragment 333

Index

FIGURES:
- Arthur's candle-bearer 331, 332, 337, 339, 341
    - and Arthur's foot-holder 340
    - and poet 340
- Arthur's foot-holder 331, 332, 338, 341
    - and Arthur's candle-bearer 340
- Austin, Private 347, 350, 351
    - mother of 353
- boar. See under motifs in SL
- Brasso 281–2, 283, 291, 304, 308, 388n19
    - and Lugo 281–2, 291
    - and NCO of 'The Fatigue' 290
- Caesar 299, 300, 301, 302, 306, 308
- Celtic chief 263, 267, 270, 271, 273
    - and Christ 271, 273
    - and persona of 'The Wall' 272
- Christ. See under motifs in SL: Incarnation, Christ, individual Paschal events
- Clitus. See personae in SL
- Crixus 350
    - and Christ 291
    - significance of name 291. See also under personae in SL, Clitus
- Elbius 298
- Fairy, Lieutenant 348, 349
- females 205
- Helige, Balder 348
- Ilia 265, 270
- Irene 268, 270
- Juno 277, 295, 307
    - and Mary 269
- Lamb 311. See also motifs in SL, lamb of sacrifice
    - and Christ 316
    - and Ram 317
- Lucifer, Private 350, 351
- Lugo 274, 277, 278, 280, 281
    - and Brasso 281–2, 291
    - and Christ 280
- Lupa. See figures in SL, wolf
- Mars 264, 265, 335
- Mary 315, 317
    - and Tellus 280
- Mary Magdalene 340
- Minotaur 350
- NCO of 'The Fatigue' 304
- Norman castellan 331, 334
- Norman sentries 331, 332, 335, 340
    - and Arthur/Christ 334
    - and poet-persona of 'Balaam's Ass' and Arthur's priest 334
    - and Roman sentries of 'The Fatigue' 334
- Oenomaus 274, 277, 278, 279, 280, 281
    - significance of his name 279
- paleolithic lord 332, 337
- Pluto and Plutus 270
- Plutus 268, 270, 274
- Ram 309, 311, 312, 313, 315, 317, 318–20
    - and boar. See under motifs in SL, boar
    - and Lamb 311, 317
    - and Mars 319
    - wife of 311
    - and wolf 319
- Remus. See under figures in SL, Romulus and
- Roman sentries of 'The Fatigue' 285, 289, 290, 291, 389n26. See also figures in SL, Crixus
- Romulus 265
    - and Christ 286
    - and Remus 255, 274, 285
- Sejanus 285, 286, 287, 291
    - as narrative reflectors 285. See also figures in SL, Crixus
- sergeant in 'The Tribune's Visitation' 295
- Tellus (goddess) 274, 275, 277, 280–1, 282, 283, 387n10
    - and Queen of the Woods 283. See also archetypes in SL, earth mother

FIGURES:
- Tiberius 286, 287, 291
- Tutelar (goddess) 309-21. See also archetypes in SL, earth mother
  and Arthur 327
  and Joyce's Anna Livia Plurabelle 311
  and Mary 315
  and Tribune 309
- Twrch Trwyth. See motifs in SL, boar
- wolf, Roman, and Mars 319

Fitzstephen, William Life of Becket 219
Flora (goddess) 21, 217-18, 219, 221, 247, 254, 327
folk songs. See individual titles; In Parenthesis, songs in
Ford, Ford Madox 154
form. See also individual titles: form of, movement in, structure of; Jones: imagination of (spatial), form in poetry of
- abstract 12-13
  in Celtic art 12
  centricity 12-13
  circularity 12
  in Jones's work 13
- geometrical 12, 148
- metamorphic 8
Foster, Stephen 'There's a Good Time Coming' 196-7
Fowler, W. Warde The Roman Festivals 391n52
Francis of Assisi, St 141, 262
- 'The Canticle of the Sun' 87
- response to nature 94
Francis de Sales, St
- Introduction to the Devout Life 104
- response to nature 94
Frank, Joseph 13, 28
Frazer, Sir James 141, 206, 296
- edition of Ovid's Fastorum libri sex 387n7

- The Golden Bough
  copies owned by Jones 371n32
  influence on The Anathemata 181, 183
  read by Jones 27, 30
Freud, Sigmund 56, 203-6, 306, 307, 320
- influence on Jones 7
- neo-Freudians 292
- Totem and Taboo 204, 205
Fry, Roger
- influence on Jones 6, 11
- and post-impressionism 10, 11, 65, 148
Frye, Northrop 203
- on anatomy 371n31
- on epic 54
Fussell, Paul, on In Parenthesis 94-5, 106, 346, 377n9, 378n14
- attempted refutations of 376n27

Galatea 233
Galileo 315
Gall, Sally M. See Rosenthal, M.L.
Gammer Gurton's Needle 349
Gauguin, Paul 10
Gawain and the Green Knight 326, 328
- Jones on 391n49
Genesis 265
Geoffrey of Monmouth 111, 216
- Historia regum Britanniae 372n4
Gilby, Fr Thomas 250
Gill, Eric 193, 194, 332
- influence on Jones 6, 9, 11, 23
Gill, Petra 14, 21, 204, 331
The Gododdin 57
- as elegy, contrasted with In Parenthesis 42
- and In Parenthesis 96, 119
- Jones on 117-8
Goebbels, Joseph 286
Goethe, Johann Wolfgang, and Industrial Revolution 313
golden bough 138, 140, 147

Golding, William *Pincher Martin* 173
Gracchus, Gaius 193
Gracchus, Tiberius 161, 193, 212
Grail-quest. See under archetypes in A, in *IP*
gratuity
- and metaphysical significance 71–2
- and utility, Jones's essays on 372n42. See also under motifs in A, in *IP*, in *SL*
Graves, Robert 49
- *Goodbye to All That* 377n8, 388n17
- poetry of, and mythology 363
- *The White Goddess* 141–2
  Jones on 378n15
Gray, John 332, 374n28
Gray, Nicolete 205
Greene, Graham, on *In Parenthesis* 3
Gregory the Great 172
Grenfell, Julian 55
Griffith, Llewelyn Wyn *Up to Mametz* 43, 44, 49
Griffith, W.J. *A Short Analysis of Welsh History* 372n4
Grisewood, Harman 6, 11, 50, 207, 223
- on *The Anathemata* 152
- on Jones and fascism 382–3n56
Gwythyr and Gywnn 325
- in *The Mabinogion* 384n7
Gywnn. See Gwythyr

Hagreen, Philip 98, 104
Hague, René 6, 148, 240
- on *The Anathemata* 158, 218, 379n18, 380n23, 380n24, 382n55, 385n14
- on Jones 204
- on 'The Sleeping Lord' fragment 392n70
- translator of *Chanson de Roland* 81–2
- typesetter of *In Parenthesis* 373n10
Hales, John 56

Hanson, Jack 21
Hardy, Thomas 362
- *The Dynasts* 383n11
Harriet Monroe Prize 258
Hartrick, A.S. 12
Hawker, R.S. 'The Song of Western Men' 349
Heaney, Seamus 96
- on *The Anathemata* 152, 365, 378n1
- and Jones's influence 361
Hector, 337. See also under figures in A
Hegel, G.W F. 64, 300, 307
- and history in *The Anathemata* 182
Heidegger, Martin 60
Helen Argive 187. See also under figures in A
Helen Camulodunum 85, 111. See also Helena, Flavia Julia
Helena, Flavia Julia 219. See also figures in A
- and Britannia 219
- and Mary 220
Henry II 50
Henry VI 222
Hepworth, Barbara 14
Herbert, George 35, 348, 371n40
Hereward the Wake 185
Hermes. See Mercury
Hilaria, Roman feast of 296, 297, 302, 305, 307
Hill, Geoffrey 394n13
- *Mercian Hymns* 361, 362
Hills, Paul 13
Hilton, Walter 348
history. See also under Jones, David
- and imagination 55
- relation to literature 95
- Welsh sense of, contrasted to English sense of 110
Hitchcock, Alfred 19
Hitler, Adolf 193, 194
Hodgkin, E.C. 369n1

Hodgkins, Frances 14
Hogarth, William 216
Holloway, John, on *The Anathemata* 155–6
Holy of Holies 315
Holy Week as dramatization of Christ's Passion 131
Home, Gordon *Roman London* 385n12
Homer 207, 338, 362, 363
- *Iliad* 392n61
    affinity with *In Parenthesis* 148
- *Odyssey* 80, 245, 247. *See also* Odysseus; Penelope
    and *The Anathemata* 152, 254
    and *The Cantos* 363
    and *In Parenthesis* 144
Homeric epic 187
- and medieval romance 231
Honeyman, Stanley 226, 369n1
Hooker, Jeremy 121, 365
- on *The Anathemata* 154, 155, 156, 378n4
- on 'The Fatigue' 389n24
- on *In Parenthesis* 377n6
- and Jones criticism 372n2
Hopkins, Gerard Manley 318, 361, 364
- alluded to 56
- 'The Bugler's First Communion' 81
- and Catholicism 5
- 'Hurrahing at Harvest' 391n53
- influence on Jones 11, 26, 30, 33–4, 35, 36
- language, affinity with that of *In Parenthesis* 53
- and nature 94
- 'Pied Beauty' 313
- Welsh affinity 371n40
- 'The Wreck of the Deutschland' 233
Hughes, Colin 388n16
- on *In Parenthesis* 44, 373n12
Hughes, Fr Daniel 49, 104
Hughes, Ted 394n13
Hulme, T.E. 5, 263
- influence on Jones 9, 11, 12

- and modernism 34
'The Hunt.' *See under The Sleeping Lord*
Hutchins, Patricia *James Joyce's World*, Jones's reading of 381n47
Huxley, Aldous *Brave New World* 306
Hwyel Dda, Laws of 324, 335
Hygca 348
'Hymn on the Morning of Christ's Nativity.' *See* Milton, John

In Parenthesis 38–150, 152, 153, 289, 337. *See also under* archetypes; fictional modes; figures; motifs; personae
- accepted for publication 3
- admired by contemporary writers 3
- allusions in
    and tone and context 121, 122, 123
    use of 28, 38, 40, 54–5, 58, 60. *See also under* fictional modes in *IP*, associative
- archetypal shell-explosion in 46, 60
- archetypes in. *See under* archetypes in *IP*
- and 'Balaam's Ass' 354–5, 355–6
- battle in, and Christ's Passion 131–2
- characterization in 17, 51, 58–9. *See also under* figures in *IP*
    relation of figures to actual prototypes 46–58
- characters, economy of 58–9
- Christmas dawn in 129–30, 242
- chronology 28, 32, 42–5
- composition of. *See also IP*, Dai's boast in
    early stages 142–4
    excluded material 84
    method of 40, 44, 52–3, 368, 372n3: as analogous to painting 8–9; death of Jenkins 82
    period of 14, 372n1

- culture in
  war as criticism of 59
- Dai's boast in 110–6, 119, 142, 147, 170, 343. *See also* figures in *IP*, Dai Greatcoat
  affinity with Taliesin of 112
  anamnesis in 111
  Arthur in 111, 113
  Bran in 111
  as centre of *In Parenthesis* 111, 120, 148, 343
  as challenge to reader 114–15
  Christ crucified in 112, 113
  as *composition en abîme* 108
  composition of 111, 170
  context of 109
  fictional modes, shifting 40
  and Grail-quest 114–15, 339
  and metamorphic form 112
  as monologue 31
  morality of being a soldier in 113–14
  and myth 55
  point of view in 108
  read by Dylan Thomas 109
  as riddle 112
  Triad pattern in 109, 111–12
- definite articles, use of 27
- and documentary 99
- as epic. *See IP*, genre of
- fictional modes in. *See under* fictional modes
- form of. *See also IP*: movement in, structure of
  accumulative 116
  affinity with shape of the Mass 59, 133–4
  dialogical tension 62, 116, 120, 146–51: and mannerist distortion 149
  double exposure 82
  metamorphic 29, 60, 112, 117–18
  and motifs, interweaving of 62, 63–4, 117
  spatial 148
  structures, intermediate 146
  symbolic correspondences in 34, 146. *See also* figures in *IP*
  time-spans, corresponding 146
- format, early plans for 373n10
- frontispiece drawing 63, 139
- genre of. *See also IP*, subgenres in
  and autobiography 45–50
  and characterization 58
  and commemoration 49–51
  and documentary 38, 42–51, 52–3
  epic 52–3, 80, 95, 148, 368: and ritual associations 121; significance of Dai's boast 108
  and narrative 42–61
  poetry 38
- and *Iliad. See under* Homer
- illustrations intended for 102
- importance of 367–8
- initial format of 373n10
- and Jones's painting 53
- language in, and Cockney 52–3
- as modernist work 41–2
- motifs in. *See* motifs
- movement in 147, 148
- mythos of
  and dialogical tension 62
  sacred 119–50: Queen of the Woods as primary symbol of 120
  secular 62–118, 119, 120: Dai Greatcoat as primary symbol of 120; relation to sacred mythos 149
- narrative time in 21, 38–42, 43, 110–11
  mythic 148
- national tradition invoked in 56–7, 95–100, 347
- past, relation to present in 63, 94–116
- and Perse's *Anabase* 26–7
- personae in. *See* personae
  and plot 51, 59

- points of view in 17, 32, 40–52
    first person 40: reverie 41 (*see also* fictional modes in *IP*, meditative); shifting 19
- primal shell-burst in 138, 173
    and fertility 87
    and *Georgics* 4 124–5
- sacrifice in 106
- setting, pastoral 362. *See also IP*, subgenres in
- and Shakespeare's history plays. *See under* Shakespeare
- songs in
    'Barbara Allen' 85, 140, 147
    'Casey Jones' 129
    '*Corpus Christi* Carol' 96
    'Es ist ein' Ros' entsprungen' 47
    'Glory, Glory Hallelujah' 136
    'The Golden Vanity' 85
    'Jesu lover of my soul' 136
    'John Barleycorn' 137
    'Johnny I hardly knew ye' 86
    'The Low Low Lords of Holland' 85
    'Mademoiselle from Armentières' 85
    'O dear what can the matter be' 86
    'Officers' wives' 73
    'Of Hector and Lysander' 101
    'Old soldiers never die' 112
    'O my I don't wantter die' 75, 100
    'On Ilkley Moor baht'at' 86
    'Onward Christian Soldiers' 129
    'Poor Jenny' 85
    '*Sospan Fach*' 85
    Salve regina 72
    'Thora' 43, 71
    'Tipperary' 7
- stand-to, significance of 123
- structure of
    centred 108, 111, 147–9. *See also* motifs in *IP*, circular journey
    and images 147–8
    and metamorphic form 115
    and motifs 119, 120–1, 122, 125
    parenthetical 120, 136, 147–8
    spatialized 148
- subgenres in
    anatomy 54, 56–7, 95
    history 40, 51. *See also IP*, and documentary
    myth 40, 42, 58–60, 63, 64, 84, 95, 107. *See also under* Arthur; Camlan; personae in *IP*, Dai Greatcoat; figures in *IP*, Queen of the Woods; *IP*, subgenres in, realism; motifs in *IP*
    pastoral 47, 116, 128, 129, 130, 145: dark pastoral 362
    realism 9, 38–9, 40, 50, 51, 58, 60, 95, 99: and myth 64, 107, 118
    romance 40, 106 (*see also* Camlan; *Chanson de Roland*, Roland): and associative mode 102
- themes in. *See* motifs in *IP*
- tone of 51. *See also IP*, language in
    and allusion 121, 122, 123
    objectivity in 42
- types in. *See IP*, characterization in
- and *Ulysses*. *See under* Joyce
- and *The Waste Land*. *See under* Eliot
Irenaeus of Lyons 6
Irene (goddess). *See under* figures in *SL*
Isaiah, dyed garments of. *See* motifs in *IP*, liturgical, Lent
Israelites, wandering in wilderness 75. *See also* Exodus

Jack o' the Green 137–8, 326
Jenkins, Joseph John 57
Jeremiah 263
John Barleycorn 137
'John Barleycorn' 230

John of the Cross 214
'John Peel' 213–14
Johnson, Samuel 228
Johnston, John H. 48, 133
– on *In Parenthesis* 54, 373–4n24, 376n24, 377n3
– Jones on 374n24
Jonah 244
Jonathan. *See under* motifs in *IP*, friendship
Jones, Alice (the poet's mother) 77, 204–5, 374–5n11
Jones, David
– allusion, use of 18. *See also under* allusions; fictional modes in *IP*; individual titles
– on *The Anathemata* 154–5, 169, 172, 190, 201
– Anglo-Saxon poetry, his reading of 371n38
– on art and religion 195
– and Catholicism 4–6, 120, 369n4. *See also* Jones, poetry of, and Christianity
– and Clitus 283–4
– combat experience of 42–8, 43–8, 50–1, 145, 344
– and Eddington, Arthur 173
– and *Henry V* 100
– historical sense of 5, 6, 55
  and imaginative presence 109
  mythic 360
– imagination of
  analogical 8, 14, 36
  associative 14, 41
  ritual 55
  spatial 12, 25
– influences on
  intellectual 6–7
  literary 25–36
– Jerusalem, his visit to 32
– and Joyce. *See also under* Joyce
  affinity with 25

– language, sense of 20, 26, 30–1, 33, 34, 88, 364–5
– and Lewis Carroll's Alice books 374n10
– and literary sources 366
– and mannerists 149
– as modernist 25, 35, 360–1, 362
– and monastic life 123
– movement, importance to 25
– neurosis of 203–6
– and objectivity (aesthetic) 4–5, 10, 11
– and paganism and Judaism (in relation to Christianity) 120
– as poet, importance of 36, 360, 368, 394n13
– as poetic innovator 361–2
– poetry of
  aesthetic lapses of 364
  allusive reflectors in 361
  and Christianity 363–4
  composition, method of 7, 9, 13, 25. *See also* individual titles
  dark pastoralism, development of 361–2
  debate in 362
  distortion, use of 35
  fictional modes and artistic potential in 24
  form in: metamorphic 361 (*see also* individual titles: form of, movement in; fictional modes, movement between); 'open' 362
  influence on subsequent poets 360–1, 367
  language. *See* Jones, language, sense of
  monologue, use of 31–3, 361
  movement in 35
  mythic method, reversal of 361
  mythology, use of 363
  narrative movement miming narrated movement in 361

poetic form miming non-poetic
  forms in 361
point of view in 19
structure as symbolic in 361, 368
symbolic catalogues in 361
symbolic transference in 361
symbolism in 361–3: archetypal
  14; associative 9–10, 13 (see
  also individual titles, subgenres
  in); Eucharist as analogous to
  10, 24 (see also anamnesis);
  and objectivity 10–11; as 'sign'
  10; and structure 11–12; in
  visual art 10
tone in 20–1, 27
topological rhyming in 361
transparency of monologues in
  361
unity of poems 362, 367. See also
  individual titles, form in
– and Pound, affinity with 25, 265–6
– prose of
  'Art in Relation to War' 340
  The Dying Gaul 343
  Epoch and Artist 343
  'Introduction to The Rime of the
    Ancient Mariner' and The
    Anathemata 236, 242–3, 248
  'The Myth of Arthur' 329, 339,
    343
– as prototype for figures in In Paren-
  thesis 45, 48, 50
– as religious poet 318. See also Jones,
  poetry of, and Christianity
– and social class 74–5
– and Spengler 374n7
– structure, importance for 11–13
– technique. See Jones, poetry of
– and the Tribune 308–9
– unity, importance for 25
– visual art of
  Curtained Outlook 14
  The Garden Enclosed 13, 15, 21,
    149

  illustrations for 'Rime of the An-
    cient Mariner' 92
  Merlin Land 14
  Petra im Rosenhag 21, 22, 149
  Tristan ac Essyllt 19
– as visual artist
  development of 8–16
  distortion, use of 24–5
  form, metamorphic, use of 18, 20
  formative influences on 9–13, 18
  influence on his poetry 7–25, 29
  and mannerism 24
  perspective, use of 14–21, 15–16
– and Wales
  history of, early interest in 372n4
  poetry of, his ability to read in
    Welsh 370n24
  Triads, reading of 376n31
Jones, Harold (the poet's brother) 205
Jones, Huw Ceiriog and Diana 391n55
Jones, Mary E., on In Parenthesis
  375n24, 377n9
Jonson, Ben 228
Joseph (biblical) See motifs in IP, li-
  turgical, Lent
Joyce, James
– allusions, use of 4
– Anna Livia Plurabelle 29, 141–2
– Anna Livia and Elen Monica 227
– and catalogues 229, 361
– and Catholicism 5
– and Dublin 228
– Finnegans Wake 36, 345. See also
  Joyce, Anna Livia Plurabelle
  alluded to 185, 186
  and The Anathemata 30
  Finn MacCool in 331, 391n53
  and Jones: affinity with Jones's
    poetry 25, 363; influence on
    29–30, 33; read by 382n51
– and modernism 360, 361
– A Portrait of the Artist as a Young
  Man 62
– Ulysses 36

aesthetically flawed 364, 393n5
and *In Parenthesis* 29, 53
and Jones, as possible influence on 30
Molly Bloom 141: and Elen Monica 227
'mythic method' 27
and subjective time 173
Jung, Carl G. 203
— and mythology 363
Jupiter 138
Juvencus *englynion* 348

Kant, Immanuel 65
Keats, John 149
— and Jones's sense of language 26
— 'Ode on a Grecian Urn' 120
Kierkegaard, Sören, and Industrial Revolution 313
'King Cophetua and the Beggar Maid' 352
Kipling, Rudyard 52, 58
Knight, W.F. Jackson
— *Cumaean Gates* 220, 235, 236, 385n21
  Jones's reading of 388n15
  quoted, on imperial Rome 269–70
  on the troia 195, 383n58
— influence on Jones of 6
— *Vergil's Troy* 231
  Jones's reading of 383n62, 384n8
  on mazes 272

Lamkin 349
Lancelot 102, 106
— and Gwenhwyfar in *The Anathemata* 230
'Land of Hope and Glory' 196
Langland, William 216
— influence on Jones of 33
— *Piers Plowman* 57, 276, 330, 349
  Jones on 391n51
Larkin, Philip 367
Latin ballads, loss of 299

Lawrence, D.H.
— *Lady Chatterley's Lover* 362
— *Women in Love* 362
Levinson Prize for 'The Tutelar of the Place' 390n38
Lewis, Saunders 336
Lewis, Wyndham 13
Liddell, Alice 77
Liddell and Scott *Latin Dictionary* 388n18
'The Lion and the Unicorn' 78–9
Llewellyn, Richard *How Green Was My Valley* 313
Llwyd, Dafydd 375n12
Llywelyn (last Welsh prince) 96–7, 147, 283, 335, 337
— and Arthur 187
— and Edward VIII 372n2
— evoked in 'The Dream of Private Clitus' 278–9
— and Maimed King 96
London as city of the imagination 228. *See also* figures in A, Elen Monica
London Times (source for Gwenhwyfar's description) 229
Longinus 111
Lovelace, Richard 348
Lowell, Robert *Notebook 1967–68* 367
Lowes, John Livingstone 142
— *The Road to Xanadu* 118
  influence on Jones of 7
  as source for *In Parenthesis* 370n7
Lucilius 297

The Mabinogion 60, 91–2, 108, 118, 384n7. *See also* names of figures
— 'Bran the Blessed' 111, 113, 116
— enchantment in 64
— Jones's reading of 390n48, 392n73
— 'Kulhwch and Olwen' 91–2, 108, 118, 321, 325, 328, 333, 345, 350, 384n7

- 'Math Son of Mathonwy' 340
- 'Maxen Wledig' 111
- 'Peredur son of Efrawg' 339
- 'Pwyll Prince of Dyfed' 324, 325–6, 328, 384n7
- and setting of Gwenhwyfar in *The Anathemata* 229
- and structure of 'The Sleeping Lord' fragment 342

MacArthur, General Douglas 185

Macaulay, Thomas Babington *The Lays of Ancient Rome*
- 'The Battle of Lake Regillus' 77–8, 252
    recited by young Jones 78
- 'The Lay of Horatius' 298–9, 389n30
    recited by young Jones 78

MacDiarmid, Hugh 227, 360, 365
- on Jones as poet 3–4

McLaren, Hamish *The Private Opinions of a British Bluejacket* 31. See also Taplow

McLuhan, Marshall 60

Mac Og 60–1
- as Celtic counterpart to Apollo 88

'Maiden in the mor lay' 247

Maimed King. See under archetypes in *A*, in *IP*, in *SL*

Malaprop, Mrs 227

'Maldon' 60

Malory, Thomas, 343
- *Morte D'Arthur* 27, 116, 147, 328, 339, 351, 360
    Agravaine 113
    allusions to 41, 87, 90–1, 97–8, 105
    Balin and Balan 141: in Dai's boast 114
    Beaumains as a type 104–5
    Dai de la Cote male taile 112, 115
    enchantment in 64
    Gwenhwyfar 230, 231
    and history 56

and *In Parenthesis*, as possible model for 59
Maimed King 63
white hart in 104
Vinaver edition of 385n17

Manawydan (the god) 240, 244

Mandeville, Sir John 631

mannerism in visual art 149. See also under *In Parenthesis*, form of; Jones, David
- and distortion 24

Mann, Thomas 56

Map, Walter 50

Maritain, Jacques
- influence on Jones 10, 11
- *The Philosophy of Art* 65
    O'Connor translation read by Jones 370n11

Marlowe, Christopher *Doctor Faustus* 385n22

Mars, 298. See also figures in *A*, in *SL*; motifs in *IP*
- as anti-fertility god 138

Marx, Karl 75, 292, 306, 307

Marxism 250, 290

Mary. See also figures in *A*, in *SL*
- and Ilia 286
- and Juno 269

Mary Rose (the ship) 246

Mass, the 221. See also under motifs in *A*, in *IP*; motifs in *SL*, Eucharist
- and Christ's Passion 131–3
- and the form of *In Parenthesis*. See *In Parenthesis*, form of
- relation of Offertory to Consecration 134, 135

Math (the god) 338, 340

Matisse, Henri 10

Matteotti, Giacomo 193

Matter of Britain, the 5. See also Arthur; Camlan; Wales
- in *In Parenthesis* 95–8, 57, 116
- Jones's contribution to 343

– in Jones's prose 369n2. See also Jones, David, prose of
Melpomene 135, 142, *143*
Melville, Herman *Moby-Dick*
– and 'The Dream of Private Clitus' 388n15
– influence on Jones 30
– and *In Parenthesis* 59, 105, 116
– as possible model for *In Parenthesis* 59
Meninsky, Bernard 13
Merchant, Paul 54
Mercury (Hermes) 135, 278
Merleau-Ponty, Maurice 310
Merlin 57, 347, 354
metaphysical poets. *See also* individual names
– influence on Jones 34–5
– as Welsh in affinity 371n40
Miller, Dr Crichton 204
Milton, John 106, 362, 363, 368
– allusion to 'On His Blindness' 174
– *Comus* 144–5, 216, 362, 378n16
– 'Hymn on the Morning of Christ's Nativity' 88, 128, 129, 145, 330
– *Paradise Lost* 248, 256, 350
Minos 125
modalities. *See* fictional modes
modernism. *See also* names of painters, writers
– in literature 13, 25–31, 33–4, 227, 360–8
   reaction against 367
– in visual art 13–14, 16, 18, 19, 24
Moloch 135
Moncrieff, C.K. Scott, translation of *Chanson de Roland* 82
Monet, Claude 19
Moore, Henry 14
Moses 122
Mother Earth. *See* archetypes, earth mother
MOTIFS:
   See also figures; personae

in *The Anathemata*
– Advent, cosmic 175. *See also* motifs in A, apocalypse
– Agelastos Petra 187, 208
– Ancient Mariner 243–5
– apocalypse 182, 197–200
   symbolized in prehistory 197–8
– art 159, 174, 206, 233, 255. *See also* motifs in A: sculpture, symbolic forms
   in Lascaux caves 232
   and propaganda 196–7
   and religion 195–6
   and ritual 178
   and sacrament 179
– barley 177, 232. *See also* Demeter; figures in A, Gwenhwyfar
– battle, cosmic 384n7
– burial 160, 211, 214, 223, 235, 252
   and sleepers 212, 214
– chalice. *See* motifs in A, cup
– Christ. *See also* motifs in A, divine Light
   cross of 243, 380n27: exaltation of 164; as fertility symbol 211; as libra 389n28; as mast 236–7; as maypole 167; topological 220
   as keel 236
   Passion of 241, 242
– Christianity and paganism 225
– Church 254. *See also under* motifs in A, voyaging
   and earth 236
   as institution 249–50
   city 206, 208, 254. *See also under* archetypes in A, bride of God; motifs in A: voyaging, individual cities
   and earth 220
   and woman 217, 221
– culture-phases
   correspondences between 183–97
   Dark Ages 183, 185: and the modern West 197

MOTIFS:
- Dorians 183, 184
- fifth-century Athens and late Middle Ages 188–90
- and the Incarnation 197, 200
- Middle Ages 154, 215–28
- modern 184, 190, 249
- prehistoric 184
- and paschal events 183
- Rome (see also motifs in A, Rome): Christian 167; imperial 184, 193–4; imperial, and modern West 190–7
- sixth-century Greece and thirteenth-century Europe 186–8
- cup/chalice 177–8, 211, 241, 242, 253
  - and Gwenhwyfar 232
- death 174. See also motifs in A, burial
- dogs
  - Argos 212–13
  - of Arthur 213
  - Gelert 213
  - Ranter 213
  - Ringwood 213
  - of Theseus 213
  - Toby 213
  - True 213
- divine Light 160–1, 166–7, 176, 177, 178, 182, 220, 221, 234, 235
- 'Dorian' 183–4, 247
- dying gods 180, 188
- earth, the. See also under motifs in A, voyaging
  - and city 220
  - geological formation of 231–2
  - as ship 167
- Eucharist 159, 161, 166, 173, 176–7, 255. See also motifs in A: Last Supper, Mass
  - and Gwenhwyfar 233
  - relation to Incarnation, 172, 174, 175, 181
  - and the Mary 251, 253
  - and symbolic art 180
- evolution, human 160, 175–7
- fascism 184, 193–4, 196
- food 174, 177. See also motifs in A, Eucharist
- fore-time. See motifs in A, prehistory
- Grail-quest 339. See under archetypes in A; motifs in A, voyaging
- gratuity and utility 158–9, 182, 184, 188, 190, 191, 192–3, 194, 197, 250
  - Jones on 182
- Gregorian chant 159, 160, 196
- history, western 183–200
- Holy Thursday. See motifs in A, Last Supper
- hunt 230, 390n45. See also motifs in A, voyaging
  - as sacrifice 178
- imperialism 183, 191–4, 198–9, 246–51
  - Athenian 237
  - British 247: and Roman 196
- Incarnation 186, 188
  - and Eucharist 181. See also under motifs in A, Eucharist
  - and evolution 176
  - and typology 206
- Jews, the 157, 194
- keel 166–7, 235–6
- Last Supper 159, 161, 168, 174, 180, 255. See also motifs in A: Christ, Eucharist, Mass
  - and Incarnation 174
- libation 178, 241, 253
- limestone 178, 232. See also motifs in A, sculpture
- Logos 236. See also motifs in A: Christ, divine Light
- London 215–28, 254. See also figures in A, Elen Monica
  - and earth mother 216, 217
  - Roman 217–20

MOTIFS:
 as Troy Novaunt 216, 220
- magic 250–1
- margaron. See motifs in A, pearl of great price
- marriage
 cosmic 208–9
 eschatological 215, 221
- Mass, the 158–9, 160, 167, 172, 242, 255
- maypole 167, 169, 180
- metamorphosis 167, 183, 218, 229. See also motifs in A, Sturm und Drang
 of language 185
 of Mars 191–2
 and setting of *The Anathemata* 255
- moon and Gwenhwyfar 230–1
- Nazis. See motifs in A, fascism
- Oedipal relationships 198, 224, 250
- paganism. See under archetypes in A
- pearl of great price 209, 244, 251–2
- prehistory 159–61, 176, 177–81, 182
 and apocalypse 197–8
 and Gwenhwyfar 231–2
- propaganda. See under motifs in A, art
- questing. See also archetypes in A, Grail-quest; motifs in A, voyaging
 and hunting 214
 and voyaging 241
- redemption. See also under motifs in A, sex
 as retroactive 242
- ritual 174, 255. See also under motifs in A, art
 sacrifice 178
 traditions of 179–80, 206
- Rome (the city) 254. See also under motifs in A, culture-phases and London, See motifs in A, London

 prehistoric 160, 161, 175
- sacrament 250
- sacrifice 208–9, 223. See also motifs in A, libation
- sculpture. See also motifs in A, limestone
 Athena 161, 167, 189, 232
 and Gwenhwyfar 232, 233
 Kore 161, 186, 232
 kouroi 161
 Venus of Willendorf 177, 186, 210, 232
- seige engines 192–3, 210–11, 269, 311
 and fertility symbols 210
- sex 174, 176, 203, 206–15, 230, 240, 247, 250. See also motifs in A: marriage, pearl of great price, voyaging and redemption 207–15
- ships. See motifs in A, voyaging
- smiling 188
- stone. See motifs in A, sculpture
- *Sturm und Drang* 199, 231
- Suffering Servant 208, 213, 236
- symbolic forms and tradition, 178
- troia 164, 195–6, 208, 221
- Troy 161, 198, 199, 207–8, 208, 220, 244, 245, 254
- Troy Novaunt. See under motifs in A, London
- utility. See motifs in A, gratuity and utility
- voyaging 20, 164–7, 234–54. See also archetypes in A, bride of God; archetypes in IP, Ancient Mariner; motifs in A: Ancient Mariner, church, city
 ancient Greek 161
 of captains with Bradshaw and Elen Monica 234–5
 of Christ 242–3. See also motifs in A, voyaging: of Church, of the Supper room as ship
 of Church 234, 235, 236–7, 241, 246. See also figures in A,

MOTIFS:
    Siren; motifs in A, voyaging (of
    Christ, of the *Mary*, of Sup-
    per room as ship)
  continuity of courses 234–5. *See
    also* motifs in A, voyaging,
    direction of
  of cosmic ship 235–7, 254: cap-
    tain of 240–1
  direction of 234–5, 240
  earth as ship. *See under* motifs in
    A, earth
  and eschatological marriage 234,
    240, 246. *See also* motifs in
    A, sex
  of God 234
  of Greek ship 235, 236, 237, 240,
    241, 242, 245: and Phoenician-
    Phocaean ship 379n19
  and land of the dead. *See* motifs
    in A, voyaging, direction of
  and Manawydan. *See* figures in A
  and Mannan mac Lir. *See* figures
    in A
  of the *Mary* 153, 166, 190, 226,
    227, 243, 245–6, 249–53: and
    the Eucharist, *see* motifs in A,
    Eucharist; source for 386n23
  of Mediterranean captain 224
  of Nelson's *Victory* 209
  of Phoenician-Phocaean crew
    153, 214, 234, 235, 237–8, 241,
    242, 243, 245: and Greek ship,
    see motifs in A, voyaging, of
    Greek ship
  of soul 234
  of the Supper room as ship 235,
    236, 241
– wars, world 163, 167, 223, 312
– Waste Land 210, 211–12
    and death 212
    renewal of 255
in *In Parenthesis*
– animal 60–1, 104, 113
    and Arthur 116
    birds 93, 94
    and *The Brothers Karamazov*
     375n18
    and Dai Greatcoat. *See under*
     personae in *IP*
    infantrymen as sheep 122
    insects 93, 94, 147: bees 91, 92,
     94, 123–5
    rats 92–3, 94, 147: and Arthur
     61, 92–3; and Coleridgean
     water-snakes 93
– apocalypse 67, 96, 116, 125, 126–8,
  140
  battle as 127–8
– art 47, 64–5, 67, 70–1, 113
– Arthur 57, 60–1
  antithetical Arthur figures 116
  in Dai Greatcoat's boast 111, 113
  as rat. *See under* motifs in *IP*,
    animal
  as saviour 92, 94, 113
– childhood's end 76–9
– circular journey 45, 79, 119, 248,
  267
– class, social 72, 74–5. *See also* mo-
  tifs in *IP*, rank
– death and sex 85–91
– dehumanization 67–72, 121
  and Dai Greatcoat. *See under*
   personae in *IP*, Dai Greatcoat
   resisted 104
– disaccommodation 72–80, 114–15,
  127
– Ezekiel's bones 147
– fall, the 63, 65, 76
– fertility 46, 87–8, 90, 123–4, 125,
  131. *See also* Saturnalia
  and bees 91
  and resurrection 124–5
  rites of. *See under* motifs in *IP*,
    liturgical
  as symbolic of culture 103–4
– and form. *See In Parenthesis*, form of

MOTIFS:
- friendship 80–3, 103, 104
    David and Jonathan 80, 102
    Roland and Oliver 81–3
- golden bough 80
- gratuity 80, 103, 104, 113, 119, 123, 290
    and Ancient Mariner's conversion 93
    and entertainment 70–1
    and play 67, 70
    and utility 47, 64–72
    and the warden of stores 75
- hell 60–1, 68, 79–80, 119, 127. *See also* Dante
    as Celtic and Coleridgean seascapes 92
    Hades and initiation 125–6, 135–6
    road to 80
- heroism 67, 101–6, 113, 119, 375–6n24
    metaphysical significance of 105–6
    and sanctity 139
    and virtue 104–5
- homelessness. *See also* motifs in *IP*, disaccommodation
    nomadic existence of infantrymen 75–6
- infantrymen as children 76
- initiation. *See* Eleusis; motifs in *IP*, hell
- Israelites 75. *See also* Exodus
    rebellious under Rehoboam 73
- Johnny (in folksongs) 85–6
- Joseph (biblical) 130
- judgment. *See* motifs in *IP*, apocalypse
- liturgical
    Advent 125–6: biblical straight way 127
    ambiguity of 121–2
    artillery and resurrection 124–5, 130

baptism 125, 126, 134
Christmas 128–30, 131: relation to Good Friday 132, 135
Divine Office and artillery 123
Easter Vigil 128, 130
Eleusinian rites 125–7, 135–6, 140
eucharists, symbolic 122, 133, 147
fertility rites 136–41
Good Friday 125, 128, 131–3. *See also* motifs in *IP*, Suffering Servant
Hebrew sacrifice 134
human sacrifice 135
initiation 125–6, 135–6
Kyrie 134
Lent 122. *See also* motifs in *IP*, Joseph
Mass, the 122. *See also* motifs in *IP*, liturgical, eucharists, symbolic
Midsummer rites 136–7
Nativity 125
Passover 133
perversion of 124
Quam oblationem 377n13
Queen of the Woods, ritual of 140
ritual: military 121, 122; religious 120–41
sacraments, metaphorical 122
sacrificial rites 133
significance of, changing 125
and structure. *See In Parenthesis*, structure of
- Maimed King. *See under* archetypes in *IP*
- Mars
    object of metaphoric worship 122–3
    perverse fertility god 88
- mechanization 68–9, 71. *See also* motifs in *IP*, dehumanization
- metaphysical significance of 119
- Midsummer. *See* motifs in *IP*, liturgical

MOTIFS:
- monastic 123
- moon 41, 69–70, 88, 107
- nature 91–4. *See also* motifs in *IP*: animal, fertility, order
- order 46, 61, 104, 119
    metaphysical 91, 94, 113
    perversion of 91–2
- pastoral. *See In Parenthesis*, subgenres in
- rank, military 72–5. *See also* motifs in *IP*, class (social)
- scapegoat 72. *See also* motifs in *IP*, Waste Land
- sex 69, 83–90, 103, 104
    and fertility 87–90
    idealization of 85
    perversion of 84, 87, 88–9
- and structure. *See In Parenthesis*, structure of
- Suffering Servant 74, 132–3
    as type of the infantryman 105, 106
- Troy, fall of 97–8, 106
- utility. *See under* motifs in *IP*, gratuity
- war
    relation to ordinary life 62–3
    the tradition of 94–116
- Waste Land 63–4, 66, 83, 91–2, 104
    and Dai's boast 111, 114–15
    and modern civilization 103–4
    personified by infantrymen 90
- weaving, imagery of 376n36
- whited sepulchre 67, 72, 147
- wisdom 70

in *The Sleeping Lord*
- apocalypse 309, 321, 326, 328, 339, 350
- art 358, 359. *See also* Ara Pacis; poetry
    architectural 279, 342
    Celtic 321, 327
    Gothic 279
    pictorial 291–2
    semiotic 292–3
- Arthur 259. *See also* under figures in *SL*
- baptism. *See* motifs in *SL*, initiation
- battle, cosmic 325, 326, 327, 330
- boar 321, 326, 327, 332, 335, 336, 337, 338, 339, 359
    and Högemann 350
    and the Mill 359
    and Ram 321, 335, 336
- Calvary
    and sacred city 286–7
    and secular city/world 276, 287, 293
- Celts, decline of 260, 334, 335–7
    and decline of West 337
- childhood 274, 277, 309, 311, 319–20
    and childlikeness 320
    and folk liturgy 311–12
    and play 310
    and the primitive 313
- Christ 271, 272, 273, 306, 307, 311, 316, 333, 341
    and Apollo 289
    and Arthur 327–8, 330, 340, 342
    and Clitus and Lugo 280
    cross of 262, 286, 293, 359: and Ara Pacis 286; and sacred city 286; topological 267
    crucifixion of 284, 285, 291
    and fire, hearth, *mundus* 342
    Passion of 262, 277, 280, 284, 288, 289, 297, 333, 338, 355, 359: and structure of 'The Fatigue,' and of Roman poems 294
    and Romulus 286
    and Sejanus 287
    and sun 289
    and Tribune 297
- Christian dialectic 288, 289, 354, 357
    synthesis as wedding 311
- city of God. *See* motifs in *SL*, sacred city

423 Index

MOTIFS:
- communism 300–1
- conversion. See motifs in *SL*, metamorphosis
- cross. See under motifs in *SL*, Christ
- culture, death and rebirth of 278
- culture-phases 299
    Dark Ages and modern West 335, 337, 341
    modern West, decline of 260
    Rome, imperial, and modern West. See under motifs in *SL*, Rome
- dancing 314–15, 318. See also motifs in *SL*, troia
- darkness 273, 289, 301–2, 307, 317, 341, 359
- dehumanization 285, 289–90, 292, 294, 301, 302, 305–8. See also motifs in *SL*, darkness
    and Tribune 298, 301, 302, 305–8
- dialectic. See motifs in *SL*, Christian dialectic
- dreaming 274–84
- dying god 264, 288, 296, 338
- Easter 305, 341
- Eucharist 292
- fascism 300–1
- femininity 278, 280–1, 309, 310–11, 340. See also under archetypes in *SL*: earth mother, mother; figures in *SL*: Tellus, Tutelar
    and home 312
    and masculinity 268–70
- fertility, vegetable 288–9, 316, 323, 336, 339, 358
- fire 316, 339, 340, 341, 342, 352–3, 355, 359. See also motifs in *SL*: hearth, light, sun
- friendship 273, 281, 290–1
- gratuity and utility 262, 281, 291, 294, 295, 296, 297–302, 304, 309, 312–13, 318–19. See also motifs in *SL*: art, friendship, poetry
- Hades 263, 267, 268, 270, 272, 277, 278, 308, 328, 330, 359. See also motifs in *SL*, initiation
- harmony, cosmic 266–7. See also motifs in *SL*, dancing
- hearth 316, 317, 335, 341, 342, 359. See also motifs in *SL*: fire, light
    as symbol of tradition 316
    and Vestal flame 316
- heaven and earth 314–15, 317
- hell. See motifs in *SL*, Hades
- Holy Spirit 353
- home 272, 274, 303, 309, 312, 316. See also motifs in *SL*, hearth
    and heights 317
    and tradition 317, 318
    and the universe 315
- imperialism. See also figures in *SL*, Ram
    British 302
    fascist 302
    Roman 266, 299, 302
    Soviet 302
- Incarnation 327, 338. See also motifs in *SL*, Christ
- initiation 272, 277–8, 285, 297, 301, 305, 306, 308, 358
- interrelation of 358–9. See also *The Sleeping Lord*, form of
- Jerusalem
    and imperial Rome 271, 273, 276, 286
    as omphalos 271
- labyrinth. See motifs in *SL*, maze
- lamb of sacrifice 276, 282. See also figures in *SL*, Lamb
- Last Supper 333
- light 289, 301, 307, 317, 340. See also motifs in *SL*: fire, hearth
- masculinity. See motifs in *SL*, femininity
- maypole 311, 314–15
- maze 264, 265, 270, 271, 273, 278, 285, 286, 287, 289, 315, 350. See also

MOTIFS:
  motifs in SL: triumph, troia; *The Sleeping Lord*, 'The Wall'
    and initiation 272
    as prison 387n9
  - metamorphosis 204–5, 274, 276–7, 280, 287, 322, 323, 330, 347, 352–3, 354. *See also* motifs in SL, dehumanization
    cultural 282–3, 292–3, 307, 322
    emotional 327
    spiritual 323, 329
  - Mill, the 344, 345, 349, 351, 352, 353, 356
    and boar 359
  - Minotaur 287. *See also* motifs in SL, boar
    and Ram 359
  - *mundus* 342, 387n8
  - necessity 301
  - Oedipal relationships 316
  - Passover 284, 296, 305
  - photosynthesis 288
  - place. *See* motifs in SL, home
  - poetry 292, 340, 358. *See also* motifs in SL, art
    and prayer 318–19, 358
    and propaganda 299
    and 'The Sleeping Lord' fragment 331
    and 'The Tutelar of the Place' 309, 318, 319, 321
    and Tribune 294, 295, 300, 303, 307
  - positivism. *See* motifs in SL, gratuity and utility
  - power 286, 311, 359. *See also* motifs in SL, imperialism
  - prayer 310, 317, 352, 358
  - prison 270, 290. *See also* motifs in SL, maze
  - redemption 329, 330, 356
  - ritual 295, 296, 297, 301. *See also* motifs in SL: Eucharist, initiation

folk 314
sacrifice: human 270, 302, 306 (*see also* motifs in SL: Christ [Passion of], dehumanization);
  ritual 295–6
- Rome, imperial 280, 284. *See also* motifs in SL: city, secular world
  fall of 278–9
  and fascism 268, 286
  and Jerusalem. *See under* motifs in SL: Jerusalem
  and modern West 268, 283, 286, 317
  as omphalos 271
- sacred city 264, 266–7, 273, 278, 286, 353, 359
  and Arthur's war band 329
  and dance 314–15
  and heights 317
  and secular world 287, 289, 292, 293
- scapegoat 330
  soldier as 346, 353, 355
- secular city 266, 317, 319
- secular world 284, 285–6, 291
  and sacred city. *See under* motifs in SL, sacred city
- seige engines 309, 311. *See also* figures in SL, Ram; motifs in SL, home
- sex 264, 269
  and death 352
- Suffering Servant 280
- sun 325, 359
- synthesis, Christian 292–3
- totalitarian state 299, 300, 359
- transfiguration. *See* motifs in SL, metamorphosis
- triumph 263, 267, 270, 293
  as maze 264, 265
- troia 264, 270, 271, 272, 273, 285, 315, 317–18, 358. *See also* motifs in SL: triumph, *via dolorosa*
- Troy, fall of 265, 337
- utility. *See under* motifs in SL, gratuity and utility
- *via dolorosa* 271, 273

MOTIFS:
- Waste Land 272, 336, 337, 339, 359
  and Grail-quest 340
  renewal of 323
- wedding 316, 359. See also motifs in SL: Christian dialectic, synthesis (Christian)
  of heaven and earth 317
- West, modern, decline of 260
- wisdom 304
- wolf 282
  Roman 265, 266. See also archetypes in SL, mother
- World War I 272, 283
Munby, J.E. A History of the 38th (Welsh) Division 43, 373n14
Mussolini, Benito 286
mythos (defined) 62

'Narrows, The' 258, 393n74
Nelson, Admiral Horatio 89. See also under figures in A
Nemi, Priests of 138
New Jerusalem 221
Newman, John Henry 186
Nicholson, Ben 14, 24
Nicodemus 320
Nike 220
Noah 241, 244
Noah's Ark 252, 386n31
Noon, William T., on The Anathemata 381n49

objectivity
- aesthetic importance of. See under Jones, David
- and tone 20
O'Brien, Flann At Swim-Two-Birds 347
'O Come, O Come, Emmanuel' 130
O'Connor, Fr John. See also Maritain
- and Browning 31
October Games, Roman 296
Odin and Christ 131, 132, 206, 212, 213

Odysseus 214, 235, 244-5
- evoked in The Anathemata 212
- monologue of 254
Odyssey. See Homer
Oedipal complex
- and Jones. See Jones, David, neurosis of
- in Jones's poetry. See motifs (in A, SL), Oedipal relationships
Oenghus. See Mac Og
'Of Noble Race Was Shenkin' 350
Olson, Charles Maximus Poems 366-7
Olwen, Jones's reading about 375n17
'Oranges and Lemons' 222-3, 320
Origen 377n5
Orwell, George Nineteen Eighty-four 302, 306, 307, 320
Ossa and Pelion 175. See also motifs in SL, apocalypse
Ovid Fastorum libri sex 387n7, n11
Owen, Wilfred 347
Oxford Book of Twentieth-Century Verse 367

painting. See also Jones, David: visual art of, as visual artist
- as analogous to poetry 8-25
- chiaroscuro in 18-19
- perspective in 16-17
  and transparency 18
  and window views 18
- tone in 19, 20
Palmer, Samuel 24
Pannonian mutiny 279, 297
Paradise Lost. See Milton
Patrick, St 185, 339
Paul St 33, 277, 301, 306, 307, 308, 390n37
Pearl
- and 'The Dream of Private Clitus' 276, 277
- poet, influence on Jones 33
Pelham, Prudence 85, 102, 204, 374n10

Penelope 142, 212
Penllyn, Tudur 375n12
Pentecost 191
Perse, St John *Anabase*, as influence on Jones 26–7, 33
Persephone 126, 211, 215, 270, 278, 279
PERSONAE:
in *The Anathemata*
- anonymous Roman 161
- Attic top-tree boy 162
- Bradshaw, Eb 163–4, 196, 202–3, 212, 227, 236
    and Elen Monica 209, 227
    and Eric Gill 194
    Jones on 202
- Elen Monica 164, 168, 189–90, 198, 202–3, 205, 207, 212, 214–28, 240, 243–7, 253, 254, 343
    as actress 227
    and Aphrodite 216
    and Athens 216
    and Bradshaw, Eb. *See under* Bradshaw
    and Celtic associations 223–4
    and Chaucer's Wife of Bath 227
    and Christ's Passion 215
    and Churchill 223
    and England 217, 223
    and Eucharist 215
    and Flora 217–18
    and Gwenhwyfar 215, 229, 231, 234
    Jones on 223
    and Joyce's Anna Livia, Molly Bloom, 227
    and Lady of the Lake 223
    and Mary 226
    and Mother Earth 216
    as poet 227
    and Sheridan's Mrs Malaprop 227
    Siren, impersonation of 248
    and triple goddess 224
- Greek sailors 166
- Marged 167, 190, 215
- Phoenician-Phocaean sailors 162
- primary 156–7, 215, 228, 255
- secondary 157. *See also* individual personae in *A*
in *In Parenthesis*
- Dai Greatcoat 29, 107–116, 146–9, 228. *See also In Parenthesis*, Dai's boast in
    and Abel 113
    and abolition of point of view 17
    and Ancient Mariner 115, 244
    and animal motifs 113
    as archetypal soldier 63, 108, 109, 110–16
    as artisan 113
    and Ball 115
    and Cain 112
    as central figure of *In Parenthesis* 115
    continuous return of 119
    and David (biblical) 112
    death of, probable 42, 115
    and dehumanization 114
    as inanimate object 112–14
    and Jones 48, 109
    as primary symbol of secular mythos 120
    and Queen of the Woods 120, 147, 148
    and Roland 115
    as scapegoat 114
    and Socrates 111
    sources of 108, 112
    and Wandering Jew 112
- primary
    and meditation 41
- secondary. *See In Parenthesis*, language in
in *The Sleeping Lord* 259, 263, 358
- 'A, a, a, Domine Deus,' persona of 261–2
- Arthur's priest 331, 332–3, 337, 341, 342, 345

PERSONAE:
    and Arthur's bard 333
    and Dai Greatcoat 343
    and Elen Monica 343
    and poet-persona of 'The Sleeping Lord' fragment 334, 340
- 'Balaam's Ass,' primary persona of 354
    and the Ancient Mariner 346, 347
    and Merlin 347
    as Private Shenkin 344, 347, 350, 351–2, 354: and Jones 344
- Clitus 274–84, 304
    and Christ 280
    and Crixus 280
    and Jenkins of *In Parenthesis* 283
    and David Jones 283–4, 388n20
    and persona of 'The Tutelar of the Place' 320
    and persona of 'The Wall' 374
    psychology of 280–1, 311
    referred to in 'Balaam's Ass' 350
    and Tribune 308
- 'The Fatigue'
    NCO in 284, 285, 287, 288, 291: and Brasso 290
    Nodens 346, 349, 350
    poet-persona of 292, 332, 340: and Arthur's bard 333; and Arthur's candle-bearer 340; and Arthur's priest 333, 334, 340
- 'The Hunt,' persona of 323
- Lavinia 346, 354
- 'The Sleeping Lord' fragment, poet-persona of 331, 332, 333
    and Arthur's priest 334, 340
- Tribune 294–309, 354. *See also* figures in *SL*, Tutelar
    and Big Brother 302, 307
    and Brasso 304, 308
    and Cain 302
    and Christ 297, 306
    and Clitus 308
    and Grand Inquisitor 306, 307

    and Jones 308–9
    and NCO of 'The Fatigue' 304
    as poet. *See* motifs in *SL*, poetry
    psychology of 310–11
    as rhetorician 298, 302–3, 308
- 'The Tutelar of the Place,' persona of 309, 313–14, 316, 317–18, 319
    and Clitus 320
    and Jones 319
    as poet. *See* motifs in *SL*, poetry
    and Tutelar 317–18
- 'The Wall,' persona of 263, 264, 278
    and Celtic chief 272
    and Christ 272, 273
    and Clitus 374
perspective in visual art 16–17
Phidias 161
physics, atomic. *See also* Eddington, Arthur
- and form of *The Anathemata* 153–4
- and imagery of 'The Tutelar of the Place' 315, 316
Picasso, Pablo 10, 14, 53
Pilate, Pontius 196, 297, 300, 302
Plato 23, 189, 203
Plutarch 136, 265
- *Florilegium* 126
Pluto 270
Plutus 268, 270, 274
Poe, Edgar Allen 'To Helen' 385n22
poetry as analogous to painting 8–25
Poetry (Chicago) 258
point of view 16–21. *See also* individual titles; perspective in visual art
- abolition of 17–18
- editorial omniscience 17
Polymnia 188
Pope, Alexander 228
- *The Dunciad* 393n11
post-impressionism. *See also* Fry, Roger
- as influence on Jones 10–11, 65, 206
Poulter, Leslie 46, 47, 386n29
Pound, Ezra 34, 54, 360
- *The ABC of Economics* 31

- and *The Anathemata*, his knowing of 3
- *The Cantos* 364, 368
  and *The Anathemata* 152, 363, 365–7
  Aphrodite in 141–2
  Demeter in 141–2
  form of 366–7
  and Jones: his admiration for 25; his first reading of 31
  juxtaposition in 155
  and mythology 363
  point of view in 20
  symbolic motifs in 156
- 'Hugh Selwyn Mauberley' 345
- and Jones, affinity with 25, 365–6
- *Personae* 392n69
- 'Portrait d'une Femme' 227
- *The Spirit of Romance* 31

Preiddeu Annwn. See under Taliesin
Pre-Raphaelites 9
Price, Valerie 204
Prise-Davies, Brigadier L.A.E. 49, 51
Proserpine. *See* Persephone
Proust, Marcel 27, 156
- *Combray* 173
Pryderi in *The Mabinogion* 342
Psalm 23 135
Purcell, Henry 348
Pwyll 325, 328
- in *The Mabinogion* 384n7
Pygmalion 233

Rabelais, François 361
Ragantona (the goddess) 328, 384n7
Raine, Kathleen 380n34
Rawlinson, General Henry 52
Rees, Alwyn and Brinley Rees *The Celtic Heritage* 391n53
Rees, Samuel 379n19, 391n56
Rehoboam 73
Rembrandt van Rijn 149
Rhiannon 328, 384n7

Rhys, John *Studies in Arthurian Legend* 384n7
- and David Brynmor-Jones *The Welsh People* 372n4
Richard II 103–4
Richey, Colonel George 393n76
Rime of the Ancient Mariner. See Coleridge
ritual, religious
- relation to life 120–1
- relation to war 121
Robbe-Grillet, Alain 108, 154
'Robin Hood' 348
Röhm, Ernst 194
Roland 102, 106. *See also Chanson de Roland*
Rolle, Richard 348
romance
- Arthurian 187
  and Homeric epic 231
- as genre 98, 102, 346
Romulus. *See under* figures in *SL*
Rosenthal, M.L. and Sally M. Gall on *The Anathemata* 158, 378n5, 379n15, 381n49, 385n18
'Rule Britannia' 299

Sabina 144–5
Sassoon, Siegfried 49
Saturnalia 88, 136, 271, 296, 302
Scannell, Fr Kevin 391n54
Scheffler, Johann 172
Schorer, Mark 390n43
Sejanus. *See under* figures in *SL*
Seven and Five Society 14
'79 Jones 50
Shakespeare, William
- *Hamlet* 89, 198
- *1 Henry IV* 99–100, 216
- *2 Henry IV* 47, 349
  Master Shallow 56
- *Henry V* 41, 99–101, 216, 379n20
  parts memorized by young Jones 41, 100

- history plays
    alluded to 346, 348
    and *In Parenthesis*, affinity with 33
    relation to history 56
    and London 228
- *Julius Caesar* 105
- *King Lear* 216, 199
- *Macbeth* 147
- *A Midsummer Night's Dream* 213, 349
- *The Tempest* 124, 252
- *Troilus and Cressida* 209, 385n22
- *Twelfth Night* 89, 146, 147

'Shallow Brown' 241
Shelley, Percy Bysshe 363
Sherry, Vincent B., Jr, on *In Parenthesis* 112, 113, 376n27, 376n35
Shirley, James 'Death the Leveller' 139, 141
Shovell, Sir Clowdisley 196, 249
Silkin, John, on *In Parenthesis* 377n3, 378n14
'Sing a Song of Sixpence' 311
Sisyphus 119, 267
Skelton, John 33
'The Sleeping Beauty' 88–9, 147
The Sleeping Lord 258–359. See also archetypes; fictional modes; figures; motifs; personae
- 'A, a, a, Domine Deus' 259, 261–3
    allusive syntax of 263
    and 'Balaam's Ass' 343
    publication history of 387n3
- and *The Anathemata* 258
- Ara Pacis in 274, 279, 280, 281
    and the cross 276
- Arthurian poems in 259, 261, 320–43, 358. See also *SL*: 'The Hunt,' 'The Sleeping Lord' fragment
    and 'Balaam's Ass' 344
    and form of *The Sleeping Lord* sequence 357
    and the modern West 344

and 'The Tutelar of the Place' 309
- 'Balaam's Ass' 259, 260, 343–57. See also *The Book of Balaam's Ass* manuscript
    and 'A, a, a, Domine Deus.' See under *SL*, 'A, a, a, Domine Deus'
    and *The Anathemata* 343
    ballads, alluded to in 348–9
    composition of: intended change to text 351; period of 343; place of 392n67
    early drafts of 259, 350, 393n74
    and 'The Fatigue' 354
    and *Finnegans Wake* 345
    form of 344–5, 356–7 (see also *SL*, 'Balaam's Ass,' movement in): dialogic 345, 347, 353–4, 355, 357; litany 352, 354, 355; metamorphic 354; and refracted consciousness 356; rhetorical 351–2
    genre of: anatomy 261, 345; dark pastoral 345, 358
    and *In Parenthesis* 343, 344, 354–6
    and Joyce, affinity with 29
    and 'Kulhwch and Olwen' 345
    language of 356, 357: metamorphic 356
    as monologue 32
    movement in 345–6: see *SL*, 'Balaam's Ass,' form of
    nursery rhymes, alluded to in 348
    points of view in 347, 356
    and Roman poems 350
    and *The Sleeping Lord* sequence 343–4
    tone of 345, 347
    and 'The Tribune's Visitation' 354
    and 'The Wall' 354

– Christian dialectic in 358. *See also under* individual titles, form of: dialectical, dialogical synthesis 254, 354
– chronological arrangement in 259–60
– culture-phases in
  correspondence between 260, 263
  medieval and modern 334
  modern 261–3
  Rome, imperial and modern 32, 344: in 'The Dream of Private Clitus' 283; in 'The Fatigue' 285, 286, 290; in 'The Tribune's Visitation' 294, 300, 302, 306–7; in 'The Tutelar of the Place' 312–13, 320; in 'The Wall' 268
– 'The Dream of Private Clitus' 270, 273–84, 297, 308, 312, 320
  contexts in 274, 276–7, 278
  and 'The Dream of the Rood' 276
  early drafts of 259
  circular form in 273
  genre of (narrated dream-vision) 274, 276, 279, 282: significance of 274, 282–3
  imagery of 358
  language of 273, 283
  manuscript drafts of 274, 280
  and *Moby-Dick*. *See* Melville
  as monologue 274
  publication history of 387n13
  setting of 274
  structure of 291, 357: significance of 278
  and 'The Tutelar of the Place' 320
  and 'The Wall' 273, 278
– 'The Fatigue' 280, 284–94, 296, 318
  allegory in 288
  and *The Anathemata* 294
  early drafts of 288, 294, 304
  form of, metamorphic 284
  language of 290
  movement in 285
  points of view in 284–5
  publication history of 388n21
  and the Roman poems 284, 293–4
  setting of 271, 284, 358n22, 389n26
  structure of 284, 285, 332: centric 292, 294; and Christ 294; significance of 291–2; and theme 357
  theme of 284
  tone of 284–5
– form of 259–61, 357. *See also* SL, movement in
  dialectical 260–1
  double exposure 265
  metamorphic 273, 295, 359
  motifs, interrelation of 358–9
  topological rhyming 264, 271, 276, 286
– genres in 357–8
  pastoral 358, 362
– history, perspective on. *See* SL, culture-phases in
– 'The Hunt' 213, 321–30, 33
  allusions, use of 324
  Arthur in 21
  Celtic society in 321–3, 327
  coda of 322, 328
  early drafts of 330, 391n50
  form of 321–2, 328: significance of 323; syntactical 330
  genre of: anatomy 322, 323; duality of 322; and symbolism 322
  and Jones: his introduction to 350; recorded reading of 321
  language of 327, 358
  narrative time in 21
  point of view in 323, 328: abolition of 18; shifting 19
  publication history of 390n43
  setting of 260: and 'The Sleeping Lord' fragment 330–2, 343
  structure of 357: and theme 357

tone of 323
- 'Hush a by baby' in 319
- importance of 368
- 'Jack and Jill' in 311
- Judas in
    and Caiaphas, dialogue of 259
    monologue of 259
- language of 357. See also individual titles
- manuscript material excluded from 259
- movement in 343
- past as narrative present in. See under SL, settings of
- positive reception of 3
- Roman poems in 259, 260, 261, 263–320, 358, 359. See also SL: 'The Dream of Private Clitus,' 'The Fatigue,' 'The Tribune's Visitation,' 'The Tutelar of the Place,' 'The Wall'
    and The Anathemata 386n1
    and 'The Fatigue' 284, 293–4
    form of 293–4: and Christ 294; dialogical 260
    manuscript drafts of 280
    and modern West 344
    as monologues 32–3
    tone in 284
    and 'The Tutelar of the Place' 309
- Rome, imperial in
    and modern West. See motifs in SL: culture-phases, imperialism
- as sequence 258–61, 368
- settings of 259. See also SL, genre of, dark pastoral
    past as narrative present in 361
- 'The Sleeping Lord' fragment 258, 260, 330–43, 358, 359
    and The Anathemata 331
    and Arthur's hall and basilica 392n66
    form of 330, 333 (see also 'The Sleeping Lord' fragment: movement in, structure of): and subjective time 342
    history, perspective on 334
    and 'The Hunt.' See SL, 'The Hunt'
    importance of 343
    language of 333
    movement in 331, 332, 333, 334
    points of view in 331, 334
    settings of 330–2
    and The Sleeping Lord sequence 334
    source for 392n64
    structure of 332, 334, 341–4, 357: and that of The Anathemata 333; and Arthur's hall 342; centric 333; and 'The Fatigue' and the Roman poems 294; and The Mabinogion 342; significance of 331, 342–3
    subjective time in 332–3
    symbolism in 331
    tone in 332
- tone of 358
- 'The Tribune's Visitation' 259, 294–309, 310, 313, 316, 318, 320, 358
    and 'Balaam's Ass' 354
    cyclic imagery in 296–7
    and Easter Vigil 305
    form and content 295
    Jones on 244
    language of 294, 302, 320: metaphorical 303
    manuscript drafts of 304
    'Mass' of the Tribune, the 305–6
    movements, rhetorical 295–7. See also personae in SL, Tribune, as rhetorician
    and painting by Jones 308
    points of view in 295, 308
    publication history of 389n29
    setting of 297
    structure of 357

tone of 295, 308
and 'The Tutelar of the Place'
  260, 309–11, 313–14, 317, 320
– 'The Tutelar of the Place' 258, 304,
  309–321, 335, 336, 340–1, 359
  and 'Ash Wednesday' 319
  circular images in 312, 315: and
    atomic physics 315, 316
  and 'The Dream of Private
    Clitus' 320
  faults of 358
  form of 319, 358. See also movements in
  Jones on 390n38
  language of 320, 358
  movements, rhetorical 309
  nursery associations in 320
  publication history 387n6
  setting 260, 297, 309, 319
  significance of in The Sleeping
    Lord sequence 309, 358
  structure and theme 357
  and 'The Tribune's Visitation'
    260, 309–11, 313–14, 317, 320
– Wales, modern, in 335–7
– 'The Wall' 258, 263–74, 286, 293,
  301, 314, 358
  and The Anathemata 258
  and 'Balaam's Ass,' 354
  form of 264
  manuscript drafts of 280, 386n2
  as monologue 274
  movement in 264
  publication history of 387n6
  setting of 264, 272
  structure of: bi-centric 267, 273;
    centric 278; rhetorical question as maze 264–5; significance of 267–8, 278, 281–2; and
    triumphal route as maze 264
  themes of: circular present 267;
    disaccommodation 267; dislocation of space and time 264, 265; past contrasted with

present 265–6, 268, 270; teleological past 267
tone of 264
Smart, Christopher 33
Snowdon, Mt 199
Somme, battle of the 52, 66
– as archetypal battle 95–6
– and Crécy 110
– and decline of civilization 97
Song of Roland. See Chanson de
  Roland
– in Dai's boast 112–13
– inspiration of In Parenthesis 98
Song of Songs 13–14, 191, 207, 209,
  221
songs. See individual titles or authors;
  In Parenthesis, songs in
Southey, Robert 'The Battle of Blenheim' 98–9
Spartacus 279
spatial imagination 8, 12, 13
Spears, Monroe K. 366
Spencer, Stanley 24, 318, 343
Spender, Stephen 25
Spengler, Oswald 27, 33, 206, 279, 334
– on culture and civilization, the distinction between 64
– The Decline of the West 186, 195,
  196, 299
  and The Anathemata, influence
    on 181–3, 190
  and Jones 6: read by him 193,
    374n7, 381n48, 383n57, 383n59
– and determinism 301
– and history, modern, definition of
  345
– on 'home' 303
– and The Sleeping Lord, form of
  260
– on World War I 66
Spenser, Edmund The Faerie Queene
  362
Stalin, Joseph 194
'Stanzas of the Graves' 391–2n60

Staudt, Kathleen Henderson 371n41, 383n56
Stern, Karl *Flight from Woman* 310, 387n14
Sterne, Laurence *A Sentimental Journey* 349
Stevenson, Bill, Dr 203, 204, 205
Stow, John *Survey of London* 219, 225
Strauss, Johann 195
Stravinsky, Igor *Petrushka* 68
structure. *See under* Jones, David; individual titles
Summerfield, Henry 343
Susanna (biblical) 247
Swift, Jonathan 'A Description of a City Shower' 217
symbolism. *See also* individual authors and titles
– archetypal, relation to point of view 18
symbolists, French 13

Tacitus 277
Taliesin 35, 92, 108, 262–3. *See also under In Parenthesis*, Dai's boast in
– *Preiddeu Annwn*, 'The Harrowing of Hades' 60–1, 92, 329
Tammuz 72, 180
Taplow (of Hamish Maclaren's *The Private Opinions of a British Bluejacket*) 82
technology. *See under* motifs (in *A*, *IP*, *SL*), gratuity and utility
Te Deum, alluded to 176
Tellus. *See* figures
Tenniel, John 78
Tennyson, Alfred Lord
– *The Idylls of the King* 5, 393n11
– 'Ulysses' 97
Terpstra, John, on the 'Sleeping Lord' fragment 334, 335
Theseus 287
– as Christ-figure 213
Thomas Aquinas, St 65

Thomas, Dylan 26, 394n13
– reads Dai's boast 109
'Thomas Rhymer' 349
Thwaite, Anthony 367
Tiberius. *See under* figures in *A*, in *SL*
Tillyard, E.M.W. 54
Tolstoy, Leo *War and Peace* 105–6
Traherne, Thomas 35, 371n40
triad (defined) 109
– Welsh Triads 111, 324, 350
triple goddess. *See under* Celts, myth
Tristan 207, 212
Troy Novaunt. *See under* motifs in *A*, London
Tullus 265
Turati, Filippo 193
Turner, J.M.W. 19, 24, 216
Twrch Trwyth (Great Boar) 92, 147. *See also* motifs in *SL*, boar
Tyler, Wat 56

Uccello, Paolo 'Rout of San Romano' 83
Utility and gratuity 64–72. *See also under* motifs in *A*, in *IP*, in *SL*

Vanabride (or Frey) 210
Van Gogh, Vincent 10
Varley, John 348
Varro 348
Varus 277
Vaughan, Henry 35, 348, 371n40
Venus 210, 215, 218, 247, 338. *See also* figures in *A*, Aphrodite
Vermeer, Jan 17
Vesta 252
Vibulenus 297
'Vidi aquam' 221, 241, 253
Virgil 263, 299, 338
– *Aeneid* 196, 197, 256, 267
  Book 6 80, 292n61
– Fourth Eclogue 185, 197
  and Augustus 383n61
– *Georgics* 191

– *Georgics* 4 echoed 124–5
visual art. *See* Jones, David: visual art of, painting; as visual artist
von Hugel, Baron 6, 370n6
Vortigern 77

Wales. *See also* Arthur; Celts, myth; Dying Gaul; Matter of Britain
– folk tales of 117. *See also* individual titles
– history of 55
  and *In Parenthesis* 41, 95–8
  Jones's early interest in 372n4
– mythos of 360
  compared with English mythos 56–7
– poetry of. *See also cynghanedd*; individual authors
  Jones's reading of it in Welsh 370n24
– significance in Jones's poetry 5
Waley, Arthur 34
Wall, Bernard 285
Wallace, Vincent *Maritana* 349
Ward, Elizabeth 376n27, 382–3n56, 383n59, 391n56
– on *The Anathemata* 153, 155, 156, 185–6, 203, 365
– on *In Parenthesis* 44, 66, 373n12, 376n27, 378n14
War poets. *See* World War I, poets of
Waste Land, the 27. *See also* archetypes (in *A*, *IP SL*), Maimed King; Eliot, *The Waste Land*; motifs (in *A*, *IP*, *SL*), Waste Land
Watkins, Vernon 258
Weil, Simone 291, 300
Westminster School of Art 9, 10, 13

Weston, Jessie L. *From Ritual to Romance* 27, 389n25
'When the stars begin to fall' 200
Whethamstede, John 164
Whitman, Walt 33, 371n35
'Who's afraid of the big bad wolf' 319
Widsith 108
Wilde, Oscar *The Picture of Dorian Gray* 57
Wild Hunt, the 325
Wilhelm, Kaiser 131
Wilkes, John *The Roman Army* 388n19
William the Conqueror 313
Williams, Gwyn, on *The Anathemata* 155
Williams, William Carlos 3, 227
– *Paterson* 36, 364, 366–7
Wolfe, Charles 'John Moore' 89
Wolfram von Eschenbach *Parzival* 139
Wood, Christopher 14
Wordsworth, William 94
– 'Harry Gill and Goody Blake' 349
– Preface to *Lyrical Ballads* 303
– *The Prelude* 393n11
World War I, poets of 362
Wyatt, Thomas 56
– 'They flee from me' 87, 222

'Yankee Doodle' 216
Yeats, W.B. 364, 365
– admiration for *In Parenthesis* 3
– historical schema of 182
– Jones on 23
– meeting with Jones 3, 369n1
– poetry, point of view in 20
– symbolism, sense of 10, 13